MASTERING THE ART OF
PLANT-BASED COOKING

VEGAN RECIPES, TIPS,
AND TECHNIQUES

MASTERING THE ART OF

Plant-Based
Cooking

JOE YONAN

PHOTOGRAPHS BY ERIN SCOTT

TEN SPEED PRESS
California | New York

CONTENTS

RECIPE LIST

BUILDING BLOCKS

BREAKFAST & BRUNCH

APPETIZERS & SNACKS

SALADS

SOUPS & STEWS

BOWLS

SIDE DISHES: GRAINS, BEANS & VEGETABLES

SAVORY BAKING: PIZZA, BREADS & MORE

DESERTS & DRINKS

Chamomile Bourbon
Milk Punch (page 467),
during its straining

INTRODUCTION

Of all the eating trends over the last few decades, none has gotten more traction—or press—than the move toward plant-based cooking.

But the truth is, vegetarian and vegan diets date back millennia, to the Buddhism and Jainism of the Indian subcontinent and to ancient Greece. According to some (disputed) reports, Pythagoras abstained from animal foods. (Would that make veganism the true Pythagorean theorem?) In the seventeenth century, Francis Bacon catalogued a long history of vegetarian Spartans, Indians, a Jewish sect of Essenes, and various Christian ascetics "who had lived unusually long lives," according to Tristram Stuart's fascinating book, *The Bloodless Revolution.* And there's evidence that much earlier than Pythagoras, despite the claims of a certain trendy diet, humans during the Paleolithic era subsisted mostly on plants.

Modern iterations of this way of eating have deep roots, some of them intertwining. In India, which has the world's largest proportion of vegetarians, meat-free eating is most widely practiced among the upper caste. India's religious traditions all teach compassion for animals, and ancient ideas connect spirituality to low-resource living, which includes rejecting animals as food. India has also had a strong influence on the rest of the world, with Mahatma Gandhi and other prominent Indians preaching the gospel of vegetarianism on trips to the West.

Given the two nations' relationship, India's ideas have had a particularly strong effect on Britain. There, in keeping with ideas of plant-based eating as a form of spiritual cleansing, a vegetarian community called the Concordium established itself in the mid-nineteenth century at mystic James Pierrepont Greaves's utopian Alcott House. Originally, "vegetarian" connoted abstention from all animal products, but at Britain's Vegetarian Society, the term was loose enough to allow for dairy and egg consumption until the Vegan Society spun off in the mid-twentieth century, coining the name "vegan" from the first and last letters of the word "vegetarian" because its founders believed veganism to be "the beginning and end" of vegetarianism: where it got its start and its natural conclusion.

In the United States, meanwhile, the Seventh-day Adventist Church encouraged vegetarianism starting in the mid-1800s, and that movement—along with Jamaican Rastafarianism and the Nation of Islam—helped lead to a growth in plant-based eating in the Black community. Sylvester Graham, father of the graham cracker, bridged the worlds of religion and public health around the same time, when, as the cholera epidemic headed toward America, he drew crowds interested in his ideas that a vegetarian diet was not only outlined by God but also the best way to prevent disease. Much later, the idea of avoiding animal products for environmental reasons got a big boost from Frances Moore Lappé's 1971 blockbuster book *Diet for a Small Planet,* and in the decades that followed, the health arguments from such books as T. Colin Campbell's *The China Study* in 2005 and the documentary *Forks Over Knives* in 2011 converted plenty of readers and viewers.

Now, it's been five years since *The Economist* declared 2019 the "year of the vegan," and endorsements by Ellen DeGeneres, Al Gore, Tom Brady, Natalie Portman, Mike Tyson, Beyoncé, and more have given the movement celebrity cred.

But what's really grown over the last decade or two is not the number of people who label themselves vegan or vegetarian; that has stayed mostly static at between 2 and 6 percent of the population, depending on the survey. What keeps increasing is the number who are eating more plant-based meals. In the same ways that people say, "Let's go get Italian tonight," now it might be "Let's go to that vegan place."

One of the longest-running, most statistically sound surveys on the topic is from the Vegetarian Resource Group, whose studies have found that while the number of vegetarians has ticked up to 6 percent, with half of those vegan, the percentage who say they sometimes eat vegetarian or vegan meals jumped from 36 percent in 2015 to 63 percent in 2022. The trend is even more striking among younger generations: *Forbes* magazine reported a few years back that fully three-quarters of Gen-Z'ers said they were cutting down on meat consumption.

What difference does it make? Well, "vegan" is a lifestyle and a commitment, while "plant-based" is just dinner. Or a product like all those alt-milks that have taken over grocery dairy aisles. So-called tech meats like the Beyond and Impossible burgers aren't even targeting vegans and vegetarians; they're after the omnivores who, whether it's for their own health or the planet's, have vowed to nudge their diet away from meat, one burger at a time. In 2020, Bloomberg estimated that in the decade leading to 2030, the number of plant-based foods in supermarkets would increase fivefold.

Meanwhile, in my role as the food editor at a national newspaper, I see many separate but overlapping strains of modern plant-based cooking. I see hippie, post-punk, and cutting-edge. I see comfort, wellness, natural and whole foods, African diasporic, Middle Eastern. And of course I see the original vegetarians and vegans, including Indian, Chinese, Korean, Japanese, and other Asian cuisines influenced by Buddhist or other ancient religious traditions, along with precolonial Central and South American and Indigenous. In this book, I bring them together with the aim of helping codify plant-based cooking as not a lifestyle, not a philosophy, but . . . a cuisine.

I'm a longtime participant in this way of cooking and eating—but as more of an expat than a native. I'm a journalist by trade, a formal student of French and Italian cooking, a former certified competitive

barbecue judge, and a West Texas native of Assyrian descent who has traveled (and traveled to eat) in Asia, Central and South America, Europe, Canada, and much of the United States. Unlike some plant-based cooks and eaters, I didn't flip a switch and jump headlong into a vegan diet. I've been moving in fits and starts in that direction for decades, eating less and less meat until one day in 2012 when I realized I didn't want it at all. I surprised even myself when I opened my freezer to start brainstorming for a dinner party and realized it was full of meat I had been buying from the farmers market—and not cooking.

The process sped up from there. When I first publicly announced that I was vegetarian, I called it my "second coming out" because I realized that the reactions, especially from chefs, colleagues, and other food-obsessed friends, were similar to the ones I had gotten the first time, when I came out as gay: How did this happen? Where did we go wrong? Is it just a phase? I joke, but a dozen years later, the last question has answered itself.

That doesn't mean my diet stopped evolving. At first, I depended heavily on eggs and dairy products on the mistaken assumption that I needed them to create something satisfying. But over the years, they have taken up less and less space in my cooking—and are now virtually absent. If it weren't for recipe and ingredient tastings that I want to be able to engage in for work, and if it weren't for the rare instances when a restaurant menu (particularly when I'm traveling) offers no other palatable options, I'd be more of a purist about it.

In that sense, I'm surely like a lot of readers of this book: forever interested in the myriad ways to make plant-based meals delicious—vibrant in flavor, interesting in texture, wholesome and nourishing to eat—and perhaps less interested in claiming an identity, as helpful as that can be for those who want to.

As a longtime food editor and writer, I've dived into the complexities of regional cuisines in virtually every place I've been—and plenty I haven't. So I know firsthand, professionally and personally, that a cuisine is defined by its history, its practitioners, often its geography. Since plant-based cooking is practiced all over the world, it has many under-pinnings, making it particularly rich and complex. It borrows from cuisines everywhere, but in the same way that American cooking is made up of influences from all the immigrants who have come (or been brought) here, along with Native Americans, plant-based cooking is made up of traditionally vegetable-focused cuisines the world over along with interpretations that turn meat-focused cuisines more fully toward vegetables.

Sometimes this involves looking back as much as forward. Take Mexican cooking, for example. When I talked with Eddie Garza, author of the 2016 book *Salud!,* he explained that the presence of lard, cheese, and other animal products represented the influence of Spain on Mexico. Before colonization, the Mesoamerican diet was primarily grains, legumes, and vegetables—all of which remain crucial to the nation's cuisines. (Nico Vera, a Peruvian-born cook and writer, explains more about this phenomenon in his essay on page 224.) Similarly, Bryant Terry, among others, has spoken many times about how modern "soul food" is disconnected from the traditionally agrarian and, yes, plant-based diets of his African ancestors.

These days, one of the challenges of plant-based recipes, cookbooks, foods, and articles is the term itself. Strictly speaking, "based" doesn't mean "exclusive," so technically, "plant-based" doesn't necessarily mean that something is vegan, free of animal products. And plenty of authors and manufacturers use that loophole to apply the term to foods or recipes that are plant-forward but not plants *only*. That's not what I'm doing in this book. When I say "plant-based," I mean vegan, and that's what all the recipes in this book are.

Can plant-based cooking be defined by something other than what it's missing? It's a difficult question to answer, and one that I've seen many people struggle with. At *The Washington Post*, where I edit food coverage, my colleagues know better than to suggest a headline that includes the idea that something vegan or vegetarian is so good, "you won't miss the meat." The meat shouldn't have anything to do with it; a pasta dish with a mushroom Bolognese is good because mushrooms themselves are so good, especially when layered with aromatic vegetables and concentrated tomatoes. Plant foods deserve accolades because of their own outstanding qualities; love them for what they are, not for what they're not.

Plant-based cooking puts vegetables, fruits, legumes, nuts, seeds, grains, herbs, and spices first, and applies creative techniques and combinations to bring out their best flavors and most satisfying, intriguing textures. But because animal products are so ingrained in our food culture, plant-based cooking can't fully escape references to them; that's why this book includes recipes for plant-based cheeses, milks, butter, creamy sauces, and burgers, and for dishes whose traditional version includes meat or another animal product. I sometimes call for store-bought versions of those products, especially the butters and milks, out of a sense of convenience and appreciation for the top quality of some of my favorite brands. But I don't include recipes that use the high-tech meat analogs, mainly because, even though I consume them from time to time, they are highly processed ingredients that someone interested in the from-scratch mentality of plant-based cooking (that is, the art of it) doesn't need. On the other hand, I do celebrate the long tradition of such plant-based protein staples as tempeh, seitan, and tofu, so not only will you find scores of recipes that use them, I also want you to know how satisfying (and superior) they can be to make yourself.

This book draws inspiration from the work of some of the world's best plant-based cooks to present a guide to, as the title indicates, mastering the cuisine—an ongoing process. This is for people who want to learn how to cook better plant-based food, in the same way they would pick up Andrea Nguyen's stellar *Into the Vietnamese Kitchen,* Diana Kennedy's groundbreaking *The Cuisines of Mexico,* or Eileen Yin-Fei Lo's encyclopedic *Mastering the Art of Chinese Cooking* to understand the basics—and beyond—of those cuisines. It is for those who want to improve their plant-based cooking skills for whatever reason—and for however many meals they desire, from a special-occasion dinner party to a weeknight dinner and every frequency in between. Moreover, these skills are applicable far beyond vegan meals. Learning these techniques will help in all kinds of cooking, as almost all modern meals contain plants in some form or amount or another.

My goal here is to provide you with as vibrant a spectrum of plant-based possibilities as I could imagine. And I didn't do it alone; I'm fortunate enough to be able to work with some of the best recipe developers around, and I enlisted their time and energy to come up with their smartest possible takes, ones that I guided from conception through testing and onto these pages, along with a wealth of my own ideas. Many of these recipes and techniques were born out of all the wisdom I have been able to gather from chefs and other authors, editors, and colleagues during my many years of writing about vegetarian (and other) cooking for *The Post*, and in my previous books, which have been devoted more and more specifically to plant-based cooking as the years went by.

As with any kind of cooking, though, this all begins with you, with your ingredients, in your kitchen. Now that you've got this book in your hands, let's take a look at the key elements of successful, satisfying, nourishing, and delicious plant-based cooking: the foundational foods, equipment, and techniques.

INGREDIENTS

Your cooking can only be as good as your ingredients, and in the plant-based kitchen, of course, that means plants: fruits, vegetables, fungi, grains, legumes, nuts, and seeds—and all the products that can be made with and from them.

FRUITS AND VEGETABLES: These are the attention-getters of the plant-based kitchen, for good reason. They bring the freshness of the seasons and the nutrients of the earth onto your plate, sometimes (but not always) after a stop at your countertop, skillet, oven, blender, or so on. I could write dozens of books going into the details of how to select, store, and prep almost any produce you can think of—and many you can't—but many other outstanding books have done this bedrock work already (see the Bibliography, page 471, for examples). Most of my produce tips in this book will be scattered throughout the relevant recipes, focusing on

techniques and strategies I think are particularly unique to this cuisine.

Here are my top-level thoughts: Try to find the freshest produce you can, cook or otherwise preserve what is most perishable as quickly as you can, and learn how best to store the rest. (For a great back-pocket preservation technique, check out Julia Skinner's Lacto-Fermented Vegetables on page 73.) Because the plant-based kitchen concerns itself with the environmental impact of cooking, seek out certified organic produce—or, even better, produce grown by farmers committed to regenerative practices. Aside from that, don't scoff at frozen; in many cases, at many times of the year, it'll taste better because of how quickly it was frozen after harvest than what is sold as "fresh."

GRAINS: They are the behind-the-scenes workhorses, adding heft, nutrition (hello, fiber!), and texture that can turn vegetables into meals. They're always there when you need them, but you can also increase their utility by getting into the habit of cooking them in batches and storing them in the refrigerator or freezer for easy weeknight accessibility. While you'll find a variety of grains in these recipes, from rice to quinoa to wheat berries, I encourage you to seek out your own favorites, learn your favorite ways of cooking them, and branch out here and there as you see fit. (For one of my favorite ways of cooking many grains, see Diana Yen's brown-rice method on page 210.)

Perhaps the most useful grain is the humble oat, the basis for many a morning meal—hot, cold, crunchy, or creamy—but also possessing the power to morph into perhaps the easiest-to-make nondairy milk of all (see page 17). The result can go just as easily into your coffee or matcha as it can act as a silky base for ice cream (see Tahini Ice Cream, page 436). You can turn other grains, such as rice or quinoa, into nondairy milk, too, but oat's advantage is that it requires no cooking or even soaking beforehand.

BEANS: I'm on record as a confirmed legumaniac; my last book, 2020's *Cool Beans*, is an ode to what I call the world's most versatile plant-based protein. Like grains, their shelf stability (either dried or in a can) makes them one of your best partners in the kitchen, while their nutrient density has earned them a well-deserved reputation as key to health and even longevity. Here's the upshot: If it weren't for beans, I don't think I would be able to maintain—let alone enjoy—eating a primarily plant-based diet, and I can never understand it when I meet the rare vegan or vegetarian for whom they're not a staple.

You'll find beans throughout this book, in both dried and canned form, because while cooking the former grants you an amazing bonus—the delicious cooking liquid, great for both storing them and using as a rich stock—the latter can help you get the incredible benefits of beans as quickly as it takes to fiddle with a can opener or pop a top.

- **AQUAFABA:** By now, you've probably heard that the liquid from canned beans (particularly no-salt-added chickpeas) is magical in its own right, as the aquafaba that can whip up as glossy as egg whites (see Aquafaba Cardamom Pavlovas, page 414). It can also act as an emulsifier in such recipes as Soft Spreadable Butter (page 21) and Silky Aquafaba Mayonnaise (page 46), can help bread crumbs stick to tofu in Korean-Style Curry (page 177), and helps bind Lentil-Chickpea Meatballs (page 330). It's so useful, you should get in the habit of saving it every time you open a can of chickpeas; it lasts for a few days in the fridge, but a better bet is to pour it into ice cube trays for freezing, then transfer them to a zip-top bag and freeze for up to 6 months.

NOODLES AND PASTA: By slightly processing grains in traditional ways virtually all over the world, manufacturers make much of their hearty nutrition even more readily accessible. While you'll get the most nutrition out of the whole grain or a whole-grain noodle or pasta, even the "white" version carries some benefits (beyond deliciousness). Noodles and pasta are so ingrained into so many plant-based foods you'll find an entire chapter of those recipes here. You can get started by making Fresh "Egg" Pasta (page 240) and see where it leads.

MUSHROOMS: They're earthy, packed with umami, and boast a variety of firm textures that help them stand in for meat, poultry, or seafood. (See Fried Oyster Mushroom Sandwiches, page 285, Trumpet Mushrooms au Poivre, page 339, and more.) But they bring their own fun-guy (get it?) attitude to any

cooking, especially once you learn how to harness their unique properties.

NUTS AND SEEDS: Like beans, these are nutritional powerhouses (hello, protein!) that bring a welcome crunchy finishing touch to any salad, grain bowl, or so much more. But once you soak, blend with water, and strain out the solids, virtually any raw nut or seed can transform into a nondairy milk (see page 17). While oat milk is easier to make, nuts and seeds offer an unbeatable variety of flavors. They can also turn into beautiful spreadable butters and positively indulgent plant-based ice cream (see Dreamy Nut or Seed Butter Ice Cream, page 437). I prefer to have raw (unroasted, unsalted) nuts on hand because they last longer in the freezer that way and taste so fresh when I toast them myself as part of making a recipe.

Perhaps the most versatile is the **cashew** (botanically the seed of a drupe fruit), whose fat content and texture help it blend (without needing to be strained) into a wonderfully creamy, rich sauce that can play different parts on the skim-milk-to-heavy-cream continuum depending on the proportion of water to cashew. It also requires less soaking time than most other nuts; if you have a high-powered blender, you can often skip the soaking altogether. Note that the cashew industry is notorious for horrific working conditions, terribly low pay, and the use of toxic pesticides, so please seek out organic cashews that are also Fair Trade certified. They are harder to find, but worth it; I regularly order Beyond the Nut brand.

COCONUT MILK AND CREAM: In some ways the fruit of the coconut palm is an entire food production system of its own. What we eat is considered the endosperm, which is thin and milky when the coconut is unripe (coconut water) and hardens into the white "meat" as the fruit matures. The meat can be flaked and dried, or combined with water and turned into milk or cream—and sold in cans. The popular oil is made from coconut milk. Along with cashew milk, coconut milk is perhaps the most common, useful, and delicious plant-based substitute for dairy milk, and in its canned form is incredibly convenient. Look for brands without stabilizers, and keep in mind that "coconut cream" can come either from cans labeled that, or from canned coconut milk that has separated (which is helped along by chilling). Also be aware that PETA has alleged rampant cruelty to monkeys that are forced to pick coconuts in parts of Thailand; go to peta.org for an updated list of brands that do not rely on animal labor.

OTHER STORE-BOUGHT NONDAIRY PRODUCTS: This universe of ingredients could be the subject of its own book, and it is difficult for me at this writing to be definitive about a category that is constantly changing and some of whose best products are local or regional in availability. For the most part, I look for products with the fewest number of ingredients, as close to homemade as possible. Don't be afraid to try new things, but also feel free to stick to your tried and true favorites. (The latest: "precision dairy" products that use fermentation, not animals, to produce actual milk proteins that can become milk or cheese.)

- **MILKS:** Soy milk is the original, and if you have access to an Asian market, you owe it to yourself to try imported brands that will be a revelation in flavor. Almond milk long ago supplanted soy as the star, but critics point out that the crop requires large amounts of water, and as a result, at the time of writing this book, pistachio milk was becoming all the rage in California. Oat milk has been the darling of baristas for years, since its natural viscosity makes it foam and combine nicely in coffees without curdling. But you'll find all sorts of other options, too— flaxseed, walnut, and pecan among them—along with higher-tech milks that promise something closer to the flavor and other qualities of cow's milk, and in some cases with a long ingredient list to help achieve it.

- **YOGURT:** You'll find versions based on soy, almond, and oat milk, but as of this writing, in my mind nothing has beaten the flavor and texture of yogurts made from coconuts rather than coconut milk, such as Cocojune brand. But you can also get great results from the fabulous two-ingredient recipe for Creamy Coconut Yogurt (page 23).

- **BUTTER:** Earth Balance was the most widely available for many years, but as with other parts of the nondairy category, many other brands have gotten into the game, using cashews, oats, coconut, and other ingredients as their base. The game-changer was Miyoko's cultured butter, which was the first I tasted that I could eat by itself on a piece of crusty bread and be perfectly happy, and which works beautifully in sweet baking. That company was founded by the wonderful Miyoko Schinner, who contributed a recipe for her own all-purpose spreadable butter (see page 21).

- **CHEESE:** This is perhaps the most complicated of all the nondairy categories in the supermarket refrigerator case, and that's no doubt because the challenge of making a vegan version of something that has so many unique qualities has been formidable, with mixed results. For the most part, I find that I'd rather find richness and flavor through other techniques rather than depending on store-bought vegan cheeses, but sometimes you just really want something, say, melty between two slices of bread or on top of lasagna or enchiladas. Because these brands change so frequently— ones I once disliked have become favorites after improving their formulas, while others have done the opposite—I hesitate to name brands, but I'll give a shout-out to Miyoko's for its liquid mozzarella (a brilliant invention, perfect for pizza), Violife for its slices and shreds, and Daiya for its meltability (at least as long as it doesn't change formulas again). For pure snacking and sprinkling and dolloping, try one of the DIY cheeses by Schinner and others (see pages 25 to 32).

NUTRITIONAL YEAST: It's been a staple of vegan cooking for decades, largely because its umami gives it a cheesiness that is easy to sprinkle on popcorn and vegetables or to act as a finishing touch much in the way Parmesan does. Some brands are fortified, which is helpful for vegans who wouldn't otherwise have a good source of vitamin B_{12}. One of my go-to uses is to very heavily coat asparagus, broccoli, or cauliflower with it, along with oil, salt, and pepper; the "nooch" helps crisp and caramelize the edges and adds that cheesy flavor. (Find an elevated version of this idea, using bread crumbs and asparagus, page 363.) It also combines well with spicy elements to make what I call Nacho Nooch (page 45).

TOFU: It's the king of the plant-based kitchen, no doubt; and if you do doubt, that probably means you are stuck on some preconceived and, frankly, outdated idea of what tofu is and could be. For one thing, as we longtime fans know, there is no single tofu, but a whole category of products in a range of textures, from custardy to firm, silken to puffy, whose roots are so deep in all manner of Asian cooking you'd be subject to ridicule if you referred to it as a meat substitute in that part of the world. Consider exploring forms of store-bought tofu that might be new to you. I use silken tofu as the base for sauces and dressings (Creamy Herby Tofu Dressing, page 65) and as a delicious appetizer with powerful toppings (Silken Tofu with Ginger-Marinated Tomatoes, page 161). Firm or extra-firm tofu is so well suited to baking, frying, and braising. And in Asian markets, fermented tofu adds just the funk you need for a plant-based homemade cheese (Basic Melty Cheese, page 25), while fried tofu puffs are simply a blast to put on anything you'd like. If you've never made your own tofu, I encourage you to give it a whirl, with my multipronged recipe (see page 75) that results in beautiful soy milk, tofu, and a shelf-stable protein powder. If you're interested in tofu that's not soy-based, you might have noticed pumpkin seed and fava bean versions in grocery stores; I show you how easy the pumpkin seed version is on page 18; I hope you try it.

TEMPEH: Fermenting makes this form of soy protein even more nutritious than tofu, and it's also becoming common to see versions of it in stores made from other legumes and grains. The most widely available grocery store brands are good, but if you get a chance to sample anything that's made fresher and closer to where you live (and probably sold frozen), do yourself a favor and snap it up: The texture and flavor will be superior. I had never thought it would be within reach to make it myself, until I met Julia Skinner, author of *Our Fermented Lives*, and she shared her tempeh recipe (page 79), which is a part of my rotation every few months.

SEITAN: I find much of the widely available seitan to be somewhat rubbery, but more and more products are proving that this traditional wheat-based protein nugget can be a welcome addition to the plant-based kitchen. I prefer versions that are as close to unflavored as possible, so I can do my own seasoning according to the recipe I'm using. And—surprise!—I do also make it myself. After struggling with attempts based on the easier technique of using vital wheat gluten, which makes a beautiful holiday roast (see page 323), I went back to the way my sister Rebekah always made it, kneading and rinsing wheat flour (and repeating and repeating) until you're left with the sticky gluten that you can form and season. Rich Landau of Vedge restaurant helped talk me through an adjustment to the technique that makes for something even softer, perfect for grilling (see Grilled Seitan, page 310).

MISO: When you're trying to add a hit of umami depth to, well, anything, miso—along with its punchier Korean counterpart, doenjang—is almost always the answer. It's the not-so-secret secret to plant-based polenta (see page 211), mac and cheese (see page 230), dressings and sauces. Stir a little white miso into risotto at the end of cooking, and you'll see. There are some stellar misos available, including my favorite brand, South Mountain, which makes misos from a variety of legumes. As always, though, you can also make it yourself; White Miso (page 83) takes little effort except patience.

DRIED SEAWEED: More and more attention has been paid over recent years to the nutritional—and eco-friendly—qualities of seaweed, which is worth exploring and adding to your diet. The king, IMHO, is dried kombu, which I use not only to help soften (and reduce the gas-inducing effects of) beans but also to bring a taste of the ocean to so many plant-based dishes, including Beet Ceviche (page 126).

SPICES: Spices and spice blends are one of the fastest, easiest ways to change the flavor profile of just about anything you're cooking, and they can help you cook your way across the globe. My collection of spice blends (see pages 37 to 45) are easy to make and store, but you should feel free to home in on the ones that make you happiest. As for individual spices, it's hard for me to pick my favorites, but the ones I find most useful in the plant-based kitchen are those that carry hints (or larger doses) of smoke,

Opposite: Pumpkin Seed Tofu (page 18)

pepper, and heat, as those are flavors that don't necessarily come naturally to fruits and vegetables on their own. Think: cumin, smoked paprika, ground chipotle, black and white pepper, among others. I'm also a lover of kala namak, the black salt traditional in Indian cooking that gives a sulfurous flavor to tofu scrambles and other egg-like dishes.

CONDIMENTS: As with spice blends, these shortcut geniuses give you the instantaneous benefit of complex flavors that were developed days or weeks or months before—either by someone else if they're store-bought, or by you if they're DIY. My pantry and fridge wouldn't be complete without such condiments as gochujang, Salsa Macha (page 48), Chinese-Style Chili Crisp (page 53), Thai curry paste, and various other dressings, spreads, and dips.

OILS: There is a segment of plant-based cooks who eschew cooking oils, but that doesn't include me, nor is it reflected in this book, because I have read countless analyses by scientists and nutrition experts I respect who find no evidence for the idea that oils themselves should be avoided. In fact, there is plenty of evidence to the contrary. While details get pretty complicated rather quickly, it's no doubt true that certain oils are less healthful than others because of their high levels of saturated fat. For most uses, I rely on extra-virgin olive oil, avocado oil, safflower oil, and others that are high in healthy monounsaturated fat, and save ones such as coconut oil for special, occasional uses (such as baking). Your choice of oil might depend on its flavor (or lack thereof) and its smoke point. Generally, refined oils have neutral flavor and higher smoke points, making them good for higher-temperature cooking, such as frying, while less-refined oils, such as virgin coconut oil and unrefined nut oils, have more flavor and lower smoke points, making them better for lower-temperature or raw cooking. In many cases in this book, you can substitute your favorite oil once you keep in mind those principles.

FERMENTS: I hope I don't have to tell you how good fermented foods such as kimchi, sauerkraut, lacto-fermented pickles, and yogurt are for your gut biome. But I want to convince you that you should make room for a variety of homemade and store-bought versions of them, depending on what your time allows. They add sharpness, depth, and bite to almost anything you use them for. Note that most traditional store-bought kimchis include nonvegan ingredients, such as shrimp paste and/or fish sauce, so check the ingredient labels or make it yourself (Clean-Out-the-Fridge Kimchi, page 71). If you're a regular kombucha drinker, as I am, consider getting into the habit of brewing your own (see page 463); with practice it'll take you just 30 minutes a week to produce three big bottles you can flavor to your liking.

THICKENERS, EMULSIFIERS, AND LEAVENERS: Especially in plant-based baking, some recipes need to do at least one of the functions otherwise provided by eggs, which bring (and hold) batters together, help them rise, and provide structure. Baking powder and baking soda are great leaveners, while chia seeds, flaxseeds, tapioca, and other starches can help with the thickening and emulsifying. Aquafaba, the liquid from canned chickpeas, can be a ringer for whipped egg whites, and I find it works better in those types of applications—meringues, pavlovas (see page 414), and the like—than in cakes and cookies. See particular recipes for the recommended ingredients, and avoid substitutions unless you're willing to undergo some trial and (hopefully tasty) error.

SWEETENERS: Highly refined cane sugar is sometimes made with bone char and therefore isn't appropriate for the plant-based kitchen. But an easy way to find vegan-friendly sugar is to simply look for the organic label. Other less-refined sweeteners, such as coconut sugar, raw cane sugar, and maple syrup, offer more depth of flavor, but keep in mind that nutritionally there is no truly "healthy" sugar, and that includes agave syrup, which is often used as a vegan substitute for honey. For a homemade honey substitute, I developed a wonderful Wild-flower Cider Syrup (page 35), inspired by a traditional New England product called boiled cider.

EQUIPMENT AND SUPPLIES

Every kitchen needs a good, large cutting board; a selection of pots and pans that suit your favorite ways of cooking; sharp knives, particularly a chef's knife and a paring knife; mixing bowls, whisks, spatulas, and other cooking utensils; and sheet pans, muffin tins, cake and pie pans. That's just a start. But the following things are particularly helpful when you're cooking plant-based foods, including items that will help you cut down on plastic use and waste.

GRATERS: A box grater helps you break down so many vegetables for cooking, and it can be so much faster to do this than to cut them into small pieces by hand. For garlic, rather than mincing, I love to use a Microplane grater—or a garlic press. And for ginger, I treasure my little ceramic ginger grater, which separates the fiber from the pungent juice with ease.

Y-SHAPED PEELER: This will let you easily dispatch even the toughest peels, such as those on winter squash.

EXTRA-LARGE SHEET PAN: Most ovens can't hold what restaurant chefs call a full sheet pan, so we settle for the standard half-sheets. But if you can find a jumbo-sized pan, which is 15 × 20 inches (38cm × 50cm), such as one sold by King Arthur Baking, I recommend it for roasting vegetables. The extra space allows you to roast, say, a large head's worth of cauliflower florets without their overlapping, which is key to getting them browned and crisp-edged rather than steaming them.

COMPOSTABLE PARCHMENT PAPER: Use these to line your half-sheet pans and save on cleanup without adding waste.

DIGITAL SCALE: Precision leads to reliable success, which is why all the recipes in this book use weights for everything but the smallest amounts.

NUT-MILK BAG: Plant-based cooking calls for a lot of squeezing and straining. Sure, you can use cheesecloth, but nylon mesh bags designed for this purpose are easier to clean and last longer.

HIGH-POWERED BLENDER: Before you strain, you blend—a lot. Using a high-powered blender, such as a Vitamix, helps your cashew creams become smooth and increases the yield of your nut milks.

MASON JARS: They're not just for canning. I use mason jars to store dried goods in my pantry and leftovers in the fridge.

CANNING FUNNELS: See mason jars, above. These funnels fit snugly into standard jars and have both a wide opening and a wide spout that allow you to easily ladle beans, soups, stews, and more right into the jars without spillage.

COTTON VEGETABLE-STORAGE BAGS: I use Vejibag brand for virtually all my fresh produce for at least part of its lifespan. You wet them, squeeze out the excess water, and put the produce in, and they seem to keep just enough moisture to extend the life of most anything. The only drawback: You can't tell what's inside at a glance, although sometimes, when I'm feeling particularly on top of things, I'll attach a little label with a rubber band.

SILICONE STRETCHY LIDS AND REUSABLE ZIP-TOP BAGS: These are so handy anytime you would normally use plastic wrap or disposable zip-top bags, single-use plastic that is clogging our oceans, among other problems.

DUTCH OVENS AND OTHER OVENPROOF POTS WITH LIDS: Besides their typical uses, these are especially helpful for avoiding the need for aluminum foil to cover baked goods. Just bake with a lid instead!

COMPOST BUCKET AND OTHER SUPPLIES: I try to keep food waste to a minimum by using up as much of the produce as I can in the moment—and compost the rest. If you have access to a municipal compost program, consider yourself lucky. If not, and you have a backyard, you can easily set up a simple compost pile. If your space is more limited, look into tumblers or, for an even smaller and quicker method, a vermicomposting system. I'm seeing more and more companies marketing small appliances that purport to create "instant" compost, when what they are really creating is a finely ground product that can be added to your garden—or other composting system—but doesn't (yet) contain all the rich microbial activity that true compost does.

CONTRIBUTORS

MAUREEN ABOOD is author and creator of MaureenAbood.com and the cookbook *Rose Water & Orange Blossoms: Fresh & Classic Recipes from My Lebanese Kitchen.*
maureenabood.com

WOONHENG CHIA is a Malaysia-born home cook who shares her passion for plant-based meals with an Asian twist.
woonheng.com

EMILY CODIK is a journalist living in Rio de Janeiro, Brazil, where she creates recipe videos for social media. She is from the Dominican Republic.
Instagram: @emilycodik

ANGEL GREGORIO is the owner of The Spice Suite, a growing community-centric spice boutique, and Black and Forth, a multiuse commercial development that helps Black women expand their businesses, both in Washington, DC.
thespicesuite.com

KRISTEN HARTKE is a journalist and recipe developer, and was recipe tester for not only this book, but also for Joe Yonan's *Cool Beans.* She teaches food journalism at American University in Washington, DC.
kristenhartke.com

HAWA HASSAN is the founder of Basbaas Sauce, a line of condiments inspired by her home country of Somalia, and author of *In Bibi's Kitchen*, which shares recipes and stories from grandmothers in eight African countries.
basbaasfoods.com

JESSICA HYLTON-LECKIE writes the award-winning vegan food blog Jessica in the Kitchen. She is based in Jamaica.
jessicainthekitchen.com

CHRISTIAN IRABIÉN is a DC chef with a multicultural background and the founder of Amparo Fondita, a restaurant that celebrates local, seasonal plant-based ingredients and showcases the flavors of contemporary Mexican cuisine.
muchasgraciasdc.com

SARAH JAMPEL is a recipe developer, writer, and editor based in Vermont, where she's the Test Kitchen and Recipe Development Manager at King Arthur Baking Company.
sarahjampel.com

ALICIA KENNEDY is a food and culture writer living in San Juan, Puerto Rico. She is the author of *No Meat Required: The Cultural History and Culinary Future of Plant-Based Eating.*
alicia-kennedy.com

ASHA LOUPY, based in Oakland, California, is a writer and recipe developer, and recipe editor for the spice company Diaspora. Her work has appeared in *Bon Appétit*, Food52, *Martha Stewart Living*, Kitchn, *The Washington Post*, and Epicurious.
fromheadtotable.com

JOY MANNING is a Philadelphia-based writer whose work has been nominated for a James Beard Award and an IACP award, and anthologized in *The Best Food Writing* series.
Instagram: @joymanning
joymanning.com

TRACYE MCQUIRTER, MPH, is the author of *By Any Greens Necessary* and *Ageless Vegan* and founder of the 10 Million Black Vegan Women Movement.
byanygreensnecessary.com

KIANO MOJU is a recipe developer, host, video producer, and the visionary behind the nonprofit Jikoni Recipe Archive, who is known for her distinctive Afri-Cali cooking style.
kianomoju.com

JOANNE LEE MOLINARO is the *New York Times* bestselling author of *The Korean Vegan* and the personality behind social media accounts with more than five million followers.
thekoreanvegan.com

MIYOKO SCHINNER is an epicurean activist out to end cruelty to animals and climate change by connecting our palate to our future. She is the founder of Miyoko's Creamery and Rancho Compasión and the author of six books.
youtube.com/@thevegangoodlifewithmiyoko

ALEXANDRA SHYTSMAN is a plant-based recipe developer, food writer, and photographer based in Brooklyn, New York.
Instagram: @thenewbaguette
alexandrashytsman.com

JULIA SKINNER, PhD, is the author of the award-winning *Our Fermented Lives*, a writing and creative coach, and the founder of the food history and fermentation organization Root. She splits her time between Atlanta, Georgia, and Cork, Ireland.
juliacskinner.com

ALI SLAGLE is the author of the James Beard Award–nominated cookbook *I Dream of Dinner (so you don't have to)* and a frequent contributor to *The New York Times* and *The Washington Post*.
alislagle.com

DORA STONE, a native of Mexico, is a graduate of the Culinary Institute of America and the chef and photographer behind the vegan Mexican recipe blog DorasTable.com.
dorastable.com

NICO VERA is a chef and journalist from Peru on a mission to veganize his country's creole cuisine one dish and origin story at a time.
piscotrail.com

K. N. VINOD is a chef whose acclaimed restaurants include Indique and RASA in Washington, DC.
chefvinod.com

BRIGID WASHINGTON is the author of *Caribbean Flavors for Every Season*. Her work has appeared in *Bon Appétit*, Epicurious, *Food & Wine*, *The New York Times*, and more. She is a dual citizen of Trinidad and Tobago and the United States.
withbrigid.com

DIANA YEN is a food stylist and recipe developer, and the author of *A Simple Feast*. Her projects with leading food and lifestyle brands focus on the simplicity and elegance of everyday meals.
studioalacarte.co

BUILDING BLOCKS

One of the quickest ways to get a sense of just how far plant-based cooking has come is to stroll through the average supermarket and marvel at just how many vegan butters, milks, yogurts, cheeses, meats, mayos, and more you now have to choose from. The category is changing so quickly that it's almost futile to recommend particular brands, but one thing that will never change is this: Few products will be as good as the versions you make at home, where you can customize them to your liking and where their freshness and flavor make them irresistible. But the building blocks of a plant-based kitchen go beyond replacements for animal products: Spice blends, sauces, stocks, and seasonings can help you infuse vegan dishes with the flavors of the world.

Endlessly Customizable Nut or Seed Milk

The genius of this master recipe for plant-based milk is that it works across a variety of nuts and seeds, from almonds to hazelnuts to sesame seeds. You can even mix them! Plus, at home you'll have the choice to make it filtered or unfiltered. Use unfiltered milk in oatmeal and porridges, or filter the milks for preparations such as stews, curries, or drinks.

Achieving the texture of your dreams takes practice. The standard ratio is 1 part nuts and seeds to every 4 parts of liquid. However, coconut milk benefits from a ratio of 2:4, or even 3:4.

Makes about 1 quart

Time: Weekday

Storage: Refrigerate unfiltered milk for up to 3 days and filtered for up to 4 days. Shake before using.

1 cup (see Notes) nuts, such as raw almonds, raw cashews, skin-on hazelnuts, walnuts, pecans, pistachios, Brazil nuts, and/or sesame seeds, pumpkin seeds, or 2 cups (180g) unsweetened coconut flakes
4 cups (950ml) water, at room temperature
½ teaspoon fine sea salt

IN A BOWL, COMBINE the nuts and/or seeds with enough water to cover by 2 inches (5cm). Soak at room temperature for 8 hours or overnight.

Rinse and drain the nuts and/or seeds. In a high-powered blender, combine the nuts and/or seeds, 4 cups (950ml) water, and salt. Start blending at low speed, gradually increasing to high, until the milk is frothy and creamy, about 1 minute.

For filtered milk, set a sieve over a large bowl and arrange a nut-milk bag on top (see page 16). Pour the milk into the bag and squeeze with your hands to strain. (Alternatively, use a very thin kitchen towel: Place the kitchen towel over the sieve and carefully pour in the milk. Gather the corners of the towel and squeeze to strain.) Pour the milk into a sealable jar, cover, and refrigerate. Refrigerate or freeze the leftover pulp for adding to smoothies, oatmeal, or other porridge.

For unfiltered milk, pour into a sealable jar, cover, and refrigerate.

COOK'S NOTES

- If you need homemade milk in a hurry, blend 4 tablespoons almond or other nut butter with 4 cups (950ml) room-temperature water. You won't even have to strain it.

- The gram weight of 1 cup will vary by nut/seed, so it's easier to use the volume measure. However, the weights will be in the range of 100 to 150 grams.

Oat Milk

Perhaps the easiest plant-based milk to make is oat milk, as it requires no soaking, only brief blending, and very little squeezing. In fact, the less you blend and squeeze, the less you bring out the oats' mucilaginous (aka slimy) qualities. That makes it fast, too. Note that oat milk works so well in baked goods, where its natural sugars help with browning and flavor, but if you heat it by itself—say, before stirring into coffee or tea—it will start to thicken.

Makes about 1 quart

Time: Weekday

Storage: Refrigerate for up to 5 days.

1 cup (90g) old-fashioned rolled oats
4 cups (950ml) cold water
½ teaspoon fine sea salt
1 tablespoon maple syrup (optional)
1 teaspoon vanilla extract (optional)

IN A HIGH-POWERED BLENDER, combine the oats and water and blend on high speed for no more than 30 seconds.

Set a sieve over a large bowl and arrange a nut-milk bag on top. Pour the milk into the bag, tie it closed, and let the oat milk drip through the bag and sieve and into the bowl. (Alternatively, use a very thin kitchen towel: Place the kitchen towel over the sieve and carefully pour in the milk. Gather the corners of the towel and let the milk drip through.) Stir in the salt, maple syrup (if using), and vanilla (if using). Pour into a sealable jar, cover, and refrigerate.

Refrigerate or freeze the leftover pulp for adding to smoothies, oatmeal, or other porridge.

Pumpkin Seed Tofu

I'm a fan of a store-bought pumpkin seed tofu called Pumfu, and was amazed when I looked at the ingredients to find only two ingredients: pumpkin seeds and water. So couldn't I make it myself? Inspired by Miyoko Schinner's delectable (and simple) Fluffy Pumpkin Seed Ricotta (page 31), I started playing around—and found another simple way to make a tofu that's not only a godsend for people who are allergic to soy, it's delectable in its own right. Unlike traditional tofu (see page 75), which requires you to first make soy milk—which involves straining the soybeans out— this leaves in the ground-up pumpkin seeds, giving it a slightly crumbly (but very pleasant) texture. And the flavor! The only complaint I have about it is that I usually eat so much of it right off the roasting or frying pan that it never makes it to the table. Not a bad problem to have.

This tofu is best cooked by roasting or pan-frying (see Note), as it's just slightly too crumbly to hold up well in stews.

Makes 6 to 8 servings

Time: Weekend

Storage: Refrigerate, still in the nut-milk bag or wrapped in cheesecloth and in an airtight container, for up to 1 week. Freezing not recommended.

    2 cups (260g) raw pumpkin seeds
    4 cups (950ml) water
    1 teaspoon fine sea salt
    2 tablespoons fresh lemon juice

SET A FINE-MESH SIEVE over a bowl and line it with several layers of cheesecloth or a nut-milk bag.

In a high-speed blender, combine the pumpkin seeds, water, and salt and puree on high speed for 2 minutes, until you see no specks.

Pour into a medium saucepan and cook over medium heat, stirring occasionally with a silicone spatula—and being sure to scrape the bottom of the pan to avoid scorching—until the mixture starts to gently bubble, 10 to 15 minutes. You should see the mixture start to form small curds.

Stir in the lemon juice and continue gently stirring, being careful not to break up the curds, until they separate a little more from the liquid, 2 to 3 minutes.

Spoon or pour the mixture into the cheesecloth-lined sieve or the nut-milk bag, smooth the top, and close the cheesecloth, layering it on top as neatly and tightly as possible. Set a small smooth-bottomed plate on the cheesecloth and top it with a small can of beans or tomatoes to gently press about 20 minutes, until the "whey" has mostly stopped dripping out. (If you have a tofu-making press, that works well here, too, but you might need to work in two batches.)

Leaving the tofu in the cheesecloth or nut-milk bag, transfer it to an airtight container and refrigerate until firm, at least 2 hours. (You can store it like this for up to 1 week.)

COOK'S NOTE: When you're ready to cook it, carefully unwrap the tofu on your countertop and cut it into cubes. If you'd like to roast it, preheat the oven to 450°F (230°C). Transfer the cubes to a sheet pan, drizzle with olive oil, and sprinkle with salt and the spices or spice mix of your choice, making sure to carefully turn it over to season and oil top and bottom. (I particularly like it with Cajun Seasoning, page 38, Jerk Spice, page 41, Garam Masala, page 40, or Ras el Hanout, page 42.) Roast until golden brown, 10 to 12 minutes. If you'd like to pan-fry it, use salt but leave off the spices. In a large skillet (preferably nonstick), heat ¼ cup (60ml) olive oil over medium-high heat. Add the tofu cubes and cook until browned on the bottom, about 5 minutes. Flip the cubes and cook on the other side until browned, 4 to 5 minutes.

Pumpkin Seed Tofu
before roasting

Soft Spreadable Butter

We've all heard that water and oil don't mix, but that's exactly what buttery spreads are. The key to combining the two is an emulsifier, such as lecithin. In this recipe, Miyoko's Creamery founder Miyoko Schinner uses aquafaba, the starchy water from a can of chickpeas, as a more accessible (albeit weaker) emulsifier. The key to whipping this into creamy goodness is all about the process and temperature of the ingredients. If you don't have a thermometer, no problem—the process will fix it even if the mixture doesn't emulsify immediately, and the butter firms up to just the right texture upon its final chilling. This butter's best use is for spreading on toast, biscuits, and other baked goods. You can also use it for cooking, and it works well for some baking—cakes, muffins, and some cookies—but not as well for flaky pastries, as the water content is too high.

Makes about 2 cups

Time: Weekend

Storage: Refrigerate for up to 1 month.

> 1¼ cups (300ml) refined coconut oil, melted, at about 80°F (27°C)
> ¾ cup (180ml) sunflower, avocado, olive, canola, or other liquid oil of choice, refrigerated for at least 2 hours
> 6 tablespoons plain nondairy yogurt, cold from the fridge
> ¼ cup (60ml) aquafaba (liquid from a can of no-salt-added chickpeas; see page 6), refrigerated for at least 2 hours
> ½ teaspoon fine sea salt, plus more to taste

IN A BLENDER, COMBINE the warm coconut oil, cold sunflower oil, yogurt, aquafaba, and salt and process until emulsified, creamy, and thick. Taste and add more salt if needed. If the mixture doesn't come together, no need to fret; just pour it into a dish and put it into the freezer for about an hour. When it starts to solidify around the edges, pour it back in the blender and process again. It should emulsify then.

Pour the mixture into a storage container and refrigerate. The butter will set and firm up as it chills.

Rich Almond-Coconut Creamer

This recipe uses the biggest knock against nut milk to its advantage: that it separates. In this case, that's exactly what we want, so it'll emulsify nicely in hot drinks. Once chilled, this almond-coconut milk will develop a thicker, creamier layer on top. Scoop it out and transfer it to a separate container. That's your creamer; it'll be more luscious than a typical nut-milk recipe, without the need to boil it or add thickeners. What remains is a wonderful milk you can use wherever you'd like.

Temperature matters here. For the best results, stir the cold creamer directly into coffee or tea, or warm the creamer gently (boiling may cause it to separate again) and whisk it to froth before adding to your drink. If the creamer does separate, simply whip it up again in the blender.

Makes about 1 cup creamer + 4 cups almond-coconut milk

Time: Weekend

Storage: Refrigerate for up to 4 days.

> 6 cups (1.4L) water, at room temperature
> 2 cups (280g) raw almonds, soaked for 8 hours or overnight, rinsed and drained
> 1½ cups (135g) unsweetened coconut flakes
> Pinch of fine sea salt
> 2 pitted dates (optional)

IN A HIGH-POWERED BLENDER, combine the water, almonds, coconut flakes, salt, and dates (if using). Blend, starting at low speed and quickly increasing to high, until creamy, about 1 minute.

Set a sieve over a large bowl and arrange a nut-milk bag on top. Pour the milk into the bag and squeeze with your hands to strain. (Alternatively, use a very thin kitchen towel: Place the towel over the sieve and carefully pour in the milk. Gather the corners of the towel and squeeze to strain.)

Pour the creamer into a wide container, cover, and refrigerate until completely chilled and the creamer separates into two layers, about 6 hours.

Scoop out the top layer and transfer it into a separate container. Refrigerate or freeze the leftover pulp and thinner milk for adding to smoothies, oatmeal, or other porridges.

Smooth Almond Crema

Nut-based sauces have been used for centuries in Mexican cooking—perhaps most famously in the classic dish chiles en nogada—but nuts and seeds also thicken other beloved sauces, such as mole (see page 313) and pipián (see page 56). That's why making a crema out of almonds comes so naturally, especially if you're looking for an option to all those cashews, which are so commonly used in plant-based cooking to make creamy sauces but can be expensive and plagued with fair-trade and labor issues (see Ingredients, page 6). Use anywhere you want a tart dose of creamy richness, particularly on tacos, enchiladas, and bean-based grain bowls.

Makes 2 cups

Time: Weekday

Storage: Refrigerate for up to 3 days; freeze for up to 3 months: first in ice cube trays, then transfer to zip-top bags.

Boiling water
1¼ cups (140g) slivered almonds
2 garlic cloves, peeled and halved
1 cup (240ml) cold water, plus more as needed
¼ cup (60ml) avocado oil or olive oil
1 tablespoon fresh lime juice, plus more to taste
1 teaspoon nutritional yeast
1 teaspoon fine sea salt, plus more to taste

IN A HEATPROOF BOWL, pour enough boiling water over the almonds to cover by 1 inch (2.5cm). Let soak for 1 hour, then drain.

In a high-powered blender, combine the soaked almonds, garlic, cold water, oil, lime juice, nutritional yeast, and salt and process first on low speed and then gradually increase to high, continuing until very smooth, 3 to 4 minutes. Scrape down the sides of the blender and puree again briefly to incorporate.

If the sauce is already the consistency of thick cream, taste, and season with more salt and/or lime juice as needed, then use immediately (it will be warm from the blender) or transfer to a jar and refrigerate. If the sauce is too thick, turn the blender speed to low, and with the motor running, gradually stream in more water, 1 to 2 tablespoons at a time, until the sauce is the right consistency.

Sweetened Condensed Coconut Milk

Making sweetened condensed milk at home is easier than expected: All you have to do is combine full-fat coconut milk—this is not the time to use low-fat—with granulated and brown sugar and cook it slowly. The result is luscious, silky, spoonable, pourable, and mixable. Use it in your favorite desserts or stir a spoonful into your cup of coffee for the ultimate morning pick-me-up.

Makes 1 cup

Time: Weekday

Storage: Refrigerate for up to 10 days.

1 (13.5-ounce/400ml) can full-fat coconut milk
¼ cup (50g) organic cane sugar
2 tablespoons lightly packed light brown sugar
Pinch of fine sea salt

IN A SMALL SAUCEPAN, combine the coconut milk, organic cane sugar, brown sugar, and salt (making sure there is at least 3 inches [7.5cm] of space from the lip of the pan to the surface, as it will bubble up when cooking). Mix well and bring to a boil over medium-high heat. Reduce the heat to medium-low and cook, stirring occasionally, until reduced by half, 35 to 45 minutes.

Allow to cool to room temperature, transfer to an airtight container, and refrigerate until fully cooled before using.

Tangy Coconut Cashew Buttermilk

This recipe by Kristen Hartke is a riff off a plant-based yogurt I created for my 2020 cookbook, *Cool Beans*. Kristen was my recipe tester for the book—all 125+ recipes!—and when she made the yogurt recipe, she immediately thought that if it was a little thinner, it might make a great vegan version of buttermilk. She gave her theory a try, adding water and lemon juice to the mixture, and it yielded a fantastic buttermilk substitute; the full-fat coconut milk gives the fattiness needed to give buttermilk biscuits and pancakes both lift and moisture, while the fermentation process provides that distinctly sour flavor.

Makes about 1 quart

Time: Weekend

Storage: Refrigerate for up to 1 week.

½ cup (65g) raw cashews, soaked in water for 2 hours and then drained

2 (13.5-ounce/400ml) cans full-fat coconut milk

⅓ cup (80ml) water

2 tablespoons fresh lemon juice

1 vegan probiotic capsule (preferably with 10 billion live active cultures, such as Jarrow Probiotic or Culturelle)

WASH AND DRY A 1-quart (1L) mason jar, rinse it in boiling water, and let dry and cool to room temperature.

In a high-powered blender, combine the soaked cashews, coconut milk, water, and lemon juice and puree until very smooth. Strain through a fine-mesh sieve to remove any remaining solids. Pour into the jar and sprinkle the contents of the probiotic capsule over the top and stir gently to combine. Cover the top of the jar with a piece of cheesecloth, secure it with a rubber band (or the metal ring from the mason jar lid), and let it sit in a warm spot for 48 hours.

Taste, and if it has a good tart flavor, cover the container and refrigerate; if it's not tart enough, let it sit another 24 hours and taste again. As it chills, the mixture will thicken and the whey will separate, so stir well when ready to use. If the mixture is overly thick, thin it with a tablespoon or so of plant-based milk to the desired texture before using.

Creamy Coconut Yogurt

Store brands of coconut yogurt have proliferated, but making your own is much simpler than you might think, requiring just two ingredients. Probiotic capsules do all the heavy lifting to kick-start the fermentation process in the coconut milk. For the best results, make sure to use coconut milk that's smooth and creamy to begin with. (An easy way to check at the grocery store is to give the can a shake, and if it sounds liquid-y inside it should be good.)

Makes about 1 quart

Time: Weekend

Storage: Refrigerate for up to 1 week.

2 (13.5-ounce/400ml) cans full-fat coconut milk

4 vegan probiotic capsules (preferably one with 10 billion live active cultures, such as Jarrow Probiotic or Culturelle), or 4 tablespoons store-bought vegan plain coconut yogurt

Optional add-ins: Wildflower Cider Syrup (page 35), agave or maple syrup, fruit jam

WASH AND DRY A 1-quart (1L) mason jar, rinse it in boiling water, let dry, and cool to room temperature.

Shake the cans of coconut milk before opening, then open the cans and pour the milk into the jar. Add the powder from the probiotic capsules (or the store-bought coconut yogurt) and stir with a wooden spoon until smooth. Avoid using a metal spoon so it doesn't react with the probiotics.

Cover the jar with a piece of cheesecloth and secure in place with a rubber band or the ring from the mason jar lid. Let the yogurt sit in a warm place (at least 75°F/24°C or warmer) for 24 to 48 hours, until it is thick and tangy. A warmer environment will help the yogurt ferment faster. If your kitchen is cold, you can also place the jar in the oven with the light on.

Once you are satisfied with the tartness of the yogurt, you can refrigerate it as is, or sweeten it with agave if you wish, or layer it in smaller jars with jam. The yogurt will continue to thicken and set as it chills.

Basic Melty Cheese

This cheese has the texture of Muenster and, despite its mildness, is full of umami and character. It can stand in for any kind of cheese: cheddar, Swiss, or anything in between. The fermented tofu and sauerkraut juice create the depth of flavor that can otherwise be achieved only through fermentation. It can be dressed up or down in a variety of dishes—sandwiches, mac and cheese, enchiladas—or tossed in hot pasta. You can adjust the flavor by adding such flavorings as liquid smoke, onion and garlic powder, or jalapeños, as in the variations that follow.

Makes 1 pound

Time: Project

Storage: Refrigerate for up to 6 weeks.

>
1 cup (120g) raw cashews

⅔ cup (160ml) sauerkraut juice (drained from a jar of raw fermented sauerkraut with active probiotics; see Notes)

2 tablespoons plain nondairy yogurt

1 cube plain Chinese fermented bean curd or tofu (see Notes), or use 2 cubes for a stronger cheese

1 teaspoon fine sea salt

⅓ cup (80ml) refined coconut oil, melted

½ cup (120ml) plus 2 tablespoons water

1 tablespoon agar-agar powder

¼ cup (35g) tapioca starch dissolved in ¼ cup (60ml) water

LINE A SMALL BOWL with compostable plastic wrap or have on hand a 1 to 2 silicone baking molds that total 4 cups (1L) in capacity.

Wash and dry a 1-quart (1L) mason jar, rinse it in boiling water, and let dry and cool to room temperature.

In a high-powered blender, combine the cashews, sauerkraut juice, yogurt, fermented tofu, and sea salt. Process on high speed until smooth and creamy, 1 or 2 minutes. Transfer the mixture to the mason jar, cover with a lid, and place in a warm window or other location with a temperature of 70°F (21°C) or higher. Let it sit for 24 to 72 hours to ferment, until it has achieved a sharpness to your liking. (The cooler the location, the longer it will take.)

Whisk the melted coconut oil into the fermented cheese mixture until it is fully incorporated.

In a small pot, whisk together the water and agar-agar. Cover, bring to a boil over medium heat, and cook until completely dissolved and the mixture drips off your whisk like molten glass. This could take 2 to 3 minutes or longer. The agar-agar must reach about 205°F (96°C) to activate its gelling properties, so be patient.

Add the cheese mixture all at once into the agar-agar and use a whisk to mix well. Whisk the tapioca starch mixture into the pot. Continue to cook, stirring with the whisk, until it becomes as thick as cooked polenta, stretchy, and shiny.

Pour the mixture into the lined bowl or mold and refrigerate overnight to firm up.

It can be used immediately, or you can let it firm up through an aging process; just wrap in wax paper or parchment and leave in the fridge for a couple of weeks until the desired hardness is achieved. (You can refrigerate it for another month after that.)

VARIATIONS

Sharp Cheddar

Add 2 tablespoons nutritional yeast and 1 tablespoon miso to the mixture in the blender. The rest of the recipe is the same.

Pepper Jack

When you add the fermented cheese to the agar-agar, add ½ cup chopped brined jalapeños. The rest of the recipe is the same.

Smoked Gouda

When you add the fermented cheese to the agar-agar, stir in 1 teaspoon liquid smoke. The rest of the recipe is the same.

COOK'S NOTES

- Make sure the sauerkraut is raw, actually fermented, and not pasteurized; its label should indicate that it contains live active cultures or probiotics, which you need to create the right flavor during this cheese's aging.

- Chinese fermented bean curd or tofu is a creamy, delicious product sold in cubes in jars: It is tofu that has been marinated in brine for months, achieving a smooth, spreadable, cheese-like texture and flavor. You can buy this in Asian grocery stores or online. Buy the plain one, not the spicy.

Velvety Tofu Cream Cheese

The combination of tofu and coconut oil makes a great base for a creamy spread, with lemon juice and miso providing a little tartness and umami—all elements of classic cream cheese. Be sure to use refined coconut oil, which has a neutral flavor. And while this spread is excellent by itself, you can also customize it by mixing in any ingredients you like—it's a blank canvas!

Makes 2½ cups

Time: Weekend

Storage: Refrigerate for up to 2 weeks.

1 (14-ounce/397g) block firm tofu, drained
½ cup (120ml) refined coconut oil, melted
2 tablespoons fresh lemon juice
1 teaspoon white miso, homemade (page 83) or store-bought
1 teaspoon fine sea salt

CRUMBLE THE TOFU INTO a food processor or blender. Add the coconut oil, lemon juice, miso, and salt and process on high until completely smooth, scraping down the sides of the container occasionally; this will take a few minutes, especially as the melted coconut oil can briefly clump.

When smooth and velvety in texture, transfer the mixture to an airtight container and chill until firm, about 4 hours.

VARIATIONS

Scallion Dill Tofu Cream Cheese

Add 4 finely sliced scallions, 4 finely chopped sprigs of dill, and 1 teaspoon garlic powder.

Maple Walnut Tofu Cream Cheese

Add ½ cup (60g) finely chopped toasted walnuts and ¼ cup (60ml) maple syrup.

Smoky Red Pepper Tofu Cream Cheese

Add ½ cup (120g) finely chopped roasted red peppers and 1 teaspoon smoked paprika.

Zesty Jalapeño Tofu Cream Cheese

Add ¼ cup (60g) finely chopped jalapeño, 1 teaspoon grated lime zest, and 2 teaspoons fresh lime juice.

Lemon-Brined Tofu Feta

Brining tofu cubes in a mixture of lemon, pickle brine (this is no-waste cooking!), and dill gives it the tart brightness of feta.

Makes 1 cup

Time: Weekend

Storage: Refrigerate for up to 2 weeks.

8 ounces (225g) firm, water-packed tofu, drained but liquid reserved
2 or 3 sprigs fresh dill
Several strips lemon zest
½ cup (120ml) fresh lemon juice (from 3 to 4 lemons)
⅓ cup (80ml) pickle brine (from any jar of pickles you have)
1 teaspoon fine sea salt

CUT THE TOFU INTO ½-inch (1.3cm) cubes. Pack the cubes loosely into a 12-ounce (355ml) jar or other lidded container, tucking in the sprigs of dill and lemon zest strips.

In a small bowl, whisk together the lemon juice, pickle brine, and salt. Pour the liquid into the jar with the tofu. If the tofu is not submerged in the liquid, use the reserved tofu water to cover. Place the lid on the jar and shake lightly, then refrigerate for at least 3 days before eating.

Creamy or Crumbly Almond Queso Fresco

When food blogger Dora Stone went vegan, giving up cheese was the hardest thing. She never liked the processed cheese substitutes and was generally frustrated with complicated vegan cheese recipes. Sound familiar? That's why her recipe for this cheese is perfect. Thanks to fatty almonds, the result is a creamy queso fresco reminiscent of fresh farmer cheese. This recipe also shows you how to turn it into a crumblier cheese. Note that the nutritional yeast, which adds a nutty flavor, also gives this cheese a light-yellow color. So if you prefer your cheese to be white, omit it. Use it fresh for snacking or to fill chiles rellenos, or crumbly for sprinkling on enchiladas, tostadas, sopes, chilaquiles, salads, grain bowls, and more.

Makes 1 cup

Time: Weekend

Storage: Refrigerate the fresh version for up to 4 days and the baked, crumbly version for up to 3 months.

Boiling water

1¼ cups (140g) slivered almonds

1 garlic clove, peeled but whole

4½ teaspoons avocado oil or olive oil

2 teaspoons fresh lemon juice, plus more to taste

2 teaspoons brine from a jar of olives

1 teaspoon nutritional yeast

½ teaspoon fine salt, plus more to taste

IN A HEATPROOF BOWL, pour enough boiling water over the almonds to cover. Let soak for 1 hour, then drain.

In a food processor, combine the soaked almonds, garlic, oil, lemon juice, olive brine, nutritional yeast, and salt. Process until the mixture gets a creamy, slightly grainy texture similar to that of ricotta cheese and starts to gather into a bigger ball, about 3 minutes. Taste and season with more salt and/or lemon juice as needed. Scrape down the sides of the bowl and process for 1 more minute.

Place a fine-mesh sieve over a bowl and line it with two layers of moistened cheesecloth. Transfer the almond mixture to the cheesecloth. Gather the corners of the cloth and twist the top gently, forming a cheese ball and draining any excess liquid if there is any.

Refrigerate 6 to 8 hours or overnight (still set in the sieve over the bowl), then unwrap the cheese to use and transfer it to an airtight storage container.

If you want a crumbly cheese, preheat the oven to 325°F (160°C). Press the unwrapped cheese into a flat disk about 1¼ inches (3cm) thick. Transfer to a baking dish and bake until the cheese starts to brown on top, for about 10 minutes. Flip and bake until the cheese is golden brown all over, 10 more minutes. Let cool, then crumble with your hands into a bowl to use immediately or transfer to a storage container.

Umami-Packed Cashew Parm

This simple sprinkle is just the thing to use to top your pasta dishes, salads, and more. Use in Lentil-Chickpea Meatballs in Tomato Sauce (page 330), Ceci e Pepe (page 228), and anywhere you want a little salty, nutty, cheesy hit.

Makes scant 1 cup

Time: Weekday

Storage: Room temperature for up to 2 weeks.

¾ cup (100g) raw cashew halves or pieces

1 tablespoon nutritional yeast

½ teaspoon garlic powder

¼ teaspoon fine sea salt

IN A FOOD PROCESSOR, pulse the cashews, nutritional yeast, garlic powder, and salt until the mixture is the texture of coarse sand. Use immediately or transfer to a jar for storage.

Goat-Style Cheese Rolled in Herbs

Easy to make and absolutely lovely, this slightly crumbly "goat cheese" can be as mild or tangy as you like depending on how long you ferment it. Feel free to change up the herbs based on what is available, adding in a few chile flakes for a bit of heat, or lemon zest for some added perkiness. You can also leave out the herbs and instead roll the cheese in a coating such as smoked paprika or black pepper, or just leave it plain and serve it topped with lemon marmalade, a beautiful combination.

Makes 1 pound

Time: Weekend

Storage: Refrigerate for up to 3 weeks, freeze for up to 3 months.

CHEESE

1½ cups (195g) raw cashews, soaked in water for 2 to 4 hours, then drained

¼ cup (60ml) water

¼ cup (39g) fermented raw sauerkraut with active probiotics, in juice (see Note, page 25)

¼ cup (60ml) Creamy Coconut Yogurt (page 23) or other nondairy yogurt, plain and unsweetened, plus more if needed

2 tablespoons unsweetened coconut cream

½ teaspoon fine sea salt

½ cup (120ml) refined coconut oil, melted

HERB MIXTURE

½ cup (25g) finely chopped fresh parsley

2 tablespoons finely chopped fresh tarragon

1 tablespoon finely chopped fresh marjoram or oregano

1 tablespoon flaky sea salt, such as Maldon

WASH AND DRY A 1-quart (1L) mason jar, rinse it in boiling water, and let dry and cool to room temperature.

Make the cheese: In a blender, combine the drained cashews, water, sauerkraut, yogurt, coconut cream, and salt and blend until smooth, about 60 seconds or longer, depending on the strength of your blender. Add the coconut oil and process again until very smooth. (It's important to add the coconut oil after blending the initial ingredients to prevent it from hardening in the blender, which can happen if the temperature of all the other ingredients combined is below 76°F/24°C.) Using an instant-read thermometer, make sure that the temperature does not exceed 110°F (43°C) after processing. If it does, allow it to cool to that or below, then add an additional 2 tablespoons yogurt and very briefly blend to combine.

Pour the mixture into the sterilized mason jar, secure with a lid, then set in a warm place (ideally between 85° and 110°F (29° and 43°C) to ferment for 12 to 24 hours. The warmer the temperature, the faster the fermentation. Suggested places are outside on a warm day, in a sunny window, near a fireplace or in a yogurt maker or an oven with the light turned on. Taste after 12 hours to see if it has achieved the desired tang of goat cheese. Transfer the container to the refrigerator and allow it to set for a full 24 hours.

Prepare the herb mixture: In a bowl, whisk together the parsley, tarragon, marjoram, and flaky salt. Spread out on a clean surface or sheet of compostable parchment paper.

On a clean surface, spread a sheet of compostable plastic wrap or parchment paper. Scoop out half the hardened cheese and put it on the sheet, loosely wrap the plastic or parchment around it, and form a log about 4 inches (10cm) long. Remove the log from the sheet and roll it in the herbs. Repeat with the remaining cheese (of course, you can just make one long log if you like). Wrap the logs tightly in plastic wrap or parchment and refrigerate until serving.

Cashew Queso

As a transplanted Texan who avoids cheese, I sometimes—okay, often—get a hankering for real Tex-Mex–style queso, the dip traditionally made in home kitchens with just two ingredients, Velveeta and Ro-Tel brand canned tomatoes with green chiles. My plant-based version depends on a few vegan pantry all-stars: raw cashews for the creamy base, nutritional yeast for nutty flavor, miso for umami, and turmeric for color. Potato starch adds the gooeyness that all queso should have, and I don't think I could call this recipe queso without a can of those tomatoes and chiles. Queso is best served with tortilla chips and margaritas, but it's also delicious as a substitute for enchilada sauce for rolled tortillas, or even to make mac and cheese.

Makes 4 to 5 cups (8 to 10 servings)

Time: Weekday

Storage: Refrigerate for up to 4 days. Freezing not recommended.

- 2 cups (260g) raw cashews, soaked overnight (see Note) and drained
- 2 cups (470ml) plus 1 tablespoon warm water
- ½ cup (40g) nutritional yeast
- 2 tablespoons potato starch
- 1 teaspoon ground turmeric
- 1 teaspoon fine sea salt, plus more to taste
- 1 (10-ounce/283g) can diced tomatoes with green chiles (such as Ro-Tel brand), or 1 cup canned diced tomatoes plus ¼ cup chopped pickled jalapeños
- 1 tablespoon red wine vinegar
- 1 tablespoon white miso, homemade (page 83) or store-bought
- Tortilla chips, for serving

IN A BLENDER, COMBINE the cashews, 2 cups (470ml) of the water, the nutritional yeast, potato starch, turmeric, and salt. Puree until smooth.

Transfer the mixture to a small saucepan. Stir in the tomatoes/green chiles (plus all their juices) and the vinegar and slowly heat the mixture over medium-low heat without bringing it to a boil, stirring and scraping the sides and bottom of the pan occasionally with a silicone spatula to avoid scorching. (If you heat the mixture too fast, without stirring, it can get clumpy.) When it is hot but not bubbling, reduce the heat to low.

In a small bowl, whisk the miso with the remaining 1 tablespoon water until smooth. Stir into the queso,

taste, and add more salt if needed. Keep on low heat, stirring occasionally, for serving. (You can also transfer it to a slow cooker for serving, if you'd like to keep it warm for a party.)

Serve hot with tortilla chips.

COOK'S NOTE: If you are using a Vitamix or other high-powered blender, skip soaking the cashews.

Fluffy Pumpkin Seed Ricotta

Here's an incredibly simple cheese without the addition of any oils and packed with protein and fiber. It's light and delicious in dishes such as lasagna and stuffed shells. Be forewarned, however—it's tinted the palest green! You can tell your friends you got it on your trip to the moon, which as we all know is made of cheese.

Makes about 1½ pounds (3½ cups)

Time: Weekday

Storage: Refrigerate for up to 1 week. The leftover "whey" can be refrigerated for up to 5 days or frozen for up to 3 months.

- 1 cup (130g) raw or sprouted pumpkin seeds
- ⅔ cup (85g) raw cashews
- 4 cups (950ml) water
- 1 teaspoon fine sea salt

IN A HIGH-POWERED BLENDER, combine the pumpkin seeds, cashews, and water and process until very smooth.

Transfer the mixture to a saucepan over medium-low heat. Heat the nut milk, scraping the bottom and side with a silicone spatula occasionally, until it comes to a boil, which can take up to 1 hour. As it heats up, it will form tiny curds and solidify, with the boiling bubbles formed from the "whey" or water.

When the whole mass has formed curds, set a large fine-mesh sieve over a bowl and pour the mixture into the sieve. Let the mixture drain for about 1 hour, or until it stops dripping. (Use the leftover "whey" liquid instead of nut milks in smoothies, porridges, and oats.)

Stir in the salt and transfer to a storage container.

Alpine-Style Aged Cheese

This lovely, mild cheese with a nutty flavor is your payoff for a few weeks of patience, as that's how long it takes to achieve the right firmness. The actual cheesemaking is relatively easy, however, and you'll end up with a cheese that can be used in all sorts of dishes, from raclette and fondue to a grilled cheese with apples. It's also fantastic just eaten plain.

Makes about 1½ pounds

Time: Project

Storage: Refrigerate for up to 4 months.

1½ cups (195g) raw cashews, soaked for 3 to 4 hours in tepid water and drained

⅓ cup (34g) frozen young coconut, thawed (see Note)

⅓ cup (52g) fermented raw sauerkraut with active probiotics, in juice (see Note, page 25)

6 tablespoons (60g) potato starch or tapioca starch

¼ cup (35g) pine nuts

2 tablespoons plain nondairy yogurt, plus more if needed

2 tablespoons nutritional yeast

1 teaspoon fine sea salt

⅔ cup (160ml) refined coconut oil, melted

½ cup (120ml) water

1 tablespoon agar-agar powder

BRINE

4 cups (950ml) boiling water

⅓ cup (80g) fine salt

LINE A SMALL BOWL with plastic wrap or have on hand 1 to 2 silicone baking molds that total 4 cups (1L) in capacity. Wash and dry a 1-quart (1L) mason jar, rinse it in boiling water, and let dry and cool to room temperature.

In a high-powered blender, combine the soaked cashews, coconut, sauerkraut, potato starch, pine nuts, yogurt, nutritional yeast, and salt. Process until the mixture is thick, creamy, and sticky and no dry patches of starch remain. Using an instant-read thermometer, make sure that the mixture doesn't exceed 110°F (43°C), or the cultures in the sauerkraut and yogurt could die and the cheese will not ferment. If your mixture is hotter than that, don't fear. Let it cool to 110°F (43°C) or below, add another 2 tablespoons of yogurt, and briefly blend just to combine.

Pour the mixture into the sterilized mason jar, cover with cheesecloth, and place in a warm location (between 85° and 110°F/29° and 43°C) for 12 to 24 hours. Locations to ferment can be a sunny window, by a fireplace, outdoors on a sunny day, in an oven with the light turned on, in a yogurt maker, etc. If you are fermenting it outdoors or in a warm part of the house, you can help retain the temperature by wrapping the container in a towel. If your only options are cooler spots, you might need to let the mixture ferment longer.

Taste the mixture after 12 hours to see if it has achieved the right amount of sharpness. If it still tastes like cashews, keep fermenting until it starts tasting cheesy and has your desired level of sharpness. Alpine cheeses tend to be fairly mild, so don't overferment.

Transfer the mixture to a 1-quart (1L) heavy-bottomed pot over medium heat. Cook the mixture, stirring constantly and scraping the bottom and sides with a silicone spatula, until it is as thick as cooked polenta, smooth, glossy, and very stretchy. Transfer the mixture to the blender.

Add the coconut oil and pulse for 15 to 20 seconds to incorporate the oil. Do not overprocess or you could lose the stretchy texture formed by the starch.

In the same pot, whisk together the water and agar-agar powder. Cover, bring the mixture to a boil over medium heat. This could take 3 to 4 minutes. The agar-agar must reach 205°F (96°C) for it to be activated—if you don't have a thermometer, just cook it until the mixture is boiling rapidly and drips like caramel from a spatula or whisk.

Quickly pour the agar-agar into the mixture in the blender and process again for 5 to 10 seconds, just until fully incorporated and the mixture is smooth, stretchy, and glossy. Pour the mixture into the lined bowl or prepared mold. Refrigerate the cheese for at least 8 hours until firm.

Make the brine: In a container large enough to hold the cheese, combine the boiling water and salt and set aside at room temperature. (If you are in a hurry, you can dissolve the salt in a cup of boiling water, then add ice and water to bring it up to 4 cups.)

After the cheese is fully firm, unmold it. Put the cheese in the brine and let it sit for 10 minutes. Flip the cheese over and let it sit for another 10 minutes. Remove the cheese from the water and place on a wire rack to drain until it is dry, at least 1 hour or longer.

Loosely wrap the cheese in compostable parchment paper or cheesecloth and place in the refrigerator on a wire rack for 2 to 4 weeks to age. Flip the cheese twice a week and swap out the parchment or cheesecloth if it becomes moist. The cheese will get firmer over time.

When the cheese has achieved a firmness to your liking, wrap tightly in beeswax paper for storage. You can also keep aging it to become firmer and firmer by keeping it in parchment or cheesecloth.

COOK'S NOTE: Young coconut—not the same as shredded coconut—can be purchased frozen either online or in Asian grocery stores or some natural foods stores.

Charred Allium Dashi

Dashi is the backbone of many Japanese dishes, from miso soup and okonomiyaki to oyakodon and shabu shabu. Awase dashi—traditionally made with dried kombu and dried bonito (tuna) flakes—is delicate, with subtle salinity and umami. Here, dried shiitake mushrooms fill in for bonito flakes, and a secret savory ingredient gets added: leek tops (the dark green ones that often end up in the compost bin). Broiled until just starting to char, they bring a little smokiness and gentle sweetness to the broth without overwhelming it with oniony flavor.

Use wherever dashi is called for, such as the base of soups or to cook rice.

Makes 6 cups

Time: Weekday

Storage: Refrigerate for up to 4 days or freeze for up to 3 months.

Dark-green tops from 1 leek (115g), rinsed well and dried

5 or 6 dried shiitake mushrooms

6 cups (1.4L) filtered water

2 (5-inch/13cm) pieces dried kombu

POSITION A RACK 6 INCHES (15cm) from the broiler and preheat the broiler for 15 minutes.

Pull the leek top apart and arrange the individual leaves in an even layer. Broil until the edges start to char and parts of the greens start to blister, 4 to 5 minutes. Transfer the leek tops to a large pot.

Add the dried shiitakes and water to the pot and bring to a simmer over medium-high heat. Turn off the heat, add the kombu, gently stir, making sure everything is submerged, and steep for 20 minutes.

Pour through a fine-mesh sieve. Save the mushrooms and kombu for another use (see Note).

COOK'S NOTE: Don't throw away the rehydrated mushrooms or kombu. Both are great thinly sliced and added to salads or miso soup.

Wildflower Cider Syrup

Since vegans avoid honey (an animal by-product), plant-based cooking often depends on alternatives. The idea for this recipe first came to me when I tasted a bee-free honey product several years ago; when I flipped it over to read the label, I saw: apples. So *that's* why it reminded me of boiled cider, a favorite syrup-like ingredient from my many years of living in New England. I also remembered how easy it was to make—just boil apple cider down for hours—and how long it keeps (almost indefinitely). I got another great idea from the blog Get Set Vegan, whose recipe uses whole apples, sugar, and—another lightbulb moment—chamomile tea bags to add that floral element all good honey possesses. So now I add tea (a chamomile-lavender combination is my current favorite) to the cider for the first bit of boiling, then take it out before the syrup starts reducing, and love the result. Use this, obviously, anywhere you'd use honey, but be forewarned: Its extra tang makes it even better.

Makes 2 cups

Time: Weekend

Storage: Refrigerate for up to 3 months.

1 gallon (3.8L) apple cider
4 chamomile or other floral tea bags

POUR 2 CUPS (470ML) OF the cider into a 5-quart (5L) or larger pot (such as a Dutch oven), stick a chopstick in and use a piece of masking tape or a marker to mark the level of the liquid. Set 5 small spoons on a plate in the freezer. (You'll use the chopstick and spoons later to help judge when your cider has reduced enough.)

Set the pot over medium-high heat, pour in the remaining cider, and add the tea bags. Bring to a boil and boil for 10 minutes, skimming off any impurities that bubble up, then remove the tea bags.

Boil the syrup until it reduces to almost 2 cups (470ml), using the chopstick to gauge, 1½ to 2 hours. When the bubbles are so small, vigorous, and foamlike that it's difficult to see the depth of the liquid, reduce the heat to medium or medium-low, as much as needed until they are gentle.

As the syrup gets closer to being finished, it speeds up, so watch carefully to keep it from reducing too much, at which point it can turn bitter and as sticky as taffy. Test the syrup by dipping in one of the spoons from the freezer, set it on the plate, and return it to the freezer for a few minutes (similar to testing whether a jam has gelled). If it has the consistency of thick honey, it's ready. If it's too thin, cook a little longer and test again.

Transfer the syrup to a sterilized glass jar or jars and refrigerate.

Vegetable Scrap Stock

This recipe takes vegetable odds and ends that are usually thrown away and turns them into a delicious stock that deepens the flavor of cooked grains, soups, and stews.

Whenever you peel a carrot, chop some garlic, or slice an onion, transfer the scraps to a bag in the freezer. When you have enough scraps, you can roast them, perhaps with miso, resulting in an umami-packed stock—a technique similar to that of *Bon Appétit*'s Andy Baraghani. But if you are short on time, you can skip that step and go straight to the stockpot.

Avoid using bitter greens (such as arugula, watercress, and kale), cruciferous vegetables (such as broccoli, cauliflower, and cabbage), and other strongly flavored scraps (such as chiles, beets, and woodsy herbs), which can dominate the stock's taste. Other than that, it's hard to go wrong with scraps for your stock. Still, I suggest starting with onion, garlic, celery, and carrot scraps for your first stock, then adding other scraps in future batches, learning how the flavor changes as you go.

Makes about 6 cups

Time: Weekend

Storage: Refrigerate for up to 5 days or freeze for up to 3 months.

- 1 pound (450g) vegetable scraps, such as garlic tops, bottoms, and skins; onion tops, bottoms, and skins; carrot tops, bottoms, and peel; celery leaves and bottoms
- 1 tablespoon red or white miso (optional), homemade (page 83) or store-bought
- ½ tablespoon black peppercorns (optional)
- 1 bay leaf (optional)
- 10 cups (2.4L) water

PREHEAT THE OVEN TO 350°F (180°C).

Arrange the vegetable scraps in a flat layer on a sheet pan. Add the miso (if using) and massage it into the scraps with your hands. Roast until the scraps have taken on color and have shrunk and shriveled, about 1 hour.

Transfer the scraps to a large soup pot or Dutch oven. Add the peppercorns and bay leaf, if using. Add the water and bring to a boil over high heat. Reduce to a simmer and cook for at least 30 minutes or longer for stronger stock.

Set a sieve over a large bowl and carefully pour the stock over the sieve without pressing the scraps down; this keeps any grit from getting through. Compost the scraps.

Allow the stock to cool before transferring into sealable containers.

Veg Bouillon

Along with making scrap stock, this DIY bouillon cube is my strategy for avoiding store-bought vegetable broth. This technique mashes up two good recipes: One from Miyoko's Creamery founder Miyoko Schinner, who smartly employs miso for umami; and one from America's Test Kitchen, which uses leeks for mild onion flavor and tomato paste for even more umami.

Makes 1¾ cups (14 bouillon cubes)

Time: Weekday

Storage: Freeze in ice cube trays until solid, then transfer to zip-top bags and freeze for up to six months.

- 2 leeks, white and light green parts only, chopped and washed thoroughly (1½ cups/113g)
- 2 carrots, peeled and cut into ½-inch (1.3cm) pieces (⅔ cup/85g)
- ¼ cup (72g) white miso, homemade (page 83) or store-bought
- 1 cup (30g) lightly packed fresh parsley leaves and thin stems
- 3 tablespoons tamari
- 2 tablespoons tomato paste
- 1 tablespoon onion powder
- 1 tablespoon granulated garlic
- 1 tablespoon celery seeds

IN A FOOD PROCESSOR, combine the leeks, carrots, miso, parsley, tamari, tomato paste, onion powder, granulated garlic, and celery seeds and puree until smooth.

Transfer the mixture to small ice cube trays, using 2 tablespoons per cube, and freeze.

To use, combine 1 cube with 1 cup (240ml) boiling water and let sit until the cube melts. Whisk to combine and use however you would use vegetable broth. (If desired, you can pour the broth through a fine-mesh sieve to strain out the solids.)

Advieh

This is the great Najmieh Batmanglij's simple, beautiful version of the Iranian spice blend from her magnum opus, *Food of Life*, and I can't imagine trying to improve on it. Advieh's deceptively simple combination of floral notes and warmth makes it quite possibly the most complex thing to come from four ingredients that I've ever tasted. Use in rice, sprinkle on roasted vegetables, stir into soups and stews, and more.

Makes about ½ cup

Time: Weekday

Storage: Cool, dark place in an airtight container for up to 3 months.

> ½ cup (10g) dried organic rose petals, plus more if needed
> 2 tablespoons ground cinnamon
> 2 tablespoons ground cardamom
> 2 tablespoons ground cumin

IN A DEDICATED SPICE or clean coffee grinder, grind the rose petals until fine. You should have about 2 tablespoons. (If you end up with less, grind some more petals, and if you end up with more, save it for the next batch.)

In a small bowl, mix together the ground rose petals, cinnamon, cardamom, and cumin.

Baharat

This is one of those spice blends that is adapted widely from region to region, family to family, throughout the Levant. The thrust with this version is to achieve the recognizable fragrance and flavor of Middle Eastern food. Baharat packs a ton of flavor, so start with a pinch, tasting and adding more if needed. Use it on roasted vegetables, any cooked legume, or mixed with olive oil and lemon as a marinade. A dusting on hummus lands you a favorite dip with authentic Arabic flavor.

Makes about ⅔ cup

Time: Weekday

Storage: Cool, dark place in an airtight container for up to 3 months.

> 2 tablespoons ground cumin
> 2 tablespoons ground coriander
> 2 tablespoons ground nutmeg
> 2 tablespoons sweet paprika
> 4 teaspoons ground cardamom
> 1 tablespoon freshly ground black pepper
> 1 teaspoon ground cinnamon
> 1 teaspoon ground cloves

IN A MEDIUM BOWL, whisk together all the ingredients until combined.

Berbere

This fiery bedrock of Ethiopian cuisine is becoming more available in stores, but it can vary in heat and composition. So if you want freshness and consistency, make your own. This quick version uses all ground spices and yields enough to make two batches of the classic lentil dish Misir Wat (page 179), with a couple tablespoons left over. Toss vegetables, tofu, or tempeh with it before roasting or grilling, stir a little into a vinaigrette, or use it to coat Roasted Pumpkin Seeds (page 117).

Makes about ½ cup

Time: Weekday

Storage: Cool, dark place in an airtight container for up to 1 month.

4 tablespoons ground New Mexico chile

2 tablespoons sweet paprika

1 teaspoon cayenne pepper

½ teaspoon ground cardamom

½ teaspoon ground coriander

½ teaspoon ground cumin

½ teaspoon ground ginger

½ teaspoon mustard powder

½ teaspoon granulated onion

¼ teaspoon ground allspice

¼ teaspoon ground cinnamon

¼ teaspoon ground cloves

¼ teaspoon garlic powder

¼ teaspoon ground nutmeg

IN A SMALL SKILLET, combine all the spices and cook over medium heat, stirring constantly, until fragrant, about 4 minutes. Let cool completely before storing.

Cajun Seasoning

I've long felt a connection to the foodways of Louisiana, especially the Cajun and Creole cooking of New Orleans. Not only have I regularly visited the Crescent City since my college years in Texas, but one of my dearest friends, Edouard Fontenot, hails from Cajun country, and so do the grandparents of my husband, Carl, who was born and raised in Houston. Edouard is one of the best cooks—and gardeners—I know, so when I was looking for a homemade substitute for Carl's beloved Tony Chachere's brand seasoning, I knew whom to ask. Edouard's grandmother used fresh garlic and scallions in her fairly simple mix of just six total ingredients, but over the years Edouard has added a few more—and when he gives it as gifts he subs in granulated garlic and onion powder for the fresh vegetables. That's the way I immediately started making it, because I want something I can keep in my spice cabinet, not the fridge or freezer. Use this whenever and wherever you want to bring a spicy Louisiana kick to your cooking: red kidney beans, roasted tofu, rice and other grains, vegetables, soups, on popcorn, and on Roasted Pumpkin Seeds (page 117).

Makes about ⅔ cup

Time: Weekday

Storage: Cool, dark place in an airtight container for up to 3 months.

2 tablespoons fine sea salt

2 tablespoons granulated garlic

1 tablespoon ground black pepper

1 tablespoon cayenne pepper

1 tablespoon onion powder

1 tablespoon sweet paprika

1 tablespoon dried thyme

2½ teaspoons dried oregano

2½ teaspoons ground white pepper

IN A SMALL BOWL, whisk together all the ingredients until combined.

Chinese Five-Spice Powder

This spice blend, a staple in Chinese cooking, can bring a touch of warming sweetness to a wealth of dishes, including roasted or braised tofu, broths, even snacks like roasted nuts or popcorn. It is also a beautiful substitute for cinnamon or pumpkin pie spice mix in baked goods. This recipe is based on one in Eileen Yin-Fei Lo's *Mastering the Art of Chinese Cooking*.

Makes a scant ½ cup

Time: Weekday

Storage: Cool, dark place in an airtight container for up to 3 months.

- 10 whole star anise
- 5 (2½-inch/6.5cm) cinnamon sticks
- 1 tablespoon aniseed or fennel seeds
- 1½ teaspoons whole cloves
- 1½ teaspoons Sichuan peppercorns

USE A MALLET OR rolling pin to break the star anise and cinnamon sticks into pieces.

Set a medium skillet over medium-high heat, add the spices, and immediately reduce the heat to medium. Toast the spices, shaking the pan frequently, until very fragrant, 1 to 2 minutes, adjusting the heat as needed to prevent burning. Transfer the spices to a bowl and let cool completely.

Transfer the mixture to a dedicated spice grinder or clean coffee grinder and process to a coarse powder.

Dukkah

This Egyptian spice-and-nut blend is one of those mixes, like za'atar, that is delicious eaten on its own, perhaps as a dip with bread you've first dunked in olive oil. But you'd be missing out if you didn't also sprinkle it liberally on salads, such as Avocado Salad with Dukkah Croutons & Harissa Dressing (page 150), roasted vegetables, and soups, where it becomes more than a seasoning: It's a garnish! Feel free to use blanched/peeled hazelnuts instead of the almonds; they're more traditional, but they're harder to find, and I'll do anything to avoid having to peel the hazelnuts myself. You can also substitute other nuts; pistachios are particularly nice here. This is adapted from Egypt native Claudia Roden's recipe in *The Oldways Table* and *A Middle Eastern Feast*.

Makes about 2 cups

Time: Weekday

Storage: Cool, dark place in an airtight container for up to 1 month.

- ¾ cup (58g) coriander seeds
- ½ cup (60g) sesame seeds
- ¼ cup (30g) cumin seeds
- ⅓ cup (45g) unsalted roasted almonds
- ¼ teaspoon fine sea salt, plus more to taste
- ⅛ teaspoon freshly ground black pepper

IN A LARGE DRY skillet, toast the coriander, sesame, and cumin seeds over medium heat, shaking and stirring the pan frequently, until fragrant, about 2 minutes. Transfer them to a food processor.

Add the almonds, salt, and pepper and process until they are finely crushed but not pulverized. (You want to be careful not to turn this into a paste.) Taste and add more salt if needed.

Garam Masala

In Hindi, *garam* means "warm" and *masala* means a "spice mixture." As soon as you taste this freshly made blend from DC chef K.N. Vinod, you'll understand why. Most people incorrectly assume that garam masala is always ground, but in fact in India and in Indian markets it's also sold as a whole spice mix. Keep that in mind when playing around with this versatile blend: For instance, bloom the whole spices in hot oil and then add to rice before steaming, or use them to infuse liquor for cocktails. The powder is typically used to finish a dish and in marinades; try it sprinkled on roasted tofu or tempeh, on Roasted Pumpkin Seeds (page 117), or even on popcorn (perhaps combined with nutritional yeast).

Makes ¾ cup

Time: Weekday

Storage: Cool, dark place in an airtight container for up to 1 month.

2 tablespoons coriander seeds
1 tablespoon cumin seeds
1 tablespoon green cardamom pods
1 teaspoon fennel seeds
1 teaspoon black peppercorns
1 teaspoon whole cloves
2 bay leaves
2 small pieces mace
2 whole star anise
2 small cinnamon sticks
¼ teaspoon freshly grated nutmeg

IN A SMALL SKILLET, combine all the spices except the nutmeg. Cook over low heat, shaking the skillet frequently, until they turn fragrant and some of them start to lightly brown in spots, about 2 minutes.

Transfer them to a dedicated spice grinder and let cool. Once they're cool, grind them to a fine powder. Stir in the nutmeg.

Milaga Podi

This Indian spice mix, also known as gunpowder, gets its name from its heat: *Podi* means "powder" in several South Indian languages such as Tamil and Malayalam, while *milaga* means "chile." Podis are made in various permutations, with various combinations of chile, lentils, seeds, and more—some even incorporate nuts, coconut, and/or tamarind.

Combine a small amount of the finished podi with oil to make into a paste, spread onto flatbread, or use as a marinade for tofu or tempeh.

This mix can also be used dry: Sprinkle on stewed beans, roasted cabbage or potatoes, steamed eggplant, and sautéed mushrooms. You can find all the ingredients in a good Indian market, such as the Patel Brothers.

Makes 1 cup

Time: Weekday

Storage: Cool, dark place in an airtight container for up to 1 month.

2 tablespoons toor dal (aka arhar dal; dried split yellow pigeon peas)
2 tablespoons chana dal (dried split chickpeas)
2 tablespoons urad dal (split peeled matpe beans)
2 tablespoons roasted chana dal (roasted split chickpeas)
3 dried red chiles, preferably Kashmiri
2 tablespoons white sesame seeds
2 tablespoons basmati rice
¼ teaspoon black peppercorns
⅛ teaspoon asafetida (aka hing)
¼ teaspoon fine sea salt, plus more to taste
2 sprigs fresh curry leaves (optional)

IN A MEDIUM CAST-IRON or other heavy-bottomed skillet, combine all the ingredients. Cook over low heat for about 10 minutes, stirring occasionally, until the ingredients become very fragrant, and the rice starts to take on a light golden color.

Transfer to a bowl to prevent further cooking and let cool slightly. Transfer to a spice mill or clean coffee grinder and process just until coarsely ground.

Jerk Spice

Jerk seasoning, native to Jamaica, is known for its fiery combination of Scotch bonnet peppers and allspice. This take on the rub is made with pantry staples and offers a delightful marriage of opposites—heat and sweet, with warming undertones. Use it on Stewed Jerk Lentils (page 179), or anywhere you'd like a taste of the Caribbean, in any other bean dish, on popcorn (perhaps with nutritional yeast), or sprinkled on tofu, tempeh, or your favorite vegetable before (or after) roasting.

Makes a scant ½ cup

Time: Weekday

Storage: Cool, dark place in an airtight container for up to 3 months.

    2 tablespoons ground allspice
    2 teaspoons light or dark brown sugar
    2 teaspoons ground cinnamon
    2 teaspoons granulated garlic
    2 teaspoons ground ginger
    2 teaspoons ground nutmeg
    2 teaspoons dried thyme
    2 teaspoons fine sea salt
    ½ teaspoon cayenne pepper

IN A SMALL BOWL, whisk together all the ingredients until combined.

Peri Peri

This blend from Angel Gregorio, creator and curator of The Spice Suite in Washington, DC, is a vibrant, citrusy, and slightly spicy take on the classic South African mix. Use it for any vegetable or bean dish, as a rub for roasted or grilled tofu or tempeh, on popcorn, or on Roasted Pumpkin Seeds (page 117). Angel loves to mix it into a little olive oil and some smoked balsamic vinegar to brush on vegetables or other foods after grilling.

Makes ½ cup

Time: Weekday

Storage: Cool, dark place in an airtight container for up to 3 months.

    1½ tablespoons onion powder
    1 tablespoon smoked paprika
    1 tablespoon ground cumin
    1 tablespoon garlic powder
    1 tablespoon dried oregano
    1½ teaspoons dehydrated granulated lemon peel
    1½ teaspoons bird's-eye chile flakes
    1½ teaspoons freshly ground black pepper
    1 teaspoon fine sea salt

IN A SMALL BOWL, whisk together all the ingredients until combined.

Ras el Hanout

"I like to think of spices the way a painter thinks of paint," the great Moroccan chef Mourad Lahlou wrote in his 2011 cookbook *Mourad*. You interpret the "painting" as you go, adding a little more of this or that, depending on the effect you're after. In fact, Morocco's *ras el hanout* translates from the Arabic as "top of the shop," meaning it's a blend of a vendor's best spices and therefore customizable depending on anyone's tastes. Lahlou, owner of the San Francisco restaurants Aziza and Mourad, told me he usually works with a half-dozen versions of ras el hanout in his kitchen at any one time. Sure enough, when I asked him for a recipe, he developed a new take from the ground up, offering this gorgeous and fragrant blend that is heavy on the warming spices we crave in fall and winter.

Use this in bean and root vegetable stews and soups, sprinkle on roasted vegetables, on popcorn, and on Roasted Pumpkin Seeds (page 117). It's particularly wonderful sprinkled on roasted or stewed tomatoes.

Makes about 1 cup

Time: Weekday

Storage: Cool, dark place in an airtight container for up to 3 months.

> ⅓ cup (28g) coriander seeds
> 2 tablespoons green cardamom pods
> 1 tablespoon plus 1 teaspoon cumin seeds
> 2 teaspoons whole cloves
> 2 teaspoons fennel seeds
> 1 teaspoon black peppercorns
> 3 tablespoons dried rosebuds
> ¼ cup (25g) sweet paprika
> ¼ cup (19g) ground turmeric
> 1 tablespoon plus 1 teaspoon Marash or Aleppo pepper flakes
> 1 tablespoon freshly grated nutmeg

IN A SMALL SKILLET, combine the coriander, cardamom, cumin, cloves, fennel seeds, and peppercorns and toast over medium-high heat until fragrant, about 2 minutes. Transfer the toasted spices to a dedicated spice grinder, add the dried rosebuds, and process until finely ground.

Transfer to a small bowl and stir in the paprika, turmeric, Marash pepper, and nutmeg. Mix until thoroughly combined.

Shichimi Togarashi

This spicy, fragrant Japanese blend makes frequent appearances at ramen shops, where patrons shake it on their bowls to taste. The first time I tasted it, in Tokyo, I was hooked, as I'm such a citrus fan and the version I tasted was brimming with orange peel. When I started making it myself, I was inspired by LA chef Niki Nakayama's take, and made my own adjustments. Use this on Creamy Sunflower Ramen (page 175) or any other soups, on popcorn and salads, or to spice Roasted Pumpkin Seeds (page 117) or Crunchy Kale Chips (page 114).

Makes about ½ cup

Time: Weekday

Storage: Cool, dark place in an airtight container for up to 3 months.

> 2 large (7 × 8-inch/18cm × 20cm) sheets roasted nori
> 2 tablespoons red pepper flakes
> 2 tablespoons white or black sesame seeds (or a mixture)
> 1 tablespoon granulated dried orange peel
> 1 teaspoon ground sanshō pepper, Sichuan peppercorns, or lemon pepper
> ½ teaspoon ground ginger

USE YOUR FINGERS TO crumble the nori into the smallest pieces possible into a small bowl. Add the pepper flakes, sesame seeds, orange peel, sanshō pepper, and ginger and whisk to combine.

From the top: Dukkah (page 39), Berbere (page 38), Cajun Seasoning (page 38), Shichimi Togarashi (opposite), and Peri Peri (page 41)

Smoky Mezcal Sazón

There's really something special about DC chef Christian Irabién's sazón, his version of the variable seasoning so crucial to Latin American kitchens. Irabién, who owns the stellar Mexican restaurant Muchas Gracias, adds his own special touch, stirring in joven (young) mezcal to punch up the smoky flavors. If you don't drink alcohol, fear not: In the dehydrating step, the alcohol evaporates.

Sprinkle this on tofu, tempeh, and vegetables before roasting, use it on popcorn or Roasted Pumpkin Seeds (page 117), and throw a tablespoon or two into rice before steaming.

Makes about 1 cup

Time: Weekend

Storage: Cool, dark place in an airtight container for up to 3 months.

    2 tablespoons granulated onion
    1 tablespoon granulated garlic
    2 tablespoons smoked paprika
    1 tablespoon plus 1½ teaspoons ground cumin
    1 tablespoon plus 1½ teaspoons ground coriander
    1 tablespoon ground allspice
    1 tablespoon ground chipotle
    1 tablespoon ground ginger
    1 tablespoon ground turmeric
    1 tablespoon fine sea salt
    2 teaspoons freshly ground black pepper
    6 tablespoons mezcal joven, plus more if needed
    1 tablespoon fresh lime juice
    ¼ cup packed (55g) dark brown sugar (optional)

IN A MEDIUM BOWL, combine the granulated onion, granulated garlic, all of the spices, the salt, and pepper and whisk until thoroughly combined. Add the mezcal and lime juice and stir until the mixture is evenly moistened and is the consistency of wet sand. (If it's too dry, add 1 tablespoon of mezcal at a time if needed.)

Preheat the oven to 200°F (90°C).

Pour the mixture onto a small sheet pan and use a spatula to spread it as thin as possible. Use a fork to poke holes all over the mixture.

Bake the sazón until hard and dry all the way through, 3 to 4 hours. Let cool, about 30 minutes.

Break the sazón into small chunks and press it through a fine-mesh sieve or grind it into a powder in a dedicated spice grinder. If you want to turn it into a sticky, sweet, and spicy dry rub for grilled or roasted vegetables, stir in the brown sugar.

Za'atar

This Middle Eastern spice blend is herbaceous and tart, earthy and bright, which makes it perfect for sprinkling on roasted vegetables, on hummus and other dips, and, traditionally, on pita or other flatbread that you've brushed with olive oil. Like so many other such blends, the proportions, and even the ingredients, vary from region to region, family to family, cook to cook. Its name doubles as the name for the wild thyme that is traditionally included, and if you can find that, definitely substitute for the thyme listed here. I like a particularly sumac-heavy version of za'atar, but if you aren't a tartness fiend like me, feel free to cut it back a little—just promise me you'll try my version first. Sprinkle on hummus and other dips, on popcorn, on avocado toast, on Roasted Pumpkin Seeds (page 117), or use to season pita crisps (see Herby Cashew-Tahini Dip with Za'atar Pita Crisps, page 120).

Makes a heaping ½ cup

Time: Weekday

Storage: Cool, dark place in an airtight container for up to 3 months.

    1 tablespoon sesame seeds
    4 tablespoons sumac
    3 tablespoons dried thyme
    1 tablespoon ground cumin
    1 teaspoon fine sea salt

IN A SMALL DRY skillet, toast the sesame seeds over medium heat, shaking the pan occasionally, until they become fragrant and lightly browned, about 2 minutes. Immediately transfer them to a bowl to cool completely.

Stir in the sumac, thyme, cumin, and salt.

Nacho Nooch

Nutritional yeast is a powerhouse in the vegan pantry: It brings a touch of cheesiness and umami to so many dishes and is often used as a finishing touch, à la Parmesan. When I saw a store-bought brand that had added chiles and other spices to its "nooch," I started sprinkling it on everything—and soon wanted to make my own. Try this on popcorn, spiced nuts, Crunchy Kale Chips (page 114), or Roasted Pumpkin Seeds (page 117); on roasted potatoes, broccoli, or other vegetables; on salads, in tacos—anywhere you want to make something a little more cheesy, spicy, or smoky.

Makes about 1 cup

Time: Weekday

Storage: Cool, dark place in an airtight container for up to 1 month.

¾ cup (60g) nutritional yeast

2 tablespoons smoked paprika

1 tablespoon ground red New Mexico chiles or ancho chiles

2 teaspoons fine sea salt

1 teaspoon ground cumin

1 teaspoon garlic powder

1 teaspoon onion powder

1 teaspoon freshly ground black pepper

¼ teaspoon cayenne pepper, plus more to taste

IN A BOWL, USE a fork to whisk together all the ingredients. Taste and add more cayenne if you'd like.

Seaweed Gomasio

My sister Rebekah has been making iterations of this since she started getting into macrobiotic cooking in the 1970s, when gomasio (a simple blend of sesame seeds and salt) was seen as a way to restore balance if you were too far on one side of the acid/alkaline or yin/yang spectrum. Even if you're not into that, it adds a delicious bit of salty, nutty texture to salads, rice, raw or cooked vegetables, soups, and more. It can also be a way to reduce your reliance on table salt if you're concerned about sodium, as the fat from the sesame seeds coats the salt and carries its flavor. I've followed Rebekah's lead and have sprinkled it on my meals anytime I visit her and her husband, Peter, in southern Maine, and then started making it myself when I saw how much cheaper (and better!) it was than the store-bought stuff. Rebekah sometimes adds seaweed to her gomasio, and I love that for its pop of umami—not to mention minerals.

Makes 1½ cups

Time: Weekday

Storage: Cool, dark place in an airtight container for up to 3 weeks.

¾ cup (90g) sesame seeds

2 tablespoons dried seaweed flakes, dulse, kombu, wakame, arame, or a combination

1½ teaspoons fine sea salt

IN A MEDIUM SKILLET, combine the sesame seeds, seaweed flakes, and salt and toast over medium heat, shaking the pan frequently, until the sesame turns medium brown and the mixture is very fragrant, about 5 minutes. Transfer to a bowl to cool completely.

Transfer the mixture to a small food processor, dedicated spice grinder, or clean coffee mill. Process until coarsely ground. (If you want your gomasio to have more texture, you can grind just half of it and mix it with the remaining unground mixture.) Transfer to an airtight container.

Silky Aquafaba Mayonnaise

Creamy, dreamy mayonnaise without the egg? It's not only possible—it's even better. Thanks to the magic of aquafaba (see page 6), luscious, egg-free mayo is at your fingertips. And without the flavor of egg yolk, this canvas can serve as a fabulous vehicle for your favorite flavors. Have fun with it: Try using flavored olive oils, cutting the neutral oil with sesame oil, and blending in other punchy ingredients (see Variations at right).

Aquafaba mayonnaise thickens when refrigerated, so plan to make it at least 1 hour before you want to serve it, and stir to recombine in case of any separation.

Use this wherever you'd use mayo, and in Fideuà de Verduras with Lemon Aioli (page 234) and Grand Aioli Platter with Espelette Aioli (page 318).

Makes 1 cup

Time: Weekday

Storage: Refrigerate for up to 1 week.

> 2 tablespoons aquafaba
>
> 1 heaping tablespoon canned no-salt-added chickpeas (see Notes)
>
> 1½ teaspoons white wine vinegar
>
> 1 teaspoon Dijon mustard
>
> ¼ teaspoon fine sea salt, plus more to taste
>
> ½ cup (120ml) plus 2 tablespoons neutral oil, such as canola, avocado, or grapeseed
>
> 2 tablespoons olive oil

IN A TALL CONTAINER big enough to fit an immersion blender, combine the aquafaba, chickpeas, vinegar, mustard, and salt. Use the immersion blender to blend until smooth.

In a spouted measuring cup (or other vessel that is easy to pour from), combine the canola oil and olive oil. Then with the blender running (see Notes), very slowly drizzle the oil into the aquafaba mixture, increasing the stream if you'd like as an emulsion forms. Taste and adjust seasonings, as necessary.

Transfer to a small serving bowl and refrigerate for at least 1 hour to overnight.

VARIATIONS

Aioli

Add 1 large garlic clove, chopped, and switch the proportions of the oils, using ½ cup (120ml) plus 2 tablespoons olive oil and 2 tablespoons canola oil.

Espelette Aioli

Add 4 large garlic cloves (chopped) and ½ teaspoon ground Espelette pepper, smoked paprika, or Aleppo pepper. Switch the proportions of the oils, using ½ cup (120ml) plus 2 tablespoons olive oil and 2 tablespoons canola oil.

Lemon Mayonnaise

Add the finely grated zest of 2 lemons (about 2 teaspoons packed) to the base before blending.

Double-Lemon Mayonnaise

Add the finely grated zest of 2 lemons (about 2 teaspoons), replace the vinegar with 2 teaspoons lemon juice, and substitute ¾ cup (180ml) lemon olive oil for the canola and olive oils.

Jalapeño Mayonnaise

Replace the canola and olive oil with ¾ cup (180ml) jalapeño olive oil (try the one from Enzo Olive Oil Company or Calivirgin), and fold in 2 tablespoons finely chopped pickled jalapeños after blending. (Note that you'll need to stir to re-emulsify the mayo before using.)

Sambal Sesame Mayonnaise

Replace the Dijon mustard with 2 teaspoons sambal oelek, add a pinch of organic cane sugar to the aquafaba base, and substitute toasted sesame oil for the olive oil.

COOK'S NOTES

- If you have a mini food processor, feel free to use that instead of an immersion blender. A standard blender doesn't work as well because it requires more volume and the mixture tends to get too hot to emulsify.

- Since the mayo uses just a little bit of a can of chickpeas, store the rest in their liquid (aquafaba) for up to 5 days, or freeze for up to 3 months.

Zucchini "Guacamole" Salsa

Blogger Dora Stone came up with this salsa—a riff on the guacamole salsa so popular with taqueros (taco vendors)—out of necessity. Whenever she wanted to make it, she would find herself short on avocados, which she has to hide from her kids if she wants to eat any. But she always had zucchini, and therefore this clever salsa. She realized that a combination of zucchini and avocado oil created something unbelievably creamy that would fool even the most fervent taco connoisseurs. Bonus: It's cheaper to make than the avocado version, and the zucchini runs no risk of turning brown, instead staying bright green even after a couple days.

Makes 2 cups

Time: Weekday

Storage: Refrigerate for up to 2 days.

> 1 medium zucchini (about 6 ounces/180g), cut crosswise into quarters
>
> 4 medium tomatillos (9 ounces/250g total), husks removed
>
> 4 tablespoons avocado oil or other neutral vegetable oil
>
> 1 to 2 large jalapeño peppers (2 to 3 ounces/74g total), stemmed and cut into large chunks
>
> ½ medium white onion (60g), cut into large chunks
>
> 1 large garlic clove
>
> ¼ cup (10g) chopped fresh cilantro
>
> ½ teaspoon fine sea salt, plus more to taste

IN A MEDIUM SAUCEPAN, combine the zucchini and tomatillos with water to cover. Bring to a boil over medium-high heat, then reduce the heat to a simmer and cook until the green of the tomatillos has turned dull and the zucchini is tender, about 6 minutes. Drain and transfer to a blender.

Meanwhile, in a small skillet, heat 1 teaspoon of the avocado oil over medium heat until it shimmers. Add the jalapeños, onion, and garlic and cook, stirring, until the jalapeños start to blister and the onion begins to brown, about 4 minutes. Remove from the heat, let cool in the pan for a few minutes, then transfer to the blender.

Add the cilantro and salt to the blender and puree until smooth. With the machine running at a low speed, remove the lid plug and slowly stream in the remaining 3 tablespoons plus 2 teaspoons oil. Slowly increase the speed to medium and blend until the sauce has thickened, about 15 seconds. Taste and season with more salt if necessary. Let cool.

Serve at room temperature or chilled.

Chunky Molcajete Salsa

There's something magical about a salsa made in a molcajete, a mortar and pestle made out of volcanic rock used in Mexico since pre-Hispanic times. It is one of those kitchen tools that gets passed down from generation to generation. A couple of years ago, food blogger Dora Stone asked her mother if she could have her molcajete, and her mother replied: "No! I'm not dead yet!" Of course, she bought her own—and will now have at least two to bequeath her own children one day. The beauty of this salsa comes from the blackening of the tomatoes and peppers, which gives it a smoky flavor that complements the sweetness and spiciness of the salsa. Despite the name, if you don't have a molcajete, you can puree this salsa in a blender or food processor, but it will be a little thinner in texture.

Makes 1½ cups

Time: Weekday

Storage: Refrigerate for up to 3 days.

- 4 Roma tomatoes (1 pound 2 ounces/515g total)
- ¼ white onion (63g)
- 2 garlic cloves, unpeeled
- 2 serrano peppers (30g)
- 1 teaspoon fine sea salt, plus more to taste
- ¼ cup (10g) chopped fresh cilantro (optional)

HEAT A CAST-IRON SKILLET or comal over medium-high heat. Add the tomatoes, onion, garlic, and serrano peppers to the pan. Cook until the garlic starts to lightly brown, about 2 minutes. Transfer it to a molcajete (or food processor) and keep cooking the remaining vegetables, turning them as needed, until they are charred and blistered all over, 8 to 10 minutes.

Add the salt to a molcajete (mortar) and grind it and the garlic down with the tejolote (pestle) in a circular motion around the entire molcajete, until a thick paste forms. Add the chiles one at a time and grind them down until they form a coarse puree. Add the tomatoes one at a time and keep grinding until you have a thick puree. (If you are using the food processor, cut the tomatoes, garlic, and serranos into chunks and transfer them to the food processor. Add the salt and pulse until pureed but still a little chunky.)

Finely chop the charred onion and add it to the salsa along with the cilantro and mix well. Taste and season with more salt if needed. Serve warm or cold.

Salsa Macha

Salsa macha is a spicy oil-based sauce made with dried chiles, seeds, and nuts. The name comes from the word *macho*, implying that you have to be strong and brave enough to eat it. It is originally from Veracruz, but every region of Mexico has its own version. This take uses a blender rather than the traditional molcajete, the country's beloved lava rock mortar and pestle. The chile paste sinks to the bottom of the container; either stir it up before you use it, or just use some of the oil off the top.

Makes a generous 2 cups

Time: Weekday

Storage: Refrigerate for up to 2 weeks.

- ⅓ cup (45g) raw pumpkin seeds
- ⅓ cup (50g) blanched unroasted peanuts
- ¼ cup (40g) sesame seeds
- 1 cup (420ml) olive oil
- 2 ounces (60g) dried árbol chiles, stemmed
- 5 garlic cloves, cut into large pieces
- ½ teaspoon fine sea salt, plus more to taste

HEAT A LARGE SKILLET over medium heat. Add the pumpkin seeds and toast, shaking the pan occasionally, until they begin to brown and pop, about 3 minutes. Transfer to a plate. Add the peanuts to the skillet and toast, shaking the pan occasionally, until golden brown, about 2 minutes. Transfer to the plate with the pumpkin seeds. Add the sesame seeds to the skillet and toast, shaking the pan occasionally, until golden brown, about 1 minute. Transfer to the plate with the peanuts and pumpkin seeds.

Pour the oil into the same skillet and heat over medium heat. Add the chiles and fry, stirring, until blackened in some spots, about 2 minutes. Transfer the chiles to a blender or food processor. Add the garlic to the skillet and fry, stirring, until golden brown, about 1 minute. Transfer to the blender. Remove the pan from the heat and let the oil cool for 10 minutes, then pour it into the blender.

Process at low speed until the chiles have broken down, but are not completely pureed, about 1 minute. Stir in the salt, pumpkin seeds, peanuts, and sesame seeds and process briefly until the nuts and seeds are finely chopped, but not pureed. Taste and season with more salt if necessary. Transfer to a container and let cool.

Romesco Sauce

I've been making some version of this classic Spanish sauce—a close cousin to the Middle Eastern dip Muhammara (page 52)—for many years, and over time my method has gotten simpler and simpler. Now I throw virtually everything onto a sheet pan, roast it all for a short time at high heat, and puree with a little smoked paprika, cayenne, and vinegar. (Since it all goes into the food processor, I don't bother separately roasting and peeling the peppers, either.) Trust me, it tastes every bit as vibrant and can't-stop-eating good as the stuff that requires multiple pans and bowls. Use this as a condiment for wraps, a topping for roasted vegetables (it's a particularly stunning match with cauliflower, broccoli, and other brassicas), and a dip for pita chips or crudités. You can even thin it out with water into an excellent cold soup; just make sure to taste and adjust the seasoning.

Makes 3 cups

Time: Weekday

Storage: Refrigerate for up to 2 weeks (drizzle with olive oil to cover first) or frozen (without extra olive oil) for up to 3 months.

3 large red bell peppers (1¼ pounds/567g total), cut into 2-inch (5cm) chunks

1 cup lightly packed (57g) bread cubes (2 to 3 small slices)

2 large plum tomatoes (8 ounces/227g total), cut into thick slices

6 garlic cloves, unpeeled

1 cup (142g) raw almonds

¼ cup (60ml) olive oil, plus more for serving and storage

1 teaspoon fine sea salt, plus more to taste

2 teaspoons sweet or hot smoked Spanish paprika (pimentón dulce or picante)

½ teaspoon cayenne pepper (optional)

1 tablespoon sherry vinegar or red wine vinegar, plus more to taste

PREHEAT THE OVEN TO 500°F (260°C).

On a sheet pan, toss together the bell peppers, bread, tomatoes, garlic, almonds, olive oil, and salt. Roast, stirring or tossing occasionally, until the mixture browns in spots and the garlic is tender, about 15 minutes. Let cool slightly.

Peel the garlic and add to a food processor. Add the bell peppers, bread, tomatoes, almonds, smoked paprika, cayenne (if using), and vinegar. Puree until mostly smooth but with a little chunky texture. Taste and season with more salt and/or vinegar if needed.

Drizzle with olive oil before serving.

Muhammara

This Middle Eastern red pepper/walnut dip is so much like Romesco Sauce (page 51) that I make it virtually the same way, with simple ingredient swaps. Use this as a condiment for wraps, a topping for roasted vegetables, and a dip for pita chips or crudités.

Makes 1½ to 2 cups (8 servings)

Time: Weekday

Storage: Drizzle with olive oil to cover, then refrigerate for up to 2 weeks. Freeze (without extra olive oil) for up to 3 months.

- 3 large red bell peppers (1¼ pounds/567g total), cut into 2-inch (5cm) chunks
- 2 large plum tomatoes (8 ounces/225g total), cut into 2-inch (5cm) chunks
- 6 medium garlic cloves, unpeeled
- 1 cup (100g) walnuts
- ¼ cup (60ml) olive oil, plus more for serving and storage
- 1 teaspoon fine sea salt, plus more to taste
- 1 cup lightly packed (57g) bread cubes (2 to 3 small slices)
- 2 teaspoons Aleppo pepper flakes
- 1½ teaspoons ground cumin
- 2 tablespoons pomegranate molasses, plus more for serving
- 1 tablespoon fresh lemon juice, plus more to taste

PREHEAT THE OVEN TO 500°F (260°C).

On a sheet pan, toss together the bell peppers, tomatoes, garlic, walnuts, olive oil, and salt. Roast, stirring or tossing occasionally, for 5 minutes. Add the bread and continue roasting until the mixture browns in spots and the garlic is tender, about 15 minutes. Let cool slightly.

Peel the garlic and transfer to a food processor. Add the bell peppers, tomatoes, walnuts, bread cubes, Aleppo flakes, cumin, pomegranate molasses, and lemon juice. Puree until mostly smooth but with a little chunky texture, scraping down the side of the bowl partway through if needed. Taste and season with more salt and/or lemon juice if needed.

Drizzle with olive oil and pomegranate molasses before serving.

Rose Harissa

This fiery condiment from Tunisia boasts such complexity of flavor that you'll want to try it on everything: slathered on roasted vegetables, dolloped into soups or on hummus, smeared on or in breads for sandwiches and wraps, and so much more. The recipe varies from village to village and household to household. The rose petals and rose water add a floral hint that slightly softens the punch.

Makes 1¼ cups (20 servings)

Time: Weekday

Storage: Refrigerate for up to 2 weeks or freeze for up to 3 months.

- 4 large ancho chiles (60g)
- 3 to 4 dried guajillo chiles (17g)
- Boiling water
- 1 tablespoon cumin seeds
- 1 tablespoon coriander seeds
- 1 tablespoon fennel seeds
- ¼ cup (60ml) olive oil, plus more for storage
- 3 garlic cloves, crushed
- 3 tablespoons fresh lime juice (from 1 to 2 limes)
- 1 canned chipotle pepper in adobo sauce
- 2 teaspoons Aleppo or Urfa pepper flakes, or ½ teaspoon red pepper flakes
- 1 teaspoon dried rose petals
- 1 teaspoon fine sea salt, plus more to taste
- ¼ teaspoon rose water

BREAK OR CUT OPEN the dried chiles, remove and compost the seeds and stems, and tear or break the flesh into 1-inch (2.5cm) pieces. Transfer them to a small heatproof bowl, cover them with boiling water, and let them sit until soft, at least 10 minutes.

In a dry skillet, combine the cumin, coriander, and fennel seeds and toast over medium heat, shaking occasionally, until they are very fragrant, 3 to 4 minutes. Transfer them to a mini food processor or a blender.

When the chiles are soft, drain them and add to the food processor or blender, along with the olive oil, garlic, lime juice, chipotle, Aleppo pepper, rose petals, salt, and rose water. Puree until mostly smooth, scraping down the bowl if needed. Taste and add more salt if needed.

Use immediately or transfer to a jar, cover with a thin layer of olive oil, and refrigerate.

Pesto How You Like It

This template allows you to easily throw together pesto-style sauces with the ingredients you have on hand. Choose from a wide variety of herbs or greens: classic basil, of course, but also parsley, arugula, spinach, chard, or kale, farmers market finds such as amaranth leaves and dandelion greens, or a mixture of all of the above. Because the size and shape of these ingredients make uniform volume measurements tricky, use the weights as your guide if at all possible. Use almost any nut or seed, such as pine nuts, almonds, walnuts, cashews, pistachios, or sunflower seeds. As you make more and more batches, your confidence for improvising will grow. This pesto is fairly thick in texture. The finishing ingredient when you add it to hot pasta is a few spoons of starchy cooking liquid. Use in: Nearly-Any-Vegetable Coconut Soup (page 171), Fresh "Egg" Pasta (page 240), and Ricotta Tortellini (page 246).

Makes about 1 cup

Time: Weekday

Storage: Refrigerate for up to 3 days. To freeze: Pour a film of oil on the surface of the pesto inside a container and freeze for up to 3 months.

1 garlic clove, halved

About ⅓ cup (48g) nuts or seeds (see Headnote)

¼ cup (20g) nutritional yeast

1 teaspoon fine salt

5 ounces (140g) herbs or greens (4 to 6 cups packed)

⅓ cup (80ml) olive oil

2 tablespoons fresh lemon juice

IN A FOOD PROCESSOR, process the garlic until finely chopped. Add the nuts or seeds, nutritional yeast, and salt. Process until finely chopped, about 30 seconds. Add the greens and process until a smooth paste forms, scraping down the sides of the bowl as needed. With the processor running, stream the olive oil and lemon juice through the tube until combined.

Chinese-Style Chili Crisp

If you haven't heard about Chinese chili crisp in the last few years, then you haven't been reading major food publications, where writers have been waxing poetic about these jars of spicy, crunchy goodness. I based my recipe on the flavor of the most widely available store-bought chili crisp, made by Lao Gan Ma, but instead of MSG I get plenty of umami by adding dried shiitake mushrooms and miso. Use this anywhere you want a hit of salty heat: on noodles or rice, in soups, on roasted vegetables, drizzled onto hummus and other dips, in tacos and so, so, much more. Even ice cream!

Makes 1¼ cups

Time: Weekday

Storage: Refrigerate for up to 2 weeks.

¼ cup (23g) unsalted roasted soybeans

½ cup (14g) dried Chinese chiles (aka Japones peppers, Tianjin, or Tien Tsin chiles), stemmed

2 tablespoons (20g) dried minced onion

4 large garlic cloves, smashed

½ ounce (14g) dried shiitake mushrooms, broken into pieces

3 inches (7.5cm/57g) fresh ginger, peeled and cut into ½-inch (1.3cm) pieces

1 teaspoon Sichuan peppercorns

¾ cup (180ml) sesame or peanut oil

2 tablespoons red miso

2 teaspoons light or dark brown sugar

½ teaspoon fine salt, plus more to taste

IN A SMALL FOOD processor, pulse the soybeans a few times to break them up. Add the chiles, onion, garlic, mushrooms, ginger, and Sichuan peppercorns and process briefly, until the mixture is the size of large red pepper flakes.

Set a fine-mesh sieve over a heatproof bowl.

In a small saucepan, combine the mixture and sesame oil and cook over medium heat until the mixture turns brown and crispy, 10 to 15 minutes. Pour the mixture into the sieve and let the solids cool to room temperature in the sieve. (This will keep them crisp longer.) When the oil in the bowl is room temperature, too, stir the solids back in, along with the miso, brown sugar, and salt. Taste and season with more salt if needed.

Roasted Tomato Ketchup

If you've ever tried to make ketchup at home, you know how long it can take—and how frustrating it can be: After hours of cooking down your tomato puree until it seems thick enough, you pour it into jars and cool it, only to open it later and find...thick tomato sauce. My keys to a great homemade ketchup are to start with a plum tomato variety, such as Roma or San Marzano, and to begin by roasting the tomatoes, which helps get rid of much of the moisture, making your final round of cooking on the stovetop a much shorter affair. You'll also keep the skins on; they add body to the final condiment. This version uses a fairly short list of warming spices, plus coconut sugar and balsamic vinegar for that sweet-tart edge.

Makes 1½ to 2 cups (16 servings)

Time: Weekend

Storage: Refrigerate for up to 3 weeks or freeze for up to 6 months.

3 pounds (1.4kg) plum tomatoes, cut into ½-inch (1.3cm) chunks

1 yellow onion, cut into ½-inch (1.3cm) chunks

6 garlic cloves, unpeeled

½ cup (120ml) olive oil

1½ teaspoons fine sea salt, plus more to taste

1 teaspoon freshly ground black pepper

1 teaspoon ground cinnamon

1 teaspoon sweet or hot smoked paprika (Spanish pimentón, dulce or picante)

1 teaspoon ground allspice

½ cup (80g) coconut sugar

¼ cup (60ml) balsamic vinegar, plus more to taste

PREHEAT THE OVEN TO 400°F (200°C).

On a large sheet pan, combine the tomatoes, onion, and garlic, spreading them out so they're as close to one layer as possible. Drizzle with the olive oil and sprinkle on the salt, pepper, cinnamon, smoked paprika, and allspice. Toss gently with a spatula to thoroughly coat.

Roast until most of the thin, watery liquid has evaporated and the tomatoes are very soft and browned in spots, about 1 hour.

Let cool slightly, then pick out the garlic and squeeze it out of its peels into a high-powered blender or food processor. Transfer the rest of the mixture to the blender or food processor and puree until very smooth.

Pour the sauce into a large deep nonreactive skillet (not cast iron). Set over medium heat and stir in the coconut sugar and vinegar. Put a splatter guard on top and cook, stirring and scraping the bottom occasionally to prevent scorching, until the sauce has turned a deep brick-red and is very thick with big lava-like bubbles, 30 to 60 minutes, depending on how much moisture was left in the tomatoes after roasting. (A test: When you run a spoon or rubber spatula through the ketchup and along the bottom of the pan, the gap and the sauce should stand separately, and the sauce should not run to fill the gap.)

Taste and add more salt and balsamic vinegar if needed. (Since you're tasting the ketchup hot but will be eating it cold later, go for slightly overpowering flavors, because they'll be muted when the temperature drops.)

Transfer to a glass jar, let cool, and refrigerate.

Masala Breakfast
Potatoes (page 92)

Pipián Verde

This beautiful pumpkin seed sauce—tangy, spicy, earthy, and full of greens—is one of Oaxaca's famous seven moles, but this version is more typical of central Mexico. The type of greens used varies according to the region. If you are able to find quelites (wild greens such as lamb's-quarters, watercress, or purslane) and fresh epazote, it will really make a difference in the flavor. Serve it over hearty vegetables, your favorite meat substitute, as a sauce for enchiladas or tacos, or with the Whole Roasted Beets with Mole (page 337). You can also use this as the base for green pozole.

Makes 4 cups

Time: Weekend

Storage: Refrigerate for up to 4 days; freeze for up to 3 months.

- ⅔ cup (95g) raw pumpkin seeds
- 6 tomatillos (1 pound 2 ounces/520g total), husks removed
- 1 poblano pepper (4½ ounces/132g)
- ½ medium white onion (85g)
- 3 medium garlic cloves, unpeeled
- 1 to 2 serrano peppers
- 1 cup (2 ounces/57g) greens, such as spinach, Swiss chard, radish greens, or a combination
- 1 cup (48g) chopped romaine lettuce
- ½ cup (16g) fresh cilantro with tender stems
- 1 sprig fresh epazote (optional)
- ¼ teaspoon dried Mexican oregano
- ¼ teaspoon ground cumin
- 1 cup (240ml) Vegetable Scrap Stock (page 36) or store-bought vegetable broth, plus more if needed
- 1 teaspoon fine sea salt, plus more to taste
- ¼ teaspoon freshly ground black pepper
- 1 teaspoon avocado oil

HEAT A LARGE SKILLET over medium heat. Stir in the pumpkin seeds and toast them until they begin to brown and pop, about 3 minutes. Remove from the pan.

Position an oven rack in the highest position and turn the broiler to high. Place the tomatillos, poblano, and onion on one side of a large ovenproof skillet or sheet pan and place the garlic and serrano(s) on the other side. Broil until they have begun to char and soften on one side, about 3 to 4 minutes for the garlic and serrano and 5 minutes for the remaining vegetables. Then flip and continue broiling until they start to char and soften on the other side, 3 to 5 minutes. (You may need to remove the garlic and serranos from the pan a few minutes before the other vegetables.)

Transfer the poblano pepper to a bowl, cover with a plate, and let sit for 5 minutes. When it's cool enough to handle, use your hands to peel the pepper and remove the stems and seeds. Peel the garlic. Transfer the peeled poblano, garlic, tomatillos, onion, and serranos to a blender. Add the greens, romaine lettuce, cilantro, epazote (if using), oregano, cumin, vegetable stock, salt, and black pepper. Blend until smooth. Add a little stock if needed to help the sauce blend. Taste and add more salt if needed.

In a large Dutch oven or heavy-bottomed pot, heat the oil over medium heat until it shimmers. Add the sauce and bring to a simmer. Reduce the heat to medium-low and cook, stirring every few minutes to make sure it doesn't stick to the bottom of the pot, until the sauce turns an army-green color and is thick enough to coat the back of your spoon, about 15 minutes. Use immediately or refrigerate or freeze.

Mole Coloradito

This is the result of food blogger Dora Stone's quest for the right way to make mole, the complex sauce that is one of the treasures of Mexican cuisine. It wasn't taught in her Culinary Institute of America curriculum, and she found it intimidating until she obsessively researched it on her own and cracked the code. One of her favorite ways of serving the sauce—often called just "coloradito"—is with a stew of ayocote beans, but you can also use it to make mole enchiladas (see Enchiladas Five Ways, page 311) or you can serve it over your favorite vegetables. This makes quite a bit of mole, but resist the urge to halve the recipe. Once you taste it, you'll wish you had made the whole thing.

Makes 6 cups (12 servings)

Time: Weekend

Storage: Refrigerate for up to 4 days or freeze for up to 3 months.

- 8 ancho chiles (145g total), stemmed, seeded, and rinsed
- 6 dried guajillo chiles (30g total), stemmed, seeded, and rinsed
- 4 cups (950ml) boiling water
- ⅓ cup (50g) sesame seeds
- 1-inch (2.5cm) piece cinnamon stick, preferably Ceylon
- 6 black peppercorns
- 1 allspice berry
- 2 whole cloves
- 1 bay leaf
- 5 tablespoons avocado oil or other neutral vegetable oil
- 2 ounces (57g) crusty white bread, such as Mexican bolillo or French boule, sliced
- ¼ cup (35g) raw almonds
- 2 tablespoons raisins
- 3 Roma tomatoes (15 ounces/420g total)
- 4 medium garlic cloves, unpeeled
- ½ medium white onion (110g)
- ½ teaspoon dried Mexican oregano
- ¼ teaspoon dried thyme
- 1 (90g) tablet Mexican chocolate (such as Ibarra or Nestlé Abuelita brand), cut into pieces
- 1 tablespoon grated piloncillo or brown sugar
- 1 teaspoon fine sea salt, plus more if needed
- 1½ cups (350ml) Vegetable Scrap Stock (page 36) or store-bought vegetable broth, plus more as needed

HEAT A LARGE HEAVY skillet over medium heat. Toast the ancho and guajillo chiles in the dry skillet until lightly toasted and fragrant, 30 seconds per side. (Be careful not to burn them or the mole will be bitter.) Transfer the chiles to a heatproof bowl. Pour the boiling water over them and let them soak and soften for 15 minutes. Reserving 2 cups (470ml) of the soaking liquid, drain the chiles and transfer them and the reserved soaking liquid to a blender.

In the same skillet still over medium heat, add the sesame seeds, cinnamon, peppercorns, allspice, cloves, and bay leaf and toast until fragrant, about 1 minute. Transfer to the blender.

Pour 3 tablespoons of the avocado oil into the skillet. Add the bread, almonds, and raisins and toast, stirring, until the bread turns golden brown, the almonds darken in spots, and the raisins puff up, about 2 minutes. Transfer them to the blender.

Turn the oven broiler to high.

Place the tomatoes, garlic, and onion in a cast-iron or other large ovenproof skillet or sheet pan and broil until the garlic has browned, about 2 minutes. Remove the garlic, flip the rest of the vegetables, and continue broiling until they have begun to char and soften, about 4 minutes. Peel the garlic and transfer it and the remaining vegetables to the blender. Add the oregano, thyme, chocolate, piloncillo, and salt to the blender.

Process until smooth. (If your blender is struggling, you can do this in two batches.) Press through a fine-mesh sieve.

In a Dutch oven or other heavy-bottomed pot, heat the remaining 2 tablespoons oil over medium-low heat until it shimmers. Pour in the mole and fry the sauce, stirring, until it bubbles and turns darker red, about 5 minutes.

Pour in the vegetable stock and stir to combine. When it starts to bubble, reduce the heat to low, cover, and simmer gently, stirring every 5 minutes to prevent sticking, until the mole becomes the consistency of thick heavy cream, about 20 minutes. If the mole is too thick, add more vegetable stock, ¼ cup (60ml) at a time, until you achieve that consistency. Taste and add more salt if needed. The mole will thicken as it cools.

Use immediately or cool for storage.

Tomato Choka

Peak summer tomatoes star in this Trinidadian recipe, which sings with bright flavors and brims with effortless ease. You roast the tomatoes on an open flame, mash, and salt them, then scald them further by pouring over hot olive oil, garlic, and onion. Fresh herbs and a touch of hot chile add zing. Serve with Pumpkin Chapatis (page 399), Bing (page 397), or another flatbread.

Makes 2 to 4 servings

Time: Weekday

Storage: Refrigerate for up to 2 days.

4 large tomatoes (1½ pounds/680g total)

1 teaspoon fine sea salt, plus more to taste

¼ cup (60ml) olive oil

4 large garlic cloves, finely grated or pressed

½ medium white onion (85g), thinly sliced

½ cup (30g) chopped scallions

½ cup (20g) chopped fresh cilantro

½ Scotch bonnet or habanero pepper, stemmed and chopped

Flatbread, for serving

PREHEAT A GAS OR charcoal grill to high (or turn a gas-range burner on high). Grill the tomatoes (or set them directly over the gas flame), rotating a few times so that each side of the tomato comes into contact with the flame, until charred and starting to collapse, 10 to 15 minutes. The tomatoes should be cooked through, with the center still a little firm. (Alternatively, preheat the oven broiler to high and broil the tomatoes.)

Transfer the tomatoes to a bowl and remove the skin (compost it). Use a large fork to thoroughly mash the tomatoes until the texture is like a thin pico de gallo. Stir in the salt.

In a skillet, heat the olive oil over medium heat until it shimmers. Add the garlic and onion and cook until the onions have wilted, about 3 minutes.

Pour the hot oil, garlic, and onion over the tomatoes. Add the scallions, cilantro, and Scotch bonnet and stir to combine. Taste and season with more salt if needed. Serve immediately with flatbread.

Chunky Garlic Paste

Garlic is a cornerstone of Korean cuisine: It makes it into most banchan (side dishes) and stews, and, of course, can play a huge role in Korea's most iconic dish—kimchi. As a result, many Korean fridges and freezers are stocked with jars and jars of prepeeled and mashed garlic (presumably because it's easier than mincing 10 pounds of garlic). Back in the 1980s, Shim Young-Soon, one of South Korea's most popular cooking instructors, developed a premade garlic paste—one that could be dropped into a pot of broth or stir-fried with some vegetables to add outstanding flavor while cutting down on the prep time. This is TikTok star Joanne Lee Molinaro's fresh and fiery take, adding apple, onion, and gochugaru (Korean chile flakes) for a complex, spicy stroke of umami brilliance.

Makes 1½ cups

Time: Project

Storage: Freeze for up to 3 months.

1 cup (140g) peeled garlic (from about 3 bulbs)

1 cup (160g) chopped apple

¾ cup (85g) chopped red onion

2 tablespoons fine sea salt

2 tablespoons water

1 tablespoon gochugaru (Korean chile flakes)

IN A FOOD PROCESSOR, combine all the ingredients and blend until you achieve a chunky paste.

Refrigerate for 1 week to let the flavors meld before freezing in ice cube trays.

Miso Sesame Dressing

There's nothing like miso for a hit of umami: This fermented soy paste (sometimes made from a variety of other legumes and grains) is a VIP in the plant-based pantry. It also forms the base for this outstanding salad dressing, which can be customized with a variety of vibrant herbs, fruits, and vegetables (optional add-ins below). I like to limit myself to one add-in per go-round, but I forgive you if you can't contain yourself.

Makes about 1 cup (6 to 8 servings)

Time: Weekday

Storage: Refrigerate for up to 1 week.

¼ cup (60ml) unseasoned rice vinegar

3 tablespoons white or yellow miso, homemade (page 83) or store-bought

1 tablespoon toasted sesame oil

2 teaspoons finely grated fresh ginger

2 teaspoons agave syrup or maple syrup

2 teaspoons white or black sesame seeds

1 teaspoon Dijon mustard

2 tablespoons water

4 tablespoons Optional Add-In (list follows)

IN A SMALL BOWL, whisk together the vinegar, miso, sesame oil, ginger, agave syrup, sesame seeds, and mustard. Whisk in the water until smooth. If desired, whisk in one of the optional add-ins.

OPTIONAL ADD-INS (4 TABLESPOONS)
- Mashed fresh berries (raspberries, strawberries, blueberries, or blackberries)
- Freshly squeezed orange or apple juice (instead of the water)
- Finely grated carrot
- Finely chopped cherry or grape tomatoes and their juices
- Finely grated beet
- Finely chopped scallions
- Finely chopped fresh parsley or mint

Tahini Dressing

Tahini sauce is the workhorse of the Middle Eastern kitchen: Where would falafel, among many other dishes, be without it? The classic—little more than tahini, water, lemon, garlic, and salt—is a fine enough salad dressing on its own. However, I like to dress it up a little further with a touch of date syrup to take the edge off the tahini's bitterness, along with some of the spices (cumin and coriander) you find in falafel wraps. As with most salad dressings, this one can be tweaked according to your preferences—see the optional add-ins for a jumping-off point.

Makes about 1 cup before add-ins (8 servings)

Time: Weekday

Storage: Refrigerate for up to 1 week.

½ cup (120ml) well-stirred tahini

¼ cup (60ml) warm water, plus more as needed

2 tablespoons fresh lemon juice

2 tablespoons olive oil

1 teaspoon date syrup, agave syrup, or maple syrup (optional)

1 garlic clove, grated

½ teaspoon ground cumin

¼ teaspoon ground coriander

½ teaspoon fine sea salt, plus more to taste

1 or 2 Optional Add-Ins (list follows)

IN A SMALL BOWL, whisk together the tahini and warm water until smooth. (If the mixture seizes up, keep whisking, adding a little more water as needed, until it smooths out.) Whisk in the lemon juice, oil, date syrup (if using), garlic, cumin, coriander, and salt. If desired, stir in one of the optional add-ins. Taste and add more salt if needed.

OPTIONAL ADD-INS
- 1 teaspoon Aleppo or Urfa pepper flakes
- 4 tablespoons finely chopped fresh parsley, mint, or dill
- 4 tablespoons finely chopped sour pickles
- 2 tablespoons toasted black or white sesame seeds

Toum

When a *Washington Post* colleague first showed me how to make this fluffy Lebanese garlic dip many years ago, I was floored: There's really no mayo in it? Nope—but it's made in a similar way to mayo, with garlic cloves and oil forming a tight emulsion as it's pureed. I've seen some descriptions of it as being akin to vegan aioli, but that really doesn't do its punch justice. This dip—which you can use as a sandwich spread, with crudités, chips, or as the base for roasted vegetables—has an exponentially higher amount of garlic than aioli (as in, more than ten times as much), so it packs an unbeatable intensity. Now that I grow my own garlic, I make it regularly. Try using it instead of (or in addition to) mayonnaise in a potato salad or coleslaw, and you may never go back. This version is based on the one Joseph Chemali, chef-owner of Shemalis Cafe and Market in DC, shared with *The Post*, but also based on versions by Maureen Abood in *Rose Water & Orange Blossoms* and Sohla El-Waylly on Serious Eats.

Make sure to use the freshest, firmest garlic possible, and don't skip the step of taking out the inner germ, which will prevent the toum from being bitter. Also, don't rush the pouring of the oil, or the mixture could separate. This works best in a mini food processor or using an immersion blender; if you only have a larger food processor, consider doubling the recipe—and giving half to a grateful friend.

Makes about 2 cups

Time: Weekday

Storage: Refrigerate for up to 3 weeks.

> 1 cup (142g) peeled garlic cloves
> (from about 3 bulbs)
>
> ½ teaspoon fine sea salt
>
> 1½ cups (350ml) neutral vegetable oil, such as sunflower or canola, plus more as needed
>
> 2 tablespoons fresh lemon juice
>
> 3 tablespoons ice water

TO TAKE OUT THE germs from the garlic, use a sharp paring knife to cut a slit in a clove, slightly off center near the root end, open up the clove, and pull and cut off the little sprout you should see in the center. (Compost the sprouts.)

Transfer the garlic and salt to a small food processor (or the blending cup or a canning jar if using an immersion blender) and process until smooth. Scrape down the sides of the bowl if needed.

While the machine is running, pour in a very thin stream, very slowly and gradually, ¾ cup (180ml) of the oil. The mixture will look like loose mashed potatoes. Scrape down the bowl. Add 1 tablespoon of the lemon juice and continue processing, streaming in another ½ cup (120ml) of the oil, then the remaining 1 tablespoon lemon juice. The mixture should be turning lighter and whiter.

With the machine still running, slowly stream in the ice water, then the remaining ¼ cup (60ml) oil. Process until it's white and fluffy. If it isn't, slowly stream in a little more oil at a time to reach the right consistency.

Use immediately or transfer to an airtight container for storage.

Clean-Out-the-Fridge Vinaigrette

It's so easy to make your own quick vinaigrette, and you probably have all the ingredients in your fridge and pantry. I've listed Variations (at right) some of them fairly classic, some less so—but you should think of this recipe as your dressing template and fill in the blanks with whatever you've got on hand. You may never buy salad dressing again. (You'll note that while the classic proportion is 3 parts oil to 1 part vinegar, I prefer a 2:1 ratio for a tarter, lighter dressing, with a little sweetener added if need be, here and there.) The emulsifiers here are sticky condiments—mustard, miso, mayo, jam—that help hold the dressing together, while also adding flavor. The key is to taste as you go and adjust—not just the salt and pepper, but any other ingredient you'd like—until the result is something great. You'll know you're there when you want to spoon it straight out of the jar rather than wait until you have a salad to toss it with.

Makes ⅔ cup (5 to 6 servings)

Time: Weekday

Storage: Refrigerate for up to 1 week.

> ¼ cup (60ml) **oil**
>
> 2 tablespoons **acid** (vinegar or citrus juice)
>
> 1 tablespoon **emulsifier**
>
> 1 teaspoon **flavoring**
>
> 1 teaspoon **sweetener** (optional)
>
> 2 tablespoons chopped fresh **herbs**, or 2 teaspoons dried herbs
>
> Pinch of fine sea salt, or to taste
>
> A few grinds of black pepper

IN A SMALL JAR, combine all the ingredients and shake until thoroughly combined. Taste and add more salt, pepper, or any other ingredient if needed.

VARIATIONS

Italian-Style Vinaigrette
- **Oil:** Olive oil
- **Acid:** Balsamic or red wine vinegar
- **Emulsifier:** Dijon mustard
- **Flavoring:** Garlic
- **Sweetener:** Agave syrup or Wildflower Cider Syrup (page 35)
- **Herbs:** Basil

Japanese-Style Vinaigrette
- **Oil:** Untoasted sesame oil
- **Acid:** Rice vinegar
- **Emulsifier:** Yellow or white miso
- **Flavoring:** Toasted sesame oil, sesame seeds, or Seaweed Gomasio (page 45)
- **Sweetener:** None
- **Herbs:** Shiso or mint

Greek-Style Vinaigrette
- **Oil:** Olive oil
- **Acid:** White wine vinegar or champagne vinegar
- **Emulsifier:** Brown mustard
- **Flavoring:** Chopped Kalamata olives
- **Sweetener:** Agave syrup or Wildflower Cider Syrup (page 35)
- **Herbs:** Dill

Chinese-Style Vinaigrette
- **Oil:** Peanut oil
- **Acid:** Chinese black vinegar
- **Emulsifier:** Store-bought vegan mayo or Silky Aquafaba Mayonnaise (page 46)
- **Flavoring:** Chinese-Style Chili Crisp (page 53)
- **Sweetener:** None
- **Herbs:** None

Mexican-Style Vinaigrette
- **Oil:** Neutral vegetable oil
- **Acid:** Lime juice
- **Emulsifier:** Apricot jam
- **Flavoring:** Store-bought salsa or Chunky Molcajete Salsa (page 48)
- **Sweetener:** None
- **Herbs:** Cilantro or mint

Middle Eastern–Style Vinaigrette
- **Oil:** Olive oil
- **Acid:** Lemon juice
- **Emulsifier/flavoring:** Pomegranate molasses
- **Sweetener:** None
- **Herbs:** Parsley

Creamy Herby Tofu Dressing

I've been making variations on this formula for a perfectly balanced, creamy, herb-packed, vegan salad dressing for a decade now. The use of shelf-stable silken tofu makes this a great back-pocket recipe; by swapping in whatever soft leafy herbs you have, along with the acid and oil, you can shift the dressing's flavors (and its shade of green), but its character and versatility remain (see Suggested Combinations below). Use this to dress greens, roasted vegetables, potatoes—or as a dip for crudités.

Makes 2 to 2½ cups (16 servings)

Time: Weekday

Storage: Refrigerate for up to 2 weeks.

> 12 ounces (340g) soft silken tofu (preferably from a shelf-stable package, such as Mori-Nu brand), drained
> 1 large or 2 small garlic cloves, peeled but whole
> 1 cup (30g) lightly packed soft herbs
> 2 tablespoons fresh lemon or lime juice
> ¼ cup (60ml) vinegar
> ¼ cup (60ml) oil
> ½ teaspoon fine sea salt, plus more to taste

IN A BLENDER OR food processor, combine all the ingredients and puree until smooth, stopping to scrape down the sides as needed. Taste and add more salt if needed.

Transfer to a container with a tight-fitting lid.

SUGGESTED COMBINATIONS

> 1 cup parsley + 2 tablespoons lemon juice + ¼ cup rice vinegar + ¼ cup olive oil + 1 tablespoon chopped fresh ginger
>
> 1 cup basil + 2 tablespoons lemon juice + ¼ cup red wine vinegar + ¼ cup olive oil
>
> 1 cup cilantro + ¼ cup lime juice + ¼ cup peanut oil
>
> 1 cup dill + 2 tablespoons lemon juice + ¼ cup red wine vinegar + ¼ cup olive oil + 1 teaspoon agave syrup
>
> 1 cup mint + 2 tablespoons lime juice + ¼ cup apple cider vinegar + ¼ cup sunflower oil + ¼ teaspoon red pepper flakes

Smoky, Sweet, Peppery Marinade for Vegetable Crisps

With the right marinade, prep, and baking time, you can turn thinly sliced vegetables, mushrooms, and more (see pages 66 to 68) into a smoky-sweet snack, salad topping, brunch side, or sandwich element reminiscent of bacon. The following choose-your-own-adventure set of recipes can help you meet your every whim.

The texture will vary along the spectrum of crisp to chewy depending on the base you pick and how long you cook it: On the crispiest side are rice paper, shiitakes, and coconut flakes; on the chewy side are tempeh, tofu, and portobellos; and in the middle, with crispy edges and slightly chewy centers, are the eggplant and carrots. Given their size, the coconut flakes make something more akin to bacon bits.

The timing will depend on the thinness of your pieces, so if you don't cut them all evenly, some will get dark faster than others. The darker, the crispier—and the uglier!—so watch them carefully and mind that trade-off.

Ingredient amounts are the same for all the crisps except the coconut: Since it is already high in fat, there's no need for oil. Also, the marinating needs no time—the flavor soaks in during the baking.

Makes a little more than ¼ cup

Time: Weekday

Storage: Refrigerate for up to 5 days.

> 2 tablespoons toasted sesame oil (omit for the coconut crisps)
> 1 tablespoon maple syrup
> 1 tablespoon tamari
> 1 tablespoon tomato paste
> 1 teaspoon liquid smoke (preferably hickory flavor) or Spanish smoked paprika (pimentón)
> 1 teaspoon garlic powder
> ½ teaspoon freshly ground black pepper

IN A SHALLOW BAKING dish, whisk together the oil (if using), maple syrup, tamari, tomato paste, liquid smoke, garlic powder, and black pepper.

Smoky Carrot Crisps

Try these on salads, toss them into pasta, use them to scoop dips, or, for double-carrot action, pair them with roasted carrots or a carrot slaw.

Makes 36 to 48 strips (about 6 servings)

Time: Weekday

Storage: Room temperature in an airtight container for up to 1 week. (They're best within a few days and will become less crisp as the days pass.)

> 3 medium carrots (about 9 ounces/265g total), scrubbed and trimmed
> Smoky, Sweet, Peppery Marinade for Vegetable Crisps (page 65)
> Fine sea salt

POSITION RACKS IN THE middle and the top and bottom thirds of the oven and preheat the oven to 325°F (160°C). Line three sheet pans with compostable parchment paper or silicone baking mats.

Hold a carrot flat on the cutting board with one hand and use the other to run a sharp Y-shaped peeler from tip to tail, pressing the peeler gently to get even slices. Repeat until you've peeled through about half of the carrot, then flip it over and finish peeling from the other side. Stop when you're left with the nub of the stem end, which you can save for snacking, salads, soups, or broth.

Transfer the carrot strips to the dish of marinade, stirring to thoroughly coat.

Transfer the carrot strips and marinade to the sheet pans, laying the strips out one at a time to avoid overlapping. Pour or brush on any extra marinade in the dish.

Bake for 10 minutes, then use a fork or tongs to flip over each carrot strip. Switch racks and rotate the sheets front to back and bake until they curl up and darken around the edges, another 10 to 15 minutes, checking every few minutes to ensure that they don't start to burn.

Remove from the oven, sprinkle with a little salt, and let them cool on the sheets, where they will crisp up.

Smoky Coconut Crisps

These are best on baked potatoes, salads, tacos, and soups—anywhere you want little crunchy bits. Unlike some other crisps, they also stay very crunchy in storage.

Makes 2 cups (8 servings)

Time: Weekday

Storage: Room temperature in an airtight container for up to 1 week.

> 2 cups (113g) large unsweetened coconut flakes
> Smoky, Sweet, Peppery Marinade for Vegetable Crisps (page 65), but made without oil
> Fine sea salt

PREHEAT THE OVEN TO 325°F (160°C). Line a sheet pan with compostable parchment paper or a silicone baking mat.

Toss the coconut flakes in the marinade until thoroughly coated.

Transfer the coconut with all the marinade to the sheet pan and spread into a single layer (as much as possible; some clumping is fine).

Bake for 6 minutes, then stir and toss and bake until the coconut is browned but not burned, another 6 to 8 minutes.

Remove from the oven, sprinkle with a little salt, and let cool on the sheet, where they will crisp up.

Smoky Eggplant Crisps

Slightly leathery (in a good way) after you store them, these make a great topping (or scoops!) for hummus, baba ghanoush, or other dips.

Makes 4 servings

Time: Weekday

Storage: Room temperature in an airtight container for up to 1 week. These have their best texture within a day or two of making, after which they get a little like fruit leather (which is not unpleasant in the least).

> 1 small oblong eggplant (10 ounces/285g), such as Asian varieties, or a thin Italian baby, stemmed but not peeled
>
> Smoky, Sweet, Peppery Marinade for Vegetable Crisps (page 65)
>
> Fine sea salt

POSITION RACKS IN THE top and bottom thirds of the oven and preheat the oven to 325°F (160°C). Line two sheet pans with compostable parchment paper or silicone baking mats.

Use a mandoline to cut the eggplant into lengthwise slices a little less than ⅛ inch thick. (Alternatively, you can use a sharp Y-shaped peeler to peel off strips or a chef's knife to get slices as thin as possible.)

Brush the strips with the marinade, then lay the strips on the sheet pans in one layer, arranging them so they're not overlapping.

Bake for 15 minutes, then use a fork or tongs to flip over each strip. Switch racks and rotate the sheet pans front to back and bake until the strips have darkened around their edges and started to get crisp, another 10 to 15 minutes, checking every few minutes to make sure they don't burn.

Remove from the oven, sprinkle with salt, and let cool on the sheets, where they will continue crisping up.

Smoky Mushroom Crisps

When made with shiitakes, these are wonderfully crisp; with portobellos, they're satisfyingly chewy and a little sticky, with crisp edges (at least when they're fresh). Either way, of course, they're packed with umami. Use them to top pasta dishes, soups (such as White Bean Soup with Crispy Shiitake Bacon, page 184), grain bowls, mac and cheese, and more.

Makes 4 servings

Time: Weekday

Storage: Room temperature in an airtight container for up to 1 week. (Shiitakes keep their crispness longer, while portobellos have their best texture after they first cool and get softer in storage.)

> 8 ounces (225g) fresh shiitake or portobello mushrooms
>
> 2 batches Smoky, Sweet, Peppery Marinade for Vegetable Crisps (page 65)

POSITION RACKS IN THE top and bottom thirds of the oven and preheat the oven to 325°F (160°C). Line two sheet pans with compostable parchment paper or silicone baking mats.

Remove the mushroom stems, if they're attached, and compost or save for making Vegetable Scrap Stock (page 36). Cut the caps into slices ⅛ inch (3mm) wide.

Working in batches, gently toss the mushrooms in the marinade until thoroughly coated. Transfer the mushrooms and as much marinade as possible to the sheet pans, making sure they're in one layer and no overlapping at all. Brush or pour on any remaining marinade.

Bake until the mushrooms have shrunk considerably and turned very dark brown with black edges, 20 to 25 minutes. (Halfway through baking, switch racks and rotate the sheets front to back.) Note that particularly if you're using portobellos, the smaller pieces will be finished before any larger ones, so you may want to remove them as they're ready.

Let cool on the sheet pan.

Smoky Rice Paper Crisps

These require a little more prep than the other crisps here, but you'll be rewarded in something that retains its crunch even after a week of storage. Try them on sandwiches!

Makes 4 servings

Time: Weekday

Storage: Room temperature in an airtight container for up to 1 week.

8 (6-inch/15cm) rice paper spring roll wrappers
Smoky, Sweet, Peppery Marinade for Vegetable Crisps (page 65)
Fine sea salt

POSITION RACKS IN THE top and bottom thirds of the oven and preheat the oven to 325°F (160°C). Line two sheet pans with compostable parchment paper or silicone baking mats.

Prepare a shallow bowl of room-temperature water. Dip one wrapper briefly into the water, let the excess water run off, and lay it flat on a cutting board. Dip a second wrapper in the water and set it on top of the first wrapper. Using a sharp knife or kitchen shears, cut each round into 6 strips. Repeat with the remaining wrappers until you have 24 strips in total.

Dredge a strip in the marinade, turning it over to coat both sides, then lay it on the sheet pan. Repeat with the remaining strips, arranging them so they're not overlapping. Pour or brush any extra marinade on top.

Bake for 12 minutes.

Use a fork or tongs to flip over each strip. Switch racks and rotate the sheet pans front to back and bake until the strips have bubbled and started to get dry and crisp on the edges, another 10 to 12 minutes.

Remove from the oven, sprinkle with salt, and let cool on the sheets, where they will continue crisping up.

Smoky Tempeh Crisps

These are crispy on the edges and a little crumbly when you bite into them, making them just the thing for adding a hit of flavor (and protein!) to grain bowls, salads, and more.

Makes 4 servings

Time: Weekday

Storage: Refrigerate for up to 1 week.

8 ounces (225g) tempeh, homemade (page 79) or store-bought
2 batches Smoky, Sweet, Peppery Marinade for Vegetable Crisps (page 65)
Fine sea salt

POSITION RACKS IN THE top and bottom thirds of the oven and preheat the oven to 325°F (160°C). Line two sheet pans with compostable parchment paper or silicone baking mats.

Cut the tempeh in half crosswise and then cut each half into slices ⅛ inch (3mm) thick or (if possible) thinner.

Carefully dredge the pieces (to avoid crumbling), one at a time, in the marinade, coating on both sides and letting a little of the excess drip off. Then lay each piece on a sheet pan, keeping them from overlapping or even touching.

Bake until golden brown and dry to the touch, 10 to 15 minutes. Flip each piece over, switch racks, and rotate the sheet pans from front to back and bake until deep brown with blackened edges, about 10 minutes. (The smaller and thinner pieces will cook faster, so you might want to remove them as they're done.)

Remove from the oven, sprinkle lightly with the salt, and let cool on the sheet pans.

Opposite, clockwise from the top: Smoky Coconut Crisps (page 66), Smoky Carrot Crisps (page 66), Smoky Tempeh Crisps (this page), and Smoky Mushroom Crisps (page 67)

Smoky Tofu Crisps

Using prebaked tofu lets you cut it thinner than if you started with the fresh curd. It also speeds up the process, cutting out the time it would take to press the extra moisture out of the tofu so it can absorb the marinade and end up crisp in parts and chewy in others. Use these to make TLTs, of course.

Makes 4 servings

Time: Weekday

Storage: Refrigerate in an airtight container for up to 1 week.

> 7 ounces (200g) baked tofu (preferably a neutral flavor such as "savory")
>
> 2 batches Smoky, Sweet, Peppery Marinade for Vegetable Crisps (page 65)

PREHEAT THE OVEN TO 325°F (160°C). Line a sheet pan with compostable parchment paper or a silicone baking mat.

Use a sharp knife to cut the tofu into 1/16-inch (2mm) pieces. (Any thinner than that and they will start to fall apart.)

Dredge each piece in the marinade, turning to coat it thoroughly, and then lay it on the sheet pan. Repeat with the remaining tofu, being careful to not overlap or let the pieces even touch. (You'll have some marinade left, which you'll use to brush the tofu when you flip the pieces halfway through baking.)

Bake until the tofu is golden brown and dry on top with dark edges, about 20 minutes. Use a spatula or tongs to gently flip the pieces, brush with the remaining marinade, and bake until the tofu is deeply browned and turning black on some of the edges, 20 to 25 minutes.

Remove from the oven and let cool on the sheets.

Popcorn Tempeh

Indonesia's great gift to the world, tempeh, is made for crumbling into irregular pieces for added texture and crunch. As you break up the block, smaller pieces (usually individual soybeans) will fall into the pan and get extra crispy. These craggy pieces are made for pan-frying: You end up with a variety of interesting textures, as well as nooks and crannies for seasoning to settle into. The result resembles popcorn: crispy jagged orbs, plus smaller, extra-crispy bits that sink to the bottom of the bucket. So why not season tempeh as you would popcorn? Once the tempeh crumbles are cooked, shake them in a mixture of nutritional yeast and garlic powder, as this recipe calls for. Or try Nacho Nooch (page 45), or season them however you like to flavor your popcorn: with dried chile, nori, everything bagel seasoning, and so on. It's a quick and fun way to add protein to meals, as you would with crispy chickpeas. Add to salads, tacos, or grain bowls, or pop them right into your mouth by the handful.

Makes 4 servings

Time: Weekday

Storage: Refrigerate for up to 5 days, and add more seasonings to taste when you reheat.

> 2 tablespoons neutral oil, plus more as needed
>
> 1 (8-ounce/225g) block tempeh, homemade (page 79) or store-bought
>
> 1/2 teaspoon fine sea salt, plus more to taste
>
> 1/4 teaspoon freshly ground black pepper, plus more to taste
>
> 1 tablespoon nutritional yeast, plus more to taste
>
> 1/2 teaspoon garlic powder

IN A LARGE CAST-IRON skillet, heat the oil over medium-high heat until it shimmers. Crumble the tempeh into the skillet in pieces the size of popped popcorn kernels (smaller pieces will fall off, and that's okay—good, even). Add the salt and pepper and cook, undisturbed, until deeply golden underneath, 1 to 2 minutes. Stir and cook, stirring occasionally, until browned all over, another 3 to 5 minutes. Add more oil as needed if the pan looks dry.

Remove from the heat, add the nutritional yeast and garlic powder, and toss to coat. Taste and season with more salt, pepper, and nutritional yeast if needed.

Clean-Out-the-Fridge Kimchi

Kimchi purists, please look the other way: This recipe breaks the rules, but the result is an easy small-batch technique that turns end-of-the-week fridge scraps such as bruised fennel bulbs, cauliflower, and weeks-old radishes into a tangy, spicy, lacto-fermented product.

First you soak napa cabbage in a salt brine, then drain and use it as a base to kick-start the fermentation. As for the pepper flakes, if you can't get your hands on Korean gochugaru, try substituting Aleppo chile flakes. Toss your scrap veggies into the mix and pack everything in jars to sit at room temperature. Every day, you'll burp your kimchi baby and taste it; the flavor becomes tangier by the day. Once you're happy with the results, place the jars in the fridge and you'll have the perfect sidekick for grain bowls, eggs, and stews for weeks to come.

Makes about 6 cups

Time: Project

Storage: Refrigerate for up to 1 month.

- 1 small head napa cabbage (2 pounds/910g), halved, cored, and cut crosswise into 2-inch (5cm) pieces
- ¼ cup (55g) sea salt, plus more to taste
- 6 medium garlic cloves, finely grated or pressed
- 3-inch (7.5cm) piece fresh ginger, peeled and grated (about 2 tablespoons)
- 3½ tablespoons gochugaru (Korean chile flakes) or Aleppo pepper flakes, plus more to taste
- 1½ teaspoons organic cane sugar
- 1 tablespoon soy sauce or tamari
- 2 teaspoons white miso, homemade (page 83) or store-bought
- 2 scallions, cut into 2-inch (5cm) pieces
- 1 pound (450g) mixed vegetables (any combination of radishes, carrots, cauliflower, fennel, asparagus, green beans, bell peppers, turnips), cut into bite-size pieces

WASH AND DRY TWO 1-quart mason jars, rinse them in boiling water, and let dry and cool to room temperature.

Place the cabbage in a large bowl and coat with salt, massaging it with your hands. Add cold water to cover the cabbage, and let it soak for 1 hour. Rinse thoroughly (up to three times) and drain the cabbage. Set aside to drain in a colander for 10 to 15 minutes.

While the cabbage is soaking, in a small bowl, combine the garlic, ginger, chile flakes, sugar, soy sauce, and miso, stirring it into a smooth paste.

Transfer the cabbage to a large bowl and add the chile paste, scallions, and vegetables. Wearing gloves, use your hands to combine everything until everything is coated in the chile paste. Taste and season with more salt and chile flakes if needed.

Pack the kimchi into the sterilized jars, pressing down and letting the liquid that releases cover the vegetables, leaving 1 inch (2.5cm) of space at the top. More liquid will release as the jar sits, so don't add water. Seal the jars with lids.

Let sit at room temperature to ferment for 1 to 5 days. The kimchi will get more sour as it ferments, and warmer environments speed up the fermentation time. Check it daily, opening the lid to "burp" the kimchi, giving it a taste and adding a splash of soy sauce or salt to season if needed. Use a spoon to press the veggies down, submerging them under the liquid as much as possible. (Don't worry if it's not fully submerged all the time; as long as you see bubbles, it's fermenting.)

Refrigerate once you're satisfied with the flavor. The kimchi will continue to slowly age in your refrigerator and be delicious for up to 1 month.

Lacto-Fermented Vegetables

Many beloved foods—including sauerkraut, kimchi, yogurt, full sour pickles, and fermented hot sauces—are the result of lacto-fermentation, in which lactic acid bacteria eat the starches in a food, acidifying the liquid and helping keep harmful microbes at bay for long-term storage. It's the original veggie pickling, requiring just salt and water, rather than the salt-water-vinegar brine we use for quick pickles, and it's one of Julia Skinner's favorite ways to add living foods to her diet.

Unlike the sauerkraut-making process, where cabbage is salted and then massaged to release its juices and form its own brine without added water, this method calls for you to mix up a simple brine first. (Brine made with 2% to 5% salinity will kick off the lacto-fermentation process; the best-tasting range for most veggies is around 3% to 4%.)

You can ferment just about any vegetable or fruit you wish, but you might not like the result. Summer peaches will ferment, for example, but they will get overly soft quickly and may not be appetizing to eat whole. If you run into a ferment that tastes good, but doesn't have the best texture, don't despair, and don't throw it away: Puree it in a blender to make a tangy sauce for your savory dishes or desserts.

Carrot sticks, celery, and bell peppers turn out great using this method. For most vegetables, all you'll need is the brine, the veggies, and a bit of time. But for cucumbers, which are infamous for getting soft, adding something tannic—a grape leaf or a pinch of black tea leaves—to your brine will keep them crisp.

If you want to make hot sauce, pack whole chiles and whole garlic cloves in a jar, pour the brine over the chiles, and ferment until the chiles soften before blending to the desired consistency.

EQUIPMENT
Fermentation weight or weights (purchased online, or use baggies of dried beans or salt, boiled and cooled rocks, or ceramic ramekins)
1-quart (1L) mason jar with lid

Makes 1 quart

Time: Project

Storage: Refrigerate, fully submerged in the brine, for up to 2 weeks for softer vegetables or several months for hot sauce or dense root vegetables such as carrots.

2 tablespoons (28g) fine sea salt (see Notes)
4 cups (950ml) room-temperature (see Notes) water, 65° to 80°F (18° to 27°C)
Vegetables, whole or cut into sticks
1 grape leaf or ½ teaspoon black tea leaves (optional; for fermenting cucumbers)

CLEAN A 1-QUART (1L) glass jar, its lid, a bowl, whisk, and any other utensils you're using with hot, soapy water before starting, and let air-dry or dry with a clean kitchen towel.

In a bowl, whisk the salt into the water until dissolved.

Fill the quart jar with vegetables. Pack them tightly for hot sauce, but don't smash them together too tightly when making whole pickles.

Pour the brine over the top of the vegetables, making sure they are completely covered. Use a fermentation weight if needed to keep them submerged.

Screw on the lid and set the jar on a plate or tray (to avoid staining your countertops) at room temperature and out of direct sunlight. Allow to ferment, making sure to "burp" your jar each day as it ferments by loosening the lid and then tightening it again. This helps to release any built-up gas.

Also check once a day to be sure the vegetables are still submerged. If you find your veggies are floating up and you can't get them to stay down, just give the jar a shake once or twice a day, which will disrupt the brine's surface and keep mold from forming.

Continue to check for signs of mold, and use a clean utensil to pull out a piece to taste for doneness. (Never put your fingers into the jar.) Once the vegetables have a flavor you like, they're done.

COOK'S NOTES
- You can use a salt other than fine sea salt, but make sure to weigh out the 28 grams and not use the tablespoon measure to make up for any differences in saltiness by volume. Also make sure the salt has no anticaking agents or other additives that can inhibit fermentation and adversely affect flavor and potentially compromise safety.

- Be sure to use room-temperature water to avoid killing the beneficial microbes on the vegetables.

Soy Milk, Tofu & a Bonus

These recipes are more than just related: I don't think it makes sense to do one without the other. For one thing, the best homemade tofu comes from homemade soy milk—because the latter is fresh, has only two ingredients (soybeans and water), and tastes better than virtually anything you can buy. Second of all, if you're going to go to the trouble of making your own soy milk, you might as well make a decent-size batch so you can use some of it for drinking and some of it to make tofu.

I used the word "trouble," but the truth is, none of this is difficult. Making the milk requires one step further than, say, almond milk, in that after the typical soaking, blending, and straining, you cook the soy milk, in part, to make it more digestible. (Remember that uncooked beans can cause gastric distress.) And it's worth it: What you get will be the best soy milk you've ever tasted, and you can use it anywhere you would use any plant-based milk: in drinks, over granola, in overnight oats and smoothies—and, of course, to make tofu.

Best of all, you don't have to do this all at once. After soaking the soybeans, you can refrigerate them for 2 days before doing anything with them. And after you make the soy milk and divide it in half, you can proceed with the tofu immediately, or refrigerate or freeze the soy milk and come back to that when it's convenient. Just get it back to the required temperature, and you're good to go.

The thing that I hope will strike you the first time you make tofu is this: Why haven't I done this before? Once you've cooked the soy milk, you just cool it down a little, add a coagulant (I prefer the traditional Japanese nigari, which is simply magnesium chloride, but lemon juice and vinegar work, too), wait for the curds to separate, then spoon them into a cheesecloth-lined press, and ... press. I've got a Japanese bamboo tofu-pressing box for this, but you can use other setups, even just a cheesecloth-lined fine-mesh sieve.

As is the case with the soy milk, the texture and flavor will be better than any tofu you can buy, because you've controlled the ingredients and because nothing is fresher than tofu you make at home. It's also adaptable: Use more or less coagulant, press for a longer or shorter amount of time, and your tofu will be firmer or softer—but still firm enough for frying, roasting, braising, and stewing, or even for crumbling, binding with plant-based mayonnaise and seasonings for a killer tofu salad. I've given you a coagulant amount and pressing time that results in a medium-firm tofu. (For custardy silken tofu, see page 78.)

I feel a little like one of those TV pitchmen when I write: Wait, that's not all! You also get a bonus recipe, for a protein powder made with okara, the pulp that's left when you strain the soy milk from the beans.

EQUIPMENT NEEDED

Nut-milk bag

Cheesecloth or muslin

Tofu mold (or fine-mesh sieve and a plate; see Notes)

Soy Milk

Makes 12 servings (12 cups)

Storage: Refrigerate the soy milk for up to 5 days or freeze for up to 6 months.

2½ cups (1 pound/450g) non-GMO organic soybeans (see Notes)

22 cups (5.2L) filtered water

IN A LARGE BOWL, combine the soybeans with 6 cups (1.4L) filtered water. Cover and soak overnight, 8 to 12 hours. Drain and rinse the soybeans, which will have gone from round to oblong.

Transfer about one-quarter of the beans to a blender, add 4 cups (950ml) water, and blend until very smooth, at least 1 minute. Set a nut-milk bag over a Dutch oven or stockpot and pour the mixture into the bag. Close the bag and squeeze it, twisting as needed, until you've pressed out as much of the soy milk as possible into the pot. Empty the pulp (okara) into another bowl or storage container. Repeat with another one-quarter of the soybeans and 4 cups (950ml) water, blending and squeezing. Repeat twice more to finish the soybeans.

Set the pot of soy milk over medium heat and heat to 212°F (100°C), using a silicone spatula to gently stir and scrape the bottom so it doesn't stick or scorch. This could take as long as 15 or 20 minutes. Adjust the heat as needed, including taking the milk off the heat if it threatens to bubble over. Once the milk reaches 212°F (100°C), reduce the heat to keep the soy milk at a simmer and cook, stirring, for 15 minutes. (This step makes the soy milk digestible.) As you simmer it, skim off any foam and periodically use tongs, chopsticks, or your skimmer to remove the skin (yuba) that forms. (Save this for a cook's treat, eating it as is or cutting it into strips and pan-frying.)

If making tofu right away, set aside half of the soy milk (about 6 cups/1.4L) and let cool to between 160° and 175°F (70° and 80°C); if making the tofu later, refrigerate the soy milk. Pour the remaining soy milk into a storage container or containers, let cool for a few minutes, then refrigerate or freeze.

Firm Tofu

Makes 20 ounces (4 to 6 servings)

Storage: Refrigerate the tofu, submerged in cold water, for up to 5 days, changing the water every day or two, or freeze for up to 6 months. (FYI, freezing will change the texture, in a way that many people, including me, love: It makes it spongier and better able to soak up marinades.)

6 cups (1.4L) soy milk

1 cup (240ml) warm filtered water

2 teaspoons powdered nigari (magnesium chloride), or 2 tablespoons fresh lemon juice or distilled white vinegar

IF YOU'VE JUST MADE the soy milk, cool it to between 160° and 175°F (70° and 80°C). If it's been refrigerated, heat it to that temperature.

In a bowl, stir together the warm water and nigari (or lemon juice or vinegar), then immediately pour it into the hot soy milk and gently stir it in. Allow the milk to sit undisturbed until curds form, 5 to 15 minutes.

Line a tofu press (see Notes) or fine-mesh sieve (or other mold with holes in it) with cheesecloth. Spoon the curds into the tofu press or sieve and set over a bowl. Fold the fabric over the curds and top with the tofu press. (Or top with a small plate and add a large can of tomatoes or beans or other small weight of about 1½ pounds/454g). Let the tofu drain until it holds together, 20 to 30 minutes.

Transfer the tofu, still in its cheesecloth, to a bowl or storage container filled with cold water. Carefully unwrap the tofu, remove the cloth, let it sit for 30 minutes, then remove and drain. (This removes any remaining bitter or sour flavor from the coagulant.)

COOK'S NOTES

- I love the Japanese cypress tofu mold that I bought as part of a kit from Cultures for Health, CulturesForHealth.com. The site also sells nigari, nut-milk bags, and other fermentation supplies.

- Look for the Iowa-based Laura Soybeans at LauraSoybeans.com.

Silken Tofu

To make this glorious fresh tofu pudding, I follow my friend Andrea Nguyen's recipe in her book *Asian Tofu*. It requires gypsum (calcium sulfate) for a beautiful soft texture that doesn't form separate curds. I like to make it in individual ramekins, which fit on a steamer rack in a stockpot, and to top with soy sauce, scallions, grated ginger, and roasted peanuts for serving.

Makes 6 appetizer servings

Storage: Refrigerate for up to 3 days. Freezing not recommended.

> 1½ teaspoons gypsum (calcium sulfate)
> 2 teaspoons filtered water, plus more for steaming
> 3 cups (700ml) soy milk, chilled or at room temperature

SET A STEAMER RACK over 2 inches (5cm) of water in a large pot, bring water to a boil, and reduce to a simmer.

In a small bowl, stir together the gypsum and water until dissolved. Pour the mixture into the soy milk and stir to thoroughly combine.

Pour the soy milk mixture into six 4-ounce (120ml) ramekins and, working in batches if needed, set them on the steamer rack, cover with the lid slightly ajar (to prevent condensation from dripping down), and steam the soy milk until it has set, 15 to 20 minutes. (It should jiggle and a toothpick in the center should leave a tiny hole; it might seep liquid a little around the edges, and that's fine.)

Remove the ramekins, cool to room temperature, and then cover and refrigerate for at least 4 hours and up to 3 days. When ready to unmold, run a knife around the edge and unmold onto a plate.

Okara Protein Powder

Use 2 tablespoons to turn a smoothie into a protein shake, sprinkle on granola, stir into muffin or pancake batter, or use in other baked goods. You can also blend it with nutritional yeast, garlic powder, and salt to make a Parmesan substitute for pasta and other dishes.

Makes 1 cup powder (8 servings)

Storage: Refrigerate for up to 2 weeks or freeze for up to 3 months.

> 2 cups okara (soybean pulp)

PREHEAT THE OVEN TO 300°F (150°C). Line a sheet pan with a silicone baking mat or compostable parchment paper.

Spread out the okara in as thin a layer as possible. Bake, stirring and breaking it up every 20 minutes, until the okara has turned golden brown and dry, 40 to 50 minutes.

Turn off the oven and leave the okara in the oven as it cools for further drying.

Transfer the okara to a food processor or dedicated spice grinder, working in batches if needed, and process to a powder.

Tempeh

Tempeh is one of my favorite soybean products. The fermentation improves digestion, and I love its texture and flavor—especially when it's fresh and homemade, a wildly superior product to what you find on grocery store shelves. Originally from Indonesia, it requires a little practice—and even trial and error—but once you get the hang of it, the results are well worth the effort. As I learned from fermentation geek Julia Skinner, the steps are fairly straightforward: You cook the beans (and they don't have to be soybeans), toss with a starter and vinegar, then wrap them into packets and let them ferment for about 2 days, until they're enrobed in a beautiful white mat of mold. The tricky part is keeping them at the right temperature to let the mold do the right thing.

The most time-consuming part is dehulling the beans, which can be painstaking. That's why, when Berkeley tempeh maker Philip Gelb told me he uses daal because the beans are already hulled and split, it was a game changer. Now my favorite beans to use are chana daal, widely available in Indian markets, and split mini fava beans, found in Middle Eastern markets. If you find already split and dehulled soybeans (see Note), snap them up.

Traditionally, tempeh is made by wrapping the beans in banana leaves for fermentation, which help naturally regulate the tempeh's moisture and temperature. But especially when you're starting out, I recommend zip-top bags, which let you more easily check the progress. (You poke holes for critical air circulation.) This is one of the few exceptions to my no-plastic rule in this book, but you can wash and reuse the bags a few times—and invest in reusable silicone bags if you plan to make a lot of tempeh.

The tempeh starter, made at least in part with *Rhizopus oryzae* spores, needs to be somewhat above room temperature to grow. You can use specialty fermentation chambers (such as bread-proofing boxes or dehydrators) or makeshift ones, but it's easiest to work with something you already have: your oven, turned off but with the oven light on, or a gas oven with a pilot light. You will need to experiment to find the setup that works best for you, depending on how hot your light is and where it is in the oven and by checking the temperature periodically with an instant-read thermometer. You can also supplement the heat with a kombucha fermentation mat (see page 463) or other gentle-heating element.

The big commitment is the several days you need to keep your oven off, so put a note on or near your oven controls to remind you not to turn it on, just in case.

EQUIPMENT

4 (1-quart/1L) plastic or silicone zip-top bags (not the kind with stay-flat bottoms)

Instant-read thermometer

Kombucha fermentation mat or heating pad (optional)

Wire cooling rack

Makes four 7- to 8-ounce (200 to 225g) blocks (about 8 servings)

Time: Project

Storage: Refrigerate in an airtight container for up to 5 days or freeze for up to 4 months.

1 pound (450g) dried soybeans or your bean of choice, soaked overnight and drained

2½ tablespoons distilled white vinegar

1 teaspoon powdered tempeh starter (see Note)

IF THE BEANS ARE whole, split and dehull them by picking up small handfuls and squeezing them between your thumb and forefinger. You want to get as many hulls off as you can. Discard the skins by covering the beans with water by several inches, then swirling them with your hand, letting the beans settle, carefully pouring off the water with the skins that have floated, and repeating as many times as needed. If you use a dehulled/split legume, like daal, skip this step.

In a Dutch oven or large saucepan, combine the beans with enough water to cover by 2 inches (5cm). Bring them to a boil, reduce the heat to low so the liquid is at a bare simmer, and cook, covered, until the beans are very tender without being mushy (they should hold their shape but squish easily when gently pressed between your fingers), about 1 hour for soybeans and 25 to 40 minutes for most daal, depending on the variety. For other beans, consult cooking-time charts online (or in *Cool Beans*); check them early and often.

Line a large sheet pan with a clean kitchen towel. Drain the beans and transfer to the towel-lined pan, gently spreading them into one layer. Lay another clean towel on top and pat gently to remove any excess moisture. The beans should be dry to the touch. Let cool to just above room temperature.

Transfer the beans to a large bowl. Sprinkle the vinegar over the beans and gently fold until evenly coated. Repeat with the tempeh starter, gently folding to evenly coat the beans.

RECIPE CONTINUES ON NEXT PAGE

Use a paring knife to poke holes every inch or two on both sides of the bags. Divide the beans among the bags. Press out the air, then fold the top half of each bag down so all your beans are in the bottom half and to shape them into a compact rectangular block 1 to 1½ inches (2.5cm to 4cm) thick. Seal the zippers.

Place the packets on a wire cooling rack, which helps air circulate more evenly and keeps the tempeh from getting soggy. Unfold the bags, keeping the beans in their neat shapes and avoiding overlapping bags.

Make sure the oven is off and cooled, turn the oven light on, and place the rack of tempeh on the rack closest to the oven light (or pilot light if you have a gas oven with no oven light).

After 2 hours, carefully open each bag and insert the tip of a clean instant-read thermometer into the center of the beans, which should be between 85° and 91°F/29° and 32°C. If they're cooler than that, put a fermentation mat or heating pad on the lowest setting on the rack directly under the beans. If they're warmer than that, move them away from the oven light or pilot light by one or two racks. Check the temperature again in 1 hour, and adjust the tempeh's distance from the light and/or the setting on the fermentation mat until you hit the range.

After 12 hours, check on the tempeh: You want to see a bit of light, fuzzy growth, which means the spores are multiplying. Check the moisture: Make sure the bottom of the tempeh isn't soggy; if it is, make sure you have enough holes poked in the bag, and flip the bag over. Take the temperature of the beans again, and if it has increased, that's a good sign: It means the beans are generating heat from the fermentation. Turn off the oven light and/or heating mat, and leave the tempeh in the oven.

Checking every few hours if possible, let the tempeh sit undisturbed until it has a clear white mat of mold around it, and it holds its shape firmly, about another 12 to 36 hours. As soon as it does, immediately transfer each bag to a separate zip-top bag without holes in it, press out the air, and refrigerate if using soon, or freeze. (If your tempeh is slightly marbled with a darker mold, especially around the bag holes, that's fine, but a lot of dark mold means your tempeh has gone past the point of being delicious and has sporulated. Next time, keep a closer eye on it and transfer it to the fridge or freezer as soon as you have a dense, white snowy mat.)

COOK'S NOTE: Find tempeh starter at Cultures for Health, CulturesForHealth.com. Find split and dehulled soybeans at Révolution Fermentation, RevolutionFermentation.com.

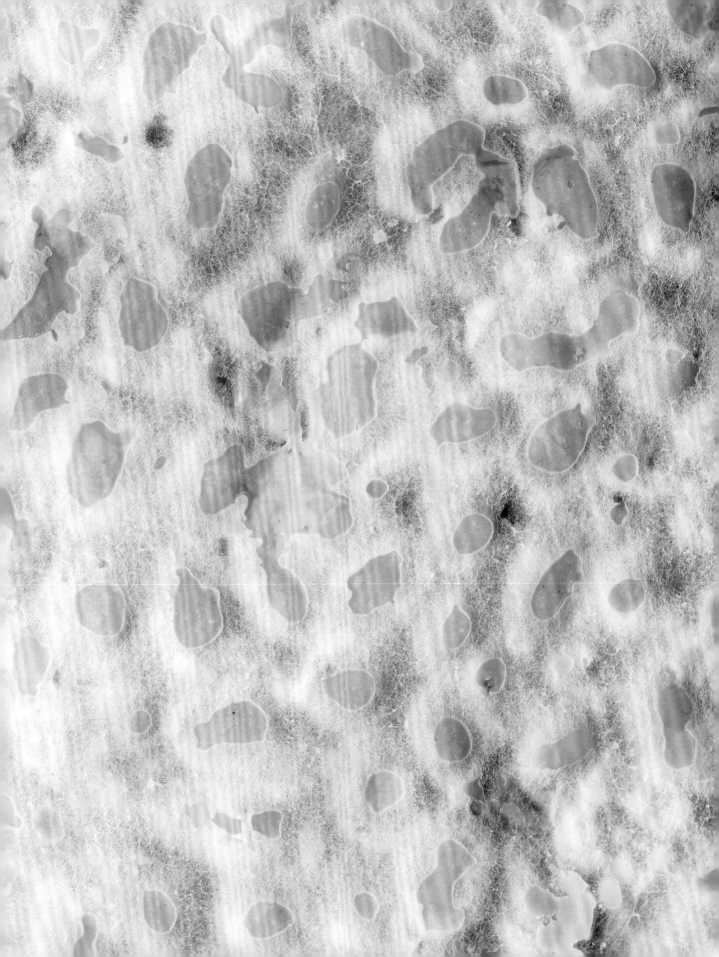

White Miso

Miso is an incredibly versatile ingredient in the plant-based pantry, as it adds such depth and umami thanks to its fermentation. It's an example of an amino paste, a savory fermented paste often (but not always) made with beans. This recipe for Japanese-style white miso—the lightest and quickest to make—from Julia Skinner is a great introduction to the process and results in a particularly versatile miso.

Japanese miso is made with soybeans, koji (the mold spores used to make shoyu, sake, and amazake), and salt. It's simple to do, but there are a few key strategies: First, make sure you get the proportions of salt and koji to beans right, and second, separate the fermenting miso paste from the outside world. (See the equipment list for how to do this.) Use a nonreactive, nonmetal vessel: A glass jar lets you keep a close eye on the project and work in smaller batches.

By thoroughly pureeing the beans and koji, you get the best texture and prevent pathogenic microbes from thriving in the gaps. Finally, thoroughly wash all jars and utensils with hot, soapy water right before using.

You can substitute other beans if you're soy intolerant or simply want to experiment. How long you let it sit is up to you: In Julia's Atlanta climate, 1 to 3 months is the sweet spot for white miso, but your results may differ. Like any living food, miso will ferment faster in warmer weather and slower in cooler weather.

EQUIPMENT
Cheesecloth

Fermentation weight or weights (purchased online, or use plastic bags filled with dried beans or salt, boiled and cooled rocks, or ceramic ramekins)

1-quart (1L) glass mason jar or two 2-cup (475ml) jars

Makes about 1 quart

Time: Project

Storage: Refrigerate for up to 6 months.

1 cup (185g) dried soybeans (to yield roughly 2 cups/250g cooked beans), soaked overnight and drained

2 cups (250g) rice koji or barley koji (see Note)

5 tablespoons (69g) fine sea salt, plus more for sprinkling and as needed

IN A DUTCH OVEN or large saucepan, combine the soybeans with enough water to cover by 2 inches (5cm). (Or use an Instant Pot or other pressure cooker and cover them by 4 inches of water.) Bring to a boil, then reduce the heat to medium-low and cook until very tender, 1 to 3 hours for soybeans, less for other bean varieties. (In a pressure cooker, cook them on high pressure for 45 minutes, then let the pressure naturally release. The timing will vary depending on the age of the beans, so return them to pressure and cook in 5- to 10-minute increments, using manual release, until they are very tender.)

Drain the beans, reserving 1 cup of the cooking water, and let cool to room temperature.

Transfer the beans to a food processor and add the koji and salt. Process until they form a thick paste. If it's too dry to form a dense ball without cracking, add the reserved cooking water, 2 tablespoons at a time, until it forms a thick paste.

Pack the soybean mixture into the clean glass jar(s) using the back of a clean spoon or ladle, pressing down after each addition to remove any air bubbles. Leave about 2 inches (5cm) of headspace at the top of the jar(s) so the miso and liquid don't leak out.

Cut a piece of cheesecloth slightly larger than the mouth of the jar, fold in the edges, and place directly on top of the soybean mixture. Sprinkle a thin layer of salt on the cheesecloth, paying special attention to spread it all the way to the edges. This helps to keep unwanted molds from growing on top. Place a fermentation weight on top of the salt and seal the jar with a lid.

Check the miso every few days, looking for signs of unwanted mold growth or large air pockets. If it's a fuzzy white mold, scrape it off and sprinkle on a bit more salt. If it's colorful or black mold, toss the miso and try again. If the miso is bubbling away and forming large air pockets, press it down again with a clean utensil, then reapply the cheesecloth, salt, and weight. Don't worry if a small amount of caramel-colored liquid floats to the top: This is tamari, which you can pour off like soy sauce.

After 2 to 3 weeks, taste the miso. If you're happy with the flavor, it's ready. If it still tastes like beans more than miso, give it more time, tasting it once a week until ready.

COOK'S NOTE: Look for rice koji in local markets and at South River Miso, SouthRiverMiso.com. Barley koji is available from Cultures for Health, CulturesForHealth.com.

BUILD A NOURISHING PLANT-BASED MEAL

By Tracye McQuirter, MPH

Whether it's a one-bowl meal, a sandwich, a wrap, a savory pastry, or any other culinary delight, a few simple guidelines can help you build a nutritious plant-based meal.

The first is to start with whole plant foods, which are closest to their natural state and contain the essential fiber, vitamins, minerals, and other nutrients that are the foundation of a healthy vegan diet.

The essential building blocks are vegetables, fruits, beans, whole grains, and nuts. When we create our meals from these core foods, we're rewarded with endless ways to enjoy delicious dishes that promote our health and longevity.

So how much of these core foods should we eat each day? Here's what that can look like for a person eating about 2,000 calories and exercising 30 minutes each day:

- Vegetables: 2 to 3 cups
- Fruits: 2 cups
- Beans: 1½ cups
- Whole grains: 1½ cups
- Nuts: ¼ cup

VEGETABLES

These can be split into two categories: dark leafy greens and other vegetables.

Dark leafy greens are the healthiest foods on the planet. They give us the most protection against chronic diseases, including heart disease and stroke—the top killers in the nation. So it's essential to eat them every day; aim for 1 cup cooked or 2 cups raw. That includes greens like arugula, beet greens, bok choy, collards, dandelion greens, kale, mustard greens, broccoli rabe, spinach, Swiss chard, and turnip greens.

In the other-vegetables category, you'll get the most nutrition bang for your buck if you eat at least 1 cup of cancer-fighting cruciferous vegetables each day. These include broccoli, Brussels sprouts, cabbage, cauliflower, kale, mustard greens, and turnip greens. You may notice these last three are also dark leafy greens, making it even easier to up your nutrition game.

You also should eat about 1 cup of raw or cooked colorful vegetables each day, choosing from among things such as bell peppers, carrots, corn, green beans, mixed frozen veggies, mushrooms, purple potatoes, radishes, sea vegetables, sweet potatoes, and zucchini.

FRUIT

Fruits can also be split into two categories: berries and other fruits.

Berries are the most nutritious fruits, containing powerful disease-fighting antioxidants and health-promoting fruit pigments, which give berries their vibrant colors. The darker the berry, the healthier the fruit! Choose from blackberries, blueberries, goji berries, raspberries, strawberries, and more. Aim for ½ cup daily.

For other fruits, eat 1 cup each day, about the equivalent of an apple, a banana, an orange, or a pear. For dried fruits, such as dates and raisins, one serving is about ½ cup.

BEANS

These protein-packed powerhouses are central to a healthy vegan diet. On average, we need to get 50 to 70 grams of protein each day. Fortunately, vegans get more than enough protein from plant foods. In fact, the largest study in history of people who eat plant-based diets was published in the *Journal of the Academy of Nutrition and Dietetics* in 2013 and showed that the average vegan gets 70 percent more protein than the recommended daily allowance. Beans, as well as nuts, have the highest amounts of protein of all plant foods.

With their wide variety, it's easy to eat 1½ cups of beans every day. Whether it's black beans, red lentils, or yellow split peas; tofu or tempeh; red pepper hummus or roasted chickpeas, beans should be a foundational part of most meals.

WHOLE GRAINS

Whole grains are the healthiest because they retain their nutrient-dense fiber, vitamins, and minerals. Choose intact whole grains first, which means the only ingredient is the grain itself. Think brown rice, black rice, wild rice, oats, quinoa, millet, bulgur, and amaranth.

Your next best choices are ingredients made from whole grains, such as whole-grain pasta, whole-grain tortillas, whole-grain bread, and whole-grain cereal.

Eating 1½ cups of whole grains each day is as simple as eating a bowl of oatmeal for breakfast and a side of brown rice, quinoa, or whole-grain pasta with lunch and dinner. Also, remember that one large whole-grain tortilla or one slice of whole-grain bread equals ½ cup whole grains. Eat your favorite whole-grain sandwich, and you're two-thirds of the way there.

NUTS

A handful of protein-rich nuts each day is key to promoting longevity. Add them as a main protein to meals, eat them as snacks, spread 2 tablespoons of nut or seed butter onto toasted whole-grain bread, or use them to make creamy sauces for savory or sweet dishes. Nuts offer delicious versatility.

EAT THE RAINBOW

One other important guideline to keep in mind when building a nutritious vegan meal is to focus on colors. Or as I like to say, health is in the hue. The variety of colors in plants comes from phytochemicals, protective compounds that can help prevent and/or reverse major chronic diseases, including heart disease, stroke, certain cancers, and diabetes. So the color of your food absolutely matters.

Strive to eat a variety of brightly colored vegetables, fruits, beans, nuts, and whole grains each day. You can start by adding at least three colors of food to each meal. Whether it's red onions, orange bell peppers, purple eggplant, brown walnuts, green lentils, or tricolor quinoa, be sure you're eating from the rainbow daily.

So what do all these guidelines translate to on a typical 9-inch (23cm) plate? It can mean something as simple as filling half your plate with vegetables, one-quarter with beans, and one-quarter with whole grains. Just keep it colorful.

One last note: These guidelines are meant to help you get into the practice of building nutritious vegan meals but aren't meant to be rigid. Instead, the goal is for them to become intuitive, so you are free to focus on the art of creating nutritious and delicious vegan meals.

Tracye McQuirter, MPH, is the author of *By Any Greens Necessary* and *Ageless Vegan* and founder of the 10 Million Black Vegan Women Movement.

BREAKFAST & BRUNCH

The traditional diner-style American breakfast is laden with animal products, but plant-based cooks can have fun reinventing it. Silken tofu makes a beautifully creamy scramble, as do pureed mung beans (the ingredient in one of the first high-tech supermarket egg substitutes, Just Egg). Oats play a starring role in the plant-based kitchen at breakfast time, as the makings of granola, oatmeal, and overnight oats, while baked goods such as scones and quick breads are tasty ways to start the day.

Lemon Blueberry Scones

Scones first made their appearance in Scottish recipe books in the sixteenth century, and American biscuits are certainly descended from them, but a scone always feels like a special treat. If you are used to the dry, crumbly scones that are often found in coffee shops, these are the complete opposite: tender, moist, packed with fresh blueberries, and slightly sweet. Enjoy them topped with a spoonful of whipped coconut cream and a dollop of raspberry jam—and accompanied by a cup of tea, of course.

Makes 12 scones

Time: Weekend

Storage: Refrigerate for up to 1 week.

2½ cups (313g) all-purpose flour, plus more as needed

1 tablespoon baking powder

½ teaspoon fine sea salt

8 tablespoons (4 ounces/113g) cold unsalted plant butter, such as Miyoko's, cut into cubes

¼ cup (50g) organic cane sugar

Grated zest of 1 lemon

⅔ cup (160ml) Nut Milk (page 17), Oat Milk (page 17), Soy Milk (page 75), or store-bought plant-based milk

1 cup (130g) blueberries

TOPPING

1 tablespoon (14g) unsalted vegan butter, melted

Coarse sugar, for sprinkling

PREHEAT THE OVEN TO 425°F (220°C). Line a sheet pan with compostable parchment paper.

In a large bowl, combine the flour, baking powder, and salt and stir well. Add the cold butter and cut it in with a pastry blender or rub it in with your fingers until the mixture looks like fine granules. Add the sugar and lemon zest and toss to mix. Add the milk and stir with a fork until a soft dough forms. Shape the dough into a ball, put on a lightly floured board, and knead gently 10 to 12 times, just to form into a cohesive dough.

Pat the dough into a large rectangle about 1 inch (2.5cm) thick. Spread the blueberries across the top of the dough, pressing in lightly. Fold the dough in half, pressing down, then pat out again into a large rectangle 1 inch thick. Then fold in half again. Divide in half and pat each piece into a 6-inch (15cm) round about 1 inch (2.5cm) thick. Cut each round into 6 wedges. Place the wedges on the prepared sheet pan so that they are almost touching and refrigerate for 15 minutes before baking. (These can also be refrigerated overnight before baking; if you do this, add 5 minutes to the baking time that follows.)

Brush the tops of the scones with melted butter and sprinkle lightly with coarse sugar.

Bake until they rise and start to become golden brown on top, 12 to 14 minutes. Transfer to a wire rack to cool for at least 30 minutes before serving.

Zucchini-Apple Breakfast Bread

In this not-too-sweet loaf, grated apple and zucchini bring moisture, while rolled oats give it a hearty texture. The ground flaxseed also provides structure in the absence of eggs (you can skip the flax, but your loaf might be a little bit squatter and wetter). If you'd like to experiment with incorporating whole wheat flour, start out by using it to replace ½ cup (63g) of the all-purpose flour, then increase from there. You can also substitute coconut or olive oil for the canola oil if you'd like another element of flavor. If you have two loaf pans, double the recipe, then keep one well-wrapped in the freezer—you'll be glad to have it.

Makes one 8½ × 4½-inch (21.5cm × 11.5cm) loaf
(8 servings)

Time: Weekend

Storage: Keep at room temperature, wrapped well, for up to 3 days, or refrigerate for up to 1 week.

Vegetable oil, for the pan

1 medium zucchini (6½ ounces/190g)

½ medium apple (3½ ounces/ 100g)

¾ cup (173g) Nut Milk (page 17), Oat Milk (page 17), Soy Milk (page 75), or store-bought plain plant-based milk

1 tablespoon flaxseed meal (see Note)

½ cup (100g) organic cane sugar, plus 1 tablespoon for sprinkling

¼ cup (45g) pure maple syrup

1 teaspoon vanilla extract

1 teaspoon apple cider vinegar

⅓ cup (80ml) vegetable oil

1⅔ cups (207g) all-purpose flour

⅓ cup (30g) rolled oats, plus 1 tablespoon for sprinkling

1 teaspoon baking powder

½ teaspoon baking soda

¼ teaspoon fine sea salt

1 teaspoon ground cinnamon

½ teaspoon ground ginger

POSITION A RACK IN the middle of the oven and preheat the oven to 350°F (180°C). Lightly grease an 8½ × 4½-inch (21.5cm × 11.5cm) loaf pan with vegetable oil and line it with compostable parchment paper so that it has overhang on both long sides to act as a sling.

Set a clean kitchen towel on a cutting board or sheet pan. Grate the zucchini onto the towel using the large holes of a box grater. Grate the apple half onto the towel, then gather the towel into a pouch and squeeze firmly to expel excess moisture.

In a medium bowl, whisk together the milk, flaxseed meal, sugar, maple syrup, vanilla, and vinegar to combine. Add the oil and whisk until the oil is emulsified (not separated or beading at the top).

In a large bowl, whisk together the flour, ⅓ cup (30g) of the oats, the baking powder, baking soda, salt, cinnamon, and ginger. Add the milk mixture, and, using a rubber spatula, fold it into the dry ingredients until no dry spots remain. Squeeze the zucchini and apple once more, then add to the batter and stir to combine.

Transfer the batter to the prepared pan, spread evenly, then sprinkle with the remaining 1 tablespoon oats and 1 tablespoon sugar.

Bake until a cake tester inserted comes out clean and the bread is brown and well risen, 50 minutes to 1 hour 5 minutes.

Let the bread cool in the pan on a wire rack until cool enough to handle, 15 to 20 minutes. Lift it out of the pan using the parchment sling and let cool completely on the rack before slicing.

COOK'S NOTE: If you don't want to buy flaxseed meal, you can make your own by grinding whole flaxseeds. Start with 1½ tablespoons whole flaxseeds, grind in a dedicated spice grinder, and measure out 1 tablespoon of meal.

PB&J Granola

This breakfast-meets-childhood-favorite will please kids and adults alike. Peanut butter brings a wallop of nuttiness that's reinforced by a little tahini. Coconut oil and maple syrup lend just enough sweetness, while cinnamon and a hearty dose of freshly grated nutmeg add a little spice. (Fun fact: Adding nutmeg makes sweets taste extra buttery without the actual butter.) And if you're a granola-cluster lover like I am, there's reason to rejoice: A flax egg—flaxseed meal bloomed in a little water—helps bind the granola together to create those crunchy clusters.

Stepping in for the jelly is a mix of sweet and tangy freeze-dried berries—try a mix of raspberries and strawberries—plus dried sour cherries. Eat with plain yogurt and fresh berries for extra jammy goodness, use it as an ice cream topper, or eat as is, straight out of the jar.

Makes 10 cups

Time: Weekend

Storage: Cool, dark place in an airtight container for up to 1 month.

2 tablespoons flaxseed meal (see Note)

¼ cup (60ml) water

⅔ cup (160ml) coconut oil, melted

½ cup (125g) peanut butter

¾ cup (180ml) maple syrup

2 tablespoons tahini

1¼ teaspoons fine sea salt

1½ teaspoons ground cinnamon

¾ teaspoon freshly grated nutmeg or ½ teaspoon preground nutmeg

3 cups (270g) rolled oats

1 cup (150g) unsalted dry-roasted peanuts

1 cup (130g) raw pumpkin seeds

1 cup (95g) raw, skin-on sliced almonds

1½ cups (45g) freeze-dried berries, such as raspberries or strawberries

1 cup (145g) dried sour cherries

PREHEAT THE OVEN TO 300°F (150°C). Line a sheet pan with a silicone baking mat or compostable parchment paper.

In a small bowl, combine the flaxseed meal and water, mix well, and set aside for 5 to 10 minutes to make a flax egg.

In a large bowl, combine the coconut oil, peanut butter, maple syrup, tahini, salt, cinnamon, nutmeg, and flax egg mixture and whisk until smooth. Add the rolled oats, peanuts, pumpkin seeds, and almonds and stir to coat in the peanut butter mixture. Pour the granola mixture onto the sheet pan and spread into an even layer.

Bake, stirring halfway through, until deeply golden and toasted, 45 minutes to 1 hour.

Remove from the oven and gently pat down the hot granola with a spatula. (This will facilitate the formation of clusters as the granola cools.) Cool completely at room temperature.

Gently break apart the granola and add it to a large bowl. Add the freeze-dried berries and dried cherries and gently toss to combine. Transfer to an airtight container for storage.

COOK'S NOTE: If you don't want to buy flaxseed meal, you can make your own by grinding whole flaxseeds. Start with a scant 3 tablespoons whole flaxseeds, grind in a dedicated spice grinder, and measure out 2 tablespoons of meal.

Sweet Potato Maple Sesame Spread

Sweet but not too sweet, this versatile spread matches the natural sugariness of sweet potatoes against the earthy bitterness of tahini. It's also a great template to customize to your own tastes. While lemon adds a jolt of brightness, it can easily be swapped out for orange. If you're a fan of warm spices—like ginger, nutmeg, cloves, and cinnamon—a pinch of each would be great and will nudge your spread into pie filling territory. Try this mixed into plant-based yogurt or oatmeal, spread on toast, or added to a smoothie—or just eat it by the spoonful.

Makes ¾ cup

Time: Weekday

Storage: Refrigerate for up to 1 week or freeze for up to 6 months.

> 1 large or 2 small sweet potatoes (12 ounces/340g total), scrubbed
> 2 tablespoons tahini
> 1½ tablespoons maple syrup
> ¼ teaspoon fine sea salt, plus more to taste
> 1 teaspoon finely grated lemon zest
> 1 teaspoon fresh lemon juice, plus more to taste
> Toasted white or black sesame seeds, for serving

IN A MEDIUM POT fitted with a steamer basket or insert, bring 1 to 2 inches (2.5cm to 5cm) of water to a boil. Place the sweet potatoes in the steamer, cover, reduce the heat to a simmer, and steam until fork-tender, 25 to 30 minutes. (Alternatively, you can use an Instant Pot: Put the sweet potatoes in a steamer basket in the pot, set to 7 minutes high pressure, quick-release the pressure manually, and check the sweet potatoes. If they're not fork-tender, reseal and set to 1 minute at high pressure, and repeat until they're tender.)

Carefully remove the sweet potatoes from the steamer and let cool. When they're cool enough to handle, remove the skins, which should slip right off. (Compost the skins.)

In a food processor, combine the sweet potatoes, tahini, maple syrup, salt, lemon zest, and lemon juice. Puree until totally smooth. Taste and season with more salt and lemon juice if needed.

Sprinkle with toasted sesame seeds for added crunch.

Masala Breakfast Potatoes

This spin on the classic American breakfast dish adds a little kick from the spices and vibrant color from the turmeric. Fresh herbs and lemon juice brighten the crisp potatoes even further. These are stellar when combined with Roasted Tomato Ketchup (page 54), as pictured on page 55.

Makes 4 to 6 servings

Time: Weekday

Storage: Refrigerate for up to 3 days.

> 6 russet potatoes (2 pounds/910g), cleaned and cut into ½-inch (1.3cm) cubes
> 1 medium red onion, diced
> 1 red, yellow, or orange bell pepper, diced
> 4 garlic cloves, finely grated or pressed
> 1 jalapeño pepper, sliced
> 2 tablespoons olive oil
> 1½ teaspoons garam masala, homemade (page 40) or store-bought
> 1½ teaspoons cumin seeds
> 1 teaspoon fine sea salt, plus more to taste
> ½ teaspoon ground turmeric
> 2 tablespoons fresh lemon juice
> ½ cup (20g) chopped fresh cilantro

PREHEAT THE OVEN TO 425°F (220°C). Line a sheet pan with compostable parchment paper.

In a large bowl, combine the potatoes, onion, bell pepper, garlic, jalapeño, oil, garam masala, cumin, salt, and turmeric and toss to combine. Spread onto the lined sheet pan.

Roast until the potatoes are tender and slightly crisp around the edges, about 40 minutes, rotating the pan front to back halfway through.

Remove from the oven, and while the potatoes are still hot, toss them with the lemon juice and cilantro. Taste and season with more salt if needed.

Chile-Glazed Sweet Potato & Tempeh Hash

For this one-pan meal, you don't have to steam or boil the sweet potatoes first. Instead, you cut them into small pieces, then cook them covered with a bit of water so that they steam and tenderize. After that, add tempeh and sliced onion to the pan, cook until browned, and pour in a sweet-spicy-salty sauce that reduces into a glaze almost instantaneously. Baby arugula provides a great dose of green, but you could use baby spinach or kale in its place, or simply eat this on its own.

Makes 4 servings

Time: Weekday

Storage: Refrigerate for up to 5 days.

2 small sweet potatoes (14 ounces/400g total), scrubbed and cut into ½-inch (1.3cm) cubes

2 to 3 tablespoons olive oil

3 tablespoons water

¼ teaspoon fine sea salt, plus more to taste

1 (8-ounce/225g) block tempeh, homemade (page 79) or store-bought, crumbled into small pieces less than 1 inch (2.5cm)

1 small yellow onion, thinly sliced

2 tablespoons soy sauce, plus more to taste

1½ teaspoons Dijon mustard

2 teaspoons sriracha, plus more to taste

1 tablespoon maple syrup, plus more to taste

1 large garlic clove, chopped

Freshly ground black pepper

2 scallions, thinly sliced

¼ cup (10g) chopped fresh cilantro leaves and tender stems

2 cups (28g) baby arugula

1 lime, cut into wedges

IN A LARGE NONSTICK skillet, combine the sweet potatoes, 1 tablespoon of the olive oil, the water, and salt. Bring to a simmer over medium-high heat, then reduce the heat to medium-low, cover, and cook until the sweet potatoes are fork-tender, 6 to 7 minutes.

Uncover, increase the heat to medium-high, and cook until the water has evaporated. Add another 1 tablespoon olive oil and cook the sweet potatoes, stirring frequently, until they start to brown, 3 to 4 minutes, adding the remaining 1 tablespoon olive oil if the pan looks dry.

Add the tempeh and onion and cook, stirring occasionally and adjusting the heat as needed, until the onion is softened and browned, the tempeh is golden brown all over, and the sweet potato is deeply browned, 8 to 10 minutes.

Meanwhile, in a small bowl, stir together the soy sauce, mustard, sriracha, maple syrup, garlic, and a generous amount of black pepper. Taste and season with more soy, sriracha, and/or maple syrup to taste.

Reduce the heat to medium, add the sauce, and stir constantly until the tempeh is coated, 15 to 20 seconds. Remove from the heat. Taste and season with more salt if needed. Add the scallions and cilantro and stir to combine.

Serve each portion with a handful of baby arugula and lime wedges for squeezing over everything.

Pineapple Macadamia Oats

It's a shame to think most people cook their oats in water. Using homemade nut milks (see page 17) opens a whole new world of flavors. Macadamia nuts, in particular, are excellent for cooking oats. If you have a powerful blender, they're soft enough to blend without the need for soaking, so you don't have to plan ahead. And in a world overrun with almond milk, macadamia milk is a refreshing change of pace, especially when paired with gorgeous fruit such as pineapple.

The key to making any pineapple-oat dish is to cook the pineapple first—and of course to use the ripest fruit you can get your hands on. How much agave syrup you'll need will depend on your preference and the sweetness of the fruit. Be sure to taste a bite of the pineapple with the finished oats before serving. Then you'll know how much agave to drizzle on top—if any at all.

Makes 4 servings

Time: Weekday

Storage: Refrigerate the stovetop oatmeal or overnight oats and cooked pineapple separately for up to 5 days.

1 teaspoon coconut oil

½ pineapple, peeled and cut into ½-inch (1.3cm) cubes (11 ounces/310g)

1 teaspoon vanilla extract

½ cup (65g) macadamia nuts, preferably soaked at room temperature for 2 hours, rinsed and drained

2 tablespoons agave syrup or Wildflower Cider Syrup (page 35), plus more for serving

½ teaspoon fine sea salt

3½ cups (830ml) water for stovetop oats; 2 to 2⅔ cups (470ml to 630ml) for overnight oats, depending on how thick you want them

2 cups (180g) rolled oats

Unsweetened coconut flakes or unsweetened shredded coconut, for serving

IN A MEDIUM SAUCEPAN, melt the coconut oil over medium heat. Add the pineapple and cook, undisturbed, until browned on one side, about 5 minutes. Add the vanilla, stir to combine, and transfer to a bowl. Hold on to the saucepan if you are making stovetop oats.

In a blender, combine the macadamia nuts, agave, and salt. Add whichever amount of water you need depending on if you are making stovetop oats or overnight oats. Start blending at low speed and quickly increase to high, blending until creamy, about 1 minute.

For stovetop oats: In the saucepan where the pineapple was cooked, combine the oats and macadamia milk. Bring to a boil over high heat, then reduce to a low boil and cook until the oats begin to break down and start to thicken, 3 minutes for looser oats and 4 to 5 minutes for thicker oats. Remove from the heat and allow to cool until it reaches your desired consistency, 5 to 15 minutes. Sample the oats and add more agave to taste. Divide among four bowls and top with the cooked pineapple, coconut flakes, and a drizzle of agave.

For overnight oats: Divide the oats and macadamia milk among four sealable jars. Cover and refrigerate for 8 hours or overnight. Sample the oats and add more agave to taste. To serve, top with the cooked pineapple, coconut flakes, and a drizzle of agave.

Pumpkin-Ginger Oats

While you certainly can use store-bought pumpkin puree to make these oats, the flavor will be more delicate if you go another route: steaming fresh cubed squash such as butternut, then blending it with soaked cashews and spices. This way, the other flavors in the pot—nutmeg, turmeric, dates, ginger—have some room to shine and don't rush at you like a pumpkin pie.

Makes 6 servings

Time: Weekend

Storage: Refrigerate without the toppings for up to 5 days.

¼ butternut squash (9 ounces/250g), peeled, seeded, and cubed (or 1 cup/245g canned unsweetened pumpkin puree)

3½ cups (830ml) water

1 teaspoon freshly grated nutmeg, plus more for serving

½ teaspoon ground turmeric

½ teaspoon fine sea salt

2 inches (5cm) peeled fresh ginger

6 pitted Medjool dates (see Notes), chopped, plus more for serving

¼ cup (40g) cashew pieces, soaked at room temperature for 2 hours (see Notes), rinsed and drained

2 cups (180g) rolled oats

Chopped pecans and date syrup or maple syrup, for serving

IN A MEDIUM SAUCEPAN fitted with a steamer basket or insert, bring 2 to 3 inches (5cm to 7.5cm) of water to a boil over high heat. Arrange the squash inside the steamer, cover, and steam until soft, about 15 minutes. (Alternatively, you can put the squash cubes in a microwave-safe bowl, add 4 tablespoons water, cover with a plate that fits on the bowl, and microwave for 4 to 5 minutes, until the squash is tender. Be careful of the steam when checking.)

When the squash is ready, transfer it to an upright blender. (If making stovetop oats, empty the saucepan and set it aside.) Add the 3½ cups (830ml) water, the nutmeg, turmeric, salt, ginger, dates, and cashews to the blender and blend, starting at low speed and gradually increasing to high, until creamy, 1 to 2 minutes.

For stovetop oats: Pour the squash/cashew mixture into the reserved saucepan. Add the oats and bring to a boil over high heat. Reduce to a low boil and cook until the oats begin to break down and start to thicken, 3 minutes for looser oats and 4 to 5 minutes for thicker oats. Remove from the heat and allow to cool until it reaches your desired consistency, 5 to 15 minutes. Serve in bowls topped with pecans, chopped dates, nutmeg, and a drizzle of date syrup or maple syrup.

For overnight oats: Divide the oats among four sealable jars and stir in the squash/cashew mixture. Cover and refrigerate for 8 hours or overnight. Sample the oats and add more sweetener to taste. To serve, top with the pecans, dates, nutmeg, and a drizzle of date syrup or maple syrup.

COOK'S NOTES

- Seek out the plumpest dates you can find, which blend far more easily than those that have dried out. If you can find only dried-out dates, hydrate them before blending. Combine the dates with hot water in a small bowl and let stand for 10 minutes before draining them and adding to the blender.

- If you have a high-powered blender such as Vitamix, you can skip soaking the cashews.

Roasted Apple Cinnamon Oats

These hearty breakfast oats taste like dessert but are mostly sweetened by fruit. The trick is to use roasted apples twice: as a topping *and* in the almond milk used to cook the oats. Why roasted apples? They have a deeper flavor than simmered ones and keep their shape far better, too.

Rather than using store-bought milk, this recipe takes full advantage of the almonds and their pulp: Slivered almonds are soaked overnight, then blended with the apples, cinnamon, and water to make a thick, unfiltered milk.

Depending on the time of year or what you're craving, you can serve the oats hot or cold. Cook the oats on the stovetop for a warming breakfast in the winter or soak them in the refrigerator for overnight oats that are perfect on the go or in the summer.

Makes 4 to 6 servings

Time: Weekend

Storage: Refrigerate the stovetop oatmeal or overnight oats and remaining roasted apples separately for up to 5 days.

1 cup (110g) sliced or slivered almonds

2 pounds (910g) sweet-tart apples (about 4 large), such as Fuji or Gala, peeled, cored, and diced

1½ teaspoons ground cinnamon, plus more for serving

3 tablespoons maple syrup, plus more for serving

¾ teaspoon fine sea salt

3½ cups (830ml) water for stovetop oats; 2 to 2⅔ cups (470ml to 630ml) for overnight oats, depending on how thick you want them

2 cups (180g) rolled oats

Almond butter, for serving

IN A SMALL BOWL, soak ½ cup (55g) of the almonds for 8 hours or overnight. Rinse and drain.

Preheat the oven to 400°F (200°C).

In a 12-inch (30cm) baking dish, combine the apples, ½ teaspoon of the cinnamon, 1 tablespoon of the maple syrup, and ¼ teaspoon of the salt. Bake the apples until soft and juicy, about 40 minutes.

Once the apples go in, spread the remaining ½ cup (55g) almonds on a small sheet pan or in an ovenproof skillet. Transfer to the oven and roast until lightly browned, 5 to 6 minutes. Immediately transfer them to a plate to cool and to prevent burning on the pan.

Remove the apples from the oven. Transfer 1 cup (170g) of the roasted apples to a blender. Add the amount of water required for the style of oatmeal you are making, along with the soaked almonds, the remaining 1 teaspoon cinnamon, remaining 2 tablespoons maple syrup, and remaining ½ teaspoon salt. Blend, starting at low speed and gradually increasing to high, until creamy, about 1 minute.

For stovetop oats: In a medium saucepan, combine the oats and almond/apple milk and bring to a boil over high heat. Reduce to a low boil and cook until the oats break down and start to thicken, 3 minutes for looser oats and 4 to 5 minutes for thicker oats. Stir in another 1 cup (170g) of the roasted apples, remove from the heat, and allow to cool until the oats reach your desired consistency, 5 to 15 minutes.

Sample the oats and add more sweetener to taste. Serve in bowls topped with the remaining roasted apples, some almond butter, the toasted almonds, and a drizzle of maple syrup.

For overnight oats: Divide the oats and apple/almond milk among four to six sealable containers. Cover and refrigerate for 8 hours or overnight. Sample the oats and add more sweetener to taste. Serve in bowls topped with the remaining roasted apples, some almond butter, toasted almonds, and a drizzle of maple syrup.

COOK'S NOTE: If you're pressed for time, you can make a similar breakfast with store-bought unsweetened applesauce, though it won't have quite as much apple flavor.

Cacao Hazelnut Oats

These are fantastic on their own, but if you have the time, they're even better with a drizzle of homemade hazelnut butter (see Note). Hazelnuts blend more easily than almonds, making them a great base for milks and butters. The only catch: For the creamiest butter, buy blanched hazelnuts, whose skins have been removed, or follow the instructions in the Note for removing the skins before blending.

Makes 4 servings

Time: Weekend

Storage: Refrigerate for up to 5 days.

3½ cups (830ml) water for stovetop oats;
2 to 2⅔ cups (470ml to 630ml) for overnight oats, depending on how thick you want them

½ cup (70g) blanched hazelnuts, soaked 8 hours or overnight, rinsed and drained

1 banana, plus more for serving

¼ cup (20g) cacao powder

3 tablespoons maple syrup, plus more to taste and for serving

1 teaspoon vanilla extract

½ teaspoon fine sea salt

2 cups (180g) rolled oats

Fresh strawberries or raspberries, chopped toasted hazelnuts, and hazelnut butter (optional; see Note), for serving

IN A BLENDER, COMBINE the water (use the amount required for the style of oats you are making), hazelnuts, banana, cacao, maple syrup, vanilla, and salt. Start blending at low speed and quickly increase to high, blending until creamy, 1 to 2 minutes.

For stovetop oats: In a medium saucepan, combine the oats and hazelnut mixture. Bring to a boil over high heat, then reduce to a slow boil and cook until the oats begin to break down and start to thicken, 3 minutes for looser oats and 4 to 5 minutes for thicker oats. Remove from the heat and cool until the oats reach your desired consistency, 5 to 15 minutes. Taste and add more maple syrup if desired. Serve immediately with sliced banana, berries, chopped toasted hazelnuts, hazelnut butter (if using), and a drizzle of maple syrup.

For overnight oats: Combine the oats and hazelnut mixture in a sealable container. Cover and refrigerate for 8 hours or overnight. Sample the oats and add more maple syrup to taste. Serve in bowls topped with sliced banana, berries, chopped toasted hazelnuts, hazelnut butter (if using), and a drizzle of maple syrup.

COOK'S NOTE: To make hazelnut butter, preheat the oven to 350°F (180°C). Put 2 cups (280g) hazelnuts on a small sheet pan and toast until fragrant and warm, about 10 minutes. Transfer them to a food processor and puree until you have a gorgeous, pourable paste. (If you have only skin-on hazelnuts, transfer them to a kitchen towel to rub off as much skin as possible.) Season with salt and store in a cool, dry place for a few weeks, though it's highly doubtful the butter will make it that long. It's delicious on oats like these, on toast, or even served with fresh berries or bananas for a quick snack.

Soft & Creamy
Tofu Scramble

This take on the classic tofu scramble uses two types of the soybean curd for a combination of creamy and firmer textures. Turmeric gives a little color, and perhaps the most important ingredient—kala namak (see Note)—lends that sulfurous, eggy flavor. By stirring it in right before serving, you preserve its taste, which gets dulled by cooking.

Makes 4 to 6 servings

Time: Weekday

Storage: Refrigerate for up to 3 days.

2 tablespoons grapeseed oil or another neutral oil

1 small yellow onion (5 ounces/140g), cut into ¼-inch (6mm) dice

4 garlic cloves, finely grated or pressed

1 (14-ounce/397g) block medium-firm tofu, crumbled into small pieces

1 teaspoon ground turmeric

½ teaspoon smoked paprika

1 teaspoon fine salt

12 ounces (340g) silken tofu, drained and lightly mashed with a fork

½ teaspoon kala namak (black salt; see Note), plus more to taste

IN A LARGE SKILLET, heat the oil over medium-high heat until it shimmers. Stir in the onion and cook until it starts to soften, 2 to 3 minutes. Stir in the garlic and cook until aromatic, about 30 seconds. Stir in the medium-firm tofu, turmeric, smoked paprika, and salt and cook, stirring occasionally, until the tofu starts to brown, about 3 minutes. Stir in the silken tofu just until heated through, about 30 seconds.

Remove from the heat and stir in the kala namak. Taste and season lightly with more kala namak as needed. Divide among serving plates and serve warm.

COOK'S NOTE: Kala namak (aka black salt or Himalayan black salt) has been used for centuries in Ayurvedic cooking in India but has gained popularity in vegan cooking because its sulfurous aroma and flavor evoke that of eggs.

Mung Bean Scrambled "Eggs"

When the Eat Just company released Just Egg, its liquid vegan egg substitute, it wowed many customers with its taste and texture—and caused some of us to wonder if we could imitate the product at home. Theirs is made with protein from split mung beans, which plant-based cooks have used for dal, dosas, and more, so it seemed doable. Sure enough, this combination of soaked beans, coconut milk, thickeners, and flavorings behaves in the pan much like whisked eggs do—and the result is something of a custardy, soft-scrambled texture that works beautifully on toast with a side of any of the vegetable crisps (pages 66 to 70), wrapped in tortillas, stirred into fried rice, or added to all manner of sandwiches and bowls. The important ingredient is kala namak (aka black salt or Himalayan black salt; see Note, page 99). My version was inspired by the great Dana Shultz of Minimalist Baker fame, whose stroke of genius here was to include white rice flour, which helps the scramble firm up.

To turn these into a fancy brunch dish, do what recipe tester Kristen Hartke did: Steam the batter in lightly oiled ramekins for about 3 minutes until just set, and serve the savory custard with mushroom duxelles and chives.

Makes 6 to 8 servings

Time: Weekday

Storage: Refrigerate for up to 3 days. The batter can be refrigerated for up to 1 week.

1 cup (195g) dried split mung beans, soaked overnight, drained, and rinsed

1 (13.5-ounce/398ml) can unsweetened coconut milk, light or full-fat

¼ cup (40g) white rice flour

1 tablespoon nutritional yeast

1 tablespoon tapioca starch

1 tablespoon olive oil

1 teaspoon aluminum-free baking powder

1 teaspoon garlic powder

½ teaspoon onion powder

½ teaspoon smoked paprika

½ teaspoon ground turmeric

½ teaspoon fine sea salt, plus more to taste and more for finishing

4 tablespoons (56g) Soft Spreadable Butter (page 21) or store-bought unsalted vegan butter, such as Miyoko's

1½ teaspoons kala namak (aka black salt)

IN A HIGH-POWERED BLENDER, combine the mung beans, coconut milk, rice flour, nutritional yeast, tapioca starch, olive oil, baking powder, garlic powder, onion powder, smoked paprika, turmeric, and salt. Taste and season with more salt as needed. Blend on high speed until very smooth. It should be the consistency of thin pancake or crepe batter; if it's too thick, add a little water.

In a large nonstick skillet, melt 1 tablespoon of the butter over medium-low heat. Add ½ cup (120ml) of the egg mixture, cover, and cook until the edges start to look dry, 1 to 2 minutes. Push the mixture to one side of the pan, breaking it up into "curds." Cover and cook until another 1 to 2 minutes, until the mixture looks like, well, eggs! Sprinkle with a little of the kala namak and a little more salt, if desired. Transfer to a plate and continue with the rest of the mixture, adding more butter to the pan as you do.

Serve warm.

Mung Bean Scrambled "Eggs" with Smoky Carrot Crisps (page 66)

Flaky Biscuits with Shiitake Gravy

Biscuits and gravy is a classic American breakfast dish, an easy way to stretch a few ingredients into a filling meal at the start of a busy day. In this take, shiitake mushrooms add deep flavor to the creamy gravy, which should be liberally spiced with black pepper. And if you've never made biscuits before, let these now become part of your regular repertoire. They are always a crowd-pleaser!

Makes six 2½-inch (6.5cm) or eight 2-inch (5cm) biscuits (6 to 8 servings)

Time: Weekday

Storage: Refrigerate the gravy for up to 3 days. Store the biscuits at room temperature in an airtight container for 1 day.

BISCUITS

3 cups (375g) all-purpose flour, plus more for dusting

1 teaspoon fine sea salt

1 tablespoon baking powder

1 cup (240ml) Creamy Coconut Yogurt (page 23) or store-bought plain vegan yogurt

2 tablespoons Nut Milk (page 17), Oat Milk (page 17), Soy Milk (page 75), or store-bought plain plant-based milk

8 tablespoons (112g) store-bought unsalted vegan butter, chilled and cut into ½-inch (1.3cm) cubes, plus 1 tablespoon, melted

SHIITAKE GRAVY

4 tablespoons (56g) Soft Spreadable Butter (page 21) or store-bought unsalted vegan butter, plus more as needed

8 ounces (225g) fresh shiitake mushrooms, stems composted (or saved for stock), caps cut into ½-inch (1.3cm) squares

2 tablespoons all-purpose flour

2 cups (470ml) Nut Milk (page 17), Oat Milk (page 17), Soy Milk (page 75), or store-bought plain plant-based milk, plus more as needed

½ teaspoon fine sea salt, plus more to taste

¼ teaspoon freshly ground black pepper, plus more to taste

MAKE THE BISCUITS: Preheat the oven to 450°F (230°C).

In a large bowl, whisk together the flour, salt, and baking powder. In another bowl, whisk together the yogurt and milk. Add the chilled butter cubes to the flour mixture, working it into the flour with your fingers quickly until the mixture resembles coarse cornmeal. Pour the yogurt mixture over the top, using a fork and/or your hands to mix it into the flour to form a slightly sticky dough.

Dust the countertop lightly with flour and turn the dough out onto it. Using a bench scraper if you'd like, pat the dough out into a rectangle about 1 inch (2.5cm) thick, then fold the bottom half of the dough up toward the center, and the top half of the dough down over the top of the folded dough (like folding a letter). Pat the dough out again into a rectangle 1 inch (2.5cm) thick. Fold again and pat out again into a rectangle 1 inch (2.5cm) thick. Dip a 2- or 2½-inch (5cm or 6.5cm) round biscuit cutter into flour and cut the dough into biscuits. Gather any scraps and pat them together gently into a rectangle 1 inch (2.5cm) thick and continue cutting. Shape any remaining scraps into the last biscuit with your hands. (If you don't have a biscuit cutter, you can cut the rectangle into 8 square biscuits.)

Transfer the biscuits to a sheet pan and chill in the freezer for 15 minutes.

Brush the tops of the biscuits with the melted butter and bake until risen and lightly browned on top, about 15 minutes. (Do not open the oven door while they are baking or they won't rise as high!)

Meanwhile, make the shiitake gravy: In a large skillet, melt the butter over medium-high heat. Add the mushrooms and cook, stirring only occasionally, until they start to brown and crisp, about 5 minutes. Use a slotted spoon to transfer the mushrooms to a bowl.

If needed, add more butter to the pan until you have about 2 tablespoons. Stir in the flour and cook, stirring, for 1 minute, then slowly pour in the milk as you whisk, cooking until it begins to thicken, 4 to 5 minutes. Stir in the mushrooms, salt, and pepper. Taste and season with more salt and pepper if needed. Reduce the heat to low and cover to keep warm. (If it gets too thick, whisk in more plant-based milk, 1 tablespoon at a time, until it is your desired consistency.)

When the biscuits are done, remove from the oven and allow to cool on the pan for 10 minutes.

Split the biscuits and top with gravy. Serve hot.

Fluffy Pancakes

As helpful as flaxseeds, aquafaba, and the like can be in the plant-based kitchen, plenty of traditional recipes that usually use eggs don't need a substitute. Pancakes are a great example, because most of the leavening is done by baking powder and/or soda, and they don't require much structure. The secret to these, which puff beautifully, is a combination of leaveners, goosed by a little vinegar. A generous amount of vanilla plus a little sugar gives them a family-friendly appeal, and they also take beautifully to Variations (see right).

Makes 4 servings (8 to 10 pancakes, depending on the variation)

Time: Weekday

Storage: Refrigerate for up to 4 days or freeze for up to 3 months.

- 1½ cups (188g) all-purpose flour
- 1 tablespoon baking powder
- 1 tablespoon organic cane sugar
- 1 teaspoon baking soda
- ½ teaspoon fine sea salt
- 1¼ cups (300ml) Nut Milk (page 17), Oat Milk (page 17), Soy Milk (page 75), or store-bought plant-based milk
- 4 tablespoons (56g) Soft Spreadable Butter (page 21) or store-bought unsalted vegan butter, melted and cooled, plus more for serving
- 1 tablespoon apple cider vinegar
- 1 tablespoon vanilla extract
- 2 to 3 teaspoons neutral oil
- Maple syrup

PREHEAT THE OVEN TO 200°F (90°C). Set a large sheet pan in the oven while it heats.

In a large bowl, whisk together the flour, baking powder, sugar, baking soda, and salt. Add the milk, melted butter, vinegar, and vanilla and whisk until just combined, with lumps but no dry spots.

Heat a large skillet over medium heat and brush the skillet with 2 teaspoons of oil.

Scoop about ⅓ cup (80ml) batter onto one side of the skillet and repeat on the other side. Cook the pancakes until bubbles form and pop along the edges and they are lightly browned on the bottom, 1 to 2 minutes. Use a spatula to flip them over and cook on the other side until puffed and lightly browned, 1 to 2 minutes. Transfer to the sheet pan in the oven.

Repeat to make more pancakes, brushing the skillet with a little more oil, as needed. Serve hot with butter and maple syrup.

VARIATIONS

Some additions taste great merely stirred into the batter, while for others I add them to the uncooked side of the pancakes in the skillet right after pouring in the batter. This way the add-ins brown, toast, and/or soften on the bottom. Make sure to flip those pancakes one more time when you serve them, so the additions are showcased on top.

Blueberry Lemon Cardamom Pancakes

Stir 1 cup (130g) blueberries, 1 tablespoon finely grated lemon zest, 1 tablespoon fresh lemon juice, and 1 teaspoon ground cardamom into the batter.

Banana Walnut Pancakes

Cut 3 ripe bananas into ¼-inch (6mm) slices and very coarsely chop ½ cup (50g) walnuts. Right after you pour the batter into the skillet, place a layer of bananas on top and sprinkle with walnuts.

Apple Cinnamon Pecan Pancakes

Thinly slice 2 large apples and very coarsely chop ½ cup (50g) pecans. Whisk 1 teaspoon ground cinnamon into the dry ingredients. Right after you pour the batter into the skillet, place a layer of apple slices on top and sprinkle with pecans.

Pumpkin Five-Spice Pancakes

Whisk 1 tablespoon Chinese Five-Spice Powder (page 39) into the dry ingredients. Stir ½ cup (122g) unsweetened pumpkin puree into the batter.

Cherry Pistachio Pancakes

Pit and halve 1 pint (210g) sweet cherries and very coarsely chop ½ cup (60g) pistachios. Right after you pour the batter into the skillet, place a layer of cherry halves on top and sprinkle with pistachios.

Matcha Raspberry Pancakes

Sift 1 tablespoon culinary-grade matcha over the dry ingredients, and whisk to combine. Fold 1 pint (250g) raspberries into the batter.

Chocolate Hazelnut Pancakes

Coarsely chop ½ cup (70g) hazelnuts. Whisk ¼ cup (23g) Dutch process cocoa powder into the dry ingredients. Fold ½ cup (120g) vegan chocolate chips into the batter. Right after you pour the batter into the skillet, sprinkle with hazelnuts.

Coconut Milk & Cardamom Doughnuts (Mahamri/Mandazi)

This slightly sweet Kenyan fried dough is best served warm as breakfast, afternoon treat, or dessert.

Makes about 24 doughnuts

Time: Weekend

Storage: Best eaten right away, but can be stored at room temperature for up to 2 days.

> 2 cups (250g) all-purpose flour, plus more for rolling
>
> ½ cup (100g) organic cane sugar
>
> 2 teaspoons instant yeast
>
> 1 teaspoon ground cardamom, freshly ground if possible
>
> ¾ cup (180ml) canned full-fat coconut milk
>
> Neutral vegetable oil, for deep-frying

IN A LARGE BOWL, combine the flour, sugar, yeast, and cardamom. Pour in the coconut milk. Using a wooden spoon, slowly incorporate the flour mixture into the liquid. Once a loose dough forms, turn out onto a clean floured work surface and knead until it forms a smooth dough, 3 to 5 minutes. The dough will be quite sticky.

Return the dough to the bowl, cover with a plate, and leave in a warm place until it has risen by about 50 percent, about two hours.

Pour 2 inches (5cm) neutral oil into a Dutch oven or other wide deep pan and heat over medium-high heat until it reaches 350°F (177°C) on an instant-read thermometer, then reduce the heat slightly to maintain that temperature.

While the oil is heating, turn the dough out onto a lightly floured surface and roll out into a large rectangle about 12 × 8 inches (30cm × 20cm) and ½ inch (1.3cm) thick. Divide the dough in half and then cut each half into 12 equal squares about 2 inches (5cm) each for a total of 24 squares. Cover them with a damp kitchen towel and let rest for 20 minutes.

Working with a few pieces at a time to avoid overcrowding, slip the dough into the oil and fry until golden brown and puffed, about 1 minute per side.

Serve hot with coffee or tea.

Kingston Cornmeal Porridge

There's a reason global reggae superstar Bob Marley soulfully sang about the appeal of cornmeal porridge in his classic hit "No Woman No Cry." In the Caribbean, cornmeal porridge is a beloved breakfast tradition that blooms with warm spices, vanilla, and sweetness. This recipe goes one step further by using coconut water and coconut milk to impart depth and dimension. It's lovely with ripe mango, bananas, or star fruit, but however you eat it, this porridge is a frugal way to give you the energy to go the distance.

Makes 2 to 4 servings

Time: Weekday

Storage: Refrigerate for up to 5 days.

> 2½ cups (600ml) coconut water, plus more as needed
>
> 1½ cups (350ml) canned full-fat coconut milk
>
> ¾ cup (135g) fine yellow cornmeal
>
> 3 tablespoons organic cane sugar
>
> ½ teaspoon fine sea salt, plus more to taste
>
> ¼ teaspoon ground cinnamon
>
> ¼ teaspoon ground nutmeg
>
> ½ teaspoon vanilla extract
>
> Fresh mango, bananas, star fruit, or other tropical fruit, for serving

IN A MEDIUM SAUCEPAN, combine the coconut water and coconut milk and bring to a boil over medium heat. Slowly, about ¼ cup (45g) at a time, whisk the cornmeal into the boiling liquid, stirring for 2 minutes after each addition, until all the cornmeal has been added.

Reduce the heat to low and simmer, stirring occasionally, until the porridge is very thick and viscous, about 2 minutes. Stir in the sugar, salt, cinnamon, nutmeg, and vanilla and cook for a few seconds to let the flavors meld. Taste and season with more salt if needed. If the porridge seems too thick, stir in a splash of more coconut water.

Serve hot topped with fruit.

Butternut Squash Rice Porridge

In Korea, nothing says "I love you" quite like a bowl of juk, or rice porridge. Juk is a lot like risotto, only you use glutinous rice, not Arborio, and the rice is cooked well past the point of its Italian counterpart. But as with risotto, you need to stand over your pan of rice, stirring repeatedly to develop the requisite starches that impart the desired creaminess. Besides for breakfast, juk is also typically made for someone who is ill—kind of like chicken soup in the United States. This butternut squash juk includes sticky rice balls for pockets of mochi-like chewy texture.

Makes 6 to 8 servings

Time: Weekend

Storage: Refrigerate for up to 3 days.

2 cups (370g) glutinous white rice (aka sweet white rice)
1 cup (160g) sweet white rice flour
Pinch of sea salt, plus more to taste
2¼ cups (508g) mashed roasted butternut squash
⅓ cup (80ml) hot water
1 tablespoon toasted sesame oil
4 cups (950ml) Vegetable Scrap Stock (page 36) or store-bought vegetable broth
2 cups (470ml) cold or room-temperature water
3 tablespoons brown rice syrup

IN A BOWL, COMBINE the rice and 6 cups (1.4L) cold water and set aside to soak.

While the rice is soaking, mix together the sweet white rice flour, sea salt, ¼ cup (56g) of the butternut squash, and the hot water. Knead the dough until you have a smooth ball.

Roll the dough into 4 logs that are about 12 inches (30cm) long and ½ inch (1.3cm) in diameter. Using a sharp knife, cut the logs crosswise into ½-inch (1.3cm) pieces. Roll each piece into a small ball and place them in a bowl. When you are finished rolling all the dough, cover the bowl and set the rice balls aside.

Drain the soaked rice. In a large deep pan or Dutch oven, heat the sesame oil over medium heat until it shimmers. Add the drained rice and cook, stirring, until you notice a little bit of white film on the bottom of the pan, about 1 minute.

Add the remaining 2 cups (452g) butternut squash, the vegetable stock, water, and brown rice syrup. Bring the mixture to a boil and then reduce the heat and simmer, stirring with a wooden spoon, for 20 minutes.

Add the rice balls and continue stirring until the liquid has been completely absorbed and the rice is breaking apart, about 40 minutes. Taste and season with more salt if needed.

Mango Almond Milk Smoothie

The addition of black pepper may come as a surprise here, but turmeric and pepper, besides being natural anti-inflammatories, are a natural pairing in savory dishes and delicious in sweet drinks. Along with the fresh ginger, the pepper amps up the drink's wake-me-up factor.

Almond milk will let the flavors sing, but other varieties—such as coconut, cashew, or oat—will certainly get the job done. Just be sure to use mango frozen at its peak ripeness. That'll make it feel like you're truly drinking sunshine in a glass.

Makes 1 smoothie

Time: Weekday

Storage: Not recommended (see Note, page 109).

¾ cup (180ml) almond milk, homemade (page 17) or store-bought
½-inch (1.3cm) fresh ginger, peeled and chopped
1 teaspoon fresh lime juice
½ teaspoon ground turmeric
Pinch of ground cardamom
Pinch of freshly ground black pepper
Pinch of fine sea salt
1 cup (110g) chopped ripe mango, frozen
1 pitted date (optional)

IN A HIGH-POWERED BLENDER, combine the almond milk, ginger, lime juice, turmeric, cardamom, pepper, salt, frozen mango, and date (if using). Start blending at low speed and gradually increase to high, blending until creamy, about 1 minute.

Pour into a tall glass and serve cold.

Avocado Basil Smoothie

Green smoothies aren't for everyone: Drinking kale for breakfast can definitely be advanced plant-based eating. But this drink is different. It doesn't have kale or spinach, instead getting its hue from Hass avocados and basil. It's loaded with healthful fats that keep you satisfied all morning, while the pineapple and coconut water offer a burst of freshness. Just make sure to freeze the pineapple and chill the coconut water and avocado for the best result. (If you haven't planned ahead, just be prepared to add 4 or 5 standard ice cubes.)

This recipe is inspired by a smoothie once served at JugoFresh, a Miami juice shop that earned a cult following before closing a few years ago. And while you can certainly skip the toppings, they served it with a sprinkling of hempseeds, chia seeds, and goji berries—a pop of color and texture that adds a special touch.

Makes 1 smoothie

Time: Weekday

Storage: Not recommended (see Note, page 109).

1 cup (240ml) coconut water, chilled, plus more to taste

2 teaspoons maple syrup

½ teaspoon vanilla extract

Pinch of fine sea salt

¼ cup (8g) lightly packed fresh basil leaves

¼ Hass avocado, chopped and chilled

¼ cup (30g) chopped fresh pineapple, frozen

Goji berries, hemp hearts, and chia seeds, for serving

IN A BLENDER, COMBINE the coconut water, maple syrup, vanilla, salt, basil, avocado, and frozen pineapple. Start blending at low speed and gradually increase to high, blending until the basil is fully incorporated, about 1 minute. The smoothie will be quite thick; add more coconut water if you prefer a looser consistency.

Pour immediately into a tall glass and sprinkle with goji berries, hemp hearts, and chia seeds. Serve cold.

Chocolate Protein Shake

Chickpeas may seem like they don't belong anywhere near a smoothie, but in this recipe they play two very important roles. They add a protein boost without the need to splurge on specialty vegan protein powders—most of which are loaded with unpronounceable, unnecessary ingredients and can be quite expensive. They also give the drink a milkshake-like thickness. The best part? You probably already have all the ingredients on hand.

Feel free to play around with the recipe: Drained and rinsed canned chickpeas are absolutely fine to use here, but try to find the no-salt-added variety if you can. While plant-based milk lends more flavor, you can get away with using cold water in a pinch, since the peanut butter and chickpeas get the creaminess down on their own. Cacao, bananas, and peanut butter are a classic combination, but you could substitute other nut butters, such as cashew or almond, for the peanut butter. Make sure you've frozen the banana and chilled the chickpeas in advance, but if you haven't and want to make this, plan to add 4 or 5 standard ice cubes to get things chilled and frothy.

Makes 1 shake

Time: Weekday

Storage: Not recommended (see Note, page 109).

1 cup (240ml) Nut Milk (page 17), Oat Milk (page 17), or store-bought plain plant-based milk

1 tablespoon creamy natural peanut butter, plus more for serving

1 tablespoon raw cacao powder

1 pitted date

Pinch of fine sea salt

¼ cup (40g) cooked chickpeas, chilled

1 ripe banana, cut into 8 pieces and frozen

Crushed unsalted or salted roasted peanuts, for serving

IN A BLENDER, COMBINE the milk, peanut butter, cacao powder, date, salt, chickpeas, and frozen banana. Start blending at low speed and gradually increase to high, blending until creamy, about 1 minute.

Use a spoon to spread a dollop of peanut butter inside a tall glass. Pour in the smoothie, top with crushed peanuts, and serve cold.

COOK'S NOTE: If you'd like to make any of the drinks (see page 107 and opposite) in advance for (almost) a workweek's worth of smoothies, feel free to scale it up by 4, freeze leftovers in ice cube trays, and reblend with more plant-based milk each morning when you're ready to drink one.

Berry Smoothie Bowl

Acai bowls are an Instagram darling for a reason: The dark-purple smoothies serve as a blank canvas for gorgeous toppings of fruits, nuts, and seeds. But behind the health benefits touted by influencers and marketers is a harsh, hidden reality. Much of the acai fruit itself is harvested by children in Brazil's forests, with few labor protections available to families and a fair-trade certification process that industry experts say has fallen woefully short.

Why not use frozen blackberries and blueberries (along with banana) in your bowl instead? Once you've nailed the blending technique, keep the banana, but dream up other flavors with frozen strawberries, mango, pineapple, dragon fruit, peaches, or cherries. Watery fruits, such as watermelon, apples, pears, grapes, and citrus, don't work as well.

You don't need a high-powered blender with a tamper, such as Vitamix, to get the job done. A regular blender works just as well, though it does require more finessing. Whatever you do, resist the urge to add more milk. If the blender stalls, stop mixing and use a spatula or wooden spoon to stir by hand before continuing. That's the secret to making a smoothie bowl that's as thick and luscious as ice cream.

Makes 2 smoothie bowls for dessert or as a snack, 1 for breakfast

Time: Weekday

Storage: Not recommended.

1 cup (115g) frozen blueberries

1 cup (105g) frozen blackberries

1 ripe medium banana (100g), cut into 8 pieces and frozen

½ cup (120ml) Nut Milk (page 17), Oat Milk (page 17), Soy Milk (page 75), or store-bought plant-based milk, chilled

SUGGESTED TOPPINGS

Sliced fresh fruit, such as banana, strawberries, kiwifruit, and mango

Chopped nuts

Hemp hearts

Flaxseed meal

Shredded or flaked unsweetened coconut

Granola

Maple syrup

Nut butter

REMOVE THE FROZEN BERRIES and banana from the freezer and allow them to thaw slightly on the counter for 5 to 10 minutes.

Using a high-powered blender: In the blender, combine the milk, blueberries, blackberries, and banana. Turn the blender on at low speed, then quickly increase to medium, using a tamper to push the fruit toward the blade and release any air bubbles. Once the mixture has started to incorporate, increase to medium-high speed, continuing to use the tamper as needed. (This might take some time and vigorous use of the tamper—be patient!) Blend until the smoothie takes on a "swirl" shape at the top, about 1 minute; do not overblend or the fruit will melt.

Using a regular blender: In the blender, combine the milk, blueberries, blackberries, and banana. Use the crush ice or pulse function to break the frozen fruit up into smaller chunks, stopping to stir if the blender stalls. Start blending at the lowest speed and gradually increase to medium, stopping to mix with a spatula or wooden spoon as needed, three or four times. If necessary, remove the lid while blending and use a wooden spoon to gently push the fruit down, keeping the spoon very far from the blade. Blend until the smoothie is thick and creamy, 1 to 2 minutes; do not overblend or the fruit will melt.

To serve, divide the smoothie between two bowls and use a spoon to create swooshes across the surface. Arrange the toppings on top and serve immediately.

COOK'S NOTE: Be sure to have the ingredients prepped before blending, including the toppings; that will keep the smoothie bowl from melting too quickly.

3

APPETIZERS & SNACKS

This chapter is for the nibblers among you—I know who you are, because I'm one of you. We get most excited about a restaurant's apps menu of crispy, crunchy little bites, and would prefer to spend all our time at a party as close to the chips and dips as possible. We're also not above dips for dinner, one of the most satisfying and somehow rebellious-seeming ways to eat, especially on a night when we cooks are all out of ideas (or energy).

Crunchy Kale Chips Your Way

These are lighter, with a more delicate crunch, than the supermarket version—not to mention so much less expensive. But the best part of making these is that you're free to use any toppings you please. If you want to go classic, try sprinkling them with cheesy nutritional yeast (or Nacho Nooch, page 45), a seedy furikake blend or Shichimi Togarashi (page 42) if you'd like more Asian flavors, or top them with finely shredded coconut and curry powder for an interesting twist.

These chips take a little TLC and monitoring; you need to start paying attention halfway through the cooking time. You'll rotate the pan, and perhaps move some pieces around if you see that the outer chips are cooking faster than the middle ones. Taking a little extra care while cooking these will ensure a rewarding bowl of crunchy snacks at the end. Note that you can use either lacinato or curly kale, but the latter will result in a lacier texture.

Makes 4 servings

Time: Weekday

Storage: These are best eaten immediately, but can be stored at room temperature in an airtight container for up to 3 days.

1 small bunch lacinato or curly kale (6 ounces/188g)

1 tablespoon olive oil

½ teaspoon fine sea salt

Assorted toppings: nutritional yeast, furikake, or coconut curry (1:1 ratio of fine coconut flakes to curry powder)

POSITION RACKS IN THE top and bottom thirds of the oven and preheat the oven to 300°F (150°C).

Using your hands, pull the kale leaves off the midribs and stems and tear them into 3-inch (7.5cm) pieces. (Compost the stems/midribs or save them for your green smoothies.) Wash and dry the leaves thoroughly, spinning them in a salad spinner and patting them dry with clean kitchen towels.

Transfer the kale leaves to a large bowl and add the olive oil, tossing until well coated. Sprinkle on the salt and toss to combine. Spread the kale leaves in a single layer on two large sheet pans, being careful not to overcrowd the pans.

Bake for 12 minutes, then switch racks and rotate the pans front to back and use a spatula to gently toss the kale pieces around to help them cook more evenly. Continue to bake until crispy, another 5 to 13 minutes, checking every few minutes and tossing with a spatula as needed.

Remove from the oven and sprinkle the chips with your topping of choice while they're warm (which helps the toppings stick). Let the chips rest on the sheet pans to continue to crisp and cool.

Crispy Fried Spicy Tofu Nuggets with Ranch-ish Dressing

If you haven't tried this double-freezing technique, prepare to be astounded: It transforms tofu into a spongier, chewier, meatier product that does a beautiful job mimicking chicken, especially when you fry it. This recipe gives you the option of three spicy treatments—Cajun, jerk, or peri peri—and offers a quick ranch-like dressing for dipping. You need to plan for this, because the freezing-and-thawing process, while simple, takes a couple of days, but you can get a head start by always keeping a package of medium-firm tofu in the freezer.

Makes 4 servings

Time: Project

Storage: Refrigerate for up to 3 days.

1 (14-ounce/397g) package medium-firm tofu, unopened

2 cups (470ml) Coconut Cashew Buttermilk (page 23), or 1½ cups (350ml) Creamy Coconut Yogurt (page 23) or store-bought vegan yogurt mixed with ½ cup (120ml) water

1 tablespoon poultry seasoning

2 teaspoons fine sea salt, plus more to taste

½ cup (120ml) Silky Aquafaba Mayonnaise (page 46) or store-bought vegan mayo

½ cup (25g) chopped fresh parsley, mint, or dill, or a combination

1 tablespoon fresh lemon juice

½ teaspoon freshly ground black pepper

2 cups (330g) potato starch

Neutral vegetable oil, for frying

2 tablespoons Cajun Seasoning (page 38), Jerk Spice (page 41), or Peri Peri (page 41), plus more to taste

FREEZE THE TOFU IN its package until solid, about 8 hours.

Thaw overnight or all day in the refrigerator, then repeat, freezing until solid and thawing thoroughly.

Remove the tofu from the package, wrap it in a clean kitchen towel, and gently squeeze as much of the water out as possible. Tear the tofu into nugget-size pieces.

In a bowl, combine 1 cup (240ml) of the buttermilk or yogurt/water mixture, poultry seasoning, and 1 teaspoon of the salt and whisk to combine. Add the tofu and toss to thoroughly coat.

In another bowl, combine the remaining 1 cup (240ml) buttermilk or yogurt/water mixture with the mayo, chopped herbs, lemon juice, remaining 1 teaspoon salt, and the pepper and whisk until smooth. Refrigerate the ranch-ish dressing until ready to use.

Pour the potato starch into a large shallow bowl. Working with one piece at a time, lift the tofu out of the buttermilk mixture and let the excess drip off, then toss it in the potato starch until coated all over. Transfer to a sheet pan or platter.

Set a wire rack over a sheet pan next to the stovetop. Pour 2 inches (5cm) oil into a Dutch oven and heat over medium-high heat until it reaches 375°F (190°C).

Working in batches to avoid overcrowding, carefully add the nuggets to the oil and fry, turning as needed, until lightly golden and crispy all over, 3 to 4 minutes. Use a slotted spoon to transfer the nuggets to the wire rack. Repeat until all the nuggets are cooked, then transfer the nuggets to a large bowl and toss with the chosen spice blend until coated.

Serve hot with the ranch-ish dressing for dipping.

Roasted Pumpkin Seeds

The next time you're cooking a pumpkin or other winter squash, you might be tempted to toss those seeds. Instead, you can turn them into a tasty, crunchy snack. If you've tried this before and found it to be too much of a hassle separating the seeds from the goopy, stringy pulp, or found the end result too chewy and woody rather than crisp, this recipe might change your mind. Boiling the pulp in salt water helps separate it from the seeds. It also seasons the seeds and tenderizes them—so they crisp up in the oven.

Adjust the amount of water and salt based on the volume of seeds and pulp you get—more from larger sugar pumpkins, less from smaller butternut or acorn squash. I've listed seasoning options, but feel free to use whatever spice mixture you like. Play around!

Makes 1 cup (8 servings)

Time: Weekday

Storage: Room temperature in an airtight container for up to 2 weeks.

> 4 cups (950ml) water
> 2 teaspoons fine sea salt
> 2 cups seeds and pulp from a freshly cut pumpkin or other winter squash (such as sugar pumpkin, kabocha, acorn, or butternut)
> 1 tablespoon olive oil
> 1 tablespoon seasoning (see options at right)

PREHEAT THE OVEN TO 325°F (160°C).

In a large saucepan, combine the water and salt and bring to a boil over medium-high heat. Add the seeds and pulp and reduce the heat slightly so the water is at a steady but not-too-vigorous boil. Cook until the seeds have darkened and started to become tender and the pulp has separated from them, about 15 minutes.

Drain the water, rinse and pick out the seeds, and discard any remaining big pieces of pulp. (From a 4-pound sugar pumpkin, you'll get about 1 cup seeds.)

Spread the seeds out onto a clean kitchen towel, add another kitchen towel on top, and pat them dry. Transfer them to a bowl and toss with the olive oil and seasoning of your choice. Spread out in one layer on a sheet pan.

Roast, stirring occasionally, until crisp and light golden brown, 10 to 30 minutes (depending on their size).

Let cool on the sheet, where they will get even crisper.

SEASONING OPTIONS

> Smoked paprika
> Garlic powder
> Onion powder
> Madras curry powder
> Any seasoning blend in the book (see pages 37 to 44)
> Nacho Nooch (page 45)
> Seaweed Gomasio (page 45)

Spicy Fried Plantains

West African spicy fried plantains, called kelewele, are traditionally made by tossing bite-size pieces in a spicy paste before frying. This version uses dried spices for a quicker path to snacking. The key is using ripe plantains, yellow and covered with little black spots, rather than green or black ones.

Makes 2 to 4 servings

Time: Weekday

Storage: Room temperature in an airtight container for up to 3 days.

> Sunflower or other neutral vegetable oil, for deep-frying
> 1 tablespoon water
> 1 teaspoon onion powder
> ½ teaspoon cayenne pepper
> ½ teaspoon ground ginger
> 2 ripe plantains (yellow with black spots), peeled and cut into ½-inch (1.3cm) cubes (about 2 cups)
> Salt

POUR 2 INCHES (5CM) OIL into a Dutch oven and heat the oil over medium-high heat until it reaches 350°F (177°C) on an instant-read thermometer. Arrange a wire rack over a sheet pan and set it next to the stove.

While the oil is heating, in a bowl, whisk together the water, onion powder, cayenne, and ginger. Add the plantain cubes and toss to thoroughly coat.

Once the oil is hot, working in batches if necessary to avoid overcrowding, fry the plantains, turning as needed, until golden brown on all sides, 4 to 5 minutes. Transfer to the wire rack and sprinkle with salt while hot. Repeat with the remaining plantains and serve hot.

Caramelized Onion Dip

Made by the traditional method, caramelizing onions takes the better part of an hour, or even more, meaning you'd need to make this recipe while you're busy with another task in the kitchen, so you're always close to the pan. But a pinch of baking soda speeds things up dramatically by increasing the pH, causing the onions to brown and soften in a mere 10 to 15 minutes. The baking soda results in a jammier texture that works perfectly for such a dip as this (and less perfectly if you want the onions to still have a bit of a bite, as in a pizza topping). Note that although it's always best to judge doneness by color, texture, and taste, each onion, depending on its freshness, seems to have a mind of its own.

To make this dip luscious and creamy, soaked cashews are used as the base, with a dash of nutritional yeast, which adds an umami punch. Serve it as an appetizer with chips or slather it on baked potatoes for a side dish.

Makes about 2 cups

Time: Weekday

Storage: Refrigerate for up to 3 days.

Boiling water

1 cup (130g) raw cashews

2 tablespoons olive oil

2 large yellow onions (1 pound/450g total), thinly sliced

¾ teaspoon fine sea salt, plus more to taste

⅛ teaspoon baking soda

¼ cup (60ml) dry white wine, such as Sauvignon Blanc

1 garlic clove, peeled but whole

1 tablespoon nutritional yeast

1 tablespoon fresh lemon juice

1 teaspoon Dijon mustard

¼ teaspoon freshly ground black pepper, plus more for garnish

Minced chives or sliced scallions, for garnish

Potato or pita chips, for serving

IN A MEDIUM BOWL, pour the boiling water over the cashews to cover by 1 inch, and let them soak while you caramelize the onions.

In a Dutch oven, warm the olive oil over medium-low heat until it shimmers. Mix in the onions, ½ teaspoon of the salt, and the baking soda. Cook until the onions turn deep golden brown and are sweet and very soft, 10 to 15 minutes, stirring frequently and mixing in a splash of water as needed to deglaze the bottom of the pan. Rotate the pan if certain areas are browning faster than others.

Once the onions are caramelized, stir in the white wine and cook until the wine has largely evaporated, about 1 minute. Remove the pot from the heat and let it cool slightly.

Drain the cashews, reserving ¾ cup (180ml) of the water. Transfer the cashews and reserved water to a high-powered blender. Add the garlic, nutritional yeast, lemon juice, mustard, black pepper, and the remaining ¼ teaspoon salt. Blend until creamy and thick, about 30 seconds. Pour the cashew sauce into a bowl.

Roughly chop the caramelized onions and add to the cashew sauce. Stir, taste, and season with more salt if needed. Refrigerate until slightly chilled, about 2 hours.

Spoon into a serving bowl and garnish with minced chives and more black pepper. Serve with chips.

Smoky Squash & Tahini Dip

Slathered on rice cakes or toast, this is an excellent snack that'll get you out of a hummus rut. To turn it into an easy lunch, swipe over a thick slice of toasted sourdough and layer it with arugula and cherry tomatoes.

You can substitute other winter squashes or sweet potato, but kabocha's sweet, nutty flavor pairs beautifully with the tahini and smoked paprika. Note that you don't need a food processor here.

Makes about 1½ cups

Time: Weekday

Storage: Refrigerate for up to 3 days.

- ¼ large kabocha squash (14 ounces/400g), seeded, peeled, and cut into 1-inch (2.5cm) cubes
- 1 tablespoon olive oil, plus more for serving
- 1 teaspoon smoked paprika
- ½ teaspoon cumin powder
- 1 teaspoon maple syrup
- ¾ teaspoon fine sea salt, plus more to taste
- 1 garlic clove, finely grated or pressed
- ¼ cup (60ml) tahini
- 1½ tablespoons fresh lemon juice, plus more for serving
- ¼ cup (60ml) warm water, plus more as needed
- Minced fresh flat-leaf parsley, sesame seeds, and lemon zest, for serving

PREHEAT THE OVEN TO 425°F (220°C).

Arrange the squash on a sheet pan or in a large cast-iron skillet. Add the olive oil, smoked paprika, cumin, maple syrup, and salt and toss to coat.

Roast until the squash is very soft and lightly browned, 25 to 35 minutes.

Transfer the squash and garlic to a shallow bowl. Use a fork to mash the squash, then stir in the tahini, lemon juice, and water. Add more water, 1 tablespoon at a time, as needed to achieve a dip-like texture. Taste and season with more salt if needed.

Spoon the dip onto a serving plate and use the back of the spoon to form a shallow well in the center. Top with the parsley, sesame seeds, lemon zest, lemon juice, and a drizzle of olive oil.

Spicy-Sweet Lotus Chips

Lotus roots don't actually grow in the earth but are the "root" to the beautiful lotus flowers you see floating on the surface of water. They can be incredibly long, but you can find more manageable portions at an Asian grocery store. They are high in fiber and low in calories, making for a great snack, especially when you dust them with a combination of sweet, spicy, and savory toppings.

Makes 4 servings

Time: Weekday

Storage: Room temperature in an airtight container for up to 1 week.

- 1 (4½-inch/11.5cm) piece lotus root (see Note)
- 3 tablespoons olive oil
- 2 tablespoons gochugaru (Korean chile flakes)
- 2 tablespoons organic cane sugar
- 1 tablespoon nutritional yeast
- 1 tablespoon onion powder
- 1 teaspoon fine sea salt
- 1 teaspoon freshly ground black pepper

POSITION A RACK IN the lowest position of the oven and preheat the oven to 475°F (240°C).

Use a sharp knife or mandoline to cut the lotus root into ⅛-inch (3mm) slices.

In a large bowl, toss the lotus root slices with the olive oil. Transfer them to one or two sheet pans, without overlapping.

Bake on the lowest rack (or two lower racks if using two sheet pans) until they turn slightly brown, about 11 minutes.

Meanwhile, in a large bowl, mix together the gochugaru, sugar, nutritional yeast, onion powder, salt, and pepper.

When the lotus roots are browned, transfer them to the bowl and toss until they're evenly coated.

Serve immediately, or transfer to an airtight container for storing.

COOK'S NOTE: You can use raw lotus root or packaged boiled lotus root; both work well here.

Herby Cashew-Tahini Dip with Za'atar Pita Crisps

Everyone loves a good party-friendly dip. This tangy herbaceous one is made by pureeing cashews, tahini, lemon juice, garlic, and herbs. The perfect dunking partners are cut-up veggie sticks and homemade pita chips.

Once you've made pita chips at home, you'll never want to buy the supermarket variety again. It's simple: You just bake split-open pita rounds in a drizzle of olive oil and a sprinkling of salt and za'atar, the Middle Eastern spice blend. Using thin pita helps create delicious air bubbles and pockets. After they are cooled, you break them into shards with your hands.

Makes 4 to 6 servings

Time: Weekday

Storage: Refrigerate the dip for up to 5 days or freeze for up to 4 months. Store the chips at room temperature for up to 2 days.

PITA CHIPS

4 pita breads, preferably thin

1 tablespoon olive oil

1 teaspoon fine sea salt

1 tablespoon Za'atar (page 44)

DIP

1 cup (130g) raw cashew halves, soaked in hot water for 15 minutes and drained

¼ cup (60ml) fresh lemon juice (from 1 to 2 lemons)

1 garlic clove, minced

1 cup (20g) mixed tender herbs, such as parsley, cilantro, dill, and basil

¼ cup (60ml) well-stirred tahini

¼ cup (60ml) water, plus more as needed

½ teaspoon fine sea salt, plus more to taste

¼ teaspoon freshly ground black pepper, plus more to taste

FOR SERVING

Crudités, such as radicchio, blanched green beans, sugar snap peas, carrots, cauliflower, radishes, and fennel

MAKE THE PITA CHIPS: Preheat the oven to 425°F (220°C).

Using a knife, cut each pita in half down the middle. Peel open each half and place on a sheet pan (like an open book). Brush the outside of each pita with the olive oil and sprinkle with the salt and za'atar.

Bake for 5 minutes. Rotate the sheet pan front to back and bake until crispy and browned, an additional 5 to 7 minutes. Remove the pan from the oven and let cool completely. Break each half into shards with your hands.

Make the dip: In a food processor, combine the softened cashews, lemon juice, garlic, herbs, tahini, water, salt, and pepper and process until smooth. Add more water, 1 tablespoon at a time, if needed to thin the dip to your desired consistency. Taste and season with more salt and pepper if needed.

Serve the dip on a platter alongside the pita chips and crudités.

Garlicky Greek Yellow Split Pea Dip

This simple dip is inspired by a classic recipe served as an appetizer or as part of a meze spread in Greece. Its traditional name is fava, but here's the funny thing: It's actually made not with fava beans, but rather with boiled yellow split peas. It's gloriously unfussy, prepared with basic ingredients and delicious with its topping of onion, capers, and a generous glug of olive oil. Spoon it into a warm pita with lettuce, tomato, and red onion for a quick lunch, or serve it swooshed onto a plate with a side of bread.

The dip thickens significantly as it cools. For the best texture and flavor, bring it to room temperature or warm it up for a few seconds in the microwave before serving. Add a splash or two of water as needed to make it spreadable again.

Makes about 3½ cups

Time: Weekday

Storage: Refrigerate for up to 4 days.

- 4 tablespoons olive oil, plus more for drizzling
- 1 medium red onion (7 ounces/200g), finely chopped
- ¾ teaspoon fine sea salt, plus more to taste
- 4 garlic cloves, finely grated or pressed
- ½ teaspoon ground cumin
- 1 cup (225g) dried yellow split peas, rinsed thoroughly and drained
- 3 cups (710ml) water
- 2½ tablespoons fresh lemon juice, plus more to taste
- Chopped capers, minced fresh flat-leaf parsley, smoked paprika, for garnish
- Warm bread, for serving

IN A MEDIUM SAUCEPAN, heat 1 tablespoon of the olive oil over medium heat until it shimmers. Measure out 2 tablespoons of the red onion and set aside for garnish. When the oil shimmers, add the rest of the red onion and ¼ teaspoon of the salt and sauté until translucent, about 4 minutes. Stir in the garlic and cumin and cook until fragrant, about 1 minute. Add the split peas, water, and remaining ½ teaspoon salt. Bring to a boil, then reduce the heat until the liquid is at a simmer and cook until the split peas are soft, about 30 minutes.

Reserving the cooking liquid, use a slotted spoon to transfer the split peas, onion, and garlic to a blender. Measure out ¾ cup (180ml) of the cooking liquid, adding water if necessary to reach that amount, and transfer it and the lemon juice to the blender. Cover with the lid and remove the center cap. Hold a kitchen towel over the hole to avoid splattering and blend, beginning at low speed and gradually increasing to medium. Drizzle in the remaining 3 tablespoons olive oil while blending and puree until the dip is creamy, about 30 seconds. If the puree is too thick, add a little more of the cooking liquid or water and blend until it is the texture of thick pancake batter. Taste and adjust seasoning. The dip will thicken as it sits.

Serve the dip warm or at room temperature. (You might taste it and season again with more salt or lemon juice just before serving if it has cooled, as the flavors will have muted.) Spoon onto a plate, spread it into a swoosh, and garnish with the reserved minced red onion, capers, parsley, smoked paprika, and a drizzle of olive oil. Serve with warm bread.

Smoky Eggplant Harissa Dip

Charring eggplants on a grill or gas stovetop until the skin blackens and the flesh is meltingly tender inside gives this dip its characteristic smoky flavor. Here, instead of the tahini you'd expect from a traditional baba ghanoush, the dip also stars harissa, a fiery North African chile paste that complements the smoky flavors.

Once the eggplant is cooked, the soft insides are scooped out and blended with toasted walnuts, garlic, lemon juice, and smoked paprika until creamy. Serve it with pita chips, grilled slices of bread, or cut-up veggie sticks for dipping.

Makes about 2 cups

Time: Weekday

Storage: Refrigerate for up to 3 days.

- 2 medium globe eggplants (12 ounces/325g each)
- 1 cup (113g) raw walnuts, roughly chopped
- 5 garlic cloves, peeled but whole
- 2 tablespoons olive oil, plus more for drizzling
- ¼ cup (60ml) fresh lemon juice (from 1 to 2 lemons)
- 1 tablespoon Rose Harissa (page 52) or store-bought harissa paste, plus more to taste
- 1 tablespoon smoked paprika, plus more for sprinkling
- 1 tablespoon agave syrup or Wildflower Cider Syrup (page 35)
- ½ teaspoon fine sea salt, plus more to taste
- Pita chips, toasted bread, or crudités, for serving

USING A GRILL: Preheat a grill to medium. Place the eggplants directly on the grates and cook, turning occasionally, until the skins are completely charred and the flesh is tender, 15 to 20 minutes.

Using a gas or electric range: Place the eggplants directly on a gas burner set to medium-high, turning occasionally with tongs until blackened and soft inside, 12 to 15 minutes. If an electric range, place the eggplants under the broiler for about the same amount of time.

Transfer the eggplants to a colander to let any excess liquid drain. Let cool for at least 15 minutes.

Meanwhile, in a dry skillet, toast the walnuts over medium-low heat, stirring occasionally, until lightly browned, about 5 minutes. Stir in the garlic and cook, stirring, until very fragrant, about 1 minute. Transfer to a bowl and let cool.

Slice the eggplants in half. Using a spoon, scoop out the soft flesh into a food processor, discarding any skins. It's fine if blackened bits of skin remain; they add smokiness to the dip. Add the garlic/walnut mixture, olive oil, lemon juice, harissa paste, smoked paprika, agave syrup, and salt and blend until creamy. Taste and season with more salt and harissa paste if needed.

Transfer the dip to a bowl and sprinkle with smoked paprika and drizzle with olive oil. Serve with pita chips, toasted bread, or crudités.

Pan con Tomate y Maíz

Pan con tomate is a beloved Catalonian dish, and as simple as summer food can get (which means as simple as any food can get). Variations abound, but the basic idea involves grating the flesh of a tomato, seasoning it with salt, then spooning it over a garlic-rubbed piece of toast. Because there are so few elements, each one has to taste its best: Pick the most aromatic, juiciest tomato. But where there is a gorgeous tomato, there is probably also corn—and basil. By shining this late-summer trifecta into the structure of pan con tomate, you get to savor each element in its purest form.

Makes 4 servings

Time: Weekday

Storage: The tomato-corn mixture can be prepared up to 1 day ahead and refrigerated. Toast the bread and plate it right before serving.

2 ears of corn (1 pound/450g total), shucked (see Note)

1 large ripe tomato, such as heirloom or beefsteak (13 ounces/377g)

Fine sea salt

Olive oil

8 (½-inch/1.3cm) slices crusty bread

1 garlic clove, halved lengthwise

A small handful of basil leaves

Black pepper

USE THE LARGE HOLES of a box grater to grate the corn kernels into a medium bowl. Wring the cobs into the bowl to get out all its milk. (Compost the spent cobs.)

Cut the tomato crosswise through the equator. Using the large holes of the box grater, grate the flesh of the tomato into the bowl with the corn until you hit the skin (compost the skins). Season the corn-tomato mixture with salt. Set aside.

In a large skillet, warm a thin layer of olive oil over medium-high heat. Working in batches and adding oil as needed, add the bread and cook until toasty and golden, about 2 minutes per side. Transfer to plates, season with salt, and rub one side with the cut sides of the halved garlic.

Spoon the tomato-corn mixture over the toast, then cover with basil leaves (hiding the tomato-corn mixture so it's a surprise to eaters). Season with black pepper and a drizzle of olive oil.

COOK'S NOTE: The easiest way to shuck corn is to use the microwave. Run water over the corncobs in their husks until soaked and microwave on high for 4 to 6 minutes, until steaming hot. Let cool slightly, then use your fingers to feel where the row of kernels ends on the wide end of the cob (opposite the silk end) and use a sharp knife to cut through those last kernels and through the cob. Holding the silk end, squeeze each cob out of the husk from that end; it should pop out clean and only slightly cooked. Rinse if needed to get more of the silks off.

Aloo Matar Tikki with Cilantro Mint Chutney

Aloo tikki are a popular snack in northern and northeastern India, as well as Pakistan. Made with potatoes flavored with warming spices, plus tangy amchur (sour mango powder), these cakes are bound with cornstarch and fried until deep golden on the outside and creamy on the inside. Served with a bright, zippy cilantro mint chutney, aloo tikki are wonderful with ice cold beers.

Makes 16 tikki (4 servings)

Time: Weekend

Storage: These are best eaten immediately, but you can fry them a couple hours ahead of time, keep them at room temperature, and reheat in a 400°F (200°C) oven until crisp, 5 to 7 minutes. Longer storage isn't recommended. You can refrigerate the potato mixture for up to 3 days before forming and frying them. The chutney can be refrigerated for up to 3 days.

CILANTRO MINT CHUTNEY

1 bunch cilantro (4 ounces/120g), leaves and stems included, roughly chopped

1 bunch mint leaves (36g), roughly chopped

1 to 2 serrano peppers, roughly chopped

1 large garlic clove, peeled but whole

½-inch (1.3cm) piece fresh ginger, peeled and roughly chopped

¼ cup (60ml) fresh lime juice

2 tablespoons olive oil

¼ teaspoon fine sea salt, plus more to taste

ALOO MATAR TIKKI

1½ pounds (680g) medium Yukon Gold potatoes, scrubbed

1 cup (170g) frozen peas, thawed

½ cup (24g) cilantro leaves and tender stems, chopped

1 serrano pepper, finely chopped

1½ teaspoons amchur or fresh lemon juice

½ teaspoon fine sea salt, plus more to taste

1 teaspoon cumin seeds

¾ teaspoon ground turmeric

½ teaspoon fennel seeds

½ teaspoon ground chiles, preferably Kashmiri

3 tablespoons cornstarch

Neutral oil, like canola or grapeseed, for shallow-frying

MAKE THE CILANTRO MINT chutney. In a blender, combine the cilantro, mint, serranos, garlic, ginger, lime juice, olive oil, and salt and blend until smooth. If the mixture is a little thick, add 1 tablespoon water at a time until you reach a thick, dippable consistency. Taste and season with more salt if needed.

Make the aloo matar tikki: Preheat the oven to 300°F (150°C).

Meanwhile, place the unpeeled potatoes in a medium pot and cover with 4 inches (10cm) of cold water. (Leaving their peels on for boiling keeps them from getting waterlogged.) Set over high heat and bring to a boil. Reduce the heat to medium-high and gently boil until the potatoes are cooked through and can easily be pierced with a knife, 20 to 25 minutes, depending on the size of the potatoes. Drain and allow the potatoes to cool for 10 minutes.

When the potatoes are cool enough to handle, peel them (composting the skins) and transfer the peeled potatoes to a large bowl. Mash with a fork into a rustic paste.

Add the thawed peas, cilantro, serrano, amchur powder, salt, cumin seeds, turmeric, fennel seeds, and chile powder to the potatoes and mix well. Add the cornstarch and mix well. Taste and season with more salt if needed.

Divide into 16 portions. With lightly oiled hands, take one portion, roll it into a ball about the size of a golf ball, and then flatten into a disk ½ inch (1.3cm) thick. Place on a sheet pan and repeat with the remaining portions.

Set a wire rack over a large sheet pan next to the stovetop. Pour ¼ inch (6mm) oil into a large skillet and heat over medium-high heat until it shimmers. Working in batches to avoid overcrowding, fry the tikki until golden brown on both sides, about 3 minutes per side. Transfer the cooked tikki to the wire rack in the sheet pan and transfer to the oven to keep warm while you fry the remaining cakes, adding more oil to the pan between batches if needed.

Serve the aloo tikki hot or warm with the chutney alongside for dipping.

COOK'S NOTE: For a party, these can be made into two-bite cocktail nibbles by halving the size of the cakes and making 32 mini cakes instead of 16 larger ones.

Beet Ceviche

Ceviche is Peru's national dish, and to purists it has five main ingredients: fish, salt, lime juice, chiles, and red onion. Writer Nico Vera's Inca ancestors prepared ceviche with tumbo, a jungle citrus, but ceviche has evolved over the past five hundred years. In the past century, Japanese families that settled in Lima transformed ceviche, and this recipe honors the legacy of Japanese-Peruvian Nikkei food culture. Nico's grandfather prepared ceviche for his family in 1940s Lima in their working-class tenement, but he could afford to use only bonito tuna; he partially cooked it in boiling water before curing it with citrus. Here, beet cubes steamed with kombu stock resemble the bonito, habanero chile peppers add heat, and sliced radishes replace the onions. Kombu stock with coconut milk makes for a savory and creamy vegan leche de tigre—the marinade in ceviche. Nori strips for garnish complete the dish. Reserve the extra coconut milk from the can for the Chamomile Bourbon Milk Punch (page 467) or freeze in ice cube trays for another use. You can prepare the kombu stock and steam the beets ahead of time (or even buy precooked vacuum-sealed beets to save a step), but toss the beets with the lime juice and mix the leche de tigre just before serving.

Makes 2 to 4 servings

Time: Weekend

Storage: Not recommended for the finished dish, but you can make the kombu stock and steam the beets up to 3 days ahead and refrigerate until you're ready to make the dish.

- 1 (4 × 6-inch/10cm × 15cm) piece dried kombu
- 2 cups (470ml) water
- ½ teaspoon fine sea salt, plus more to taste
- 1 tablespoon fresh lime juice
- 1 teaspoon canned full-fat coconut milk
- 2 medium beets (7 ounces/200g total), peeled and cut into ½-inch (1.3cm) cubes (about 1 cup)
- ½ to 1 habanero pepper, depending on your tolerance for heat
- French breakfast or other radishes, sliced into thin rounds, for garnish
- Toasted nori, cut into strips with kitchen shears, for garnish

RINSE THE KOMBU, THEN add it to a medium pot with the water and ¼ teaspoon of the salt. Let the kombu soak for 15 minutes, then bring the water to a boil, reduce to a simmer, and cook for 15 minutes, stirring initially to dissolve the salt. Turn off the heat. Remove the kombu, thinly slice it, and reserve it for garnish.

To make the leche de tigre, transfer ¼ cup (60ml) of the kombu stock to a bowl and let cool. Add the lime juice, coconut milk, and remaining ¼ teaspoon salt and whisk to combine.

Add enough water to the pot with the rest of the kombu stock in it to come just below a steamer basket. Place the steamer basket in the pot and spread the beet cubes evenly in the basket. Bring the liquid to a boil, reduce to a simmer, cover, and steam until tender, 20 to 30 minutes.

Transfer the beets to the bowl with the leche de tigre, toss to combine, and let cool.

Cut off and compost the top of the habanero. Using disposable gloves to protect your hands, slice the pepper in half lengthwise and devein. Mince half the habanero and add it to the bowl with the beets. If you want the dish milder, reserve the remaining habanero half for another use; if you want more heat, slice the remaining half into thin strips. Stir the beets, taste, and season with more salt as needed.

Divide the mixture among small bowls and serve at room temperature, or chill and serve cold. Garnish with radish rounds, the reserved habanero strips (if using), toasted nori strips, and slivers of rehydrated kombu immediately before serving.

Hearts of Palm Ceviche

This ceviche is inspired by Chiapas, a coastal state on Mexico's southern tip that is part tropical jungle, part coastline, part forest—and so rich in biodiversity and culture. In regions of Chiapas where the right palm tree grows, hearts of palm are eaten often in salads, ceviche, escabeche, and even fried in oil. Ground seaweed gives this a kiss from the ocean, but it still tastes great without it. Serve with tostadas or other chips.

Makes 4 to 6 servings

Time: Weekday

Storage: Refrigerate for up to 2 days.

2 (14-ounce/400g) cans hearts of palm, drained and chopped

2 Roma tomatoes (9 ounces/255g total), seeded and diced

½ cup (90g) finely chopped red onion

½ to 1 habanero pepper, to taste, finely chopped

¼ cup (10g) chopped fresh cilantro leaves and tender stems

1 teaspoon ground nori (see Note), or 1 tablespoon nori or dulse flakes (optional)

½ teaspoon dried Mexican oregano

¼ cup (53g) chopped Manzanilla olives

2 tablespoons olive oil

2 tablespoons fresh lime juice

¼ teaspoon fine sea salt, plus more to taste

¼ teaspoon freshly ground black pepper

½ avocado, cubed

Tortilla chips or tostadas, for serving

IN A LARGE BOWL, stir together the hearts of palm, tomatoes, red onion, habanero, cilantro, nori (if using), oregano, and olives. In a small bowl, whisk together the olive oil, lime juice, salt, and pepper. Stir this into the hearts of palm mixture. Transfer to an airtight container and let marinate in the fridge for 30 minutes to 1 hour.

Before serving, stir in the avocado, taste and add more salt if needed. Serve chilled with chips or tostadas.

COOK'S NOTE: To make ground nori, crumble a large nori sheet into a dedicated electric spice grinder and process until finely ground.

Corn & Zucchini Pakora with Tomato Tamarind Chutney

Pakora—also known as pakoda, pikora, pakodi, and bhajiya—are a popular street food and snack across the Indian subcontinent and throughout the Indian diaspora. They can be made from a variety of vegetables—from potatoes to onions and spinach—and are bound by chickpea (gram) flour that turns deliciously golden and shatteringly crispy when fried.

These pakora star two summer favorites: zucchini and corn. The chutney served alongside gets a double kick of acidity and tang from tamarind and lime juice, providing the perfect foil for the fried pakora.

Makes 4 to 6 servings

Time: Weekend

Storage: These are best eaten immediately, but you can fry them a couple hours ahead, keep them at room temperature, and reheat in a 400°F (200°C) oven until heated through and crisp, 5 to 7 minutes. Or you can refrigerate them for up to 3 days and reheat them, adding 2 to 4 more minutes to the reheating time. Refrigerate the chutney for up to 3 days.

TOMATO TAMARIND CHUTNEY

1 piece (30g) tamarind pulp, about the size of a golf ball, preferably seedless (see Note)

½ cup (120ml) boiling water

1 teaspoon cumin seeds

½ teaspoon fennel seeds

2 or 3 dried chiles de árbol, stemmed and torn into pieces

1 cup (145g) cherry tomatoes, halved

3 Medjool dates, pitted and halved

½ teaspoon fine sea salt, plus more to taste

¾ cup (180ml) water

2 tablespoons fresh lime juice, plus more to taste

PAKORA

2 medium zucchini (11 ounces/325g total), stems removed

1 cup (150g) fresh corn kernels (from 1 ear corn)

1 serrano pepper, stemmed and finely chopped

½ cup (24g) cilantro, tender leaves and stems, roughly chopped

2 tablespoons fresh mint, roughly chopped

2 tablespoons fresh dill, roughly chopped

½ teaspoon cumin seeds

½ teaspoon ground chiles, preferably Kashmiri

½ teaspoon ground turmeric

½ teaspoon asafoetida (hing)

¾ teaspoon fine sea salt

1 cup (120g) chickpea flour

¼ cup (60ml) water, plus more as needed

Canola, peanut, sunflower, or other neutral vegetable oil, for frying

MAKE THE TOMATO TAMARIND CHUTNEY: Place the tamarind in a medium bowl, cover with the boiling water, and let sit for 15 minutes. Place a fine-mesh sieve over a medium bowl and strain the soaked tamarind into the bowl. Vigorously press the tamarind through the sieve. (Compost any remaining fibrous solids or seeds.)

In a dry medium saucepan, toast the cumin seeds, fennel seeds, and chiles de árbol over medium heat until fragrant, about 30 seconds. Add the cherry tomatoes, dates, salt, reserved tamarind pulp, and water. Bring to a boil, cover, reduce the heat to low, and simmer until the tomatoes are soft, 10 to 15 minutes. Remove from the heat and allow to cool to room temperature.

Transfer the cooled mixture to a blender, add the lime juice, and blend until smooth. Taste and season with more salt and lime juice, as necessary. Transfer to a small serving bowl.

Make the pakora: Grate 1 zucchini on the large holes of a box grater into a large bowl. Slice the remaining zucchini lengthwise into strips ¼ inch (6mm) thick, then thinly slice crosswise to create little matchsticks and transfer to the bowl with the grated zucchini. Add the corn kernels, serrano, cilantro, mint, dill, cumin seeds, chile powder, turmeric, asafoetida, and salt to the zucchini and mix to combine. Add the chickpea flour and water and mix, using your hands to squeeze the vegetables gently to release any water in the zucchini and corn. You're aiming for a thick batter that holds the vegetables together. If the batter is too thick, add a tablespoon of water at a time until you reach the right consistency.

Set a wire rack over a sheet pan next to the stovetop. Pour 3 inches (7.5cm) of oil into a Dutch oven or other heavy-bottomed pot and heat over medium-high heat to 325°F (163°C). Reduce the heat slightly to maintain it.

Dip a large spoon in the oil and use it to scoop a 2-tablespoon portion of the batter, gently lowering it into the hot oil. Repeat several times to fry in batches (avoiding overcrowding). Let the pakora fry undisturbed for 3 minutes, then gently flip them and fry until deep golden, another 3 to 4 minutes. (It's perfectly okay if some of them break; they don't need to be uniform.) Transfer the pakora to the wire rack as they are ready, and repeat the frying process with the remaining batter.

Serve hot or warm with the tomato tamarind chutney alongside for dipping.

COOK'S NOTE: If you can find prepared tamarind paste (sometimes labeled "concentrate"), it already has the fiber (and seeds) removed, so you can skip the soaking/straining step. You'll need about ¼ cup (30g).

Lentil Samosa Puffs

Samosas are a common street snack in Kenya, where they are sold everywhere, including gas stations. Typically made with a thin pastry and folded into little parcels that are deep-fried, these skip all the fuss of folding and frying by using puff pastry that's easy to fill and quick to crisp up in the oven. You may have a little filling left over; eat it over rice or on baked potatoes or sweet potatoes.

Makes 18 puffs

Time: Weekend

Storage: Refrigerate for up to 5 days.

- ¾ cups (150g) large green/brown lentils
- ¾ cups (175ml) water
- ¾ teaspoon fine sea salt, plus more to taste
- 1 tablespoon olive oil
- ½ medium red onion (3 ounces/85g), finely diced
- 1 teaspoon coriander seeds
- ½ teaspoon whole cumin seeds, plus more for sprinkling
- 2 scallions, finely chopped
- 2 garlic cloves, thinly sliced
- ½-inch (1.3cm) piece fresh ginger, peeled and minced
- ½ jalapeño pepper, finely chopped
- 2 tablespoons fresh cilantro leaves and tender stems, chopped
- 1 tablespoon fresh lime juice, plus lime wedges for serving
- 2 sheets frozen vegan puff pastry, thawed (see Notes)
- 2 tablespoons Nut Milk (page 17), Oat Milk (page 17), Soy Milk (page 75), or store-bought plant-based milk
- Flaky sea salt, for garnish

PREHEAT THE OVEN TO 400°F (200°C). Line a large sheet pan with a silicone baking mat or compostable parchment paper.

In a medium pot, combine the lentils, water, and ½ teaspoon of the salt. Bring to a boil over medium-high heat, then reduce the heat to medium and cook until the lentils are tender, 15 to 20 minutes. Drain any excess liquid.

In a large skillet, heat the oil over medium-high heat until it shimmers. Add the onion and cook until softened and lightly browned on the edges, 8 to 10 minutes.

Reduce the heat to medium and stir in the coriander seeds, cumin seeds, scallions, garlic, ginger, and jalapeño. Cook, stirring, until fragrant, 1 to 2 minutes. Stir in the lentils, cilantro, and remaining ¼ teaspoon salt, cooking just enough to warm the lentils through. Turn off the heat and stir in the lime juice. Taste and season with more salt if needed.

On a lightly floured surface, gently roll each sheet of puff pastry just slightly, to even it out and smooth over any folds. Cut each sheet into 9 squares. Fill each with 1 tablespoon of filling in the center and fold over into a triangle. Pinch together the edges with a fork.

Place the folded samosa puffs on the prepared sheet pan. Brush the tops with the milk and sprinkle with cumin seeds and flaky salt.

Bake until golden brown, about 20 minutes.

Serve with lime wedges.

COOK'S NOTES

- If you'd like to make these ahead, freeze before baking for up to 3 months, and bake from frozen. Just add 5 minutes to the baking time.

- As of this writing, the most widely available vegan puff pastry in the United States is made by Pepperidge Farm, with two 9¾ × 10½-inch sheets in a 17.3oz/490g package. Dufour, known for its all-butter puff pastry, has now started selling a plant-based version sold as one 9 × 15-inch sheet in a 14-ounce package. Either works, but you'll need two packages if you use the Dufour.

Trumpet Mushroom Tiradito

Tiradito, the marriage of Peruvian ceviche and Japanese sashimi, is one of the hallmark dishes of the Nikkei cuisine that Japanese indentured workers and immigrants first cooked in early twentieth-century Lima. Though there are many variations, three important ingredients are salt, hot pepper, and citrus—all of which are combined with ginger and jalapeño in the leche de tigre, the spicy marinade that captures the essence of both ceviche and tiradito. Unlike ceviche, tiradito is traditionally sliced and sauced rather than "cooked" in the marinade. In food writer Nico Vera's version, inspired by his travels to Lima and Tokyo, a kombu stock imparts umami from the sea, a sweet potato mash balances and thickens the leche de tigre, and sliced trumpet mushroom stems resemble sashimi. This makes for a beautiful, elegant dinner-party course and is best enjoyed immediately after preparing. In the Peruvian tradition, serve extra leche de tigre in shot glasses and drink with an optional splash of pisco.

Makes 4 servings

Time: Weekend

Storage: Not recommended. The extra kombu stock and sweet potato can be refrigerated for up to 1 week or frozen for up to 3 months.

- 4 large trumpet mushrooms (9 ounces/255g total), with stems 3 inches (7.5cm) long and 1 inch (2.5cm) thick
- 1 (4 × 6-inch/10cm × 15cm) piece dried kombu, rinsed
- 2 cups (470ml) water
- ¼ teaspoon fine sea salt, plus more to taste
- 1 small garnet sweet potato (7 ounces/200g)
- 3 teaspoons toasted sesame oil
- ¼ cup (60ml) fresh lime juice, plus more to taste
- 3 tablespoons chopped red onion
- 3 tablespoons chopped celery
- 1 tablespoon chopped fresh cilantro leaves
- 1 tablespoon chopped peeled fresh ginger
- 2 medium garlic cloves, chopped
- 1 tablespoon chopped seeded jalapeño, plus more to taste and thin slices for garnish
- 1 scallion, thinly sliced, for garnish

STARTING WITH THE STEM end, slice each mushroom on the diagonal into ⅛-inch (3mm) slices, including the mushroom cap.

In a medium pot, combine the kombu, water, and salt and let the kombu soak for 15 minutes. Bring to a boil over high heat, then reduce to a simmer and cook for 15 minutes, stirring initially to dissolve the salt. Turn off the heat. Remove the kombu and compost it. Add the mushroom slices to the pot with the kombu stock and let cool to room temperature, about 1 hour.

Meanwhile, in another medium pot, combine the sweet potato with enough water to cover by 1 inch (2.5cm). Bring the water to a boil over high heat, then reduce to a simmer and cook until the sweet potato is fork-tender, 20 to 30 minutes. Drain. When the sweet potato is cool enough to handle, peel it and mash enough of the flesh to equal ¼ cup (62g). (Compost the peel and reserve the extra sweet potato for another use, such as adding to soups, smoothies, tacos, and grain bowls.)

Remove the mushroom slices from the kombu stock and pat dry with a towel. Measure ½ cup (120ml) kombu stock for the leche de tigre and reserve the remaining stock for another use, such as adding to soups and sauces.

In a large nonstick skillet, heat 2 teaspoons of the sesame oil over medium heat until it shimmers. Add the mushroom slices and cook undisturbed on one side until the edges are lightly golden, about 1 minute.

To make the leche de tigre, in a blender, combine the reserved ¼ cup (62g) sweet potato mash, ½ cup (120ml) kombu stock, the lime juice, onion, celery, cilantro, ginger, garlic, jalapeño, and the remaining 1 teaspoon sesame oil and puree on high until smooth, about 30 seconds. Taste and season with salt, more lime, and/or jalapeño as needed. Transfer ½ cup (120ml) leche de tigre into a container with a spout. Set aside the remaining leche de tigre.

Slowly pour the ½ cup of leche de tigre onto the center of each of four small plates to form a circular pool, 2 tablespoons per plate. Arrange the mushroom slices over the pools, garnish with the sliced jalapeño and scallion, and serve immediately with the reserved leche de tigre in shot glasses (with an optional splash of pisco).

4

SALADS

Salads might just be the most honest, accessible, and adaptable expression of plant-based cooking there is. As you'll soon see, they are also so much more than lettuce greens, a few chopped vegetables, and dressing. Instead, they can be low-effort ways to showcase raw and/or cooked produce in ways that bring out the most flavor and texture while combining them smartly with punchy vinaigrettes, crunchy bits, and more. To prove how versatile such produce can be in salads, this chapter begins by spotlighting four iconic ingredients, one for each time of year—asparagus, tomatoes, winter squash, and citrus—and pairing each with just a few other ingredients in three different preparations. All together, they sing a song of the seasons.

Grilled Asparagus & Fava Beans with Caper-Garlic Dressing

Here's a salad you can eat with your hands. Asparagus is delightfully sweet and golden, and takes only a few minutes on the grill over high, direct heat. The fava beans get grilled in their pods, which means you don't have to peel them—twice!—like you normally do. As the pods grill, the outsides char and the pods will start to puff: That's the beans inside steaming to tenderness. When the vegetables are done grilling, they're dressed in a salty, bright mixture of chopped capers, garlic, lemon, and olive oil. If you'd like, grab asparagus spears with your fingers and eat the fava beans like edamame, licking the dressing off the outsides as you angle for a bean inside. Instead of, or in addition to, these two vegetables, also consider snap peas, spring onions, bok choy, or any other grilling vegetable that looks good to you.

Makes 4 servings

Time: Weekday

Storage: Refrigerate for up to 2 days. Bring to room temperature and adjust seasonings before serving.

 2 teaspoons capers in brine, drained

 2 medium garlic cloves, peeled but whole

 Freshly ground black pepper

 1½ teaspoons grated lemon zest

 2 tablespoons fresh lemon juice

 3 tablespoons olive oil

 Fine sea salt

 1 bunch asparagus (1 pound/450g), woody ends trimmed

 1 pound (450g) fava beans in their pods

HEAT A GRILL TO high. (Or preheat the oven broiler.)

Chop and smash together the capers, garlic, and a few grindings of black pepper until a coarse paste forms. Add to a liquid measuring cup along with the lemon zest, lemon juice, and 2 tablespoons of the olive oil. Stir to combine. Season to taste with salt.

Spread the asparagus and fava beans on a large sheet pan. Drizzle with the remaining 1 tablespoon oil, season with salt and pepper, and toss to coat.

Grease the grill grates, then add the vegetables perpendicular to the grates over direct heat and cook, turning occasionally, until the asparagus are golden and crisp-tender and the fava beans are charred in spots and puffed, 3 to 7 minutes. (If using the broiler, keep the vegetables on the sheet pan and broil for 3 to 4 minutes per side.)

As the vegetables finish grilling, return them to the sheet pan and pour some of the dressing over. Continue until all the vegetables are done. (If you used the broiler, just let the vegetables cool slightly, then pour all the dressing onto the vegetables.)

Asparagus with Crispy Ginger & Garlic

Steaming is a surefire way to end up with bright-green, not-tough asparagus, which can then take an assertive, full-throttle dressing. This is inspired by chili crisp (see a homemade version, page 53), a Sichuan sauce heady with umami and textured from fried bits. While this recipe is minimalist, you can embellish it as you wish. Pouring hot, seasoned fat over vegetables is found in many cuisines, including Cantonese, Indian, and Appalachian traditions. By doing so, you get an exciting sizzle and the vegetables cook just a bit. Follow the format of flavorful hot oil + delicate vegetable for any number of quick side dishes.

Makes 4 servings

Time: Weekday

Storage: Best eaten fresh, so the crispy stuff stays crispy, but can refrigerate for up to 3 days.

- 2 bunches asparagus (1 pound/450g each), woody ends trimmed, cut on the bias into slices 1 inch (2.5cm) thick
- 3 tablespoons neutral oil
- 3 garlic cloves, thinly sliced
- 2-inch (5cm) piece fresh ginger, peeled, halved crosswise, and cut into thin matchsticks
- ½ teaspoon red pepper flakes, plus more to taste
- 1 tablespoon reduced-sodium soy sauce, plus more to taste

IN A LARGE POT fitted with a steamer basket or insert, bring about 1 inch (2.5cm) of water to a boil.

Add the asparagus to the steamer, cover, and cook until bright-green and crisp-tender, 2 to 4 minutes (depending on the thickness of the spears). Transfer to a platter to cool.

In a medium skillet or saucepan, combine the oil, garlic, and ginger and set over medium-high heat. Once it sizzles, reduce the heat to medium and cook, swirling occasionally, until light golden, 5 to 7 minutes. Turn off the heat and stir in the pepper flakes.

Pour the sauce over the asparagus, add the soy sauce, and toss to combine. Taste and add more pepper flakes and soy sauce if needed.

Salad of Asparagus & Snap Peas Two Ways

Asparagus and snap peas are both good raw and charred, and this salad celebrates that range: sweet, bitter, tender, crisp. First, small pieces of raw asparagus and snap peas sit in a mixture of lemon and dried apricots, their raw edges softening. Then larger pieces of asparagus and snap peas are broiled, the tops getting charred and the rest remaining snappy. To make it more substantial, consider adding Israeli couscous or whole grains.

Makes 4 servings

Time: Weekday

Storage: Not recommended for the finished salad, which is best eaten the day it's made. Can be made up to 3 hours in advance and held at room temperature.

- 2 bunches asparagus (1 pound/450g each), woody ends trimmed
- 2 cups (6 ounces/172g) sugar snap peas, trimmed
- ¾ cup (100g) dried apricots, coarsely chopped
- 1 teaspoon grated lemon zest
- ¼ cup (60ml) fresh lemon juice (from 1 to 2 lemons), plus more as needed
- Fine sea salt
- 2 tablespoons plus ¼ cup (60ml) olive oil, plus more as needed
- ½ cup (10g) mint leaves

POSITION A RACK 6 INCHES (15cm) from the broiler and preheat the broiler.

Cut the asparagus in half crosswise. Transfer the pieces with the feathery tips to a sheet pan. Thinly slice the bottom pieces on the diagonal and add to a large bowl. Transfer half the snap peas to the sheet pan, then thinly slice the remaining half on the diagonal. Add the sliced snap peas to the bowl with the asparagus and add the dried apricots, lemon zest, and lemon juice. Season with salt.

Season the sheet pan with salt and 2 tablespoons of the oil. Arrange the asparagus tips and whole snap peas in a single layer and broil until crisp-tender and charred in spots, 7 to 10 minutes. Let cool slightly.

Transfer the broiled asparagus and snap peas to the large bowl. Add the remaining ¼ cup (60ml) oil. Stir to combine, taste, and add more salt, lemon juice, and olive oil as needed. Top with the mint leaves and serve.

Tomato & Fig Salad with Smoky Chile Oil (page 141),
Tomato & Peach Salad with Rosemary-Lime Salt (page 140),
and Asparagus with Crispy Ginger & Garlic (page 137)

Tomato & Peach Salad with Rosemary-Lime Salt

This shows just how well tomatoes and peaches go with each other, especially when you dress them with rosemary oil and lime juice, then sprinkle with a finishing salt of fried rosemary and lime zest. Massaging the lime zest and fried rosemary in the salt releases their oils and makes for a fragrant, flavorful salt that can be used elsewhere, too. The almonds add good crunch, but feel free to use any nut or toasted seed; sesame seeds or nigella seeds would be great. If you want to bulk up the dish, avocado, baby greens, or couscous wouldn't be out of place.

Makes 4 servings

Time: Weekday

Storage: Not recommended.

1 lime

2 large tomatoes (12 ounces/340g each), cored and cut into ½-inch (1.3cm) wedges

4 peaches (2 pounds/910g total), pitted and cut into ½-inch (1.3cm) wedges

Flaky sea salt

2 tablespoons olive oil

1 sprig fresh rosemary

¼ cup (25g) sliced almonds

FINELY GRATE THE ZEST of the lime into a small bowl.

Arrange the tomatoes and peaches on a serving platter. Squeeze half the lime over the fruit (about 1 tablespoon) and season sparingly with flaky salt.

In a medium skillet, heat the olive oil over medium heat. Add the rosemary sprig and fry, flipping once, until the sizzling subsides and the leaves are crisp, 3 or 4 minutes. Use a slotted spoon to transfer to a plate. To the same oil still over medium, add the almonds and cook, stirring occasionally, until lightly golden brown, just a minute or two. (Almonds will continue to brown off the heat, so pull them when they are just faintly golden.) Use the slotted spoon to transfer them to the same plate. Reserve the rosemary oil.

To the small bowl of lime zest, crumble the rosemary leaves between your fingers. (Compost the stem.) Add 1 teaspoon flaky salt and massage the mixture between your hands until very fragrant.

Drizzle some of the rosemary oil from the skillet over the fruit, then top with the rosemary-lime salt and the almonds. Taste and adjust seasonings as needed, with more lime juice, oil, and salt.

Tomato-Watermelon Salad with Sumac & Lemon

Tomato and watermelon, two sweet juicy fruits, get a dose of savory tartness from olive oil, lemon, and sumac. While lemon is a high note of sourness—fresh and perky—sumac is the undercurrent: dried, fruity, with a longer, deeper drawl. Other great additions would be red pepper flakes, a crunchy vegetable like jicama or cucumbers, toasted crushed spices like coriander or cumin, seeds (sesame, nigella), and more herbs (always more herbs). Salting the fruit helps concentrate their flavors; if you taste a piece and it's not screaming summer to you, sprinkle it with a little sugar, too.

Makes 4 servings

Time: Weekday

Storage: Not recommended.

- 2 large tomatoes (12 ounces/340g each), such as heirloom or beefsteak, cut into irregular, 2-bite pieces
- 1 small watermelon (3 pounds/1.4kg), rind removed, cut into irregular 2-bite pieces
- Fine sea salt
- 2 tablespoons fresh lemon juice
- 1 tablespoon olive oil, plus more to taste
- 1 teaspoon finely grated lemon zest
- 1 teaspoon sumac, plus more to taste
- ½ cup (10g) mint leaves

ARRANGE THE TOMATOES AND watermelon on a large platter and season with salt.

Drizzle the fruit with the lemon juice and olive oil, then sprinkle with the lemon zest and sumac and scatter on the mint leaves. Taste and adjust the salt (with salt), silkiness (with olive oil), and tartness (with sumac).

Tomato & Fig Salad with Smoky Chile Oil

Since tomatoes are sweet but also acidic, you don't always need to add vinegar or citrus juice to a tomato salad. They just need some fat to balance that acidity, which here comes in the form of an oil infused with smoked paprika, cumin seeds, and pepper flakes. Warming up ground or whole spices in oil is like shaking them awake; they're practically dormant in the jar, but alive once bloomed in oil. The combination is smoky, spicy, and a little crunchy from the cumin seeds. In addition to tomatoes, this fruit salad has figs, a late-summer treat that also can teeter-totter from sweet to savory. The key to balancing the fruit and the oil is to season each element with salt. Without enough salt, the salad might not taste like much. But just like those snoozing spices in their jars, they'll come alive with proper seasoning.

Makes 4 servings

Time: Weekday

Storage: Not recommended for the finished salad. The oil can be made up to 3 days ahead and refrigerated. Bring to room temperature before drizzling over the fruit.

- 8 ounces (225g) fresh figs, halved lengthwise
- 1 pint (290g) Sungold or cherry tomatoes, halved
- Fine sea salt
- 3 tablespoons olive oil
- ½ teaspoon smoked paprika
- ½ teaspoon cumin seeds
- Pinch of red pepper flakes, plus more for garnish
- Flaky sea salt

ARRANGE THE FIGS AND tomatoes on a platter and season with salt.

In a small skillet, combine the oil, smoked paprika, cumin seeds, and pepper flakes. Cook over medium heat, swirling often, until sizzling and fragrant, 2 to 3 minutes. Remove from the heat and season with salt.

Pour over the fruit. Sprinkle with flaky salt and pepper flakes and serve immediately.

Raw Butternut Squash Salad with Apples, Dates & Ginger

Along with other hardy vegetables like Swiss chard stems, collard greens, sweet potato, and Brussels sprouts, butternut squash can be delightful raw. Shaved, thinly sliced, or cut into matchsticks, it is not unlike a carrot: sweet—but tough. By massaging the matchsticks with some salt as you would kale or cabbage, they slacken to a pleasant crunch. This salad doubles down on squash's sweetness with crisp apple and caramelly dates. When you are making a raw salad, it's always nice to add a cooked element to add pops of deepened flavor; here, the dates are charred in a hot pan to soften and add a whiff of smoke. To counter all this sweetness, ginger and lime add pep. Because the apple is coated in lime juice, it won't brown, so you can make this dish up to a day ahead.

Makes 6 servings

Time: Weekday

Storage: Refrigerate for up to 3 days.

1 small butternut squash (about 1½ pounds/680g)

1½ inches (4cm) fresh ginger, peeled, 1 inch (2.5cm) cut into thin matchsticks, the remainder finely grated

½ teaspoon fine sea salt, plus more to taste

1 green apple (about 8oz/222g), cored and cut into thin matchsticks

1 teaspoon grated lime zest

2 tablespoons fresh lime juice (from 1 to 2 limes)

5 pitted Medjool dates

2 tablespoons olive oil

PEEL THE BUTTERNUT SQUASH. Cut in half lengthwise and remove the seeds. Thinly slice the squash, then stack the slices and thinly slice them into matchsticks. (If you have a mandoline, you could pull it out now for the first thin slices, then use your knife for the matchsticks.) In a large bowl, toss the squash matchsticks and ginger matchsticks with the salt, and squeeze for a few minutes, until the squash starts to slacken.

In a medium bowl, stir together the apple, lime zest, lime juice, and grated ginger.

In a medium cast-iron skillet, cook the dates over medium-high heat, flipping occasionally, until charred in spots, 2 to 3 minutes. Let cool slightly, then rip into halves or quarters.

Add the apple mixture, dates, and olive oil to the squash and stir to combine. Taste and season with more salt if needed.

Squash & Cabbage Salad with Roasted Grapes & Olives

Roasting's special power is to sweeten and soften harsh edges: Winter squash goes from rigid to fork-tender and caramelized. Grapes go from mild (or maybe mushy or so-so) to jammy and very sweet. Kalamata olives go from salty (and maybe too intense) to gently briny. When you roast all three together, the olives and grapes collapse, the grapes release their syrupy, concentrated juices into the oil, and all the flavors sweeten and soften. That delicious roasting liquid is used as the fat in the salad dressing. For the acidic piece of the dressing, use the brine the olives are packed in: It's salty and punchy, and obviously goes well with the olives. Work the brine into the cabbage to help the rigid crucifer soften, then add more brine to taste once all the salad elements are together. Each batch of brine tastes different, so adjust the balance of sweet, salty, acidic, and fatty flavors in your salad to taste.

Makes 6 servings

Time: Weekday

Storage: Refrigerate without the mint for up to 3 days.

1 delicata squash (12 to 16 ounces/340g to 450g), cut crosswise into rings ½ inch (1.3cm) thick, seeds and pulp removed

¾ cup (115g) seedless purple grapes

½ cup (75g) pitted Kalamata olives, drained

3 tablespoons olive oil, plus more as needed

Fine sea salt and freshly ground black pepper

12 ounces (340g) red cabbage, cored and cut into ½-inch (1.3cm) pieces

2 tablespoons brine from the olive jar, plus more as needed

Fresh lemon juice (optional)

½ cup (15g) packed fresh mint leaves, torn if large

POSITION A RACK IN the lowest position of the oven and preheat the oven to 425°F (220°C).

On a large sheet pan, toss together the squash, grapes, olives, and olive oil. Season with salt and pepper and arrange in a single layer. Roast until the squash is browned and tender, 25 to 30 minutes.

Meanwhile, in a large bowl, combine the cabbage and olive brine. Season with salt and squeeze assertively until the cabbage starts to soften.

Transfer everything on the sheet pan, including the oil and grape juices, to the bowl of cabbage and toss gently to combine. Season to taste with more salt, pepper, olive oil, and olive brine, adding a little lemon juice if the olive brine isn't acidic enough. Add the mint and stir once more before serving.

Citrus & Mango Salad with Fresh Turmeric & Cucumbers (page 146), Orange & Endive Salad with Toasted Quinoa (page 148), and Raw Butternut Squash Salad with Apples, Dates & Ginger (page 142)

Winter Squash Salad with Vinegared Beets & Arugula

This is inspired by the Yam & Cheese, a sandwich at Court Street Grocers in New York that piles roasted sweet potatoes, pickled beets and red onion, whipped goat cheese, greens, and a sumac vinaigrette on a fluffy seeded roll. This salad rendition simultaneously roasts beets and winter squash, and quick-pickles the beets with vinegared shallots. Arugula adds spicy freshness, but any assertive green would work.

Makes 4 servings

Time: Weekday

Storage: Refrigerate the roasted squash and the beet-shallot mixture for up to 5 days. Bring the salad together right before serving.

> 1 medium butternut squash (2 pounds/968g) or another winter squash, peeled and cut into 1-inch (2.5cm) pieces
>
> 7 tablespoons olive oil, plus more to taste
>
> Fine sea salt and freshly ground black pepper
>
> 6 medium beets (5 ounces/140g each), peeled and cut into ½-inch (1.3cm) pieces
>
> 1 to 2 large shallots or 1 small red onion (4 ounces/115g), thinly sliced
>
> ½ cup (120ml) red wine vinegar, plus more to taste
>
> 4 packed cups (80g) arugula

POSITION RACKS IN THE top and bottom thirds of the oven and preheat the oven to 400°F (200°C).

Spread the squash on a large sheet pan, drizzle with 1 tablespoon of the olive oil, season with salt and pepper, and toss to coat. Spread the beets on a second sheet pan, drizzle with 1 tablespoon of the olive oil, season with salt and pepper, and toss to coat. Roast until tender, 25 to 30 minutes, switching racks and rotating the pans front to back halfway through.

Meanwhile, in a large bowl, stir together the shallots and vinegar. Season with salt and pepper.

Transfer the beets to the shallot mixture, add the remaining 5 tablespoons olive oil, and stir to combine. Let cool slightly, 5 to 10 minutes. Transfer the squash to a serving platter or plates.

When the vegetables are cooled slightly, top the squash with the arugula. Season with salt and pepper. Spoon the beets, shallots, and dressing over the arugula. Season to taste with salt, pepper, and more oil and vinegar.

Citrus & Mango Salad with Fresh Turmeric & Cucumbers

Here's a salad that will shake your taste buds awake. The verve is a fresh turmeric dressing guided by a salsa recipe in Cal Peternell's *Twelve Recipes* that's malleable to your tastes. It's as good on something juicy-fresh, like here, as on avocado toast, Fluffy Pumpkin Seed Ricotta (page 31), or tofu.

Makes 4 servings

Time: Weekday

Storage: Refrigerate for up to 1 day.

> 1 large lime
>
> 2 ounces (56g) fresh turmeric
>
> 1 tablespoon olive oil, plus more as needed
>
> ¾ teaspoon fine sea salt, plus more to taste
>
> ¼ teaspoon freshly ground black pepper, plus more to taste
>
> 1½ pounds (680g) mixed citrus fruits, such as 3 to 4 Cara Cara or blood oranges, white or ruby grapefruit, tangerines, or pomelos, peeled and cut into irregular pieces
>
> 2 mangoes (10 ounces/285g each), peeled and cut into irregular pieces
>
> 2 Persian (mini) seedless cucumbers, peeled if desired and cut into irregular pieces

FINELY GRATE AND JUICE the lime into a small bowl. Wearing latex gloves to keep the turmeric from staining your hands, remove any short nubs from the turmeric and finely grate them into the bowl. Peel the remaining rod of turmeric with a spoon, then halve it lengthwise and thinly slice crosswise into half-moons. Add to the small bowl. Add the olive oil, ½ teaspoon of the salt, and the pepper and stir to combine. Taste and season with more salt and pepper if needed. (The dressing can be made up to a few days ahead.)

Combine the citrus, mangoes, and cucumbers on a serving platter and sprinkle with the remaining ¼ teaspoon salt. Drizzle the turmeric dressing (including the turmeric pieces) over everything. Taste and if the mixture is too tart, drizzle lightly with more olive oil. The salad can sit out for up to 3 hours before serving.

Citrus-Avocado Salad

Citrus and avocado are a classic pairing of sweet/juicy and rich/creamy. They really don't need much enhancement besides a little salt and a thin drizzle of olive oil, plus maybe some red pepper flakes if you want a spark of heat. To make a salad exciting bite after bite with so few ingredients, variety is key. That means including different types of citrus but also creating a diversity of shapes: Cut the citrus however feels fun to you, and scoop the avocado into thin slivers with a spoon. The shape of the avocado pieces has an important purpose: The scoop elegantly carries the olive oil and citrus juice in each bite. Consider a ratio of 4 to 6 citrus fruits to 2 avocados as a starting point for four people and let the salad shift composition based on the fruit you have to play with.

Makes 4 servings

Time: Weekday

Storage: Not recommended for the finished salad. You can cut the citrus up to 3 days ahead, but wait to cut the avocado and plate it right before serving, as the avocado could risk browning otherwise.

- 2 pounds (910g) sweet mixed citrus fruits, such as 4 to 6 Cara Cara or blood oranges, white or ruby grapefruit, tangerines, or pomelos
- 2 large avocados (10 ounces/285g each)
- ½ teaspoon red pepper flakes (optional)
- Flaky sea salt
- 2 teaspoons olive oil, or more for drizzling

WORKING ONE AT A time, cut off the top and bottom of a citrus fruit and set it on one of its cut sides. Follow the curve of the fruit to cut away the peel and white pith, exposing the shiny flesh. Reserve the peels. Cut the fruit into a mixture of shapes: Cut into rounds or half-moons ½ inch (1.3cm) thick or cut into 1-inch (2.5cm) chunks, and so on. Remove the seeds. Transfer the fruit and any juice on the cutting board to a serving platter. Repeat with the remaining citrus fruits.

Halve the avocados and remove the pits. Use a spoon to scoop thin slivers of the avocado and plop them right onto the platter. Squeeze the citrus peels (which have some fruit flesh left on them) over the avocado (the acid in the citrus juice will keep the avocado from browning). Season with the pepper flakes (if using), flaky salt, and a drizzle of olive oil.

Charred Tangerine & Herb Salad

When tangerine pieces hit high heat, their insides concentrate and soften while their outsides brown and deepen in flavor. Don't bother supreming the fruit; keep the membrane intact. The other surprise is the use of large amounts of tender herbs as so much more than a garnish. You're eating the tangerines cool, so you can cook them up to 1 hour ahead, but don't dress the herbs until right before serving.

Makes 4 servings

Time: Weeknight

Storage: Not recommended.

- 6 tangerines, mandarins, or clementines (about 15 ounces/426g total)
- 3 tablespoons olive oil
- Fine sea salt
- ¼ cup (32g) pistachios, coarsely chopped
- 1 lemon
- Freshly ground black pepper
- 4 packed cups (120g) mixed tender herbs (such as mint, parsley, cilantro, and/or dill), large leaves torn in half

PEEL THE TANGERINES AND, keeping the membranes intact, separate the fruit into segments (like you're going to snack on the tangerine).

In a large cast-iron skillet, heat 1 tablespoon of the olive oil over high heat until it shimmers. Add the tangerines in a single layer and cook, undisturbed, until charred underneath, 1 to 2 minutes. Transfer to serving plates or a platter to cool and sprinkle lightly with salt.

In the same skillet, toast the pistachios over medium heat until fragrant and lightly golden, 2 to 3 minutes. Transfer to a small bowl, finely grate a little lemon zest over top, and season with salt and pepper. Toss with your hands until you smell lemon.

In a large bowl, toss the herbs with the remaining 2 tablespoons olive oil and enough lemon juice to lightly coat (about 2 tablespoons). Season with salt and pepper.

Pile the herbs on top of the tangerines, then sprinkle with the pistachios.

Orange & Endive Salad with Toasted Quinoa

Oranges and endives are such good pals because they're both so juicy. One bite of the duo feels practically thirst-quenching. The sweet fruit and slightly bitter leaves are often paired with olives, radicchio, and nuts, but here they get a sharp contrast to all that moisture from an unlikely ingredient: quinoa, the little seed that could. When uncooked quinoa is toasted over moderate heat, it gets nutty and crunchy, almost like a cracklier sesame seed. Because quinoa doesn't taste like a whole lot, it's wise to pair it with an assertive flavoring; here, red pepper flakes make it punchier, but feel free to add another seasoning after toasting—for instance, raw sugar, cumin or fennel seeds, ground cinnamon or turmeric, or toasted coconut.

Makes 4 servings

Time: Weekday

Storage: Not recommended for the finished salad. Toasted quinoa can be stored in an airtight container at room temperature for 1 week before using. Mix the salad together right before serving.

3 tablespoons quinoa, any color

Fine sea salt and freshly ground black pepper

½ teaspoon red pepper flakes

4 oranges (about 10 ounces/295g each)

5 Belgian endives, cut crosswise into 1-inch (2.5cm) pieces

1 tablespoon olive oil, plus more as needed

2 teaspoons sherry vinegar or white wine vinegar, plus more as needed

IN A DRY MEDIUM skillet, toast the quinoa over medium heat, shaking the pan occasionally, until the seeds pop like popcorn, 3 to 4 minutes. Transfer to a small bowl, season with salt and black pepper to taste and set aside to cool slightly. Stir in the pepper flakes.

Finely grate 2 teaspoons of orange zest into a large bowl. Working one at a time, cut off the top and bottom of an orange and set it on one of its cut sides. Follow the curve of the fruit to cut away the peel, pith, and membranes, exposing the fruit. Slice the fruit into rounds ½ inch (1.3cm) thick, then in quarters to create triangles; cut the pieces again if the triangles are quite large (you want them about the same size as the pieces of endive). Transfer to the large bowl with the orange zest and repeat with the remaining fruit. Squeeze any juice from the peels into the large bowl. (Compost the peels.)

Add the endive, olive oil, and vinegar to the bowl, season with salt, and gently toss (your hands might be your best tool here) to combine. Taste and add more olive oil or vinegar as needed to balance the sweetness of the orange.

Sprinkle the toasted quinoa over the salad right before serving.

Tomato-Bean Salad with Tomato Vinaigrette

A cookout-friendly salad for peak summer, this uses tomatoes in two ways: as the base of a vinaigrette and cut into large pieces to intermingle with beans. This salad gets better as it sits, which makes it a good make-ahead candidate. Let it come to room temperature before serving and add the basil and walnut mixture right before you're ready to eat to maintain respective freshness and crunch. If you don't want to cook dried beans, simply substitute with two 15-ounce (425g) cans, drained and rinsed. If you don't want to add nuts, croutons would make a good substitute. And if you're not a fan of the salty pop of capers, you can omit them entirely or add coarsely chopped olives instead.

Makes 4 to 6 servings

Time: Weekend

Storage: Refrigerate for up to 2 days.

BEANS

1 cup (see Note) dried white beans, such as gigante, lima, corona, cannellini, or navy, soaked for 6 to 8 hours or overnight, then drained

1 onion, halved

4 garlic cloves, smashed

2 dried chiles (optional), crushed

1 tablespoon olive oil

2 teaspoons fine sea salt

SALAD

2 medium tomatoes (6 to 7 ounces/170g to 200g each)

5 tablespoons olive oil

1 tablespoon sherry vinegar or red wine vinegar, plus more to taste

¼ teaspoon Aleppo pepper flakes, plus more for serving

1 small garlic clove, grated

Pinch of organic cane sugar, plus more to taste

½ teaspoon fine sea salt, plus more to taste

1 pint (290g) cherry tomatoes

½ cup (50g) walnuts, coarsely chopped

1 tablespoon capers, drained well

½ cup (15g) lightly packed fresh basil leaves, torn if large

Bread for serving

COOK THE BEANS: In a large heavy-bottomed pot, combine the beans, onion, garlic, dried chiles (if using), olive oil, and salt. Cover the beans with water by at least 3 inches. Bring to a boil over medium-high, then reduce the heat to maintain a very gentle simmer and cook, topping off water as needed, until the beans are totally creamy and tender, 45 minutes to 3 hours (start checking early, as the time could vary greatly depending on the age of your beans, whether you soaked them, and more).

Let the beans cool in their liquid as long as you can. Pluck out the onions, garlic, and chiles and compost them. Drain the beans (saving the cooking liquid to freeze and use for future beans, dips, or soups). Transfer to a large serving bowl.

Prepare the salad: Set a fine-mesh sieve over a medium bowl. Cut 1 medium tomato in half through the equator, then hold by the skin and grate on the large holes of a box grater into the sieve until you're left with only the skin. Use your hands or a spoon to press the tomato flesh through the sieve, leaving the seeds behind (and composting them, along with the skin). You should have ⅓ to ½ cup (80ml to 120ml) tomato liquid. Whisk in 3 tablespoons of the oil, the vinegar, Aleppo pepper, garlic, sugar, and ¼ teaspoon of the salt until emulsified. Pour over the beans and stir to coat. Taste and add more vinegar, sugar, and/or salt as needed.

Cut the remaining tomato into 1-inch (2.5cm) pieces. Halve any small cherry tomatoes and quarter any larger ones. Set all the tomatoes in the fine-mesh sieve, sprinkle with the remaining ¼ teaspoon sea salt, and toss to combine. Set aside to drain.

In a medium skillet, heat the remaining 2 tablespoons oil over medium heat until it shimmers. Add the walnuts and cook, stirring frequently, for 1 minute. Add the capers and cook until the walnuts are golden brown and the capers are crisp and burst, 2 to 4 minutes.

Shake the cut tomatoes to drain any excess liquid, then add to the bowl with the beans. Taste and add more vinegar, sugar, and/or salt if needed.

When ready to serve, fold in the basil and walnut-caper mixture. Sprinkle with Aleppo pepper. Serve with crusty bread for sopping up the juices.

COOK'S NOTE: The gram weight of 1 cup will vary by bean, so it's easier to use the volume measure. However, the weight of the beans will be in the neighborhood of 140 grams for the really big beans (e.g., gigantes and coronas) and around 215 grams for the smaller beans, like navy, with the rest falling somewhere in the middle.

Avocado Salad with Dukkah Croutons & Harissa Dressing

Inspired by avocado toast, this is equal parts avocado, croutons, and tender greens and herbs—in other words, the best kind of salad. The croutons are flavored with Dukkah (page 39)—a spice-and-nut blend originating in Egypt, combining nuts and sesame seeds with warming spices like cumin and coriander. A triple dose of lemon in the dressing—from zest, juice, and finely chopped preserved lemon—provides just enough acidity and brininess to cut through the natural sweetness of the avocado.

Makes 4 servings

Time: Weekday

Storage: Not recommended for the finished salad. Refrigerate the dressing for up to 5 days. Store croutons at room temperature for up to 3 days before assembling the salad.

CROUTONS

3 cups (125g) torn bite-size pieces hearty French bread, like batard or baguette

¼ cup (60ml) olive oil

2 tablespoons Dukkah (page 39) or store-bought dukkah blend

¼ teaspoon fine sea salt

DRESSING

1 teaspoon finely grated lemon zest

2 tablespoons fresh lemon juice

1½ tablespoons finely chopped preserved lemon, seeded

1 tablespoon Rose Harissa (page 52) or store-bought harissa

½ teaspoon date syrup or maple syrup

¼ teaspoon fine sea salt

¼ cup (60ml) olive oil

SALAD

2 cups (40g) lightly packed baby arugula

1 cup (50g) chopped fresh flat-leaf parsley

½ cup (15g) lightly packed cilantro leaves and tender stems, torn into bite-size pieces

½ cup (15g) lightly packed mint leaves, torn if large

½ cup (15g) lightly packed dill fronds

2 large avocados (7 ounces/200g each), cut into large chunks

Dukkah, homemade (page 39) or store-bought, for sprinkling

MAKE THE CROUTONS: Preheat the oven to 400°F (200°C).

Spread out the bread on a large sheet pan, drizzle with the olive oil, and toss to coat the bread in the oil. Sprinkle with the dukkah and salt and toss, gently pressing the spices so they adhere to the bread. Bake until golden brown and crisp, 13 to 15 minutes. Let cool to room temperature.

Make the dressing: In a medium bowl, combine the lemon zest, lemon juice, preserved lemon, harissa, date syrup, and salt. Whisk to combine and then slowly drizzle in the olive oil, continuing to whisk, until all the oil is incorporated and the dressing is emulsified.

Make the salad: In a large bowl, toss together the arugula, parsley, cilantro, mint, and dill. Add the croutons and ¼ cup (60ml) dressing and gently toss to combine, making sure not to bruise the herbs.

Arrange the dressed greens and croutons on a serving platter or divide among individual plates. Nestle the chunks of avocado in the salad, drizzle generously with the remaining dressing, and sprinkle with more dukkah. If you have extra dressing, serve it on the side.

Peach Chow

In Trinidad and Tobago, chow is a vibrant little snack made with fresh fruit—typically green or slightly underripe mangoes—that can be easily adapted to suit your taste and preferences for heat. In this version, you toss the peaches of high summer in a fiery, refreshing mix of habanero peppers, lime juice, mint, garlic, and cilantro. Mint isn't traditionally used in the chows of the Caribbean, but the clean sweetness of the herb leans into the lusciousness of the peach.

Makes 2 to 4 servings

Time: Weekday

Storage: Refrigerate for up to 3 days.

3 medium yellow peaches (1 pound/450g total), cut into ¼-inch (6mm) slices

2 tablespoons fresh lime juice

¼ cup (8g) lightly packed fresh cilantro leaves and tender stems, roughly chopped

¼ cup (about 10 large leaves) mint, stacked, rolled, and thinly sliced

3 garlic cloves, finely grated or pressed

½ small red habanero pepper, seeded, deveined, and minced

½ teaspoon fine sea salt, plus more to taste

IN A LARGE BOWL, combine the peaches, lime juice, cilantro, mint, garlic, habanero, and salt. Using a fork, toss to thoroughly combine. Taste and add more salt if needed. Serve immediately.

Caribbean Coleslaw

This crunchy slaw—sans mayonnaise—boasts some unexpected additions, which makes it polished and unique without losing its simplicity. Don't be surprised if it dethrones most of your other summertime sides.

One of the best parts is the brightness of the dressing, which gets its sweet-tart flavor from a combination of pineapple juice, lemon, Dijon mustard, and more. Even on day two, the texture of this slaw remains intact.

Makes 3 or 4 servings

Time: Weekend

Storage: Refrigerate for up to 3 days.

½ small head green cabbage (12 ounces to 1 pound/340g to 450g), cored and thinly sliced (about 4½ cups)

1½ cups (130g) grated carrots (about 2 large)

1 large red bell pepper, very thinly sliced lengthwise

¼ cup (15g) chopped scallions

¼ cup (10g) chopped fresh cilantro

½ teaspoon chopped Scotch bonnet or habanero pepper (seeded and deveined if you'd like a tamer heat)

3 tablespoons fresh lemon juice

3 tablespoons olive oil

¼ cup (60ml) pineapple juice

1 tablespoon Dijon mustard

3 garlic cloves, finely grated or pressed

2 teaspoons light or dark brown sugar

1 teaspoon fine sea salt, plus more to taste

IN A LARGE BOWL, combine the cabbage, carrots, bell pepper, scallions, and cilantro.

In a small bowl, combine the chile pepper, lemon juice, oil, pineapple juice, mustard, garlic, brown sugar, and salt. Whisk to combine.

Pour the dressing over the cabbage and toss to thoroughly coat. Taste and season with more salt if needed. Serve cold or at room temperature.

Chard Salad with Paprika Croutons & Chickpeas

This salad is a texture party. By layering various shades of crispiness, it fills your mouth with lots of shapes and bits to bite into. You have the crush of a crouton, feathery-crisp chickpeas that go creamy in the middle, little toasted sesame seeds that jangle around your mouth, and—perhaps the happiest surprise—a fresh, juicy, celery-ish crunch from chard stems. Chard is a great salad green because unlike kale, it's sweet, tender, and has stems that are pleasant to eat raw. The leaves are quite silky, which provides contrast to all the crispiness. Because this salad has so much textural excitement, the flavors can be a touch more muted: just the drawl of smoked paprika on the croutons and chickpeas, plus the sting of raw garlic and vinegar in the dressing.

Makes 6 servings

Time: Weekday

Storage: Separately refrigerate the undressed salad (without the chickpeas and croutons) and the dressing for up to 5 days. Store the chickpeas and croutons at room temperature for up to 3 days.

- 2 (15-ounce/425g) cans no-salt-added chickpeas
- 1 (7-ounce/200g) piece crusty bread, such as a baguette or boule
- 5 tablespoons olive oil
- ½ teaspoon fine sea salt, plus more to taste
- ¼ teaspoon freshly ground black pepper, plus more to taste
- 1¼ teaspoons smoked paprika
- 3 tablespoons sherry vinegar
- 1 small garlic clove, peeled but whole
- 1 bunch Swiss or rainbow chard (12 ounces/340g), washed and dried
- 1 tablespoon toasted sesame seeds

PREHEAT THE OVEN TO 400°F (200°C).

Drain the chickpeas, saving the aquafaba (see page 6). Using a salad spinner, rinse, drain, and spin the chickpeas. Lay a clean kitchen towel on a large sheet pan, pour the chickpeas on the towel, and gently roll them around in the towel to further dry.

Cut the bread into ½-inch (1.3cm) slices, then cut them crosswise into ½-inch (1.3cm) strips, then tear the strips into ½-inch (1.3cm) pieces. You should end up with 3 to 4 cups.

Scatter the chickpeas and the bread pieces on the sheet pan and toss the mixture with 2 tablespoons of the olive oil, the salt, and pepper. Spread into an even layer and cook, shaking halfway through, until golden and crisp, 22 to 25 minutes. Sprinkle with the smoked paprika, shake vigorously to fully coat, taste, and season with more salt and pepper if needed.

Meanwhile, in a large bowl, stir together the remaining 3 tablespoons olive oil and the vinegar. Finely grate in the garlic clove, taste, and season with salt and pepper.

To chiffonade the Swiss chard, stack a few leaves, then from the long side roll them up tightly into a long cylinder, like you're making a cigar. Thinly slice them crosswise, right through the stems, ribs, and all. Repeat with the remaining leaves.

When the chickpeas and croutons are ready, add the chard, sesame seeds, croutons, and chickpeas to the dressing bowl and toss to coat. Serve immediately.

Green Goddess Wedge Salad with Crispy Chickpeas

Classic wedge meets tangy, herbaceous Green Goddess. Instead of bacon bits, canned chickpeas are coated in smoked paprika, cumin, and cornstarch and roasted until extra crispy. The best way to enjoy wedge salads is as cold as possible—if you're feeling fancy, you might even chill the plates—so make sure to keep the lettuce and dressing refrigerated until you're ready to serve.

Makes 4 servings

Time: Weekday

Storage: Not recommended for the assembled salad. Refrigerate the dressing for up to 1 week, and store the chickpeas in a cool, dry place for up to 2 days. (They will lose a little crispness.)

- ¾ cup (156g) Silky Aquafaba Mayonnaise (page 46) or store-bought plant-based mayo
- 1½ teaspoons white wine vinegar
- 2 teaspoons garlic powder
- ½ teaspoon freshly ground black pepper
- 1 teaspoon finely grated lemon zest
- 2 tablespoons fresh lemon juice
- ½ cup (15g) lightly packed fresh basil leaves, roughly chopped
- ¼ cup (8g) lightly packed fresh cilantro leaves and tender stems, roughly chopped
- ¼ cup (8g) lightly packed fresh dill fronds, roughly chopped, plus more for garnish
- ¼ cup (8g) lightly packed fresh chives, roughly chopped, plus more for garnish
- 1 (15-ounce/425g) can chickpeas, drained and rinsed
- 3 tablespoons olive oil
- 1 tablespoon cornstarch
- 1½ teaspoons smoked paprika
- ½ teaspoon ground cumin
- ½ teaspoon fine sea salt
- 1 medium head iceberg lettuce, cut into 6 wedges

PREHEAT THE OVEN TO 450°F (230°C).

In a blender, combine the mayonnaise, vinegar, 1 teaspoon of the garlic powder, the pepper, lemon zest, lemon juice, basil, cilantro, dill, and chives and blend until smooth. Refrigerate the dressing for at least 30 minutes or until ready to use.

Spread the chickpeas on a sheet pan, drizzle with the olive oil, and toss to coat the beans in the oil. Sprinkle the beans with the cornstarch, smoked paprika, cumin, remaining 1 teaspoon garlic powder, and ¼ teaspoon of the salt and gently toss to coat every chickpea in the cornstarch and spices.

Bake until deeply golden and crisp, 15 to 18 minutes. Let cool for 15 minutes, then sprinkle with the remaining ¼ teaspoon salt.

To serve, arrange the wedges on a large platter or individual plates. Spoon a generous amount of the dressing over each wedge and sprinkle with crispy chickpeas. Garnish with more chopped dill and chives. Serve immediately.

Green Soba Noodle Salad

This refreshing cold noodle salad employs a few classic ideas. Like tabbouleh, the dish's flavor comes from tender greens. Arugula (though it could be cilantro, watercress, or even baby kale) is chopped with ginger, jalapeño, sesame seeds, and salt. With each stroke, the salt softens and seasons each ingredient, and the mix gets so fine that it can stick to the noodles, like pesto. The combination of crushed sesame seeds and salt recalls the Japanese seasoning gomasio (see Seaweed Gomasio, page 45), which adds subtle heft and nuttiness to each bite. After everything is chopped together, it's added to a tart dressing of lemon juice, soy sauce, and rice vinegar, which is reminiscent of ponzu. To bulk up the meal, consider adding avocado, edamame, nori, or pan-fried tofu (or marinate tofu in the dressing).

Makes 4 servings

Time: Weekday

Storage: Refrigerate the noodles and the dressing separately for up to 2 days.

- 6 cups (120g) tightly packed baby arugula
- 2-inch (5cm) piece fresh ginger, peeled and coarsely chopped
- 1 jalapeño, coarsely chopped
- 2 tablespoons toasted sesame seeds, plus more for serving
- Fine sea salt
- ½ cup (120ml) fresh lemon juice (from 3 to 4 lemons)
- ¼ cup (60ml) unseasoned rice vinegar
- ¼ cup (60ml) reduced-sodium soy sauce, plus more to taste
- 1 tablespoon toasted sesame oil, plus more for serving
- 1 pound (450g) soba noodles

BRING A LARGE POT of water to a boil for the soba.

Meanwhile, on a cutting board, combine 4 cups (80g) of the arugula, the ginger, jalapeño, and sesame seeds. Season with salt. Chop everything together until wet and homogenous. The easiest way to do this is to start with some forceful chops to break down the arugula, then rock your knife over the mixture until everything is about the same size; move the mixture around so all the bits get attention from the knife. Transfer to a large bowl and add the lemon juice, vinegar, soy sauce, and sesame oil.

Once the water boils, add the soba noodles and cook until al dente according to the package directions. Drain and rinse under cold water until cool to the touch.

Add the soba to the bowl of dressing and stir to combine. Taste and season with more soy sauce if needed. Add the remaining 2 cups (40g) arugula and stir once more. Garnish with some sesame seeds and a few drops of sesame oil.

Quick Green Papaya Salad

Refreshingly mild, crisp, and tangy, this salad—made with the underripe (green) papaya—is nuanced with the right amount of heat, citrus, and sweet to perk you up, especially during the heat of summer. The recipe is a hybridized riff on the more traditional Laotian or Thai varieties; pepper flakes add the heat, and soy sauce (as opposed to fish sauce) brings some salty depth. If you can't find green papaya (make sure it's very hard!), don't worry: Green mangoes, kohlrabi, shredded green cabbage, and broccoli stems are all fitting substitutes.

Makes 2 to 4 servings

Time: Weekday

Storage: Refrigerate for up to 3 days.

- ¼ cup packed (55g) light brown sugar
- 5 large garlic cloves, finely grated or pressed
- 3 tablespoons fresh lime juice (from 1 to 2 limes)
- 1 tablespoon soy sauce
- 1 teaspoon red pepper flakes
- ½ teaspoon fine sea salt
- ½ small green papaya (1 pound/450g)
- ½ cup (20g) chopped fresh cilantro leaves and tender stems

IN A LARGE BOWL, combine the brown sugar, garlic, lime juice, soy sauce, pepper flakes, and salt and whisk to combine.

Peel and remove the seeds and membrane from the papaya. (Compost the peel and seeds.) Grate the papaya across the large holes of a box grater. You should have about 3 cups.

Transfer the papaya to the bowl with the dressing and thoroughly toss to combine. Sprinkle with the cilantro and serve.

Sticky Shallot & Lentil Salad

A confit is food that is slow-cooked in liquefied fat, and it works beautifully with vegetables. Whether using tomatoes, leeks, carrots, summer squash—or shallot, as in this recipe—the vegetables will come out slumped and concentrated in flavor. Not only that, but the fat is infused with whatever is cooking with it. In this recipe, that's primarily shallots and some balsamic vinegar, both as sweet as can be. The vinegar gets black and sticky, like the pricey aged stuff you wish you were using, and the shallots are lightly oniony and nearly jam. Combine this whole mixture with lentils, and add parsley and celery for fresh crunch, as well as a small amount of raw shallots and balsamic from the bottle.

Makes 4 servings

Time: Weekend

Storage: Refrigerate for up to 2 days.

- ½ cup (120ml) olive oil
- ½ cup (120ml) balsamic vinegar
- 1 tablespoon Dijon mustard
- ½ teaspoon red pepper flakes
- Fine sea salt and freshly ground black pepper
- 1 pound (450g) shallots (about 8), peeled and cut lengthwise into ½-inch (1.3cm) wedges
- 1½ cups (300g) French green or black lentils
- 2 celery stalks (175g), thinly sliced
- ½ cup (25g) finely chopped fresh parsley leaves and stems

PREHEAT THE OVEN TO 300°F (150°C).

Bring a medium pot of water to a boil.

In a liquid measuring cup, stir together the olive oil, balsamic, mustard, and pepper flakes until emulsified. Season the dressing to taste with salt and black pepper.

Finely chop enough of 1 shallot (about one-quarter of the shallot) to yield 2 tablespoons. In a small bowl, combine the chopped shallot with ¼ cup (60ml) of the dressing.

In a shallow baking dish fitted with a cover and that can hold the shallots in one layer, combine the remaining shallots (keeping them in one layer) with the remaining ¾ cup (180ml) dressing and stir to combine. Cover and bake until the shallots are very soft, 1½ to 2 hours. Let cool slightly. (The shallot confit can be made up to 3 days ahead.)

While the shallots are cooking, add the lentils to the boiling water. Season with salt, reduce to a simmer, and cook until just tender, 20 to 25 minutes. Drain, shake dry, and transfer to a large bowl.

Add the shallot confit and oil, along with any liquid still in the baking dish, to the lentils. Stir to combine, then add the reserved dressing with the chopped shallots in it and stir until lightly coated. Season to taste with salt and pepper. Add the celery and parsley. Stir and taste once more, adding more salt as needed.

Broccoli Tabbouleh

After food writer Joy Manning ate a version of this salad at the Philadelphia restaurant Spice Finch, she had to ask chefs Jennifer Carroll and Billy Riddle how to make it. In the true spirit of tabbouleh, the grain—traditionally bulgur, but you can use quinoa to make it gluten-free—plays a minor role. It's the confetti of broccoli and herbs that makes this fresh salad so appealing. The tahini drizzle is rich and creamy.

You could substitute ground coriander for the whole seeds here, but toasting and grinding the spice fresh makes a big difference in the flavor and aroma. Use any combination of fresh soft herbs—parsley and basil are also good. Cherry tomatoes are the most reliably flavorful year-round, but if it's summer and you have in-season larger tomatoes, use those.

This is a great make-ahead salad because it improves with a few hours in the refrigerator. Add baked or fried cubes of tofu to make it more of a substantial meal, if you'd like.

Makes 4 servings

Time: Weekend

Storage: Refrigerate leftover tabbouleh and tahini drizzle in separate containers for up to 5 days.

TABBOULEH
⅓ cup (55g) fine bulgur
⅔ cup (160ml) hot water
1 head broccoli (12 ounces/350g)
1 teaspoon fine sea salt, plus more to taste
1 teaspoon coriander seeds, toasted and ground
½ teaspoon sweet paprika
¼ teaspoon red pepper flakes
¼ cup (60ml) olive oil
1 tablespoon fresh lemon juice
2 shallots, chopped (about ½ cup)
1 pint (290g) cherry tomatoes, quartered
¼ cup (10g) chopped fresh cilantro
¼ cup (13g) chopped fresh dill
¼ cup (13g) chopped fresh mint

TAHINI DRIZZLE
⅓ cup (75g) tahini
¼ cup (60ml) warm water
2 tablespoons fresh lemon juice
1 tablespoon olive oil
½ teaspoon fine sea salt, plus more to taste
½ teaspoon agave syrup or Wildflower Cider Syrup (page 35)
2 garlic cloves, finely grated or pressed

MAKE THE TABBOULEH: In a fine-mesh sieve, rinse the bulgur and transfer it to a small bowl. Add the hot water and let soak until the bulgur has absorbed the water, 10 to 12 minutes. Fluff with a fork.

While the bulgur is soaking, roughly chop the broccoli florets and peel the tough exterior from the stem (compost the peels). Cut everything so it fits into the feed tube of your food processor.

Using the food processor's grating disk, shred the broccoli. You should have about 7 cups of shredded broccoli.

In a large bowl, combine the salt, coriander, paprika, pepper flakes, oil, and lemon juice. Whisk to combine, then add the bulgur, broccoli, shallots, tomatoes, and herbs and toss well. Taste and season with more salt as needed.

Make the tahini drizzle: In a small bowl, whisk together the tahini, warm water, lemon juice, olive oil, salt, agave, and garlic. Taste and season with more salt as needed.

Spoon the broccoli tabbouleh onto a serving platter and drizzle the tahini sauce over the top. Serve immediately.

Roasted Mushroom Salad with Mustard-Miso Dressing

Mushrooms, roasted until dense and crisp at the edges, have a savory, bacon-like quality that works well in salads. Maitake mushrooms, also known as hen of the woods, work as well as oyster mushrooms here. You could use a silicone baking mat for easier cleanup, but it impedes the mushrooms' browning.

It takes a lot of oil to get mushrooms crisp, so pairing them with an oil-free dressing makes sense. Mustard, miso, and agave create a sharp, sweet, salty dressing that you will find many other uses for; it makes a nice dip for raw vegetables or a sauce for fried or baked tofu. If you can't get Little Gem lettuce, mâche and butter lettuce are good alternatives. You can also replace the snap peas with an equal volume of shredded carrots.

Makes 4 servings

Time: Weekday

Storage: Refrigerate for up to 3 days.

- 1 pound (450g) oyster or maitake mushrooms, base trimmed
- 6 tablespoons neutral vegetable oil
- ¼ teaspoon fine sea salt, plus more to taste
- 3 tablespoons white miso, homemade (page 83) or store-bought
- 2 tablespoons unseasoned rice vinegar
- 4 teaspoons Dijon mustard
- 1 tablespoon agave syrup or Wildflower Cider Syrup (page 35)
- 12 ounces (340g) Little Gem or other salad greens (about 12 cups), torn into bite-size pieces
- 2 cups (166g) snap peas, halved lengthwise on the bias

PREHEAT THE OVEN TO 450°F (230°C).

Tear the mushrooms into thick shreds and transfer to a bowl. Add the oil and salt and toss to thoroughly coat. Spread evenly on a sheet pan and roast until crisp at the edges, 12 to 15 minutes, stirring halfway through.

While the mushrooms roast, in a large bowl, combine the miso, vinegar, mustard, and agave. Add the salad greens and snap peas and toss to combine. Taste and season with more salt if needed.

Divide among serving bowls and top with the mushrooms.

Silken Tofu with Ginger-Marinated Tomatoes

Silken tofu can be a confusing category: The variety sold in shelf-stable packaging (not packed in water) comes in a range of silken, from soft to extra-firm. Even though they are all more luscious and softer than firm or extra-firm tofu that's not labeled as silken, it still varies in sturdiness. For this recipe, look for firm silken tofu, which will hold its shape when sliced and behaves here much like fresh mozzarella does in a Caprese salad. This recipe incorporates elements from both Caprese and Japanese hiyayakko, which contrasts the rich tofu with spicy ginger and scallions. Here, summer-ripe tomatoes are marinated with ginger and soy sauce, then combined with slices of tofu and basil. Hiyayakko is traditionally served with the seasonings balanced atop a square of the tofu, but this recipe has you slice the tofu and shingle it with tomatoes so the tomato juices can mingle with more of the tofu, Caprese-style. To make it a meal, eat over short-grain rice or with edamame and/or nori.

Makes 4 servings

Time: Weeknight

Storage: Not recommended.

- 1 pound (450g) mixed tomatoes, halved or thinly sliced depending on size
- Fine sea salt
- 2 teaspoons reduced-sodium soy sauce
- 1½-inch (4cm) piece fresh ginger, peeled, halved crosswise, and thinly sliced into matchsticks
- 12 ounces (340g) firm silken tofu
- Small handful of fresh basil leaves, for serving
- Toasted sesame oil, for serving

IN A MEDIUM BOWL, season the tomatoes with salt. Add the soy sauce and ginger and stir to combine. Set aside to marinate for at least 10 minutes or up to 3 hours.

Cut the tofu crosswise into slices ½ inch (1.3cm) thick and transfer to a platter or plates. Add the tomatoes and any liquid to the tofu, layering any tomato slices between tofu slices. Top with basil and a few dots of sesame oil.

Romesco Grain Salad

Inspired by the bold flavors of Catalonian romesco sauce—roasted peppers, tomatoes (here, in fresh and paste form), smoked paprika, garlic, and toasted nuts—this hearty grain salad is just as good warm as it is cold from the fridge the next day. Chickpeas would make a wonderful addition, or you can top it with a dollop of Creamy or Crumbly Almond Queso Fresco (page 27) or Fluffy Pumpkin Seed Ricotta (page 31). Full disclosure: Roasting the peppers, toasting the hazelnuts, and cooking the grains add some time to this recipe. To make it more weeknight-friendly, do all of that ahead of time—or use store-bought roasted peppers.

Makes 4 servings

Time: Weekend

Storage: Refrigerate for up to 3 days.

Fine sea salt

1 cup (185g) wheat berries or semi-pearled farro, rinsed

2 medium red bell peppers (6 ounces/170g each)

¾ cup (100g) blanched hazelnuts (see Note)

¼ cup (60ml) plus 1 tablespoon olive oil

1 large garlic clove, thinly sliced

½ teaspoon smoked paprika

¼ teaspoon red pepper flakes

3 tablespoons tomato paste

2 teaspoons sherry vinegar or red wine vinegar, plus more to taste

1 pint (290g) cherry tomatoes, halved or quartered

3 scallions, thinly sliced

1 cup (30g) lightly packed fresh parsley leaves and tender stems, chopped

BRING A MEDIUM POT of salted water to a boil. Add the wheat berries or farro, reduce the heat to a simmer, and cook until the grains are tender but with a little bite, 20 to 35 minutes. Drain well and transfer to a large bowl.

While the grains are cooking, turn the oven to broil.

Place the bell peppers on a small sheet pan or in a cast-iron skillet and broil, turning once and monitoring closely, as broilers can vary in intensity, until deeply charred all over, 15 to 20 minutes. Transfer to a bowl, cover with a plate, and let steam and cool.

Set the oven to 350°F (180°C). Spread the hazelnuts onto the same sheet or skillet and toast, watching closely, until they are fragrant and browned, 7 to 10 minutes. Transfer to a bowl to cool.

In a medium skillet, combine ¼ cup (60ml) of the olive oil and the garlic and cook over medium heat until the garlic starts to sizzle, 3 to 5 minutes. Add the smoked paprika and pepper flakes and cook, stirring, until fragrant and dispersed, about 30 seconds. Add the tomato paste and cook, smashing it into the oil to break up any clumps, until deep red and evenly distributed, 2 to 3 minutes. Transfer to a small bowl, add the vinegar, ¼ teaspoon salt, and the remaining 1 tablespoon olive oil and stir to combine.

Peel the skins off the bell peppers and core them. (Compost the skins and cores.) Roughly chop the flesh and add to the bowl with the grains.

Roughly chop the hazelnuts and add to the bowl with the grains. Add the tomato paste mixture, cherry tomatoes, scallions, and parsley. Taste and season with more salt and vinegar if needed. Serve warm or at room temperature.

COOK'S NOTE: If you can find only raw hazelnuts with their skins on, after toasting them, transfer to a kitchen towel, wrap up to cover, and let cool. (This will make the nuts easier to peel.) When they're cool, rub them against one another in the towel to remove as many of their skins as possible.

Mixed Bean Salad with Herb Vinaigrette

To develop flavor from green beans and cooked beans, both fairly neutral ingredients, most recipes for three-bean salads require that the ingredients sit in a dressing pumped up with vinegar and possibly aromatics like chile and shallots. This recipe maximizes flavor several ways: by smashing the green beans, which breaks down their cell walls and makes them drink up more dressing, and by adding a forest of herbs—leaves and stems alike. When finely chopped, the herb stems deliver an exciting crunch and highly concentrated flavor. It's still a salad for picnics and potlucks, but exciting enough to enter the regular rotation for weeknight lunches and dinners, too.

Makes 4 servings

Time: Weekday

Storage: Refrigerate for up to 3 days.

3 cups (see Note) drained and rinsed cooked beans, preferably a mix of types, such as kidney, chickpea, pinto, or navy (cooked from dried or from two 15-ounce/425g cans)

1 cup (50g) chopped fresh dill and/or parsley leaves or stems

3 tablespoons sherry vinegar or fresh lemon juice

1½ teaspoons ground coriander or cumin

Fine sea salt and freshly ground black pepper

½ pound (225g) green beans

¼ cup (60ml) olive oil

IN A LARGE BOWL, stir together the cooked beans, dill/parsley, vinegar, and coriander. Season with salt and pepper.

Trim the stem ends from the green beans. On a cutting board, use a meat pounder or rolling pin to pound the green beans until they split into irregular pieces. Rip them into 1- or 2-inch (2.5cm or 5cm) pieces, adding them to the large bowl of cooked beans as you go. Season the beans with salt, add the olive oil, and stir to combine all the beans with the dressing. Let sit for 20 minutes for the flavors to meld and the green beans to soften.

COOK'S NOTE: The gram weight of 3 cups will vary by type of bean, so it's easier to use the volume measure. However, the weights will be somewhere in the range of 160 to 210 grams.

Seared Cauliflower Salad

The nifty thing about brassicas like cauliflower and broccoli is they're good both raw and cooked. To get all their best sides in one dish, this recipe has you sear the cauliflower in large wedges, leaving it charred, smoky, complex, and tender in some spots and crunchy, fresh, and vegetal in others. You cut the cauliflower into florets *after*, not before, searing, then toss them in a bowl of macerated dried apricots and shallot. The warm cauliflower soaks up the prickly and sweet macerating vinegar, while parsley adds some freshness. Feel free to adjust the flavorings as you wish. Perhaps balsamic vinegar, capers, and basil; or harissa, lemon, and mint; or lime, canned chipotle in adobo, and peanuts. And so on. To make this more of a main dish, add lentils, white beans, and/or grains.

Makes 4 servings

Time: Weekday

Storage: Refrigerate without the parsley
for up to 3 days.

½ cup (105g) dried apricots, chopped

¼ cup (60ml) sherry vinegar, plus more to taste

1 shallot, thinly sliced

Fine sea salt and freshly ground black pepper

1 large head cauliflower (2 to 2½ pounds/970g to 1.1kg)

3 tablespoons olive oil, plus more as needed

½ cup (15g) lightly packed fresh parsley leaves, stems thinly sliced

IN A LARGE BOWL, stir together the apricots, vinegar, and shallot. Season with salt and pepper.

If the cauliflower has a substantial piece of stem, cut it off, peel, and cut crosswise into slices ½ inch (1.3cm) thick. Cut the head through the core into 6 to 8 wedges. The goal is to create large enough wedges that they won't fall apart when searing (they will get cut smaller after cooking).

In a large cast-iron skillet, heat 1 tablespoon of the olive oil over medium-high heat. Working in batches to avoid overcrowding, add one layer of the cauliflower wedges and stem slices cut-side down and season with salt. Cook without touching until well browned, 3 to 4 minutes. Flip to the other cut side and cook until well browned, 3 to 4 minutes. Transfer to a cutting board and continue until all the cauliflower is seared, adding more oil as needed.

Cut the cauliflower into florets. While they're still warm (so they soak up some vinegar), add to the apricot-shallot mixture and toss to combine. Add the remaining 2 tablespoons olive oil and toss to combine. Taste and season with more salt, pepper, vinegar, and olive oil as needed. Add the parsley leaves and stems and stir once more before serving.

Tuna Salad–Style Chickpea or Tofu Salad

Chickpea "tuna" salad is a smart idea that's been going around for a while: The creaminess of the salad is created by smashing the beans. But anything chickpeas can do, tofu can usually do, too, so this recipe lets you choose between them. If you go the tofu route, the salad is a little lighter and bouncy (in a good way), because the tofu is grated on the large holes of a box grater, turning into shreds that resemble tuna. Either way, you then add the salad's flavorful, crunchy stuff: mustard, red onion, celery, cornichons. Some feathery crispiness is added in the form of a handful of crushed potato chips. You might think: how extravagant and unnecessary! But these chips give each bite a great surprise of texture. Eat this salad on its own, over greens, or in a sandwich.

Makes 2 or 3 servings

Time: Weekday

Storage: Refrigerate without the chips for up to 3 days.

5 to 6 large cornichons (30g), chopped, plus 2 tablespoons brine, plus more to taste

1 tablespoon olive oil, plus more to taste

2 teaspoons Dijon mustard

Fine sea salt and freshly ground black pepper

1 (15-ounce/425g) can chickpeas, drained and rinsed, or 1 (14-ounce/397g) block extra-firm tofu

¼ cup (32g) finely chopped red onion (from 1 small red onion)

2 large celery stalks (150g), coarsely chopped

¼ cup (13g) packed finely chopped celery or parsley leaves

Handful of potato chips

IN A LARGE BOWL, stir together the cornichon brine, olive oil, and mustard until emulsified. Season with salt and pepper.

If using chickpeas: Add the chickpeas to the bowl and lightly mash with a fork. If using tofu: Pat the tofu dry. Using the large holes of a box grater, grate the tofu into the bowl of dressing.

Season with salt and pepper and stir to combine. Add the cornichons, onion, celery, and celery or parsley leaves. Stir to combine. Taste and adjust accordingly with more cornichon brine, olive oil, salt, or pepper.

Right before serving, crumble potato chips over the top.

5

SOUPS & STEWS

As the nights start to turn cool and we pull on our sweaters and scarves . . . oh, who am I kidding? I like soups and stews year-round, and I bet you do, too. Okay, maybe not a hot, hearty stew at noon on a sweltering DC summer day, but other than that, bowls of brothy goodness are at home on my table most months—and cold soups are especially welcome in August! Soups and stews can concentrate and celebrate the essential flavors of your favorite vegetables, and spices and toppings can take them into can't-stop-eating territory. This is where legumes, my favorite plant-based protein, often shine.

Nearly-Any-Vegetable Coconut Soup

For this formula, food writer and editor Sarah Jampel was inspired by her friend Caroline Lange, who is adept at turning a can of coconut milk and whatever vegetables are in her kitchen into an I-can't-believe-you-just-made-this soup. Three variation examples follow, but as long as you use lots of alliums and other flavor-bringers—herbs, chiles, ginger, spice—you're on your way to something delicious. Use your judgment: If you're making a carrot soup whose color you want to preserve, for instance, you might go lighter on the soft green herbs. Once you get the hang of the method, add what calls to you: lemongrass, curry paste, soy sauce, miso—or any of the spice blends, salsas, and other condiments from the Building Blocks chapter (page 15).

Makes 3 or 4 servings

Time: Weekday

Storage: Refrigerate, preferably without toppings, for up to 5 days and freeze for up to 6 months.

2 tablespoons **oil** (coconut, olive, vegetable, or avocado)

8 to 12 ounces (225g to 340g) **alliums** (scallions, leeks, onions), roughly chopped

2 to 6 garlic cloves, roughly chopped

½- to 1½-inch (1.3cm to 4cm) piece fresh ginger, peeled and sliced (optional)

1 hot **chile** (serrano, jalapeño, or habanero), sliced (optional)

Fine sea salt

Up to 1 tablespoon ground or whole **spices** (red pepper flakes, whole dried chiles, coriander, cumin, fennel seeds, garam masala, smoked paprika, turmeric)

Up to 1 tablespoon chopped **woody herbs** (thyme, rosemary, sage)

1 to 2 pounds (450g to 910g) fresh or frozen **vegetables** (spinach or other greens, peas, butternut/kabocha squash, carrots, zucchini/summer squash, canned tomatoes, sweet potatoes, corn, mushrooms), peeled and chopped if necessary

1 (13.5-ounce/400ml) can full-fat coconut milk

1 to 1½ cups (30g to 45g) lightly packed **tender herb leaves** (parsley, basil, dill, cilantro, tarragon)

Freshly ground black pepper

Citrus zest (optional)

1 teaspoon **acid** (fresh lemon or lime juice, or vinegar), or more to taste

TOPPING OPTIONS

Croutons

Fried shallots

Pesto How You Like It (page 53)

Salsa verde

Chimichurri

Additional herbs

Plant-based yogurt or sour cream

Crushed toasted nori

Seaweed Gomasio (page 45)

Shichimi Togarashi (page 42)

IN A LARGE SOUP pot, heat the **oil** over medium heat until it shimmers. Add the **alliums**, garlic, ginger (if using), and chile (if using). Season lightly with salt and cook, stirring occasionally, until the alliums soften and the garlic starts to brown, 4 to 7 minutes.

Add the **spices, woody herbs**, and **vegetables** and stir until the vegetables are coated and the spices are fragrant, about 1 minute. Add 2 tablespoons water, cover the pot, reduce the heat to low, and cook, stirring once or twice, until the vegetables are completely tender, 3 to 10 minutes depending on the veg you're using. (If you're cooking mushrooms here, you won't need the water yet.)

Add the coconut milk. Fill the can with water and add it to the pot. Increase the heat to bring to a simmer, then reduce it to maintain a gentle simmer and cook until the soup is hot and the flavors have melded, about 5 minutes. Remove from the heat and add the **tender herbs**.

Working in batches if needed, transfer the soup to a blender, being careful not to fill it more than halfway, remove the center cap from the blender lid, cover it with a clean kitchen towel, and puree until smooth. (Or use an immersion blender to puree directly in the pot.) Add more water as needed until you reach your desired consistency. Season to taste with salt, black pepper, **citrus zest** (if using), and the **acid**.

Divide the soup among serving bowls, add the **toppings of your choice**, and serve hot.

RECIPE CONTINUES ON NEXT PAGE

Carrot Coriander Coconut Soup

- **Oil:** Coconut
- **Alliums:** Scallions and onion
- **Chile:** Jalapeño
- **Spices:** Coriander and cumin
- **Woody herbs:** [none]
- **Vegetables:** 1 pound (450g) carrots
- **Tender herbs:** [none]
- **Citrus zest:** [none]
- **Acid:** lime juice
- **Toppings:** Sliced scallions, minced jalapeño, black pepper

Lemony Spinach Coconut Soup

- **Oil:** Olive oil
- **Alliums:** Leeks
- **Chile:** Jalapeño
- **Spices:** [none]
- **Woody herbs:** [none]
- **Vegetables:** 2 pounds (910g) fresh spinach
- **Tender herbs:** Cilantro and dill
- **Citrus zest:** Lemon zest
- **Acid:** Lemon juice
- **Toppings:** Salsa verde or chimichurri

Zucchini Thyme Coconut Soup

- **Oil:** Olive oil
- **Alliums:** Onions
- **Chile:** [none]
- **Spices:** Red pepper flakes
- **Woody herbs:** fresh thyme leaves
- **Vegetables:** 1½ pounds (680g) zucchini or summer squash
- **Tender herbs:** Cilantro
- **Citrus zest:** Lemon zest
- **Acid:** Lemon juice
- **Toppings:** Chopped toasted walnuts and fresh thyme leaves

Ajo Blanco (White Gazpacho)

When we think of chilled soups, tomato gazpacho usually comes to mind. It's certainly a summertime star, but one of my pantry-friendly favorites year-round is ajo blanco. This rich Spanish soup is made with day-old bread, almonds, garlic, and olive oil. You'll be surprised at how creamy the consistency becomes from simply blending almonds with water and bread.

It's cold and refreshing, with a kick from the garlic and a splash of sherry vinegar for acidity. Finish it off with a drizzle of olive oil and colorful garnishes.

Makes 4 to 6 servings

Time: Weekday

Storage: Refrigerate for up to 2 days.

> 2 cups (470ml) ice-cold water, plus more as needed
>
> 1 cup (140g) blanched almonds (see Note)
>
> 3 garlic cloves, roughly chopped
>
> 1 (6-ounce/170g) piece day-old baguette, torn into 1-inch (2.5cm) pieces (about 3 cups)
>
> ¼ cup (60ml) olive oil, plus more for drizzling
>
> 1½ tablespoons sherry vinegar, plus more to taste
>
> Fine sea salt and freshly ground black pepper
>
> 1 cup (145g) cherry tomatoes or grapes, halved, for garnish
>
> Chopped chives and/or chive blossoms (optional), for garnish

IN A HIGH-POWERED BLENDER or food processor, combine the cold water, almonds, garlic, bread, olive oil, and sherry vinegar. Blend on medium-high speed until smooth and creamy. The consistency should be thick enough to coat a spoon but still runny. Add water by the tablespoon as needed and season with salt, pepper, and more sherry vinegar to taste.

Transfer soup to a large bowl, cover, and chill for at least 2 hours or up to 1 day. If the soup has become thick, add water to loosen (it should be the consistency of runny pancake batter).

To serve, top each bowl with tomatoes and a drizzle of olive oil. If desired, garnish with chopped chives.

COOK'S NOTE: To blanch raw almonds, boil them in water for 1 minute, then transfer to an ice water bath. This will loosen the skins, making them easy to peel off.

Classic Chili Five Ways

I first started making a smoky version of this chili from Gena Hamshaw's *Food52 Vegan* using black beans and sweet potatoes. I have since swapped in and out many other combinations, including kidney beans and chickpeas, plantains and mushrooms, depending on what I have a taste for, turning this into more of a blueprint than a set-in-stone recipe. The key elements are beans, a starchy or "meaty" ingredient, canned tomatoes (or tomatillos), and generous spices.

Makes 6 cups (4 to 6 servings)

Time: Weekday

Storage: Refrigerate for up to 1 week or freeze for up to 3 months.

2 tablespoons olive oil

1 large yellow onion, chopped

4 garlic cloves, chopped

2 to 3 canned **chipotle peppers** in adobo sauce (depending on how spicy you want it), finely chopped, or 1 to 2 **jalapeños** or **serranos** (see Variations)

2 teaspoons ground cumin

½ teaspoon Spanish smoked paprika (pimentón)

1 teaspoon kosher salt, plus more to taste

About 1½ pounds (680g) **vegetables, fruit, or fungi** (see Variations)

1 (15-ounce/425g) can diced **tomatoes**, preferably fire-roasted, or 1½ cups (235g) canned crushed **tomatillos** (see Variations)

2 (15-ounce/425g) cans no-salt-added **beans**, drained and rinsed (see Variations)

1 cup (240ml) water

2 tablespoons fresh lime juice, plus more to taste

½ cup (18g) lightly packed fresh cilantro leaves (or parsley for the cilantro haters), chopped

2 large avocados, sliced

3 scallions, thinly sliced

IN A LARGE SOUP pot or Dutch oven, heat the oil over medium-high heat until it shimmers. Add the onion and garlic and cook until lightly browned, 8 to 10 minutes. Stir in the chipotles, cumin, smoked paprika, and kosher salt and cook just until fragrant, about 30 seconds.

Stir in the vegetables until well coated. Add the tomatoes or tomatillos, beans, and water and bring the mixture to a boil. Reduce the heat to low, cover, and cook until the flavors meld and the vegetables, fruit, or fungi are very soft, 15 to 20 minutes.

Stir in the lime juice and cilantro. Taste and add more salt and/or lime juice if needed.

Divide among serving bowls and top with the avocado and scallions.

VARIATIONS

Black Bean–Sweet Potato Chili

Chipotle peppers + peeled sweet potatoes (cut into ¾-inch/2cm cubes) + tomatoes + black beans.

Kidney Bean–Plantain Chili

Chipotles + ripe plantains (yellow with plenty of black spots, cut into ½-inch/1.3cm slices and then in half crosswise to form half-moons) + tomatoes + red kidney beans.

Adzuki-Mushroom Chili

Chipotles + sliced cremini mushrooms + tomatoes + adzuki beans.

Chickpea Chili Verde

Jalapeños or serranos + peeled Yukon Gold potatoes (cut into ¾-inch/2cm cubes) + tomatillos + chickpeas. (Note: Don't add the tomatillos until the potatoes are tender, and then cook another 5 minutes to meld the flavors.)

White Bean–Squash Chili Verde

Jalapeños or serranos + peeled and seeded butternut squash (cut into ¾-inch/2cm cubes) + cannellini or navy beans + tomatillos.

Creamy Sunflower Ramen

When I first tried chef Jonah Kim's vegan ramen at his now-closed restaurant Yona in Arlington, Virginia, it was one of those how-did-you-do-that? moments: The creamy consistency was a ringer for that of pork-based broth. Turns out his secret was high-quality Japanese soy milk, which is thicker than the conventional stuff because of a higher ratio of soybeans to water. I tried it that way and loved it, sourcing the Banrai brand at an Asian supermarket. But the first time I made sunflower milk (see Endlessly Customizable Nut or Seed Milk, page 17), the nutty flavor reminded me of that soy-based broth, so I knew I had the kind of DIY solution I like—without needing to seek out a special ingredient. If you've made the milk from Soy Milk, Tofu & a Bonus (page 75), feel free to use that here instead. For these bowls, I double down on the sunflower by using those sprouts rather than bean sprouts, and add a little kick of spice and brightness from shichimi togarashi. The other key to success: using fresh ramen noodles, if you can find them. If not, just break open whatever packages you can find—and make sure to ditch those seasoning packets.

Makes 4 servings

Time: Weekend

Storage: Refrigerate the noodles, broth, and vegetables separately for up to 5 days, or freeze for up to 3 months.

BROTH

1 cup (140g) raw sunflower seeds, soaked in water for 8 to 12 hours, drained and rinsed

2 cups (470ml) water

6 cups (1.4L) Vegetable Scrap Stock (page 36) or store-bought vegetable broth

1 teaspoon fine sea salt, plus more as needed

GARNISHES AND RAMEN

12 ounces (340g) fresh shiitake mushrooms, stems composted (or saved for stock)

2 tablespoons sunflower oil

Fine sea salt

1 pound (450g) baby bok choy, cored and thinly sliced crosswise

4 tablespoons Shichimi Togarashi (page 42)

1 pound (450g) fresh ramen noodles, such as Sun Noodle brand, divided into 4 equal portions

1 cup (35g) lightly packed fresh sunflower sprouts

PREHEAT THE OVEN TO 400°F (200°C).

Make the broth: In a high-powered blender, combine the soaked sunflower seeds and water and blend until very smooth, 30 seconds to 1 minute. Set a nut-milk bag in a bowl, pour in the sunflower milk, close the bag, and use your clean hands to extract as much of the liquid as possible, twisting and squeezing the bag over the bowl. (Compost the pulp, or save it to add to smoothies, such as in place of the peanut butter in the Chocolate Protein Shake, page 108.)

In a large saucepan, combine the sunflower milk, vegetable stock, and salt, whisking to combine. Taste and add more salt if needed. Set over medium heat, and when the mixture is very hot but not bubbling, reduce the heat to low and cover to keep hot.

Prepare the garnishes: On a large sheet pan, toss the shiitake caps with 1 tablespoon of the sunflower oil. Transfer to the oven and roast until tender, about 10 minutes. Leave the oven on. Transfer the mushrooms caps to a cutting board, cut into thick slices, and season lightly with salt.

While the mushrooms are roasting, use a salad spinner to wash and thoroughly dry the baby bok choy.

Transfer the bok choy to the same sheet pan you used for the mushrooms and toss with the remaining 1 tablespoon sunflower oil. Roast just until the greens wilt, about 3 minutes. Remove from the oven, season lightly with salt, and let the bok choy rest on the sheet pan.

Cook the ramen: Bring a medium pot of salted water to a boil over high heat.

Ladle ½ cup (120ml) of the hot broth into each of four deep bowls. Add 1 tablespoon of the shichimi togarashi to the bottom of each bowl.

Add one portion (4 ounces/115g) of ramen noodles to the boiling water. Cook until barely tender, 30 to 90 seconds. Use a spider sieve or slotted spoon to lift the noodles from the water, holding them over the pot to drain, then transfer them to one of the bowls. Repeat with the remaining noodles.

Divide the remaining hot broth among the bowls. (If it has separated or slightly curdled, don't worry: Just whisk it for a few seconds, and it'll come back together.) Top each bowl with mushrooms, roasted bok choy, and sunflower sprouts. Serve hot.

Double-Mushroom Noodle Soup

The foundation of this soup is kombu dashi, an essential Japanese broth made by soaking kombu in water until it infuses the pot with its umami essence. To this subtle broth you'll add dried mushrooms, crushed ginger, and garlic, which takes the liquid from delicate to powerful. The second burst of mushroom flavor comes from fresh mushrooms, which are seared in oil, then simmered in the soup until they're plump and meaty. (As for the dried mushrooms, once they've given their life force to the water, they're no longer flavorful.) Finish your soup with noodles, bok choy (or another green vegetable, like asparagus, edamame, or napa cabbage), and sliced scallions. If you want more protein, add a scoop of silken tofu to each bowl.

Makes 4 servings

Time: Weekend

Storage: Refrigerate the soup, bok choy, and noodles separately for up to 5 days. Freezing the finished soup is not recommended, but you can freeze the stock without the fresh mushrooms, miso, or soy sauce for up to 6 months.

- 2 (7 × 1-inch/18cm × 2.5cm) pieces dried kombu (10g)
- 8 cups (1.9L) water
- 12 ounces (340g) mixed fresh mushrooms, such as shiitake, oyster, and maitake, stems and caps separated (for shiitakes), caps torn into 1-inch (2.5cm) pieces, stems reserved
- 1 ounce (28g) mixed dried mushrooms
- 4 garlic cloves, peeled and smashed
- 2½-inch (6.5cm) piece fresh ginger, unpeeled and smashed
- Fine sea salt
- 2 baby bok choys (8 ounces/225g total), halved
- 12 ounces (340g) dried or 1 pound (450g) fresh wheat noodles, such as somen, ramen, or udon
- ¼ cup (60ml) neutral oil, such as sunflower or canola
- 2 tablespoons mirin
- 1 tablespoon soy sauce, plus more to taste
- 1½ tablespoons white or yellow miso, homemade (page 83) or store-bought
- 3 scallions, thinly sliced
- Toppings (optional): Seaweed Gomasio (page 45), Shichimi Togarashi (page 42), seaweed flakes, furikake, or crushed nori

IN A DUTCH OVEN or large soup pot, cover the kombu with the water. Let soak for 10 to 15 minutes, until the kombu is soft, pliable, and unfurled. Set the pot over medium heat and bring to a gentle simmer. As soon as you see small bubbles, remove from the heat, pluck out the kombu, and thinly slice it to reserve for garnish.

Add the fresh mushroom stems, dried mushrooms, garlic, and ginger to the pot and bring to a boil over high heat. Reduce the heat to medium-low and simmer, partially covered, until the dried mushrooms are soft and the liquid is deep brown, very fragrant, and slightly reduced, 20 to 30 minutes. Pour the broth through a fine-mesh sieve into a large bowl.

Add enough water to fill the pot at least halfway (no need to wipe it out), generously salt it, and bring to a boil. Blanch the bok choy until bright green, 30 seconds to 1 minute. Use tongs to transfer it to a colander.

Return the water to a boil, add the noodles and cook according to the package directions. Drain and rinse with cool water. Distribute the noodles among serving bowls and rinse out the pot.

Return the pot to medium-high heat. Add the oil and heat until it shimmers. Add the torn fresh mushrooms and stir to coat them in the oil. Cook, undisturbed, until they start to brown, 2 to 3 minutes. Salt lightly and continue cooking, stirring frequently, until they shrink and brown, 3 to 4 minutes.

Reduce the heat to medium, add the mirin, and stir to deglaze the pot. Pour in the stock, bring to a simmer, and add the soy sauce. Remove from the heat. To add the miso without creating lumps, either whisk it in a small bowl with a little of the stock, or add it to a small fine-mesh sieve, submerge the sieve in the broth, and use the back of a spoon to push the miso through and liquefy it. Taste and season with more soy sauce if needed. Cover to keep warm.

Ladle the hot stock over the noodles in the bowls. Top with the bok choy, sliced scallions, reserved thinly sliced kombu, and other toppings of your choice.

Korean-Style Curry

This dish, often based on a commercial mix, is usually less spicy and thicker than Indian or Thai curries, looking more like an American stew. This version uses shiitake mushrooms, a "tofu katsu" (cutlet), and sweet potato for thickening.

Makes 4 servings

Time: Weekday

Storage: Refrigerate the curry, without the tofu, for up to 1 week or freeze for up to 3 months. Refrigerate the tofu for up to 1 week; freezing them is not recommended.

CURRY PASTE

1 tablespoon olive oil

1 teaspoon cumin seeds

1 teaspoon fennel seeds

2 teaspoons ground coriander

2 teaspoons ground turmeric

1½ teaspoons garlic powder

1 teaspoon onion powder

½ teaspoon freshly ground black pepper

½ cup (65g) diced cooked sweet potato

1 cup (160g) diced apple

About ½ cup (120ml) water

CURRY SAUCE

1 tablespoon olive oil

½ cup (43g) sliced shiitake mushroom caps

½ cup (65g) diced onion

1 tablespoon minced garlic

1¼ cups (160g) diced Yukon Gold potato

1 cup (140g) diced carrot

¼ cup (60ml) soy sauce

2 cups (470ml) Vegetable Scrap Stock (page 36) or store-bought vegetable broth

½ cup (120ml) Nut Milk (page 17), Oat Milk (page 17), Soy Milk (page 75), or store-bought plant-based milk

TOFU CUTLETS

1 (16-ounce/454g) block extra-firm tofu

Neutral oil, for the sheet pan

½ cup (80g) potato starch

1 teaspoon fine sea salt

1 cup (240ml) aquafaba, Nut Milk (page 17), Oat Milk (page 17), Soy Milk (page 75), or store-bought plant-based milk

2 cups (160g) panko bread crumbs

Cooking spray

Steamed rice, for serving

PREHEAT THE OVEN TO 450°F (230°C).

Make the curry paste: In a medium saucepan, heat the oil over medium-high heat until it shimmers. Add the cumin seeds and fennel seeds and cook until fragrant, about 1 minute. Add the coriander, turmeric, garlic powder, onion powder, and pepper and cook for 1 minute, stirring constantly to prevent burning.

Add the cooked sweet potato and apple and stir until they are evenly coated. Cook until the apple begins to soften, about 1 minute.

Transfer the mixture to a blender and blend to a smooth paste, adding up to ½ cup (120ml) water as needed to get or keep the blades moving.

Make the curry sauce: In a deep pan or Dutch oven, heat the oil over medium-high heat until it shimmers. Add the mushrooms and cook until they begin to brown, about 2 minutes. Add the onion and garlic and cook until the onion is translucent, about 3 minutes. Add the potato and carrot and cook until they begin to brown, about 2 minutes.

Add the curry paste and stir until all the vegetables are evenly coated. Add the soy sauce and the vegetable stock, stirring to scrape up any browned bits with a wooden spoon. Bring the mixture to a boil, reduce the heat until the liquid is at a simmer, and cook until the potatoes are tender, about 10 minutes. Stir in the milk and cook for 1 more minute to incorporate the flavors.

Meanwhile, prepare the tofu cutlets: Slice the tofu in half crosswise and then again in half lengthwise, to make 4 cutlets.

Lightly oil a small sheet pan.

Set up a dredging station in three shallow bowls: In one bowl, whisk together the potato starch and salt. Pour the aquafaba or milk into a second. Spread the panko in the third. One by one, dredge each tofu cutlet in the potato starch, turning to coat each one well. Tap off any excess starch, then dip each cutlet in the aquafaba or milk, and then the panko. Transfer the cutlets to the oiled sheet pan as you work.

Mist the top of each cutlet with cooking spray. Bake until the panko is golden brown, about 10 minutes.

Slice the tofu cutlets diagonally and serve over rice with the curry sauce.

Misir Wat

This Ethiopian classic from Basbaas Sauce founder and cookbook author Hawa Hassan infuses red lentils with a double dose of spices: from Berbere (page 38) and from niter kibbeh (the spiced butter that also flavors Gomen, page 355). The combination gives the dish a beautifully layered, complex heat. Split red lentils can go from firm to mush in a minute, so keep a close eye on them. You want them completely tender and beginning to break down, but still with a bit of texture.

Makes 4 to 6 servings

Time: Weekday

Storage: Refrigerate for up to 5 days in an airtight container or freeze for up to 3 months.

4 cups (950ml) water

¼ cup (57g) Niter Kibbeh (page 355)

1 small red onion (4 ounces/115g), finely chopped

1 tablespoon chopped fresh ginger

3 garlic cloves, finely grated or pressed

3 tablespoons Berbere (page 38)

2 cups (370g) red lentils, rinsed and drained

3 plum tomatoes (4 ounces/115g each), seeded and chopped

1½ teaspoons fine salt, plus more to taste

2 tablespoons fresh lemon juice

½ cup (18g) lightly packed fresh cilantro leaves, coarsely chopped

IN A SAUCEPAN OR kettle, bring the 4 cups (950ml) water to a boil and keep it hot.

In a Dutch oven or large saucepan, warm the niter kibbeh over medium heat. Once it's hot, add the red onion and cook, stirring frequently, until softened, about 5 minutes. Add the ginger, garlic, and berbere and cook until sizzling, about 30 seconds. Add the lentils and tomatoes and stir to coat.

Add the salt and 3 cups (700ml) of the hot water from the pan/kettle. Increase the heat to medium-high to bring the mixture to a gentle boil, then reduce to medium so that the mixture is at a bare simmer. Cook, stirring occasionally, until the lentils are very tender but not completely falling apart, 15 to 20 minutes. (Add more of the hot water, as needed, to keep the lentils from sticking to the bottom of the pot and burning.)

Taste and season with more salt if needed. Stir in the lemon juice and cilantro and serve hot.

Stewed Jerk Lentils

Spooned over freshly steamed brown rice or starring in a soup, lentils have long been admired for their clean, nutty-earthy flavor, nutrition (they're packed with fiber and protein), and easy preparation. That makes them a must-have ingredient in plant-based cooking. This recipe takes the humble lentil to the tropics and introduces a bombastic partner: jerk spice. The resulting dish brims with energy and heat.

Makes 4 to 6 servings

Time: Weekend

Storage: Refrigerate for up to 5 days or freeze for up to 3 months.

1 pound (450g) large green/brown lentils

1 Scotch bonnet or habanero pepper

7 large garlic cloves, finely grated or pressed

½ cup (55g) chopped white onion

1 cup (55g) chopped scallions

1 teaspoon grated lime zest

2 tablespoons fresh lime juice

1 teaspoon fine sea salt, plus more to taste

¼ cup (60ml) unrefined coconut oil

¼ cup (30g) Jerk Spice (page 41)

Steamed brown rice, for serving

IN A DUTCH OVEN or other large pot, combine the lentils with enough water to cover them by 1 inch (2.5cm). Add the whole Scotch bonnet pepper. Bring to a boil over medium-high heat, then reduce the heat to a simmer, cover, and cook until the lentils are broken and soft, 30 to 45 minutes.

Carefully remove and reserve the Scotch bonnet, which should be slightly shriveled. (You're going to add it back, but you don't want it to break up when you stir, which would cause the dish to get much spicier.) Add the garlic, onion, scallions, lime zest, lime juice, salt, coconut oil, and jerk spice. Stir to combine. Return the Scotch bonnet pepper to the pot and simmer until the lentils are thick and stewy, 5 to 7 minutes. Taste and season with more salt if needed.

Fish out and compost the Scotch bonnet. Serve the lentils hot over brown rice.

Oaxaca-Style Lentil Soup

This hearty soup is smoky, savory, and just the right amount of sweet, thanks to the addition of pineapple and plantain. This unique combination might just change the way you see lentils—and it's the reason this soup is sometimes referred to as Lentils with Fruit. This recipe includes smoked paprika instead of the more traditional bacon. Serve as is or garnish with a couple of slices of fried plantain.

Makes 4 servings

Time: Weekday

Storage: Refrigerate for up to 3 days or freeze for up to 3 months.

LENTILS

1 cup (190g) large green/brown lentils, picked over and rinsed

3 cups (700ml) water

½ small white onion (96g), peeled

1 bay leaf

SOUP

2 Roma tomatoes (10 ounces/283g total), quartered

2 garlic cloves, peeled but whole

1 teaspoon avocado or another neutral oil

½ small white onion (96g), chopped

1 medium carrot (4 ounces/115g), scrubbed and cut into ½-inch dice

Pinch of ground allspice

Pinch of ground cloves

¼ teaspoon smoked paprika

3 cups (700ml) vegetable stock

1 medium-ripe (yellow with a touch of green and plenty of dark spots) plantain (8 ounces/225g), peeled and cut into ½-inch dice

¾ cup (125g) diced fresh pineapple

1 serrano pepper, seeded and chopped

3 sprigs fresh cilantro, chopped

1 teaspoon fine sea salt, plus more to taste

¼ teaspoon freshly ground black pepper

COOK THE LENTILS: In a medium saucepan, combine the lentils, water, onion, and bay leaf. Bring to a boil over medium-high heat. Reduce the heat until the liquid is at a simmer and cook, uncovered, until the lentils are beginning to soften, about 15 minutes. Drain. (Compost the onion and bay leaf.)

Make the soup: In a blender, combine the tomatoes and garlic and puree until smooth.

In a Dutch oven or large soup pot, heat the oil over medium heat until it shimmers. Stir in the onion and carrot and cook until they begin to soften, about 7 minutes. Stir in the allspice, cloves, and smoked paprika and cook, stirring occasionally, for 1 minute. Pour in the tomato puree and simmer until the puree turns deep red, about 2 minutes.

Stir in the lentils, vegetable stock, plantain, pineapple, serrano, cilantro, salt, and black pepper. Bring to a very gentle simmer and cook, uncovered, until the vegetables are very tender, about 20 minutes. Taste and add more salt if needed. Serve hot.

Dominican-Style Red Beans

Ask any Dominican what the secret is to making red beans, and you'll get a different answer every time—something that can probably be said about every recipe so closely tied to a nation's identity.

There are a few things, however, that everyone agrees upon: The beans always call for oregano, garlic, bell peppers, and some form of acid. If you can find fresh sour oranges, sold at many Latin American grocery stores and markets, their juice is fantastic as a substitute for the apple cider vinegar, though the latter will do the trick.

This recipe calls for blending a sofrito (aromatics and spices sautéed in oil) with the boiled vegetables and some of the cooked beans, bringing all the ingredients together and reducing waste. It's not a required step by any means, but it results in gorgeous, creamy beans with a smooth, flavorful broth. In addition to rice, serve these with Spicy Fried Plantains (page 117).

Makes 6 to 8 servings

Time: Weekend

Storage: Refrigerate for up to 4 days or freeze for up to 3 months.

1 large red onion (12 ounces/340g)

1 green bell pepper (5 ounces/142g)

12 garlic cloves (60g), peeled but whole

1 pound (450g) dried red beans or red kidney beans, soaked 8 hours or overnight, drained and rinsed

1 celery stalk (50g), chopped

2 teaspoons dried oregano

2 teaspoons dried thyme

1 thin strip of dried kombu (optional)

2 tablespoons olive oil

1½ teaspoons fine sea salt, plus more to taste

3 tablespoons double-concentrated tomato paste

2 tablespoons apple cider vinegar, plus more to taste

6 sprigs fresh cilantro

Steamed rice, for serving

PEEL AND HALVE THE onion. Add one half to a Dutch oven or other large pot. Mince the other half and set aside for the sofrito. Halve and seed the bell pepper. Add one half to the Dutch oven. Mince the other half and set aside with the onion for the sofrito. Put 4 of the peeled garlic cloves in the Dutch oven. Finely grate or press the remaining 8 and set aside for the sofrito.

Add the beans, celery, ½ teaspoon of the oregano, ½ teaspoon of the thyme, and the kombu (if using) to the Dutch oven. Add water to cover by 1 inch (2.5cm). Bring to a boil over high heat, reduce to a simmer, and cook until the beans are tender, 40 to 60 minutes or more, adding more hot water if needed to keep the beans barely covered. (Avoid much stirring to keep the beans from breaking.) Pluck out and compost the kombu, if using.

Meanwhile, to prepare the sofrito, in a large deep skillet, heat the olive oil over medium heat until it shimmers. Add the reserved minced onion and bell pepper and ½ teaspoon of the salt. Sauté until the onions are translucent, about 4 minutes. Stir in the reserved minced garlic and the remaining 1½ teaspoons oregano and 1½ teaspoons thyme and cook until fragrant, about 30 seconds. Add the tomato paste and vinegar and cook until the tomato paste turns a shade darker, about 2 minutes. Turn off the heat.

When the beans are ready, pluck out the boiled onion, bell pepper, celery, and garlic and transfer to a blender, Add the sofrito, 1 cup (240ml) of the bean cooking liquid, and ½ cup of the cooked beans and puree until creamy, about 30 seconds. Return the puree to the pot of beans. (Alternatively, add 1 cup/240ml of the bean cooking liquid, ½ cup/120ml of the cooked beans, and the boiled onion, bell pepper, celery, and garlic to the skillet where the sofrito is and puree with an immersion blender before returning it to the pot of beans.)

Stir in the remaining 1 teaspoon salt. Bring to a boil, reduce to a simmer, and cook without stirring until the flavors meld and the beans thicken to your liking, 10 to 20 minutes. (Fish out and compost the cilantro stems, if you'd like.) Taste and season with more salt and/or vinegar if needed and serve hot with rice.

Korean Ramyeon

In Korea, instant ramen noodles (ramyeon) are not what you expect. They are not just what college kids eat when they're down to the last few dollars of their monthly stipend, but instead come in hundreds of flavors and varieties and are typically sold by the case. As colorfully portrayed in the Oscar-winning movie *Parasite*, ramyeon are enjoyed by the rich and less-than-rich alike. This recipe from cookbook author Joanne Lee Molinaro (aka The Korean Vegan on social media) can serve as a homemade addition to your ramyeon shelf, and you can use your favorite kind of ramen noodles (including gluten-free noodles), instead of the kind that comes in the package. It has a spicy and savory broth, with hints of sweetness, plus a gorgeous rolled omelet made possible by store-bought liquid egg replacer (such as Just Egg brand).

Time: Weekday

Makes 2 servings

Storage: Refrigerate for up to 3 days.

SPICE MIX
1 tablespoon gochugaru (Korean chile flakes)
1 tablespoon nutritional yeast
2 teaspoons onion powder
2 teaspoons garlic powder
1 teaspoon smoked paprika
1 teaspoon ground cumin
1 teaspoon freshly ground black pepper
½ teaspoon ground turmeric

GYERRANMARI (ROLLED OMELET)
1 cup (240ml) liquid egg replacer, such as Just Egg
½ teaspoon fine sea salt
½ teaspoon freshly ground black pepper
1 tablespoon sunflower or other neutral vegetable oil

RAMYEON
1 tablespoon sesame oil
4 scallions, chopped, plus more thinly sliced for garnish
½ cup (70g) julienned carrot
4 large fresh shiitake mushrooms, stems composted (or saved for stock) and caps sliced (1 cup)
6 garlic cloves, finely grated or pressed
2 tablespoons soy sauce
1 teaspoon maple syrup
4 cups (950ml) water
8 ounces (225g) uncooked ramen noodles

MAKE THE SPICE MIX: In a small bowl, mix together the gochugaru, nutritional yeast, onion powder, garlic powder, smoked paprika, cumin, black pepper, and turmeric.

Make the gyerranmari (rolled omelet): In a small bowl, whisk together the liquid egg replacer, salt, and pepper.

In a small (preferably 6-inch/15cm) nonstick pan, heat the oil over medium heat until it shimmers. Pour in about half the liquid egg replacer and cook without disturbing until it is mostly set, about 2 minutes. Use a spatula or chopsticks to roll it up and over itself, rolling all the way from the left side of the skillet to the right. Leaving the roll on the right side of the pan, pour in half of the remaining egg replacer, cook it without disturbing until it is mostly set, about 2 minutes, then roll the first omelet back across the pan from right to left, picking up the next layer of "egg." Repeat once more with the remaining egg replacer, cooking and rolling back from left to right, then remove the finished gyerranmari and let it cool while you make the ramyeon.

Make the ramyeon: In a medium saucepan, heat the sesame oil over medium heat. Immediately add the scallions, carrot, mushrooms, and garlic and cook until fragrant, about 1 minute. Add the spice mixture and stir to evenly coat the vegetables. Pour in the soy sauce and maple syrup and cook, scraping the bottom of the pan to deglaze.

Add the water and increase the heat to medium-high to bring the mixture to a gentle boil. Add the noodles and cook, stirring, until they are fully cooked, about 3 minutes.

Divide the ramyeon among serving bowls. Slice the gyerranmari into pieces ½ inch (1.3cm) thick and divide among the bowls. Garnish with sliced scallions.

White Bean Soup with Crispy Shiitake Bacon

This recipe transforms an everyday pantry staple of canned white beans into a bowl of comforting soup that gets a special topping of crunchy shiitake bits. You can use the Smoky Mushroom Crisps (page 67) here, or you can do a simpler roast of shiitake slices until they become crispy, and so fragrant and earthy, they are reminiscent of truffles. Any leftover bits make for a can't-stop-eating snack or provide texture sprinkled over risotto, pasta, and baked potatoes.

Makes 4 to 6 servings

Time: Weekday

Storage: Refrigerate for up to 4 days or freeze for up to 3 months. Store the shiitake bacon at room temperature for up to 2 days, recrisping in the oven if needed.

SOUP

¼ cup (60ml) olive oil

1 medium yellow onion (8 ounces/225g), chopped

2 celery stalks (85g), chopped

1 medium carrot (3 ounces/85g), scrubbed and chopped

6 garlic cloves (29g), finely grated or pressed

2 sprigs fresh thyme

½ teaspoon fine sea salt

¼ teaspoon freshly ground black pepper

4 cups (950ml) Vegetable Scrap Stock (page 36) or store-bought vegetable broth

2 (15-ounce/425g) cans cannellini beans, drained and rinsed

SHIITAKE BACON

8 ounces (225g) fresh shiitake mushrooms, stems composted (or saved for stock), caps cut into ⅛-inch (3mm) slices

2 tablespoons olive oil

¼ teaspoon fine sea salt

Pinch of freshly ground black pepper

TO FINISH

Nut Milk (page 17), Oat Milk (page 17), Soy Milk (page 75), or store-bought plant-based milk

Fine sea salt and freshly ground black pepper

Tender sprigs fresh thyme, for garnish

Chili oil, for drizzling (optional)

PREHEAT THE OVEN TO 400°F (200°C).

Make the soup: In a large pot, heat the oil over medium heat until it shimmers. Add the onion, celery, carrot, garlic, thyme sprigs, salt, and pepper. Cook, stirring occasionally, until the vegetables are fragrant and tender, 8 to 10 minutes.

Add the vegetable stock and beans, increase the heat to high, and bring the mixture to a boil. Reduce the heat to medium and simmer until thickened, 12 to 14 minutes. (Fish out and compost the thyme stems.)

Meanwhile, make the shiitake bacon: Spread the shiitake slices into a single layer on a sheet pan, drizzle with the olive oil, sprinkle with the salt and pepper, and toss to combine. Bake until browned and crispy, 18 to 20 minutes, rotating the pan front to back and tossing the mushrooms with a spatula halfway through. Let cool on the pan; the mushrooms will continue to crisp as they cool.

To finish: Add the milk to the soup and use an immersion blender to puree it in the pot. (Alternatively, working in batches, transfer the soup to a blender, being careful not to fill it more than halfway, remove the center cap from the blender lid, cover it with a clean kitchen towel, and puree until smooth.) Taste and season with more salt and pepper if needed.

Divide the soup among bowls. Top with the shiitake bacon and garnish with thyme sprigs. If desired, add a drizzle of chili oil. Serve hot.

Chipotle-Orange Pinto Beans

These are the kinds of beans that can go either way: Cook them down until thick and creamy to serve with tortillas as a filling for tacos, enchiladas, or burritos. Or leave them loose and brothy to spoon over cilantro-speckled rice. What makes them shine in this recipe is the pairing of chipotles in adobo and the floral notes of orange juice and zest. Well, that and the copious amounts of garlic—in both the cooking liquid and the sofrito.

For the best result, sample the beans at the very end and add a dash of agave syrup, vinegar, or salt, tasting as you go, until the flavors are perfectly balanced—slightly sweet, slightly spicy, and perfectly delicious. That last step—as simple as it may seem—is what turns ordinary beans into something endlessly craveable.

Makes 8 to 10 servings

Time: Weekend

Storage: Refrigerate for up to 4 days.

1 medium white onion (7 ounces/200g)

1 large red bell pepper (6½ ounces/190g)

10 large garlic cloves, peeled but whole

1 pound (450g) dried pinto beans, soaked 8 hours or overnight, drained and rinsed

1 bay leaf

1 tablespoon plus 1 teaspoon sweet paprika

1 thin strip of dried kombu (optional)

1 pound (450g) large oranges (2 to 3)

2 tablespoons olive oil

½ teaspoon fine sea salt, plus more to taste

3 tablespoons tomato paste

⅓ cup (80g) finely chopped canned chipotle peppers in adobo sauce with their sauce (about 3 chipotles)

1 tablespoon dried oregano

2 tablespoons apple cider vinegar, plus more to taste

½ teaspoon agave syrup or Wildflower Cider Syrup (page 35), plus more to taste

1 teaspoon smoked paprika

Chopped fresh cilantro, for serving

Tortillas or rice, for serving

PEEL AND HALVE THE onion. Add one half to a large pot for the beans. Mince the other half and set aside for the sofrito. Halve and seed the bell pepper. Add one half to the pot. Mince the other half and set aside with the onion for the sofrito. Put 4 of the peeled garlic cloves in the pot, and finely grate or press the other 6 cloves and set aside separately for the sofrito.

Set the pot over high heat and add the beans and enough water to cover them by 2 inches (5cm). Add the bay leaf, 1 tablespoon sweet paprika, and kombu (if using). Bring to a boil, then reduce to a simmer and cook until the beans are tender, 40 to 60 minutes or more.

Meanwhile, finely grate the zest from the oranges until you have 1 tablespoon packed zest. Juice the oranges until you have ½ cup (120ml). Set the zest and juice aside.

To make the sofrito, in a Dutch oven or medium saucepan, heat the oil over medium heat until it shimmers. Add the reserved chopped onion and bell pepper and ¼ teaspoon of the salt. Sauté, stirring, until the onion is translucent, about 5 minutes. Stir in the minced garlic, tomato paste, chipotles, oregano, and remaining 1 teaspoon sweet paprika and cook until the sofrito begins to brown and stick to the bottom of the pan, about 2 minutes. Pour in the orange juice and vinegar, using a spoon to scrape the bottom of the pan, and cook for 3 minutes to let the flavors meld. Turn off the heat.

When the beans are ready, drain the beans, reserving their liquid, and fish out and compost the onion, bell pepper, kombu, and bay leaf. Transfer the boiled garlic cloves, the beans, and 1½ cups (350ml) of the cooking liquid to the pot with the sofrito. Use a fork to mash the boiled garlic cloves against the edge of the pot. Stir in the remaining ¼ teaspoon salt and simmer until the flavors meld and the beans thicken, about 10 minutes.

Stir in the agave syrup, orange zest, and smoked paprika. Taste and season with more agave, vinegar, and salt if needed. If you'd like to keep them brothy, sprinkle them with cilantro and serve hot with rice and/or tortillas. If you'd like them thicker for other uses, keep cooking until they're reduced and thickened to your liking. (If desired, you can mash some of them with a fork or wooden spoon to help thicken).

Broccoli Soup with Smoked Paprika & Big Croutons

The creamy base of this soup comes from boiled and pureed broccoli stalks (which normally go straight into the compost bin) along with potato and tahini—a trick picked up from my friend and "Salt Fat Acid Heat" genius Samin Nosrat. The florets do triple duty, too: Some roast in the oven, so they get nice and charred; some are briefly cooked just until bright green and then blended into the soup; the rest are added in the last few minutes. If you can't get enough smoked paprika, feel free to double the amount in the soup itself.

Makes 4 to 6 servings

Time: Weekend

Storage: Refrigerate without the croutons for 5 days or freeze for up to 6 months. Store croutons at room temperature for up to 3 days.

- 3 to 4 large heads broccoli (2½ pounds/1.1kg total)
- 6 tablespoons olive oil, plus more for serving
- 1½ teaspoons fine sea salt, plus more to taste
- 1 (5-ounce/150g) piece baguette or country-style bread, cut into 1-inch (2.5cm) cubes (about 3 cups)
- ½ teaspoon smoked paprika, plus more for serving
- 1 medium or 2 small yellow onions (8 ounces/225g), coarsely chopped
- 6 large garlic cloves (29g), coarsely chopped
- 1 sprig fresh rosemary
- ½ teaspoon red pepper flakes
- 1 medium russet potato (8 ounces/225g), scrubbed, peeled, and cut into 1-inch (2.5cm) pieces
- 5 cups (1.2L) water
- 3 tablespoons fresh lemon juice, plus more to taste
- 3 tablespoons well-stirred tahini

POSITION A RACK IN the middle of the oven and preheat the oven to 425°F (220°C).

Slice the broccoli to separate the stalks from the crowns. Trim ½ inch (1.3cm) from the bottom of the stalks, then peel the outer layer until you reach the moist, brighter green, tender inside. (Compost the scraps.) Cut the stalks into 1-inch (2.5cm) pieces, and cut the crowns into 1- to 1½-inch (2.5cm to 4cm) florets, keeping the two piles separate.

Take about 2 cups (150g) of the florets, reserving the rest, and in a medium bowl toss them with 1 tablespoon of the olive oil and ¼ teaspoon of the salt. Transfer them to one side of a large sheet pan. In the same bowl, toss the bread cubes with 2 tablespoons of the oil, ¼ teaspoon of the smoked paprika, and ¼ teaspoon of the salt. Spread them on the other side of the sheet pan.

Roast, shaking once or twice, until the croutons are crisp and golden and the broccoli is starting to brown and char, 12 to 15 minutes. Let cool on the pan and reserve for serving.

Meanwhile, in a large pot, heat the remaining 3 table-spoons oil over medium heat until it shimmers. Add the onion, garlic, rosemary, pepper flakes, remaining 1 teaspoon salt, and remaining ¼ teaspoon smoked paprika and stir to coat. Cover the pot and cook until the onion is soft and starting to take on color, 6 to 8 minutes.

Add the broccoli stalks and potato and stir to coat in the oil. Add the water, increase the heat to high, and bring to a boil. Reduce the heat to a simmer, cover, and cook until the potatoes and broccoli stalks are fork-tender, 10 to 12 minutes.

Add half the remaining broccoli florets and cook until bright green and tender, 3 to 5 minutes. Add the lemon juice and tahini. Remove the rosemary stem. Working in batches if needed, transfer the soup to a blender, being careful not to fill it more than halfway, remove the center cap from the blender lid, cover it with a clean kitchen towel, and puree until smooth. (Alternatively, remove from the heat and puree in the pot with an immersion blender). Taste and season with more salt and lemon juice if needed.

Pour the soup back into the pot (if you used a standing blender), return the heat to low, add the remaining broccoli florets, and cook until the florets are bright green and tender, 3 to 5 minutes.

Divide the soup among serving bowls. Top with the croutons, roasted broccoli, a drizzle of olive oil, and a sprinkling of smoked paprika.

Tarascan Pinto Bean Soup

This cross between a tortilla soup and a bean soup from the Mexican state of Michoacán is perfectly creamy, savory, and just the right amount of spicy. Beans add a richness that would typically come from cream. Feel free to experiment with different combinations of chiles, such as chipotle, pasilla, or both. This soup gets a riot of garnishes: fried tortilla and chile strips, avocado, Smooth Almond Crema (page 22), and Creamy or Crumbly Almond Queso Fresco (page 27).

Makes 4 servings

Time: Weekend

Storage: Refrigerate, without the garnishes, for up to 3 days or freeze for up to 3 months. Store the fried tortilla and chile strips at room temperature for up to 3 days.

- 2 ancho chiles (36g), stemmed, seeded, and rinsed
- Boiling water
- 3 Roma tomatoes (5 ounces/140g each)
- ¼ white onion (63g), peeled but left in one piece
- 2 garlic cloves, unpeeled
- 3½ cups (830ml) Vegetable Scrap Stock (page 36) or store-bought vegetable broth, plus more as needed
- 2 cups (300g to 340g) cooked pinto beans, cooking liquid reserved, or canned (from two 15-ounce/425g cans), drained and liquid reserved
- ½ cup (120ml) plus 1 teaspoon avocado or other neutral oil
- 4 (6-inch/15cm) corn tortillas, cut into strips
- 2 pasilla chiles (32g), seeded and cut into strips
- 1 bay leaf
- 1 sprig fresh thyme
- 1 teaspoon fine sea salt, plus more to taste
- ¼ teaspoon freshly ground black pepper
- 1 cup (150g) cubed avocado, for garnish
- ½ cup (120ml) Smooth Almond Crema (page 22) or store-bought vegan sour cream, for garnish
- ½ cup (56g) Creamy or Crumbly Almond Queso Fresco (page 27) or store-bought vegan feta, for garnish

HEAT A DUTCH OVEN or other deep heavy-bottomed pot over medium-high heat. Add the ancho chiles and toast until fragrant and lightly toasted, 30 seconds per side. Transfer them to a heatproof bowl, pour the boiling water over them, soak for 10 minutes, and drain. Transfer to a blender.

In the same pot over medium-high heat, combine the tomatoes, onion, and garlic. Cook, turning frequently, until they become soft and slightly charred, 8 to 10 minutes. Let cool slightly, peel the garlic, and transfer it, along with the tomatoes and onion, to the blender. Add 1 cup (240ml) of the vegetable stock and puree until smooth. Transfer the tomato/ancho puree to a bowl or measuring cup with a spout and rinse out the blender.

Add the beans and 1 cup (240ml) of their cooking liquid (or a combination of liquid from the can and more vegetable stock if using canned) to the blender. Puree until smooth, adding more cooking liquid if needed to get the mixture to the consistency of thick cream.

In the Dutch oven, heat ½ cup (120ml) of the oil over medium-high heat until it shimmers. Add the tortilla strips and pasilla chile strips and cook, stirring frequently, until crisp, 3 to 4 minutes. Use a slotted spoon to transfer to a plate. Carefully pour the hot oil into a heatproof bowl, let cool, and save for another use.

Put the Dutch oven back over medium heat, add the tomato/ancho puree and simmer until it turns dark red and thickens slightly, about 5 minutes. Stir in the bean puree, bay leaf, thyme sprig, salt, black pepper, and remaining 2½ cups (590ml) vegetable stock. Bring to a simmer and cook until it has the consistency of smooth cream and the flavors meld, about 15 minutes. (Fish out and compost the bay leaf.) Taste and season with more salt if needed.

Divide the soup among serving bowls and garnish with the fried tortilla and chile strips, avocado, almond crema, and queso fresco. Serve hot.

Beet & Quinoa Soup

Along the coast of Peru, the catch of the day often ends up in a bowl of parihuela, a seafood soup that resembles French bouillabaisse. In this version, a kombu stock imparts the flavor of the sea, and cooking the beets in the stock gives the soup a deep red color reminiscent of Peru's aji panca chile. An onion and tomato base is deglazed with white wine, while sweet peas, corn, and quinoa make the soup hearty. Roasted shiitake mushrooms give the soup extra umami, and sriracha adds heat.

Makes 4 to 6 servings

Time: Weekend

Storage: Refrigerate for up to 5 days or freeze for up to 3 months.

12 fresh shiitake mushrooms (3½ ounces/96g total), stems composted (or saved for stock), caps quartered

1 tablespoon olive oil

2 teaspoons fine sea salt, plus more to taste

2 tablespoons canola or other neutral cooking oil

½ cup (70g) finely chopped red onion (about ¼ large red onion)

2 medium garlic cloves, finely grated or pressed

1 small tomato (4½ ounces/130g), chopped (about ½ cup)

½ teaspoon freshly ground black pepper

½ teaspoon ground cumin

½ teaspoon dried oregano

¼ cup (60ml) Sauvignon Blanc or other dry white wine

8 cups (1.9L) water

About 6 pieces (29g) dried kombu, 4-inch (10cm) square or the equivalent

3 medium beets (10 ounces/300g total), peeled and cut into ½-inch (1.3cm) cubes (about 1½ cups)

¼ cup (45g) white quinoa

½ cup (65g) fresh or frozen green peas

½ cup (70g) fresh or frozen yellow corn kernels

2 tablespoons fresh lime juice, plus more to taste

Sriracha (optional)

A few fresh cilantro leaves, for garnish

Lime wedges, for squeezing

PREHEAT THE OVEN TO 425°F (220°C). Line a sheet pan with a silicone baking mat or compostable parchment paper.

In a bowl, toss the mushroom quarters with the olive oil and ½ teaspoon of the salt. Transfer them to the sheet pan and roast until they reduce in size by half and begin to brown, about 20 minutes.

In a large pot, heat the canola oil over medium-high heat until it shimmers. Add the onion and garlic and cook until the onion starts to soften, about 2 minutes. Add the tomato, black pepper, cumin, oregano, and the remaining 1½ teaspoons salt and cook until the tomato softens and the onion begins to brown, about 5 minutes. Add the white wine, deglaze the pot by scraping up any browned bits, and simmer for 1 minute. Turn off the heat and add the water to the pot.

Rinse the kombu, add it to the pot, and let it soak for 15 minutes.

Bring the liquid to a boil over high heat, then reduce the heat to a simmer and cook for 15 minutes to flavor the stock with the kombu. (Fish out and compost the kombu.)

Add the beet cubes and quinoa. Return to a simmer and cook until the beets are tender and the quinoa seeds have popped open, 20 to 30 minutes.

Remove from the heat and stir in the peas, corn, and roasted mushrooms. Cover and let the soup sit for 10 minutes to help the flavors meld. Stir in the lime juice. If you'd like to make the soup spicy, stir in some sriracha. Taste and season with more salt and lime as needed.

Divide the soup among serving bowls (being sure to ladle from the bottom so the quinoa is evenly distributed). Top with the cilantro and serve with lime wedges for squeezing at the table.

Spiced Roasted Tomato Soup

For a pureed soup packed with flavor, the oven is the way to go. Roasting vegetables before pureeing them deepens their flavor and brings out their natural sweetness. The technique works especially well with ripe farmers market tomatoes in the summer. But it can also elevate regular grocery store tomatoes, even grape or cherry varieties, making this your go-to recipe for when a tomato soup craving hits in the dead of winter.

Use this recipe and the Creamy Roasted Cauliflower Soup (opposite) as a starting point for a whole world of pureed roasted-vegetable soups; substitute or mix in other vegetables, such as butternut squash, sweet potatoes, carrots, and red bell peppers. In this case, cashews offer richness and body, while the fennel and cumin seeds add another layer of flavor.

Makes 4 to 6 servings

Time: Weekend

Storage: Refrigerate for up to 3 days, without the croutons. Store croutons in a cool, dark place for up to 3 days.

- 5 large tomatoes (2 pounds/905g total), quartered
- 1 medium red onion (8 ounces/225g), peeled and quartered
- 1 bulb garlic (55g), separated into unpeeled cloves
- 3 tablespoons olive oil
- 2½ teaspoons fennel seeds
- 2½ teaspoons cumin seeds
- 1 teaspoon fine sea salt, plus more to taste
- 2½ cups (120g) torn 1-inch (2.5cm) cubes sourdough bread
- 1½ cups (350ml) hot water
- ½ cup (65g) raw cashew pieces, soaked in warm water for 1 hour, rinsed, and drained
- 1 tablespoon nutritional yeast
- 2 tablespoons double-concentrated tomato paste
- 1½ tablespoons red wine vinegar, plus more to taste

FOR SERVING
Freshly ground black pepper
Minced flat-leaf parsley
Olive oil, for drizzling
Creamy Coconut Yogurt (page 23) or store-bought plain coconut yogurt

PREHEAT THE OVEN TO 425°F (220°C).

Combine the tomatoes, onion, and garlic cloves on a sheet pan. Drizzle with 2 tablespoons of the olive oil and sprinkle with the fennel seeds, cumin seeds, and ½ teaspoon of the salt. Toss to coat. Roast until the garlic is soft and the tomatoes have shriveled and started to brown, 50 to 60 minutes.

When the tomatoes have been in the oven for about 40 minutes, combine the bread cubes and the remaining 1 tablespoon olive oil on another sheet pan. Roast until golden and crisp, about 15 minutes. Let cool.

Pull the roasted vegetables out and let cool slightly. When they're cool enough to handle, squeeze the garlic cloves out of their skins into a blender. Add the tomatoes, onions, and any collected juices. Add the hot water, soaked and drained cashews, nutritional yeast, tomato paste, vinegar, and remaining ½ teaspoon salt. Place the lid on the blender, remove the center cap, cover with a kitchen towel, and blend until creamy, about 1 minute. Taste and season with more salt and/or vinegar as needed.

To serve: Divide the soup among serving bowls. Top with the croutons, black pepper, parsley, and drizzles of olive oil and coconut yogurt. Serve hot.

Creamy Roasted Cauliflower Soup

Roasted cauliflower gets a flavor boost from coriander and cilantro—two forms of the same plant—along with pine nuts. Like the Spiced Roasted Tomato Soup (opposite), this is tremendously adaptable. It makes an excellent lunch or light dinner when paired with a vegetable sandwich or avocado toast.

Makes 4 to 6 servings

Time: Weekend

Storage: Refrigerate for up to 3 days.

1 head cauliflower (1 pound/450g)

1 medium yellow onion (8 ounces/225g), peeled and cut into 8 wedges

4 tablespoons olive oil

1 teaspoon ground coriander, plus more for serving

1 teaspoon fine sea salt, plus more to taste

4 tablespoons pine nuts

½ teaspoon red pepper flakes

3 cups (700ml) hot water

1 tablespoon nutritional yeast

1½ tablespoons fresh lemon juice, plus more to taste

Chopped fresh cilantro leaves, for serving

PREHEAT THE OVEN TO 400°F (200°C).

Trim the cauliflower and cut it into 2-inch (5cm) pieces, including the core. Thinly slice the tender parts of the leaves and reserve them for garnish. Arrange the cauliflower and onion on a large sheet pan. Drizzle with 2 tablespoons of the oil, sprinkle with the coriander and ½ teaspoon of the salt, and toss to coat. Roast until the cauliflower and onion are tender and golden, about 40 minutes.

While the vegetables are roasting, in a small saucepan, heat the remaining 2 tablespoons oil over medium-low heat until it shimmers. Stir in 2 tablespoons of the pine nuts and toast until lightly golden, about 30 seconds. Pour the oil and pine nuts into a heatproof bowl, stir in the pepper flakes, and set aside.

When the vegetables are ready, use a spoon to transfer them to a blender. Add the hot water, the remaining 2 tablespoons (untoasted) pine nuts, the remaining ½ teaspoon salt, the nutritional yeast, and lemon juice. Place the lid on the blender, remove the center cap, cover with a kitchen towel, and puree until creamy, about 1 minute. Taste and season with more salt and lemon juice if needed.

Divide the soup among serving bowls and top with the reserved cauliflower leaves, cilantro, a little ground coriander, the toasted pine nuts, and a drizzle of the pine nut oil. Serve hot.

Brazilian Feijoada

On weekends in Brazil, families gather around the country's national dish: feijoada, a hearty black bean and meat stew they serve with rice, collard greens, sliced oranges, and farofa—a crunchy cassava-flour side dish. Even without the farofa, this plant-based version of feijoada from food writer Emily Codik—inspired by Rio de Janeiro chef Tati Lund's—feels like just as much a celebration: It replaces the meat with vegetables and smoked tofu.

Like virtually all stews, the feijoada tastes best the day after it's made.

Makes 10 to 12 servings

Time: Weekend

Storage: Refrigerate for up to 4 days.

1 pound (450g) dried black beans, soaked 8 hours or overnight, drained and rinsed

8 ounces (225g) smoked tofu (such as SoyBoy brand) or baked/marinated tofu, cut into ¾-inch (2cm) cubes

1 thin strip of dried kombu (optional)

2 tablespoons olive oil

2 medium yellow onions (15 ounces/430g total), chopped

1¼ teaspoons fine sea salt, plus more to taste

8 large garlic cloves (30g), finely grated or pressed

1 tablespoon ground cumin

2 large carrots (5 ounces/135g each), scrubbed and cut into slices ¼ inch (6mm) thick

¼ small kabocha squash (10 ounces/280g), peeled, seeded, and cut into ½-inch (1.2cm) cubes

1½ cups (350ml) water

1 teaspoon apple cider vinegar

1 teaspoon smoked paprika

FOR SERVING
2 medium oranges
Gomen (page 355) or other sautéed collard greens
Steamed white or brown rice

IN A DUTCH OVEN or other large pot, combine the beans, smoked tofu, and kombu (if using). Add water to cover by 2 inches (5cm). Bring to a boil over high heat, then reduce to a simmer and cook until tender, 50 to 60 minutes.

Meanwhile, in a large skillet, heat the oil over medium heat until it shimmers. Add the onions and ½ teaspoon of the salt and cook until translucent, about 5 minutes. Stir in the garlic and cumin and cook until fragrant, about 30 seconds. Remove from the heat.

When the beans are ready, transfer the onion mixture to the beans in the Dutch oven. Stir in the carrots, squash, water, and remaining ¾ teaspoon salt. Bring to a boil over high heat, reduce to a simmer, and cook until the vegetables are tender and the flavors meld, 15 to 25 minutes. Stir in the vinegar and smoked paprika. Taste and season with more salt if needed. Cover to keep warm.

Cut the oranges into suprêmes: Cut off a piece from the top and bottom and set an orange on one of the cut sides. Use a sharp knife to follow the curve of the fruit and cut off the peel, white pith, and membrane to expose the flesh. Cut in between the membranes to release the segments. Squeeze the juice from the leftover membranes and the peels into the collards and stir in the orange suprêmes. Serve hot with rice.

Red Kidney Bean & Jerky Stew

This bean and tofu jerky stew brings together the worlds of Peru's mountains and the city, with their Andean and Afro-Peruvian culinary traditions. For centuries, Indigenous people from the Andes dehydrated potatoes and animal protein for preservation. Meanwhile, in Lima, Afro-descendant women shaped Peru's creole cuisine. They cooked staples such as rice and beans, often as accompaniment for other traditional dishes, but here the beans are the stars of the dish. Combining them with Smoky Tofu Crisps (page 70) makes the dish a vegan Peruvian version of the popular North American chili, and the spices in the tofu crisps complement the seasoning. For the full Peruvian experience, serve the stew in a bowl with steamed rice.

Makes 4 servings

Time: Weekend

Storage: Refrigerate for up to 1 week or freeze, without the tofu crisps, for up to 3 months.

1 jalapeño pepper, stemmed and halved lengthwise

3 tablespoons canola or other neutral cooking oil

½ large red onion (175g), finely chopped

3 garlic cloves, finely grated or pressed

1 teaspoon fine sea salt, plus more to taste

½ teaspoon freshly ground black pepper

½ teaspoon ground cumin

½ teaspoon dried oregano

3 cups (530g) cooked red kidney beans or no-salt-added canned beans (from two 15-ounce/425g cans)

2 cups (470ml) water

6 sprigs fresh cilantro, plus leaves for garnish

2 tablespoons fresh lime juice, plus more to taste

12 or more pieces Smoky Tofu Crisps (page 70)

Olive oil, for drizzling

Steamed rice, for serving

REMOVE AND COMPOST THE seeds and veins from the jalapeño. Mince one half of the chile and thinly slice the other half. Set both aside separately.

In a Dutch oven or other large pot, heat the canola oil over medium-high heat until it shimmers. Add the onion and garlic and cook until the onion softens, about 5 minutes. Add the minced jalapeño, salt, black pepper, cumin, and oregano and cook until fragrant, about 2 minutes.

Stir in the beans, water, and cilantro sprigs. Bring to a boil and reduce to a simmer. Use a wooden spoon to mash some of the beans against the inside of the pot. Cook until the stew is creamy and when you swipe the spoon against the bottom of the pot it leaves a trail, 20 to 25 minutes.

Fish out and compost the cilantro sprigs and stir in the lime juice. Taste and season with more salt and lime juice if needed.

Divide the stew into bowls and top with the tofu crisps. Drizzle with olive oil and garnish with cilantro leaves and jalapeño slices. Serve hot with steamed rice.

Tomato & Red Pepper Stew

This is really a fiery, super-flavorful sauce that is the base for a plethora of Nigerian dishes, including the classic jollof rice. But when you stir in a few cups of your favorite cooked vegetables—even leftover ones—it turns into a stew that's wonderfully flexible and delicious alongside rice or eaten with bread.

Time: Weekday

Makes 4 servings

Storage: Refrigerate for up to 1 week or freeze for up to 6 months.

1½ pounds (680g) Roma tomatoes, roughly chopped (about 5 cups)

1 medium red bell pepper, roughly chopped

1 medium yellow onion, roughly chopped

1 habanero or Scotch bonnet pepper, stemmed

⅓ cup (80ml) plus 2 tablespoons sunflower oil

1 large yellow onion, thinly sliced

6 garlic cloves, thinly sliced

1 tablespoon finely grated peeled fresh ginger

2 frozen cubes Veg Bouillon (page 36), 2 crushed vegetable stock cubes, or 2 teaspoons vegetarian soup base

2 teaspoons curry powder

1 teaspoon dried thyme

1 teaspoon fine sea salt, plus more to taste

2 to 3 cups cooked vegetables of your choice

IN A BLENDER, COMBINE the tomatoes, bell pepper, chopped onion, and habanero and blend until smooth.

In a medium pot, heat 2 tablespoons of the oil over medium-high heat until it shimmers. Add the sliced onion and cook until browned on the edges, 5 to 8 minutes. Add the garlic and ginger and cook until fragrant, 1 to 2 minutes.

Pour in the tomato mixture, scraping the bottom of the pan to incorporate any browned bits. Add the bouillon cubes, curry powder, thyme, and salt. Bring to a simmer, then reduce the heat to medium-low and cook, uncovered, until the mixture has reduced and thickened slightly, about 20 minutes.

Taste and season with more salt as needed. Add the remaining ⅓ cup (80ml) oil, increase the heat to medium, and cook the sauce at a brisk simmer until it has slightly darkened and thickened, the tomatoes taste sweet, and the stew is no longer runny, about 20 minutes.

Stir in the cooked vegetables, cook a few more minutes just to heat them through, and serve hot.

Coconut-Cashew Tempeh

For tempeh that's tender and flavorful all the way through, braise it. This recipe takes a cue from Southeast Asian curries and simmers seared tempeh in coconut milk, which reduces into a creamy sauce around it. Sambal oelek, an Indonesian chile paste, counters the sweetness of the coconut milk; if you can't find it, you can substitute with sriracha, but hold back a bit on the lime juice, as sriracha tends to be more acidic. While the toasted coconut and cashew topping is crunchy and irresistible, you could skip it and go for store-bought fried shallots instead. Whatever you do, be sure to serve this with hot steamed rice, a great bed for all of the extra sauce.

Makes 3 to 4 servings

Time: Weekday

Storage: Refrigerate for up to 5 days.

4 tablespoons neutral oil, such as sunflower or canola

½ cup (65g) raw cashews, coarsely chopped

⅓ cup (30g) large unsweetened coconut flakes

½ teaspoon fine sea salt, plus more to taste

1 (8-ounce/225g) block tempeh, homemade (page 79) or store-bought

1 medium red onion (6½ ounces/180g), thinly sliced

2 large garlic cloves, chopped

1 tablespoon sambal oelek

1 tablespoon dark or light brown sugar, plus more to taste

1 (13.5-ounce/400ml) can full-fat coconut milk, well-shaken

1 tablespoon fresh lime juice, plus more to taste

Cooked jasmine rice, for serving

⅓ cup (15g) chopped fresh cilantro leaves and tender stems

Lime wedges, for squeezing

IN A LARGE SKILLET, heat 2 tablespoons of the oil over medium-high heat until it shimmers. Add the cashews and coconut flakes and cook, stirring constantly, until toasted, 1 to 2 minutes. Use a slotted spoon or spatula to transfer to a plate. (It's okay if some oil travels with the coconut and cashews and some small bits of them are left in the pan.) Sprinkle with ¼ teaspoon of the salt.

Cut the tempeh horizontally in half (like you're cutting a cake into layers) into 2 thinner slabs. Cut each slab in half lengthwise, so you have 4 long planks, then cut those planks crosswise into 4 to form 16 squares. Cut each diagonally into a triangle.

Add the remaining 2 tablespoons oil to the skillet and return to medium-high heat. Once it shimmers, add the tempeh triangles and cook on all sides until golden, tossing occasionally, 4 to 5 minutes.

Reduce the heat to medium, add the onion, and cook, stirring frequently, until softened and starting to brown, 3 to 4 minutes. Add the garlic, sambal oelek, and brown sugar and cook, stirring frequently, for 1 minute. Add the coconut milk and remaining ¼ teaspoon salt, bring to a simmer, and cook until reduced and thickened, 5 to 7 minutes. Stir in the lime juice. Taste and season with more salt, lime juice, and/or brown sugar if needed.

Spoon the tempeh and sauce over the rice, garnishing with the toasted coconut and cashews and chopped cilantro. Serve hot with the lime wedges for squeezing.

Lentil-Walnut Picadillo

Picadillo comes in many versions, but it's usually a combination of ground beef, tomatoes, raisins, and olives. This version uses chopped lentils and walnuts, a duo that works wonders as a substitute for ground beef in stews and fillings. The key is nailing the texture: Overmix those two ingredients in the food processor and you'll end up with something akin to puree. Aim for a crumbly mixture with small, visible chunks—best to err on the side of coarser pieces than mushy lentils.

Picadillo is the perfect opportunity for batch cooking. Double the recipe and freeze it in smaller portions to have future meals ready in just minutes. Serve it with white rice, avocado, and sweet plantains, or use it as a filling for baked sweet potatoes.

Makes 6 to 8 servings

Time: Weekday

Storage: Refrigerate for up to 5 days or freeze for up to 6 months.

1 cup (170g) large green/brown lentils

1 bay leaf

1 thin strip of dried kombu (optional)

½ cup (50g) walnuts

2 tablespoons olive oil

1 medium onion (7 ounces/195g), chopped

1 red bell pepper (6 ounces/180g), chopped

¾ teaspoon fine sea salt, plus more to taste

4 garlic cloves, finely grated or pressed

1 tablespoon sweet paprika

1 tablespoon ground cumin

¼ teaspoon dried oregano

2 tablespoons double-concentrated tomato paste

1½ tablespoons red wine vinegar, plus more for to taste

1 (14-ounce/395g) can crushed tomatoes

1 cup (120g) sliced green olives, preferably pimento-stuffed

½ cup (70g) raisins

Dash of maple syrup

Dash of reduced-sodium soy sauce or tamari

Chopped fresh cilantro, for serving

IN A MEDIUM SAUCEPAN, combine the lentils, bay leaf, and kombu (if using). Add water to cover by 2 inches (5cm). Bring to a boil over high heat, then reduce to a simmer and cook, uncovered, until the lentils are softened but still firm, about 10 minutes.

When the lentils are ready, drain them as thoroughly as possible and transfer to a food processor. (Fish out and compost the kombu and bay leaf.) Add the walnuts to the food processor and pulse until the mixture is coarsely crumbled, about 7 or 8 times.

Rinse and dry the saucepan that was used for the lentils. Pour in the olive oil and warm over medium heat until it shimmers. Add the onion and bell pepper, season with ¼ teaspoon of the salt, and sauté until tender, 6 to 7 minutes. Stir in the garlic, paprika, cumin, and oregano and cook until fragrant, about 1 minute. Stir in the tomato paste and vinegar and cook until thickened, about 2 minutes.

Add the crushed tomatoes, olives, raisins, and lentil/walnut mixture. Fill the empty tomato can with water and add to the pot and stir in the remaining ½ teaspoon salt. Bring to a boil, then reduce to a simmer and cook until the flavors meld and the picadillo has thickened, about 15 minutes. Taste and adjust the seasoning with maple syrup, soy sauce, vinegar, and more salt as needed to balance the flavors.

Serve hot garnished with cilantro.

6

BOWLS

Grain bowls became so ubiquitous at one point that you might have wondered what would happen to all the unused plates in the world. The universe has corrected itself, but the beauty of a bowl—a warm base of grains or noodles topped or mixed with a variety of vegetables, a sauce, maybe more—has never wavered. You'll see a variety of grains here, but a lot of quinoa, because it cooks so quickly and packs a good dose of protein. These bowls feel especially welcome at lunchtime, perhaps because they are typically easily brown-baggable and tasty even at room temperature.

Bibimbap with Spicy Tofu Crumbles

Bibimbap is the ultimate Korean comfort food and a great way to use up leftover vegetable side dishes like banchan. These bowls feature crispy tofu crumbles, carrots, spinach, and bean sprouts, but you should feel free to use whatever vegetables you have on hand. Remember that *bibimbap* means "mixed rice," so perhaps the most important step is the one you take right before eating, when you vigorously stir together the ingredients in your bowl.

Makes 4 servings

Time: Weekday

Storage: Refrigerate the rice, tofu, and vegetables separately for up to 5 days.

- 1½ cups (278g) brown rice (short-, medium-, or long-grain), rinsed
- 3 tablespoons gochujang (Korean chile paste)
- 2 tablespoons soy sauce or tamari
- 1½ tablespoons unseasoned rice vinegar
- 1 tablespoon plus 2 teaspoons toasted sesame oil
- 1 tablespoon agave syrup or Wildflower Cider Syrup (page 35)
- 1 (16-ounce/454g) block extra-firm tofu, cut into 1-inch (2.5cm) cubes
- 2 tablespoons vegetable oil
- 2 cups (220g) grated carrots
- ½ teaspoon fine sea salt, plus more to taste
- 7 cups (5 ounces/140g) baby spinach
- 2 cups (180g) fresh mung bean sprouts
- 4 teaspoons toasted sesame seeds
- 4 scallions, finely chopped

BRING A LARGE SAUCEPAN of water to a boil. Add the rice to the boiling water, reduce to a gentle boil, partially cover, and cook until the rice is tender, about 30 minutes. Drain off the remaining water and return the rice to the pot. Cover tightly and let the rice sit for 10 minutes. Fluff with a fork before serving.

Meanwhile, in a small bowl, whisk together the gochujang, 1 tablespoon of the soy sauce, the rice vinegar, 1 tablespoon of the sesame oil, and the agave syrup.

Spread a clean kitchen towel onto your workspace. Transfer the tofu cubes to it and gently use the towel to pat them dry.

In a cast-iron or other heavy skillet, heat the vegetable oil over medium-high heat until it shimmers. Add the tofu and remaining 1 tablespoon soy sauce, flipping occasionally, until browned on all sides, about 10 minutes. Use a fork to crumble it into smaller pieces in the pan, and continue cooking, stirring frequently, until it gets crispy, about 5 minutes. Transfer to a bowl to cool.

In the same skillet over medium-high heat, add the carrots and cook, stirring, until slightly softened, 1 to 2 minutes. Transfer to a bowl and season with ¼ teaspoon of the salt. Return the pan to the heat and add the spinach, cooking and stirring until it thoroughly wilts, 1 to 2 minutes. Add the remaining ¼ teaspoon salt and the remaining 2 teaspoons sesame oil. Taste and season with more salt if needed. Transfer to the bowl with the carrots, keeping them separate.

Divide the rice into serving bowls and top each with separate piles of carrots, spinach, bean sprouts, and tofu. Drizzle the gochujang sauce over each bowl and sprinkle with the sesame seeds and scallions. Serve hot.

COOK'S NOTE: This method for cooking brown rice is so easy, you'll never have to measure water or follow package directions again. You just boil it like pasta, and once the rice has cooked through, you drain off the excess water, return the hot rice to the pot, cover, and let it steam in the residual heat. Voilà! Perfectly fluffy rice that is easy to scale up or down.

Master Khichdi

"It's the ultimate Indian comfort food," chef Priya Ammu tells me, and of course she's talking about khichdi (aka khichri or kitchari), the one-pot dish of rice and legumes that is beloved for its gentle healing properties. Khichdi versions are as varied as the regions, cities, neighborhoods, and cooks in all of India. Priya is a bit of a khichdi missionary: She believes so strongly in its underestimated appeal that she even built a fast-casual pandemic-era business, Tokri, on the idea, selling four variations with different grains, legumes, and vegetables. When restrictions loosened, she closed Tokri and returned to her first love, DC Dosa, but khichdi will always have a place in her kitchen. This is her basic version, but I've also listed some variations that can help you take it in different directions.

Makes 6 servings

Time: Weekend

Storage: Refrigerate for up to 3 days or freeze for up to 3 months.

1 cup (180g) basmati rice

1½ cups (295g) yellow lentils (aka split mung beans)

3 tablespoons canola oil or olive oil

2 teaspoons cumin seeds

2 bay leaves

1 black cardamom pod

1 small yellow onion (5 ounces/140g), chopped

2 tablespoons minced or grated peeled fresh ginger

½ teaspoon asafoetida (hing)

4 cups (950ml) water

½ teaspoon ground turmeric

1 teaspoon fine sea salt, plus more to taste

USING A FINE-MESH SIEVE, rinse the rice and lentils for a few minutes under cold running water. Transfer them to a bowl, add enough water to cover by 2 inches (5cm), and soak for 2 hours. Drain.

In a large saucepan, heat the oil over medium-high heat until it shimmers. Add the cumin, bay leaves, and cardamom and sauté until very fragrant, about 1 minute. Add the onion, ginger, and asafoetida and sauté until the onions are golden brown, 7 or 8 minutes. Add the drained rice/lentil mixture and sauté until the rice and lentils are toasted slightly in the oil, about 2 minutes.

Add the water, turmeric, and salt and bring to a boil. Reduce the heat until the mixture is at a simmer, cover, and cook until the water is fully absorbed, 10 to 12 minutes.

KHICHDI VARIATIONS

Vegetables

SPINACH: Add 3 cloves chopped garlic when sautéing the onion. Add 4 cups (80g) packed baby spinach leaves when adding the drained rice/lentil mixture and reduce the water to 3½ cups (830ml).

CABBAGE: Add 3 cloves chopped garlic when sautéing the onion, Add 2 cups (180g) packed thinly sliced cabbage when adding the drained rice/lentil mixture.

CAULIFLOWER: Pan-fry or roast 4 cups (540g) cauliflower florets until browned and crisp, then fold into the finished khichdi, or layer on top before serving.

Grains

BROWN RICE: Use in place of basmati. Cook in 8 cups (1.9L) water instead of 4 for 20 to 24 minutes instead of 10 to 12.

KERALA ROSEMATTA RICE: Use the same amount of water and cooking time as basmati.

Legumes

WHOLE MUNG BEANS: Use in place of the yellow lentils, but soak separately from the rice, for 8 hours.

WHOLE BLACK URAD BEANS: Use in place of the yellow lentils, but soak separately from the rice, for 8 hours.

Mushroom Risotto with Pine Nut Butter

The first time I made cookbook author Amy Chaplin's pine nut puree and tossed it with cooked pasta and then fresh summer tomatoes, I was in heaven. And I've made it dozens of times since, for my husband and myself, for friends and family. But before I even finished making the dish that first time, I marveled at the puree's cheesy flavor and ultracreamy texture and knew I'd use it on other things, too. One of my favorite uses is to finish risotto like this simple mushroom one; it adds a beautiful richness. Note that the pine nut butter is most easily made in a mini food processor, so if you have only a larger one, consider doubling the batch and saving half for another use. You can also use a mortar and pestle.

Makes 6 servings

Time: Weekday

Storage: Refrigerate for up to 5 days or freeze for up to 3 months.

⅔ cup (100g) pine nuts

3 tablespoons olive oil

1½ teaspoons fine sea salt, plus more to taste

1 teaspoon fresh thyme leaves, plus more for garnish

8 cups (1.9L) water

1 ounce (28g) dried porcini mushrooms

2 tablespoons (28g) Soft Spreadable Butter (page 21) or store-bought unsalted vegan butter

8 ounces (225g) oyster, shiitake, cremini, or other mushrooms, cleaned, trimmed, and cut into ½-inch (1.3cm) pieces (remove the stem if using shiitakes)

2 large shallots (3 ounces/85g total), chopped

2 cups (380g) risotto rice, such as Arborio, Carnaroli, or Vialone Nano

1 cup (240ml) dry white wine

Freshly ground black pepper

IN A DEEP MEDIUM skillet or Dutch oven, toast the pine nuts over medium heat, shaking the pan occasionally, until fragrant and golden, about 5 minutes. Reserve the pan. Transfer ½ cup (65g) of the pine nuts to a mini food processor or the blending cup of an immersion blender. (Save the remaining pine nuts for garnishing the risotto.) Add the olive oil, ½ teaspoon of the salt, and the thyme and puree until smooth. Set the pine nut butter aside.

In a saucepan, bring the water to a gentle boil. Add the dried porcini, turn off the heat, cover, and let sit for 5 minutes, until the mushrooms are hydrated. Use a slotted spoon to remove the mushrooms, then finely chop them. Pour the mushroom stock through a fine-mesh sieve lined with cheesecloth into a bowl. Rinse the pot, return the strained mushroom stock to the pot, and stir in the remaining 1 teaspoon salt. Bring to a simmer over medium heat, then reduce the heat to medium-low and cover to keep hot.

Put the same skillet or Dutch oven you used to toast the pine nuts over medium-high heat. Add the butter, and once it melts and foams, add the reserved chopped rehydrated porcini mushrooms, the fresh mushrooms, and the shallots. Sauté until the fresh mushrooms soften and lightly brown, about 5 minutes.

Add the rice and stir to thoroughly coat it in the butter. Pour in the wine, bring to a boil, and cook until the liquid is reduced by at least half, 2 to 4 minutes.

Reduce the heat to medium. Stir in about ¾ cup (180ml) of the hot mushroom stock and keep stirring until the stock is mostly absorbed. Repeat with another ¾ cup (180ml) of the stock, stirring until almost absorbed, and repeat until the rice is mostly tender but remains just a little chewy in the center, 20 to 25 minutes total. You should use all but about ½ cup (120ml) of the stock.

Stir in the pine nut butter, plus more stock if needed to loosen the risotto. (Your goal: risotto that is a little runny, not stiff. It should spread on a plate when you serve it.) Taste and season with more salt if needed.

Divide among serving plates, grind some black pepper on top, and sprinkle with some thyme leaves and the reserved toasted pine nuts. Serve hot.

Wild Rice & Quinoa Bowl

One of writer Nico Vera's last memorable meals before the pandemic shutdown in 2020 was at Portland's Farm Spirit, where chef Aaron Adams's wild rice and quinoa salad was a standout. The combination of two grains native to North and South America got Nico thinking about precolonial ingredients and the meals his ancestors prepared from produce they cultivated, and it inspired this recipe. Jerky is prominent in both continents, and using Smoky Tofu Crisps (page 70) makes the bowl vegan. Likewise, Indigenous peoples on both continents cultivated maize, which they nixtamalized into hominy. Tomatoes and cranberries add color plus umami and bitterness, while the creamy avocado sauce gives a touch of sweetness, and the pumpkin seeds offer their signature crunch.

Makes 4 servings

Time: Weekend

Storage: Refrigerate the combined wild rice and quinoa, garnishes, and sauce separately for up to 5 days.

1 cup (175g) wild rice

5⅓ cups (1.26L) water

¾ teaspoon fine sea salt

⅔ cup (115g) white quinoa

1 cup (240ml) Creamy Coconut Yogurt (page 23) or store-bought plain coconut yogurt

1 small avocado, coarsely chopped

1 teaspoon maple syrup, preferably dark

½ cup (85g) canned hominy, drained

½ cup (75g) cherry tomatoes, halved and sprinkled with fine sea salt

½ cup (57g) fresh or thawed frozen cranberries

¼ cup (35g) pumpkin seeds, toasted

20 pieces Smoky Tofu Crisps (page 70)

IN A SMALL SAUCEPAN, combine the wild rice, 4 cups (950ml) of the water, and ¼ teaspoon of the salt. Bring to a gentle boil over high heat and boil, uncovered, until the water level reduces to the level of the wild rice, about 30 minutes. Reduce to a simmer, partially cover, and cook until the water evaporates completely and the grains break open, about 15 minutes. Uncover and fluff with a spoon.

Meanwhile, in another small saucepan, combine the quinoa, the remaining 1⅓ cups (310ml) of water, and ¼ teaspoon of the salt. Bring to a boil over high heat and boil, uncovered, until the water level reduces to the level of the quinoa, about 5 minutes. Reduce to a simmer, partially cover, and cook until the water evaporates completely and the grains break open, about 10 minutes. Uncover and fluff with a spoon.

In a medium bowl, mix the cooked quinoa and cooked wild rice.

In a tall container or immersion blender cup, combine the yogurt, avocado, remaining ¼ teaspoon salt, and the maple syrup. Use an immersion blender to puree the yogurt mixture into a smooth sauce.

Divide the quinoa and wild rice mixture among the serving bowls. Top each with a large dollop of sauce. Arrange the hominy, cherry tomatoes, cranberries, pumpkin seeds, and tofu crisps in each bowl. Serve warm.

Mujaddara

This Lebanese lentil dish is what recipe tester Kristen Hartke makes to give to friends at home with a new baby, as an alternative to the lasagnas that inevitably pile up after such an event. It's delicious either warm or cold and will be welcome regardless of the size (or age) of your household. The lentils provide plenty of protein and fiber, while crispy, slightly sweet, sticky onions give it lots of flavor and texture.

Makes 4 servings

Time: Weekday

Storage: Refrigerate for up to 1 week.

3 tablespoons olive oil, plus more for drizzling

2 medium onions (1 pound/450g total), thinly sliced (about 4 cups)

2 teaspoons fine sea salt, plus more to taste

½ teaspoon organic cane sugar

1 teaspoon ground cumin

½ teaspoon smoked paprika

1 cup (200g) French green lentils, rinsed and drained

3½ cups (830ml) water

½ lemon

1 cup (180g) basmati rice, rinsed and drained

1-inch (2.5cm) piece of cinnamon stick

Freshly ground black pepper

¼ cup (10g) fresh flat-leaf parsley, coarsely chopped

IN A LARGE SKILLET, heat 1½ tablespoons of the oil over medium heat until it shimmers. Add the onions and 1 teaspoon of the salt and stir to coat. Cook, stirring occasionally, until the onions wilt, about 5 minutes. Reduce the heat to low, cover, and cook until the onions are soft, translucent, and slightly golden, about 10 minutes. Uncover and stir in the sugar and another ½ tablespoon of the oil. Continue cooking over low heat, stirring occasionally, until the onions are dark golden and a bit sticky, with some strands beginning to become browned and crisp, another 10 minutes. Transfer the onions to a plate.

Using the same pan (no need to rinse or wipe it out), heat the remaining 1 tablespoon oil over medium heat until it shimmers. Sprinkle in the cumin and smoked paprika, swirling them in the hot oil for 30 seconds. Add the lentils and stir to coat, then add 2 cups (470ml) of the water and bring to a boil. Once the lentils have come to a boil, reduce the heat to low, add the cut lemon and remaining 1 teaspoon salt, cover, and cook until tender, about 25 minutes. Be sure to check occasionally to make sure the lentils are simmering. If the water evaporates before the lentils are tender, add ½ cup (120ml) water at a time as needed.

Meanwhile, in a medium saucepan, combine the rinsed rice, cinnamon stick, and remaining 1½ cups (360ml) water. Bring to a boil, then reduce to very low, cover, and simmer until all the water is absorbed, 15 to 20 minutes. Uncover, remove the cinnamon stick, and fluff the rice with a fork to separate the grains.

When the lentils are tender, fish out and compost the lemon. Taste and season with salt and pepper as needed.

To serve, spoon the rice onto a platter, then top with the lentils, drizzle lightly with some olive oil, garnish with the onions, and sprinkle with the chopped parsley.

Steamed Veggie Macro Bowl

Macro bowls have become a regular in food writer Diana Yen's lunchtime rotation when she craves something nourishing that is still hearty enough to give her energy throughout the day. These colorful bowls are typically a balance of grains, raw or cooked vegetables, a protein, healthy fat, and dressing. Fermented veggies like kimchi or sauerkraut are also a great addition.

Her recipe has a nutty brown rice base, topped with sweet kabocha squash, broccoli, and asparagus. For protein, five-spice tempeh is stir-fried until browned and crispy. The bowl is finished with a creamy miso-tahini sauce and sprinkled with furikake. Once you've learned the basics of steaming vegetables, feel free to make your own combinations with any you want to use up in your fridge.

Makes 4 servings

Time: Weekday

Storage: Refrigerate for up to 5 days.

- 1½ cups (278g) brown rice (short-, medium-, or long-grain), rinsed
- ¼ cup (60ml) well-stirred tahini
- 1 tablespoon white miso, homemade (page 83) or store-bought
- 2 garlic cloves, finely grated or pressed
- 1 teaspoon grated fresh ginger
- 2 tablespoons fresh lemon juice
- 1 teaspoon soy sauce or tamari
- 1 teaspoon agave syrup, Wildflower Cider Syrup (page 35), or maple syrup
- ½ head broccoli (9 ounces/255g), cut into 1-inch (2.5cm) florets
- ⅓ kabocha squash (8½ ounces/240g), stemmed, seeded, and cut into ¼-inch wedges
- 6 fat asparagus spears (9 ounces/255g total), tough ends trimmed, cut into 2-inch (5cm) pieces
- 3 tablespoons vegetable oil
- 12 ounces (340g) tempeh, homemade (page 79) or store-bought
- 1 teaspoon Chinese Five-Spice Powder (page 39)
- ½ teaspoon fine sea salt, plus more to taste

FOR SERVING
- Furikake, Shichimi Togarashi (page 42), Seaweed Gomasio (page 45), or toasted sesame seeds
- Sauerkraut, Clean-Out-the-Fridge Kimchi (page 71), or other fermented vegetables

BRING A LARGE SAUCEPAN of water to a boil. Add the rice to the boiling water, reduce the heat to a gentle boil, partially cover, and cook until the rice is tender, about 30 minutes. Drain off the remaining water and return the rice to the pot. Cover tightly and let the rice sit for 10 minutes. Fluff with a fork before serving.

In a small bowl, whisk together the tahini, miso, garlic, ginger, lemon juice, soy sauce, and agave syrup. Whisk in warm water, 1 tablespoon at a time, until the dressing is thick but able to be drizzled.

In a large pot fitted with a steamer basket or insert, bring 1 inch (2.5cm) of water to a boil. Arrange the broccoli, squash, and asparagus in the basket. Cover and steam until the vegetables are crisp-tender, 5 to 6 minutes. (If you are using thinner spears of asparagus, wait to add them 2 minutes into the cooking time to keep them from overcooking in the steamer.)

Meanwhile, in a large skillet, heat the oil over medium heat until it shimmers. Crumble in the tempeh with your fingers, sprinkle with the five-spice powder and salt, and cook, stirring occasionally and breaking up any large pieces with a spoon, until deep golden and crispy, 3 to 4 minutes. Taste and season with more salt as needed. Transfer the tempeh to a plate.

Divide the rice among serving bowls. Top each bowl with vegetables, tempeh, and a drizzle of miso-tahini dressing. Sprinkle with furikake, togarashi, gomasio, or sesame seeds. Add kimchi, sauerkraut, or other fermented vegetables. Serve warm.

Miso Polenta with Peas & Asparagus

Here's what gives polenta a salty, umami depth, no big heap of Parmesan necessary: white or yellow miso. Plant-based butter adds richness to both the grains and the vegetables.

For creamy polenta that won't have you standing over the stove stirring for 30 minutes, follow this trick from Maria Speck's book *Simply Ancient Grains*: Soak the polenta in hot water for 8 to 12 hours to give the cornmeal a head start at hydration. When you're ready to cook, simply whisk in more water, turn on the heat, and cook, stirring occasionally, for about 15 minutes.

When peas and asparagus aren't in season, this would be great with roasted squash, seared mushrooms, or burst cherry tomatoes.

Makes 3 to 4 servings

Time: Weekend

Storage: Refrigerate leftover vegetables and polenta separately for up to 5 days. Gently reheat polenta over low heat, adding water to loosen.

1 cup (156g) polenta

1½ cups (360ml) boiling water

1½ cups (360ml) cool water

1 teaspoon fine sea salt, plus more to taste

1 tablespoon white or yellow miso, homemade (page 83) or store-bought

2 tablespoons hot water

2½ tablespoons (35g) Soft Spreadable Butter (page 21) or store-bought unsalted vegan butter

2 teaspoons olive oil

1 large shallot (2 ounces/64g), thinly sliced

2 garlic cloves, thinly sliced

¼ teaspoon red pepper flakes

1 bunch asparagus (1 pound/450g), woody ends trimmed, cut into 2-inch (5cm) pieces

1 cup (145g) fresh or frozen peas

1 teaspoon sherry vinegar or white wine vinegar

Optional topping: Umami-Packed Cashew Parm (page 27), nutritional yeast, or store-bought vegan Parmesan (such as Violife)

AT LEAST 8 AND UP to 12 hours before cooking, in a heavy-bottomed medium saucepan, whisk together the polenta and boiling water. Cover and set aside (or let cool and refrigerate for up to 2 days).

When ready to cook the polenta, add another 1½ cups (360ml) water and ½ teaspoon of the salt and whisk to loosen the polenta. Bring to a boil over medium-high heat, whisking frequently. Once boiling, whisk constantly until the mixture thickens, 2 to 3 minutes. Reduce the heat to low, cover, and cook, stirring vigorously with a wooden spoon every few minutes, until creamy and thick, 8 to 10 minutes.

In a small bowl, whisk the miso with the hot water to dissolve. Whisk the miso mixture and 1 tablespoon of the vegan butter into the polenta. Taste and season with more salt as needed. Cover and keep warm.

In a large skillet, combine 1 tablespoon of the vegan butter, the olive oil, shallot, garlic, and pepper flakes and set over medium-high heat. Once the butter melts, cook, stirring frequently, until the shallots and garlic are soft, 1 to 2 minutes. Add the asparagus and peas and stir to coat. Add 2 tablespoons water, reduce the heat to medium, cover, and cook until the asparagus is crisp-tender and the peas are cooked through, 2 to 3 minutes. Remove from the heat and stir in the sherry vinegar, remaining ½ tablespoon vegan butter, and remaining ½ teaspoon salt.

Serve the vegetables over the polenta. If desired, top with a sprinkling of cashew Parm.

Spring Quinoa with Asparagus, Spring Onions & Peas

Turn to this recipe when spring's first asparagus appears. You'll likely be able to find spring onions—not to be confused with smaller scallions—and fresh peas then, too. You can easily swap garlic scapes for the spring onions and sliced snap peas for the peas depending on how the season shapes up where you live. The mint brings a lively, distinctly spring-feeling quality to this recipe, but use all parsley if you want to keep it to one herb. Leftovers are excellent warm, cold, or at room temperature. You can also stir them into a green salad or fold them into a wrap for something that doesn't feel like leftovers at all.

Makes 4 to 6 servings

Time: Weekday

Storage: Refrigerate, preferably without the almonds, for up to 5 days.

> 3 tablespoons olive oil
> 1 bunch spring onions (6½ ounces/183g), trimmed and chopped
> 1½ cups (255g) any color quinoa
> 2 garlic cloves, sliced
> 2 cups (470ml) water
> ½ teaspoon fine sea salt, plus more to taste
> 1 bunch asparagus (1 pound/450g), woody ends trimmed, cut into 1-inch (2.5cm) segments (see Note)
> 1 cup (125g) fresh green peas
> ¾ teaspoon grated lemon zest
> 1½ teaspoons fresh lemon juice
> ¼ cup (13g) chopped fresh parsley
> 2 tablespoons chopped fresh mint
> ⅓ cup (30g) sliced almonds, toasted

IN A POT WITH a tight-fitting lid, heat 2 tablespoons of the olive oil over medium heat until it shimmers. Add the spring onions and cook, stirring occasionally, until they start to soften, about 3 minutes.

Add the quinoa and cook, stirring, until the grains begin to darken and some of them start to pop, about 5 minutes. Add the garlic and cook until just fragrant, about 1 minute.

Add the water and salt and bring to a boil. Cover, reduce the heat to low, and cook until the quinoa is tender and the water is absorbed, 17 to 20 minutes. If water remains at the bottom of the pot after 20 minutes, remove the lid and stir until it's evaporated.

While the quinoa is cooking, bring a pot of salted water to a boil and add the asparagus. Cook for about 3 minutes, until the asparagus is just tender. Drain.

When the quinoa is done cooking, reduce the heat to low and fold in the asparagus and peas. Cover and cook until the vegetables are heated through. Off the heat, stir in the remaining 1 tablespoon olive oil, the lemon zest, lemon juice, parsley, and mint. Taste and season with more salt if needed.

Spoon onto a serving platter and sprinkle the almonds over top.

COOK'S NOTE: Especially if it's fresh from the farm or farmers market, asparagus can be sandy. Wash the asparagus by plunging it into a deep bowl of cold water and letting it soak; the sand will settle to the bottom of the bowl.

Summer Quinoa with Corn, Tomatoes, Eggplant & Pistachios

With plenty of raw tomatoes and fresh herbs, this dish rides the salad/grain bowl line. It's one of those things that is good hot, cold, or at room temperature. If local corn is in season and you have the time to shuck fresh ears for this recipe, it's well worth the effort. Frozen corn is good, too. If it's too hot to fire up the oven, feel free to grill the eggplant in thick (1-inch/2.5cm) slices, then cut it into cubes. Tomatoes of any variety work here, but Sungolds—those sunny yellow cherry tomatoes that are everywhere in summer—are a special favorite. Top with Lemon-Brined Tofu Feta (page 26), if desired.

Makes 6 servings

Time: Weekday

Storage: Refrigerate for up to 3 days, without the fresh herbs and pistachios.

1 medium eggplant (1 pound/450g), peeled and cut into 1-inch (2.5cm) cubes

5 tablespoons olive oil

1 teaspoon fine sea salt, plus more to taste

¼ teaspoon freshly ground black pepper

1 small onion (6 ounces/170g), chopped (1 cup)

1½ cups (255g) any color quinoa

2 garlic cloves, sliced

2 cups (470ml) water

1½ cups (185g) fresh or frozen corn kernels

1 pint (290g) Sungold tomatoes, halved

½ cup (20g) mixed chopped soft herbs, such as chives, basil, dill, and/or parsley

⅓ cup (45g) pistachios, toasted and chopped

PREHEAT THE OVEN TO 400°F (200°C). Line a large sheet pan with a silicone baking mat or compostable parchment paper.

In a bowl, toss the eggplant with 3 tablespoons of the olive oil, ½ teaspoon of the salt, and the pepper. Transfer to the sheet pan and roast until the eggplant is creamy and brown, 20 to 25 minutes. (This can be done 1 day ahead.)

In a pot with a tightly fitting lid, heat the remaining 2 tablespoons olive oil over medium heat until it shimmers. Add the onion and cook, stirring occasionally, until starting to soften, about 3 minutes.

Add the quinoa and cook, stirring, until the grains begin to darken and some of them start to pop, about 5 minutes. Add the garlic and cook until just fragrant, about 1 minute.

Add the water and remaining ½ teaspoon salt and bring to a boil. Cover, reduce the heat to low, and cook until the quinoa is tender and the water is absorbed, 17 to 20 minutes. If water remains at the bottom of the pot after 20 minutes, remove the lid and stir until it's evaporated.

While the quinoa is cooking, heat a dry cast-iron skillet over medium-high heat. Add the corn and cook, stirring, until charred in spots, about 5 minutes. (If you're using frozen corn, it could take longer to char, because of the extra moisture.)

When the quinoa is finished cooking, reduce the heat to low and fold in the eggplant and corn. Cover and cook until the vegetables are heated through. Off the heat, stir in the tomatoes and herbs. Taste and season with more salt if needed.

Spoon onto a serving platter and sprinkle the pistachios over top.

Summer Quinoa with Corn, Tomatoes, Eggplant & Pistachios (page 213) and Spring Quinoa with Asparagus, Spring Onions & Peas (page 212)

Fall Quinoa with Squash & Pumpkin Seeds

Thanksgiving can be a little tricky if you're following a plant-based diet. This quinoa bowl is a good dish to bring along to those holiday gatherings, as it can be a hearty entree for vegans or an appropriately festive side dish for all. It's also satisfying on any crisp fall evening.

When you toss those fresh herbs into the pot, the unmistakable Thanksgiving aroma will get you in an autumn holiday spirit. You could sub any winter squash or even sweet potato for the butternut. (Half-moons of delicata are especially fetching, and you don't even have to peel it.) Swap in pecans for the pumpkin seeds if you like. If you want to be wild, you can throw roasted Brussels sprouts in here instead of or in addition to the squash. This is good to make ahead by a day or two (just make sure not to stir too much—your roasted squash could become mashed squash). If you're taking it to a holiday dinner or potluck, you can simply reheat it in the microwave if oven space is at a premium, or bake it in a casserole dish if it's not.

Makes 4 to 6 servings

Time: Weekday

Storage: Refrigerate for up to 3 days, preferably without the parsley and pumpkin seeds.

1 small butternut squash (1 to 1½ pounds/450g to 680g), peeled (see Note), seeded, and cut into ½-inch (1.3cm) cubes (about 4 cups)

2 tablespoons olive oil

1 teaspoon fine sea salt, plus more to taste

Pinch of freshly ground black pepper

2 tablespoons (28g) unsalted vegan butter

1 small onion (4 ounces/110g), chopped (about 1 cup)

1 celery stalk (37g), chopped (about ⅓ cup)

1½ cups (255g) any color quinoa

1 tablespoon chopped fresh sage

1 teaspoon chopped fresh rosemary

1 teaspoon chopped fresh thyme

2 garlic cloves, sliced

⅓ cup (45g) dried cranberries

2 cups (470ml) water

2 teaspoons apple cider vinegar

⅓ cup (45g) pumpkin seeds, toasted

¼ cup (13g) chopped fresh parsley

POSITION RACKS IN THE top and bottom thirds of the oven and preheat to 400°F (200°C). Line two sheet pans with silicone baking mats or compostable parchment paper.

Place the butternut squash cubes on the sheet pans, drizzle with the olive oil, season with ½ teaspoon of the salt and the black pepper, and toss to coat. Roast until the squash is tender and browned, about 20 minutes.

Meanwhile, in a pot with a tight-fitting lid, melt the butter over medium heat. Add the onion and celery and cook, stirring occasionally, until they start to soften, about 3 minutes. Add the quinoa and cook, stirring, until the grains begin to darken and some of them start to pop, about 5 minutes.

Add the sage, rosemary, thyme, and garlic and cook just until fragrant, about 1 minute. Add the dried cranberries, water, and remaining ½ teaspoon salt and bring to a boil. Cover, reduce the heat to low, and cook until the quinoa is tender and the water is absorbed, 17 to 20 minutes. If water remains at the bottom of the pot after 20 minutes, remove the lid and stir until it's evaporated.

When the quinoa is done cooking, reduce the heat to low and stir in the vinegar. Gently fold in the roasted squash. Taste and season with more salt if needed.

Spoon onto a serving platter and top with the pumpkin seeds and parsley.

COOK'S NOTE: A sharp, Y-shaped vegetable peeler should be able to make relatively quick work of winter squash peeling, but if you find it difficult, one thing that can help is microwaving the squash first. Just poke holes all over it and microwave on high for 2 or 3 minutes. The exterior softens enough to make peeling easier.

Winter Quinoa with Roasted Mushrooms & Cashews

Specialty mushrooms like oyster and trumpet are available all year long, and they make for luxurious plant-based meals. You can use a mix of cremini and specialty mushrooms to keep the cost in check. Plain-Jane frozen vegetables like broccoli or cauliflower seem more glamorous when paired with these fancy fungi, and they are a good way to help you eat enough vegetables in winter, although feel free to use fresh if/when you have access to them. Tossed with quinoa and toasted cashews, this dish becomes a comforting meal.

Makes 4 to 6 servings

Time: Weekday

Storage: Refrigerate, preferably without the cashews and parsley, for up to 3 days.

6 tablespoons olive oil

½ cup (55g) chopped onion

1½ cups (255g) any color quinoa

2 garlic cloves, sliced

2 cups (470ml) water

1 teaspoon fine sea salt, plus more to taste

10 ounces (285g) frozen broccoli or cauliflower

1 pound (450g) mixed mushrooms, such as cremini, oyster, shiitake, and trumpet, trimmed and roughly torn (remove and compost the stems if you use shiitakes)

2 teaspoons fresh lemon juice

¼ cup (13g) chopped fresh parsley

⅔ cup (85g) raw cashews, toasted and chopped

POSITION RACKS IN THE top and bottom thirds of the oven and preheat to 450°F (230°C). Place two sheet pans in the oven to preheat as well.

In a pot with a tightly fitting lid, heat 2 tablespoons of the olive oil to over medium heat. Add the onion and cook, stirring occasionally, until it starts to soften, about 3 minutes. Add the quinoa and cook, stirring, until the grains begin to darken and some of them start to pop, about 5 minutes.

Add the garlic and cook just until fragrant, about 1 minute. Add the water and ½ teaspoon of the salt and bring to a boil. Cover, reduce the heat to low, and cook until the quinoa is tender and the water is absorbed, 17 to 20 minutes. If water remains at the bottom of the pot after 20 minutes, remove the lid and stir until it's evaporated.

Meanwhile, in a bowl, toss the frozen broccoli and the mushrooms with the remaining 4 tablespoons olive oil. Spread them out on the preheated sheet pans. Roast until the vegetables are lightly browned and crisp at the edges, about 15 minutes, switching racks halfway through the cooking time. Sprinkle with the remaining ½ teaspoon salt.

When the quinoa is done cooking, reduce the heat to low and fold in the roasted vegetables. Off the heat, stir in the lemon juice, parsley, and toasted cashews. Taste and season with more salt if needed. Serve warm.

Fried Rice with Vegetables

This dish is inspired by nasi goreng kampung, a Malay phrase that translates to "village" (*kampung*) "fried" (*goreng*) "rice" (*nasi*). While the traditional nasi goreng kampung that food writer WoonHeng Chia grew up with in Malaysia has a seafood element to it, this recipe uses kombu to bring a taste of the sea to the sambal. Other ways in which this fried rice stands out from the pack: shallot and kecap manis, the latter being the sweet-sticky dark soy sauce that's one of Southeast Asia's greatest gifts to the world. Both add a hint of sweetness while taming the spicy sambal.

As with all fried rice dishes, the best results come from cooked rice that has dried out some; if it's not day-old, make sure it isn't too moist and that you cool it completely before using. Either way, make sure to fluff the rice before adding it to the pan.

Makes 2 servings

Time: Weekday

Storage: Refrigerate for up to 3 days.

SAMBAL

10 dried Thai bird's-eye chiles

2-inch (5cm) piece dried kombu

Boiling water

1 medium shallot, roughly chopped

1 small tomato, chopped

3 garlic cloves, peeled but whole

1 or 2 tablespoons water, if needed

FRIED RICE

2 tablespoons neutral vegetable oil, such as canola or sunflower, plus more if needed

4 ounces (115g) firm tofu, cubed

½ teaspoon fine sea salt, plus more to taste

1 medium shallot, sliced

3 ounces (85g) green beans, trimmed and cut on the diagonal into 1-inch (2.5cm) slices

3 cups (480g) cooked and cooled or leftover white rice, fluffed

¼ teaspoon shiitake or porcini powder (optional)

¼ teaspoon kecap manis (or ¼ teaspoon soy sauce plus ½ teaspoon brown sugar)

Sliced tomato, sliced cucumber, and lime wedges, for serving

MAKE THE SAMBAL: In a heatproof bowl, combine the chiles and kombu. Pour boiling water over them to cover by 1 inch (2.5cm), and let sit for at least 5 minutes. Drain and transfer to a high-powered blender.

Add the shallot, tomato, and garlic to the blender and process, adding a tablespoon or two of water if needed, until you have a smooth paste. Set the sambal aside.

Make the fried rice: In a large skillet, heat 1 tablespoon of the oil over medium heat. Add the tofu and cook until golden brown, 4 to 5 minutes per side. Sprinkle with the salt. Transfer to a plate.

Add the sliced shallot to the same skillet, adding more oil if needed, and cook, stirring, until tender, 4 to 5 minutes. Transfer to the plate with the tofu.

Add the remaining 1 tablespoon oil to the skillet and slowly pour in the sambal. Reduce the heat to medium-low and cook, stirring occasionally, until it turns darker, about 10 minutes.

Add the green beans and cook, stirring, just until they start to become tender, about 2 minutes. Add the rice and stir-fry until heated through, about 1 minute. Add the cooked tofu and shallots along with the mushroom powder (if using), and kecap manis. Toss to combine.

Using the back of your spatula, press the rice as it cooks to loosen the grains. Stir-fry for another minute until the rice is dry. Taste and season with more salt if needed.

Serve hot with tomatoes, cucumber, and lime wedges.

Ocopa Potato Garden

For centuries, the Inca have cultivated hundreds of varieties of native potatoes in Peru's Andes Mountains. Their Andean descendants prepare potatoes in different ways: boiled, baked in earthen ovens, or cooked in stews. For a traditional potato salad, they make an ocopa sauce with dairy, hot peppers, peanuts, and huacatay—an indigenous wild mint. They pour this sauce over potatoes on a bed of lettuce, and that's how writer Nico Vera learned to prepare this dish. His modern interpretation inverts the presentation to create a potato garden, where roasted multicolored fingerling potatoes are "planted" over the sauce and garnish leaves fall over the yellow, red, and purple tubers. A plant yogurt makes the sauce vegan, and a combination of mint and parsley resembles the wild huacatay.

Makes 4 servings

Time: Weekend

Storage: Refrigerate the potatoes, garnishes, and sauce separately for up to 5 days.

1 pound (450g) fingerling potato medley, scrubbed and cut into 1-inch (2.5cm) slices

3 tablespoons olive oil

¾ teaspoon fine sea salt, plus more to taste

2 tablespoons canola or other neutral cooking oil

¼ cup (30g) chopped red onion
(from ¼ small onion)

2 tablespoons finely chopped jalapeño pepper (seeded and deveined)

2 garlic cloves, finely grated or pressed

¼ teaspoon freshly ground black pepper

¼ teaspoon ground coriander

1 cup (240ml) Creamy Coconut Yogurt (page 23) or plain coconut milk yogurt

4 tablespoons chopped fresh mint leaves

4 tablespoons chopped fresh flat-leaf parsley leaves

1 teaspoon creamy peanut butter

4 Kalamata olives, pitted and quartered, for garnish

A few green lettuce leaves, thinly sliced, for garnish

PREHEAT THE OVEN TO 425°F (220°C). Line a sheet pan with a silicone baking mat or compostable parchment paper.

In a medium bowl, toss the potatoes with 2 tablespoons of the olive oil and ¼ teaspoon of the salt. Arrange the potatoes on the sheet pan and bake until fork tender, about 20 minutes. Let cool to room temperature.

In a small skillet, heat the canola oil over medium heat until it shimmers. Add the onion, jalapeño, and garlic and cook until the onion begins to brown slightly, about 3 minutes. Add the black pepper, coriander, and remaining ½ teaspoon salt. Continue to sauté until the onion mixture becomes fragrant, about 2 minutes. Let cool slightly, then transfer to the blending cup of an immersion blender or other tall container.

To the blending cup, add the yogurt, 2 tablespoons of the mint, 2 tablespoons of the parsley, the peanut butter, and the remaining 1 tablespoon olive oil. Use an immersion blender to puree into a smooth sauce. (Alternatively, you can puree in a mini food processor.) Taste and season with more salt if needed.

To serve, scoop the sauce into the center of four small plates. Divide the potatoes among the plates, arranging over the sauce. Garnish with the olives, the remaining 2 tablespoons each of the mint and parsley, and the lettuce.

Sambal Green Bean & Tofu Stir-Fry

Made from a reduced mixture of fresh and dried chiles and spices, sambal is widely used in Indonesia, Singapore, and Malaysia in curries, nasi lemak (coconut rice), and stir-fries. While many sambals include belacan (fermented shrimp paste), this one uses kelp (aka kombu), to achieve the same oceanic umami.

This is a great stir-fry to make ahead for meal-prepping, because it tastes even better the next day and goes well with rice or noodles.

Makes 4 servings

Time: Weekend

Storage: Refrigerate for up to 3 days.

SAMBAL

2 large shallots, roughly chopped

3 garlic cloves, halved

3 fresh Thai red chiles, seeded and roughly chopped

1 (3-inch/7.5cm) piece dried kombu, softened in hot water for a few minutes and drained, then cut into 1-inch (2.5cm) pieces

STIR-FRY

1 tablespoon neutral vegetable oil, such as sunflower, plus more if needed

12 ounces (340g) firm or extra-firm tofu, cut into 1-inch (2.5cm) cubes

½ teaspoon fine sea salt, plus more to taste

8 ounces (225g) green beans, trimmed and cut into 2-inch (5cm) pieces

⅔ cup (160ml) water

1 tablespoon soy sauce, plus more to taste

1 teaspoon organic cane sugar

1½ teaspoons vegan oyster sauce or mushroom sauce

¼ teaspoon ground mushroom seasoning or shiitake or other mushroom powder

Rice or noodles, for serving

MAKE THE SAMBAL: In a food processor, combine the shallots, garlic, chiles, and kombu and process until it becomes a coarse paste. (You should still see pieces of the ingredients, so don't puree it.)

Make the stir-fry: In a large skillet, heat the oil over medium heat until it shimmers. Add the tofu and pan-fry until golden brown, a few minutes on each side. Season with the salt and transfer to a plate.

In the same skillet still over medium heat, add the sambal and sauté until the shallots soften and turn translucent, adding a little more oil if needed. Add the green beans and the pan-fried tofu and stir-fry until the green beans are browned in spots, about 1 minute.

Add the water, soy sauce, sugar, oyster sauce, and mushroom seasoning. Cover and let the mixture simmer for 1 minute for the flavors to mingle. Uncover, taste, and season with more soy sauce and/or salt if needed.

Serve warm with rice or noodles.

Stir-Fried Bihun (Rice Vermicelli)

This is Malaysia-born food blogger WoonHeng Chia's go-to dish for lunch, since it's easy to put together and helps clean out the fridge. Although the most common vegetables to use in this simple stir-fry are cabbage and carrot, feel free to add spinach, broccoli, gai lan (Chinese broccoli), or yu choy (Chinese flowering cabbage). And if you're not already a fan of rice vermicelli, this is a great way to get to know it; also known as rice stick, it's naturally gluten-free and usually made from just rice and water. The thin noodles are rehydrated in just a few minutes, making this a fabulously useful pantry staple.

Makes 2 to 3 servings

Time: Weekday

Storage: Refrigerate for up to 3 days.

4 Thai bird's-eye chiles, stemmed and thinly sliced

¼ cup (60ml) plus 1 tablespoon soy sauce, plus more to taste

8 ounces (227g) dried rice vermicelli

1 teaspoon vegan oyster sauce or mushroom sauce

1 teaspoon dark soy sauce

⅛ teaspoon freshly ground black pepper

¼ cup (60ml) water

1 tablespoon neutral oil, such as sunflower or canola

2 garlic cloves, sliced

Scant 3 ounces (80g) fresh mushrooms, sliced

1 medium carrot (3 ounces/87g), coarsely grated

8 ounces (225g) cabbage, thinly sliced

8 ounces (225g) mung bean sprouts

2 scallions, chopped

Splash of toasted sesame oil, for serving

IN A SMALL BOWL, combine the chiles with ¼ cup (60ml) of the soy sauce. Set aside.

Bring a large saucepan of water to a boil. Add the rice vermicelli and cook until soft and pliable, 2 to 3 minutes. Drain.

In another small bowl, whisk together the remaining 1 tablespoon soy sauce, the vegan oyster sauce, dark soy sauce, black pepper, and water until combined.

In a large nonstick skillet, heat the neutral oil over medium-high heat until it shimmers. Add the garlic and sauté until fragrant, about 30 seconds. Add the mushrooms and stir-fry until aromatic, about 1 minute. Push the garlic and mushrooms to one side of the pan, add the carrots and sauté just until they start to wilt, about 30 seconds. Add the vermicelli and the oyster sauce mixture and use chopsticks and/or tongs to swirl and toss the noodles in the sauce until it has been absorbed.

Fold in the cabbage and continue to toss until the cabbage starts to wilt, about 1 minute. Fold in the bean sprouts and toss for another minute, until they start to wilt. Taste and season with more soy sauce if needed.

Divide among serving plates, garnish with chopped scallions, and drizzle with sesame oil. Serve hot, with the bowl of chiles in soy sauce on the side for spooning onto the noodles as you eat.

DECOLONIZE YOUR DIET

By Nico Vera

Starting in the fifteenth century, colonization impacted all aspects of Indigenous culture in the Americas. European colonists uprooted Indigenous peoples from their homes, enslaved them, indoctrinated language and religion, and exploited natural resources for economic gain. Colonial practices destroyed Indigenous food systems and introduced foreign plants and animals, transforming many Indigenous recipes, disappearing others, and creating new dishes.

Peru's Indigenous peoples, for instance, prepared ceviche in precolonial times. But its contemporary and most traditional preparation—fish cured in lime juice with salt, red onions, and native hot peppers—is a product of colonization because Spain's colonial foodways introduced two of its ingredients: limes and red onions. Colonization also created Mexico's emblematic carnitas taco of pulled pork atop native corn tortillas after the Spanish introduced pigs to the Americas. And in the United States, dairy foods—milkshakes, ice cream, cheese, and more—became a product of colonization when Europeans brought cows to the Americas.

Before colonization, though, Indigenous cooking in the Americas was largely plant-based.

In Peru, Indigenous peoples thrived on a diet of native ingredients such as quinoa, potatoes, corn, hot peppers, and wild herbs and plants. They also used food storage methods, such as freeze-drying potatoes into chuño, which has a ten-year shelf life, in case of scarcity or drought. Quinoa, dubbed "The Mother Grain," was an important source of protein for the Inca. The Inca also cooked animal protein such as fish and llama, and they cultivated most of their foods according to seasonality and at challenging high elevations in the Andes.

In Mexico, Indigenous peoples cooked with native ingredients such as squash, beans, corn, and *xitomatl*—tomato, in the Indigenous language Náhuatl. They also developed nixtamalization, the process of treating corn with lime (calcium hydroxide) water to remove toxins produced by fungi, making the corn more workable, and increasing its nutritional value. This is the basis for making corn tortillas, tamales, tostadas, sopes, and all the other dishes that start out as masa. Some animal protein, such as birds or fish, was also part of their diet, which complemented their agricultural system, yielding diverse, nutritious foods.

In North America, Indigenous peoples developed community-based regional food systems rooted in permaculture. Here, the Three Sisters—squash, beans, and corn—complement one another nutritionally and form the foundation of Indigenous culinary traditions. They also carry spiritual significance and, when grown together, work synergistically to create fertile soil. Across North America, some animal protein, such as deer or other native game, was also part of their diet.

Today, chefs and home cooks in Peru, Mexico, the United States, and elsewhere are seeking to reconnect with their ancestral food cultures by decolonizing contemporary recipes, and in the process are unearthing the deep roots of plant-based cooking in the Americas. But what does it mean to decolonize a dish? Is it simply to cook only with precolonial Indigenous ingredients? Is it possible to undo the evolution of traditional dishes that were transformed by colonization? The answer is not that simple.

Let's take a closer look at Peru's ceviche. Precolonization, some five hundred years ago, the Inca cooked ceviche by curing fish for hours in the juice of tumbo, a jungle citrus similar to a sour orange, mixed with salt and native hot peppers. After the Spanish colonists introduced limes and red onions to Peru's cuisine, ceviche's ingredients changed. But postcolonization, Japanese indentured workers who settled in Lima transformed ceviche even further. They shortened the curing time and quickly tossed the catch of the day with salt, fresh lime juice, onions, and hot peppers. Colonization transformed the dish's ingredients and its preparation.

To strictly decolonize ceviche would mean to cook it like the Inca, without limes and without onions. It would also mean erasing the culinary contributions of Japanese culture. Should that be the goal of decolonization?

Three chefs are confronting the challenges of decolonizing recipes in different ways.

From Peru's Pacific Coast, over the Andes Mountains, and into the Amazon jungle, chef Virgilio Martinez forages for native ingredients at different elevations to create a tasting menu at his Lima restaurant, Central. He also works with farmers and producers, especially in the Andes, to feature their ingredients on his menus. And he cooks using Indigenous techniques such as pachamanca, an underground earthen oven that slow-cooks buried ingredients with hot rocks. By using native ingredients in situ, instead of re-creating traditional postcolonial dishes, Martínez is effectively cooking through a decolonization lens.

All food evolves over time. Just as immigrants adapt their cuisines to fit the ingredients of their new homeland, these chefs are showing that decolonization can be an exercise in looking to the past as a way to imagine the future.

Based in Los Angeles, Jocelyn Ramirez is a chef and author of *La Vida Verde*, a cookbook with plant-based recipes inspired by her Mexican roots. One of her recipes for tacos eschews pulled pork for shredded jackfruit, and another combines tofu, tempeh, and mushrooms to resemble chorizo. Cooking with plant-based ingredients instead of pork is one way Ramirez is decolonizing the taco. But she also builds community through her food business, Todo Verde. From cooking classes to farmers markets and other events, she is trying to bring food equity to LA neighborhoods and promote a healthy plant-based lifestyle that celebrates a shared ancestral culture.

In the United States, Oglala Lakota chef Sean Sherman, aka the Sioux Chef, is revitalizing the nutritional plant-diverse Indigenous cuisine of his ancestors. While his cooking includes some native animal proteins, it eliminates ingredients that didn't exist before colonization—such as dairy, wheat, flour, cane sugar, beef, pork, and chicken. But he also embraces a modern Indigenous perspective and cooks with nonnative plants. With a focus on education, Sherman opened the Indigenous Food Lab, a cooking school and restaurant that showcases decolonized dishes, foods, and techniques of North America's Indigenous peoples.

As a chef and former omnivore who turned vegan several years ago, I was afraid I would lose my cultural identity if I stopped eating the traditional animal-protein dishes I grew up with in Peru. But chefs such as these have shown me—and others—that cooking with plant-based ingredients can be a practice in decolonization. After experimenting with veganizing several dishes, I had a realization: The culinary essence of my country's traditional recipes is not the animal protein, but rather the combination of flavors, hot peppers, spices, textures, and stories that have shaped a dish over centuries.

Learning to cook Peru's traditional dishes with plant-based ingredients has done the opposite of what I feared it might. I haven't merely preserved my cultural identity while going vegan; I've forged an even deeper connection to my ancestral roots.

Nico Vera is a journalist and chef from Peru who is on a mission to veganize Peru's creole cuisine.

7

PASTA & OTHER NOODLES

I don't think it's just me. At some point, most plant-based eaters have probably had the following thought, or something like it: "Maybe I'm really just a carbotarian." That's because the simple mixture of wheat and water can satisfy and comfort like nothing else, whether it's in the form of Italian pasta (fresh or dried), Japanese soba, Spanish fideos, or Korean jjolmyeon. In the plant-based kitchen, smooth, creamy sauces for pasta come from coconut milk, cashews, and chickpeas, or virtually any vegetable cooked long enough to melt. Tomato-based sauces are a no-brainer, and mushrooms add umami to a long-simmered ragu. Ultimately, pastas are a natural place to showcase pretty much any member of the edible plant kingdom that you like so much you can't resist tossing it with a saucy bowl of carbs.

Ceci e Pepe

The classic pasta dish cacio e pepe seems simple on paper—after all, it's just pasta with a cheese and pepper sauce—but it requires attention to ingredients and technique to achieve silky success rather than clumpy failure. As is so often the case, pasta cooking water is the magic ingredient that pulls everything together. A trick I learned from Yotam Ottolenghi is to cook the pasta in much less water than usual, which packs it with the starch needed for emulsifying the sauce. Here, pureed chickpeas (*ceci* in Italian) lend even more starchiness (not to mention protein, fiber, and flavor) and take over for the cheese, with a little Umami-Packed Cashew Parm (page 27) and lots of freshly cracked black pepper adding even more flavor. In the spirit of Ottolenghi's recipe, I like to finish with some nontraditional za'atar, but this dish is great without it.

Makes 4 to 6 servings

Time: Weekday

Storage: Refrigerate for up to 5 days.

1 (15-ounce/425g) can chickpeas, undrained

7 cups (1.66L) water

Boiling water

1½ teaspoons fine sea salt, plus more to taste

1 pound (450g) dried bucatini or spaghetti

4 tablespoons (56g) Soft Spreadable Butter (page 21) or unsalted vegan butter

2 teaspoons freshly cracked black pepper

½ cup (55g) Umami-Packed Cashew Parm (page 27), plus more for serving

2 tablespoons fresh lemon juice, plus more to taste

2 tablespoons Za'atar (optional; page 44), for serving

IN A BLENDER OR food processor, puree the chickpeas with their liquid until smooth.

Set a colander over a large bowl.

In a wide deep sauté pan or Dutch oven, bring the water to a boil over medium-high heat. Stir in 1 teaspoon of the salt. Add the pasta and cook until al dente, stirring occasionally to keep the pasta from sticking to the bottom of the pot and adding boiling water as needed to keep it barely submerged. Drain the pasta in the colander, reserving all the pasta water in a bowl. (You should have about 2½ cups/600ml.)

Return the pan to medium heat and add the butter. Once it melts, stir in the pepper and cook until fragrant, about 30 seconds. Stir in the chickpea puree, cashew Parm, and remaining ½ teaspoon salt. Bring to a simmer and cook for a minute or so until it thickens. Add the pasta and toss to combine. Add the lemon juice and 1½ cups (350ml) of the pasta water, tossing and stirring until the pasta is coated and the sauce is silky, adding more pasta water as needed. Taste and season with more salt and lemon juice as needed.

Transfer to shallow bowls, sprinkle with more cashew Parm and the za'atar (if using), and serve hot.

COOK'S NOTE: If you have leftovers, the sauce stiffens up when the pasta is refrigerated, so you'll want to stir in hot water, ½ cup (120ml) at a time, when reheating.

Creamy Pasta with Mushrooms

This easy weeknight dish, which comes together in less than 30 minutes, is the answer to your search for the perfect creamy, rich, dairy-free pasta. The secret to this luscious sauce is coconut milk for creaminess and nutritional yeast for cheesy flavor. It is truly decadent and works wonderfully with all pasta shapes. Sautéed mushrooms give this dish an earthy finish, and lemon juice adds a tangy brightness.

Makes 4 servings

Time: Weekday

Storage: Refrigerate for up to 3 days.

2 tablespoons olive oil

1 pound (450g) mixed mushrooms, such as oyster, maitake, cremini, or shiitake (any tough stems composted or saved for stock), torn into bite-size pieces

Fine sea salt

12 ounces (340g) spaghetti or bucatini

2 tablespoons (28g) Soft Spreadable Butter (page 21) or unsalted vegan butter

2 to 3 medium shallots (6 ounces/165g total), chopped

2 garlic cloves, finely grated or pressed

½ cup (120ml) canned full-fat coconut milk, whisked until smooth

¼ cup (20g) nutritional yeast

1 tablespoon finely grated lemon zest

2 tablespoons fresh lemon juice

2 tablespoons chopped fresh flat-leaf parsley

Freshly ground black pepper

IN A DEEP SAUTÉ pan, heat the oil over medium-high heat until it shimmers. Add the mushrooms and cook, stirring occasionally, until they exude their liquid, it evaporates, and they start to brown, 7 to 8 minutes. Stir in ½ teaspoon salt, taste, and season with more salt as needed. Transfer the mushrooms to a plate.

Meanwhile, bring a large pot of salted water to a boil. Add the pasta and cook to 2 minutes shy of al dente according to the package directions. Reserving 1 cup (240ml) of the pasta water, drain the pasta.

Set the same pan you used for the mushrooms over medium heat and add the butter. Once it melts, add the shallots and garlic and cook, stirring, until softened and fragrant, about 2 minutes.

Transfer the cooked pasta to the pan. Add the coconut milk, nutritional yeast, and the reserved 1 cup (240ml) pasta water and bring to a simmer. Using tongs, gently toss the pasta with the sauce and cook until slightly thickened, about 2 minutes. Add the mushrooms, lemon zest, lemon juice, and parsley and toss to combine. Taste and season with more salt as needed.

Divide among plates and finish with generous grinds of pepper.

Cashew Mac & Cheese

Commercially made vegan cheese often includes miso and coconut oil in the ingredients; miso adds umami, while coconut oil adds a velvety texture. The sauce for this mac and cheese uses cashews as the base, while the onion, carrot, garlic, and white wine all bring that depth of flavor that we associate with cheesy goodness. You can serve this right out of the pot or go the extra mile and cover it in bread crumbs before a final bake.

Makes 6 servings

Time: Weekday

Storage: Refrigerate for up to 5 days or freeze for up to 3 months.

1¼ cups (165g) raw cashews

1 medium onion (5 ounces/140g), roughly chopped

1 medium carrot (3 ounces/85g), roughly chopped

2 garlic cloves, peeled but whole

½ cup (120ml) white wine

2 cups (470ml) water

Fine sea salt

1 pound (450g) elbow macaroni

1 tablespoon white or yellow miso, homemade (page 83) or store-bought

1 tablespoon coconut oil

2 teaspoons mustard powder

½ teaspoon smoked paprika

¼ teaspoon cayenne pepper

⅛ teaspoon ground nutmeg

½ teaspoon freshly ground black pepper, plus more to taste

Optional if baking: Oil for the baking dish and ½ cup plain bread crumbs or All-Purpose Crisp Bread Crumb Topping (page 239)

IN A SMALL SAUCEPAN, combine the cashews, onion, carrot, garlic, white wine, and water and bring to a boil over medium-high heat. Reduce the heat to medium-low and simmer until the cashews and vegetables are very tender, 20 to 30 minutes, adding more water to cover as needed.

Meanwhile, bring a large pot of salted water to a boil. Add the macaroni and cook to al dente according to the package directions. Reserving 2 cups of the pasta water, drain the macaroni and return to the pot.

Reserving the cooking liquid, drain the cashews and vegetables. Transfer the cashews and vegetables to a blender. Add about ½ cup (120ml) of the reserved vegetable cooking liquid, the miso, coconut oil, mustard powder, smoked paprika, cayenne, nutmeg, black pepper, and 1 teaspoon salt. Blend on high until smooth and creamy, adding more of the reserved cooking liquid as needed if the mixture becomes too thick. (It should be the consistency of creamy coconut milk.)

To serve, pour the cashew sauce over the macaroni in the large pot, turn the heat to medium, and stir until completely coated. Stir in some of the reserved pasta water, ¼ cup (60ml) at a time, to loosen the sauce if needed. Taste and season with more salt and/or pepper as needed.

Serve immediately or pour into an oiled 9 × 13-inch (23cm × 33cm) baking dish, top with bread crumbs or the bread crumb topping, and bake at 375°F until bubbling and lightly browned, about 30 minutes.

Everyday Walnut, Lentil & Mushroom "Red Gravy"

A traditional pot of meaty tomato sauce (aka "gravy") is typically shot through with streams of beef and pork fat. In this take, the richness so essential to the dish's character comes from walnuts, vegan butter, and olive oil for a gravy that is flavorful, hearty, and meaty but not greasy. The walnuts soften in the sauce and, when combined with lentils and mushrooms, become very meat-like. In fact, you can use this trio of ingredients, sautéed in fat and a little flavorful liquid, to replace ground beef in many dishes, including tacos and shepherd's pie. A prepared "no chicken" broth, such as those from store-bought bouillon or Veg Bouillon (page 36), adds an important savory depth of flavor here. (You can use water, but it loses something.) This sauce is terrific on Fresh "Egg" Pasta (page 240) or any dried pasta that you like. You can make it ahead (it improves with a rest period in the refrigerator).

Makes 3 cups

Time: Weekday

Storage: Refrigerate for up to 5 days or freeze for up to 1 month.

- ¼ cup (50g) cooked or canned large brown/green lentils
- ¼ cup (28g) walnut pieces
- 8 ounces (225g) cremini mushrooms, trimmed and roughly chopped
- 2 tablespoons (28g) Soft Spreadable Butter (page 21) or store-bought unsalted vegan butter
- 1 tablespoon olive oil
- 1 medium onion (5 ounces/140g), cut into small dice
- 1 small/medium carrot (2 to 3 ounces/70g), scrubbed and cut into small dice
- 1 garlic clove, finely grated or pressed
- 1 tablespoon tomato paste
- 1 tablespoon white miso, homemade (page 83) or store-bought
- ½ teaspoon dried oregano
- ½ teaspoon fine sea salt, plus more to taste
- ¼ teaspoon red pepper flakes
- ½ cup (120ml) broth made from store-bought "no-chicken" bouillon or Veg Bouillon (page 36), or water
- 1 (14-ounce/397g) can crushed tomatoes
- ½ teaspoon red wine vinegar, plus more to taste

IN A FOOD PROCESSOR, combine the lentils, walnuts, and mushrooms and pulse until finely chopped, about 10 pulses.

In a Dutch oven, melt the butter with the olive oil over medium heat. When the butter stops foaming, add the onion and carrot and cook until the vegetables soften, 5 to 8 minutes.

Add the lentil/walnut/mushroom mixture and cook until the mushrooms have exuded their liquid and brown bits stick to the bottom of the pot, about 8 minutes. Add the garlic, tomato paste, miso, oregano, salt, and pepper flakes and cook until fragrant, about 1 minute.

Add the broth and bring to a simmer, scraping up browned bits from the bottom of the pot. Add the crushed tomatoes and bring to a simmer. Simmer over low heat, partially covered, until slightly thickened and the flavors have melded, about 35 minutes.

Stir in the vinegar. Taste and season with more salt and vinegar as needed.

Fideuà de Verduras with Lemon Aioli

A Catalonian favorite, fideuà is similar to paella, but made with broken pasta instead of rice. This spring-forward version pairs toasted fideus (short noodles) with asparagus, leeks, and peas, but artichoke hearts, snap peas, and fava beans would also be lovely here. Tomato paste brings umami-rich depth, while smoked paprika and saffron provide a fragrant base.

This party-friendly dish is best served straight out of the pan, after you've given it an extra few minutes uncovered on the stovetop at the end to develop that coveted socarrat (crispy bottom). A topping of briny green olives complements the green vegetables, and don't skimp on the dollops of Lemon Mayonnaise (page 46).

Makes 4 servings

Time: Weekend

Storage: Refrigerate for up to 5 days.

Pinch of saffron

¼ cup (60ml) warm water

8 tablespoons olive oil

8 ounces (225g) angel hair pasta, broken into 1-inch (2.5cm) pieces

1 (15-ounce/425g) can chickpeas, drained

1 large leek (8 ounces/225g), white and light green parts only, thinly sliced

4 garlic cloves, finely grated or pressed

3 tablespoons tomato paste

1½ teaspoons smoked paprika

1 teaspoon fine sea salt, plus more to taste

2½ cups (590ml) Vegetable Scrap Stock (page 36) or store-bought vegetable broth

6 ounces (170g) asparagus, woody ends trimmed, cut on the diagonal into 1-inch (2.5cm) pieces, tips kept separated from the stems

1 cup (135g) frozen green peas

¼ cup (35g) Spanish green olives, such as Manzanilla or Gordal, pitted and halved

¼ cup (8g) lightly packed fresh parsley leaves, roughly chopped

Flaky sea salt, for serving (optional)

Lemon Mayonnaise (page 46)

IN A SMALL BOWL, combine the saffron and warm water and let steep for 15 minutes.

While the saffron is steeping, in a large skillet, heat 3 tablespoons of the olive oil over medium-high heat until it shimmers. Reduce the heat to medium-low and add the broken pasta, stirring to coat. Toast, stirring frequently, until deep golden brown, 5 to 7 minutes. Transfer the pasta to a medium bowl.

Return the skillet to medium-high heat, add the remaining 5 tablespoons olive oil, and heat for 30 seconds. Add the drained chickpeas and cook, stirring occasionally, until their skins start to turn golden brown and blister, 6 to 8 minutes. Add the leek and cook until it starts to soften and turn light golden, 3 to 4 minutes. Add the garlic, tomato paste, smoked paprika, and fine salt and cook until fragrant, about 2 minutes.

Add the reserved toasted pasta, saffron water, and vegetable stock, stirring to combine. Reduce the heat to medium-low, cover, and cook for 5 minutes. Stir in the asparagus stem pieces and frozen peas, arrange the asparagus tips on top of the fideuà, cover, and cook until the pasta is al dente and the vegetables are crisp-tender, 7 to 9 minutes. If you want to develop a bottom crust (socarrat), cook uncovered for 1 to 2 minutes more.

Remove from the heat and garnish with the olives and parsley. If desired, add a sprinkling of flaky salt. Serve hot straight from the pan, with the lemon mayonnaise alongside for diners to spoon onto their portions.

COOK'S NOTE: Reheat leftovers in an oiled skillet over medium-high heat until warmed through and crispy on the bottom.

Orecchiette with Garlicky White Beans & Leafy Greens

This recipe was inspired by the ubiquitous garlicky beans-and-greens side dish found at countless Italian American restaurants, with pasta added to make it a meal. Orecchiette's cuplike shape is ideal for catching the beans and garlic, but any shape you like will work. Use your favorite leafy greens here: Kale, Swiss chard, arugula, and mature spinach all work fine. Navy beans are nice here because of their small size, but cannellini and Great Northern beans are an obvious alternative. If you keep dried beans on hand, especially heirloom varieties like borlotti, cook them up for this. You can use anything that strikes you as Italian-leaning or pasta-friendly here, even chickpeas.

Makes 4 to 6 servings

Time: Weekday

Storage: Refrigerate for up to 3 days.

Fine sea salt

12 ounces (340g) orecchiette pasta

2 pounds (910g) leafy greens, tough stems removed and reserved

¼ cup (60ml) olive oil

3 garlic cloves, chopped

2 tablespoon capers, chopped

¼ teaspoon red pepper flakes

½ teaspoon grated lemon zest

1 (15.5-ounce/439g) can or 1½ cups (275g) cooked navy or other white beans, drained and rinsed

1 tablespoon (14g) Soft Spreadable Butter (page 21) or store-bought unsalted vegan butter

1 teaspoon fresh lemon juice, plus more to taste

TOPPING OPTIONS

Umami-Packed Cashew Parm (page 27)

All-Purpose Crisp Bread Crumb Topping (page 239)

Nutritional yeast, or store-bought vegan Parmesan, for serving

IN A POT OF boiling salted water, cook the pasta to al dente according to the package directions.

Meanwhile, thinly slice the greens' stems and chop the leaves, keeping them in separate piles.

In a large skillet, warm the olive oil over medium-high heat until it shimmers. Add the stems, and cook, stirring occasionally, until they soften, 4 minutes. Add the greens—it's going to seem like a ridiculous amount at first, but they cook down dramatically, so forge ahead. Add a splash of water and cover until the greens are wilted, about 5 minutes. Add the garlic, capers, and pepper flakes and cook until fragrant, about 1 minute. Add the lemon zest, white beans, and ⅛ teaspoon fine salt. Continue cooking until everything is heated through, about 5 minutes. Remove from the heat.

Reserving about ½ cup (120ml) of pasta water, drain the pasta and add to the greens in the skillet and toss. Add ¼ cup (60ml) of the pasta water and toss to coat. Add the vegan butter and lemon juice and toss again. Taste and season with more lemon juice and/or salt if needed. If you'd like it to be saucier, add the remaining pasta water 1 tablespoon at a time until you achieve your desired consistency.

Sprinkle with your choice of topping and serve hot.

Orecchiette with Melted
Broccoli Sauce (page 239)
and Bucatini with Melted
Corn Sauce (page 239)

Pasta with Melted-Vegetable Sauce

Break nearly any vegetable down into small bits—by chopping it finely by hand, in a food processor, or letting your box grater do the work—and it becomes a quick-cooking pile that can easily be turned into a delicious, almost-creamy pasta sauce. The veg gets cooked with onion, pepper flakes (skip them if you'd like!), and water until it's very tender, then finished uncovered until it becomes jammy and develops flavor. At that point, all you need is a little help from pasta water and olive oil to form a creamy emulsion. Blend it up if you'd like a totally smooth sauce, or leave it bitsy if you'd prefer some texture. Try this with cabbage, zucchini, cauliflower, broccoli, beets, kale, leeks, raw corn, or winter squash, and add as many alliums and aromatics—shallots, garlic, woody herbs, chiles (fresh, dried, crushed)—as you see fit. You'll have to adjust the amount of olive oil, pasta water, salt, and the cook time depending on the vegetable you choose. In case that's too open-ended for you, four delicious variations on the idea follow, each of which offers you more direction, including suggested pasta shapes to pair with each sauce.

Makes 4 to 6 servings

Time: Weekday

Storage: Refrigerate for up to 3 days.

Fine sea salt

5 tablespoons olive oil, plus more as needed

1 to 2 pounds (450g to 900g) vegetable of your choice, finely chopped or grated (see Variations that follow)

1 medium or 2 small yellow onions (8 ounces/225g total), finely chopped

2 garlic cloves, chopped

¼ to ½ teaspoon red pepper flakes, to taste

2 tablespoons water

1 pound (450g) dried pasta of your choice

1 tablespoon fresh lemon juice, plus more to taste

Freshly ground black pepper

Nutritional yeast or Umami-Packed Cashew Parm (page 27), for serving

BRING A LARGE POT of salted water to a boil.

Meanwhile, in another large pot or Dutch oven, heat 2 tablespoons of the oil over medium-high heat until it shimmers. Add the chopped or grated vegetables, onions, garlic, and pepper flakes and stir to coat in the oil. Stir in ½ teaspoon salt, add the water, reduce the heat to medium-low, cover, and cook, stirring occasionally until the vegetables are soft, 3 to 10 minutes, adding more water if the pan is dry and the vegetables are sticking.

Add the pasta to the boiling water and cook until al dente according to the package directions.

Add another 2 tablespoons of the olive oil to the vegetables and continue to cook, uncovered and stirring frequently, until they are soft enough to smash with a spoon, 6 to 12 minutes. Add more oil as needed to keep the vegetables from sticking. Remove from the heat if the vegetables are finished before the pasta. Stir in the lemon juice.

Reserving 1 cup (240ml) of the pasta water, drain the pasta.

If you'd like a smooth sauce: Add ¼ cup (60ml) reserved pasta water and 1 tablespoon olive oil and use an immersion blender to blend until smooth, adding more water as needed to loosen the puree if it seems too thick. (Alternatively, transfer the sauce to a standing blender and then return to the pan, reheating if needed.) Add the pasta and toss to combine, adding more pasta water as needed to create a saucy consistency.

For a chunky sauce: Set the vegetables over low heat, add the pasta, and stir to combine. Add ¼ cup (60ml) reserved pasta water and 1 tablespoon olive oil and stir vigorously until the pasta is glossy. Add more pasta water as needed to create a saucy consistency.

Taste and season with pepper and more salt and/or lemon juice as needed.

Divide among serving bowls, drizzle with more olive oil, if desired, sprinkle with nutritional yeast or cashew Parm, and serve warm.

Orecchiette with Melted Broccoli Sauce

Use 1 pound (450g) broccoli, remove the florets, and trim the toughest end off the stem. Use a vegetable peeler to peel the stem, and chop it and florets into ¼-inch (6mm) pieces. Pair with a short pasta such as orecchiette, rigatoni, or penne.

Spaghetti with Melted Spinach Sauce

Use 1 pound (450g) frozen chopped spinach or 2 pounds (910g) fresh spinach. If you'd like, toss the finished dish with baby spinach or chopped arugula or kale before serving.

Mafaldine with Melted Butternut Squash Sauce

Start with 1½ pounds (680g) butternut squash, peel and seed it, then grate it on the large holes of a box grater. (You should get about 4 packed cups.) Pair with curly or ruffled pasta such as mafaldine, farfalle, rotini, fusilli, or gemelli. Or combine with macaroni and bake.

Bucatini with Melted Corn Sauce

Start with 8 large ears corn (12 ounces/340g each), remove the husks and silks, and grate them on the large holes of a box grater. (You should get about 2 cups.) Add 2 of the cobs to the pot of pasta water while cooking the pasta, to infuse it with corn flavor. Pair with bucatini or other long pasta. Garnish with salted chopped tomatoes, charred corn kernels, and fresh basil, if you'd like.

All-Purpose Crisp Bread Crumb Topping

Bread crumbs have always been used in Italy as a more affordable alternative to cheese for topping pasta dishes. In this recipe from food writer Joy Manning, the crumbs pick up some cheesy notes from the addition of nutritional yeast. I challenge you to find a pasta dish that these morsels do not improve. Crucially, they provide that appealing browned appearance that is so often missing in such vegan casseroles as Lasagna (page 263), Eggplant Rollatini (page 260), and Cashew Mac & Cheese (page 230). Remember to add them just before serving, because they'll lose their trademark crispness sitting on top of food in the refrigerator. You can halve the recipe for small households, but once you try them, you'll want to have more on hand.

Makes ¾ cup

Time: Weekday

Storage: Refrigerate in an airtight container for up to 2 weeks.

- ¼ cup (60ml) olive oil
- ¾ cup (60g) panko bread crumbs
- 2 tablespoons nutritional yeast
- ¼ teaspoon fine sea salt
- ⅛ teaspoon garlic powder

IN A SKILLET, HEAT the olive oil over medium heat until it shimmers. Add the panko, nutritional yeast, salt, and garlic powder. Cook, stirring every minute or so, until the crumbs are evenly browned and smell toasted, 5 to 8 minutes. (You'll want to stir them more often toward the end; the browning happens fast and the crumbs can burn easily.)

Immediately transfer to a plate to stop cooking and let cool completely before using or storing.

Fresh "Egg" Pasta

Back when she was an omnivore, recipe developer Joy Manning knew only one way to make fresh pasta: You break an egg or drop a bunch of egg yolks into a well in a hill of flour, then knead. As she began exploring a plant-based version, she started by trying to replace the egg. Silken tofu, aquafaba, a soy milk/flax slurry, and store-bought liquid egg replacer all fell short. Eventually, she recruited an expert: chef Rodger Holst, co-owner of Miss Rachel's Pantry, a vegan restaurant and catering company in Philadelphia. Holst taught her to break down the substitutions: Replace the protein in the egg by using a high-protein flour (semolina instead of all-purpose or tipo "00"), and replace the egg's fat with olive oil. The last secret ingredient is elbow grease. You knead this dough by hand for an extended period to develop the gluten structure that gives the noodles their firm bite. I know some of you might wonder if you can use the dough hook on your stand mixture. Sadly, it doesn't work well. Turn on a podcast, zone out, and consider it your upper-body workout for the day.

Joy has used this technique to make all manner of pasta shapes, including strands, tubes, twists, bow ties, orecchiette, lasagna, tortellini, and ravioli.

Makes 1 pound dough (4 servings)

Time: Weekend

Storage: Tightly wrap the dough in plastic wrap and freeze it for up to 3 months; thaw before rolling out, cutting, and cooking. (Refrigeration for more than a couple of hours is not recommended.)

2 cups (320g) semolina flour

½ cup (120ml) water, plus more as needed

2 teaspoons olive oil

½ teaspoon fine sea salt

⅛ teaspoon ground turmeric (optional; for color)

ADD THE SEMOLINA FLOUR to a bowl, make a well in the center, and pour in the ½ cup (120ml) water, olive oil, salt, and turmeric (if using). Stir with a fork until it begins to come together into a rough mass of dough. Use your hands to knead it a bit in the bowl to form a crumbly, stiff ball of dough that hangs together.

Add water 1 teaspoon at a time (or even use a spray bottle full of water to mist the dough) until the dough just comes together. You want to add as little water as possible to achieve a stiff, low-hydration dough.

Cut the dough in half; it's easier to knead half at a time. Cover one half with a damp kitchen towel and knead the remaining half for about 8 minutes, until it feels elastic and a bit smoother under your palm and it's holding together well. If it seems to be sticking to your work surface, sprinkle it with a little semolina flour. (This means you added a little too much water, but it will still be okay.) The dough will remain a bit rough textured even after lots of kneading—that's okay, too. Press the dough into a disk and wrap it tightly in compostable plastic wrap. Repeat with the other half of the dough and let both halves rest in the refrigerator for at least 45 minutes and up to 2 hours. (Any longer than that and the dough relaxes too much.)

Now the dough is ready to use (or freeze for long-term storage). Keep one half of the dough covered with the plastic wrap while you shape the other half. Use a rolling pin to flatten the dough into a rectangle thin enough to feed through your pasta machine on the thickest setting. Sprinkle it with a little semolina flour to keep it from sticking when you cut it, then roll it through the pasta machine on each progressively thinner setting until you reach the desired thickness for what you want to do with it.

Unfortunately, pasta machine settings are not standard. For filled pasta shapes, roll it to one of the thinnest settings. For noodles, such as hand-cut pappardelle, you'll want it thicker, somewhere in the middle of the settings.

Whether you're making sheets, noodles, or other shapes, cook the pasta in a large pot of salted water for 3 to 6 minutes (taste for doneness or check online for cooking time guidance on a specific shape).

Rasta Pasta

Bold, fiery, thick, and creamy, this pasta—great served hot or cold—offers a taste of the beauty of cultural syncretism. In Jamaican immigrant communities from New York to London, Rasta Pasta is a treasured tradition, favored for the way two seemingly disparate worlds—Italy and Jamaica—come together in one bright and unfussy pot. It's so beloved in Jamaica, the esteemed Evita's Italian Restaurant devoted an entire menu to the dish's many variants, including a signature the restaurant dubs Reggae-toni. This version turns the typically dairy-heavy dish plant-based with the use of coconut milk, itself a Caribbean staple, keeping Rasta Pasta firmly in touch with its roots.

Makes 4 servings

Time: Weekday

Storage: Refrigerate for up to 3 days.

Fine sea salt

12 ounces (340g) penne pasta

3 tablespoons unrefined coconut oil

½ cup (60g) chopped red onion

5 garlic cloves, finely grated or pressed

1 teaspoon chopped Scotch bonnet or habanero pepper

1 teaspoon grated lime zest

1 tablespoon chopped fresh thyme

3 tablespoons Jerk Spice (page 41)

4 bell peppers (1½ pounds/680g), preferably a mix of red, green, yellow, and orange, thinly sliced

1 (13.5-ounce/400ml) can full-fat coconut milk

3 scallions, thinly sliced

BRING A LARGE POT of salted water to a boil. Add the penne and cook it 2 minutes shy of al dente according to the package directions. Reserving ½ cup (120ml) of the pasta water, drain the pasta.

Meanwhile, in a large sauté pan, heat the coconut oil over medium-high heat until it melts and starts to shimmer. Add the onion and garlic and sauté until the onion has lost some of its bright purple hue, 1 to 2 minutes. Stir in the Scotch bonnet, lime zest, thyme, jerk spice, and ½ teaspoon salt and cook, stirring, just until fragrant, a few seconds. Add all the bell peppers and cook, stirring, until they are well coated in the aromatics, about 1 minute. Stir in the coconut milk and bring to a boil. Reduce the heat to medium so the liquid is gently simmering, cover, and cook for 3 minutes to meld the flavors.

Add the cooked pasta to the sauce, reduce the heat to low, and gently toss to combine. If the sauce seems too thick, stir in some of the pasta water, ¼ cup (60ml) at a time, to thin it out. Taste and season with more salt as needed.

Divide among serving bowls, top with the scallions, and serve warm. Alternatively, let come to room temperature and refrigerate for a few hours before garnishing to serve as a pasta salad.

Tortellini in Charred Onion & Carrot Brodo

Charring onions and carrots gives such flavorful depth to a broth, it's good enough to sip. Leaving the skins on the onions helps add color, too. For this take on the classic Italian tortellini en brodo, seek out excellent vegan tortellini or make your own Ricotta Tortellini (page 246). This makes a beautifully simple, restorative, light meal as is, but it wouldn't be out of place to think about adding asparagus spears, cubed summer squash, or sliced mushrooms to the final broth.

Makes 4 servings

Time: Weekday

Storage: Refrigerate the tortellini and broth separately for up to 5 days or freeze for up to 3 months.

  2 tablespoons olive oil

  2 large yellow onions (10 ounces/285g each), unpeeled, root end trimmed, cut into eighths

  2 large carrots (4 ounces/115g each), scrubbed, trimmed, and cut into 1-inch (2.5cm) chunks

  4 garlic cloves, unpeeled

  6 cups (1.4L) water

  Fine sea salt

  2 (9-ounce/255g) packages store-bought vegan tortellini, such as Kite Hill, or 1 recipe Ricotta Tortellini (page 246)

  Freshly ground black pepper, for serving (optional)

  Calabrian chile oil or other chile oil, for serving (optional)

  Parsley or cilantro leaves, for garnish

IN A DUTCH OVEN or soup pot, heat the oil over medium-high heat until it shimmers. (Turn the vent on if you have one.) Add the onions, cut-side down, along with the carrots and garlic and cook undisturbed until blackened in spots, about 3 minutes.

Add the water, bring to a boil, reduce the heat to medium-low, cover, and cook until the carrots are soft, about 40 minutes.

Pour the broth through a sieve into a bowl (compost the solids). Rinse the pot, return the broth to the pot, and stir in 2 teaspoons salt. Taste and season with more salt as needed. Turn the heat to medium-low and cover to keep warm.

Bring a large pot of salted water to a boil. Add the tortellini and cook according to the package directions or following the instructions for Ricotta Tortellini (page 246) until tender. Drain.

Divide the tortellini among shallow serving bowls and pour the broth over them. Grind pepper over each bowl, drizzle with some chile oil (if using), and garnish with parsley or cilantro. Serve hot.

COOK'S NOTE: If you'd like, you can cook the tortellini in the broth instead of separately, but it will turn the broth a little cloudy.

Ricotta Tortellini

Here's where some of your previous efforts can pay off: You turn Fresh "Egg" Pasta (page 240) into tortellini by cutting and stuffing it with a simple mixture based on Fluffy Pumpkin Seed Ricotta (page 31) and Umami-Packed Cashew Parm (page 27). If you don't have all those at the ready, never fear: You can substitute store-bought square wonton wrappers, vegan ricotta, and vegan Parmesan. Serve these with your favorite sauce, such as Pesto How You Like It (page 53) or a simple marinara, or, for a particularly elegant dish, use for Tortellini in Charred Onion & Carrot Brodo (page 244).

Makes about 36 tortellini (4 to 6 servings)

Time: Weekend

Storage: Refrigerate for up to 3 days. Freeze formed but uncooked tortellini on sheet pans until firm, then transfer to zip-top bags and freeze for up to 3 months. Cook directly from frozen, adding 1 to 2 minutes to the cooking time.

1 cup (225g) Fluffy Pumpkin Seed Ricotta (page 31) or store-bought vegan ricotta

¼ cup (30g) Umami-Packed Cashew Parm (page 27), nutritional yeast, or store-bought vegan Parmesan

2 tablespoons finely chopped fresh flat-leaf parsley

Fine sea salt

8 ounces (225g) Fresh "Egg" Pasta (page 240)

All-purpose flour, for dusting

IN A BOWL, STIR together the ricotta, cashew Parm, parsley, and ¼ teaspoon salt. Taste and season with more salt as needed.

Divide the pasta dough into 4 equal pieces. Work with one piece at a time and use a damp kitchen towel to keep the other three pieces covered. Use a pasta machine to roll one piece into progressively thinner sheets until it is paper thin. Repeat with the remaining pieces, keeping the rolled and unrolled dough covered with the towel as you work.

Dust a large sheet pan lightly with flour. Have a small bowl of water ready for moistening the dough as needed and a shallow bowl of flour ready for dusting the tortellini as you finish shaping them.

Cut each sheet into 3-inch (7.5cm) squares.

To make each tortellini, rotate a dough square so that it's oriented like a diamond. Put 1 heaping teaspoon of ricotta filling into the middle of the diamond, then fold up the bottom point to the top to create a triangle. Use your fingers to press out any extra air around the filling, then fold the bottom straight edge up and just over the filling and then fold it up and over one more time. Dip a finger in the water and moisten the two outer points, then bring one around the other to form a ring and press together to seal. Transfer the tortellini to the bowl of flour as you work. Repeat with the remaining squares.

Gently toss and dust the shaped tortellini with flour and set them on the sheet pan.

To cook, bring a large pot of salted water to a boil. Reduce the heat so the boil is gentle, not rolling. Working in batches, use a slotted spoon to lower as many tortellini as will fit without overcrowding into the water and cook until they float, about 5 minutes. Transfer to serving dishes, add your favorite sauce and any garnishes, and serve warm.

Wild Mushroom Ragu with Mock Pappardelle

Mushrooms take center stage in this hearty, saucy ragu. Choose your favorite varieties, using at least two different fresh ones, but don't omit the dried wild mushrooms, which add intensity of flavor and contribute their savory soaking liquid.

The cut curly lasagna noodles make a good stand-in for pappardelle, which typically contain eggs, a tip we picked up from Isa Chandra Moskowitz's terrific book *I Can Cook Vegan*. When you're shopping, look for noodles extruded with a brass die (such as those labeled "trafila in bronzo" or the like in Italian and "bronze cut" or "bronze die cut" in English); it leaves a rough texture that sauce clings to well. Of course, you can make your own vegan pappardelle from Fresh "Egg" Pasta (page 240). This mushroom ragu is also very much at home spooned over polenta or baked white or sweet potatoes.

Makes 4 to 6 servings

Time: Weekday

Storage: The ragu can be refrigerated for up to 3 days or frozen for up to 1 month before you make the pasta. Leftovers of the finished dish can be refrigerated for up to 3 days.

1 cup (240ml) boiling water

½ ounce (14g) dried wild mushrooms, such as porcini or chanterelle

2 tablespoons (28g) Soft Spreadable Butter (page 21) or unsalted vegan butter

1 medium yellow or white onion, chopped (1½ cups/225g)

1 carrot, chopped (½ cup/60g)

1 stalk celery, chopped (¼ cup/28g)

Fine sea salt

¼ teaspoon freshly ground black pepper, plus more to taste

2 sprigs fresh thyme

8 ounces (225g) oyster mushrooms, chopped

8 ounces (225g) cremini mushrooms, chopped

4 ounces (115g) fresh shiitake mushrooms, stems composted (or saved for stock), caps chopped

2 tablespoons water

2 tablespoons olive oil

1 garlic clove, finely grated or pressed

1 tablespoon tomato paste

½ cup (120ml) dry sherry or red or white wine

2 tablespoons all-purpose flour

1 cup (240ml) Vegetable Scrap Stock (page 36) or broth made from Veg Bouillon (page 36) or store-bought vegan no-chicken concentrate

12 ounces (340g) wavy lasagna noodles

½ cup (25g) chopped parsley

IN A SMALL HEATPROOF bowl, pour the boiling water over the dried mushrooms and let stand for 10 minutes. Reserving the soaking liquid, drain and chop the soaked mushrooms.

In a large skillet, melt the vegan butter over medium heat. Add the onion, carrot, celery, ¾ teaspoon salt, and the pepper and cook until softened, about 10 minutes. Add the rehydrated dried mushrooms, the thyme, all the fresh mushrooms, and the water. Cover and cook until the fresh mushrooms start to soften and exude their liquid, 5 to 8 minutes. Uncover, increase the heat to medium-high, add the olive oil, and cook until the mushrooms brown and start to caramelize, 12 to 15 minutes.

Meanwhile, bring a large pot of salted water to a boil.

While the water is coming to a boil, add the garlic to the skillet of mushrooms and cook until fragrant, about 30 seconds. Add the tomato paste and cook until it slightly darkens, about 1 minute. Add the sherry, bring to a simmer, and cook, scraping the bottom of the skillet with a wooden spoon to pick up any browned bits, until the sherry has mostly evaporated, 5 to 6 minutes.

Stir in the flour. Add the reserved mushroom soaking liquid and the vegetable stock. Bring to a simmer and cook, uncovered, until thickened, 10 to 15 minutes.

While the ragu simmers, cook the lasagna noodles. For a rustic effect, break them while dry into rough quarters. For neater noodles, boil until 2 minutes shy of the package directions and remove the sheets with tongs to a cutting board. Use a pizza cutter or long knife to cut each sheet lengthwise into 4 pieces. Return the noodles to the boiling water to finish cooking.

When the noodles are done, reserve at least ½ cup (120ml) pasta water and drain the noodles.

Taste the ragu and season with more salt and pepper as needed. (Fish out and compost the thyme stems.) Transfer the noodles to the skillet of ragu and stir to coat, adding pasta water ¼ cup (60ml) at a time to loosen the ragu if desired.

Divide among serving bowls, top with the parsley, and serve warm.

Penne with Eggplant Vodka Sauce

There's nothing like the creamy spiciness of vodka sauce, perfectly warming on a chilly winter evening. Here, pureed eggplant provides that luscious silky quality.

Makes 6 servings

Time: Weekday

Storage: Refrigerate for up to 3 days.

Fine sea salt

2 tablespoons olive oil

1 medium yellow onion (6½ ounces/185g), chopped

4 garlic cloves, chopped

1 small or ½ medium Italian globe eggplant (10 ounces/285g), unpeeled and cubed (about 3 cups)

1 pound (450g) penne pasta

½ cup (120ml) vodka

1 (28-ounce/794g) can crushed tomatoes

2 tablespoons oil-packed sun-dried tomatoes (about 6 halves), chopped, plus 1 tablespoon of their oil

1 teaspoon dried oregano

1 teaspoon red pepper flakes

½ teaspoon freshly ground black pepper, plus more to taste

BRING A LARGE POT of salted water to a boil.

Meanwhile, in a large skillet, heat the oil over medium heat until it shimmers. Add the onion and sauté until softened and translucent, about 5 minutes. Add the garlic and sauté for 2 minutes. Add the eggplant, stirring to coat, then sprinkle with 1 teaspoon salt. Reduce the heat to medium-low and cook until very soft, 15 to 20 minutes.

Add the pasta to the boiling water and cook to al dente according to the package directions. Reserving 1 cup (240ml) of pasta water, drain the pasta and return it to the pot, covering to keep warm.

Stir the vodka into the eggplant mixture, reduce the heat to low, and cook until the vodka reduces and starts to evaporate, about 3 minutes. Stir in the crushed tomatoes, sun-dried tomatoes and their oil, oregano, pepper flakes, and black pepper. Remove from the heat, and using an immersion blender to puree until smooth, add some of the reserved pasta cooking water, 1 tablespoon at a time, to loosen if needed. (Alternatively, working in batches if needed, transfer the soup to a blender, being careful not to fill it more than halfway, remove the center cap from the blender lid, cover it with a clean kitchen towel, and puree until smooth.) Taste and season with more salt and pepper as needed.

Pour the sauce into the pot with the pasta and stir to coat it thoroughly. Serve warm.

Cold Chewy Korean Noodles

Jjolmyeon literally translates from Korean as "chewy noodles," a reference to the slight bite that provides for an altogether unique mouthfeel in this dish. This recipe originated in Incheon—a popular destination for expats—in the 1970s, when a restaurant wanted to find something to do with a batch of naengmyeon noodles (typically as skinny as angel hair pasta) that were mistakenly made too large by the factory. A new noodle and dish were born! While these can be served with broth or any kind of sauce, this version is the most popular way to eat jjolmyeon—with a spicy sauce made of gochujang. Crunchy vegetables enhance texture and round out the refreshing flavors of this cold noodle dish. Look for the noodles in the freezer section of well-stocked Asian supermarkets.

Makes 4 servings

Time: Weekday

Storage: Not recommended for the finished dish, but the sauce can be refrigerated for up to 1 week or frozen for up to 3 months before using in this dish.

12 ounces (340g) jjolmyeon, thawed

4 tablespoons gochujang (Korean chile paste)

2 tablespoons soy sauce

2 tablespoons unseasoned rice vinegar

¼ cup (60ml) brown rice syrup

4 tablespoons Chunky Garlic Paste (page 58)

¼ cup (60ml) water

8 ounces (225g) asparagus or thin green beans, trimmed and cut into 2-inch (5cm) pieces

1 cup (95g) shredded red cabbage

1 cup (90g) mung bean sprouts

1 cup (120g) julienned cucumber

1 cup (130g) julienned carrot

BRING A POT OF water to a boil. Add the noodles and cook according to the package directions.

Meanwhile, in a bowl, whisk together the gochujang, soy sauce, rice vinegar, brown rice syrup, garlic paste, and water.

When the noodles are done, scoop them out with a sieve (leaving the water in the pot), rinse them under cold water, and divide them among four serving bowls.

Return the pot to the heat, bring the water back to a boil, and use it to blanch the asparagus pieces until crisp-tender, 2 to 3 minutes. Pour into a sieve and run cold water over them.

Divide the sauce among the noodles. Top with the asparagus, cabbage, bean sprouts, cucumber, and carrot and serve immediately.

Soba Noodles with Cabbage & Fried Almonds

Refreshing and long-lasting, this noodle salad is perfect for a picnic or summer meal-planning. Equal parts slaw and starch, it's even tastier the next day. You massage thinly sliced cabbage with salt so it slackens, then toss it with nutty soba and a toasty sauce made of tahini, soy sauce, and rice vinegar. The salad's real treat, however, is fried almonds—they're crunchy and rich, and the oil they fry in forms the foundation of the dressing. Starting the nuts in cold oil rather than hot means they'll cook slowly and evenly and reduces the risk of burning. Top this with seared tofu planks or Popcorn Tempeh (page 70) for a protein boost.

Makes 4 servings

Time: Weekday

Storage: Refrigerate for up to 3 days.

Fine sea salt
1 small head green cabbage (1½ pounds/680g), quartered, cored, and thinly sliced
4 scallions, thinly sliced
8 ounces (225g) soba noodles
4 teaspoons toasted sesame oil
½ cup (50g) sliced almonds
¼ cup (60ml) sunflower or another neutral oil
¼ cup (60ml) tahini
3 tablespoons soy sauce
1 tablespoon rice vinegar, preferably unseasoned
1 teaspoon maple syrup
1 tablespoon finely grated fresh ginger
1 tablespoon water
½ cup (20g) chopped fresh cilantro leaves and tender stems

BRING A LARGE POT of salted water to a boil.

Meanwhile, in a large bowl, toss the cabbage with ½ teaspoon salt. Use your hands to aggressively massage it until it slackens, softens, shrinks, and starts to look shiny and wet, 1 to 2 minutes. Add the scallions and toss to combine.

Add the soba to the boiling water and cook according to the package directions. Drain well, rinse under cold water, using your hand to agitate the noodles, then drain well again. Toss with 2 teaspoons of the toasted sesame oil (to prevent the noodles from clumping).

In a medium skillet, combine the almonds and sunflower oil. Set the skillet over medium-high heat and cook, stirring frequently, until the nuts start to foam and turn golden-brown, 6 to 9 minutes. Using a slotted spoon, transfer the fried almonds to the bowl of cabbage.

Pour the oil remaining in the skillet into a small bowl or heatproof glass measuring cup. Add the tahini, soy sauce, rice vinegar, maple syrup, ginger, water, and remaining 2 teaspoons sesame oil. Whisk to combine. Taste and season with salt as needed. Remember that the dressing should be assertive, as it's going to dress a lot of noodles and cabbage.

Add the soba and dressing to the cabbage mixture and toss to thoroughly combine. Taste and season with more salt as needed. Sprinkle with the cilantro and serve.

8

CASSEROLES

The. Ultimate. Comfort. Food. That's what casseroles—bubbling and hot, creamy and cheesy—are, and in the plant-based kitchen it's easy to achieve those qualities. In some cases, you'll make use of some of the cheeses, creams, and butter in the Building Blocks chapter (page 15), and in others you'll see that richness can come from other sources, too, such as an easy béchamel based on cauliflower (see Cauliflower Cashew Béchamel, page 263) or eggplant (see Eggplant & Artichoke Pastitsio, page 264).

Baked Stuffed Shells

This is the dish food writer Joy Manning takes to Christmas dinner at her mother's house, because it fits in with the rest of her family's food, and no one complains about it being vegan because they can't tell the difference. The shells are filled with a wonderfully savory, lightly tangy concoction based on raw cashews. You can assemble it a day or two in advance and bake it right before serving. Be sure to find *jumbo* shells for this, not those labeled "large."

Makes 4 to 6 servings

Time: Weekend

Storage: Refrigerate for up to 3 days.

Fine sea salt

6 ounces (170g) jumbo pasta shells

Scant 1½ cups (190g) chopped canned or jarred artichoke hearts (packed in oil or water), drained

2 cups (260g) raw cashews (see Note), soaked overnight, drained, and rinsed

½ cup (120ml) plus 1 tablespoon Nut Milk (page 17), Oat Milk (page 17), Soy Milk (page 75), or store-bought plant-based milk

1½ tablespoons white wine vinegar

1½ tablespoons nutritional yeast

1 garlic clove, peeled but left whole

½ teaspoon onion powder

¾ teaspoon grated lemon zest (from ½ lemon)

3 cups (700ml) homemade or store-bought marinara sauce

3 tablespoons finely chopped fresh parsley

BRING A LARGE POT of salted water to a boil. Add the pasta and cook for 2 minutes shy of al dente according to the package directions. Drain, then spread onto a sheet pan until cool enough to handle.

Preheat the oven to 350°F (180°C).

Use your hands to squeeze the extra liquid out of the artichoke hearts. Transfer to a food processor. Add the cashews, milk, vinegar, nutritional yeast, garlic, onion powder, lemon zest, and ¾ teaspoon salt. Puree until completely smooth, scraping down the sides of the bowl if needed. Add the artichoke hearts and pulse until incorporated, about 5 pulses. You should have about 3 cups filling. Taste and season with more salt if needed.

Pour half the marinara sauce in the bottom of a 9 × 13-inch (23cm × 33cm) baking dish with a cover. Stuff each shell with about 2 tablespoons of the cashew ricotta mixture. (If you have a pastry bag, it can make the job easier. If not, use a small spoon.) Place the stuffed shells on top of the sauce. Pour the rest of the sauce into the baking dish, leaving some of the cashew ricotta mixture exposed.

Cover and bake until hot and bubbling and the pasta is completely cooked, about 30 minutes. Let sit for a few minutes, then top with chopped parsley and serve warm.

COOK'S NOTE: Buy raw (unroasted, unsalted) cashews online in bulk and store them in the freezer, which preserves the freshness so essential for getting this and other mixtures to be luscious and creamy.

Baked Ziti

Cheesy baked pasta has got to be the food that's closest to a big hug, particularly when it's chilly out (or let's be honest, any time of the year). This version uses homemade pumpkin seed ricotta, vegan melty cheese, and cashew Parm, but if you don't have those on hand, store-bought versions of those baked-pasta staples will help you get this on the table in no time. Just be prepared for return hugs. Note that the vegan cheese melts better if it's under the sauce, not exposed to the air.

Makes 6 servings

Time: Weekend

Storage: Refrigerate for up to 5 days or freeze for up to 3 months.

2 tablespoons olive oil

1 large onion (10 ounces/283g), chopped

4 garlic cloves, chopped

1 tablespoon dried oregano

Fine sea salt

¼ to ½ teaspoon red pepper flakes, to taste

2 (28-ounce/794g) cans crushed tomatoes

1 pound (450g) dried ziti or other tubular pasta

1 pound (450g) Fluffy Pumpkin Seed Ricotta (page 31) or store-bought vegan ricotta

8 ounces (225g) Basic Melty Cheese (page 25) or store-bought vegan mozzarella, coarsely grated or cut into ½-inch (1.3cm) pieces

½ cup (55g) Umami-Packed Cashew Parm (page 27) or grated store-bought vegan Parmesan, plus more for topping

IN A LARGE SKILLET, heat the oil over medium heat until it shimmers. Add the onion, garlic, oregano, and 1 teaspoon salt and cook until the vegetables soften, about 4 minutes. Sprinkle in the pepper flakes, stir, and cook them for just a few seconds, until fragrant. Add the tomatoes and bring the mixture to a boil.

Reduce the heat so that the sauce is at a vigorous simmer but isn't rapidly boiling. (Use a splatter screen if you have one.) Cook until the sauce has thickened and reduced slightly and the flavors have melded, 20 to 30 minutes. Taste and season with more salt as needed.

While the sauce is cooking, bring a large pot of salted water to a boil. Add the ziti and cook for 2 minutes shy of al dente according to the package directions. Drain in a colander and return to the empty pot.

Preheat the oven to 400°F (200°C).

When the sauce is ready, set a 9 × 13-inch (23cm × 33cm) baking dish on a large sheet pan and ladle enough sauce into the baking dish to just coat the bottom. Stir one-third of the remaining sauce into the pasta in the pot. Stir in one-third of the ricotta into the pasta. Spoon half the pasta mixture into the baking dish, spreading it evenly, and top with half of the melty cheese. Dollop with half the remaining ricotta. Pour half the remaining sauce evenly over the top. Repeat with the remaining pasta mixture, melty cheese, and ricotta, ending with the remaining sauce to cover. Sprinkle with the cashew Parm.

Bake until the sauce is bubbling and the cashew Parm is golden, 25 to 30 minutes. Remove from the oven and let cool for 10 to 15 minutes before serving hot.

Musaca de Cartofi (Potato Moussaka)

Most people are familiar with moussaka as a Greek dish made with sliced eggplant, but it can also be found as a potato version in Romania. This version was inspired by a recipe in Irina Georgescu's cookbook *Carpathia: Food from the Heart of Romania*, where the rich flavor of sweet paprika gives Eastern European flair to this comforting casserole. This is one of those dishes that's even better the next day, so if you have the time and patience to make it ahead of time, you'll be glad you did.

Makes 4 to 6 servings

Time: Weekend

Storage: Refrigerate for up to 3 days.

FILLING

1 tablespoon sunflower or other neutral oil

2 medium onions (1 pound/450g total), finely diced

1 carrot (3 ounces/85g), finely diced

1 (14-ounce/397g) block extra-firm tofu, drained and crumbled

8 ounces (225g) cremini mushrooms, trimmed and chopped

1 tablespoon sweet paprika

1 teaspoon fine sea salt

1 teaspoon freshly ground black pepper

1 (14.5-ounce/411g) can diced tomatoes

1 (10.75-ounce/305g) can tomato puree

POTATOES AND ASSEMBLY

2 pounds (910g) russet potatoes, peeled and cut into ⅛-inch (3mm) slices

1 teaspoon sunflower or other neutral oil, for the baking dish

3½ ounces (100g) Basic Melty Cheese (page 25) vegan cheddar cheese shreds

⅔ cup (142g) Creamy Coconut Yogurt (page 23) or store-bought vegan yogurt, preferably Greek-style

2 tablespoons (28g) Soft Spreadable Butter (page 21) or store-bought unsalted vegan butter, diced

Fine sea salt and freshly ground black pepper

MAKE THE FILLING: In a 12-inch (30cm) skillet, heat the oil over medium heat until it shimmers. Add the onions and carrot and sauté until they just begin to soften, 3 to 4 minutes. Stir in the tofu, mushrooms, paprika, salt, and pepper and cook until the tofu starts to turn light golden on the edges, about 5 minutes. Add the diced tomatoes and tomato puree, reduce the heat to medium-low, and simmer, stirring occasionally, until reduced and thickened, about 25 minutes.

Meanwhile, cook the potatoes: In a large soup pot, bring about 6 cups (1.4L) water to a boil. Add the potatoes and cook until just softened, about 5 minutes. Drain thoroughly and let cool for a few minutes.

Preheat the oven to 350°F (180°C). Lightly oil a 9 ×13-inch (23cm × 33cm) baking dish.

To assemble the dish: In a small bowl, mix the cheese and the yogurt. Arrange one-third of the potatoes in the baking dish, overlapping the slices slightly. Scatter 1 tablespoon of the diced plant butter on top and sprinkle with a little salt and pepper, then spread half the filling evenly across the top. Repeat with another layer of potatoes, the remaining diced butter, more salt and pepper, and the rest of the filling. Add a final layer of the potatoes, then spread the yogurt mixture evenly across the top.

Bake until the top begins to bubble, 30 to 35 minutes. Let sit for a few minutes and serve hot.

Cheesy Butternut Squash & Potato Bake

By balancing sweet squash against a deeply savory sauce, you get a satisfying main dish that makes an impressive dinner alongside a simply dressed salad, braised greens, or a pot of beans. Once you learn how to make the dairy-free béchamel, use it in mac and cheese or a baked cauliflower casserole. If you don't want or are sensitive to chile heat, either reduce or omit the cayenne. And be sure to use a plain nondairy milk you like the taste of: Its flavor will be apparent. You can bake this in a casserole dish with at least 3-quart (3L) capacity, a 9-inch (23cm) square baking dish, or a large ovenproof skillet; you might have to adjust your layers depending on the dish's dimensions.

Makes 6 to 8 servings

Time: Weekend

Storage: Refrigerate for up to 3 days or freeze for up to 3 months.

½ small butternut squash (14 ounces/396g), peeled, seeded, and cut into slices ¼ inch (6mm) or thinner

4 medium Yukon Gold potatoes (1½ pounds/680g total), scrubbed and thinly sliced

1¼ teaspoons fine sea salt, plus more to taste

½ teaspoon freshly ground black pepper, plus more to taste

4 tablespoons olive oil

¼ red onion or 1 large shallot (3 ounces/85g), chopped

4 garlic cloves, finely grated or pressed

¼ cup (31g) all-purpose flour

2½ cups (590ml) Nut Milk (page 17), Oat Milk (page 17), Soy Milk (page 75), or store-bought plant-based milk

½ cup (120ml) water

1½ tablespoons yellow or red/brown miso

¼ cup (20g) nutritional yeast

1 tablespoon fresh lemon juice, plus lemon wedges for serving

1 tablespoon fresh thyme leaves, plus more for garnish

½ teaspoon cayenne pepper

½ cup (40g) panko bread crumbs

COOK'S NOTE: Feel free to cube and roast the remaining butternut squash to put on grain bowls, salads, in tacos, or for Smoky Squash & Tahini Dip (page 119) or Butternut Squash Rice Porridge (page 107).

PREHEAT THE OVEN TO 350°F (180°C).

In a large bowl, toss the squash and potatoes with ¾ teaspoon of the salt and ¼ teaspoon of the pepper.

In a medium saucepan, heat 3 tablespoons of the olive oil over medium-high heat until it shimmers. (You can also do this directly in the dish you'll be baking in, if it's flameproof.) Add the onion and garlic and cook, stirring frequently, until soft and starting to brown, 2 to 3 minutes.

Reduce the heat to medium, add the flour, and whisk until it's starting to turn golden, about 30 seconds. Slowly whisk in the milk and water. Increase the heat to medium-high and bring to a simmer, stirring frequently, until the sauce is thick enough to coat the back of a spoon, 4 to 5 minutes. Remove from the heat.

In a small bowl, whisk the miso with ¼ cup (60ml) of the hot sauce until smooth, then transfer it back to the saucepan and stir to combine. Stir in the nutritional yeast, lemon juice, thyme, cayenne, ¼ teaspoon of the salt, and the remaining ¼ teaspoon black pepper. Taste—it should taste aggressive, since the vegetables are so mild—and season with more salt as needed.

Transfer about ½ cup (120ml) sauce to a 3-quart (3L) baking dish (such as an oval casserole), 9-inch (23cm) square pan, or large deep ovenproof skillet. (If you made the sauce in the dish you'll be baking in, pour all but about ½ cup/120ml sauce out into a large measuring cup.)

On top of the sauce, make a single layer of overlapping squash and potatoes (no need to be exacting!). Add ½ cup (120ml) sauce over the top, spreading evenly. Repeat with another layer of vegetables and sauce, continuing until you have used up all the vegetables and ending with ½ cup (120ml) sauce.

Cover with a lid or sheet pan and bake until the sauce is bubbling at the edges, 30 minutes. Uncover and bake until the vegetables are very soft and the sauce is thick and bubbling in the center of the dish, 30 to 40 minutes.

While the dish is baking, in a small bowl, stir together the panko, remaining 1 tablespoon olive oil, and remaining ¼ teaspoon salt.

When the casserole has about 10 minutes remaining, scatter the panko mix over the top. It should brown nicely by the time the sauce is bubbling.

Remove from the oven, scatter with thyme and more black pepper, if desired, and let cool for 10 minutes before serving warm, with lemon wedges.

Eggplant Rollatini

This is the first dinner food writer Joy Manning made the day she learned her cholesterol was high. It was inspired by the things she had on hand and her love for all things red sauce, eggplant, and Italian American. Back then, she wasn't familiar with vegan egg replacers. That first batch of rollatini was good, but adding the egg replacer or flax egg really binds them into cohesive rolls that hold their shape well and have a more pleasing, firmer texture. This is the perfect make-ahead dish because it improves overnight. It also impresses nonvegan diners when you bring it along to share or have people over for dinner. Wait until just before serving to add the bread crumb topping and fresh basil.

Makes 6 to 8 servings

Time: Weekday

Storage: Refrigerate for up to 3 days.

EGGPLANT
6 tablespoons olive oil

¾ teaspoon fine sea salt

2 medium or 3 small eggplants
(2½ pounds/1.1kg total), peeled

FILLING
1 pound (450g) firm tofu, drained

¼ cup (60ml) vegetable oil

2 tablespoons olive oil

2 tablespoons white wine vinegar

1 teaspoon fine sea salt

1 teaspoon freshly ground black pepper

1 tablespoon powdered egg replacer or flaxseed meal

10 ounces (285g) frozen spinach, thawed and squeezed dry

FOR ASSEMBLY
2½ cups (600ml) homemade or store-bought marinara

All-Purpose Crisp Bread Crumb Topping (page 239)

2 tablespoons chopped fresh basil leaves

POSITION TWO RACKS IN the upper and bottom thirds of the oven and preheat to 375°F (190°C). Line two sheet pans with silicone baking mats or compostable parchment paper. Brush each with 1 tablespoon olive oil.

Prepare the eggplant: Slice the eggplant lengthwise into slabs ¼ inch (6mm) thick. (It's better that they be a little too thick than a little too thin.) Arrange the eggplant slices on the two prepared baking sheets (some overlap is okay). Brush the eggplant with the remaining 4 tablespoons olive oil and season with the salt.

Roast the eggplant until soft, 20 to 30 minutes. Let cool.

Meanwhile, make the filling: In a food processor, combine the tofu, vegetable oil, olive oil, vinegar, salt, pepper, and egg replacer. Puree until completely smooth. Add the spinach and pulse until incorporated, 6 to 8 pulses.

Reduce the oven temperature to 350°F (180°C).

To assemble: Lay a slice of eggplant on a cutting board with the short end facing you. Place 1 to 3 tablespoons of filling (the smaller amount if the eggplant you started with are small, the larger amount if they're medium) along the bottom edge of the eggplant slice, then roll it up. Repeat with the remaining eggplant slices and filling.

Pour 1 cup (240ml) sauce into a 9 × 13-inch (23cm × 33cm) baking dish. Place the rollatini next to each other in as many rows as will fit (two if the eggplant you started with are larger, three or four if they're smaller). Top them with another 1½ cups (350ml) sauce. Cover tightly with foil.

Bake until hot all the way through and the sauce is bubbling, about 30 minutes. Let rest for 10 minutes before topping with the bread crumb topping and basil.

Eggplant Brick

Recipe tester Kristen Hartke once gave this recipe to a friend who wanted to use up a lot of eggplant. A few days later, her friend sent her a message: "I don't know whether to curse you or thank you. It was way more labor-intensive than I am used to, so I told my husband this would be the last time he had this. Then we tasted it and loved it—so I guess, along with the eggplant, I'll eat my words!" This is a special-occasion dish. Even though there are very few ingredients, it takes some time to put the components together—and you need to start the day before, because the brick needs to chill overnight before baking. The thin slices of eggplant when layered with the tomato sauce become compressed into one luscious melt-in-your-mouth mélange. Honestly, it's kind of indescribably perfect, and it's one of those dishes that tastes equally delicious hot, cold, or at room temperature, especially when served with salad and bread. You'll be glad you put in the effort.

Makes 4 to 6 servings

Time: Weekend

Storage: Refrigerate for up to 1 week or freeze for up to 3 months.

Olive or vegetable oil, as needed

2 cups (250g) all-purpose flour

1 tablespoon dried oregano

1 tablespoon grated lemon zest

1½ teaspoons fine sea salt, plus more to taste

1 teaspoon freshly ground black pepper

1 teaspoon sweet paprika

½ teaspoon smoked paprika

2 medium Italian (globe) eggplants (about 2½ pounds/550g total), cut crosswise into slices ⅛ inch thick

2 cups (470ml) store-bought marinara sauce or homemade tomato sauce (see Note)

4 tablespoons finely chopped fresh parsley

LIGHTLY OIL A 9 × 5-inch (23cm × 13cm) loaf pan.

In a large shallow bowl or pie plate, whisk together the flour, oregano, lemon zest, 1 teaspoon of the salt, the pepper, sweet paprika, and smoked paprika.

Set a wire rack over a sheet pan next to the stovetop. In a large skillet, heat ¼ cup (60ml) oil over medium heat until it shimmers. Dredge several slices of eggplant in the flour, shaking off the excess. Working in batches to avoid overcrowding, fry on both sides until crisp and browned, 1 to 2 minutes per side. Transfer to the wire rack to drain. Continue with the rest of the eggplant slices, adding olive oil, 1 tablespoon at a time, to the pan as needed. Sprinkle the fried eggplant with the remaining ½ teaspoon salt.

When all the eggplant is fried, taste the marinara sauce and season with more salt as needed.

Place several eggplant slices in the bottom of the loaf pan so that they overlap, then spread with a light layer of tomato sauce. Keep repeating the layers all the way to the top edge of the pan, ending with a final layer of eggplant slices. Reserve the remaining tomato sauce.

Cut a double layer of compostable parchment paper to fit snugly over the top of the brick, pressing it down firmly against the top layer, and refrigerate overnight.

When ready to bake the brick, preheat the oven to 350°F (180°C).

Bake the loaf, covered with the parchment paper, for 30 minutes. Remove the paper and cover the top with a layer of the reserved tomato sauce. Bake until lightly bubbling on top, another 15 minutes.

Remove from the oven and allow to set at room temperature for at least 20 minutes.

Run a table knife or offset spatula around the edges of the brick to loosen it. Invert a plate on top of the loaf pan, flip both of them over, and unmold the brick, then invert it again onto a serving platter, so the tomato sauce is still on top. Drizzle it with a little olive oil and sprinkle it with chopped parsley just before serving.

COOK'S NOTE: Use the really simple tomato sauce that gets made for Lentil-Chickpea Meatballs in Tomato Sauce (page 330).

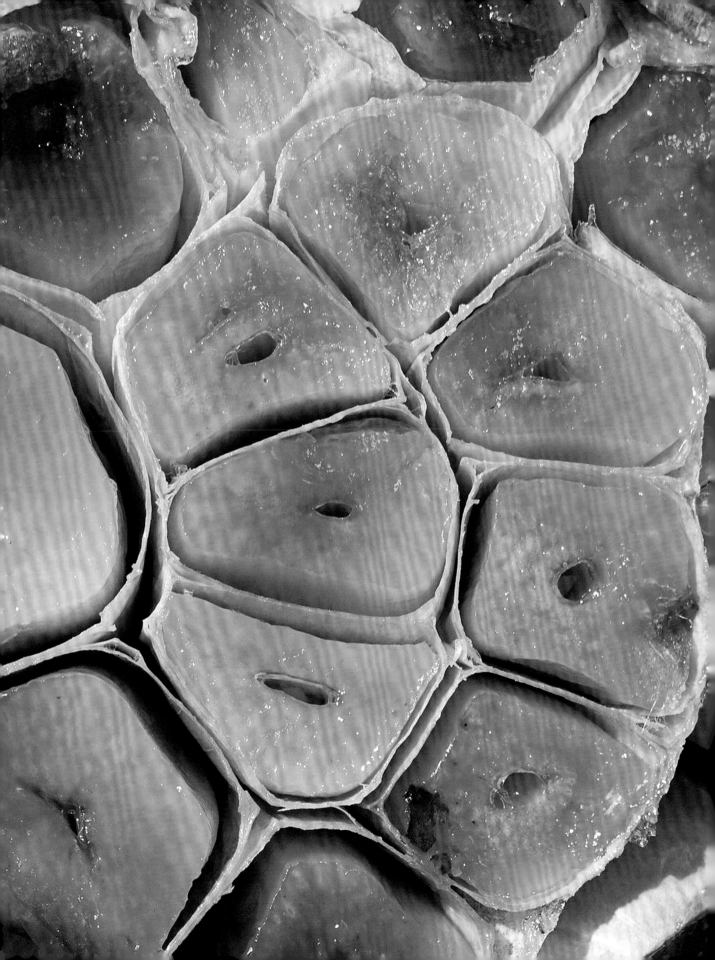

Lasagna with Cauliflower Cashew Béchamel

So much of the love lasagna gets is directed at the top layer of mozzarella, melty and browned. Vegan cheese can struggle to bubble or brown, so here's an alt-lasagna, one that resists comparisons to the iconic Italian American red-sauce cheese bomb. This one has a cauliflower-based béchamel and a cheese-ish filling made from tofu and greens.

This lasagna is more approachable if you make it over 2 or even 3 days. The filling and sauce can be made up to 3 days ahead. Once those components are in hand, it's easy: Assemble, bake, and serve.

The toppings are not optional. The golden-brown bread crumbs and fresh parsley take the baked lasagna's appearance from blah to appetizing. Top this—and many other pasta dishes—with homemade cashew Parm or store-bought vegan Parmesan, if you'd like.

Makes 6 to 8 servings

Time: Project

Storage: Refrigerate for up to 3 days.

CAULIFLOWER CASHEW BÉCHAMEL

1 garlic bulb

2 teaspoons olive oil

½ head cauliflower (14 ounces/400g), trimmed and roughly chopped (about 3 cups)

1½ cups (350ml) Vegetable Scrap Stock (page 36), store-bought vegetable broth, or water

⅔ cup (85g) raw cashews, soaked overnight and drained

2 teaspoons white miso, homemade (page 83) or store-bought

⅛ teaspoon ground nutmeg

½ teaspoon fine sea salt, plus more to taste

⅛ teaspoon garlic powder

TOFU FILLING

1 large bunch Tuscan kale (12 ounces/340g), leaves chopped and stems finely chopped

1 (15-ounce/425g) block firm tofu, drained

¼ cup (60ml) vegetable oil

2 tablespoons olive oil

2 tablespoons white wine vinegar

1 teaspoon fine sea salt, plus more to taste

1 teaspoon freshly ground black pepper

3 tablespoons nutritional yeast

1 tablespoon powdered egg replacer or flaxseed meal

FOR ASSEMBLY AND SERVING

1 pound (450g) oven-ready (no-boil) lasagna noodles

Chopped fresh parsley, for serving

All-Purpose Crisp Bread Crumb Topping (page 239)

Umami-Packed Cashew Parm (page 27) or store-bought grated vegan Parmesan

PREHEAT THE OVEN TO 350°F (180°C).

Make the béchamel: Cut off the bottom end of the garlic to expose the cloves, drizzle with the olive oil, and transfer to a small baking dish with a lid. Roast until the garlic is light brown and soft, about 1 hour.

Meanwhile, bring a pot of water to a boil. Add the cauliflower and cook until very tender, about 10 minutes. Use a slotted spoon to transfer the cauliflower to a blender. Cover the pot (you'll use the water to blanch the kale) and remove from the heat.

When the garlic is done, squeeze the roasted garlic cloves out of the skin into the blender. Add the vegetable broth, cashews, miso, nutmeg, salt, and garlic powder. Blend until completely smooth. Taste and season with more salt as needed.

Make the tofu filling: Return the same pot of water you used for the cauliflower to a boil. Add the kale leaves and stems and cook until tender, about 5 minutes. Drain, transfer the kale to a clean kitchen towel, and squeeze all the extra water out of it.

In a food processor, combine the tofu, vegetable oil, olive oil, vinegar, salt, black pepper, nutritional yeast, and egg replacer. Puree until smooth. Add the kale and pulse until it is evenly mixed in, 5 to 8 pulses. Taste and season with more salt as needed.

To assemble the lasagna: Cover the bottom of a covered 9 × 13-inch (23cm × 33cm) baking dish with about ¾ cup (180ml) of the béchamel. Top with a layer of lasagna noodles; 3 should fit. Top the noodles with about one-quarter (1 cup) of the filling. Place another layer of noodles over the filling, press them down lightly, and top with another ¾ cup (180ml) béchamel and another one-quarter of the filling. Repeat twice more, alternating noodles with ¾ cup (180ml) béchamel and one-quarter of the filling each time. Top with the final layer of noodles and the remaining ½ cup (120ml) béchamel.

Cover and bake until piping hot in the center, about 40 minutes. Let stand for 15 minutes, then top with the parsley, bread crumb topping, and vegan Parmesan. Slice and serve hot.

Eggplant & Artichoke Pastitsio

Pastitsio is often referred to as "Greek lasagna," which makes sense: It's layers of pasta and a tomato-based filling topped off with a creamy béchamel. This rendition calls on a variety of flavors—some traditional, some not—to create richness. An artichoke sauce adds a cheesy umami to the pasta base, while pureed eggplant in the béchamel offers a savory contrast.

Makes 6 servings

Time: Weekend

Storage: Refrigerate for up to 1 week or freeze for up to 3 months.

1 large Italian (globe) eggplant
(about 2 pounds/910g)

PASTA WITH ARTICHOKE SAUCE
Fine sea salt

1 pound (450g) macaroni or ziti

¾ cup (170g) canned, jarred, or frozen artichoke hearts (drained if canned/jarred, thawed if frozen)

½ cup (120ml) olive oil

MUSHROOM-LENTIL FILLING
1 tablespoon olive oil

1 small onion (5½ ounces/156g), diced

3 garlic cloves, finely grated or pressed

1 teaspoon ground cinnamon

1 teaspoon smoked paprika

8 ounces (225g) button mushrooms, trimmed and finely chopped

½ cup (60g) chopped walnuts

1 cup (200g) cooked or canned lentils, drained

1 (28-ounce/794g) can crushed tomatoes

1 teaspoon dried oregano

1 teaspoon fine sea salt

1 teaspoon freshly ground black pepper

EGGPLANT BÉCHAMEL
1 cup (240ml) Nut Milk (page 17), Oat Milk (page 17), Soy Milk (page 75), or store-bought plant-based milk

1 teaspoon white or yellow miso, homemade (page 83) or store-bought

3 tablespoons (42g) Soft Spreadable Butter (page 21) or store-bought unsalted vegan butter

¼ cup (31g) all-purpose flour

⅛ teaspoon ground nutmeg

½ teaspoon fine sea salt, plus more to taste

PREHEAT THE OVEN TO 450°F (230°C).

Pierce the eggplant in several places, transfer to a sheet pan, and roast, turning occasionally, until it's completely soft and beginning to collapse, 30 to 40 minutes. Remove from the oven and let cool for 15 to 20 minutes. Leave the oven on but reduce the temperature to 375°F (190°C).

Meanwhile, make the pasta with artichoke sauce: Bring a pot of salted water to a boil. Add the pasta and cook to al dente according to the package directions. Reserving 1 cup (240ml) of the pasta water, drain the pasta and return it to the pot.

Transfer the reserved pasta cooking water to a blender and add the artichoke hearts, olive oil, and 1 teaspoon salt. Puree until smooth, then poor into the pot and mix with the cooked pasta.

Make the mushroom-lentil filling: In a large skillet, heat the oil over medium heat until it shimmers. Add the onion and sauté until it starts to become soft and translucent, about 5 minutes. Add the garlic and sauté until fragrant, about 30 seconds. Stir in the cinnamon and smoked paprika and cook for 30 seconds. Add the mushrooms and cook until they soften and begin to brown, 5 to 7 minutes. Stir in the walnuts, lentils, tomatoes, oregano, salt, and pepper. Reduce the heat to medium-low and cook until thickened, about 15 minutes.

Make the béchamel: Scoop out the flesh of the cooled eggplant into a blender (compost the skin). Add the milk and miso to the blender and puree until smooth.

In a 2-quart (2L) saucepan, melt the butter over medium heat. Whisk in the flour and nutmeg and cook for 2 minutes, whisking constantly. Slowly pour in the eggplant puree a little at a time, whisking until completely blended. Remove from the heat and whisk in the salt. Taste and season with more salt as needed.

Fill a deep 9 × 13-inch (23cm × 33cm) baking dish with the pasta mixture. Spread the mushroom-lentil filling over the top of the pasta evenly, then spoon the eggplant béchamel over the top and smooth it out evenly with a spatula.

Bake until lightly browned and bubbling, about 30 minutes. Transfer to a wire rack and let cool for at least 30 minutes before serving.

9

FILLED & STACKED: DUMPLINGS, SANDWICHES, TACOS & MORE

These are the hand-iest of foods, the dishes you can reach out and grab, which means they're particularly fun for parties. The making of them, which in some cases is a bit laborious, can be a party in itself: When it comes to filling dumplings or tamales, many hands make quick work. But the time is worth it when you and your guests take a bite, composed so each one contains so many flavors and textures. Some of these are also built to travel, making them perfectly suited for picnics. Seemingly every culture on the planet has traditional little filled things, and many times the original version is plant-based—and if it's not, these recipes show you how easy it is to make them so.

Bok Choy Tofu Dumplings

These vegetable dumplings from food writer WoonHeng Chia feature a filling full of texture and flavor, using a mix of wood ear mushrooms, corn, and tofu. Dumplings can be boiled, steamed, fried, or pan-fried, but here WoonHeng uses a technique familiar to anyone who has made potstickers: a combination of pan-frying and steaming. And when you whisk a little flour into the steaming liquid, once it evaporates you're left with a crisp, lacy crust on one side of the otherwise-soft dumplings, adding even more texture.

Makes 4 servings

Time: Weekend

Storage: Refrigerate for up to 5 days. You can also freeze the formed dumplings for up to 6 months before cooking them; freeze them in one layer, without touching, on a sheet pan, then transfer them to a freezer-safe bag or other container. Cook from frozen.

FILLING

½ ounce (15g) dried wood ear or black fungus mushrooms

Hot water

4 ounces (115g) baby bok choy (about 6)

1 teaspoon fine sea salt, plus more to taste

1 teaspoon sunflower or other neutral oil

½ teaspoon grated fresh ginger

1 garlic clove, finely grated or pressed

1 small carrot (2 ounces/57g), coarsely grated (½ cup)

3 ounces (85g) firm tofu

1 tablespoon chopped scallion

1 tablespoon frozen corn, thawed

2 teaspoons soy sauce, plus more to taste

2 teaspoons toasted sesame oil

2 teaspoons toasted sesame seeds

¼ teaspoon freshly ground black pepper

DUMPLINGS

25 egg-free dumpling wrappers, thawed if frozen (and kept covered by a damp towel until use)

1 cup (240ml) water, plus more for forming the dumplings

1½ tablespoons all-purpose flour

1 tablespoon neutral oil

Black sesame seeds (optional), for serving

Chile oil (optional), for serving

MAKE THE FILLING: Rinse the mushrooms well and transfer to a small bowl. Cover with hot water and rehydrate until soft, 15 to 20 minutes. Rinse, pat dry, trim off the hard end, and thinly slice.

While the mushrooms are rehydrating, wash the bok choy, trim off the ends, and thinly slice the leaves and stems. Transfer to a bowl and massage the bok choy with ½ teaspoon of the salt. Let the bok choy rest for 20 minutes while the salt draws out extra moisture.

In a large nonstick skillet, heat the oil over medium heat until it shimmers. Add the ginger and garlic and sauté until fragrant, about 30 seconds. Add the carrot and rehydrated mushrooms and stir-fry until the carrots are tender, 1 to 2 minutes. Stir in another ¼ teaspoon of the salt. Transfer the mixture to a medium bowl. Rinse and dry the skillet.

Transfer the wilted bok choy to a nut-milk bag, layered cheesecloth, or a clean cotton kitchen towel and squeeze as much liquid out as possible. Transfer to the bowl with the carrot-mushroom mixture.

Add the tofu to the same bag, cloth, or towel, squeeze out its liquid, and transfer the tofu to the bowl.

Add the scallion, corn, soy sauce, sesame oil, sesame seeds, pepper, and the remaining ¼ teaspoon salt and mix until thoroughly combined. Taste and season with more soy sauce and/or salt as needed.

Make the dumplings: Fill a small bowl with water.

Place a dumpling wrapper in your palm. Wet the edges with water. Place about 1 tablespoon of filling in the middle and bring the sides together. Pleat to seal, then transfer to a plate and cover with a damp kitchen towel. Continue, keeping the unused wrappers and dumplings covered, until all the wrappers are used.

In a small bowl or liquid measuring cup, whisk the water with the flour until smooth to make a slurry.

To cook the dumplings, in the same large nonstick skillet, heat the oil over medium heat until it shimmers. Working in batches to avoid overcrowding, arrange the dumplings in one layer and pan-fry until the bottoms turn golden brown. Add enough slurry to come ¼ inch (6mm) up the side of the dumplings and cover with a lid. Cook until the liquid has evaporated and the dumplings are translucent on top, 2 to 3 minutes. Transfer the dumplings to a serving platter, and continue cooking the rest of the dumplings, adding more oil and slurry as needed.

If desired, sprinkle the dumplings with black sesame seeds and drizzle with chile oil.

Stuffed Green Chile Peppers

Many Korean meals include dishes made with cheong gochu, bright green chiles that look like skinny and long jalapeño peppers and can range in spiciness from mild to flaming hot. They're often stuffed with ground meat and eggs, but this version—made with the biggest jalapeños you can find, or small poblanos—employs a delectable combination of mushrooms, tofu, and more. You will have a little more filling than you need for this recipe; mix it with a little vegan mayo and eat on toast or in a sandwich.

Makes 8 appetizer servings (16 stuffed peppers)

Time: Weekday

Storage: Refrigerate for up to 2 days.

8 fresh green chiles, such as very large jalapeños or small poblanos, stemmed and halved lengthwise

2 tablespoons grapeseed, canola, or other neutral oil, plus more for deep-frying

10 ounces (285g) fresh shiitake mushrooms, stems composted (or saved for stock) and caps chopped

1 (16-ounce/454g) block extra-firm tofu, drained and patted dry

1½ teaspoons fine sea salt, plus more to taste

4 scallions, chopped

2 cups (330g) potato starch

1 cup (240ml) Nut Milk (page 17), Oat Milk (page 17), Soy Milk (page 75), or store-bought plant-based milk

2 teaspoons ground turmeric

1 teaspoon freshly ground black pepper

REMOVE ALL THE SEEDS and membranes from the chiles.

In a large skillet, heat the oil over medium-high heat until it shimmers. Add the shiitakes and sauté until browned, 5 to 7 minutes. Transfer to a large bowl. Mash the tofu with a fork. Using your hands, squeeze out any excess liquid. Transfer to the bowl with the shiitakes and add 1 teaspoon of the salt and the scallions. Stir until well mixed.

Stuff each chile half tightly with enough stuffing so that there is a healthy mound on top.

In a shallow bowl, combine 1 cup (165g) of the potato starch, the remaining ½ teaspoon salt, the soy milk, turmeric, and black pepper. Place the remaining 1 cup (165g) potato starch in a separate bowl.

Set a wire rack over a sheet pan next to the stovetop. Pour 2 inches (5cm) oil into a Dutch oven and heat over medium-high heat until it reaches 375°F (190°C). Adjust the heat as needed to hold that temperature.

Dredge each stuffed pepper in the dry potato starch, then dip in the wet batter and carefully add to the hot oil. Continue with the remaining peppers, working in batches to avoid overcrowding. Fry the peppers until golden brown, about 3 minutes. Transfer the peppers to the wire rack over the sheet pan. (Alternatively, you can pan-fry the peppers in a few tablespoons of oil over medium-high heat, cooking for 1 minute or so per side until they are golden brown.)

Serve hot or at room temperature.

Swiss Chard Tamales

Tamales are Mexico's love letter to corn, pockets of masa filled with the best of the harvest, wrapped in corn husks, and steamed until tender. A pre-Hispanic food, their name is derived from the Náhuatl word *tamalli*, which means "wrapped." They have always been a celebratory food, made in community for religious feasts, holidays, and other events. They are incredibly versatile and change from region to region; this version uses Swiss chard in the filling and combines it directly with the masa before steaming (rather than stuffing it inside).

If you are not planning on having a tamalada (tamal-making party), you can work ahead. Make the filling and the dough 1 day ahead, and then wrap and steam them the following day.

Makes 6 servings (24 tamales)

Time: Project

Storage: Refrigerate for up to 4 days or freeze for up to 3 months.

24 large dried corn husks, plus more for lining the steamer

FILLING

1 bunch Swiss chard (8 ounces/227g)

1 teaspoon avocado oil

¾ cup (96g) chopped onion

2 garlic cloves, finely grated or pressed

1 to 2 serrano peppers (or jalapeños for milder heat), chopped

1⅔ cups (300g) diced Roma tomatoes (from 2 to 3 tomatoes)

½ cup (62g) finely grated carrots

1 teaspoon fine sea salt, plus more to taste

½ teaspoon freshly ground black pepper

MASA

½ cup (120ml) refined coconut oil, avocado oil, or olive oil (see Notes)

½ cup (125g) Fluffy Pumpkin Seed Ricotta (page 31), Cashew Ricotta (page 387), or store-bought vegan ricotta

1½ teaspoons baking powder

1 tablespoon fine sea salt, plus more to taste

4 cups (520g) instant masa harina (see Notes)

4 cups (950ml) warm Vegetable Scrap Stock (page 36) or store-bought vegetable broth, plus more as needed

1 (12-ounce/340g) can/jar pickled jalapeño slices, drained

SOAK THE CORN HUSKS in hot water, in a large pot or in your kitchen sink. Place a plate over them to weight them down so they are completely submerged. Let them soak for at least 1 hour.

Make the filling: Strip the Swiss chard leaves from the stems. Thinly slice both stems and leaves, keeping them separate.

In a large skillet, heat the oil over medium heat until it shimmers. Add the Swiss chard stems, onion, garlic, and chiles and sauté until they begin to soften, about 7 minutes. Stir in the tomatoes and sauté until the tomatoes begin to break down and soften, about 3 minutes. Stir in the Swiss chard leaves and sauté until they cook down and become tender, about 2 minutes. Stir in the carrots, salt, and pepper. Taste and season with more salt as needed. Remove from the heat and let cool.

Make the masa: In a stand mixer fitted with the paddle, combine the oil and ricotta and beat on medium-high speed for 1 minute. Add the baking powder and salt and beat for 1 more minute to incorporate into the oil. Add 2 cups (260g) of the masa harina, pour in 2 cups (470ml) of the vegetable stock, and beat to incorporate. Once it is completely smooth, add the other half of the masa harina and vegetable stock. Beat on low speed until thoroughly mixed. Add the vegetable filling and beat for 1 minute to incorporate. The dough should have the consistency of a thick cake batter; add more vegetable stock as needed. Taste the dough and season with more salt as needed. It should be a little bit salty. For lighter and fluffier tamales, let the dough rest for 1 hour in the refrigerator. Remove the dough from the fridge and rebeat it, adding enough liquid to get it to the consistency it had before.

To set up the steamer: Remove the corn husks from the water and set on a kitchen towel. Reserve the largest husks to wrap the tamales and the small ones to line the steamer. Fill the bottom of the steamer with water, making sure the water is not touching the steamer rack. Line the rack and sides of the steamer basket/insert with corn husks. Set aside.

RECIPE CONTINUES ON NEXT PAGE

To wrap the tamales: Pull 24 pencil-thin strips off of the large corn husks and set aside (these will be used as ties). Take a husk and dry off the excess water with a kitchen towel. Place the husk in your hand with the tapered side away from you and the smooth side up. Using a spoon, spread 2 to 3 tablespoons of the dough ¼ inch (6mm) thick onto the corn husk, forming a 3- to 4-inch (7.5cm to 10cm) square. Leave a border of at least ¾ inch (2cm) on each side of the square. Place a slice of pickled jalapeño in the center of the tamal. Bring the two long sides of the corn husk together, using the masa to surround the pickled jalapeño, and roll the sides of the husk in the same direction around the tamal. If the husk is too small, fold one of the long sides toward the center, and then fold the other long side on top. Fold down the empty tapered section of the corn husk, forming a closed bottom. This will leave the top of the tamal open. Tie with a corn husk strip to secure the bottom of the tamal. Repeat this process until you run out of masa.

To cook the tamales, place each tamal in the steamer basket/insert vertically, leaning against the side of the pot, with the open end facing up. Cover them with a layer of corn husks. If the steamer is not full, fill the empty spaces with more corn husks. Cover the pot and bring the water to a boil over high heat. Reduce the heat to medium and cook for 45 minutes. To check that the tamales are cooked, take a tamal out of the steamer and try to separate the husk from the masa. If the masa separates easily from the corn husk, this means the tamales are done. If they still stick to the husks, steam for 10 more minutes and check again.

Remove the steamer from the heat and let sit, covered, for 10 minutes. Uncover and let cool for at least 1 hour. Don't be alarmed if the tamales seem really soft. As they cool, they will firm up.

COOK'S NOTES

- If you'd like, you can use ½ cup (112g) unsweetened pumpkin puree in place of the oil in the masa dough.

- If you have access to fresh masa, use 2 pounds (910g) of it instead of the masa harina and reduce the vegetable stock to ¾ cup (180ml), plus more as needed.

Empanadas Santa Rita

These crispy, savory-sweet empanadas filled with picadillo are from the northern state of Chihuahua, Mexico, and are named for Saint Rita. This interpretation fills them with mushroom and TVP (textured vegetable protein): a highly nutritious soy product that is basically defatted soy flour, a by-product of making soybean oil. These empanadas get a touch of sweetness from a bit of sugar (and anise) in the dough, a small amount of raisins in the filling, and a light dusting of sugar after they're fried.

Since making empanadas can be time-consuming, feel free to make the filling and/or the dough 1 to 2 days before using and refrigerate until you're ready to cook. Assemble and fry the empanadas right before serving.

Makes 6 to 8 servings (18 empanadas)

Time: Weekend

Storage: Refrigerate for up to 5 days. You can also freeze the assembled empanadas (on a sheet pan and not touching one another) and then transfer to zip-top bags and freeze for up to 3 months. (Thaw them thoroughly before frying.)

DOUGH

½ cup (120ml) water

½ teaspoon aniseed

½ teaspoon baking soda

4 cups (500g) all-purpose flour

½ teaspoon fine sea salt

½ teaspoon organic cane sugar

1½ tablespoons refined coconut oil or vegetable shortening, at room temperature

½ cup (120ml) Nut Milk (page 17), Oat Milk (page 17), Soy Milk (page 75), or store-bought plant-based milk, lukewarm, plus more if needed

FILLING

½ large white onion (170g)

½ cup (48g) textured vegetable protein (TVP)

1½ cups (350ml) plus 2 tablespoons water

1 bay leaf

2 tablespoons soy sauce

3 garlic cloves, 2 peeled but whole and 1 chopped

⅛ teaspoon smoked paprika

1 tablespoon avocado oil

½ cup (57g) finely chopped cremini mushrooms

½ cup (70g) diced unpeeled russet potatoes

⅛ teaspoon ground cloves

Pinch of ground cinnamon

⅛ teaspoon freshly ground black pepper

2 tablespoons slivered almonds

2 tablespoons raisins

¼ cup (35g) frozen peas

¾ cup (180ml) vegetable broth

FOR ASSEMBLY

Vegetable oil, for deep-frying

¼ cup (50g) organic cane sugar

MAKE THE DOUGH: In a small saucepan, combine the water, aniseed, and baking soda. Bring to a simmer over medium-low heat and simmer gently for 5 minutes. Remove from the heat and let steep for 10 minutes. Strain into a bowl, reserving the liquid and half of the aniseeds. (Compost the rest of the seeds.) Rinse out the saucepan.

In a large bowl, whisk together the flour, salt, and sugar. Add the coconut oil and rub the mixture in between your fingers until fine crumbs form. Pour in the anise water, reserved aniseeds, and the lukewarm milk and mix everything with your hands, bringing the dough together. If the dough is still too dry, add more milk, 1 tablespoon at a time, until the dough comes together. Knead the dough for 5 to 6 minutes until it is smooth and no longer sticky. Cover the bowl with a kitchen towel and let the dough rest at room temperature for 1 hour.

While the dough is resting, make the filling: Cut the onion half in half again. Leave one of the onion quarters whole and chop the other one.

In the same small saucepan you used for the anise water, combine the TVP, 1½ cups (350ml) of the water, the intact onion quarter, and the bay leaf. Bring to a boil over medium-high heat, then reduce the heat to medium-low and simmer for 10 minutes. Drain the

TVP (fish out and compost the onion and bay leaf). Squeeze the water out of the TVP.

In a blender, combine the soy sauce, 2 whole garlic cloves, 2 tablespoons of the chopped onion, the smoked paprika, and the remaining 2 tablespoons water. Puree the seasoning sauce until smooth.

In a large skillet, heat the avocado oil over medium heat until it shimmers. Add the rest of the chopped onion and the chopped garlic and sauté until they soften, about 7 minutes. Stir in the mushrooms and cook until they brown, about 6 minutes. Stir in the TVP and cook until it browns, 4 to 6 minutes.

Pour in the seasoning sauce from the blender and simmer until it begins to evaporate, 2 to 3 minutes. Stir in the potatoes, cloves, cinnamon, black pepper, almonds, raisins, and peas. Pour in the vegetable broth, stir, and simmer until most of the liquid has evaporated and the potatoes are tender, 10 to 12 minutes. Transfer to a bowl and refrigerate until completely cool.

To assemble: Pour 3 inches (7.5cm) oil into a Dutch oven and heat the oil over medium-high heat until it reaches 375°F (190°C).

While the oil is heating, divide the dough into 18 equal portions (about 40g each) and roll into balls. Lightly flour a surface and roll out each ball to ¼ inch (6mm) thick, turning the dough as you go to form an even, 5- to 6-inch (13cm to 15cm) round.

Place 1½ tablespoons of the cooled filling in the center of each round. Brush water around half of the outer edge of each round and fold the dough over the filling, making the edges meet. Pinch the edges to seal and crimp with a fork.

Set a wire rack over a sheet pan next to the stovetop. Carefully lower 2 empanadas at a time into the hot oil and fry until golden brown on both sides, about 3 minutes. Transfer to the wire rack and sprinkle with sugar. Repeat with the remaining empanadas. Serve hot.

COOK'S NOTE: These were designed to be fried, but if you would prefer to bake them, use the dough from the Empanadas de Piña (page 415) instead, reducing the sugar in it to ½ teaspoon, and bake at 350°F (180°C) until the bottoms are golden brown, 15 to 20 minutes.

Cabbage Rolls with Herby Rice & Shallots

There are countless iterations of stuffed cabbage across the Middle East and Europe. This version takes inspiration from dolmas (stuffed grape leaves) filled with lemony, herby rice. Here, each cabbage leaf encloses basmati rice that's mixed with dill, cilantro, currants, and jammy shallots cooked with tomato paste and smoked paprika for a super-savory undercurrent. Feel free to use whatever tender herbs you favor (mint would be great, as would parsley) and to swap out the currants for raisins—just chop them up so that they can be distributed more evenly in the rice mixture. You can also swap the almonds with the more classic pine nuts.

Makes 4 servings

Time: Weekday

Storage: Refrigerate for up to 5 days.

Fine sea salt

1 small to medium head red, green, or Savoy cabbage (1¾ pounds/794g)

1 cup (180g) basmati rice, rinsed

1 cup (30g) lightly packed fresh dill leaves, finely chopped, plus more for serving

½ cup (15g) lightly packed fresh cilantro leaves and tender stems, finely chopped, plus more for serving

5 tablespoons dried currants

1 garlic clove, grated

1 teaspoon finely grated lemon zest

3 tablespoons fresh lemon juice

1 teaspoon freshly ground black pepper

4 tablespoons olive oil

⅓ cup (30g) sliced almonds

2 large shallots (4½ ounces/128g total), thinly sliced

2 tablespoons tomato paste

½ teaspoon smoked paprika

½ cup (120ml) plus 1 tablespoon hot water

BRING A LARGE POT of generously salted water to a boil. Line a sheet pan with a lint-free kitchen towel. Cut away the stem and core of the cabbage. Gently peel away 12 to 14 large leaves, trying your best not to tear them and cutting away more of the core as needed. Cut a triangular notch in the base of each leaf to remove the thickest part of the core. Dunk the leaves in the boiling water in groups of 4 to 5 until soft and pliable, 20 to 30 seconds. Transfer to the towel-lined sheet pan. (Reserve any remaining cabbage for another use, such as slaw or stir-fry.)

Bring the water back up to a boil. Add the rice and cook until al dente, 4 to 5 minutes, then drain, rinse with cold water to stop cooking, and drain well again.

Transfer the rice to a bowl and add the dill, cilantro, 4 tablespoons of the currants, the garlic, lemon zest, 1 tablespoon of the lemon juice, the pepper, and ¼ teaspoon salt. Toss to mix until thoroughly combined.

Using the same pot you used for boiling the rice, heat 3 tablespoons of the olive oil over medium heat until it shimmers Add the almonds and cook, stirring constantly, until golden brown, 30 to 60 seconds. Remove from the heat and use a slotted spoon to remove the almonds from the oil (leaving the oil in the pan). Set aside a couple of tablespoons for garnish and mix the rest of the almonds into the rice.

Return the pot to medium heat and add the shallots. Season lightly with salt and cook, stirring frequently, until soft and jammy, 4 to 5 minutes. Add the tomato paste and smoked paprika and cook, stirring and smashing constantly, until the tomato paste is dark and evenly distributed, 1 to 2 minutes. Transfer to the rice and mix until incorporated. Taste and season with salt. Rinse the pot.

In a small bowl, combine the remaining 1 tablespoon currants, 1 tablespoon lemon juice, and 1 tablespoon hot water.

Scoop 3 tablespoons of the rice mixture into the center of each leaf. Roll it up from the notched base, folding the sides in toward the center. Place the roll seam-side down in the pot and repeat with the remaining leaves.

Add the remaining 1 tablespoon olive oil, remaining 1 tablespoon lemon juice, and remaining ½ cup (120ml) water to the pot. Bring to a simmer over high heat, then reduce the heat to low, cover, and simmer until the cabbage is completely tender and the rice is fully cooked, 15 to 20 minutes.

Meanwhile, drain the currants from the lemon water.

Serve garnished with the reserved almonds, lemon-soaked currants, and more herbs. Serve warm, at room temperature, or cold.

Kale & Caramelized Onion Turnovers

Kale loves to be balanced with something sweet, and what savory sweetness is more alluring than caramelized onions? The combination, when wrapped in phyllo, gives vegan spanakopita vibes: good in larger form as here for a meal, or you can make them smaller for a party appetizer.

Make the filling mixture up to 3 days ahead and refrigerate until you're ready to make the turnovers.

Makes 6 servings (twelve 5-inch/13cm turnovers)

Time: Weekend

Storage: Refrigerate for up to 3 days or freeze for up to 3 months. You can also refrigerate the folded pies before baking for up to 3 days or freeze for up to 3 months. Bake from frozen, adding a few minutes as needed to the baking time.

10 ounces (285g) curly kale

4 tablespoons olive oil, plus more if needed

2 small onions (8 ounces/227g total), sliced

½ teaspoon fine sea salt, plus more to taste

¼ cup (60ml) water

12 sheets frozen phyllo pastry, thawed

White and/or black sesame seeds, for garnish

SEPARATE THE KALE LEAVES from the stems. Finely chop the stems and leaves, but keep them separate.

In a large skillet, heat 2 tablespoons of the olive oil over medium-low heat. Add the kale stems, onions, and salt and cook, stirring occasionally, until the onions are very soft, sticky, browned, and caramelized. This could take as little as 40 minutes or up to 1 hour or even longer, depending on the onions.

Preheat the oven to 400°F (200°C).

Add the chopped kale leaves and the water to the caramelized onions, increase the heat to medium, cover, and cook until the kale is wilted, about 5 minutes. Uncover and cook, stirring frequently, until the kale is very tender and the water has evaporated, about 15 minutes. Taste and season with salt.

Keeping the unused phyllo covered with a damp kitchen towel as you work so it doesn't dry out, lay a sheet of phyllo on a flat work surface with one of the short sides facing you. Pour the remaining 2 tablespoons olive oil into a small bowl. Using a pastry brush, brush the surface of the pastry lightly with olive oil. (It doesn't have to be evenly coated.)

Lay another sheet of phyllo directly on top of the first and brush lightly again with oil. Repeat with a third layer.

Place a scant ¼ cup of filling in the middle of the phyllo sheet, about 1 inch (2.5cm) from the edge closest to you. Place another scant ¼ cup on either side of the first, midway between the first mound of filling and either edge of the sheet, for a total of 3 mounds.

Use a pizza cutter to cut the phyllo midway between each filling mound into 3 lengthwise strips. Starting at the end closest to you, gently fold each strip into a triangle like folding a flag: First make a 45-degree fold, bringing the bottom edge of the strip to meet one side, then a horizontal fold, then a 45-degree fold to the other side, and so on.

Repeat the process twice more with the remaining 9 sheets of phyllo and filling mixture to make 9 turnovers (a total of 12 turnovers). Brush the tops of the turnovers lightly with oil and sprinkle sesame seeds on top.

Place the turnovers on a sheet pan and bake until golden brown, about 25 minutes.

Bean & Cheese Gorditas

These popular antojitos (snacks) sold on the streets of Mexico get the name *gordita* ("little fat one") from the fact that unlike, say, quesadillas, they are made from much thicker disks of masa, griddled and then split and filled with a guisado (stew). This recipe keeps things simple with refried beans and vegan cheese, but you can also fill them with any of the three vegetable fillings in Enchiladas Five Ways (page 311).

Makes 10 to 12 gorditas

Time: Weekday

Storage: Refrigerate for up to 2 days.

1¾ cups (225g) instant masa harina

½ teaspoon fine sea salt

¼ teaspoon baking powder

1½ cups (350ml) warm water, plus more if needed

1 tablespoon avocado oil

¾ cup (175g) Refried Beans (page 372) or store-bought refried beans, warmed

¾ cup (85g) crumbled Crumbly Almond Queso Fresco (page 27) or store-bought vegan feta, such as Violife

Chunky Molcajete Salsa (page 48), Salsa Macha (page 48), Zucchini "Guacamole" Salsa (page 47), or another favorite salsa of your choice

IN A LARGE BOWL, combine the masa harina, salt, and baking powder and mix well. Pour in the water while slowly mixing the masa harina with your hand. The dough should be moist, but not sticky, like a soft Play-Doh. If necessary, add more water, 1 tablespoon at a time, until you reach the right consistency. Cover with a damp kitchen towel and let rest 15 minutes.

Uncover the dough and divide it into 10 equal portions (about 57g each) and roll into balls. Flatten each ball with your hands to make a round patty about ⅓ inch (8.5mm) thick and about 3½ inches (9cm) in diameter.

In a large cast-iron skillet or comal, heat the oil over medium-high heat until it shimmers. Add as many masa rounds as will comfortably fit in the skillet without overcrowding and cook until crisp and golden on the bottom, with brown spots, 3 to 4 minutes. Flip them over and cook until crisp and golden with brown spots on the other side, about 3 minutes. Transfer to a plate and repeat with the rest of the gorditas.

Let the gorditas cool slightly. Using a serrated knife, cut a slit in the edge about halfway around one gordita's circumference, making a pocket. Fill the gordita with 1 tablespoon of refried beans and 1 tablespoon of vegan queso fresco. Repeat with the remaining gorditas and serve immediately with salsa.

COOK'S NOTES

- Feel free to make the masa a couple of hours before and store in the fridge. When ready to use, add warm water to return it to the right consistency.

- For really crispy gorditas, instead of cooking them on a comal, deep-fry them before cutting and filling.

Fava Bean Tlacoyos

A tlacoyo is a crisp corn masa patty shaped like a football filled with beans and topped with salad or cheese, and it was the hands-down favorite antojito (snack) I ate on a street food tour of Mexico City on my honeymoon. This version is filled with a refried fava bean/chipotle puree and topped with a refreshing cactus salad, almond queso fresco, and salsa.

Pre-Hispanic in origin, tlacoyos represent Mexican cuisine in its purest form, emphasizing the basic elements of the cuisine: corn, beans, and chiles. To work ahead, you can prepare the filling the day before. You can also form and fill the tlacoyos a couple of hours before pan-frying them.

Makes 8 servings

Time: Weekend

Storage: Refrigerate for up to 3 days.

FILLING

½ cup (94g) dried peeled fava beans

3½ cups (830ml) water

¼ white onion (48g)

½ teaspoon fine sea salt, plus more to taste

1 dried chipotle chile

½ dried avocado leaf (optional)

Boiling water

½ teaspoon avocado oil

MASA

2 cups (260g) instant masa harina

½ teaspoon fine sea salt

¼ teaspoon baking powder

1½ cups (350ml) warm water, plus more if needed

CACTUS SALAD

Fine sea salt

2 cups (225g) diced fresh nopalitos (cactus paddles; see Note)

⅓ cup (35g) chopped onion

1 garlic clove, finely grated or pressed

1¼ cups (225g) diced Roma tomatoes (about 2 tomatoes)

1 small serrano pepper, minced with seeds

2 tablespoons fresh lime juice

2 tablespoons chopped fresh cilantro

¼ teaspoon freshly ground black pepper

TLACOYOS AND SERVING

2 tablespoons avocado oil

1 cup (112g) crumbled Crumbly Almond Queso Fresco (page 27)

Chunky Molcajete Salsa (page 48) or Zucchini "Guacamole" Salsa (page 47), for serving

MAKE THE FILLING: In a medium saucepan, combine the fava beans, water, onion, and salt. Bring to a boil over high heat, then reduce the heat to a simmer and cook until the beans are tender, about 45 minutes.

Heat a cast-iron skillet or comal over medium heat and toast the chipotle chile and avocado leaf (if using) briefly, about 1 minute. Place the chipotle in a heatproof bowl and pour boiling water on top. Let soak for 10 minutes, then drain.

Reserving ½ cup (120ml) of the cooking liquid, drain the fava beans and transfer to a blender. Add the soaked chipotle and avocado leaf (if using) and blend until smooth. If necessary, add some of the reserved cooking liquid to create a creamy consistency.

In a large skillet, heat the oil over medium heat. Pour in the pureed beans and cook, stirring constantly, until the beans thicken, about 5 minutes. Taste and season with more salt if needed. Remove from the heat and let cool.

Make the masa: In a large bowl combine the masa harina, salt, and baking powder and mix well. Pour in the water while slowly mixing the masa harina with your hand. The dough should be moist, but not sticky, like a soft Play-Doh. If necessary, add more water until

you reach the right consistency. Knead for 5 minutes by hand inside the bowl, cover with a damp kitchen towel, and let rest while you make the cactus salad.

Make the cactus salad: Bring a large pot of lightly salted water to a boil over high heat. Add the nopalitos to the pot, reduce the heat to medium so the water is at a gentle boil, and cook for 10 minutes, periodically skimming the foam that rises to the top. Drain in a colander and rinse under cold water. Let sit in the colander until ready to use.

In a large bowl, combine the nopalitos, onion, garlic, tomatoes, serrano, lime juice, cilantro, ½ teaspoon salt, and the black pepper. Mix to combine. Taste and season with more salt if necessary.

To form the tlacoyos: Divide the dough into 8 equal portions (about 77g each). Keeping the rest covered, flatten a portion to about ¼ inch (6mm) thick and place 1 tablespoon of the filling in the center. Fold the dough over the filling, making the edges meet. Press the edges to seal. With your hands, press the ends of the dough to form pointy tips. Flatten the tlacoyo with your hands (or use a tortilla press) to about ½ inch (1.3cm) thick. Repeat with the rest of the masa and filling.

In a large cast-iron skillet or comal over medium heat, heat 1 tablespoon of the avocado oil. Add 2 tlacoyos and cook until the edges start to dry out and change color, 3 to 4 minutes. Flip the tlacoyos; the cooked side should be crisp and with brown spots. Cook the other side until golden brown, about 3 minutes. Transfer to a platter and repeat, adding more oil as necessary, to cook the remaining tlacoyos.

To serve, divide the cactus salad evenly among the tlacoyos and sprinkle with almond queso fresco. Serve hot with salsa.

COOK'S NOTE: If you can find fresh cactus paddles preprepped—their thorns removed—that will save you some time. If not, to prepare them, choose paddles that are bright green and soft but not limp. Using gloves, rinse under cold water, being careful with the thorns. Then, using a vegetable peeler or small sharp knife, peel away the bumps and thorns and rinse again. Lay the paddle flat on a chopping board and trim about ¼ inch (6mm) around the edges and about ½ inch (1.3cm) of the thick base before dicing.

Causa Rolls with Beet & Potato

Causa is a traditional Peruvian chilled mashed potato casserole with a tuna or chicken salad middle layer. The mash is already vegan because instead of milk or butter, Peru's creole cooks mix in olive oil, lime juice, and ají amarillo (native yellow chiles). This recipe honors Nikkei, the Japanese-Peruvian food culture prevalent in Lima for more than one hundred years, by having you shape the causa like a sushi roll, filling it with a salad of beet cubes steamed with kombu stock (making them resemble the bonito tuna so popular among Lima's working class). The potatoes get a little kick from sriracha, while nori strips, avocado, and jalapeño garnish the sliced rolls.

Makes 4 servings

Time: Weekend

Storage: Not recommended, but you can make and refrigerate the potato puree 1 day in advance, until you are ready to make the dish.

2 pounds (910g) Yukon Gold potatoes, peeled and cut into 1-inch (2.5cm) pieces

1½ teaspoons fine sea salt

2 tablespoons fresh lime juice

1 tablespoon toasted sesame oil

1½ teaspoons sriracha

1 (4 × 6-inch/10cm × 15cm) piece dried kombu, rinsed

2 cups (470ml) water

2 medium beets (7 ounces/200g total), peeled and cut into ½-inch (1.3cm) cubes (about 1 cup)

½ medium cucumber (4 ounces/115g), peeled and cut into ½-inch (1.3cm) cubes (about 1 cup)

2 tablespoons Silky Aquafaba Mayonnaise (page 46) or store-bought vegan mayonnaise

3 scallions, white part only, finely chopped (about 2 tablespoons)

Toasted nori strips, for garnish

Sliced avocado, for garnish

Thinly sliced jalapeño rounds, for garnish

IN A LARGE POT, combine the potatoes with enough water to cover by 2 inches (5cm). Bring to a boil over medium-high heat, reduce the heat until the water is simmering, and cook until the potatoes are tender, about 10 minutes. Drain and let the potatoes cool slightly.

When the potatoes are cool enough to handle, use a ricer to press them into a large bowl. (A ricer gets them particularly smooth, but alternatively you can use a potato masher and try to get out as many lumps as possible.) Fold in 1 teaspoon of the salt, the lime juice, sesame oil, and sriracha. Transfer the mixture to the refrigerator to chill completely before using, at least 3 hours.

In a medium pot, combine the kombu, the 2 cups (470ml) water, and ¼ teaspoon of the salt. Let the kombu soak for 15 minutes, then set the pot over medium-high heat and bring the water to a boil. Reduce the heat until the water is simmering and cook for 15 minutes. Remove from the heat (fish out and compost the kombu).

Place a steamer basket/insert in the pot, pouring out a little of the kombu stock if need be so the basket isn't touching the water, and spread the beet cubes evenly in the basket. Bring the kombu stock to a boil over medium-high heat, reduce to a simmer, cover, and steam the beets until tender, 20 to 30 minutes. Transfer the beets to a bowl and let them cool.

When the beets are cool, add to their bowl the cucumber, remaining ¼ teaspoon salt, mayonnaise, and scallion whites and stir to combine.

Set an 11½ × 8-inch (29cm × 20cm) piece of compostable parchment paper on your work surface, with a short side facing you.

Once the mashed potato is chilled, scoop one-quarter of it, about 1 cup, on top of the parchment and shape it into a 7 × 4-inch (18cm × 10cm) rectangle centered on the parchment, with the 7-inch (18cm) side of the rectangle parallel to the long side of the parchment. (From your perspective, the mashed potato rectangle should be taller than it is wide.) Spread one-quarter of the beet and cucumber filling, about ½ cup, lengthwise down the center of the mashed potatoes.

Starting with the parchment's bottom short edge, fold it up in half to bring together the 4-inch (10cm) edges of the mashed potato. Gently peel the parchment off the mashed potato, and use your hands as needed to shape the potato into a roll with the beet filling inside. Transfer the roll to a plate. (It should be about 2½ inches/6.5cm in diameter.) Repeat to make 3 more rolls.

Slice each roll into 6 pieces and top the pieces with nori, avocado, and jalapeño. Serve immediately.

Banh Xeo

This take on Vietnamese savory turmeric crepes (typically stuffed with pork and shrimp) uses tofu, bell pepper, and bean sprouts. The crepes have an irresistibly crispy, delicate golden crust wrapped around tender herbs and lettuce leaves. Dunking them into a savory-sweet chile lime dipping sauce makes for a zippy finish.

This dish is meant to be served family-style, which means everyone digs in together and makes their own wrap at the table.

Makes 4 servings

Time: Weekday

Storage: Refrigerate for up to 2 days.

BATTER

1 cup (160g) plus 2 tablespoons white rice flour (not sweet rice flour)

1 tablespoon cornstarch

1 teaspoon fine sea salt

½ teaspoon ground turmeric

1½ cups (350ml) hot water

6 tablespoons unsweetened canned full-fat coconut milk

DIPPING SAUCE

1 serrano pepper, thinly sliced

2 garlic cloves, finely grated or pressed

3 tablespoons fresh lime juice (from 1 to 2 limes)

¼ cup (60ml) soy sauce or tamari

2 tablespoons organic cane sugar

1 tablespoon hot water, plus more as needed

FILLING AND ASSEMBLY

1 (14-ounce/397g) block extra-firm tofu, drained

3 tablespoons vegetable oil, plus more for cooking the crepes

1 tablespoon soy sauce or tamari

1 garlic clove, finely grated or pressed

1 red bell pepper (7 ounces/200g), cut into strips ¼ inch (6mm) thick

1½ cups (135g) mung bean sprouts

1 shallot, thinly sliced

¼ teaspoon fine sea salt, plus more to taste

FOR SERVING

Tender lettuce leaves, such as butter or green leaf

Fresh mint leaves

Fresh cilantro sprigs

MAKE THE BATTER: In a medium bowl, whisk together the rice flour, cornstarch, salt, and turmeric. Slowly pour in the hot water and coconut milk, whisking until combined. Cover and let the batter rest and thicken, about 30 minutes.

Make the dipping sauce: In a small bowl, whisk together the serrano, garlic, lime juice, soy sauce, and sugar. Stir in the hot water until the sugar dissolves. Taste and add another splash of water to dilute if needed.

For the filling: Using a clean kitchen towel, pat the tofu dry, lightly pressing it with your palm to squeeze out excess moisture. Cut the tofu into ¾-inch (2cm) cubes.

In a 10-inch (25cm) cast-iron or other nonstick skillet, heat 2 tablespoons of the oil over medium-high heat until it shimmers. Add the tofu and soy sauce and cook, flipping occasionally, until the tofu is browned on all sides, about 8 minutes. Add the garlic and cook, stirring, until very fragrant, about 30 seconds. Transfer to a bowl.

Return the pan to medium-high heat and heat 1 tablespoon of the oil until it shimmers. Add the bell pepper, bean sprouts, shallots, and salt and cook, stirring, until slightly softened and fragrant, 2 to 3 minutes. Taste and season with more salt as needed. Transfer to the bowl with the tofu and toss to combine.

Wipe out the pan and return it to medium heat. Add 1 teaspoon oil, swirling to coat the pan. Whisk the batter until smooth. Using a measuring cup with a spout, pour one-quarter of the batter (about ½ cup/120ml) into the pan, swirling to evenly coat the bottom. Fill in any gaps with more batter, 1 teaspoon at a time. Arrange one-quarter of the vegetable filling over half of the crepe. Cook, without disturbing, until the crepe is set and the edges are browned and crispy, about 3 minutes. Fold the crepe over and transfer to a plate. Repeat with remaining batter for the crepes, slicking the pan with some oil before each one.

To serve: Set up a platter with the lettuce leaves, herbs, and the dipping sauce. Each person can stuff or top a crepe with herbs and/or lettuce leaves, wrap the lettuce leaves around a crepe if desired, and dip into or drizzle on the sauce.

Fried Oyster Mushroom Sandwiches

It doesn't take much more than a little brine from jarred pickles, some dried nori, and a little Old Bay seasoning to bring a touch of the sea to landlocked oyster mushrooms. This recipe pairs them with a bright rémoulade sauce for even more spark.

Makes 4 servings

Time: Weekday

Storage: The fried mushrooms can be refrigerated for up to 3 days. The rémoulade sauce can be refrigerated for up to 2 weeks.

FRIED MUSHROOMS

1 pound (450g) oyster mushrooms, ends trimmed

¾ cup (180ml) Nut Milk (page 17), Oat Milk (page 17), Soy Milk (page 75), or store-bought plant-based milk

¼ cup (60ml) pickle brine

1 cup (125g) all-purpose flour

1 cup (172g) medium-grind cornmeal

1½ teaspoons sea salt

1 teaspoon ground dried nori (crushed by hand from sheets or store-bought)

1 teaspoon Old Bay seasoning

1 teaspoon garlic powder

½ teaspoon freshly ground black pepper

Neutral vegetable oil, for shallow-frying

SANDWICHES

2 tablespoons (28g) Soft Spreadable Butter (page 21) or softened store-bought unsalted vegan butter

4 sub rolls, split lengthwise

10 tablespoons Rémoulade Sauce (recipe follows)

Lemon wedges, for serving

MAKE THE FRIED MUSHROOMS: Separate the oyster mushrooms from each other, if needed. Rinse them, shake off any excess water, and place into a large baking dish in a single layer.

In a bowl, whisk together the milk and pickle brine and pour over the mushrooms. Allow the mushrooms to soak in the liquid, turning occasionally, for 15 minutes.

In a shallow dish, whisk together the flour, cornmeal, salt, nori, Old Bay, garlic powder, and pepper.

Place a wire rack over a sheet pan next to your frying station.

Pour 1 inch (2.5cm) oil into a Dutch oven and heat the oil over high heat until it reaches 350°F (177°C) on an instant-read thermometer.

Shake off the excess marinade from a mushroom, dredge it in the flour mixture, then immediately (and carefully) transfer it to the hot oil, repeating with as many more mushrooms as will fit without overcrowding the pot. Fry for about 2 minutes per side, until crispy and golden, then transfer to the wire rack to drain.

Assemble the sandwiches: Heat a griddle or large skillet over medium-high heat. Spread the softened butter on the inside of the rolls and toast, buttered-side down, on the griddle until lightly golden, 1 to 2 minutes. Transfer the rolls to serving plates and spread 2 tablespoons of the rémoulade sauce inside each sandwich. Divide the fried mushrooms among the rolls, and drizzle each sandwich with a little more sauce.

Serve immediately with lemon wedges for guests to squeeze over the inside of the sandwiches if they'd like.

Rémoulade Sauce

A great sauce to have around for dipping and spreading and for use with the Lion's Mane Mushroom Cakes (page 326). It will keep refrigerated for up to 2 weeks.

Makes about 1½ cups

1 cup (240ml) Silky Aquafaba Mayonnaise (page 46) or store-bought vegan mayonnaise

4 tablespoons Dijon mustard

2 teaspoons grated horseradish

1 teaspoon sweet paprika

1 tablespoon finely chopped fresh chives

2 tablespoons capers, roughly chopped

3 cornichons, finely diced

2 teaspoons Tabasco or other hot sauce

IN A SMALL BOWL, whisk together the mayonnaise, mustard, horseradish, paprika, chives, capers, cornichons, and Tabasco. (To make the sauce smooth as shown on the preceding page, puree it in a food processor or blender.) Refrigerate until ready to use.

Huitlacoche & Zucchini Blossom Tacos

Food writer Dora Stone first tried these tacos in the famous canals of Mexico City's Xochimilco, where vendors in the colorful boats sell street foods to floaters-by.

Huitlacoche, a black corn fungus also known as corn smut, is a wonderfully smoky and earthy delicacy that possesses both the umami of mushrooms and the sweetness of corn. It is used in tacos, tamales, soups, and stews all over Mexico.

Serve on warm blue corn tortillas with a homemade chunky salsa.

Makes 4 servings

Time: Weekday

Storage: The tacos are best eaten as soon as they're made, but you can refrigerate the filling separately for up to three days.

FILLING

1 poblano pepper (4½ ounces/130g)

1 tablespoon avocado oil

1 white onion (7 ounces/200g), chopped

2 garlic cloves, finely grated or pressed

1 serrano pepper, minced

3 cups (11½ ounces/326g) fresh huitlacoche (see Note)

⅔ cup (90g) fresh or frozen corn kernels

¼ cup (60ml) Vegetable Scrap Stock (page 36) or store-bought vegetable broth (optional)

1 cup (100g) sliced fresh squash blossoms (or substitute canned)

1 Roma tomato (5 ounces/140g), diced

½ cup (7g) chopped fresh epazote (or substitute cilantro plus ¼ teaspoon lightly crushed aniseeds)

1 teaspoon fine sea salt, plus more to taste

Freshly ground black pepper

TACOS

12 blue corn tortillas

½ cup (115g) Fluffy Pumpkin Seed Ricotta (page 31), Cashew Ricotta (page 387), or store-bought vegan ricotta

Chunky Molcajete Salsa (page 48), for serving

MAKE THE FILLING: Turn the oven to broil. Place the poblano on a sheet pan and on a rack a few inches from the broiler. Broil, turning the pepper with tongs every minute or two as needed as it chars, until all the sides are charred. (If you have a gas stove, you can do this on the open flame of a burner instead.) Transfer the pepper to a bowl and cover with a plate. Let it steam for 5 minutes, then use your hands to peel the thin skin from the poblano. Tear the stem off and remove the seedpod, then slice the poblano.

In a large skillet, heat the oil over medium heat. Add the onion, garlic, and serrano and sauté until slightly browned, about 7 minutes. Stir in the huitlacoche and corn and sauté until the corn is tender and the huitlacoche begins to release some of its liquid, about 10 minutes. If the vegetables begin to stick to the bottom of the pan, add the ¼ cup (60ml) vegetable stock and scrape the bottom of the pan to release.

Stir in the squash blossoms, poblanos, tomato, epazote, salt, and black pepper and sauté until the epazote and squash blossoms have cooked down, about 5 minutes. Taste and season with more salt as needed.

Make the tacos: Heat a cast-iron skillet or comal to medium-high heat and heat the tortillas for a few seconds on each side. Spread 2 teaspoons of the vegan ricotta on each tortilla and fill with 1½ tablespoons of the filling. Serve hot with salsa.

COOK'S NOTE: If you have a hard time finding fresh huitlacoche, substitute with a combination of one 7-ounce (198g) can huitlacoche and 1 cup (60g) sliced shiitake mushroom caps. Sauté the mushrooms with the onions.

Bake & Squash Sandwiches

This riff on Trinidad and Tobago's beachside staple, bake and shark, is not only satisfying but much more ocean-friendly. Thick slices of zucchini squash keep the sandwich filling dense, perfect for stacking between ethereal pillowy fried dough—called bake—along with Caribbean Coleslaw (page 151). This sandwich is a summer stunner.

Makes 6 servings

Time: Weekday

Storage: Refrigerate the fried bread for up to 5 days and the filling for up to 3 days, storing them separately.

BAKES

2 cups (250g) all-purpose flour, plus more as needed

1 tablespoon baking powder

½ teaspoon fine sea salt

½ teaspoon organic cane sugar

1 tablespoon plus 1 teaspoon olive oil

¾ cup (180ml) water

Vegetable oil, for frying

SQUASH

2 large zucchini (20 ounces/570g total), cut lengthwise into thirds

1 cup (240ml) canned full-fat coconut milk

1½ teaspoons fine sea salt

¼ teaspoon Tabasco or other hot sauce

1 cup (80g) panko bread crumbs

1 teaspoon Tajín seasoning, Cajun Seasoning (page 38), or Smoky Mezcal Sazón (page 44)

ASSEMBLY

1½ cups (330g) Caribbean Coleslaw (page 151) or your favorite coleslaw

MAKE THE BAKES: In a medium bowl, whisk together the flour, baking powder, salt, and sugar. Add 1 tablespoon of the olive oil and use a fork (or your fingers) to incorporate until the mixture resembles coarse cornmeal.

Create a well in the middle of the flour mixture and slowly stream in the water, stirring, until the dough comes together. Knead the dough in the bowl until it's soft and pliable, about 1 minute. If the dough is too sticky, add more flour, 1 tablespoon at a time, until it is easy to work with.

Form the dough into a ball, brush with the remaining 1 teaspoon of olive oil, and cover with a clean kitchen towel. Let rest for 20 minutes.

Transfer the dough to a lightly floured surface and use a bench scraper or knife to divide in half. Divide each half into thirds, for 6 total pieces.

Using a rolling pin, roll each piece of dough into a 6-inch (15cm) oval.

Set a wire rack over a sheet pan next to the stovetop. In a Dutch oven or deep sauté pan, pour the vegetable oil to a depth of 1 inch (2.5cm). Heat the oil over medium heat to 350°F (177°C).

Working in batches to avoid overcrowding, gently place the dough into the hot oil, fry for 10 seconds, then flip. (Flipping early in the frying allows it to puff up.) Fry until golden brown, about 30 seconds per side. Transfer the bakes to the wire rack as they are done. Fry, drain, and cool the remaining pieces. Let the oil cool slightly, then pour off all but ¼ cup (60ml) of the oil from the Dutch oven.

Fry the squash: Pat the zucchini planks dry with a kitchen towel.

In a large bowl, combine the coconut milk, 1 teaspoon of the salt, and the hot sauce. In another large bowl, stir together the panko and Tajín.

Dip a zucchini plank into the coconut milk mixture, then dredge in the panko mixture, pressing it in with your fingers to help it stick. Transfer to a platter and repeat until all the zucchini planks are breaded.

Return the Dutch oven to medium heat until the oil shimmers. Working in batches to avoid overcrowding, pan-fry the zucchini until the bottom is golden brown, about 3 minutes. Flip and pan-fry until golden brown on the second side, another 3 minutes. Transfer to the same platter, and repeat until all the planks are fried. While still warm, sprinkle them with the remaining ½ teaspoon salt.

To assemble: Set a zucchini plank in the middle of one of the bakes. Top with 4 tablespoons of the coleslaw, fold the bake around the filling, and repeat with the remaining bakes and filling. Serve warm.

Cauliflower Larb Lettuce Cups

Refreshing and crisp with bright flavors, Thai-inspired larb is a great appetizer for warmer days. This version uses lettuce wraps to scoop up the spiced roasted-cauliflower filling and then dip the cups into a zingy chile sauce. Herbs give the cups another layer of fresh flavors, and a dusting of toasted rice powder adds a nutty, crunchy finish.

This dish is just as fun to eat as it is to make, with guests helping themselves to make their own wraps.

Makes 6 appetizer servings

Time: Weekday

Storage: Refrigerate the cauliflower filling for up to 3 days.

1 large head cauliflower (3½ pounds/1.5kg)

2 tablespoons olive oil

1 teaspoon red pepper flakes

2 teaspoons ground cumin

2 teaspoons ground turmeric

1 teaspoon fine sea salt

1 tablespoon uncooked long-grain white rice

DIPPING SAUCE

1 to 2 Thai chiles, thinly sliced
(use one for mild heat, two for spicy)

3-inch (7.5cm) piece lemongrass, tough outer layers removed, finely chopped (about 2 tablespoons)

1 teaspoon finely grated lime zest

¼ cup (60ml) fresh lime juice

2 tablespoons soy sauce or tamari

2 tablespoons brown sugar

1 tablespoon water

2 teaspoons grated fresh ginger

FOR SERVING

2 scallions, thinly sliced

Bibb or butter lettuce leaves

Fresh cilantro sprigs

Fresh mint leaves

PREHEAT THE OVEN TO 425°F (220°C).

Remove the cauliflower florets from the stem, and separate into bite-size florets. Trim the stem, then use a sharp vegetable peeler to peel its tough outer skin. Cut in half lengthwise and again into thin half-moons.

On a large baking sheet, toss the cauliflower with the oil, pepper flakes, cumin, turmeric, and salt. Roast, tossing occasionally, until tender and beginning to char, 30 to 35 minutes. Let cool.

In a small skillet over medium heat, add the rice and cook, shaking the pan often, until browned, 2 to 3 minutes. Transfer the rice to a mortar and pestle or spice grinder, let cool, then grind until fine.

Make the dipping sauce: In a small bowl, combine the chiles, lemongrass, lime zest, lime juice, soy sauce, brown sugar, water, and ginger. Stir until the sugar is dissolved. Taste and dilute with more water if needed.

To serve: Transfer the cauliflower to a bowl, top with the scallions, and sprinkle with the toasted rice powder. Serve alongside the lettuce leaves, cilantro, mint, and bowl of dipping sauce. Let guests spoon the cauliflower mixture onto the leaves, garnish with the herbs, and dip in the sauce.

Sesame Tofu Cutlet Sandwiches

In this not-so-traditional but delicious preparation, extra-firm tofu is treated sort of like katsu: breaded, fried, and served in a sandwich with a crunchy slaw. If you crave the heat and tang of kimchi, try using 1 cup (150g) thinly sliced vegan kimchi in place of 1 cup (95g) cabbage.

Makes 4 servings

Time: Weekday

Storage: The fried tofu can be refrigerated for up to 3 days. The coleslaw can be refrigerated for up to 1 week.

¼ small head green cabbage (7 ounces/200g), very thinly sliced (about 2 cups)

¼ teaspoon fine sea salt, plus more to taste

¼ cup (60ml) Silky Aquafaba Mayonnaise (page 46) or store-bought vegan mayonnaise

2 tablespoons sriracha or other hot sauce

1 (14-ounce/397g) block extra-firm tofu

2 tablespoons plus ½ teaspoon soy sauce

3 teaspoons toasted sesame oil

¼ cup (20g) panko bread crumbs

¼ cup (35g) cornstarch

5 tablespoons toasted sesame seeds

6 tablespoons sunflower or other neutral oil

2 teaspoons unseasoned rice vinegar

½ cup (20g) fresh cilantro leaves and tender stems

4 hamburger buns or potato rolls or 8 slices soft bread, lightly toasted

IN A BOWL, COMBINE the cabbage and salt and massage with your hands until the cabbage is moist and starting to wilt, about 1 minute. Transfer the cabbage to a colander or fine-mesh sieve, set it over bowl, and let the cabbage drain while you proceed with the recipe.

In a small bowl, mix together the mayonnaise and sriracha.

Wrap the tofu in a clean kitchen towel and microwave for 1 minute. Unwrap, rewrap with a fresh towel, and repeat. (This helps rid it of extra moisture.)

Slice the block of tofu in half horizontally (like splitting a hamburger bun) to make 2 thinner slabs. Cut each slab in half crosswise to make 4 total rectangles.

Set up a dredging station in two shallow bowls. In one bowl, whisk together 2 tablespoons of the soy sauce and 2 teaspoons of the sesame oil. In the second bowl, whisk together the panko, cornstarch, and 2 tablespoons of the sesame seeds.

Working with one slab of tofu at a time, dip into the soy sauce mixture, turning to coat all the sides, then transfer to the panko mixture. Use your hands to press the dry mixture all over the tofu (really press it in!), then transfer to a plate or small baking sheet.

Set a wire rack over a sheet pan next to the stovetop. In a large nonstick skillet, heat the oil over medium-high heat until it shimmers. Add the tofu in a single layer and fry, flipping once and reducing the heat as needed, until browned and crispy, 2 to 3 minutes per side. (It's okay if some sesame seeds escape during this process—most should stick.) Transfer to the wire rack.

Give the cabbage a final squeeze, discard any liquid that has drained, and return it to the bowl. Add the rice vinegar, cilantro, remaining 3 tablespoons sesame seeds, remaining 1 teaspoon sesame oil, and remaining ½ teaspoon soy sauce. Taste, and season with more salt as needed.

To assemble the sandwiches, spread both sides of the buns with the mayo mixture. Add a piece of tofu, then top with the slaw and the top buns. Serve warm.

The Ultimate Real-Veggie Veggie Burgers

In an age of high-tech products meant to mimic the exact texture and flavor of beef burgers, many of us longtime vegans and vegetarians have missed something: veggie burgers that actually include—and even celebrate—vegetables, legumes, fungi, and other stars of the edible, delicious plant kingdom. I've played around with veggie burger recipes for more than a decade, and my favorites are those in which such ingredients play a visible, starring role. The trick is always about texture. Too many such recipes result in something mushy or falling apart (or both), but long ago, with the help of chef Brian Van Etten, I cracked the code, and while I've been tinkering around the edges of the idea ever since, the basic approach remains. You cook a pound of mushrooms with aromatic vegetables and spices, combine with a can's worth of mashed beans and other flavorings, and bind with flour. There's no food processor involved—nor should there be, because you want to keep, not obliterate, the texture of these delicious ingredients. The key to keeping them intact is a little make-ahead magic: You bake them first, which helps to firm up and set them. Then you refrigerate or freeze until you're ready to cook, pan-frying or grilling them to crispy-edged perfection.

The other key may seem surprising, but it's true. It's best to only lightly toast the buns, if at all, because the softer the bun, the less likely it is to crush the patty when you eat the burger.

This is a master recipe, offering you plenty—or should it be planty?—of options for ingredient swaps that will take them in different, but always flavor-packed, directions. The wiggle room comes in the choice of spices, mushroom and bean varieties, nuts or seeds, and acidic or other flavorings. Feel free to substitute any of these with your own combinations; as long as the proportions remain, it'll work.

Makes 6 servings

Time: Weekend

Storage: The cooked burgers can be refrigerated for up to 5 days. After baking, you can refrigerate the patties for up to 1 week or freeze in silicone zip-top bags for up to 6 months. Thaw before pan-frying or grilling.

2 tablespoons olive oil

1 cup (128g) chopped onion (yellow, white, or red) or shallots

3 garlic cloves, chopped

1 tablespoon **spices** (see Variations)

1 teaspoon fine sea salt, plus more to taste

1 pound (450g) **mushrooms**, trimmed if needed and chopped (see Variations)

1½ cups (265g) cooked **beans** or 1 (15-ounce/425g) can no-salt-added beans, drained and rinsed (see Variations)

½ cup **nuts** (50g to 70g depending on the nut), chopped, or whole seeds (60g to 70g, depending on the seed; see Variations)

1 tablespoon liquid aminos (such as Bragg), coconut aminos, tamari, or soy sauce

¾ cup (93g) all-purpose flour or (75g) chickpea flour

¼ cup (20g) nutritional yeast or Nacho Nooch (page 45)

1 to 2 tablespoons **acid or other flavorings** (see Variations)

¼ cup (60ml) grapeseed, sunflower, or other neutral vegetable oil

6 soft hamburger buns, very lightly toasted if desired

Accompaniments: Lettuce, tomato, pickles, sliced onions, and other **condiments** of your choice (see Variations)

PREHEAT THE OVEN TO 375°F (190°C). Line a large sheet pan with compostable parchment paper.

In a large skillet, heat the olive oil over medium-high heat until it shimmers. Add the onion and garlic and sauté until they are tender and lightly browned, 3 to 4 minutes. Stir in the **spices** and salt and cook, stirring, just until fragrant, about 30 seconds. Add the **mushrooms** and cook, stirring occasionally, until the mushrooms exude their liquid and it evaporates and they start to brown, 6 to 8 minutes. Remove from the heat and let cool for a few minutes.

In a large bowl, lightly mash the **beans** with a fork, leaving some whole. When the mushroom mixture has cooled, add it to the bowl, along with the **nuts or seeds**, aminos, flour, nutritional yeast, and **acid and other flavorings** and stir to thoroughly combine. The mixture will be very sticky. Taste and add more salt if needed.

RECIPE CONTINUES ON NEXT PAGE

Lightly oil a ½-cup (120ml) measure. Scoop 6 heaping portions onto the parchment, then wet your hands and use them to pat and shape the mixture into large patties, about 4 inches (10cm) across and ½ to ¾ inch (1.3cm to 2cm) thick.

Bake the patties until firm and dry on the outside, 20 to 30 minutes, flipping them over about halfway through. Transfer to a wire rack to cool.

In a large skillet, heat the vegetable oil over medium-high heat until it shimmers. Add as many patties as will fit without overcrowding and fry until crisp on the bottom, 3 to 4 minutes. Carefully flip them over and fry until crisp on the other side, 3 to 4 minutes. Transfer to a platter. (Alternatively, you can cook them on a gas or charcoal grill over medium-high heat for about the same timing.)

Build the burgers with your preferred accompaniments and **condiments**. Serve hot.

Southwest Veggie Burgers

- **Spices:** 2 teaspoons ground cumin + 1 teaspoon chipotle chile powder
- **Mushrooms:** Cremini
- **Beans:** Pinto, red kidney, or black
- **Nuts/seeds:** Toasted pumpkin seeds
- **Acid/other:** 2 tablespoons fresh lime juice
- **Condiments:** Cashew Queso (page 31), pickled jalapeños

Curried Veggie Burgers

- **Spices:** Madras curry powder or Garam Masala (page 40)
- **Mushrooms:** 12 ounces (340g) oyster + 4 ounces (115g) shiitake caps
- **Beans:** Chickpeas
- **Nuts/seeds:** Walnuts
- **Acid/other:** 1 tablespoon white miso + 1 tablespoon unseasoned rice vinegar
- **Condiments:** Sambal Sesame Mayonnaise (page 46)

Mediterranean Veggie Burgers

- **Spices:** 2 teaspoons Za'atar (page 44) + 1 teaspoon smoked paprika
- **Mushrooms:** 12 ounces (340g) cremini or oyster + 4 ounces (115g) chanterelles
- **Beans:** Cannellini or chickpeas
- **Nuts/seeds:** Almonds or pistachios
- **Acid/other:** 2 tablespoons red wine vinegar or sherry vinegar
- **Condiments:** Aioli (page 46), Rose Harissa (page 52)

Tofu Summer Rolls with Cucumber, Herbs & Pickled Onions

The Vietnamese name for summer rolls is *gỏi cuốn*, which translates literally to "salad rolls"—a very apt description considering that the bulk of the filling consists of herbs, lettuce, and fresh vegetables. While pork and shrimp are traditional fillings, this recipe uses pan-fried tofu instead. Pickled onions, also veering away from the classic, add acid and mild heat, and the rice noodles offer substance (and a delightfully slippery texture). These are perfect for hot summer evenings when you really don't feel like cooking anything, especially if you prepare the tofu and the rice noodles well in advance.

Makes about 12 rolls (4 servings)

Time: Weekday

Storage: Best eaten while fresh, but can be refrigerated, wrapped in a damp towel, and sealed in an airtight container, for up to 3 days.

PICKLED ONIONS

¼ large or ½ small red onion (78g), thinly sliced

¼ cup (60ml) unseasoned rice vinegar

¼ cup (60ml) hot water

¼ teaspoon organic cane sugar

¼ teaspoon red pepper flakes

¼ teaspoon fine sea salt

PEANUT SAUCE

½ cup (130g) natural peanut butter, well-stirred

7 tablespoons hot water

1½ tablespoons soy sauce

1½ teaspoons sriracha

1½ teaspoons unseasoned rice vinegar

¼ teaspoon organic cane sugar, plus more to taste

¼ teaspoon fine sea salt, plus more to taste

ASSEMBLY

3 ounces (85g) rice vermicelli

1 (16-ounce/454g) block firm or extra-firm tofu, drained and patted dry

2 tablespoons neutral oil, plus more as needed

¼ teaspoon fine sea salt, plus more to taste

12 rice paper rounds

1 small head Bibb or butter lettuce, separated into leaves

3 Persian (mini) cucumbers, thinly sliced on a diagonal

1¼ cups (20g) tender herbs, such as dill, mint, basil, and cilantro

MAKE THE PICKLED ONIONS: In a small bowl, combine the onion, vinegar, water, sugar, pepper flakes, and salt. Let it sit while you proceed with the recipe.

Make the peanut sauce: In a medium bowl, whisk together the peanut butter, hot water, soy sauce, sriracha, rice vinegar, sugar, and salt until smooth. Taste and season with more salt and/or sugar as needed.

To assemble: In a pot of boiling water, cook the rice vermicelli according to the package directions. Drain well, rinse with cold water, and drain again. Using kitchen shears, cut the pile of noodles in thirds crosswise.

Cut the tofu into 1 × 2-inch (2.5cm × 5cm) rectangles about ½ inch (1.3cm) thick. Pat them dry. In a large nonstick skillet, heat the oil over medium-high heat until it shimmers. Working in batches to avoid over-crowding, add a single layer of tofu and cook until golden brown on the bottom, 2 to 3 minutes. Flip and cook until golden brown on the other side, 2 to 3 minutes. Transfer to a plate or baking sheet and sprinkle with the salt. Repeat with the remaining tofu.

Drain the onions.

Fill a wide shallow bowl with room-temperature water. Working with one rice paper round at a time, submerge until pliable but not floppy or soft, 5 to 10 seconds. Lift out of the water, letting any excess drain off, and place on a large plate or cutting board. In the center of the round, make a small horizontal pile of a piece of torn lettuce, a couple of slices of cucumber, a few pickled onion slices, a mix of herbs, and a small handful of noodles. Lean a few planks of tofu along the bottom of the pile.

Fold in the left and right sides, then start with the side nearest to you and roll away from you tightly, using the stability of the tofu to help. (You can also make a wrapper with an open top by folding the left side in before adding the filling.) Repeat with remaining rice paper rounds and fillings.

Serve with the peanut sauce for dipping.

COOK'S NOTE: The peanut sauce is open to customization: Add grated garlic and ginger, use a fresh chile instead of sriracha, or thin it out with a little hot water and toss it with the noodles.

Crispy Tacos with Potatoes

These golden tacos are the stuff of dreams: a homey combination of mashed potatoes and crispy tortillas, served with crunchy, creamy, and spicy toppings and traditionally served during Lent. You can make the mashed potatoes ahead of time (or use leftovers) and then fill the tortillas right before frying. Note that these don't store well as leftovers, which is just another excuse to finish them shortly after they're fried—as if you needed a reason.

Makes 4 servings

Time: Weekday

Storage: Not recommended for the finished tacos. The mashed potato filling can be refrigerated for up to 5 days before assembling and frying.

POTATO FILLING

3 medium russet potatoes (2 pounds/910g total), scrubbed and cut into chunks

1 tablespoon fine sea salt, plus more to taste

1 tablespoon garlic powder

1 tablespoon nutritional yeast

1 teaspoon smoked paprika

¼ teaspoon freshly ground black pepper

TACOS

12 corn tortillas

½ cup (120ml) peanut, sunflower, or other neutral oil

1 head romaine lettuce, cored and thinly sliced

2 large Roma tomatoes, cored and diced

½ medium red onion, thinly sliced

½ cup (56g) Creamy or Crumbly Almond Queso Fresco (page 27) or store-bought vegan feta

½ cup (120ml) Smooth Almond Crema (page 22)

½ cup (120ml) Chunky Molcajete Salsa (page 48) or your favorite salsa

MAKE THE POTATO FILLING: In a heavy pot, combine the potatoes, salt, and enough cold water to cover the potatoes by 1 inch (2.5cm). Bring to a boil over medium-high heat, then reduce the heat and simmer the potatoes until soft and cooked through, about 20 minutes. Reserving 1½ cups (350ml) of the cooking water, drain the potatoes.

Set a ricer or food mill over a large bowl and pass the potatoes through it into the bowl, leaving the skins behind. (Or, for a more rustic filling, you can keep the skins in and mash the potatoes in the bowl with a fork or potato masher.) Stir in the garlic powder, nutritional yeast, smoked paprika, pepper, and ¾ cup (180ml) of the potato water. Taste and season with more salt as needed. The potatoes should be creamy; if they're too dry, stir in some of the remaining potato water until you reach the desired consistency.

Make the tacos: Microwave the tortillas, 4 at a time, on high for 1 minute until they are soft and pliable.

Top each tortilla with 2 heaping tablespoons of the potato filling and fold in half.

In a large skillet, heat the oil over medium-high heat until it shimmers. Working in batches to avoid overcrowding, add a few of the tacos and fry until golden brown and crispy, 6 to 7 minutes per side. (Alternatively, you can cook these in an air fryer: Set it to 400°F/200°C and cook for 15 minutes, flipping them halfway through.)

Transfer to a serving platter and top with the lettuce, tomatoes, onion, queso fresco, crema, and salsa. Serve hot.

10

KNIFE & FORK: CENTER OF THE PLATE MAINS

Sometimes it doesn't seem all that long ago that the definition of dinner was protein (read: meat or seafood), starch, and side vegetable. How things have changed! Vegan and vegetarian cooks have been calling for a return of the vegetable to the center of the plate for decades, and we have long known that protein can come from plenty of plants. But now we're just as likely to eat a main-course salad, grain bowl, or pasta as we are a collection of nibbles (dips for dinner!), having stretched that dinner definition to its very limits. This chapter is for those who want a bit of a throwback, who still want to dig into the main attraction on their plate, whether there's a starch and a side or not.

Cauliflower with Korma-Inspired Sauce

The creamy, nutty, spicy, and warming sauce that accompanies these cauliflower steaks is inspired by korma, a North Indian gravy with countless variations that is usually made with yogurt, spices, and blended nuts or seeds. The nuttiness comes from almond butter, inherently creamy and toasty, a trick picked up from Varu Chilakamarri, author of *Indian Cuisine for the Busy Vegetarian*.

If you don't want to go to the trouble of searing and roasting cauliflower steaks (which makes for a beautiful presentation but takes some time), this would be just as good with roasted cauliflower florets. Toss the florets with vegetable oil and salt, then roast at 350°F (180°C) for 30 to 40 minutes, stirring two or three times, until starting to char. Toss with the sauce and serve over rice. To cut back on time, you could also make the sauce a day ahead and reheat gently when ready to serve.

Makes 4 servings

Time: Weekday

Storage: Refrigerate for up to 4 days.

1 large head cauliflower (2¼ pounds/1kg)

5 tablespoons vegetable or canola oil

¾ teaspoon fine sea salt, plus more to taste

1 medium red onion (8 ounces/225g), thinly sliced

5 garlic cloves, finely grated or pressed

2-inch (5cm) piece fresh ginger, finely grated

1 teaspoon garam masala, homemade (page 40) or store-bought

¼ to ½ teaspoon ground red chiles, to taste

½ teaspoon freshly ground black pepper

¼ teaspoon ground cardamom

1 (14.5-ounce/411g) can whole peeled tomatoes

¼ cup (60ml) water

3 tablespoons almond butter

2 tablespoons unsweetened coconut cream

¼ cup (8g) lightly packed fresh cilantro leaves and tender stems, coarsely chopped

⅓ cup (47g) almonds, toasted and coarsely chopped

Steamed basmati rice, for serving

1 lemon, cut into wedges

PREHEAT THE OVEN TO 350°F (180°C).

Remove the tough outer leaves from the cauliflower (leave the tender inner leaves) and trim the bottom of the stem. Rest the cauliflower stem-side up and cut it into 2 or 3 steaks 1 to 1½ inches (2.5cm to 4cm) thick, going from bottom to top through the core. Keep the rest of the cauliflower in chunks or florets as big as possible.

In a large skillet, heat 2 tablespoons of the vegetable oil over medium-high heat until it shimmers. Add the cauliflower, both the steaks and any florets, sprinkle with ¼ teaspoon of the salt, and cook, pressing down occasionally and rotating the pan for even heat, until charred and browning, 6 to 7 minutes. Flip, add another 1 tablespoon of the oil, sprinkle with another ¼ teaspoon of salt, and continue to cook until the second side is charred and browning, 4 to 5 minutes. (If any small florets cook more quickly, remove them sooner.) Transfer to a baking sheet, reserving any tiny florets that have broken off for serving, and bake until fork-tender, for 12 to 16 minutes.

Meanwhile, return the skillet to medium heat. Add the remaining 2 tablespoons oil and the red onion and cook, stirring occasionally, until starting to brown, about 10 minutes. Scoop out about 4 tablespoons and set aside for serving.

Add the garlic and ginger to the onions still in the pan and cook, stirring constantly, until fragrant, about 1 minute. Add the garam masala, ground chiles, black pepper, cardamom, and remaining ¼ teaspoon salt and cook, stirring constantly, until fragrant, about 30 seconds. Add the tomatoes and water and bring to a simmer, breaking up tomatoes with the back of a spoon. Cook, stirring occasionally, until thick and starting to stick to the bottom of the pot, 4 to 5 minutes.

Remove from the heat and add the almond butter and coconut cream. Use an immersion blender (or transfer to a blender or food processor) to puree until smooth. Taste and season with more salt as needed.

To serve, spread a generous amount of korma sauce on a large platter, reserving some sauce to serve on the side. Nestle the cauliflower in the sauce, then sprinkle with the reserved red onions, the cilantro, and almonds. Serve with rice, lemon wedges, and the extra sauce.

Crispy Sesame Chickpea Tofu with Pea Sprout Salad

Chickpea tofu, a popular Burmese dish, is more akin to polenta than conventional tofu: It's a porridge made with chickpea flour and water (plus a little turmeric for color and earthy flavor), poured into a dish, and cooled until firm. You can cut it into cubes and eat it like that, but frying it results in a deeply golden, crisp exterior and creamy interior.

This recipe goes a step further, coating the tofu with sesame seeds, added for texture and nuttiness. These triangles act as large, protein-rich croutons on a bright, crunchy salad.

Makes 4 to 6 servings

Time: Weekend

Storage: Not recommended for the finished dish, but you can make the chickpea tofu and refrigerate up to 3 days before frying. The dressing can be refrigerated for up to 3 days.

CHICKPEA TOFU

2 cups (180g) chickpea flour

1 teaspoon fine sea salt, plus more to taste

1 teaspoon ground turmeric

4½ cups (1.05L) water

2 teaspoons toasted sesame oil

1 tablespoon canola oil, plus more for shallow-frying

3 tablespoons white sesame seeds

3 tablespoons black sesame seeds

SALAD

¼ cup (60ml) rice vinegar, preferably unseasoned

1 tablespoon soy sauce

½-inch (1.3cm) piece fresh ginger, peeled and grated

1½ teaspoons organic cane sugar

¼ teaspoon fine salt, plus more to taste

½ teaspoon freshly ground black pepper

⅓ cup (80ml) canola oil

½ medium head red cabbage (8 ounces/225g), finely shredded

2 cups (2 ounces/55g) pea sprouts

½ cup (18g) lightly packed fresh cilantro leaves

½ cup (18g) lightly packed dill fronds, torn into bite-size pieces

Sambal oelek, sriracha, or gochujang, for serving (optional)

MAKE THE CHICKPEA TOFU: In a large pot, whisk together the chickpea flour, salt, turmeric, and 1½ cups (350ml) of the water. Let sit for 15 minutes.

Whisk in the remaining 3 cups (700ml) water, place over medium-high heat, and bring to a boil, whisking occasionally. Reduce the heat to medium-low, partially cover, and cook, whisking frequently, until the mixture has thickened and the raw chickpea flour taste has cooked out, 12 to 15 minutes. Taste and season with more salt as needed. Turn off the heat and whisk in the sesame oil.

While the chickpea mixture is cooking, oil an 8-inch (20cm) square baking pan with the canola oil. Sprinkle the white and black sesame seeds in an even layer over the bottom of the pan.

Spoon the cooked chickpea mixture over the sesame seeds and rap the pan on the counter to create an even layer and remove any air bubbles. Let cool at room temperature for 1 hour or cover and refrigerate overnight.

Loosen the edges of the cooled chickpea tofu and carefully flip onto a cutting board. Cut the tofu in half and then cut each half into 3 rectangles. Cut each rectangle diagonally to create a total of 12 triangles.

Set a wire rack over a sheet pan next to the stovetop. Pour ¼ inch (6mm) canola oil into a large nonstick skillet and heat over medium heat until it shimmers. Add the tofu pieces seed-side down, working in batches so as not to overcrowd the pan. Fry the tofu until deep golden brown, about 3 minutes. Flip the pieces and fry until golden brown on the other side, about 4 minutes. Transfer the tofu to the wire rack and let cool for 15 minutes.

Meanwhile, make the salad: In a medium bowl, whisk together the vinegar, soy sauce, ginger, sugar, salt, and pepper until the sugar is dissolved. While whisking, slowly drizzle in the canola oil until an emulsified dressing forms. Taste and season with more salt as needed.

Immediately before serving, toss the cabbage in the bowl with the dressing. Add the pea sprouts, cilantro, and dill and gently toss.

To serve, arrange the salad on a large platter or individual plates and nestle the chickpea tofu wedges on top. Serve with sambal oelek, if desired.

Herby Falafel

I've long warned: If you see a falafel recipe that uses canned or precooked chickpeas, back away and look for another recipe. True falafel—with its characteristic crunchy exterior and fluffy interior—can never come about that way. Instead, dried chickpeas are the key; you soak them overnight, then pulse in the food processor with other ingredients. Similarly, purists like me shy away from baking instead of frying falafel. But recipe developer Joy Manning told me about her way of sizzling falafel in the oven on a well-oiled sheet pan instead of giving a dunk in a bubbling pot of oil. I immediately saw the appeal.

One issue with baking, though, is that it's harder to get the falafel to hold together. Joy's solution is to add a little flour to the mix, and to handle the falafel balls carefully.

So here's the best of both worlds: An excellent recipe for traditionally made fried falafel, green inside from parsley and cilantro, plus a great variation for baking them instead.

Sandwiches are an obvious pick for these falafel, and they're excellent wrapped in Bing (page 397) with your favorite pickles, hummus, tahini, and whatnot, or over a pile of shaved raw cabbage with a drizzle of Tahini Dressing (page 59).

Makes 4 to 6 servings

Time: Weekday

Storage: Refrigerate for up to 3 days or freeze for up to 3 months.

- 1 generous cup (200g) dried chickpeas, soaked overnight and drained
- 1 small onion (5½ ounces/156g), chopped (about 1 cup)
- 1 cup lightly packed (30g) fresh parsley leaves (about 1 small bunch)
- 1 cup lightly packed (30g) fresh cilantro leaves and tender stems (about 1 small bunch)
- 1 teaspoon fine sea salt
- 3 garlic cloves, peeled but whole
- 1 teaspoon ground cumin
- 1 teaspoon baking powder
- Peanut, sunflower, or other neutral oil, for frying

IN A FOOD PROCESSOR, combine the chickpeas, onion, parsley, cilantro, salt, garlic, cumin, and baking powder and pulse—do not let the motor run continuously!—until the mixture is very finely chopped but not pasty, with the ingredients the size of broken grains of rice.

Use a #40 disher (cookie scoop) or 1-tablespoon measure to scoop 2 tablespoons of the mixture and transfer it to one hand. Gently squeeze it in your hand to form an oblong ball and transfer it to a platter or cutting board. Repeat with the remaining falafel. (The less you touch and otherwise fuss with them, the better they'll hold together.)

Let them rest while you heat the oil.

Set a wire rack over a sheet pan next to the stovetop. Pour 3 inches (7.5cm) oil into a Dutch oven (do not use a shallower pot, which can lead to messy splatters as you fry). Heat the oil over medium-high heat to between 350° and 360°F (177° and 182°C). Adjust the heat as necessary to maintain it.

Working in batches of 4 to 5 falafel to avoid over-crowding, use a slotted spoon to carefully lower each ball into the oil, which should immediately bubble around them. Try to place them so they don't touch and cook until deep brown all over, 3 to 4 minutes. Use the slotted spoon to transfer them to the wire rack to drain. (If desired, you can put the wire rack setup in a 200°F/90°C oven so the falafel stay warm as you fry them.)

Serve warm.

VARIATION

Baked Falafel

Add ¼ cup (31g) all-purpose flour to the chickpea mixture in the food processor. Preheat the oven to 450°F (230°C) with a rack in the lowest possible position and a sheet pan on the rack to preheat along with the oven.

After forming the falafel, remove the hot baking sheet from the oven and brush it liberally with olive oil. Gently transfer the falafel to the baking sheet and do not move them once you have put them down, or they might break up. Bake on the lowest rack until the edges brown, 8 to 10 minutes, then gently turn them over (resisting the impulse to flatten them; the texture is lighter and better if you don't) and bake on the second side until browned, about 5 minutes.

Creamy Butter Mushrooms

This is a plant-based take on one of the most popular ways to cook seafood in Malaysia. Curry leaves and spicy Thai chiles add heat and a unique flavor to these crispy, battered mushrooms tossed in a creamy sauce. It's a delicious dish for mushroom lovers—and anyone who might harbor any doubts about them.

If you can't find oyster mushrooms, king oyster, lion's mane, or shiitake mushrooms work well as an alternative. Serve the mushrooms on their own, wrapped with butter lettuce, or over rice.

Makes 2 to 3 servings

Time: Weekday

Storage: While these are best served immediately after cooking, the fried mushrooms can be refrigerated separately from the sauce for up to 3 days. When ready to serve, bake or air-fry the mushrooms to crisp them up and then toss with the heated sauce.

BATTER

½ cup (80g) white rice flour (not sweet rice flour)

½ cup (63g) all-purpose flour

¼ teaspoon fine sea salt

¼ teaspoon freshly ground black pepper

1 cup (240ml) water

FRIED MUSHROOMS

1 cup (240ml) neutral oil

6 ounces (180g) oyster mushrooms, trimmed and torn into bite-size pieces

SAUCE

3 tablespoons (42g) Soft Spreadable Butter (page 21) or unsalted vegan butter

Handful of fresh curry leaves

2 fresh Thai chiles, chopped

1 cup (240ml) Nut Milk (page 17), Oat Milk (page 17), Soy Milk (page 75), or store-bought plant-based milk

½ tablespoon organic cane sugar

½ teaspoon fine sea salt

MAKE THE BATTER: In a bowl, whisk together the rice flour, all-purpose flour, salt, and pepper. Measure out ⅓ cup (50g) of the dry ingredients and set aside in a separate bowl for dredging. Whisk the water into the remaining dry ingredients to make a thin batter.

Set a wire rack over a sheet pan next to the stovetop. In a 3-quart (3L) saucepan, heat the oil over medium-high heat until it reaches 350°F (177°C). Reduce the heat slightly to maintain it.

Toss the mushrooms with the reserved dry flour mixture until they are well coated.

Once the oil is heated, dip the mushrooms in the wet mixture and fry in small batches until golden, 1 to 2 minutes per side. Transfer the fried mushrooms to the wire rack to drain. This will keep the mushrooms crispy while you prepare the sauce.

Make the sauce: In a nonstick skillet, melt the butter over medium heat. Temper the curry leaves by cooking them for a few seconds in the butter until aromatic, then add the chiles and sauté for a few more seconds. Add the milk, sugar, and salt and cook, stirring, until the sugar has melted. Continue to cook until the sauce starts to thicken. Remove from the heat.

Add the fried mushrooms to the sauce and quickly toss to combine. Transfer to a plate and serve warm.

Family-Style Tofu

As the name implies, this is a common tofu dish in most Chinese households and can be found at many Chinese restaurants as one of the options for vegetarians and vegans. Every household or restaurant has their own secret recipe, but the common ingredients include carrot, mushrooms, and spices. This version braises the tofu in a simple aromatic sauce whose flavors it absorbs.

Silken tofu is also a good option for this dish. If you can't find dried wood ear mushrooms, look for the rehydrated version at major grocery stores. Serve the tofu on its own or over rice.

Makes 2 to 3 servings

Time: Weekend

Storage: Refrigerate for up to 2 days.

  ¼ cup (4g) dried wood ear mushrooms

  1 tablespoon vegan oyster sauce

  2 tablespoons soy sauce

  1 teaspoon organic cane sugar

  Pinch of ground white pepper

  1 (14-ounce/397g) block firm tofu, drained and sliced lengthwise into strips 1 inch (2.5cm) thick

  1 tablespoon neutral oil, plus more as needed

  2-inch (5cm) piece fresh ginger, peeled and thinly sliced

  1 small carrot, scrubbed and thinly sliced

  3 garlic cloves, thinly sliced

  2 cups (470ml) plus 3 tablespoons water

  1 teaspoon cornstarch

  2 scallions, chopped

IN A LARGE BOWL, soak the dried wood ear mushrooms in room-temperature water until they are rehydrated, about 1 hour. Drain the water and remove the tough core from each mushroom. Slice into strips.

In a small bowl, whisk together the oyster sauce, soy sauce, sugar, and white pepper until the sugar has dissolved.

Pat the tofu dry. In a nonstick skillet, heat the oil over medium heat until it shimmers. Add the tofu and pan-fry until golden brown on all sides, 6 to 8 minutes total. Transfer to a plate.

Using the same skillet still over medium heat, sauté the ginger slices until aromatic, adding a little more oil if needed. Add the carrot and garlic and stir-fry for a few more seconds. Add 2 cups (470ml) of the water and the oyster sauce mixture to the pan and bring to a boil. Add the mushrooms and tofu and cover the pan with a lid. Let the mixture simmer until the carrot is tender, 5 to 10 minutes.

In a small bowl, make a cornstarch slurry by mixing the cornstarch with the remaining 3 tablespoons water. Remove the cover from the pan and swirl in the cornstarch slurry, tossing to thoroughly coat the mushrooms and tofu in the sauce. Fold in the scallions. Serve warm.

Gochujang Tofu with Edamame-Mint Puree

This recipe was inspired by one that chef Daniel Biron serves at his Rio de Janeiro restaurant Teva, where he sources from a small producer a surprisingly firm, dense tofu that stands up beautifully to the dish's bold flavors. If you get into making your own tofu (see page 75), here's a great place to use it. This recipe loads it up with flavor: A sauce made with gochujang (Korean red chile paste), molasses, ginger, and mirin (sweet Japanese rice wine) results in a delightful mix of sweet and savory that pairs perfectly with the edamame-mint puree.

Makes 4 servings

Time: Weekday

Storage: The finished dish is best eaten immediately. The gochujang sauce and edamame puree can be made up to 3 days ahead and stored separately in the refrigerator.

GOCHUJANG SAUCE

1-inch (2.5cm) piece fresh ginger, peeled and grated

2 garlic cloves, grated

½ cup (128g) tomato paste (regular, not double-concentrated)

1½ tablespoons gochujang

2½ tablespoons reduced-sodium tamari or soy sauce

2 tablespoons mirin

2 tablespoons balsamic vinegar

2½ tablespoons molasses

1½ teaspoons toasted sesame oil

TOFU

2 tablespoons olive oil

2 (14-ounce/397g) blocks extra-firm tofu, each block cut into four lengthwise slabs and thoroughly patted dry

⅛ teaspoon fine sea salt

⅛ teaspoon freshly ground black pepper

EDAMAME-MINT PUREE

1 tablespoon olive oil

1 cup (55g) chopped scallions

1 garlic clove, minced

4 cups (620g) frozen shelled edamame

2 cups (470ml) room-temperature water

¾ teaspoon fine sea salt, plus more to taste

½ cup (10g) firmly packed fresh mint leaves

1 tablespoon fresh lime juice

FOR SERVING

White sesame seeds

Sliced fresh mint leaves

Chopped scallions

MAKE THE GOCHUJANG SAUCE: In a medium saucepan, combine the ginger, garlic, tomato paste, gochujang, tamari, mirin, balsamic vinegar, molasses, and sesame oil. Bring to a simmer over medium-high heat, reduce the heat, and cook until slightly thickened, about 4 minutes. Remove from the heat.

Prepare the tofu: In a cast-iron or other nonstick skillet, warm the olive oil over medium-high heat. Season the tofu with the salt and pepper. Add to the skillet and sear until golden, 2 to 3 minutes per side. Turn off the heat. Transfer the gochujang sauce to the skillet, toss gently to coat, and allow to sit while preparing the edamame-mint puree.

Make the edamame-mint puree: Rinse and dry the saucepan used for the gochujang sauce and set it over medium heat. Add the oil and heat until it shimmers. Stir in the scallions and garlic and cook until fragrant, about 1 minute. Add the edamame, water, and ¼ teaspoon of the salt. Bring to a boil over high heat, reduce to a simmer, and cook partially covered until the edamame are tender, about 10 minutes. Remove from the heat and drain, reserving ¾ cup (180ml) of the cooking liquid.

Transfer the cooked edamame, reserved cooking liquid, mint leaves, and the remaining ½ teaspoon salt to a blender. Begin blending at low speed, gradually increasing to medium, until the mint is fully incorporated, about 1 minute. The puree should be the consistency of hummus. Pour the puree back into the saucepan. Stir in the lime juice. Taste and season with more salt if needed.

Return the skillet with the tofu and gochujang sauce in it to medium heat and warm until the sauce is glossy and the tofu is hot. If needed, warm the edamame-mint puree over medium heat, adding a splash of water if it has thickened too much.

To serve, spoon the puree onto a plate and arrange the tofu and gochujang sauce on top. Serve immediately sprinkled with sesame seeds, mint, and scallions.

Jerk Tofu

The spicy Jamaican jerk sauce on this tofu from food writer Jessica Hylton-Leckie is the real deal. Jessica was born and raised in Jamaica, so preserving the Jamaican culture in language, arts, and food is one of her priorities. With a combination of Scotch bonnet peppers, pimento (allspice), nutmeg, soy sauce, thyme, and other seasonings, jerk sauce is Jamaica in a bottle. You get hints of sweet and salty, as well as lots of spicy and a kick of flavor.

Makes 4 servings

Time: Weekend

Storage: Refrigerate for up to 4 days. The Jerk Sauce can be refrigerated for up to 2 weeks.

> 1 (16-ounce/450g) block extra-firm tofu, drained
> ⅓ cup (80ml) Jerk Sauce (recipe follows)
> Lime wedges, for serving

WRAP THE TOFU IN a clean kitchen towel and microwave for 1 minute. Unwrap, rewrap with a fresh towel, and repeat. (This helps rid it of extra moisture.)

Slice the block of tofu in half crosswise, then cut each half lengthwise into 4 equal slices to give you 8 rectangles.

Using a fork, poke some holes into each tofu slice before placing it in a zip-top bag or a food storage container. Pour the jerk sauce over the tofu, seal or cover tightly, and gently shake the container or the bag to ensure all the pieces are coated. Marinate for at least 3 hours and up to overnight.

Preheat the oven to 450°F (230°C). Place a cast-iron grill pan or an oven-safe skillet in the oven as it preheats.

Remove the tofu from the container and place on the grill pan. Roast for 15 minutes, until the tofu is blackened in spots and crisp on the edges. (Alternatively, the tofu can be grilled over medium heat on an outdoor grill until both sides are seared and fully cooked, 5 to 8 minutes on each side.)

Serve with lime wedges on the side.

Jerk Sauce

Fabulous on tofu (at left), the sauce can also be used as a marinade for grilled vegetables, to spice up quinoa or rice, or as a sandwich spread.

Makes 1 cup

> 4 Scotch bonnet peppers (about 3¼ ounces/92g total), preferably organic (see Note)
> 1 medium red or yellow onion (8 ounces/225g), chopped
> 6 garlic cloves, peeled but whole
> 5 scallions, trimmed and cut into thirds
> ¼ cup (60ml) distilled white vinegar
> ¼ cup (60ml) soy sauce
> 2 tablespoons neutral vegetable oil
> 1 tablespoon grated fresh ginger
> 2 tablespoons whole dried allspice (pimento) berries or 1 teaspoon ground allspice
> 2 tablespoons brown sugar
> 1 tablespoon freshly ground black pepper
> 1½ teaspoons sea salt
> 1 teaspoon freshly grated nutmeg
> 7 sprigs fresh thyme

IN A BLENDER, COMBINE the Scotch bonnets, onion, garlic, scallions, vinegar, soy sauce, oil, ginger, allspice, brown sugar, black pepper, salt, nutmeg, and thyme and puree until smooth. Store in an airtight container in the refrigerator.

COOK'S NOTE: Organic Scotch bonnet peppers are much hotter and larger than their conventionally grown siblings, so if you're not using organic, you may want to add up to 3 more. The sauce is very spicy, so use fewer peppers for a milder sauce. Adjust accordingly for your taste buds. If you're not sure, start with just one, and work your way up. If you can't find Scotch bonnet peppers, habanero peppers are a good substitute. The flavor of the jerk sauce will differ slightly.

Mochiko Tofu

This plant-based version of the Hawaiian favorite subs in super-firm tofu for the traditional chicken. Super-firm tofu, which you buy already pressed, is sturdy enough to stand up to the thicker mochiko batter, but if you can't find it, you can use extra-firm tofu and remove some of the moisture (see Note). The batter is a sweet, umami-rich combination of soy sauce, sake, sugar, plenty of garlic and ginger, and of course, mochiko (Japanese sweet rice flour).

Start this a day or two before you want to fry it, to give the tofu time to marinate in the batter before you wrap it with nori strips and then fry it to deep golden perfection. Eat over steamed rice with extra green onions sprinkled on top, or serve with Sambal Sesame Mayonnaise (page 46) for dipping.

Makes 4 servings

Time: Weekend

Storage: Best eaten immediately, but leftovers can be refrigerated for up to 2 days and reheated in an air fryer or oven to maintain crispness.

1 (16-ounce/454g) block super-firm (pressed) tofu (or extra-firm tofu; see Note), drained

⅓ cup (80ml) soy sauce

2 tablespoons sake

1-inch (2.5cm) piece fresh ginger, peeled and finely grated

2 garlic cloves, finely grated or pressed

1 scallion, finely chopped

2 tablespoons organic cane sugar

½ teaspoon fine sea salt

½ cup (80g) mochiko flour

2 nori sheets, cut into 2½ × 1-inch (6.5cm × 2.5cm) strips

Canola oil, for frying

Flaky sea salt, for finishing

1 large lemon, cut into wedges

SLICE THE TOFU IN half lengthwise, then cut crosswise to create planks ½ inch (1.3cm) thick. Using a clean kitchen towel, pat dry. Place in a single layer in a 9 × 13-inch (23cm × 33cm) baking dish.

In a medium bowl, whisk together the soy sauce, sake, ginger, garlic, scallion, sugar, and salt until the sugar is dissolved. Whisk in the mochiko flour until smooth, then pour over the tofu. Gently flip the tofu so both sides are coated in the mochiko batter, cover, and refrigerate for at least 4 hours to as long as 48 hours.

Remove the tofu from the refrigerator 15 minutes before frying. Take one strip of nori and wrap it around the center of a piece of tofu and then return to the batter, flipping to fully coat the nori. Repeat with the remaining tofu.

Set a wire rack over a sheet pan next to the stovetop. Pour 1 inch (2.5cm) oil into a Dutch oven or large saucepan and heat the oil over medium-high heat to 350°F (177°C). Adjust the heat to maintain this temperature.

Working in batches so you don't overcrowd the skillet, fry the tofu, flipping it halfway through, until deep golden, 4 to 5 minutes. Transfer the tofu to the wire rack.

To serve, pile on a serving plate, sprinkle with flaky salt and nestle lemon wedges around the tofu. Serve hot.

COOK'S NOTE: If using extra-firm tofu, before slicing it, wrap the block in a clean kitchen towel and microwave for 1 minute, then unwrap, wrap with another clean towel, and microwave again for 1 minute. This helps expel water and is faster than pressing.

Grilled Seitan

The boom in from-scratch bread baking at home has caused another boom: in DIY seitan, thanks to the increased availability of vital wheat gluten, which is used in bread baking to supercharge loaves' elasticity, rise, chew, and crumb. It's true that using vital wheat gluten is much quicker than the traditional process of repeated washing, rinsing, and kneading of flour, but it can create a musty—and, for lack of a better word, gluten-y—flavor that I find off-putting.

I remembered the best seitan I ever tasted was from Vedge restaurant in Philadelphia, where chef Rich Landau turned it into the most beautiful crispy-edged, juicy pieces. Rich later told me he didn't make his own but used a custom seitan from the late Ray Reichel (of Ray's Seitan). Rich had hoped to document the recipe firsthand, but Ray died during the COVID pandemic, taking his secrets with him. Thankfully, Rich remembered enough of what he learned from Ray so he could coach me through trials that led to success. The bonus: Ray's method also happens to be much quicker and easier than the traditional.

You start with bread flour, as many traditional seitan recipes do, but you knead, rinse, and wash only briefly, repeating just a few times, leaving much more of the starch in the seitan before proceeding with the resting and boiling steps. After it cools in its cooking liquid, you tear it into pieces, run it through an umami-packed marinade, and flash it on a hot grill. It works like a dream.

This is seitan that's not trying to be anything else: It's charred and crispy on the outside, juicy inside, and it makes the most delicious tacos, grain bowls, skewers, or whatever you'd like to eat it on or with.

Makes 6 servings

Time: Weekend

Storage: The grilled seitan is best when first cooked and is a little gummy when cold, but you can refrigerate it for up to 3 days and reheat it under the broiler, being careful not to burn it.

SEITAN

6 cups (810g) white bread flour

2 cups (470ml) water

4 cups (950ml) vegetable broth

¼ cup (60ml) tamari

2 (5- to 7-inch/13cm to 18cm) pieces dried kombu

MARINADE

¾ cup (180ml) sunflower oil or other neutral vegetable oil

1 tablespoon tamari

1 tablespoon Dijon mustard

1 tablespoon fresh rosemary leaves

1½ teaspoons balsamic vinegar

1½ teaspoons vegan Worcestershire sauce

1½ teaspoons mixed whole peppercorns

¼ teaspoon annatto (achiote) seeds (optional)

1 garlic clove, peeled but whole

Fine sea salt, for sprinkling on the seitan

MAKE THE SEITAN: In a large bowl, combine the flour and water and stir until a shaggy ball of dough forms, adding a little more water if the dough seems too dry to come together. Transfer it to a clean bowl, cover with room-temperature water, and let it rest for at least 30 minutes and up to 2 hours.

Meanwhile, in a Dutch oven or soup pot, combine the broth, tamari, and kombu. Bring to a boil over medium-high heat, then reduce the heat to a simmer and cook for 15 minutes to meld the flavors. Remove from the heat. Fish out and compost the kombu. Cover to keep warm.

Once the dough has rested, pour out the excess water, set a colander inside the bowl, and transfer the dough to the colander. Set the bowl in the sink. Fill the bowl with cold tap water, and, working in the colander, knead, stretch, and pull the dough under the water for a minute or so, drain, and repeat two more times. (The water will start off opaque white but become a little less so as you repeat the steps; it will still remain quite cloudy and will not run clear.) Drain and let the dough sit in the colander to rest for at least 30 minutes and up to 2 hours.

Bring the tamari broth to a gentle boil, add the seitan dough, and return to the boil. Stir it vigorously for a few seconds, then let it gently boil, without stirring, for 30 minutes. Turn off the heat, and let the dough cool in the broth to room temperature. (If desired, you can transfer it to an airtight container and refrigerate for up to 2 days.)

Make the marinade: In a high-powered blender, combine the oil, tamari, mustard, rosemary, vinegar, Worcestershire sauce, peppercorns, annatto, and garlic and blend until smooth and emulsified. Transfer to a small bowl.

Build a two-zone fire in a charcoal grill or preheat a gas grill to high on one side and leaving the other on medium or medium-low (if possible; see Note) for keeping the pieces warm before serving.

While the grill is preheating, transfer the seitan to a fine-mesh sieve and rinse and drain it, then pat dry with a clean kitchen towel. (You can save the broth for sipping or for soups; freeze for up to 3 months.)

When the grill is ready (the coals are glowing with white ash, but there are no large flames), tear the seitan by hand into 1- to 2-inch (2.5cm to 5cm) pieces. (Doing this by hand instead of cutting with a knife results in more uneven surfaces that get crispy and coated with the marinade.) Once all the seitan is pulled into pieces, transfer them to the marinade, stir briefly to coat, then use long-handled tongs to transfer them to the grill. (You want to avoid leaving the seitan sitting in the marinade for more than 15 or 20 minutes, as its acids can cause the seitan to get too soft.)

Working in batches if necessary, sear the seitan for 1 to 2 minutes per side, until slightly charred and crisp, working quickly to keep from burning them. Transfer them to a plate or platter as they are finished, sprinkling them with fine salt while they're still hot.

Serve warm.

COOK'S NOTE: If you don't have access to an outdoor charcoal or gas grill, you can make this on a stovetop grill pan or cast-iron skillet over high heat. Just remember to turn your exhaust fan and smoke alarms off, or at least open some windows.

Enchiladas Five Ways

Enchiladas are one of the best-known Mexican dishes—and one of the most misunderstood. There is a place and a palate for a baked enchilada casserole covered in melted gooey cheese, but in most Mexican homes, enchiladas are a simple dish of stuffed corn tortillas bathed in a flavorful sauce and topped with crema and a sprinkle of fresh cheese. And here's perhaps the most surprising part: Enchiladas covered in a chile-heavy sauce aren't even the only kind. In fact, as Dora's Table blogger Dora Stone demonstrates with this wonderful array, enchiladas are not just a dish, but a category of dishes, and they include incredible variations whose names are based on the sauce: Besides enchiladas rojas (red chile sauce), there are enfrijoladas (black bean sauce), enmoladas (mole sauce), entomatadas (tomato sauce), and encacahuatadas (spicy peanut sauce), to name a few.

The key to a good vegan enchilada is a hearty vegetable filling, plus a homemade almond crema and almond queso fresco. (If you don't have those on hand or the time to make them, feel free to substitute store-bought vegan sour cream and vegan feta.)

Here, Dora unlocks an entire world of vegan enchiladas, with recipes for five sauces and three fillings, allowing you to mix and match. All the fillings work with all the sauces, but I've noted which are especially well matched.

To make ahead, prepare the sauce and filling the day before, and assemble and cook right before serving.

Makes 4 servings

Time: Weekend

Storage: The completed enchiladas don't store well, but you can refrigerate leftover sauce and filling in separate containers for up to 5 days and reheat before assembling.

RECIPE CONTINUES ON NEXT PAGE

Sauce of choice at right and on pages 313 to 314

12 corn tortillas

Filling of your choice (pages 314 to 315), warmed

1 cup (115g) crumbled Crumbly Almond Queso Fresco (page 27) or store-bought vegan feta, such as Violife

½ cup (120ml) Smooth Almond Crema (page 22) or store-bought vegan sour cream

ADDITIONAL TOPPINGS (OPTIONAL):

½ cup (85g) sliced white onion

½ cup (57g) sliced radishes

2 cups (110g) shredded romaine lettuce

IF THE SAUCE WAS made ahead, reheat it in a large skillet.

Heat the tortillas on a comal, in a dry skillet, or in the microwave until they are soft and pliable. If using a comal or skillet, heat it over medium-high heat until smoking and cook the tortillas for 30 seconds per side. Or microwave 4 tortillas at a time on high for 30 seconds to 1 minute, until they're hot.

Use tongs to dip the tortillas in the heated sauce, transfer to a plate, and place 1 tablespoon of the filling in the center of the tortilla. Roll the tortilla tightly around the filling. Repeat this process with the rest of the tortillas.

To serve unbaked: Set 3 of the filled tortillas on each of four plates. Pour some sauce on top and top with almond crema, almond queso fresco, and any other optional toppings.

To serve broiled: Turn on the oven broiler to low. Fill and roll the enchiladas as directed. Pour ½ cup (120ml) of the sauce in the bottom of a 9 × 13-inch (23cm × 33cm) baking dish and arrange the rolled tortillas seam-side down over the sauce. Pour the remaining 1½ cups (350ml) sauce over the rolled tortillas and give the baking dish a little shake to distribute them. Drizzle with the almond crema and almond queso fresco, and broil for 3 to 5 minutes to lightly brown the cheese. Add any additional toppings, if using, and serve hot.

Enfrijolada (Black Bean) Sauce

Makes 3 cups

1 dried pasilla chile, stemmed and seeded

1 small dried avocado leaf (optional; see Note)

2 (15-ounce/425g) cans or 3 cups (630g) cooked black beans, drained

1½ cups (350ml) Vegetable Scrap Stock (page 36) or store-bought vegetable broth

½ teaspoon fine sea salt, plus more to taste

2 tablespoons avocado oil

½ medium white onion (85g), chopped

2 garlic cloves, finely grated or pressed

HEAT A LARGE CAST-IRON skillet over medium heat until it starts to smoke. Add the chile and avocado leaf (if using) and toast for about 30 seconds per side, until the chile is pliable and fragrant.

Transfer the chile and avocado leaf to a medium saucepan over medium-high heat. Add the beans, vegetable broth, and salt and bring to a simmer. Remove from the heat and let the mixture sit (for at least 10 minutes) to soften the chile.

Return the cast-iron skillet to medium heat and heat 1 tablespoon of the avocado oil until it shimmers. Add the onion and garlic and sauté until they soften, about 7 minutes.

Transfer the sautéed onion and garlic to a blender. Add the bean mixture to the blender and puree until smooth.

In the cast-iron skillet, heat the remaining 1 tablespoon oil over medium-high heat until it shimmers. Pour in the bean puree and bring to a simmer. Taste and season with more salt as needed.

COOK'S NOTE: Look for dried avocado leaves in Latin supermarkets.

Entomatada (Tomato) Sauce

Makes 3 cups

1½ pounds (680g) Roma tomatoes
1 to 2 jalapeño peppers, stemmed
¼ large white onion (57g), cut into large chunks
2 garlic cloves, peeled but whole
½ teaspoon fine salt, plus more to taste
¼ teaspoon freshly ground black pepper
1 tablespoon avocado oil
1 bay leaf

IN A MEDIUM SAUCEPAN, combine the whole tomatoes and jalapeños and add water to cover by 1 inch (2.5cm). Bring to a boil, then reduce the heat to medium-low and gently simmer until the tomatoes are soft, about 15 minutes.

Drain the tomatoes and chiles and transfer them to a blender. Add the onion, garlic, salt, and pepper to the blender and puree until smooth.

In a large skillet, heat the oil over medium heat until it shimmers. Pour in the sauce and stir in the bay leaf. Reduce the heat to low and simmer the sauce until it turns a darker shade of red, about 6 minutes. Remove and compost the bay leaf. Taste and season with more salt as needed.

Enmolada (Mole) Sauce

Makes about 3½ cups

3 cups (700ml) Mole Coloradito (page 57)
Vegetable Scrap Stock (page 36) or store-bought vegetable broth

IN A LARGE SKILLET, heat the mole over medium heat. Whisk in enough stock so that the mole has the consistency of a cream soup: thick but pourable.

Enchilada Rojas (Red Chile) Sauce

Makes 3 cups

20 dried guajillo chiles (160g total), stemmed and seeded
4 ancho chiles (45g total), stemmed and seeded
½ large white onion (120g), cut into large chunks
4 garlic cloves, peeled but whole
½ teaspoon dried Mexican oregano
2 teaspoons fine sea salt, plus more to taste
½ teaspoon freshly ground black pepper
1 tablespoon avocado oil

HEAT A LARGE CAST-IRON skillet over medium heat until it starts to smoke. Working in batches to avoid overcrowding, add one layer of guajillo and ancho chiles and toast for about 30 seconds per side, until the chiles are pliable and fragrant. Repeat with the remaining chiles.

Transfer the chiles to a medium saucepan over medium-high heat, add water to cover by 1 inch (2.5cm), and bring to a simmer. Reduce the heat to medium and simmer until the chiles are soft, 10 to 15 minutes.

Reserving 3 cups (710ml) of the chile soaking liquid, drain the chiles. Transfer the chiles to a blender and add the onion, garlic, oregano, salt, pepper, and 2 cups (470ml) of the chile soaking liquid. Puree until smooth, adding more of the soaking liquid if needed to get a smooth, pourable sauce. Taste and season with more salt as needed. If desired, strain the sauce through a fine-mesh sieve to make it extra-smooth.

In a large skillet, heat the oil over medium heat until it shimmers. Pour in the sauce, bring it to a simmer, and cook until it thickens and turns a deep red color, about 6 minutes.

Encacahuatada (Peanut) Sauce

Makes 3 cups

16 dried guajillo chiles (110g total), stemmed and seeded

2 large Roma tomatoes (9 ounces/255g)

2 cups (300g) unsalted roasted peanuts

2 to 3 canned chipotle peppers in adobo sauce

4 garlic cloves, peeled but whole

¼ teaspoon ground cloves

2 teaspoons fine sea salt, plus more to taste

½ teaspoon freshly ground black pepper

1 tablespoon avocado oil

HEAT A LARGE CAST-IRON skillet over medium heat until it starts to smoke. Add the chiles and toast for about 30 seconds per side, until the chiles are pliable and fragrant. Transfer the chiles to a medium saucepan and add water to cover by 1 inch (2.5cm). Bring to a simmer over medium-high heat, reduce the heat slightly, and simmer gently until the chiles are soft, about 10 minutes. Reserving the soaking water, drain through a fine-mesh sieve. Transfer the chiles to a blender. Add 2 cups of the soaking water, and save the rest for another use. (If you don't quite have 2 cups, add enough water to get you there.)

In the same skillet you used to toast the chiles, cook the whole tomatoes over medium-high heat until they are slightly blackened on all sides, about 6 minutes. Transfer the tomatoes to the blender.

Add the peanuts, chipotle peppers, garlic, ground cloves, salt, and black pepper. Puree until smooth. Taste and season with more salt as needed. If desired, strain the sauce through a fine-mesh sieve for a super-smooth texture.

In a large skillet, heat the oil over medium heat until it shimmers. Pour in the sauce and cook until it thickens a bit and the color dulls, about 6 minutes.

Hearty Greens & Hominy Filling

Best with: Encacahuatada (Peanut) or Enfrijolada (Black Bean) Sauce.

Makes 3½ cups

1 bunch Swiss chard (8 ounces/225g)

1 tablespoon avocado oil

1 pound (450g) oyster mushrooms, trimmed and torn into bite-size pieces

½ cup (120ml) Vegetable Scrap Stock (page 36) or store-bought vegetable broth

3 garlic cloves, finely grated or pressed

1 (15-ounce/425g) can white hominy, drained and rinsed

1 teaspoon fine sea salt, plus more to taste

¼ teaspoon freshly ground black pepper

REMOVE THE SWISS CHARD leaves from the stems. Thinly slice the stems, chop the leaves, and keep the two separate.

In a large skillet, heat the oil over medium-high heat until it shimmers. Stir in the mushrooms and Swiss chard stems and sauté until the mushrooms are golden brown, 5 to 6 minutes.

Reduce the heat to medium-low, add the garlic, and cook until fragrant, about 1 minute. Stir in the Swiss chard leaves and vegetable broth. Cover and cook until the Swiss chard fully wilts, 2 to 3 minutes.

Stir in the hominy, salt, and pepper. Taste and season with more salt as needed.

Shiitake & White Bean Filling

Best With: Enmolada (Mole), Enchilada Rojas (Red Chile), or Encacahuatada (Peanut) Sauce.

Makes 4 cups

1 tablespoon avocado oil

1 medium white onion (7 ounces/200g), thinly sliced

2 garlic cloves, finely grated or pressed

8 ounces (225g) fresh shiitake mushrooms, stems composted (or saved for stock), caps cut into large pieces

2 (15-ounce/425g) cans or 3 cups (600g) cooked navy or other white beans, drained

½ cup (120ml) Vegetable Scrap Stock (page 36) or store-bought vegetable broth

1 teaspoon fine sea salt, plus more to taste

¼ teaspoon freshly ground black pepper

IN A LARGE SKILLET, heat the oil over medium heat until it shimmers. Add the onion and sauté until tender and translucent, about 5 minutes.

Stir in the garlic and cook until fragrant, about 1 minute. Stir in the shiitake mushrooms and sauté until they begin to brown, about 6 minutes.

Stir in the beans, vegetable stock, salt, and pepper. Reduce the heat to low and simmer gently until most of the liquid evaporates, about 4 minutes.

Taste and season with more salt as needed.

Zucchini & Black Bean Filling

Best with: Entomatada (Tomato) or Enchilada Rojas (Red Chile) Sauce.

Makes 3 cups

1 poblano pepper (4 ounces/115g)

1 tablespoon avocado oil

½ large white onion (113g), chopped

2 garlic cloves, finely grated or pressed

1 cup (140g) fresh or frozen corn kernels

½ cup (118ml) Vegetable Scrap Stock (page 36) or store-bought vegetable broth, plus more if needed

1 cup (115g) diced zucchini

1 (15-ounce/425g) can black beans, drained and rinsed

1 teaspoon fine sea salt, plus more to taste

¼ teaspoon freshly ground black pepper

TURN THE OVEN TO broil. Place the poblano on a sheet pan and on a rack a few inches from the broiler. Broil, turning the pepper with tongs every minute or two as needed as it chars, until all the sides are charred. (If you have a gas stove, you can do this on the open flame of a burner instead.) Transfer the pepper to a bowl and cover with a plate. Let it steam for 5 minutes, then peel the thin skins from the poblano. Tear the top off and remove the seedpod, then chop the poblano.

In a large skillet, heat the oil over medium heat until it shimmers. Add the onion and sauté until tender and translucent, about 5 minutes.

Stir in the garlic and cook until fragrant, about 1 minute. Reduce the heat to low and stir in the corn and vegetable broth. Cover and cook until the corn is tender, about 3 minutes.

Uncover, stir in the zucchini and poblano, and sauté until the zucchini is tender but not completely soft, about 4 minutes. If the vegetables are sticking to the pan, add a little more vegetable stock.

Stir in the black beans, salt, and pepper. Taste and season with more salt as needed.

From the top: Shiitake & White Bean Filling (page 315) with Enchilada Rojas (Red Chile) Sauce (page 313), and Hearty Greens & Hominy Filling (page 314) with Encacahuatada (Peanut) Sauce (page 314)

Grand Aioli Platter with Espelette Aioli

This recipe is French-style entertaining at its simplest and best: an array of market-fresh vegetables with an aioli spiked with mild, fruity, slightly spicy Espelette pepper for dipping. This could have gone just as easily in the Appetizers & Snacks chapter (page 113), but traditionally it is a meal's centerpiece, not a nibble.

You can really choose whatever vegetables you'd like, but make sure they're as fresh as possible. This array focuses on easy-to-find produce, but if you have access to a farmers market or your own garden, let what looks best guide you. (For inspiration, see our purple array on the following page.) In spring, consider blanched baby artichoke hearts, tender Tokyo turnips, snap peas, and asparagus. At the height of summer, try different types of cucumbers, the tiniest pattypan squash you can find, and wedges of heirloom tomatoes. Whatever the mix, you want about 2 pounds (910g) of vegetables in total. Don't forget the ice-cold rosé.

Make sure to whip up the aioli a couple hours in advance, so it can fully chill before serving.

Makes 6 to 8 servings

Time: Weekday

Storage: Refrigerate leftovers for up to 3 days.

Espelette Aioli (page 46)

6 ounces (170g) boiled or steamed baby Yukon Gold potatoes, halved

6 ounces (170g) baby carrots (4 to 6), scrubbed with tops left on and halved lengthwise

6 ounces (170g) radishes (1 small bunch), such as French breakfast or Easter egg

2 Persian (mini) cucumbers (3 ounces/85g each), cut into spears

2 small heads Little Gem lettuce (3 ounces/85g each), quartered

1 cup (5 ounces/150g) cherry tomatoes

1 large lemon, cut into wedges

Flaky sea salt, for serving

SET A BOWL OF Espelette aioli on a large platter and arrange the vegetables around it. Serve with a small bowl of lemon wedges and a pinch bowl of flaky salt for your guests to use as they'd like.

For the Grand Aioli Platter with Espelette Aioli, you can use the recipe as a mere suggestion. Here we arranged the platter by shades of purple, with cauliflower, radishes, carrots, and Belgian endive.

Hariyali Jackfruit Biryani

Hariyali (which means "greenery" in Hindi) is a green masala, typically made with chicken or lamb and hailing from the Hyderabad region of India. This recipe marinates meaty young jackfruit in a creamy, spicy masala overnight (note that you'll need to plan for that), then mixes it with fried potatoes and layers it with rice and shallots. The result: a dish tasty enough for family dinner and stunning enough for a party centerpiece.

Makes 4 to 6 servings

Time: Weekend

Storage: Refrigerate for up to 4 days.

HARIYALI MASALA

2 cups lightly packed (96g) fresh cilantro, leaves and stems roughly chopped

2 cups lightly packed (80g) fresh mint leaves, roughly chopped

1 (5.4-ounce/160ml) can unsweetened coconut cream

5 tablespoons Creamy Coconut Yogurt (page 23) or plain coconut yogurt

2 tablespoons fresh lemon juice

3 garlic cloves, roughly chopped

1 to 2 serrano peppers, roughly chopped

1-inch (2.5cm) piece fresh ginger, peeled and finely grated

1½ teaspoons garam masala, homemade (page 40) or store-bought

1½ teaspoons fine sea salt

½ teaspoon ground turmeric

1 (14-ounce/397g) can jackfruit in brine, drained and pulled into ½-inch (1.3cm) pieces

BIRYANI

2 cups (360g) basmati rice, preferably extra-long and aged (see Note)

½ cup (120ml) canola oil

5 large shallots (2 ounces/60g each), thinly sliced

1 to 2 large Yukon Gold potatoes (8 ounces/225g), scrubbed, halved lengthwise, and sliced into ½-inch (1.3cm) half-moons

3 tablespoons fine sea salt

½ teaspoon cumin seeds

5 whole cloves

3 green cardamom pods

1 bay leaf

Pinch of saffron steeped in 2 tablespoons water

1 large lemon, cut into wedges

MAKE THE HARIYALI MASALA: In a blender, combine the cilantro, mint, coconut cream, coconut yogurt, lemon juice, garlic, chiles, ginger, garam masala, salt, and turmeric. Puree until smooth. (It should be a little thinner than Greek yogurt.) Transfer the mixture to a medium bowl, add the jackfruit, and mix well. Cover and refrigerate overnight or at least 6 hours.

Preheat the oven to 375°F (190°C).

Make the biryani: Place the basmati rice in a fine-mesh sieve and rinse well. Transfer to a medium bowl, cover with water, and soak for 30 minutes.

Meanwhile, set a wire rack over a sheet pan next to the stovetop. In a large skillet, heat the oil over medium-high heat until it shimmers. Add half the shallots, and fry, stirring occasionally, until golden brown, 5 to 7 minutes. Using tongs or a slotted spoon, transfer the shallots to the wire rack. Repeat with the other half of the shallots, leaving the oil in the pan.

Working in batches if needed to avoid overcrowding, carefully add the potatoes to the skillet in a single layer and fry until deeply golden on both sides, 3 to 4 minutes per side. Transfer the potatoes to the wire rack. (Reserve the shallot-infused oil for another use.)

In a Dutch oven, bring 6 cups (1.4L) water to a boil over medium-high heat. Add the salt, cumin, cloves, cardamom, and bay leaf and boil for 1 minute. Add the rinsed rice and boil until just barely al dente, 5 to 6 minutes. Drain, keeping the whole spices with the rice.

Remove the jackfruit from the refrigerator and transfer the mixture, including all the marinade (masala), into the pot you cooked the rice in. Add the potatoes and stir to combine. Bring to a boil over medium-high heat, reduce the heat to medium-low, cover, and cook until the potatoes are soft, about 10 minutes. Turn off the heat and transfer half the masala into a bowl, leaving the potatoes and jackfruit.

Sprinkle half the parboiled rice in an even layer over the mixture in the pot. Sprinkle one-third of the fried shallots and the remaining half of the masala over the rice and top with the remaining half of the rice. Spoon the saffron water over the rice and sprinkle with the remaining half of the rice. Spoon the saffron water over the rice and sprinkle with the remaining fried shallots.

Cover and bake for 35 minutes. Remove from the oven and let sit, covered, for 15 minutes before serving.

Spoon large portions into a shallow serving bowl. Serve hot with lemon wedges for squeezing at the table.

COOK'S NOTE: Good rice is key. Look for aged, extra-long basmati at Indian markets or online.

Leek-Wrapped Seitan Roast

Usually the argument for making a plant-based version of a meat dish is to provide those who are new to vegan dishes with something that looks and tastes familiar. But lifelong vegans and vegetarians can love these dishes just as much, simply because they taste delicious. Recipe tester Kristen Hartke's adult daughter, who was raised on a plant-based diet and has never eaten a "real" roast of any kind, absolutely loves it when Kristen makes a seitan roast for holiday dinners. This version is redolent with mushrooms and earthy spices and, when wrapped with leeks, makes a stunning centerpiece for any special occasion. Serve with roasted potatoes, carrots, and/or other vegetables, and a crisp salad.

Makes 6 servings

Time: Weekend

Storage: Refrigerate for up to 3 days.

4 tablespoons olive oil, plus more as needed

10 ounces (285g) cremini mushrooms, sliced

2 tablespoons dry sherry

2 cups (260g) vital wheat gluten

1 teaspoon granulated onion

1 teaspoon garlic powder

1 teaspoon celery seeds

1 teaspoon ground sage

1 teaspoon freshly ground black pepper

1 teaspoon fine sea salt, plus more as needed

½ teaspoon ground bay leaf

½ teaspoon sweet paprika

½ teaspoon smoked paprika

½ teaspoon dried thyme

8 ounces (225g) firm or extra-firm tofu, drained

1¼ cups (300ml) Vegetable Scrap Stock (page 36) or store-bought vegetable broth, plus more if needed

¼ cup (60ml) soy sauce

¼ cup (20g) nutritional yeast

4 cups (950ml) water

2 large leeks

IN A LARGE SKILLET, heat 2 tablespoons of the oil over medium heat until it shimmers. Add the mushrooms and sauté until softened and lightly golden and any liquid that has released from the mushrooms has evaporated, about 10 minutes. Add the dry sherry and deglaze the pan for a few minutes, until the sherry has mostly evaporated but the mushrooms are still moist. Remove from heat and allow the mushrooms to cool slightly.

In a large bowl, whisk together the vital wheat gluten, granulated onion, garlic powder, celery seeds, sage, black pepper, salt, ground bay leaf, paprika, smoked paprika, and thyme.

Transfer the mushrooms and their juices to a blender and add the tofu, stock, soy sauce, and nutritional yeast. Puree until smooth.

Make a well in the center of the dry ingredients and pour the pureed tofu mixture into it, then use a fork to combine the ingredients until a dough begins to form; if the dough is still dry, add additional broth or water, 1 tablespoon at a time, until the dough comes together. Knead the dough inside the bowl until it is cohesive and springy, about 3 minutes. Cover with a kitchen towel and let it rest for 30 minutes.

Set a wire rack in a sheet pan next to the stovetop. In a large deep sauté pan or 3-quart (3L) saucepan, bring the water to a boil over medium-high heat.

Trim off the root end of the leeks, separate the leaves, reserving any of the thin ones in the very center for another use. (You can chop them, along with any leftover leeks, freeze, and use them anywhere you'd start with chopped onions.) Rinse them well, and pat them dry. Add several leek leaves at a time to the boiling water and blanch for 30 seconds to 1 minute, until they become soft and pliable. Use tongs or a slotted spoon to transfer them to the rack to drain. Continue until the leaves from both leeks are blanched. Reduce the heat under the pan to medium-low and cover to keep hot; you'll use this water to make a water bath for the roast.

RECIPE CONTINUES ON NEXT PAGE

Let the leeks cool enough to handle. If you want to get fancy, you can weave the leeks together at this point to create a woven mat to place on top of the seitan loaf when you are ready to roast it.

Preheat the oven to 350°F (180°C).

Turn the seitan dough from the bowl out onto a 12 × 18-inch (30cm × 46cm) piece of compostable parchment paper. Shape the seitan into a slightly rounded loaf 8 or 9 inches (20cm or 23cm) long and 5 inches (13cm) high, with the loaf running lengthwise on the parchment. Rub the loaf all over with 1 tablespoon of the olive oil and sprinkle lightly with salt. Lay the leeks individually on top of the loaf (or the entire woven mat, if you are using that method), lining them up so that the entire visible surface of the loaf is covered with the leeks. (You do not need to have the leeks covering the bottom of the loaf, just the top and sides. You may have leeks left over, but it's nice to start with more than you need so you can pick the best ones for the decoration.) Brush the remaining 1 tablespoon olive oil over the leeks and sprinkle lightly with another pinch of salt.

Bring the two long sides of the parchment paper up over the top of the loaf and fold them together so that the paper is snug—but not tight—over the top of the loaf, then tuck the ends of the paper underneath the loaf. Place the wrapped loaf inside a baking dish or large loaf pan that is at least 4 inches (10cm) deep and slightly larger than the loaf itself. Place that dish inside a large roasting pan or baking dish that is at least 3 inches (7.5cm) deep.

Place the roasting pan on a pulled-out oven rack and carefully pour 2 inches (5cm) of the leek-boiling water into the large outer roasting pan (not inside the smaller pan that contains the loaf), to create a water bath. Bake for 1 hour, adding more boiling water to the large outer roasting pan in order to keep it at 2 inches.

After 1 hour, remove the smaller pan containing the loaf from the water bath and open up the parchment paper to reveal the top of the roast. Brush lightly again with olive oil and return the pan to the water bath, then return the setup to the oven. Continue cooking until the leeks are golden and lightly crisp, about 20 minutes, adding more boiling water to the water bath if necessary.

Remove the roast from the oven and let it cool for 15 minutes before slicing and serving.

Tofu Shakshuka

This recipe for a traditionally egg-filled dish is based on chef Michael Solomonov's version from his cookbook *Zahav: A World of Israeli Cooking*. It's based on tofu, but because this is truly all about the sauce, it is equally wonderful with big white beans (like giant limas or Royal Corona), chickpeas, or rounds of firm polenta. One big advantage tofu has over eggs is that you can make this dish a day ahead and it only improves overnight in the refrigerator. Just add the fresh cilantro before serving. For a less spicy dish, omit the jalapeño seeds.

Makes 4 servings

Time: Weekday

Storage: Refrigerate for up to 5 days or freeze for up to 3 months.

¼ cup (60ml) olive oil, plus more for drizzling

1 large onion (10 ounces/280g), chopped

2 large red bell peppers (1 pound/453g total), chopped

1 jalapeño pepper, diced (seeded for less heat)

4 garlic cloves, chopped

1 tablespoon sweet paprika

1½ teaspoons ground cumin

1½ teaspoons ground coriander

½ teaspoon smoked paprika

1 teaspoon fine salt, plus more to taste

1 (28-ounce/794g) can crushed tomatoes

1 cup (240ml) Vegetable Scrap Stock (page 36), store-bought vegetable broth, or water

¾ teaspoon organic cane sugar

2 tablespoons nutritional yeast

1 (14- to 16-ounce/400g to 450g) block firm tofu, drained and cut into ½-inch (1.3cm) cubes

½ cup (20g) chopped fresh cilantro

Bread, for serving

IN A LARGE SKILLET, heat the olive oil over medium heat until it shimmers. Add the onion, bell peppers, and jalapeño and cook until softened, about 10 minutes. Add the garlic, sweet paprika, cumin, coriander, smoked paprika, and salt and cook until the spices are fragrant, about another minute.

Add the crushed tomatoes, stock, sugar, nutritional yeast, and tofu. Simmer uncovered over low heat, stirring occasionally, until the sauce has thickened, 10 to 15 minutes. Taste and season with more salt as needed.

Stir in the cilantro, divide among serving bowls, drizzle with olive oil, and serve hot with bread.

Lion's Mane Mushroom Cakes

Lion's mane mushrooms look like pillowy white fluff balls, but when shredded they surprisingly mimic lump crabmeat in texture and appearance. Their flavor is mild and not overly mushroomy, making them the perfect canvas for lots of herbs and other punchy flavors.

This play on crab cakes uses aquafaba mayonnaise as a binder. If you don't have any Lemon Mayonnaise (page 46) on hand, substitute store-bought vegan mayo and stir in 2 teaspoons finely grated lemon zest.

Eat with a simply dressed salad and a zippy rémoulade sauce on the side, or make mini cakes and dollop the rémoulade on top as a bite-size cocktail party appetizer.

To make ahead, you can refrigerate the formed cakes for up to 2 days before pan-frying.

Makes 2 main-course servings or 4 appetizer servings

Time: Weekday

Storage: Refrigerate the mushroom cakes for up to 3 days and the rémoulade for up to 1 week.

8 ounces (225g) lion's mane mushrooms, trimmed

½ cup (120ml) Lemon Mayonnaise (page 46)

½ cup (50g) panko bread crumbs

2 tablespoons finely chopped fresh parsley

2 tablespoons finely chopped fresh chives, plus more for garnish

2 tablespoons finely chopped fresh dill, plus more for garnish

½ teaspoon fine salt, plus more to taste

1 tablespoon canola oil

2 tablespoons (28g) Soft Spreadable Butter (page 21) or store-bought unsalted vegan butter

¾ cup Rémoulade Sauce (page 285), preferably left chunky

TEAR THE MUSHROOMS INTO small to medium shreds (aim for the consistency of lump crabmeat) and place them in a large bowl. Add the lemon mayonnaise, panko, parsley, chives, dill, and salt and mix well. Taste and season with more salt as needed. Refrigerate for at least 15 minutes, to help the cakes hold together.

Divide the mixture into 8 equal portions and form into patties ½ inch (1.3cm) thick.

Set a wire rack over a sheet pan next to the stovetop. In a large nonstick skillet, heat the oil over medium-high heat until it starts to shimmer. Add the butter, and once it melts, add as many mushroom cakes as will fit without overcrowding the skillet. Reduce the heat to medium and cook until deep golden brown on the bottom, 3 to 4 minutes. Flip the cakes and cook until deep golden brown on the other side, 3 to 4 minutes. Carefully transfer to the wire rack to drain. (They are delicate, so be careful to not break them as you move them.)

Carefully transfer the cooked mushroom cakes to a serving plate or individual plates. Garnish with fresh chives and dill and serve warm, with the rémoulade sauce on the side.

COOK'S NOTE: These are a little loose on the edges, as a high-quality crab cake should be, but if you want them firmer, mix 2 tablespoons water with 1 tablespoon flaxseed meal, let sit for 5 minutes, then stir into the mixture before forming and pan-frying.

Steamed Eggplant with Black Bean Sauce

If you've never tried steamed eggplant, please do: It turns the vegetable soft and custardy without making it mushy. I prefer to use skinny Asian eggplants for this, but you can substitute baby Italian eggplants—or big ones, cut into large cubes instead of rounds. (Keeping the peel on helps the steamed eggplant keep its shape.) The topping is a vast simplification/riff on Chinese fermented black bean sauce, using prepared black bean garlic sauce plus a can's worth of decidedly nontraditional conventional black beans, a combination I first explored for my cookbook *Cool Beans*. Red pepper flakes, peanuts, and scallions add crunch and punch. Serve with noodles, rice, or another grain of your choice.

Makes 4 servings

Time: Weekday

Storage: Refrigerate for up to 4 days.

¼ teaspoon fine sea salt

1 pound (450g) long skinny Asian eggplant (2 to 3), unpeeled and cut into rounds 1 inch (2.5cm) thick

2 tablespoons safflower, grapeseed, or other neutral oil, plus more for greasing the steamer

1 (15-ounce/425g) can black beans, drained and rinsed, or 1½ cups (300g) cooked black beans

4 scallions, thinly sliced

4 large garlic cloves, chopped

½ teaspoon red pepper flakes

½ cup (120ml) mirin

¼ cup (60ml) water

3 tablespoons black bean garlic sauce

1 tablespoon hoisin sauce

1 tablespoon unseasoned rice vinegar

½ cup (75g) unsalted roasted peanuts, chopped

Cilantro leaves, for garnish

LIGHTLY SALT THE EGGPLANT rounds on both sides. Use a little oil to lightly grease a steamer basket/insert and set it into a pot with 1 to 2 inches (2.5cm to 5cm) of water in it. Bring the water to a boil over medium heat. Add the eggplant, carefully stacking if needed. Cover and steam until the eggplant is very soft when pierced with a fork or skewer but still holds its shape, 15 to 20 minutes.

Meanwhile, in a large skillet, heat the oil into over medium-high heat until it shimmers. Add the beans and cook, stirring, for 1 minute. Stir in about three-quarters of the scallions (saving the remaining one-quarter for garnish), garlic, and pepper flakes and cook until fragrant, about 30 seconds. Stir in the mirin, increase the heat to high, and cook until it mostly evaporates, 4 to 5 minutes. Reduce the heat to medium-high. Stir in the water, black bean sauce, and hoisin. Bring to a boil, reduce the heat to medium, and simmer, stirring occasionally, until the sauce has thickened and reduced slightly, 4 to 5 minutes. Remove from the heat and stir in the vinegar. Cover to keep warm.

Divide the steamed eggplant among serving plates, spoon the black bean sauce over the top, and garnish with the peanuts, reserved scallions, and cilantro. Serve warm.

Lentil-Chickpea Meatballs in Tomato Sauce

Crisp on the outside, tender in the middle, these meatballs are perfect over your favorite starchy bed, such as polenta or pasta. And if you have leftover cooked lentils on hand, the meatballs come together fairly quickly—the hardest part is waiting for them to firm up in the freezer and again in the oven. (You can also freeze them and save them for later; just add 5 minutes to the bake time.) Searing them in olive oil gives them a delicious crust, so don't skip this step.

The dried herbs add a nice flavor but aren't essential. If your meatball mixture seems too wet, add more panko by the tablespoon until you can easily shape it into balls. (Dampening your hands with water will help!)

Makes 4 servings

Time: Weekend

Storage: Uncooked meatballs can be frozen for up to 3 months (add 5 minutes to the bake time). Cooked sauce can be refrigerated for up to 1 week. Refrigerate cooked meatballs in tomato sauce for up to 5 days.

SAUCE

2 (28-ounce/794g) cans whole peeled tomatoes

¼ cup (60ml) olive oil, Soft Spreadable Butter (page 21), or store-bought unsalted vegan butter

½ medium or 1 small yellow onion (3½ ounces/100g), halved

1 teaspoon fine sea salt, plus more to taste

MEATBALLS

1 (15-ounce/425g) can no-salt-added chickpeas, undrained

1½ cups (245g) cooked and cooled large green/brown lentils, or 1 (15.5-ounce/439g) can (see Note), drained

½ medium or 1 small yellow onion (3½ ounces/100g), roughly chopped

½ cup (55g) Umami-Packed Cashew Parm (page 27), nutritional yeast, or store-bought vegan Parmesan

6 tablespoons panko bread crumbs

1 teaspoon dried basil

1 teaspoon dried thyme

½ teaspoon dried oregano

1 teaspoon fine sea salt, plus more to taste

¼ teaspoon freshly ground black pepper

TO FINISH

6 tablespoons olive oil

Polenta, pasta, or bread, for serving

¼ cup (30g) Umami-Packed Cashew Parm (page 27), nutritional yeast, or store-bought vegan Parmesan

MAKE THE SAUCE: In a medium saucepan, combine the tomatoes, oil or butter, onion, and salt. Bring to a boil over medium-high heat, then reduce the heat to maintain a bare simmer and cook, uncovered, stirring occasionally to break up the tomato chunks, until the sauce has reduced and is flavorful, 35 to 40 minutes. Taste and season with more salt as needed. Remove from the heat.

Make the meatballs: Reserving the liquid (aquafaba), drain the chickpeas and transfer to a food processor. Add ¼ cup (60ml) of the aquafaba, the lentils, onion, cashew Parm, panko, basil, thyme, oregano, salt, and pepper. Pulse in short intervals, stopping to scrape down as necessary, until the mixture comes together into clumps and holds together when pressed but still maintains some texture, 30 to 45 seconds. Taste and season with more salt as needed.

Line a sheet pan with parchment or a silicone baking mat or lightly oil. Divide the lentil mixture into 12 portions (about 57g each) and roll into balls (oiling your hands first is helpful), transfer to the sheet pan, then freeze until firm, about 20 minutes.

Preheat the oven to 350°F (180°C).

To finish: In a large nonstick skillet, heat the oil over medium-high heat until it shimmers. Add the chilled meatballs. Cook, turning carefully with tongs, until all sides are browned, 6 to 8 minutes. Adjust the heat as needed and don't be worried if some of the meatball mixture falls into the oil.

Return the meatballs to the sheet pan and bake until cooked through and firmer, 25 to 30 minutes. (They'll still be a little delicate.)

Reheat the sauce. Divide the meatballs over polenta, pasta, or bread, then spoon the sauce on top. Sprinkle with the cashew Parm and serve hot.

COOK'S NOTE: Canned lentils work well here, but if you want to start from scratch, cook ¾ cup (150g) dried lentils in enough water to cover by 2 inches (5cm) until tender, 30 to 45 minutes.

Spice-Rubbed Eggplant with Bulgur & Olives

This recipe is a simplified, vegan version of a favorite from Yotam Ottolenghi, a vegetable cookery virtuoso. While eggplant can be a tricky beast, scoring it speeds up the cooking process, ensuring the outside doesn't dry out before the insides are tender, while also creating cavities for a flavorful oil to penetrate. And then there are the chickpeas. The key to crispiness is twofold: First, dry them out thoroughly using a kitchen towel. Second, cook them *without* oil until they're hardened and then add oil and continue cooking until crisp. Bulgur is nice in this dish because it's quick-cooking and the grains are small and soft, not competing in texture with the crunchy chickpeas, meaty olives, or custardy eggplant. But feel free to swap it out for another grain like couscous, quinoa, or even orzo.

Makes 4 servings

Time: Weekday

Storage: Refrigerate for up to 4 days. (Note that the chickpeas will lose their crispness once refrigerated.)

4 small or 2 medium Italian eggplants (1½ pounds/680g total), halved lengthwise

1 (15.5-ounce/439g) can chickpeas, drained and rinsed

¼ cup (60ml) olive oil

2 garlic cloves, finely grated or pressed

Fine sea salt

2 teaspoons ground coriander

1 teaspoon ground cumin

¼ teaspoon smoked paprika

¼ cup (35g) coarse bulgur

¾ cup (180ml) plus 2 tablespoons water

2 tablespoons tahini

1 tablespoon fresh lemon juice, plus more to taste

½ cup (85g) Castelvetrano olives, pitted and roughly chopped

½ cup (14g) fresh cilantro, roughly chopped

Pomegranate molasses, for serving (optional)

POSITION RACKS IN THE top and bottom thirds of the oven and preheat the oven to 400°F (200°C).

Score the cut side of each eggplant with crisscrossing diagonal cuts about 1 inch (2.5cm) apart, being sure not to go so deep that you hit the skin. Transfer to a sheet pan.

Wrap the chickpeas in a lint-free kitchen towel, then pat gently to thoroughly dry. Transfer to a separate sheet pan (some of the papery translucent skins of the chickpeas will have separated; feel free to leave them).

In a small bowl, combine the olive oil, garlic, ¾ teaspoon salt, the coriander, cumin, and smoked paprika in a small bowl. Measure out 1 tablespoon and set aside for roasting the chickpeas. Distribute the rest of the oil/spice mixture over the eggplant and then rub into the cuts.

Transfer the eggplant to the bottom rack and the chickpeas to the top rack. Roast the eggplant until it begins to collapse and is completely tender when poked with a paring knife or cake tester, 25 to 40 minutes (depending on its size).

Roast the chickpeas until very dry, about 15 minutes. Pull out, add the reserved oil/spice mixture and stir to coat. Return to the oven until crisp and browned, 8 to 10 minutes.

Meanwhile, in a small saucepan, combine the bulgur, ¾ cup (180ml) of the water, and a pinch of salt. Bring to a boil over medium-high heat. Reduce the heat to low, cover, and simmer for 10 minutes. Remove from the heat, let sit for 5 minutes, stir to fluff, then cover to keep warm.

In a small bowl, combine the tahini, lemon juice, remaining 2 tablespoons water, and a pinch of salt. Taste and season with more salt and/or lemon juice as needed.

Add the crisp chickpeas (being sure to scrape in any oil from the baking sheet), olives, and cilantro to the bulgur and stir to combine. Season with salt to taste.

Transfer the eggplant to a serving platter. Drizzle with about half the tahini sauce, then distribute the bulgur and drizzle with the remaining tahini sauce. Finish with a drizzling of pomegranate molasses, if desired.

Skillet Spanakopita

When you start spanakopita on the stove, the phyllo gets an opportunity to get crisp on the bottom before the dish gets finished off in the oven—so there's no soggy phyllo! This slightly rustic (and a little spicy) version of the Greek standard lets you use a variety of greens, if you'd like, in addition to spinach and bakes it with thinly sliced lemons for an extra punch. Another crucial ingredient is the delicious homemade lemon-brined tofu feta, but if you don't have time to make it, store-bought plant-based feta works well, too.

Makes 4 to 6 servings

Time: Weekday

Storage: Refrigerate for up to 1 week or freeze for up to 3 months.

1 pound (450g) baby spinach, kale, or other leafy greens (or a combination)

2 tablespoons olive oil, plus more for brushing

1 small red onion (6 ounces/170g), thinly sliced

3 garlic cloves, finely grated or pressed

½ to 1 teaspoon red pepper flakes, to taste

½ teaspoon ground nutmeg

1 cup (115g) crumbled Lemon-Brined Tofu Feta (page 26) or store-bought vegan feta

½ bunch fresh dill (2 ounces/57g), coarsely chopped

1 tablespoon grated lemon zest

Fine sea salt and freshly ground black pepper

8 frozen sheets phyllo dough, thawed

½ lemon, thinly sliced, seeds removed

1 tablespoon sesame seeds

1 teaspoon nigella seeds (optional)

PREHEAT THE OVEN TO 400°F (200°C).

Wash and spin-dry the greens, and thinly slice them. (For the larger greens, keeping them attached to their stems, and working in batches if needed, stack the leaves, roll them up lengthwise like a huge cigar, and very thinly slice them.)

In a large pot, heat 1 tablespoon of the olive oil over medium heat until it shimmers. Add the onion and sauté until it begins to soften, about 2 minutes. Add the garlic, pepper flakes, and nutmeg and cook, stirring, until fragrant, about 1 minute. Stir in the greens and cook until wilted and any excess moisture has evaporated, 5 to 15 minutes (depending on the hardiness of the green variety you're using). Remove from the heat.

Stir the lemon-brined tofu feta, dill, and lemon zest into the greens. Season to taste with salt and pepper and let cool slightly.

Brush a 10-inch (25cm) ovenproof skillet with the remaining 1 tablespoon olive oil. Brush a sheet of phyllo lightly with olive oil, then nestle it inside the skillet, with the ends hanging over the edge of the skillet. Continue layering the remaining sheets of phyllo, brushing with olive oil, overlapping, and gently pressing them inside the skillet so that there's an even amount of phyllo hanging over the edge of the perimeter of the pan. Don't worry if the phyllo sheets crack or rip; you can simply patch them together in the pan, brushing with olive oil so that they stick together, but plan on working quickly so they don't dry out too much.

Spoon the greens inside the phyllo and top with the sliced lemons. Fold the overhanging phyllo loosely on top of the greens toward the center of the pan (there will still be greens and the sliced lemons visible in the center). Brush lightly with olive oil and sprinkle with the sesame seeds and nigella seeds (if using).

Place the skillet on the stovetop over medium heat and cook for 5 minutes. Move to the oven to bake until the phyllo is golden on top, 12 to 15 minutes.

Cool in the pan on a rack for 10 minutes before slicing and serving. Serve hot, cold, or at room temperature.

Twice-Cooked Sweet Potatoes with Cilantro & Tamarind

This recipe is directly inspired by chaat, a category of Indian snacks that are symphonies of textures and flavors. Many include an herb chutney, a tamarind chutney, yogurt, red onion, and a crunchy topping. Here, the base of the chaat is twice-cooked sweet potatoes, which get soft in the oven and then charred and caramelized when they hit the stove. Peanuts serve as a crunchy topper. This treatment turns chaat into a main course, but you can also serve this as a starter or side if you'd like.

Chaat masala is a distinctively tart, irresistible, and hard-to-describe spice mix that often contains amchoor (green mango powder), asafoetida (hing), and black salt (kala namak). It's worth seeking out (and sprinkling on all manners of vegetables and proteins), but if you can't find it, skip it (then make a note to yourself to order some!). The yogurt offers a creamy, cooling contrast to the punchy green sauce and tangy tamarind.

Makes 2 to 4 servings

Time: Weekday

Storage: Refrigerate for up to 3 days.

- 2 sweet potatoes (1½ pounds/680g total), scrubbed
- ¾ cup (180ml) Creamy Coconut Yogurt (page 23) or store-bought plant-based Greek-style yogurt
- 2 tablespoons fresh lime juice
- ½ teaspoon fine sea salt, plus more to taste
- ½ teaspoon organic cane sugar
- 1 cup (30g) lightly packed fresh cilantro leaves and tender stems
- ½ cup (15g) lightly packed fresh mint leaves
- ½ large or 1 small jalapeño, cut into 3 or 4 pieces
- 5 tablespoons olive oil
- 3½ teaspoons water
- 2 tablespoons tamarind chutney
- ¼ cup (38g) salted roasted peanuts, chopped
- 1 tablespoon finely chopped red onion or shallot
- Chaat masala, for sprinkling

PREHEAT THE OVEN TO 350°F (180°C).

Microwave the sweet potatoes on high for 2 minutes. Transfer to a sheet pan and bake until fork-tender, 25 to 30 minutes. (Alternatively, bake without microwaving until tender, 45 minutes to 1 hour or more.) Allow to cool slightly, then halve the potatoes lengthwise.

In a small bowl, mix the yogurt with 1 tablespoon of the lime juice, ¼ teaspoon of the salt, and ¼ teaspoon of the sugar. Taste and season with more salt as needed. Spread evenly on a rimmed serving platter or shallow bowl.

Gather the cilantro, mint, and jalapeño in a pile on a cutting board. Add the remaining ¼ teaspoon of the salt and finely chop, corralling the pile as it spreads out. Transfer to a small bowl and add 3 tablespoons of the olive oil, the remaining 1 tablespoon lime juice, remaining ¼ teaspoon sugar, and 1½ teaspoons of the water. Stir to combine. Taste and season with more salt as needed.

In a small bowl, thin the tamarind chutney with the remaining 2 teaspoons water.

In a large skillet, heat the remaining 2 tablespoons olive oil over medium-high heat. Working in batches to avoid overcrowding, add the sweet potatoes, cut-side down, and cook, undisturbed, until beginning to char, 3 to 5 minutes. Transfer to the serving platter and repeat with the remaining sweet potatoes.

Drizzle the sweet potatoes with the tamarind chutney, dollop with the cilantro-mint mixture, and top with the peanuts and red onion. Sprinkle generously with the chaat masala and serve warm or at room temperature.

Whole Roasted Beets with Mole

I got this idea from DC chef Tom Madrecki, who served a version at his hit supper club many years ago. The beets don't need to be peeled before roasting, which blackens the skin and makes them easy to slice through. They're not the most attractive when they come out of the oven, but that changes once they're coated in sauce and diners cut in to see a striking combination of colors. Tom's dish combined red beets with a dark mole, but I realized that pumpkin seed mole would be just as stunning with golden beets. So I give you a few ways to go here: Make the plum mole if you have red beets and the pumpkin seed mole if you have golden beets—or mix and match. Or, perhaps best of all, if you have already made one of the more involved moles in this book—Mole Coloradito (page 57) or Pipián Verde (page 56)—use one or both here. Serve this with your favorite plant-based protein, if you'd like.

Makes 4 servings

Time: Weekend

Storage: Refrigerate the mole for up to 1 week or freeze for up to 6 months. Refrigerate the roasted beets for up to 5 days. Warm both before serving.

> 4 medium red or golden beets (a little larger than tennis balls, about 2 pounds/910g total)
>
> 1 tablespoon olive oil
>
> Mole of choice (1 cup/240ml): Plum Mole (recipe follows), Pumpkin Seed Mole (recipe follows), Mole Coloradito (page 57), or Pipián Verde (page 56)
>
> **FOR SERVING**
>
> Yellow rice, Garlic-Infused Jasmine Rice (page 360), or another favorite grain
>
> Small beet green leaves (optional), for garnish
>
> Pumpkin seeds, sesame seeds, and cilantro leaves (if using Pumpkin Seed Mole or Pipián Verde), for garnish
>
> Cashews, prunes, and pomegranate seeds (if using Plum Mole or Mole Coloradito), for garnish

PREHEAT THE OVEN TO 500°F (260°C). Line a large sheet pan with compostable parchment paper or a silicone baking mat.

Trim off any small root tails from the beets and trim off any remaining stem. Scrub the beets thoroughly under running water, using a small brush if needed to remove any trace amounts of dirt. Dry, transfer to the sheet pan, and drizzle with the oil, rubbing to coat them.

Roast until the beets are barely tender and a skewer pierces them with just a little resistance, 1 hour to 1 hour 45 minutes, depending on the size and age of the beets.

To serve, divide the rice or other grains among four serving plates, nestle a beet in the middle of each bed of grains, and pour about ¼ cup (60ml) of your preferred mole on each beet to coat, plus more if you'd like. Garnish with the small beet leaves if you have them. Add some pumpkin seeds, sesame seeds, and cilantro if using the pumpkin seed mole or pipián verde. Add some cashews, prunes, and pomegranate seeds if using the plum mole or mole coloradito. Serve warm.

Plum Mole

Use on any roasted or steamed vegetables, in enchiladas, and more.

Makes about 2 cups

- 10 ounces (285g) plum tomatoes (4 medium or 2 large), quartered
- 2 to 4 large shallots (5 ounces/142g total), peeled and quartered
- ½ cup plus 2 tablespoons (75g total) raw cashews
- 4 large dried chile peppers, such as ancho, pasilla, or guajillo
- 1 garlic clove, peeled but whole
- 1 canned chipotle pepper in adobo sauce
- ½ cup (85g) dried plums (prunes), quartered
- 1 ripe banana, cut into chunks
- 1 teaspoon fine sea salt, plus more to taste
- 1 tablespoon olive oil

POSITION AN OVEN RACK in the closest position to the broiler element or flame and turn on the broiler.

Arrange the tomatoes and shallots on a small sheet pan and broil them until charred all over, turning them a time or two, about 15 minutes. Scrape them into a food processor.

Turn the oven to 500°F (260°C).

Place the cashews on a small sheet pan and roast until lightly browned and fragrant, about 5 minutes. Immediately transfer them to the food processor with the tomato mixture.

Heat a medium skillet over high heat. Add the dried chiles and heat for just a few minutes on each side, until their flesh goes brown and turns pliable. Transfer them to a small bowl and barely cover with water and soak until soft, about 15 minutes. Use tongs to remove the chiles. Strain and reserve the soaking water.

Tear the chiles open, compost the stems and seeds, and transfer the remaining flesh to the food processor, along with the garlic, chipotle, prunes, banana, and salt. Puree until smooth.

Return the skillet you used for the chiles to medium heat and pour in the 1 tablespoon oil. Add the paste and cook, stirring constantly and scraping the bottom of the pan, until the paste darkens slightly and thickens, 5 to 10 minutes.

Stir in the chile-soaking water ¼ cup (60ml) at a time to create a thick but pourable, saucelike consistency, adding more water if needed. Taste and season with salt as needed. Refrigerate for up to 1 week or freeze for up to 6 months.

Pumpkin Seed Mole

Use on any roasted or steamed vegetables, in enchiladas, and more.

Makes about 2 cups

- 5 to 6 large tomatillos (14 ounces/400g total), husks removed
- 1 jalapeño pepper, stemmed
- ½ cup (65g) pumpkin seeds
- ¼ cup (40g) toasted sesame seeds
- 1 cup (36g) lightly packed fresh cilantro leaves and stems
- ¼ cup (60ml) water
- 1 garlic clove, peeled but whole
- 3 tablespoons Wildflower Cider Syrup (page 35) or maple syrup, plus more to taste
- 2 tablespoons olive oil
- 1 teaspoon fine sea salt, plus more to taste
- ½ teaspoon ground ancho chiles
- ½ teaspoon ground cumin

POSITION AN OVEN RACK in the closest position to the broiler element or flame and turn on the broiler.

Arrange the tomatillos and jalapeño on a small sheet pan and broil until lightly charred and the tomatillos are very soft, 5 to 10 minutes. Scrape them into a food processor.

Turn the oven to 500°F (260°C).

Spread the pumpkin seeds on a small sheet pan and roast until lightly browned and fragrant, 3 to 5 minutes. Add the sesame seeds and roast for another 30 seconds to 1 minute, just until they start to brown. Immediately transfer the pumpkin and sesame seeds to the food processor with the tomatillo mixture.

Add the cilantro, water, garlic, cider syrup, oil, salt, ground chiles, and cumin. Puree until smooth. Taste and season with more cider syrup and salt as needed. Refrigerate for up to 1 week or freeze for up to 6 months.

Trumpet Mushrooms au Poivre

Steak House Night doesn't have to actually involve steak. Mushrooms can deliciously stand in, and while the mushroom that gets the most attention for such a role is the portobello, trumpet mushrooms—with their extra-firm texture—deserve the spotlight, too. Halved, scored, and seared, these mushrooms are served with an au poivre sauce that'll have you licking the plate. The sauce is a savory combination of caramelized shallots, vegetable stock, Dijon mustard, a splash of brandy and, of course, plenty of coarsely ground black pepper. A little cashew cream adds a silky lusciousness, while taking the edge off the sharp black pepper.

Makes 4 servings

Time: Weekend

Storage: The mushrooms are best eaten immediately, but they can be refrigerated for up to 2 days. The cashew cream can be refrigerated up to 5 days in advance.

MUSHROOMS AU POIVRE

1 pound (450g) trumpet mushrooms, trimmed

6 tablespoons canola or other neutral vegetable oil

½ teaspoon fine sea salt, plus more to taste

2 tablespoons (28g) Soft Spreadable Butter (page 21) or store-bought unsalted vegan butter

1 tablespoon coarsely ground black pepper

2 medium shallots (2½ ounces/75g total), finely chopped

1 garlic clove, finely grated or pressed

⅓ cup (80ml) brandy or Cognac

1½ cups (350ml) Vegetable Scrap Stock (page 36) or store-bought vegetable broth

⅓ cup (80ml) Cashew Cream (recipe follows)

2 teaspoons Dijon mustard

¼ cup (12g) parsley, roughly chopped

½ lemon

Flaky sea salt, for finishing

PREHEAT THE OVEN TO 275°F (140°C). Place a sheet pan in the oven to preheat.

Slice the mushrooms in half lengthwise. Using a paring knife, score diagonally across the cut side of the mushroom, going only about ¼ inch (6mm) in. Then score diagonally the other direction to create a crosshatch. Repeat with the remaining mushrooms.

In a large skillet, heat 2 tablespoons of the oil over medium-high heat until it shimmers. Working in batches to avoid overcrowding, add the mushrooms cut-side down and cook until deep golden, 4 to 6 minutes. Flip and cook until light golden on the second side, 2 to 3 minutes. Transfer to the sheet pan in the oven to keep warm. Repeat with the remaining mushrooms, adding more oil to the skillet for each batch as needed.

Reduce the heat to medium and add the butter to the skillet. Once it melts, add the pepper and cook, stirring frequently, until fragrant, about 30 seconds. Add the shallots and garlic and sauté until they start to soften and turn light golden, 2 to 4 minutes. Add the brandy and cook until the liquid has reduced by half, 2 to 3 minutes. Add the vegetable stock, increase the heat to medium-high, and simmer until the sauce has reduced by about one-third, 5 to 7 minutes.

Reduce the heat to low, stir in the cashew cream and mustard, and cook for another minute to heat through. Taste and add more salt as needed.

Spoon the sauce onto a serving platter and top with the warm mushrooms. Garnish with parsley and squeeze the lemon over the whole dish. Finish with a sprinkle of flaky salt. Serve warm.

Cashew Cream

The cashew cream keeps for 5 days and can be swirled into pasta sauces, added to smoothies, stirred into coffee, eaten with fresh fruit, and more.

Makes a generous 1 cup

¾ cup (100g) raw cashews

Boiling water

⅓ cup (80ml) water, plus more as needed

½ teaspoon fine sea salt

PLACE THE CASHEWS IN a heatproof bowl and pour boiling water over them to cover by 1 inch (2.5cm). Let soak for 30 minutes.

Drain and rinse the cashews, then transfer to a blender. Add the ⅓ cup (80ml) water and salt and puree until smooth. You're looking for a silky, spoonable texture, a little thicker than heavy whipping cream; if the mixture is too thick, add 1 tablespoon water at a time until you reach the right consistency. Refrigerate until ready to use.

Steamed Silken Tofu with Blackberry Chile Sauce

Some people view tofu as a subpar stand-in for meat, but anyone who takes the ingredient seriously knows it has so much potential. This is especially true when you try kinds of tofu beyond extra-firm. Silken tofu, as this recipe shows, feels a lot like panna cotta or a very firm pudding. This recipe pairs it with an intense sauce that hits all the flavor points as the tofu dissolves in your mouth.

Makes 4 servings

Time: Weekday

Storage: Refrigerate for up to 1 week.

1 (16-ounce/454g) block silken tofu

½ cup (120ml) water

¼ cup (60ml) soy sauce

2 tablespoons sesame seeds

1½ tablespoons maple syrup

1 tablespoon mirin

1 tablespoon unseasoned rice vinegar

½ teaspoon freshly ground black pepper

1 tablespoon vegetable oil

3 garlic cloves, thinly sliced

3 scallions, thinly sliced, plus more for garnish

2 tablespoons gochugaru (Korean chile flakes)

5 large blackberries, halved, plus more for garnish

½ Fresno or jalapeño pepper, seeded and thinly sliced

CAREFULLY REMOVE THE SILKEN tofu from the packaging and place it on a plate. Allow it to sit for about 5 minutes. Drain the excess liquid at the bottom of the plate.

In a pot fitted with a steamer basket or insert, bring 1 to 2 inches (2.5cm to 5cm) of water to a boil over medium heat. Once the water starts to boil, place the tofu in the steamer, cover, and steam until a knife inserted in the center comes out warm to the touch, about 6 minutes.

While the tofu is steaming, in a medium bowl, mix together the water, soy sauce, sesame seeds, maple syrup, mirin, rice vinegar, and black pepper.

In a small pan, heat the oil over medium-high heat until it shimmers. Add the garlic, scallions, and gochugaru and cook, stirring constantly, until very fragrant, about 30 seconds (being careful to not let the gochugaru burn). Add the soy sauce mixture and the blackberries and cook until the sauce begins to thicken, about 3 minutes.

When the tofu is finished steaming, transfer it carefully from the steamer to a cutting board and carefully slice the block in half lengthwise and then into pieces ½ inch (1.3cm) thick.

Transfer the tofu to a serving platter, spoon the blackberry sauce over the top, and garnish with chopped scallions, sliced chile peppers, and more blackberries.

Whole Roasted Carrots with Lemony Tahini Sauce

This recipe for sweet spice-coated carrots paired with a nutty tahini dressing and lots of fresh herbs employs the technique of steam-roasting that makes the vegetables fork-tender. When you add water to the pan, then cover it, the carrots steam, cooking through before their exteriors brown. Use this same method for other hardy vegetables that tend to toughen up before tenderizing, such as beets, parsnips, and potatoes.

If you're working with a mix of small and large carrots, halve any bigger ones lengthwise—that will help them cook at the same rate. While two people can easily finish this dish as a main, you can stretch it out by serving it with flatbread or an herby chickpea salad. This would also be delicious with pine nuts instead of walnuts.

Makes 2 main-course servings or 4 side-dish servings

Time: Weekday

Storage: Refrigerate for up to 4 days; the tahini sauce will taste more garlicky over time.

- 1 pound 2 ounces (510g) carrots (507g), 1 to 1½ inches (2.5cm to 4cm) in diameter, scrubbed
- 2 tablespoons plus 2 teaspoons olive oil, plus more for drizzling
- 1 teaspoon cumin seeds, lightly crushed
- 1 teaspoon coriander seeds, lightly crushed
- ¼ teaspoon cayenne pepper
- Fine sea salt
- ½ cup (120ml) water
- ¼ cup (56g) tahini, well-stirred
- 4 tablespoons fresh lemon juice (from 1 to 2 lemons)
- ½ garlic clove, finely grated or pressed
- ⅓ cup (30g) raw walnuts
- ¼ cup (10g) lightly packed fresh cilantro leaves
- ¼ cup (13g) lightly packed fresh mint leaves, torn if large
- Aleppo pepper flakes, for sprinkling

PREHEAT THE OVEN TO 400°F (200°C).

In a 9 × 13-inch (23cm × 33cm) baking pan (or any other ovenproof vessel where the carrots fit in a single layer), combine the carrots, 2 tablespoons of the olive oil, the cumin seeds, coriander seeds, cayenne, and ¼ teaspoon salt. Toss with your hands until the carrots are well coated in spices. Carefully add ¼ cup (60ml) of the water to the pan (avoid dousing the carrots directly). Cover the pan tightly with a lid or an inverted sheet pan, and roast until the carrots are tender, 15 to 20 minutes.

Carefully remove the cover, directing hot steam away from your face. Increase the oven temperature to 425°F (220°C) and return the carrots to the oven until they are fall-apart tender and are starting to brown, 12 to 15 minutes, flipping them over halfway through.

Meanwhile, in a small bowl, whisk together the tahini, remaining ¼ cup (60ml) water, 2 tablespoons of the lemon juice, the remaining 2 teaspoons olive oil, the garlic, and a pinch of salt until smooth. Add more water as needed to loosen the tahini sauce so it's easy to drizzle. Taste and season with more salt if needed.

When the carrots are nearly done, add the walnuts to a small baking sheet and toast, watching carefully (they burn quickly!), until they're a few shades darker and very fragrant, 4 to 5 minutes. Let cool slightly, then coarsely chop.

Transfer the carrots to a serving platter, scraping to drizzle with any oil and spices left in the baking dish. Drizzle with the tahini sauce, then top with some of the toasted walnuts and herbs. Drizzle with more tahini sauce, then add the remaining nuts, cilantro, mint, and more sauce. (You may have more tahini sauce than you need for this, but it's great on all manner of roasted vegetables, salads, grain bowls, and more.) Drizzle with the remaining 2 tablespoons lemon juice and some olive oil. Sprinkle with Aleppo pepper.

Whole Roasted Cabbage with Potatoes & White Beans

This has all the elements of a great cabbage stew, but since you present the glorious crucifer whole and cut it into wedges at the table, it's in a much more celebratory, dinner-party-worthy format. Roasting cabbage this way turns the exterior dark, charred, and even a little crispy in parts and leaves the interior silky and nutty. Cutting a deep X in the top before roasting, first under cover and then exposed, helps get the spiced oil in between some of the leaves.

Makes 4 main-course servings or 8 side-dish servings

Time: Weekend

Storage: Refrigerate the cabbage and the potato mixture separately for up to 1 week or cut the cabbage into pieces, stir into the potato mixture, and freeze for up to 3 months.

¼ cup (60ml) plus 1 tablespoon olive oil, plus more for drizzling

2 tablespoons Ras el Hanout (page 42), Garam Masala (page 40), or Madras curry powder

1 tablespoon dark or light brown sugar

2 teaspoons fine sea salt, plus more to taste

1 medium head green cabbage (2¼ pounds/1kg)

½ cup (120ml) dry white wine

1 yellow onion (8 ounces/227g), chopped

4 garlic cloves, chopped

1 (15-ounce/425g) can cannellini or other white beans, or 1½ cups (270g) cooked beans, plus ½ cup (120ml) cooking or can liquid

1 (14.5-ounce/411g) can diced tomatoes

1 large russet potato (12 ounces/340g), scrubbed and cut into ½-inch (1.3cm) chunks

Fresh parsley leaves, for serving

Flaky sea salt, for serving

PREHEAT THE OVEN TO 450°F (230°C).

In a small bowl, whisk together ¼ cup (60ml) of the oil, 1 tablespoon of the ras el hanout, the brown sugar, and 1 teaspoon of the salt. Trim the bottom of the cabbage to give it a stable base, then cut a deep X across the top, going about halfway through the cabbage, being careful not to cut all the way through the core so the cabbage stays intact.

Transfer the cabbage to a Dutch oven or stockpot large enough to hold it with the lid on. Brush the cabbage all over with some of the spiced oil mixture, then drizzle the rest into the opening created by the X on top. Cover and roast for 40 minutes.

Uncover and pour in the wine. Carefully baste the cabbage with the wine and any other accumulated liquid, and continue roasting until a skewer inserted all the way through the cabbage meets with little resistance, 25 to 30 minutes. (Don't worry if the cabbage isn't super tender all the way through; it provides textural interest to have some of the leaves remain a little firmer and others softer.)

While the cabbage is roasting, in a large skillet, heat the remaining 1 tablespoon oil over medium-high heat until it shimmers. Add the onion and garlic and cook until the onion turns translucent, about 4 minutes. Add the remaining 1 tablespoon ras el hanout and remaining 1 teaspoon salt and cook, stirring, until the spices are very fragrant, about 30 seconds. Add the beans and their liquid and the tomatoes and bring to a boil. Add the potatoes, cover, and cook, stirring occasionally, until the potatoes are fork-tender, about 20 minutes. Taste and add more salt if needed. Cover to keep warm.

When the cabbage is tender, carefully transfer it to a large serving platter. Spoon the potato-bean mixture all around the cabbage, sprinkle it with parsley, and drizzle with olive oil. Cut along the sections into 4 wedges if serving as a main course or into 8 wedges if serving as a side dish, and serve hot.

Whole Roasted Romanesco with Romesco

If you haven't seen fractal-patterned romanesco cauliflower (sometimes called romanesco broccoli), I bet it's only a matter of time. The best way to showcase this incredible shape is to keep the vegetable whole, and the best way to roast it is covered in a Dutch oven, steaming it in its own juices and getting it tender before you uncover to facilitate browning. The perfect pairing, because of its flavors and name, is Spanish romesco sauce.

Makes 4 to 6 servings

Time: Weekday

Storage: Refrigerate for up to 5 days. Freezing is not recommended.

6 tablespoons olive oil, plus more for drizzling

4 garlic cloves, finely grated or pressed

1 tablespoon finely grated lemon zest

1 teaspoon fine sea salt

½ teaspoon Spanish smoked paprika (pimentón)

1 large head romanesco cauliflower (2 to 3 pounds/910g to 1.4kg)

2 cups (470ml) Romesco Sauce (page 51)

⅓ cup (35g) slivered or sliced almonds, toasted

PREHEAT THE OVEN TO 400°F (200°C). Put a Dutch oven or large ovenproof stockpot in the oven while it heats. (If you don't have one big enough to accommodate the cauliflower, use foil instead of a lid.)

In a large bowl, stir together the oil, garlic, lemon zest, salt, and smoked paprika.

Trim the cauliflower's stem end so it can stand upright. Transfer it to the bowl with the marinade and brush the cauliflower all over with the oil mixture.

Remove the pot from the oven and gently place the cauliflower inside. Cover and roast for 20 minutes. Uncover and continue roasting until a skewer goes in easily, 10 to 15 minutes.

Spread the romesco sauce onto a serving platter. Nestle the cauliflower in the middle of the sauce, drizzle with olive oil, sprinkle with the almonds, and serve warm. (Cut into wedges, if you'd like, or let guests spear off their own florets and swipe them through the sauce.)

Whole Roasted Celery Root with Cider Glaze

So what if it looks, well, a little gnarly? Celery root (aka celeriac) is one of my favorite vegetables, and its mild celery flavor takes on a little sweetness when you roast it, which also brings out its buttery texture. I first got the idea for this treatment from Yotam Ottolenghi and Ramael Scully's beautiful book, *NOPI*, but I like to add a shiny, sticky apple cider glaze to enhance its dramatic appearance and add a little sweet-tartness, along with some diced apples and walnuts.

Time: Weekend

Makes 4 servings

Storage: Refrigerate for up to 5 days. Freezing is not recommended.

1 medium-large celery root (1½ to 2 pounds/680g to 910g)

1 tablespoon olive oil

1 teaspoon fine sea salt, plus more for serving

½ cup (120ml) apple cider

1 tablespoon brown sugar

1 tablespoon (14g) Soft Spreadable Butter (page 21) or store-bought unsalted vegan butter

⅓ cup (60g) diced unpeeled Granny Smith or other tart apple

¼ cup (30g) chopped toasted walnuts

Celery leaves or parsley leaves, for garnish

PREHEAT THE OVEN TO 375°F (190°C).

Trim the bottom, with its hairy roots, off the celery root, and rinse it clean. Transfer it to a Dutch oven, brush it with the olive oil, and sprinkle with the salt.

Roast until a skewer goes in easily, 1½ to 2 hours.

While the celery root is roasting, in a large skillet, combine the cider, brown sugar, and butter. Set over medium heat. Once the butter melts, increase the heat to high and cook until the cider has reduced slightly and formed a sticky glaze, 4 to 5 minutes. Remove the cider glaze from the heat.

When the celery root is ready, transfer it to a serving plate and carefully pour the cider glaze over it to fully coat it. Sprinkle with a little salt, the apple, walnuts, and celery leaves. Cut into wedges and serve warm.

Tempeh Goreng

Tempeh goreng (Malay for "fried tempeh") is one of blogger WoonHeng Chia's favorite dishes to make when she goes back home to Malaysia, because the tempeh sold at the local morning market is so fresh and affordable. That means, naturally, that if you make your own Tempeh (page 79), this is an ideal use for it. The crucial step in her recipe is to slice the tempeh thinly so the pieces stay crispy after they are fried. Peanuts and potato slices add more layers of texture. To maintain all this crunch, each ingredient is cooked separately before they're all tossed together with the sauce. Serve this sweet and salty meal with a bowl of warm rice, or as a snack without.

Makes 4 servings

Time: Weekday

Storage: Refrigerate for up to 3 days.

- 2 tablespoons warm water
- 1 tablespoon soy sauce, plus more to taste
- 1 tablespoon organic cane sugar
- 1½ teaspoons kecap manis (sweet Indonesian soy sauce; see Note)
- ½ teaspoon fine sea salt
- Neutral vegetable oil, such as sunflower, for deep-frying
- 1 pound (450g) tempeh, homemade (page 79) or store-bought, cut into ⅛-inch (3mm) slices
- 1 medium russet potato (8 ounces/225g), scrubbed and cut into ⅛-inch (3mm) slices
- ⅓ cup unroasted peanuts
- 1 medium shallot, thinly sliced
- 3 garlic cloves, thinly sliced
- 5 fresh Thai red chiles, cut into 1-inch (2.5cm) slices
- 1 jalapeño pepper, thinly sliced lengthwise
- 2 tablespoons Thai sweet chili sauce (optional)

IN A SMALL BOWL, whisk together the water, soy sauce, sugar, kecap manis, and salt until combined.

Set a wire rack over a sheet pan next to the stovetop. Pour 1 inch (2.5cm) neutral oil into a Dutch oven or wok and heat the oil over medium-high heat to 350°F (177°C). Reduce the heat to medium and adjust the heat as needed to maintain that temperature.

Working in batches if necessary to avoid overcrowding, add the tempeh slices and fry, stirring occasionally, until the edges turn crispy and golden brown, about 5 minutes. Use a slotted spoon or Chinese spider to transfer the tempeh to the wire rack to drain.

Using the same pot and oil, add the potato slices and fry, stirring occasionally, until the edges turn crispy and golden brown, 7 to 8 minutes. Transfer the potato slices to the wire rack to drain.

Add the peanuts and fry until they just start to turn a tiny bit darker, 1 to 2 minutes. (Keep in mind that the peanuts will keep cooking while they cool down.) Using a slotted spoon, transfer them to a plate to cool.

Pour out all but 1 tablespoon of oil in the pot and return it to medium heat. Add the shallot and stir-fry until translucent, 1 to 2 minutes. Add the garlic and stir-fry until aromatic, about 1 minute. Add the Thai chiles and jalapeño and stir-fry until they start to become tender, 2 to 3 minutes.

Return the fried tempeh, potato, and peanuts to the pot and add the reserved sauce. Toss to combine. Remove from the heat. If using Thai sweet chili sauce, add it and toss to combine. Serve hot.

COOK'S NOTE: If you can't find kecap manis, you can substitute 1 teaspoon brown sugar plus ½ teaspoon soy sauce.

FIRST, DO NO HARM

By Joanne Lee Molinaro

Oftentimes, when I tell people I am vegan, they look me up and down and say, "Vegan? But you're Korean—how is that possible?" To some degree, I understand the incredulity: I had to create an entire blog to convince even myself that one could adapt Korean cuisine to be plant-based. I would soon learn that the skepticism that initially drove me to delve into the "veganization" of my favorite Korean dishes was, in part, premised upon a very limited understanding of Korean cuisine.

First, like many people, I associated Korean food with Korean barbecue: those rich, indulgent, special-occasion meals that my family and I would have a handful of times a year. In actuality, my diet growing up was probably 70 percent plant-based already, because of the abundance of fresh produce from our own yard. My grandmother, a farmer her whole life, cultivated a beautiful garden packed with fresh squash, sesame leaves (perilla), chiles, corn, tomatoes, cucumbers, and nameless "namools," edible grass or leaves that ultimately found their way onto our bapsang, or table. But for whatever reason, I had forgotten this aspect of my diet (or, at least, stored it away) and had bought into the notion that Korean food equaled grilled meat.

Second, I was completely unaware of Korean temple food, a type of cuisine that has been endemic to the Korean peninsula by way of Buddhist monks for more than sixteen hundred years. While South Korea is often thought of as a Judeo-Christian country (due in some part to American missionaries who began arriving on the peninsula in the late 1800s, as well as a fraught relationship with the Catholic church dating back to the Joseon Dynasty), nearly a quarter of South Koreans identify as Buddhist.

In Korea, temple cuisine is meat- and fish-free, and, with the exception of dairy in some dishes, plant-based. But, in addition to omitting meat and other animal products, temple cuisine also excludes alliums—onions, leeks, garlic, scallions—based on the idea that such foods can prevent clarity of mind and spirit. A typical bapsang of temple cuisine is composed of numerous small dishes, or banchan, even more so than the average Korean meal, which generally consists of a number of banchan that satellite around a bowl of rice and perhaps one "main" dish (such as grilled meat or fish).

These small dishes include a variety of pickled vegetables; seasoned shoots, roots, and greens; noodles bathing in a clear and refreshing broth; delightfully crunchy and chewy savory pancakes with arteries of carrot and cabbage. Food is prepared directly from the vegetation cultivated on-site or locally. Virtually no part of a plant goes wasted, and each is prepared in such a way as to maximize flavor, texture, and mouthfeel, and to cleanse the spirit. They are flavored with combinations of dozens of sauces, some that are brewed and fermented over decades, achieving the kind of intensity and clarity of flavor that would make a sommelier proud.

Often described as "minimalist," temple food is sometimes mischaracterized as "simple." However, much of the cuisine was derived from dishes that were served out of the royal kitchen. When the royal maids who prepared the king's meals retired, they often became nuns at a local Buddhist temple. Not surprisingly, they took all the knowledge and skill they gained in royal court and applied that to the dishes they prepared in their humbler kitchens.

Indeed, the precision and skill involved with preparing a meal in the "temple fashion" has been getting noticed in the upper echelons of the food world. Eric Ripert, a Michelin three-star chef and owner of one of the world's top restaurants, Le Bernardin, has lauded Jeong Kwan-sseunim, one of the best-known South Korean Buddhist monks in the world, as an exceptional chef. Jeong Kwan-sseunim was featured in the season three opener of Netflix's popular *Chef's Table*, during which food writers such as Jeff Gordinier waxed poetic about Sseunim's mastery over sauces and the power of fermentation: the two pillars of temple cuisine. In 2016, her Balwoo Gongyang became the first Korean-style temple food restaurant to receive a coveted Michelin star.

In 2019, I had the honor of meeting with Jeong Kwan-sseunim for tea in her home, at the very top of the Baegam Mountain, or Baegam-san, where the Chunjinam Hermitage seemed to grow right out of the rocks like a cluster of touch-me-not blossoms. The hermitage was a study in juxtaposition, with the humblest of dingy structures squatting side by side with ornate Buddhist temples, brightly painted and gilded. Onggi, large earthen clay pots teeming with the bacteria necessary to ferment sauces, soybeans, and cabbage, studded the corners of small living quarters, casting their long shadows across stone paths that had recently been swept with handmade broomsticks.

Upon arriving, Jeong Kwan-sseunim seated us at a large table in one of the monastery's buildings, what looked to be a communal dining area. Without speaking, she began to prepare tea, her movements swift and efficient. After pouring tea for us, she asked me a few questions about myself, why I was visiting Korea. Luckily, my sister-in-law was there to fill in the unfortunate gaps in my Korean speaking skills. I explained to her that my "mission" was to show the world that Korean food could easily be veganized and that part of why I wanted to meet her was to discuss her cuisine.

Jeong Kwan-sseunim studied me the way a bird might study the sea or a bee might study the tight bud of a blossom. I felt myself growing smaller as her gaze cut through my ingratiating smiles and honorifics, before she finally said:

> "'Vegan' is just a label. It doesn't really mean anything."

I bobbed my head enthusiastically, as if it were exactly what I'd known all along, while inside, I wondered if my visit with her was doomed from the start.

Jeong Kwan-sseunim continued to explain the history of Buddhism in Korea, its tenets, and above all, the commitment to avoid causing harm to any living thing. Her hands were small and hardy, just like my grandmother's had been, and she used them to peel back the words I had grown so accustomed to deploying to define myself: Korean, vegan, girl, cook. Instead, as we sipped our tea and nibbled on rice crackers on the slopes of Baegam-san, she replaced all my words with a truth as round and hard as an acorn:

> "You mustn't harm living things because when you do, you harm yourself."

At its heart, the beauty of temple food is its intentionality. Because temple food isn't just about restricting your diet, losing weight, lowering your cholesterol, reducing your carbon footprint, and reducing animal suffering. It's actually about all of that and more. As the Jogye Order of Korean Buddhism writes in *Buddhist English (Elementary 1)*, "Everything we do, think or say"—including what and how we eat—"has an effect on the world around us and on us. Change will happen to us anyway, but through the choices we make about how to behave, we can change ourselves, and the world around us, for the better."

Joanne Lee Molinaro is author of the bestselling cookbook *The Korean Vegan*.

11

SIDE DISHES: GRAINS, BEANS & VEGETABLES

These are your main-course partners, the dishes that help you build heft and satisfaction on your table. This chapter is heavy on rice and other grains, because in the plant-based kitchen, that might be all you need to add to a vegetable-focused entree, but there are plenty of other ideas to help you mix and match as you see fit.

Grilled Vegetables with Miso Butter

This dish is a perfect example of less is more—a few simple ingredients that come together to create something special, with minimal effort. The smokiness of grilled vegetables gets an umami punch when topped off with a dollop of plant butter that's been blended with miso and lemon zest. Make it your own by using any vegetables you like!

Makes 4 servings

Time: Weekday

Storage: Refrigerate the butter for up to 1 month or freeze for up to 6 months. Refrigerate the vegetables for up to 3 days.

4 tablespoons (56g) Soft Spreadable Butter (page 21) or store-bought unsalted vegan butter, at room temperature

1 tablespoon white or yellow miso, homemade (page 83) or store-bought, at room temperature

1 teaspoon grated lemon zest

½ teaspoon ground white pepper

Olive oil (preferably a spray for easier coating)

1 small sweet potato (6 ounces/170g), scrubbed and sliced into ¼-inch (6mm) rounds

1 large zucchini or summer squash (11 ounces/312g), cut lengthwise into planks ½ inch (1.3cm) thick

12 ounces (340g) cherry tomatoes (preferably on the vine for easier grilling)

8 ounces (225g) shishito peppers

Fine sea salt

IN A SMALL BOWL, combine the butter, miso, lemon zest, and white pepper and stir until thoroughly combined. Refrigerate until the vegetables are ready.

Prepare a charcoal grill for hot direct grilling, or heat a gas grill to high. (Alternatively, you can use a grill pan on the stove, heated over medium-high heat.) Spray or lightly rub olive oil on all the vegetables, then sprinkle very lightly with salt. Place the vegetables on the grill, being sure to place more tender or thinly cut vegetables toward the outside edges, where the grill is less hot, and thicker vegetables toward the hottest part in the center of the grill. (If your cherry tomatoes and/or shishito peppers are so small they risk falling through the grates, use a grill basket or a cast-iron skillet directly on the grates.)

Keep a close eye on the vegetables as you grill them, reducing the flame, turning, and/or moving the vegetables as necessary so they get lightly charred but not burnt; don't move the vegetables more than necessary, so that they do get a nice char and begin to soften.

Grill the vegetables until tender, then transfer to a serving platter. Place spoonfuls of miso butter on top of the vegetables while they are still hot from the grill, so that the butter melts and coats the vegetables. Serve immediately.

Roasted Winter Squash with Fried Hazelnuts, Rosemary & Lemon

Winter squash come in so many shapes and sizes: What can you do with all of them, especially the ones that are hard to peel? If you roast them whole, the insides steam to tender, and the peels soften so much that they can be eaten (or easily peeled off and composted). Ripping up the roasted squashes creates fun, organic shapes and craggy edges, the ideal spots for an assertive dressing of hazelnuts, rosemary needles, and thinly sliced lemon zest, all three fried in olive oil. With just the addition of lemon juice, the dressing is greater than the sum of its parts: earthy, fruity, slightly bitter—good on squash, yes, but also kale, mashed potatoes, white beans, and more.

Makes 4 servings

Time: Weekend

Storage: Refrigerate for up to 3 days, preferably with the squash separate from the dressing.

- 3 to 4 pounds (1.4kg to 1.8kg) winter squash (see Note), such as acorn, butternut, kabocha, Honeynut, Koginut, or red kuri, scrubbed
- ½ cup (120ml) olive oil, plus more for coating the squash and drizzling
- Fine sea salt
- 1 lemon
- ½ cup (70g) blanched hazelnuts, coarsely chopped
- 2 tablespoons packed rosemary leaves
- Freshly ground black pepper

PREHEAT THE OVEN TO 425°F (220°C).

Prick the squash with a knife in several places all over. Transfer to a baking dish or sheet pan, lightly coat with olive oil, and season with salt. Roast, turning halfway through, until a knife slides easily through, 30 minutes to 1 hour, depending on the type and size of the squash. Let cool slightly.

Meanwhile, use a vegetable peeler to remove a few thick strips of zest from the lemon. Thinly slice the zest crosswise into thin strips until you have 1 tablespoon. Transfer to a small heatproof bowl.

In a small skillet or saucepan, combine the ½ cup (120ml) oil, the hazelnuts, and rosemary. Cook over medium-high heat, swirling often, until the rosemary is crisp and the hazelnuts are lightly golden, 3 to 4 minutes. Pour over the lemon zest and let cool.

When the squash has cooled slightly, cut or tear it in half and scoop out the seeds. (Save them, if you'd like, for Roasted Pumpkin Seeds, page 117.) Break or cut the squash into 2- to 3-inch (5cm to 7.5cm) pieces and transfer to a platter.

Halve and squeeze the zested lemon and add 2 to 3 tablespoons lemon juice to the hazelnut-rosemary mixture. Add salt and pepper to taste and spoon over the squash.

COOK'S NOTE: The squashes can be roasted up to 4 days ahead; refrigerate them whole so they don't dry out. Reheat in a 350°F oven until warm before cutting.

Gomen

These Ethiopian greens get their complex seasoning from niter kibbeh, a spiced butter. Traditionally, it needs to be skimmed and clarified, but the lack of milk solids makes vegan butter an easier process. While collards are the traditional greens for this dish, feel free to use kale, mustard greens, or any sturdy green you like.

Makes 4 servings

Time: Weekday

Storage: Refrigerate for up to 5 days or freeze for up to 3 months.

- 2 bunches collard greens (12 ounces/340g each)
- 3 tablespoons niter kibbeh, store-bought or homemade (recipe follows)
- 1 medium red onion (8 ounces/225g), chopped
- 1 tablespoon chopped fresh ginger
- 2 garlic cloves, finely chopped or grated
- 1 jalapeño or Fresno chile, chopped
- 1 teaspoon fine sea salt, plus more to taste
- 1 cup (240ml) water
- 2 tablespoons fresh lemon juice

TRIM THE TOUGH STEMS from the collards, wash and dry the leaves, and stack them. Roll them lengthwise, then cut crosswise into ½-inch (1.3cm) shreds. Compost the stems..

In a large Dutch oven, heat the niter kibbeh over medium heat. Add the onion and cook, stirring occasionally, until softened, about 5 minutes. Add the ginger, garlic, and jalapeño and cook until sizzling, about 30 seconds. Add the collards and salt. Toss to coat the collards in the niter kibbeh and cook until they begin to wilt, 2 to 3 minutes.

Add the water and bring to a simmer. Cover and cook, stirring once or twice, until the collards are very tender, but still slightly soupy, about 15 minutes. (Add a little more water, if needed, to keep some liquid in the bottom of the pot.) Taste and season with more salt if needed. Stir in the lemon juice and serve hot.

Niter Kibbeh

Niter kibbeh has many uses—including in Misir Wat (page 179). It will keep, covered, in your refrigerator for more than a month. Use it to sauté vegetables or tofu or stir into cooked beans or grains.

Makes about 1 cup

Time: Weekday

Storage: Refrigerate for up to 1 month or refrigerate for up to 3 months.

- 8 ounces (225g) Soft Spreadable Butter (page 21) or store-bought unsalted vegan butter
- 1-inch (2.5cm) piece fresh ginger, thinly sliced
- 4 garlic cloves, sliced
- 5 green cardamom pods
- 5 whole cloves
- 1 cinnamon stick
- 1 teaspoon cumin seeds
- 1 teaspoon black peppercorns
- ¼ teaspoon ground turmeric

IN A SMALL SAUCEPAN, combine the butter, ginger, garlic, cardamom, cloves, cinnamon, cumin, peppercorns, and turmeric. Set over medium-low heat, and once the butter melts, bring to a simmer over medium heat and cook for 5 minutes. Remove from the heat and let cool to room temperature in the pan.

Strain through a very fine-mesh sieve (see Note) into a jar. Use right away or refrigerate or freeze.

COOK'S NOTE: Use the leftover niter kibbeh solids to flavor rice, stirring them into the dry grains before adding liquid and salt and steaming.

Agrodolce Radicchio

To tame the brilliant bitterness of radicchio, this recipe douses it in *agrodolce* (literally "sour-sweet" in Italian) made from simmering vinegar (that's the sour) with maple syrup and dates (that's the sweet). Red pepper flakes bring the heat, and Castelvetrano olives, added at the end, provide that last missing element: saltiness. (They're juicy, too!) Feel free to dress this dish up with herbs: Parsley, mint, and/or dill would be welcome additions. Eat it with braised white beans or chickpeas, slow-cooked greens, or simply cooked squash or sweet potatoes, which would be a mild counterpart to all the bold flavors.

Makes 4 servings

Time: Weekday

Storage: Refrigerate for up to 5 days.

- ½ cup (50g) raw walnuts
- 2 medium heads radicchio (9 ounces/255g each), cut into 2-inch (5cm) wedges
- 3 tablespoons olive oil, plus more for drizzling
- ¾ teaspoon fine sea salt
- ¾ cup (180ml) apple cider vinegar
- ¼ cup (60ml) maple syrup
- ¼ teaspoon red pepper flakes
- 5 Medjool dates, pitted and torn or chopped
- ¼ cup (40g) pitted Castelvetrano olives, cut or torn in half
- Flaky sea salt, for finishing

PREHEAT THE OVEN TO 350°F (180°C).

Spread the walnuts on a baking sheet and toast until very fragrant and a shade darker, 8 to 10 minutes. Transfer to a cutting board to cool slightly, then coarsely chop.

Increase the oven temperature to 400°F (200°C).

Spread the radicchio wedges on a large sheet pan, drizzle with the olive oil, and sprinkle with ½ teaspoon of the fine salt. Toss gently to coat. Roast until wilted, tender, and charred on the edges, 12 to 15 minutes, turning halfway through with tongs. (If you'd like the radicchio to be a little more charred, turn the oven to broil and broil very briefly, watching carefully.)

Meanwhile, in a small saucepan, combine the vinegar, maple syrup, pepper flakes, dates, and remaining ¼ teaspoon fine salt. Bring to a boil over medium heat. Reduce the heat to medium-low and simmer the agrodolce until syrupy and reduced, 8 to 10 minutes.

Transfer the radicchio to a platter. Spoon the agrodolce over the radicchio, then top with the dates, olives, and walnuts. Drizzle with a little olive oil, sprinkle with the flaky salt, and serve warm.

Iranian-Style Jeweled Cauliflower Rice

Even though my Assyrian grandparents were refugees from the same part of the world, I didn't taste the traditional version of this, one of the great dishes of Iran, until I met Najmieh Batmanglij. Naj is the grande dame of Persian cooking, and her rice was the crowning glory of a table at a charity event hosted by Joan Nathan, the grande dame of Jewish cooking. (It was a two-dame night!) The dish consists of twice-cooked rice, scented with orange blossom water, and topped with almost-candied orange peels and carrots plus a chewy, crunchy mix of super-tart dried barberries, pistachios, and more. The topping glistens—these are the jewels of the name—and the textures and flavors sing. With apologies to the traditions of Naj and my own grandmother, I've adapted it to use riced cauliflower, just the thing for those who crave something a little less starchy and a little more healthful. Because barberries can be tricky to find, I'm calling for golden berries, which carry a similar pucker-inducing tartness that cuts through the sweetness of the carrots and their syrup. Bonus: It comes together more quickly than the original, and it's just as stunning on the table.

Makes 8 servings

Time: Weekday

Storage: Refrigerate for up to 3 days.

2 large oranges

7 tablespoons organic cane sugar

1 teaspoon saffron

3 tablespoons orange blossom water

1 head cauliflower (2½ to 3 pounds/1.1kg to 1.4kg), trimmed and cut into 2-inch (5cm) pieces

2 teaspoons fine sea salt, plus more to taste

2 tablespoons olive oil

½ cup (55g) sliced or slivered almonds, toasted

½ cup (65g) pistachios, toasted and chopped

½ cup (2½ ounces/75g) dried golden berries, dried barberries, or dried unsweetened cranberries

½ cup (2½ ounces/75g) dried cherries or golden raisins

3 large carrots (12 ounces/340g total), scrubbed and cut into 2-inch (5cm) matchsticks

4-inch (10cm) cinnamon stick

2 teaspoons freshly ground cardamom

1 cup (240ml) water

USING A VEGETABLE PEELER, peel wide strips of zest off the oranges. Stack and slice the strips crosswise into thin slivers. Bring a small pot of water to a boil over medium-high heat. Add the orange zest slivers and boil for 1 minute, then drain and rinse with cold water.

In a mortar and pestle (or a wooden spoon and a small bowl), combine 1 tablespoon of the sugar and the saffron. Crush the mixture until it forms a powder. Stir in 2 tablespoons of the orange blossom water.

Working in batches as needed, transfer the cauliflower pieces to a large food processor and pulse just until the cauliflower is reduced to the size of grains of rice. Scoop it into a Dutch oven or other pot large enough to comfortably hold it. Stir in the salt.

In a large skillet, heat 1 tablespoon of the oil over medium heat until it shimmers. Add the almonds and pistachios and sauté until the nuts become fragrant, about 1 minute. Add the golden berries and cherries and toss with the nuts until coated with oil and warmed through. Transfer to a bowl.

In the same skillet over medium heat, combine 2 tablespoons of the saffron/orange blossom water mixture, 1 tablespoon of the sugar, and the remaining 1 tablespoon oil. Add the carrots and orange zest slivers and sauté until the carrots just start to wilt, about 2 minutes. Add the remaining 5 tablespoons sugar, the cinnamon stick, cardamom, and water. Increase the heat to high to bring to a boil. Reduce the heat to medium and simmer the carrots until they are just tender and the liquid has become syrupy, about 10 minutes.

Set a sieve over the Dutch oven containing the cauliflower rice and pour the carrot mixture into the sieve. Toss and stir the carrots so as much liquid as possible drains into the rice. Add the remaining 1 tablespoon plain orange blossom water to the rice and stir until the syrup and orange blossom water are evenly distributed throughout the rice. Taste and season with more salt if needed.

Set the Dutch oven over medium-low heat, cover, and cook until the cauliflower rice has just lost its crunch but is not mushy, 10 to 15 minutes. Stir in the remaining 1 tablespoon saffron/orange blossom water mixture.

Scoop the rice onto a large platter and top with the carrot-orange mixture and the dried fruit/toasted nut mixture. Serve warm.

Harvest Rice

Korean harvest rice is meant to represent the bounty of autumn. While such recipes often include beans (black soybeans, kidney beans, or chickpeas), this one is a little more fruit forward, thanks to dried jujube fruit (aka red dates or Chinese dates), and highlights some of the starchier items of fall, such as sweet potato (the wonderful yellow-fleshed Korean variety) and roasted chestnuts. It also includes far less soaking time and can be whipped up in under 2 hours—and that includes the soaking time for the jujubes. What results is a hearty, sweet, and sticky rice dish that could *almost* serve as dessert—except a sprinkle of salt keeps it squarely in the savory realm.

Makes 4 servings

Time: Weekend

Storage: Refrigerate for up to 1 week.

> 6 to 7 medium dried jujube fruits (70g) or pitted Medjool dates
> Boiling water
> 1 cup (190g) short-grain brown rice
> 1 cup (180g) sweet brown rice
> ½ cup (100g) pearled barley
> ¼ cup (45g) black rice
> 1 Korean or Japanese sweet potato (11 ounces/300g), peeled and cut into 1-inch (2.5cm) chunks
> ¼ cup (40g) diced peeled roasted chestnuts
> ½ teaspoon fine sea salt
> 4½ cups (1.1L) water

IN A SMALL HEATPROOF bowl, cover the jujubes with boiling water and soak for 1 hour. Drain.

In a large fine-mesh sieve, combine the short-grain brown rice, sweet brown rice, barley, and black rice and rinse several times, to remove most of the exterior starch, until the water running through is almost clear. (It won't be completely clear because of the black rice.)

In a Dutch oven, combine the jujubes, rice mixture, sweet potato, chestnuts, salt, and water. Bring to a boil over high heat. Reduce the heat to low, cover, and cook until the rice is tender but not mushy, 50 to 55 minutes. (Alternatively, you can cook in a rice cooker, using the "brown rice" setting.) Serve hot.

Garlic-Infused Jasmine Rice

On the menu of his DC restaurant Muchas Gracias, chef Christian Irabién describes this side dish as "jasmine rice with all of the garlic." And it certainly tastes that way: Garlic perfumes and infuses seemingly every one of the soft grains, resulting in a side dish that's become one of my go-to recipes. Make sure to chop the garlic very finely, or grate it: That's the key to spreading its flavor throughout.

Makes 4 to 6 servings

Time: Weekday

Storage: Refrigerate for up to 3 days or freeze for up to 3 months.

> 2 tablespoons olive oil
> ¼ cup (65g) diced white onion
> 8 large garlic cloves, finely chopped or grated
> 2 bay leaves
> 2 cups (360g) jasmine rice
> 3 cups (700ml) water
> ½ lime or lemon
> 1½ teaspoons fine sea salt, plus more to taste

IN A MEDIUM SAUCEPAN, heat the oil over medium heat until it shimmers. Add the onion, garlic, and bay leaves and sauté until the onion turns translucent but has not taken on any color, about 3 minutes.

Stir in the rice and cook, stirring, until the rice is glossy and coated and the onion is evenly distributed, about 3 minutes.

Add the water, lime or lemon half, and salt. Stir only once to incorporate the liquid (stirring more will cause the rice grains to release their starch and become clumpy). Reduce the heat to medium-low, cover, and cook until all the liquid is absorbed, about 15 minutes. Turn off the heat, leave the lid on, and let the rice sit for 10 minutes. Fish out and compost the lemon and bay leaves. Taste and season with more salt if needed. Serve hot.

Homestyle Mexican Rice

This is one of the first things blogger Dora Stone ever learned how to make. The aroma of the rice cooking takes her back to her mother's kitchen and the taste of the crunchy toasted rice her mother would give her to snack on while she cooked. The toasting is key for other reasons: It keeps the rice from clumping and adds a nutty flavor. Feel free to use canned tomatoes instead of fresh in this recipe. Dora also likes to use vegan "no-chicken" bouillon paste instead of salt because the flavor reminds her of a popular chicken bouillon powder that is used extensively in Mexico.

Makes 4 servings

Time: Weekday

Storage: Refrigerate for up to 3 days or freeze for up to 3 months.

2 cups (300g) diced Roma tomatoes or 1 (14.5-ounce/411g) can diced tomatoes

½ cup (65g) chopped white onion

1 garlic clove, peeled but whole

1 tablespoon vegetable oil

1½ cups (270g) basmati or other long-grain white rice

2¼ cups (532ml) Vegetable Scrap Stock (page 36) or store-bought vegetable broth

½ cup (65g) frozen peas

½ cup (70g) diced carrot

1 serrano pepper (optional), seeded and finely chopped

1 teaspoon vegan no-chicken bouillon paste (such as Better Than Bouillon), or 1 teaspoon fine sea salt

1 large sprig fresh cilantro

Fine sea salt

IN A BLENDER, COMBINE the tomatoes, onion, and garlic and process until smooth.

In a medium saucepan, heat the oil over medium heat until it shimmers. Add the rice and cook, stirring constantly, until the rice is golden brown and smells toasty, 2 to 3 minutes.

Add the pureed tomatoes and bring to a simmer. Reduce the heat to medium-low and cook, stirring constantly, until the sauce starts to darken, about 2 minutes. (Use a splatter screen if needed.)

Stir in the vegetable stock, peas, carrots, serrano (if using), and bouillon paste or salt. Add the cilantro sprig. Increase the heat to high and bring to a boil. Reduce the heat to low, cover, and cook until the rice absorbs all the liquid, about 20 minutes. Remove from the heat but leave the rice covered to rest for 10 minutes, then uncover and fluff with a fork.

Taste and season with salt if needed. Serve hot.

Asparagus with Nutritional Yeast Bread Crumbs

Stir nutritional yeast and a little dried chile into some toasted panko bread crumbs for a crispy, umami, light topping for seared asparagus. Searing instead of roasting requires more attention from you, which is good because you can better gauge whether your asparagus is done or not. Because asparagus come in various thicknesses, use your fingers to see if they're done: A squeeze at the thickest part should result in a slight give.

Makes 4 servings

Time: Weekday

Storage: Refrigerate the asparagus and store the panko separately at room temperature, both for up to 5 days.

  ¼ cup (60ml) olive oil
  ½ cup (40g) panko bread crumbs
  ½ teaspoon fine sea salt, plus more to taste
  ¼ cup (20g) nutritional yeast
  ½ teaspoon red pepper flakes, plus more to taste
  1 bunch asparagus (1 pound/(450g), tough ends trimmed

IN A LARGE CAST-IRON skillet, heat 2 tablespoons of the oil over medium heat until it shimmers. Add the panko and salt and cook, stirring, until golden, 3 to 5 minutes. Transfer to a small bowl and stir in the nutritional yeast and pepper flakes. Taste and season with more salt and/or pepper flakes if needed.

Wipe out the skillet. Add the remaining 2 tablespoons oil over medium-high heat. Add the asparagus and cook, tossing occasionally, until crisp-tender and charred in spots, 3 to 5 minutes. Season with salt, transfer to a plate, then sprinkle over the panko.

COOK'S NOTE: The nutritional yeast bread crumbs are also great on roasted vegetables, pasta, lentils, soup, and more.

Garlic Chive Kimchi

One common misconception is that there is just one kind of kimchi: cabbage kimchi. The truth is, there are hundreds of varieties, and at its core, kimchi is simply a pickled vegetable, often seasoned with gochugaru (Korean chile flakes). This recipe takes garlic chives and "kimchi-ifies" them for the next time you need a little pop in your salad, sandwich, or rice bowl. You can eat these immediately after making, or for a more fermented, funkier flavor, let the mixture sit for a few days. Like all kimchi, it gets even better with time.

Makes about 8 cups (12 to 16 servings)

Time: Project

Storage: Refrigerate for up to 1 month.

  1 pound (450g) garlic chives (see Note), trimmed and cut into 3-inch (7.5cm) pieces
  3 tablespoons gochugaru (Korean chile flakes)
  1½ tablespoons unseasoned rice vinegar
  1½ tablespoons maple syrup
  1½ tablespoons fine sea salt
  1 teaspoon freshly ground black pepper

IN A LARGE BOWL, combine the garlic chives, gochugaru, rice vinegar, maple syrup, salt, and pepper and mix until the chives are evenly coated.

Serve some immediately, if desired, and transfer the rest to an airtight container and let it sit for 3 days at room temperature, then serve.

COOK'S NOTE: If you can't find garlic chives, aka Chinese chives, substitute the greens from scallions plus 2 grated or pressed garlic cloves.

Soy & Maple–Glazed Korean Sweet Potatoes

Korean or Japanese sweet potatoes look and taste different from the bright orange variety you see in most Western grocery stories. Their skin is dark purple, while their flesh is a light yellow. They impart more nuttiness than sweetness, and because of their lower moisture content, they are great for glazing, as the sticky-sweet glaze plays off their natural starchiness. This recipe relies on two other staples of the Korean pantry—soy sauce and doenjang (fermented soybean paste)—to inject intense umami, for a result that you might want to make for every meal, including breakfast.

Makes 2 servings

Time: Weekday

Storage: Refrigerate for up to 1 week.

Sunflower or other neutral vegetable oil, for greasing the pan

10 ounces (285g) Korean or Japanese sweet potatoes, peeled and cut into 1-inch (2.5cm) chunks

¼ cup (60ml) maple syrup

1½ tablespoons soy sauce

1½ teaspoons doenjang (Korean fermented soybean paste) or red miso

2 tablespoons (28g) Soft Spreadable Butter (page 21) or store-bought unsalted vegan butter

1 tablespoon toasted sesame seeds

POSITION A RACK IN the lowest position in the oven and preheat to 475°F (240°C). Lightly oil a sheet pan.

Meanwhile, in a medium saucepan, combine the sweet potatoes with enough water to cover by several inches. Bring to a boil over medium-high heat, reduce the heat to medium, and cook the sweet potatoes until they are almost, but not quite, cooked all the way through, about 20 minutes. (A skewer inserted in one should encounter a touch of resistance in the center.)

Drain the potatoes and transfer them to the oiled sheet pan.

Return the empty saucepan to medium heat. Add the maple syrup, soy sauce, doenjang, and butter and stir to combine. Bring to a boil and cook until the sauce thickens, 2 to 4 minutes.

Brush the sauce all over the potatoes, flipping them as needed. You'll have some sauce left over, which you'll use to continue brushing on the potatoes as they cook.

Bake the potatoes on the lowest oven rack until they start to brown, about 10 minutes. Turn the potatoes over, brush with more glaze, and bake until deeply browned and fork-tender, 5 more minutes.

Brush with the remaining glaze, sprinkle with the sesame seeds, and serve hot.

Green Pilau

Pilau (aka pilaf) is a fragrant rice dish with variations found throughout East Africa, the Middle East, India, and neighboring countries. Spice blends and flavorings can vary greatly. This amazingly fragrant green pilau gets its vibrant hue from blended spinach and herbs.

Makes 6 to 8 servings

Time: Weekday

Storage: Refrigerate for up to 3 days or freeze for up to 3 months.

8½ cups (6 ounces/170g) baby spinach, roughly chopped

¾ cup (30g) chopped fresh cilantro

2 cups (470ml) Vegetable Scrap Stock (page 36) or store-bought vegetable broth

1 teaspoon fine sea salt

3 tablespoons sunflower oil

1 medium yellow onion (8 ounces/225g), thinly sliced (about 1 cup)

4 garlic cloves, finely grated or pressed

1 tablespoon finely grated fresh ginger

1 jalapeño, finely chopped

1 cinnamon stick

1 teaspoon ground cumin

¾ teaspoon ground cardamom

½ teaspoon smoked paprika

½ teaspoon ground cinnamon

½ teaspoon freshly ground black pepper

⅛ teaspoon ground cloves

8 ounces (225g) red potatoes, peeled and cut into ½-inch (1.3cm) chunks

2 cups (360g) basmati rice, rinsed

1½ cups (200g) frozen green peas

IN A BLENDER, COMBINE the spinach, cilantro, ½ cup (120ml) of the vegetable stock, and the salt. Puree until smooth.

In a medium saucepan, heat the oil over medium-high heat until it shimmers. Add the onion and sauté until soft and brown, about 10 minutes. Stir in the garlic, ginger, jalapeño, cinnamon stick, cumin, cardamom, smoked paprika, ground cinnamon, black pepper, and cloves and cook until very fragrant, about 1 minute.

Add the potatoes and the remaining 1½ cups (350ml) vegetable stock. Bring to a boil, then reduce the heat to medium, cover, and cook until the potatoes are almost but not quite tender, about 10 minutes.

Stir in the rice and spinach mixture, increase the heat to medium-high to bring to a simmer, then reduce the heat to medium-low, cover, and cook until the rice is tender and has absorbed the liquid, about 15 minutes.

Turn off the heat and stir in the peas. Cover and allow to steam for another 5 minutes. Fluff with a fork and serve hot.

Curried Chinese Long Beans

In Trinidad and Tobago, Chinese long beans (bodi), are a bastion of versatility. Here they are curried, a traditional way of enjoying them there. If you don't have easy access to long beans, this preparation also works wonderfully with conventional green beans. Serve this with brown rice, roti, naan, or your favorite flatbread, such as Bing (page 397) or Pumpkin Chapatis (page 399).

Makes about 4 cups (2 to 4 servings)

Time: Weekday

Storage: Refrigerate for up to 4 days.

> 3 tablespoons vegetable oil
> ½ cup (70g) chopped shallot (from 1 large shallot)
> 4 garlic cloves, smashed and chopped
> 1 tablespoon grated fresh ginger (from 1-inch/2.5cm piece of peeled ginger)
> ½ small Scotch bonnet or habanero pepper, seeded, deveined, and chopped
> 1 tablespoon Madras curry powder
> 1⅓ cups (320ml) water
> 1 pound (450g) Chinese long beans or green beans, trimmed and cut into 2-inch (5cm) pieces
> 1 cup (180g) chopped tomato (1 to 2 large plum tomatoes)
> 2 teaspoons fine sea salt
> ½ teaspoon freshly ground black pepper

IN A LARGE SKILLET, heat the oil over medium-high heat until it shimmers. Add the shallot, garlic, ginger, and Scotch bonnet pepper and sauté until the shallot is tender, about 2 minutes. Reduce the heat to low. Stir in the curry powder and cook, stirring, until fragrant, about 1 minute.

Add ⅓ cup (80ml) of the water, stir to combine, and cook for another 30 seconds. Add the beans and the remaining 1 cup (240ml) water, stir to combine, and increase the heat to medium-high to bring to a simmer. Reduce the heat to medium-low, cover, and cook until the beans are tender and most of the water has evaporated, 12 to 15 minutes. If it's still a little soupy looking, uncover and cook for a few more minutes to drive off extra liquid.

Stir in the chopped tomato, salt, and black pepper. Serve hot.

Jamaican Rice & Peas

A quintessential Jamaican side dish, rice and peas (the latter word being what islanders use to refer to beans) is almost a requirement at any get-together there. Traditionally plant-based, it's also one of the easiest Jamaican dishes to prepare. Note that the dish isn't really spicy—as long as you are careful to not puncture the Scotch bonnet pepper during cooking.

Makes 6 servings

Time: Weekend

Storage: Refrigerate for up to 3 days or freeze for up to 3 months.

> 1 cup (185g) dried red kidney beans, soaked overnight, rinsed, and drained
> 3 to 4 cups (700ml to 950ml) water
> 2 cups (370g) long-grain white rice, rinsed
> 1 (13.5-ounce/400ml) can full-fat coconut milk
> 3 scallions, halved crosswise
> 2 garlic cloves, peeled and left whole
> 1 Scotch bonnet pepper or habanero pepper, left whole
> 1 teaspoon allspice berries (aka pimento berries)
> 1 teaspoon fine sea salt, plus more to taste
> A few sprigs fresh thyme

IN A 3-QUART (3L) saucepan, combine the kidney beans with water to just cover, about 3 cups (700ml). Bring to a boil, then reduce the heat to medium so the liquid is at a brisk simmer. Cook the beans until tender, 30 minutes to 1 hour, adding as much of the remaining 1 cup (240ml) water as needed to keep them barely covered as the liquid evaporates.

When the beans are tender, stir in the rice, coconut milk, scallions, garlic, Scotch bonnet, allspice, salt, and thyme sprigs.

Cover the pot and bring to a boil over medium-high heat. Reduce the heat to medium and cook for 15 minutes, then reduce the heat to low and cook until the rice is fully cooked, 5 to 10 minutes. (Check occasionally to see if the liquid is evaporating before the rice is cooked, and if so, add a little extra water, ¼ cup/60ml at a time, as needed.)

Remove from the heat and let the rice sit, covered, for 10 minutes. Taste and season with more salt as needed. (Fish out and compost the seasonings.) Serve hot.

Rice Pilaf with Herbs & Pomegranate

This side dish is pretty enough to have a starring role on your table. What really makes this pilaf is the toppings: a handful or two of fresh herbs, tart, crunchy pomegranate seeds, fried shallots, and fried pine nuts. Trust me: It's hard to refrain from eating those shallots and pine nuts while the pilaf is cooking.

Because rice is one of the main components of the dish, it is best made with good-quality, aged basmati rice. You can find it at your local Indian market or online.

Makes 4 to 6 servings

Time: Weekday

Storage: Refrigerate for up to 5 days.

4 ounces (115g) angel hair pasta

¼ cup (60ml) olive oil

2 large shallots, very thinly sliced

2 garlic cloves, smashed and peeled

1 cup (180g) basmati rice, rinsed and drained well

2⅓ cups (550ml) Vegetable Scrap Stock (page 36) or store-bought vegetable broth

½ teaspoon fine sea salt

1 bay leaf

¼ cup (35g) pine nuts

½ cup (70g) pomegranate seeds (aka arils; see Note)

¼ cup (5g) fresh mint leaves, torn

¼ cup (9g) dill fronds

¼ cup (7g) flat-leaf parsley

TAKING A SMALL HANDFUL at a time, break the angel hair pasta into ½-inch (1.3cm) pieces (you're aiming for them to be a little longer than the rice).

In a large heavy-bottomed pot, heat the oil over medium-high heat until it shimmers. Add the shallots, stirring to coat in the oil, and arrange in a single layer. Reduce the heat to medium and fry the shallots until deeply golden, 7 to 9 minutes. Place a fine-mesh sieve over a medium heatproof bowl and pour the shallots into the sieve, so the bowl catches the oniony olive oil.

Return the pot to medium-low heat. Add 3 tablespoons of the shallot-infused oil and the broken angel hair pasta to the pot and gently toast the pasta, stirring frequently until lightly browned, 6 to 8 minutes. Add the garlic and cook for another minute.

Increase the heat to medium-high and add the rice, stock, salt, and bay leaf. Stir well and bring to a boil. Reduce the heat to low, cover, and cook for 18 minutes. Remove from the heat and let rest, covered, for 10 minutes.

While the rice is resting, heat a small skillet over medium heat and add the remaining 1 tablespoon shallot oil. Add the pine nuts and toast, stirring frequently, until lightly golden, 1 to 2 minutes. Remove from the heat and transfer to the sieve with the fried shallots.

To assemble, uncover the rice pilaf and gently fluff with a fork. Transfer to a shallow serving bowl or platter and sprinkle with half the fried shallot/pine nut mixture. Sprinkle the pomegranate seeds and herbs over the pilaf and finish with the remaining half of the shallot/pine nut mix. Serve warm or at room temperature.

COOK'S NOTE: Pomegranate seeds spoil quickly but freeze beautifully, so if you like to use them (and you should!), keep a cup or two in an airtight container in the freezer for up to 1 year.

Ugali

A staple in Kenyan cuisine, ugali is made of white cornmeal and can be served alongside any savory dish. This recipe results in a porridge dense enough to cut with a knife. Traditionally, it is eaten with your hands; you pull off a piece of it, make an indentation, and use it to scoop up some stew.

Makes 2 to 4 servings

Time: Weekday

Storage: Refrigerate for up to 1 week.

  4 cups (950ml) water
  2 tablespoons (28g) Soft Spreadable Butter (page 21) or store-bought unsalted vegan butter
  1 teaspoon fine sea salt
  2 cups (320g) fine white cornmeal

IN A 3-QUART (3L) saucepan, bring the water to a boil over medium-high heat. Stir in the butter and salt and reduce the heat to medium-low.

While whisking constantly, slowly stream in the cornmeal. Once you've added all the cornmeal, switch to a wooden spoon and reduce the heat to low. Cook, stirring constantly, until the excess liquid has cooked off and the ugali begins to firm up, a white film has formed along the sides and bottom of the pan, and steam is coming off the bottom, 10 to 15 minutes.

Turn the ugali onto a plate by holding a plate over the pan and flipping both together. Cover the ugali with the upside-down pot to keep it warm until ready to serve. (If the ugali doesn't easily release, put it back on the heat for a few minutes and try again.)

Cut the ugali into wedges and serve warm.

COOK'S NOTE: Cut leftovers into ½-inch (1.3cm) slices and pan-fry in a little oil.

Pickled Spicy Garlic Scapes

Garlic scapes are the long curly stalks that grow from the necks of hardneck garlic plants, and gardeners and farmers remove them to send more of the plant's energy to the bulbs. Their texture is a little bit like that of green beans, but the flavor is much more powerful, and when you're lucky enough to come across them at the farmers market (or if you grow your own like I do), you'll want to pounce on them for this easy, delicious recipe. When the scapes are steeped in salt water over a period of days, the bitterness seeps out and all that remains is a lovely tartness. In fact, they taste so good, you can eat them with just a bowl of rice, without dressing them with anything at all. However, this sauce—based on garlic, Korean gochujang, and rice vinegar—requires so little work and looks so impressive, you might as well give it a whirl. These fiery scapes can be enjoyed with rice or porridge, on grain bowls, or just as a snack.

Makes 4 cups (8 servings)

Time: Project

Storage: Refrigerate for up to 1 month.

  1 pound (450g) garlic scapes
  8 cups (1.9L) water
  2 tablespoons fine sea salt
  2 tablespoons garlic paste (store-bought or made from finely grating 6 cloves)
  1½ tablespoons gochujang (Korean chile paste)
  1 tablespoon rice vinegar, preferably unseasoned

CLEAN THE GARLIC SCAPES and trim off any extra tough parts. Cut the scapes into 3-inch (7.5cm) pieces. Place them in a large bowl.

In a 4-quart (4L) or larger pot, bring the water to a boil over high heat. Turn off the heat and stir in the scapes and the salt. Transfer to a bowl, cover, and let the scapes soak in the salt water at room temperature for about 3 days, until they begin to turn yellow, slightly bendable, and sweet to the taste.

Drain the scapes and transfer to a bowl. Add the garlic paste, gochujang, and rice vinegar and stir vigorously, until the scapes are evenly coated.

Serve immediately or transfer to an airtight container for storage.

Okonomiyaki Sweet Potato Fries

This is a playful spin on okonomiyaki, a Japanese street food classic. The dish is typically savory cabbage pancakes topped with a sweet-savory sauce, loaded with mayonnaise, bonito, and nori. In this version, crispy sweet potato sheet pan fries are traded in for the pancakes, with layers of creamy vegan mayonnaise, okonomiyaki sauce, furikake (sesame seeds and nori), and scallions on top.

   This includes instructions for a homemade okonomiyaki sauce, but if you have access to a good Asian market, you might find vegan okonomiyaki sauce there. The sauce is ketchup based, with sweetness from brown sugar, plus mirin and soy sauce for an umami kick.

Makes 4 to 6 servings

Time: Weekday

Storage: Refrigerate the fries, preferably separately from the sauce and toppings, for up to 5 days.

OVEN FRIES

4 large sweet potatoes (2¼ pounds/1kg total), scrubbed and cut into "fries" ¼ inch (6mm) thick

3 tablespoons olive oil

1 teaspoon fine sea salt

½ teaspoon freshly ground black pepper

OKONOMIYAKI SAUCE

⅓ cup (80ml) ketchup

3 tablespoons soy sauce

2 tablespoons dark brown sugar

1 tablespoon mirin

FOR SERVING

4 tablespoons Silky Aquafaba Mayonnaise (page 46) or store-bought vegan mayo, whisked with a little water to loosen

Furikake seasoning

Thinly sliced scallions

PREHEAT THE OVEN TO 425°F (220°C).

Make the oven fries: On a large sheet pan, toss the sweet potatoes with the oil, salt, and pepper. Spread the fries out in a single layer, making sure not to overlap any or overcrowd the pan. (If needed, divide the fries between two sheet pans.)

Bake until the sweet potatoes are lightly browning, 12 to 15 minutes. Gently toss with a spatula and bake until crispy, another 10 to 12 minutes.

Meanwhile, make the okonomiyaki sauce: In a small saucepan, whisk together the ketchup, soy sauce, brown sugar, and mirin. Bring to a boil over medium-high heat, then reduce the heat until the sauce is at a simmer, stirring frequently until the sugar dissolves and the mixture thickens slightly, 1 to 2 minutes.

To serve: Transfer the fries to a large platter or individual plates and drizzle with the warm okonomiyaki sauce and some mayonnaise. Sprinkle with the furikake and scallions. Serve immediately.

Refried Beans

The beautiful simplicity of refried beans will get you every time. They're absolutely the best slathered on a warm flour tortilla. In Mexico, they are eaten at every meal, even breakfast! Traditionalists say that they must be fried in lard, but historians point out that the original refried beans must have been fried with another kind of fat or with no fat at all, since the colonizers were the ones who brought pigs to Mexico. These are best made from beans cooked from scratch, but in a pinch you can use canned beans and the liquid from the can, or vegetable broth.

Makes 4 servings

Time: Weekday

Storage: Refrigerate for up to 3 days or freeze, preferably without the queso fresco topping, for up to 3 months.

> 4 cups cooked and drained pinto or black beans (680g for pinto or 740g for black)
>
> ¾ cup (180ml) reserved bean cooking liquid, plus more as needed
>
> 1½ tablespoons avocado oil or other neutral vegetable oil
>
> ⅓ cup (45g) minced white onion (from ½ medium onion)
>
> 2 garlic cloves, finely grated or pressed
>
> 1 teaspoon fine sea salt, plus more to taste
>
> ¼ teaspoon freshly ground black pepper
>
> ½ cup (56g) Crumbly Almond Queso Fresco (page 27) or store-bought vegan feta

IN A BLENDER, COMBINE the beans and the cooking liquid and puree until smooth. (Alternatively, you can place the beans in a large bowl and use a potato masher to mash the beans into a puree.) Add more cooking liquid as needed to adjust the consistency of the beans to your preference, but remember: They will thicken in the pan the longer you cook them, so it's better to start with them looser.

In a large skillet, heat the oil over medium heat until it shimmers. Add the onion and garlic and sauté until the onion is soft and slightly browned, about 7 minutes. Pour in the pureed beans, salt, and pepper and cook, stirring constantly, until the beans thicken, about 5 minutes. (If they get too thick, stir in more bean cooking liquid until they're just how you want them.) Taste and add more salt if needed.

Sprinkle the queso fresco on top and serve hot.

Spicy Thai Basil & Ginger Mushrooms

Thai basil—which has a slightly spicy, licorice-y flavor and aroma—adds a delicious touch to any dish, including this quick mushroom side. This uses king oyster mushrooms because of their uniquely firm, almost crunchy texture, and because their low moisture means they absorb sauces so well—especially when scored.

Makes 4 servings

Time: Weekday

Storage: Refrigerate for up to 4 days.

> 2½ tablespoons soy sauce, plus more to taste
>
> 1 teaspoon organic cane sugar
>
> 1 tablespoon toasted sesame oil
>
> 1¼ pounds (567g) king oyster mushrooms, cleaned with a brush or damp towel and cut into rounds 1 inch (2.5cm) thick
>
> 2 tablespoons neutral vegetable oil, such as sunflower
>
> 1-inch (2.5cm) piece fresh ginger, peeled and thinly sliced
>
> 4 garlic cloves, sliced
>
> 4 fresh Thai red chiles, cut into 1-inch (2.5cm) pieces
>
> 2 scallions, cut into 1-inch (2.5cm) pieces
>
> ¼ cup (8g) packed fresh Thai basil leaves

IN A SMALL BOWL, whisk together the soy sauce, sugar, and sesame oil until combined.

Using a sharp knife, lightly score the mushroom rounds on each side.

In a large skillet, heat 1 tablespoon of the vegetable oil over medium heat until it shimmers. Add the mushrooms and fry until the edges turn slightly golden, 2 to 3 minutes per side. Transfer to a bowl.

In the same skillet still over medium heat, heat the remaining 1 tablespoon vegetable oil. Add the ginger and sauté until fragrant, 1 to 2 minutes. Add the garlic and chiles and sauté until fragrant, a few seconds.

Return the mushrooms to the skillet and add the scallions. Swirl in the reserved sauce, quickly toss to combine, taste, and add more soy sauce if needed.

Add the whole Thai basil leaves, toss just to combine, and serve warm.

Sukuma Wiki (Sautéed Collard Greens)

These thinly sliced and lightly sautéed greens are a classic East African preparation. In Swahili, *sukuma wiki* means "to push the week," a reference to the affordability of a bundle of greens and their help in getting food on the table until a cook's next paycheck. Collard greens are most commonly used, but other dark leafy greens can be prepared the same way. Traditionally the stems are removed, but if you'd like to use them rather than composting, you can finely chop them and add them with the tomatoes, cooking until tender before adding the greens.

Makes 2 to 4 servings

Time: Weekday

Storage: Refrigerate for up to 4 days.

- 1 pound (450g) collard greens
- 2 tablespoons sunflower or olive oil
- 2 medium tomatoes (10 ounces/285g total), cored and cut into ½-inch (1.3cm) cubes
- 2 garlic cloves, thinly sliced
- ½-inch (1.3cm) piece fresh ginger, peeled and finely chopped
- 1 teaspoon fine sea salt, plus more to taste

REMOVE THE STEMS FROM the collard greens and compost them. Wash and dry the leaves.

To chiffonade-cut the greens, working in batches, stack the leaves into a neat pile. Roll them lengthwise into a tight bundle, like an oversize cigar. Holding the bundle tightly, thinly slice the cigar crosswise into ribbons ⅛ inch (3mm) wide.

In a large skillet, heat the oil over medium heat until it shimmers. Add the tomatoes, garlic, and ginger and cook, stirring, until the tomatoes release their juices, about 2 minutes.

Add the greens, stirring to help wilt them down. Once the greens have turned a bright green, 3 to 4 minutes, stir in the salt. Continue cooking the greens, stirring occasionally, until they darken and become tender, about 10 minutes. Taste and season with more salt if needed. Serve hot.

Braised Mushrooms with Bok Choy

This simple, elegant dish features mushrooms braised in a delicate, light sauce and served over crisp-tender bok choy. It is often served at Chinese wedding banquets, with the bok choy arranged like a flower petal and the mushrooms in the center. Goji berries, which also signify life, add a little color.

Makes 3 to 4 servings

Time: Weekday

Storage: Refrigerate the mushrooms (with their sauce) and the bok choy separately for up to 3 days.

- 1 teaspoon cornstarch
- 3 tablespoons warm water
- 2 tablespoons sunflower or other neutral oil
- 4 garlic cloves, thinly sliced
- 1 pound (450g) baby bok choy, halved and rinsed (quartered if large)
- ¼ teaspoon fine sea salt, plus more to taste
- 2-inch (5cm) piece fresh ginger, peeled and julienned
- 9 large shiitake mushroom caps, stems composted, or dried shiitake caps, rehydrated
- 1 tablespoon soy sauce, plus more to taste
- ½ tablespoon vegan oyster sauce
- ¼ teaspoon organic cane sugar
- ¾ cup (180ml) Vegetable Scrap Stock (page 36) or store-bought vegetable broth
- 1 teaspoon dried goji berries

IN A SMALL BOWL, whisk together the cornstarch and water.

In a large skillet, heat 1 tablespoon of the oil over medium heat until it shimmers. Add half the garlic and sauté until fragrant, about 1 minute. Add the bok choy and salt and stir to coat the bok choy with the oil. Cover and let the bok choy steam just until it is cooked through but still maintains a little crunch, 30 seconds to 1 minute.

Uncover, swirl in 1 tablespoon of the cornstarch slurry, and toss the bok choy to coat. Taste and season with more salt if needed. Transfer the bok choy to a serving plate, arranging it in a circular pattern if you'd like. Cover to keep warm.

Return the skillet to medium heat and heat the remaining 1 tablespoon oil until it shimmers. Add the ginger and the remaining garlic and sauté until aromatic, about 1 minute. Add the mushrooms and cook until they start to soften, 1 to 2 minutes. Add the soy sauce, oyster sauce, sugar, and vegetable stock. Bring to a simmer and cook until the sauce is reduced by half, 2 to 3 minutes.

Stir in the goji berries. Taste and season with more soy sauce if needed. Swirl in the remaining cornstarch slurry and toss to combine.

Spoon the mushrooms and all the sauce on top of the bok choy, keeping it in the middle if you'd like, for a decorative look. Serve warm.

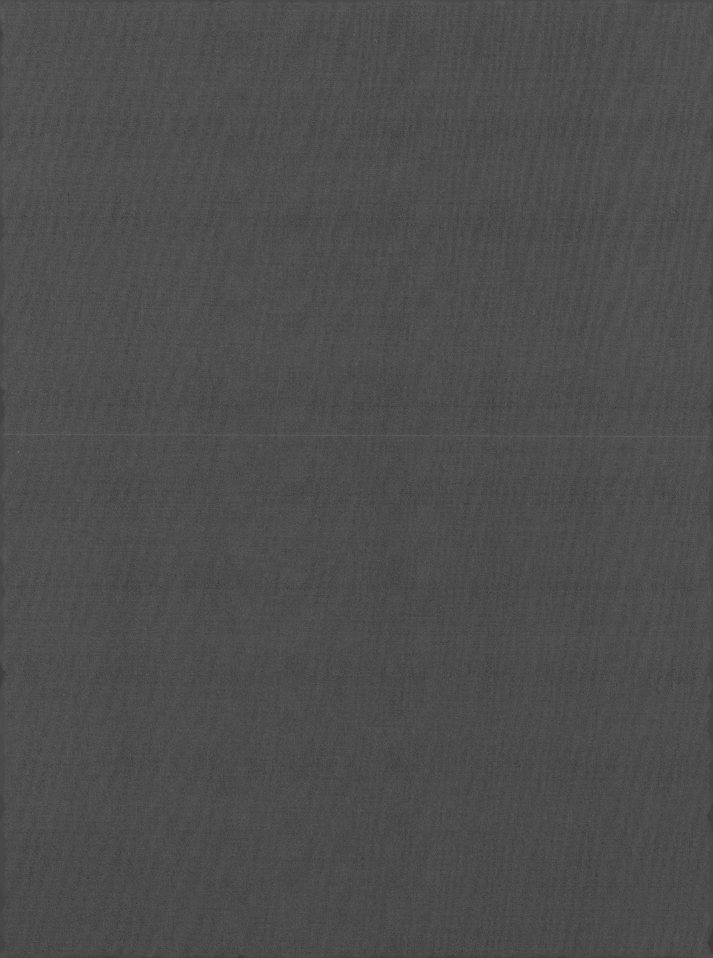

12

SAVORY BAKING: PIZZA, BREADS & MORE

Especially at its most elemental level, savory baking is so friendly to the plant-based approach, because, well, the grains that make up so many flours are nothing if not plants. Flatbreads need nothing to lift them, of course, but when you want a rise, it can usually come from yeasts and other baking leaveners, with no need for eggs. Vegan butter can make beautifully flaky pie crusts, and plant-based cheeses can melt on pizzas—or you can lean on a white sauce based on cauliflower (see White Pizza with Crispy Cauliflower & Shiitakes, page 379).

Socca Pizza

Like so many travelers to France, food writer Diana Yen had socca for the first time while wandering around a farmers market in Nice. It was chilly outside and a woman was making the delicious chickpea flatbreads in a large pan over a fire. When Diana dug into her warm, paper-wrapped socca—it was perfectly crispy on the outside with a tender center—she knew she wasn't just in France, she was in heaven.

Yen's one-skillet pizza is inspired by the traditional socca of her dreams but topped with pesto, shaved asparagus, peas, tangy lemon slices, and melty vegan cheese. You'll get the pan very hot in the oven before pouring the batter in to create a crispy bottom. It's much faster and easier than making traditional pizza dough and, bonus: It's gluten-free. If you don't have chickpea flour, you can make your own by blitzing dried chickpeas in a food processor or blender until fine.

Makes one 10-inch pizza (4 servings)

Time: Weekday

Storage: Refrigerate for up to 2 days.

1⅓ cups (125g) chickpea flour

1⅓ cups (320ml) water

3 tablespoons plus 4 teaspoons olive oil

1 garlic clove, finely grated or pressed

¾ teaspoon fine sea salt, plus more to taste

4 ounces (115g) asparagus (about 4 spears), bottom 1 inch (2.5cm) trimmed off

½ lemon, thinly sliced, seeds removed

2 tablespoons green peas, thawed if frozen

Freshly ground black pepper

¼ cup (60ml) Pesto How You Like It (page 53) or your favorite store-bought vegan pesto

3½ ounces (100g) Basic Melty Cheese (page 25) or store-bought vegan shredded white melting cheese

Fresh sprigs thyme, for garnish

IN A LARGE BOWL, whisk together the chickpea flour, water, 2 tablespoons of the olive oil, the garlic, and ½ teaspoon of the salt. It should be the consistency of pancake batter. Let the batter rest at room temperature for 25 minutes.

Place a 10-inch (25cm) cast-iron skillet or oven-proof nonstick skillet in the oven and preheat to 425°F (220°C).

Once your batter has rested, carefully remove the hot skillet from the oven. Add 2 teaspoons of the olive oil, swirling to coat the bottom. Pour in the batter (it should sizzle), return the skillet to the oven, and bake until the socca is firm and the edges are turning golden brown, 8 to 10 minutes.

While the socca is baking, use a vegetable peeler to create long ribbons of asparagus by drawing the peeler from the base to the tip of the stalk. (It helps to set the spear on a cutting board as you hold the base.) In a bowl, combine the asparagus ribbons, lemon slices, peas, 2 teaspoons of the olive oil, the remaining ¼ teaspoon salt, and pepper and toss to combine. Taste and season with more salt and pepper if needed.

Remove the socca from the oven. Position an oven rack in the highest position and turn the oven to broil.

Brush the top of the socca with the remaining 1 tablespoon oil. Set the skillet on the oven rack and broil until the socca starts to brown in spots, 3 to 4 minutes.

Remove the skillet from the oven and use a spoon to spread the pesto over the socca. Top with shredded cheese, the asparagus/lemon slice mixture, and thyme sprigs. Return the skillet to the broiler and broil until the cheese is bubbling and the socca is crisp underneath (check the bottom by gently lifting with a spatula), 5 to 8 minutes.

Let the pizza cool slightly before removing from the pan. Slice and serve warm.

White Pizza with Crispy Cauliflower & Shiitakes

It takes the perfect white vegetable to make the perfect white pizza. Tester Kristen Hartke's recipe uses cauliflower in a creamy béchamel sauce, then turns riced cauliflower into a spicy, crispy topping. Start with a large cauliflower head, about 2 pounds (910g), to make sure you have enough.

This may look like a project, but it's easily divisible into pieces: Make the dough, sauce, and toppings ahead of time, then assemble and bake right before serving.

Makes one 14-inch pizza (4 servings)

Time: Weekend

Storage: Refrigerate for up to 1 week. Refrigerate the béchamel for up to 1 week or freeze for up to 3 months.

DOUGH

1 cup (125g) all-purpose flour, plus more as needed

1 tablespoon instant yeast

⅔ cup (160ml) hot water (about 125°F/52°C), plus more as needed

1 tablespoon plus 1½ teaspoons olive oil

1½ teaspoons barley malt syrup or light agave syrup

⅔ cup (120g) semolina flour or fine cornmeal

2 teaspoons dried oregano

¾ teaspoon fine sea salt

CRISPY CAULIFLOWER & SHIITAKE TOPPING

8 ounces (225g) riced cauliflower

3 tablespoons olive oil

¾ teaspoon fine sea salt

½ teaspoon freshly ground black pepper

¼ teaspoon red pepper flakes

¼ teaspoon garlic powder

8 ounces (225g) fresh shiitake mushrooms, stems composted (or saved for stock), caps sliced

¼ teaspoon dried thyme

ASSEMBLY

2 tablespoons all-purpose flour

1 tablespoon semolina flour or fine cornmeal

¾ cup (180ml) Cauliflower Béchamel (recipe follows)

1 tablespoon dried oregano

1 tablespoon olive oil

1 teaspoon flaky sea salt

MAKE THE DOUGH: In a food processor, combine ½ cup (63g) of the all-purpose flour, the yeast, and the hot water and pulse until completely combined. Add the olive oil, barley malt syrup, semolina flour, oregano, and salt and pulse to combine. Add the remaining ½ cup (63g) all-purpose flour and blend until the dough forms a ball, adding more flour as necessary until you get a soft dough that isn't sticky. If the dough is too dry, add 1 teaspoon of hot water at a time until it becomes pliable. Process the dough for about 30 seconds. (If you don't have a food processor, don't despair. You can use a large bowl and your clean hands to mix up the dough—it'll just take an extra 10 minutes of kneading until it becomes pliable.)

Lightly flour a countertop and turn the dough out onto the counter. Knead the dough for another 30 seconds, until it feels smooth, then cover it with an overturned large bowl and let it rest until it's lightly puffed and softened, about 20 minutes.

While the dough is resting, make the cauliflower and shiitake topping: Preheat the oven to 425°F (220°C).

In a large bowl, toss the cauliflower with 2 tablespoons of the olive oil, ¼ teaspoon of the salt, ¼ teaspoon of the black pepper, the pepper flakes, and garlic powder until thoroughly combined.

In another large bowl, toss the mushrooms with the remaining 1 tablespoon olive oil, the remaining ½ teaspoon salt, the remaining ¼ teaspoon pepper, and the thyme until the mushrooms are coated.

Place the cauliflower on one half of a large sheet pan and the mushrooms on the other half, spreading both out evenly. Roast until the cauliflower and mushrooms are beginning to turn brown and crisp, 10 to 15 minutes. Allow to cool slightly before using.

To assemble: Position a rack in the lowest position and preheat the oven to 500°F (260°C). If you have a pizza stone, make sure to place it on the bottom rack of the oven as it preheats; if you don't have a pizza stone, use an overturned large sheet pan instead.

In a small bowl, mix the 2 tablespoons of flour and 1 tablespoon of semolina and use the mixture to lightly dust a countertop.

RECIPE CONTINUES ON NEXT PAGE

Take the pizza dough and loosely form into a ball in your hands, then gently flatten into a disk on the countertop. Pick up the disk and hold it between your fingertips, leaving about 1 inch (2.5cm) at the edges, constantly turning the disk in a circular motion to allow the disk to lightly stretch down toward the countertop as you turn it. When the disk is about an 8-inch (20cm) round, place it on the countertop and use your fingertips to continue stretching it into a larger round, being sure to leave a thicker 1-inch lip. Continue stretching out the dough, leaving the lip, until you have about a 13-inch round.

Take a sheet of compostable parchment paper and gently slide it underneath the shaped pizza dough.

Spoon about ½ cup (120ml) of the béchamel on the prepared dough, using the back of the spoon to spread it evenly across the surface, leaving the lip empty and adding up to ¼ cup (60ml) more sauce as needed to evenly coat the crust. Spread the crispy cauliflower bits evenly over the pizza, then arrange the shiitake crisps on top. Sprinkle with the oregano. Brush the lip with the olive oil and sprinkle the flaky sea salt on the lip all the way around the pizza.

Slide the pizza with the parchment paper onto a pizza peel, wire rack, or another upside-down sheet pan, then slide the pizza—with the parchment paper—onto the heated pizza stone or sheet pan.

Bake until the crust is puffed and golden and the surface is bubbling, 10 to 12 minutes. Slide the pizza with the parchment back onto the peel, rack, or sheet pan you're using and transfer to a cutting board.

Remove the parchment, then let the pizza cool for 10 minutes. Cut into wedges with a knife or pizza wheel and serve hot.

COOK'S NOTE: The dough can be wrapped in compostable plastic wrap and refrigerated for up to 3 days or frozen for up to 3 months. Thaw and/ or bring to room temperature before using. (You can also shape the dough and freeze the crust on a sheet pan lightly dusted with flour, then wrap tightly and freeze for up to 3 months. Top and bake the frozen crust, adding time as needed.)

Cauliflower Béchamel

Cauliflower béchamel is for more than just pizza: Spoon the warmed sauce over grilled asparagus, mix it into 2 cups (240g) of hot cooked macaroni and sprinkle with toasted garlic bread crumbs, or spread on top of planks of seared tofu and broil for a couple of minutes until bubbling and golden. Or make another pizza or two, of course!

Makes a scant 2 cups

  10 ounces (285g) cauliflower florets

  3 ounces (85g) white or yellow onion

  ¼ cup (15g) nutritional yeast

  1 tablespoon Nut Milk (page 17), Oat Milk (page 17), Soy Milk (page 75), or store-bought plant-based milk

  1 garlic clove, peeled but whole

  1 teaspoon fine sea salt

  1 teaspoon za'atar, homemade (page 44) or store-bought

  ⅛ teaspoon ground nutmeg

IN A 2-QUART (2L) saucepan, combine the cauliflower florets, onion, and water to cover by 1 inch (2.5cm). Bring to a boil over high heat. Reduce the heat to medium and simmer until soft, 15 to 20 minutes.

Drain completely, then transfer to a blender while still hot. Add the nutritional yeast, milk, garlic, salt, za'atar, and nutmeg and process until completely smooth. (If you taste it at this point, the garlic will still be fairly sharp, but the flavor will mellow as the sauce cools to room temperature.) Refrigerate the béchamel for up to 1 week or freeze for up to 3 months.

Mushroom Keema Matar Parathas

There are many types of paratha throughout South Asia, as well as across the Indian diaspora. Every house will (truthfully!) say their paratha are the best. Made with a blend of all-purpose and whole wheat flours and stuffed with a bold, spicy filling of ground mushrooms and peas, this version doesn't result in the paper-thin, flaky type, but instead is tender, pliable, and so delicious. Enjoy hot, slathered with your favorite lightly salted vegan butter with a little achaar (Indian pickles) on the side.

Note that you'll need to allow 1 hour for the dough to rest before filling, forming, and cooking the parathas.

Makes 6 servings

Time: Weekend

Storage: Refrigerate for up to 5 days or freeze for up to 3 months.

FILLING

2 tablespoons canola or other neutral vegetable oil

4 ounces (115g) cremini mushrooms, thinly sliced

2 medium shallots (3½ ounces/100g total), chopped

½-inch (1.3cm) piece fresh ginger, peeled and chopped

1 serrano chile, chopped

2 garlic cloves, chopped

¾ teaspoon garam masala, homemade (page 40) or store-bought

½ teaspoon fine sea salt

¼ teaspoon ground turmeric

¼ teaspoon red chile powder, preferably Kashmiri

1 tablespoon tomato paste

½ cup (120ml) water

¼ cup (35g) frozen peas, thawed

¼ cup (10g) fresh cilantro, roughly chopped

PARATHAS

1½ cups (188g) all-purpose flour

¾ cup (95g) whole wheat flour

1 teaspoon fine sea salt

4½ tablespoons canola or other neutral vegetable oil, plus more for the workspace

¾ cup (180ml) water, plus more as needed

4 tablespoons (56g) lightly salted vegan butter, melted

2 tablespoons chopped fresh cilantro

MAKE THE FILLING: In a large skillet, heat 1 tablespoon of the oil over medium-high heat until it shimmers. Add the mushrooms, spreading them out in a single layer. Cook, undisturbed, until they start to turn golden on one side, 3 to 4 minutes. Continue to cook, stirring occasionally, until the mushrooms are browned, 2 to 3 minutes more.

Push the mushrooms to the side, add the remaining 1 tablespoon canola oil to the empty spot in the pan and add the shallots, ginger, and serrano chile. Reduce the heat to medium and cook, stirring occasionally, until the shallots are soft and starting to turn golden, 4 to 5 minutes.

Add the garlic, garam masala, salt, turmeric, chile powder, and tomato paste and continue to cook until the spices are toasted and the tomato paste starts to brown, 2 to 3 minutes. Stir in the water, reduce the heat to medium-low, and cook until the sauce has reduced to a thick paste coating the mushrooms, 8 to 10 minutes.

Add the peas and cook for another 2 minutes. Turn off the heat, stir in the cilantro, and let cool for at least 10 minutes.

Transfer the cooled mushroom/pea mixture to a food processor. Pulse into a very coarse paste, transfer to a medium bowl, and, if needed, cool to room temperature.

Meanwhile, make the paratha dough: In a medium bowl, whisk together the all-purpose flour, whole wheat flour, and salt. Add 1½ tablespoons of the oil and mix in with your fingers. Add the water and gently mix with your hands until a shaggy dough forms. (If the dough is too dry, add 1 tablespoon of water at a time until it comes together.)

Transfer to the counter and knead until the dough comes together into a smooth ball, 4 to 5 minutes. Divide into 6 equal portions and roll each portion into a ball, place on a plate, cover with a clean kitchen towel, and let rest at room temperature for 1 hour.

Preheat the oven to 300°F (150°C). Place a large sheet pan in the oven.

To stuff and form the parathas, lightly oil your counter or other workspace. Take one ball of dough and roll it into a 5-inch (13cm) round. Place a scant tablespoon of mushroom filling in the middle and gather the dough around the filling, pinching the dough together to seal. Flatten into a disk and gently start to press and stretch into a thinner round. Gently roll, using a rolling pin, moving from the outside to the center, until you have a paratha 6 to 7 inches (15cm to 18cm) in diameter (don't worry if some of the filling bursts out). Place the stuffed paratha on a large sheet pan, cover with a clean kitchen towel, and repeat with the remaining dough balls.

To cook the parathas, heat a large skillet over medium-high heat. Add 1½ teaspoons of the oil and swirl to coat the pan. Add one paratha and cook for 1 minute on the first side, flip and cook the second side for 2 minutes. Flip again, brush the top with melted butter and cook until the dough is completely cooked through, 30 seconds to 1 minute. Transfer to the sheet pan in the oven to keep warm while cooking the remaining parathas, coating the pan with 1½ teaspoons of oil each time.

Brush with more melted butter, sprinkle with cilantro, and serve hot.

Everyday Lentil Wraps

Red lentils are the secret pantry ingredient for easy, high-protein wraps that can be used alongside many dishes. After soaking the lentils in water for a few hours to soften, you puree them with water and salt in a blender, then cook them up crisp and puffy in a skillet, much like pancakes.

These take well to all manner of add-ins and variations at right, depending on how you want to use them: Add curry powder if they're accompanying a chickpea stew, spinach if you're looking to add a boost of healthy greens, or kimchi to make into stand-alone savory pancakes. These naturally gluten-free wraps can also be used anytime in place of tortillas for tacos and burritos, wraps for falafel, or for dipping into saucy stews.

Makes 8 servings

Time: Weekend

Storage: After cooling, store in an airtight container at room temperature for up to 1 day or refrigerate for up to 3 days. Or layer wraps between sheets of waxed paper in an airtight container and freeze for up to 2 months.

1⅓ cups (255g) red or split yellow lentils
2⅔ cups (630ml) water, plus more as needed
1 teaspoon fine sea salt
2 teaspoons vegetable oil

IN A BOWL, COMBINE the lentils and water. Let sit for 3 hours or up to overnight to soften.

In a blender, combine the lentils, soaking water, and salt. Puree until smooth and the mixture is the consistency of pancake batter. Add water, 1 tablespoon at a time, to thin out the batter if needed.

In a nonstick medium skillet, heat the oil over medium-high heat until it shimmers. Using a ladle, pour ¼ cup (60ml) batter into the pan. Using the back of a spoon and working outward from the center in rapid concentric circles, quickly spread the batter into a 6-inch (15cm) round. Cook until the bottom has browned, about 2 minutes. Flip over and cook an additional 1 to 2 minutes. (The wraps will puff up to about ¼ inch/6mm thick while cooking.)

VARIATIONS

Curry Wraps

Add 2 teaspoons curry powder to the other ingredients in the blender before pureeing.

Spinach Wraps

Add 1 cup (35g) spinach to the other ingredients in the blender before pureeing.

Kimchi Pancakes

Add ¼ cup (60ml) kimchi brine and 2 tablespoons soy sauce to the other ingredients in the blender before pureeing. Fold in 1 cup (160g) chopped kimchi. After cooking, top the pancakes with sliced scallions and 1 teaspoon toasted sesame seeds. In a small dish, combine soy sauce and rice vinegar to taste for dipping.

Colorful Veg-Infused Corn Tortillas

Classic corn tortillas are one of the world's great foods, an icon of Mexican and other Latin American cuisines, and perfect just the way they are. But if you're making them from scratch (well, using widely available masa harina, that is), here's a fun way to add vibrant color and flavor by incorporating vegetables.

It does take some practice getting the texture of the dough right, as well as finding the right heat to cook them on. Whichever of these veg purees you want to incorporate, make sure the total amount of puree plus water equals 1½ cups (350ml) for every 2 cups (260g) of masa harina.

Makes twenty 5-inch tortillas

Time: Weekend

Storage: Refrigerate for up to 5 days.

> Vegetable options: 2 small carrots (4½ ounces/125g total), or 1 small red beet (3½ ounces/100g), or 3½ cups (70g) baby spinach
> 2 cups (260g) masa harina, plus more for sprinkling
> ½ teaspoon fine sea salt

CHOOSE THE VEGETABLE YOU want to use to for the puree.

For carrot puree

Peel the carrots (compost the peels or reserve for another use) and cut into 1-inch (2.5cm) chunks. In a small pot, combine the carrots with enough water to cover by 1 to 2 inches (2.5cm to 5cm). Cover, bring to a boil, reduce the heat to medium, and simmer until the carrots can be pierced easily with a knife, about 20 minutes. Reserving the cooking water, drain the carrots.

For beet puree

Scrub the beet and place in a small pot. Add enough water to cover by 1 to 2 inches (2.5cm to 5cm). Cover, bring to a boil, reduce the heat to medium, and simmer until the beet can be pierced easily with a knife, about 20 minutes. Reserving the cooking water, drain the beet, and when cool enough to handle, peel (composting the peel) and cut into 1-inch (2.5cm) chunks.

For spinach puree

Bring a few inches of water to a boil in a medium pot. Stir in the spinach and cook until completely wilted, about 1 minute. Reserving the cooking water, drain the spinach.

For all the tortillas

Transfer the cooked, drained vegetables to a blender or food processor. (Or leave them in the pot and use an immersion blender.) Add 1¼ cups (300ml) of the reserved cooking water and puree until completely smooth. (You should have about 1½ cups/350ml veg puree; if you have less, stir in a little more water until you do. If you have more, reserve any extra for another use, such as blending into smoothies.)

In a large bowl, whisk together the masa harina and salt. Add the vegetable puree and stir until a thick mass forms and there are no large dry spots of flour left.

Turn the dough out onto a counter sprinkled with masa harina and knead for 5 minutes. The final dough should be soft, smooth, not dry, and not stick to your hands, kind of like Play-Doh. (If the dough is too sticky, incorporate more masa harina.) Place it back in the bowl, cover with a damp kitchen towel, and let rest for 30 minutes.

When you are ready to cook the tortillas, preheat a cast-iron or other heavy skillet (such as a comal or steel or iron crepe pan) over medium-high heat.

Divide the dough into 4 equal portions, then divide each of those portions into 5 equal pieces. Keeping the remaining dough covered with a damp kitchen towel as you work, roll each piece into a ball and flatten them slightly into thick disks with your fingers. Keep the disks covered with the towel.

Line a tortilla press with parchment paper and use it to press each disk into about a 5-inch (13cm) round. (If you don't have a tortilla press, place a ball of dough into a folded piece of parchment paper, and firmly press down with a small skillet or glass pie plate. To make the tortilla thinner, use a rolling pin to gently press and stretch the dough outward while it is still in the folded parchment.)

Depending on the size of your skillet, cook up to 3 tortillas at a time, about 1 minute per side. Brown spots should appear on the bottom of the tortilla within 1 minute of cooking; if they do not, your skillet may not be hot enough. Keep the cooked tortillas wrapped in a clean, dry kitchen towel (or tortilla warmer, if you've got one).

Choose-Your-Own-Adventure Rustic Galette with Cashew Ricotta

This savory rustic galette looks impressive no matter what you put on it, and who doesn't love flaky, buttery dough? The cashew "ricotta"—a puree of soaked cashews, miso, and lemon juice—works well in lasagna, crostini, and more, and you can make it up to 4 days in advance. If you have Fluffy Pumpkin Seed Ricotta (page 31) on hand, feel free to use that here, or store-bought vegan ricotta. The ricotta is the base of the galette, while you can choose lots of options for toppings.

Makes 8 servings

Time: Weekend

Storage: Refrigerate leftovers for up to 4 days.

DOUGH

2¼ cups (280g) all-purpose flour, plus more for dusting

½ teaspoon fine sea salt

½ cup (109g) refined coconut oil, chilled if needed so it's scoopable (see Note), not liquid

½ cup (120ml) ice water

CASHEW RICOTTA

1 cup (130g) raw cashew halves or pieces

Boiling water

1 tablespoon fresh lemon juice, plus more to taste

2 teaspoons white miso, homemade (page 83) or store-bought

1 small garlic clove, peeled but whole

¼ teaspoon fine sea salt, plus more to taste

¼ cup (60ml) water

TOPPING OPTIONS

- 1 large cleaned leek (8 ounces/225g), cut into half-moons and sauteed in olive oil until golden (about 1 cup)
- 1 pound/450g (4 small) onions, thinly sliced and caramelized (about 1½ cups)
- 12 ounces (340g) cremini, oyster, and/or chestnut mushrooms, trimmed, sliced and sauteed in olive oil until tender (about 1½ cups)
- 8 ounces (225g) asparagus (1 small bunch), thinly sliced on the bias and tossed in olive oil (about 2 cups)
- 2 heirloom tomatoes (about 1½ pounds /680g), cut into ½-inch-thick slices
- A combination of two or more of the above

MAKE THE DOUGH: In a large bowl, whisk together the flour and salt. Add the coconut oil and incorporate it into the flour by mashing with a fork until the dough is roughly the size of peas (it's okay if some pieces are larger or smaller). Gradually sprinkle in the ice water while tossing the mixture with the fork. The dough will appear dry and shaggy, but don't worry; just mix lightly until the water is incorporated.

Turn the dough out onto the counter. Working quickly, gather the dough and knead it a few times to shape it into a disk, being careful not to overwork the dough. Wrap in beeswax wrap and refrigerate for 30 minutes (or up to several days). Don't worry if the dough seems too dry at this point; it will hydrate fully in the fridge.

Make the cashew ricotta: In a small heatproof bowl, cover the cashews with boiling water. Soak for at least 30 minutes.

Drain the cashews and transfer to a food processor or high-powered blender. Add the lemon juice, miso, garlic, and salt. Pulse until everything is broken down. Add the water and puree until the mixture is creamy and homogeneous. Taste and season with more lemon juice and/or salt if needed. (The ricotta can be made up to 4 days in advance.)

Preheat the oven to 375°F (190°C). Line a baking sheet with parchment paper.

To assemble, take the dough out of the fridge and let rest at room temperature for a few minutes before rolling. Sprinkle a bit of flour on the counter, rolling pin, and dough to prevent sticking. Roll the dough into a rectangular-ish shape about ¾ inch (2cm) thick and fold it into thirds (like folding a letter for an envelope). Roll out again, then fold again, this time meeting the two short ends in the middle (so it looks like an open book). Finally, roll the dough into a rectangle ¼ inch (6mm) thick. Transfer to the lined baking sheet. If the dough starts to feel wet or sticky at this point, return it to the fridge to firm up for a few minutes.

Spread the ricotta on the dough in an even layer, leaving a 2-inch (5cm) border of dough all around. Spread the topping of your choice over the ricotta. Fold the dough border in over the fillings.

Bake until the crust is lightly golden, 50 to 60 minutes.

Cool for 5 minutes before slicing and serving.

COOK'S NOTE: The coconut oil needs to be at a scoopable consistency; if it's liquid, freeze for up to 15 minutes.

Chickpea Black Pepper Crackers

These gluten-free crackers have a sweet-savory personality, thanks to the cheesy flavor of nutritional yeast and mild sweetness of cornmeal, making them akin to homemade Cheez-Its. A pinch of bright yellow turmeric tricks you into thinking these crackers are cheesier than they actually are. Coarsely ground black pepper lends a bit of heat. This recipe is virtually failproof and can blend seamlessly into your weekly meal prep.

Makes about 40 crackers

Time: Weekday

Storage: Store in an airtight container in a cool, dark place for up to 10 days.

1 cup (90g) chickpea flour

¼ cup (45g) fine or medium-grind cornmeal

1 tablespoon nutritional yeast

½ teaspoon baking powder

½ teaspoon garlic powder

½ teaspoon fine sea salt

½ teaspoon coarsely ground black pepper

⅛ teaspoon ground turmeric (optional; for color)

3 tablespoons extra-virgin olive oil

3 tablespoons water, plus more as needed

Flaky sea salt, for finishing

PREHEAT THE OVEN TO 350°F (180°C).

In a food processor, combine the chickpea flour, cornmeal, nutritional yeast, baking powder, garlic powder, salt, pepper, and turmeric (if using). Pulse to combine.

In a small cup, combine the oil and water.

With the motor running, stream the oil/water mixture gradually into the food processor. Process until the dough forms a ball against the side of the bowl, stopping to scrape down the sides as needed. Add a little more water, 1 teaspoon at a time, if the dough is too dry to form a ball.

Turn the dough out onto your counter and press into a ball with your hands. Cover with a kitchen towel and let rest for 10 minutes.

Place the dough on a sheet of compostable parchment paper or a silicone baking mat and gently flatten with your hands. Roll out into a rectangular-ish shape about ⅛ inch (3mm) thick. Using a sharp knife, score into desired shapes without cutting through the dough. (To get about 40 crackers, make them about 2½ inches/6.5cm square.) Transfer the dough on the parchment or silicone to a large sheet pan.

Bake until the edges are golden brown and the center looks dry, 15 to 20 minutes. While it's still warm, sprinkle with flaky sea salt.

Let cool completely on the sheet pan before breaking up into crackers.

Vegetable Pot Pie

For some of us, pot pie brings back warm memories of sinking a fork into the crust and seeing the creamy filling start to dribble out as the steam releases. This version uses both a top and a bottom crust, and parbaking the bottom crust helps keep it crisper. A lemon-thyme salt adds the perfect finishing touch.

Makes 4 to 6 servings

Time: Weekend

Storage: Refrigerate for up to 1 week. Before baking, you can tightly wrap and freeze the whole pie for up to 3 months; bake from frozen, adding up to 20 minutes to the baking time.

PIE CRUST

2½ cups (313g) all-purpose flour, plus more for dusting

1 teaspoon fine sea salt

1 cup (8 ounces/225g) Soft Spreadable Butter (page 21) or store-bought vegan butter, chilled and cut into cubes

1 cup (240ml) ice water

FILLING

2 tablespoons canola or other neutral oil

1 pound (450g) cremini mushrooms, trimmed and quartered

1 teaspoon fine sea salt, plus more to taste

1 large onion, chopped

2 medium carrots, halved lengthwise and cut into ½-inch (1.3cm) slices

2 celery stalks, halved lengthwise and cut into ½-inch (1.3cm) slices

1 small fennel bulb, quartered and cut into ¼-inch (6mm) slices

8 ounces (225g) baby new potatoes, scrubbed and quartered

3 fresh sage leaves

1 fresh or dried bay leaf

½ teaspoon freshly ground black pepper, plus more to taste

1 tablespoon olive oil

2 tablespoons all-purpose flour

1 cup (240ml) Vegetable Scrap Stock (page 36) or store-bought vegetable broth

¼ cup (60ml) Nut Milk (page 17), Oat Milk (page 17), Soy Milk (page 75), or store-bought plant-based milk

1 cup (130g) frozen green peas

2 tablespoons fresh thyme leaves

1 teaspoon grated lemon zest

1 tablespoon flaky sea salt

MAKE THE PIE CRUST: In a food processor, combine the flour and salt and pulse to combine. Add half the chilled butter cubes and pulse a few times. Add the remaining cubes and pulse until the mixture begins to look like sand with a few larger chunks of vegan butter remaining. Drizzle in the ice water, about 1 tablespoon at a time, while pulsing, just until the dough begins to come together in large clumps. You may need to use only about half of the ice water. (If you don't have a food processor, you can use a large bowl and a fork or a pastry cutter.)

Lightly dust a countertop with flour and turn the dough out onto it. Quickly pat into a round and fold in half, then pat out and fold in half again. Cut the dough in half, form each into a disk about 1 inch (2.5cm) thick, then wrap in parchment paper and refrigerate for at least 30 minutes (and up to 3 days) before using.

Divide the dough into 2 equal portions. On the flour-dusted countertop, roll each portion of dough into a 12-inch (30cm) round. Place one of them into a 9-inch (23cm) deep-dish pie plate, gently pressing it into the corners of the dish without stretching. Trim the overhang to about ½ inch (1.3cm).

Place the second round of dough on a sheet pan. Cover both crusts with parchment and refrigerate for at least 30 minutes. (You can wrap them in parchment for storage up to 3 days.)

Preheat the oven to 425°F (220°C).

Prick the bottom crust all over with a fork. Line with parchment paper and pie weights (dried rice or beans, coins or clean pebbles) and bake until light golden brown all over, 15 to 20 minutes. Remove from the oven and let cool on a rack while you prepare the filling.

Reduce the oven temperature to 400°F (200°C).

Make the filling: In a large skillet, heat 1 tablespoon of the canola oil over medium-high heat until it shimmers. Add the mushrooms and allow them to cook for 5 minutes without stirring. Stir to coat in the oil and cook until browned all over and the juices have been released, 3 to 4 minutes. Stir in ¼ teaspoon salt. Transfer the mushrooms to a plate.

Add the remaining 1 tablespoon canola oil to the skillet. Add the onion, carrots, celery, fennel, potatoes, sage, and bay leaf. Season with the remaining ¾ teaspoon salt and the pepper and stir to coat. Then cook over medium heat until the potatoes and carrots are fork-tender, about 10 minutes.

Drizzle the olive oil over the cooked vegetables, tossing to coat, then sprinkle the flour over the top and toss again. Cook for a minute or two, stirring, to remove the raw flour taste. Stir in the vegetable broth and milk, stirring over medium heat while the liquid thickens to a creamy consistency. Taste and season with more salt and/or pepper as needed. Allow to cool for 15 minutes, then stir in the peas and mushrooms.

In a small bowl, combine the thyme leaves, lemon zest, and flaky salt. Use a wooden spoon to gently smash the ingredients together until well combined and fragrant. (You can also use a mortar and pestle for this.)

Fish out and compost the bay leaf. Spoon the filling into the parbaked pie shell, smoothing it evenly in the pie dish. Top with the second round of chilled pie dough, tucking the edges against the edges of the bottom crust to seal, then crimp the edges with your fingers or the tines of a fork. Using a sharp knife, cut a 1-inch (2.5cm) X in the center of the top crust, then dust the top with the thyme/lemon zest mixture.

Bake until the top crust is deep golden brown and the filling is bubbling, 30 to 40 minutes.

Transfer to a rack to cool for at least 10 minutes before serving.

Seeded Brown Rice Crackers

These seedy crackers are better than anything you can find in a supermarket. They're packed with nutrient-dense seeds, contain zero refined grains, and are ridiculously satisfying to crunch down on. Lacy, light, and crisp, they're also sturdy enough to withstand thick dips like hummus and guacamole. Use the seed crumbs at the bottom of the container as a topping for soups, salads, and toasts.

Makes about forty 2-inch crackers

Time: Weekday

Storage: Store in an airtight container in a cool, dark place for up to 10 days.

2 cups (400g) cooked and cooled short-grain brown rice (see Note)

1 tablespoon extra-virgin olive oil

1 tablespoon soy sauce or tamari

1 tablespoon water

½ teaspoon fine sea salt

1 cup (130g to 140g) sunflower seeds or pumpkin seeds, or a mix

¼ cup (35g) black or white sesame seeds

¼ cup (40g) chia seeds

POSITION RACKS IN THE top and bottom thirds of the oven and preheat the oven to 325°F (160°C).

In a food processor, combine the rice, olive oil, soy sauce, water, and ¼ teaspoon of the salt. Blend until the rice is broken down into a mushy, slightly chunky paste.

In a large bowl, stir together the sunflower and/or pumpkin seeds, sesame seeds, chia seeds, and the remaining ¼ teaspoon salt. Add the rice mixture. Using a rubber spatula or a spoon, stir until a thick, homogeneous dough forms and there are no loose seeds left at the bottom of the bowl. Let rest for 10 minutes.

Place half of the dough on a large sheet of parchment paper, divide it into 2 rectangular-ish mounds, and space them a few inches apart. Cover with another sheet of parchment paper. To flatten the mounds, place a baking sheet or roasting pan on the top piece of parchment, and firmly press down. Then use a rolling pin to gently press and stretch the dough toward the edges of the parchment, until the dough is about ⅛ inch (3mm) thick. (The final shape of the dough doesn't matter.)

Remove the top parchment and slide the dough with the bottom parchment onto a baking sheet. Repeat with the other half of the dough. (If you have only one baking sheet, bake one batch at a time, keeping the remaining dough covered with a towel.)

Bake for 25 minutes. Then switch racks and rotate the baking sheets front to back. Continue baking until the crackers are fragrant and have golden brown edges, about 20 minutes more.

Remove from the oven and cool completely.

Break the crackers into shards and serve.

COOK'S NOTE: If you don't have already cooked brown rice, start with 1 cup (190g) uncooked rice and cook it according to the package directions, or look for frozen or shelf-stable cooked brown rice.

No-Knead Multigrain Sourdough Boule

If you appreciate the tangy flavor and hearty crust of sourdough loaves and are ready to jump into the deep end, this no-knead boule is the perfect gateway recipe.

Inspired by and adapted from recipes by Jim Lahey and Posie (Harwood) Brien, this loaf incorporates nutty spelt flour, sunflower seeds, and steel-cut oats. For anyone experienced with sourdough, it's a snap, and for you newbies, it's straightforward enough to make the planning and time worth the effort, especially once you taste it.

Compared to a traditional sourdough boule, this dough is wetter, less structured, and gets surprisingly puffy. Resist the urge to add more flour.

Makes 1 large loaf

Time: Weekend

Storage: Store leftover bread in an airtight container at room temperature for up to 2 days, or refrigerate for up to 10 days. To freeze, wrap slices in several layers of beeswax wrap, and freeze for up to 3 months.

⅓ cup (45g) sunflower seeds

¼ cup (40g) steel-cut oats

Boiling water

2½ cups (313g) all-purpose flour

1½ cups plus 1 tablespoon (180g) spelt flour

1¾ teaspoons fine sea salt

½ cup (100g) ripe sourdough starter (see Note)

1⅓ cups (315g) lukewarm water, plus more if needed

ABOUT 12 HOURS BEFORE you want to bake the bread (either early morning for an evening bake or late evening for a morning bake), combine the sunflower seeds and oats in a small heatproof bowl and add enough boiling water to cover by about 1 inch (2.5cm). Let stand at room temperature for 1 hour.

Drain and rinse the soaked seeds and oats.

In a medium bowl, whisk together the all-purpose flour, spelt flour, and salt.

In a large bowl, combine the starter and lukewarm water and whisk until the starter is completely dissolved. Add the flour mixture and the seed mixture. Stir with a bowl scraper or rubber spatula just until a lumpy, shaggy mass forms and there are no large dry spots. Add a little more water, 1 tablespoon at a time,

if needed. You're not kneading the dough here, just making sure the flour is fully incorporated.

Cover the bowl with beeswax wrap or a plate and let rest at room temperature for 1 hour.

Next, fold the dough: Starting at the edge of the bowl farthest from you, grab the dough with your hand, stretch it upward, and fold it over onto itself. Then give the bowl a quarter-turn and repeat the folding motion a total of four times (think of it like making an envelope).

Cover the bowl again and rest the dough at room temperature until it is doubled in size, light, and bubbly, 8 to 10 hours.

After this rise, gently turn the dough out onto a floured surface; the dough will be puffy, stringy, and wet—do not add more flour. Repeat the four-time folding motion again. Continue picking up and gently stretching the edges of the dough and folding them over the center to encourage the dough into a round shape.

Place a lint-free kitchen towel near the dough, generously coat it in flour, and rub the flour into the towel with your hands (this helps prevent the dough from sticking to the towel). Then, using a bench scraper or spatula, invert the dough onto the floured towel so it is seam-side down. Drape another lightly floured, lint-free towel over the dough and let it rest until almost doubled in size, about 1½ hours.

About 40 minutes before the end of the rising time, preheat the oven to 450°F (230°C) with a 5-quart (5L) or larger Dutch oven and its lid in the oven to preheat.

After the rise, remove the top towel from the dough, sprinkle a little flour over the dough, and lay a piece of parchment paper on top. Swiftly flip the dough onto the parchment paper (so it is seam-side up) and remove the remaining towel. Carefully place the dough with the parchment paper into the preheated Dutch oven and cover tightly with a lid.

Bake for 20 minutes. Then remove the lid and bake until the crust is a deep golden brown all over, about 25 minutes more.

Remove from the oven and transfer the bread to a rack. Cool completely before slicing.

COOK'S NOTE: Don't have a sourdough starter of your own? See if a local bakery will sell you some, or find out if there are fellow bakers in your area who wouldn't mind sharing. Or to learn how to DIY; KingArthurBaking.com is a great source.

Classic Corn Bread with optional add-ins of corn kernels and pickled jalapeños

Classic Corn Bread

This light, fluffy corn bread doesn't require any flaxseeds or other egg substitutes. The key is pairing the cornmeal with bread flour, whose extra protein and gluten give it structure. This corn bread uses a small amount of sugar, a tradition that developed at least in part because modern supermarket cornmeal doesn't have the sweet, vibrant flavor of those old Southern brands. If you have access to great stone-ground cornmeal (try anything local, or Anson Mills mail order), feel free to eliminate the sugar here. Either way, the most challenging thing about this recipe is resisting the urge to eat most of the slab while it's still warm, so I don't blame you one bit if you give in. If you'd like, make this into muffins instead, and try one or more of the optional additions listed at right.

Makes 12 servings

Time: Weekday

Storage: Room temperature, wrapped in beeswax wrap, for up to 2 days, refrigerate for up to 5 days, or freeze for up to 1 month.

1 tablespoon neutral vegetable oil, for the pan

1¼ cups (190g) medium-grind yellow cornmeal

1 cup (135g) bread flour

¼ cup (50g) sugar

2 teaspoons baking powder

1 teaspoon baking soda

½ teaspoon fine sea salt

1¼ cups (300ml) Nut Milk (page 17), Oat Milk (page 17), Tangy Coconut Cashew Buttermilk (page 23), or store-bought plant-based milk or buttermilk

¼ cup (56g) Soft Spreadable Butter (page 21) or store-bought unsalted vegan butter, melted

1 teaspoon apple cider vinegar

Optional additions (at right)

GREASE AN 8- OR 9-inch (20cm or 23cm) square baking pan with the oil. Position a rack in the middle of the oven, place the pan on the rack, and preheat the oven to 400°F (200°C).

In a large bowl, whisk together the cornmeal, bread flour, sugar, baking powder, baking soda, and salt.

In a liquid measuring cup, stir together the milk or buttermilk, melted butter, and vinegar.

Pour the milk mixture into the flour mixture and whisk until smooth, then whisk for another 10 seconds or so (to help develop the flour's gluten). Carefully remove the hot pan from the oven and scrape the batter into the pan, using a spatula to spread it evenly.

Bake until the corn bread is dark brown around the edges and a tester inserted in the center comes out clean, 15 to 20 minutes. (It will take a little longer in the smaller pan.)

Transfer the pan to a wire rack to cool for about 10 minutes. Use a knife to loosen the edges if needed, turn out, and cut into squares. (If it sticks, just cut the squares out of the pan.) Serve warm or at room temperature.

OPTIONAL ADDITIONS

Fold one or more of these into the batter right before baking:

- 1 cup (140g) fresh or frozen corn kernels
- 1 cup (130g) fresh or frozen blueberries
- ½ cup (45g) sliced pickled jalapeños
- ½ cup (25g) chopped fresh parsley or cilantro leaves

Bing

There are so many versions of bing, the Chinese flatbread: Many, such as scallion pancakes, are unleavened, and get their flakiness from the way the dough is folded and rolled. This version, based on the one I first tried at the now-defunct Momofuku CCDC in Washington, is different: It's yeasted, and so soft and fluffy as to be downright pillowy. When I tried it with their pimiento cheese and other dips, I hardly wanted to eat anything else on the table. The restaurant group first served it at Majordomo in Los Angeles and, much to my delight, published the recipe on their website.

I've taken a few tiny liberties, barely tweaking the amounts and using instant yeast instead of dry active, which simplifies the method a little. All in all, this recipe is a good reminder of just how simple flatbreads can be to make—and how delicious the result. This might remind you of a particularly puffy naan, and you can use it anywhere you'd use naan, or any other flatbread: with dips, soups, stews, to make wraps, or to just eat warm. That's what I couldn't stop doing the first time I tasted these—and the first (and every) time I've made them since. They freeze particularly well, meaning you can feel free to make the whole batch even if you're just cooking for one or two, and microwave them directly from frozen.

Makes 8 bing (8 servings)

Time: Weekend

Storage: Refrigerate for up to 1 week or freeze for up to 6 months.

> 3½ cups (440g) all-purpose flour, plus more for rolling
>
> 2 tablespoons sugar
>
> 1¾ teaspoons instant yeast
>
> 1 teaspoon fine sea salt
>
> 1 cup plus 2 tablespoons (266g) warm water
>
> ¼ cup (60ml) olive oil, plus more for oiling the bowl and brushing the flatbreads
>
> ½ cup (120ml) sunflower, canola, or other neutral oil
>
> Flaky sea salt, for finishing (optional)

IN THE BOWL OF a stand mixer, whisk together the flour, sugar, yeast, and salt.

In a small bowl or liquid measuring cup, combine the water and olive oil.

Snap on the dough hook, turn the mixer to medium-low, and slowly pour in the water/oil mixture. Once it is all poured in, increase the mixer speed to medium-high and knead until the dough is very smooth and a little tacky, 7 to 10 minutes. (Alternatively, you can knead the dough by hand for 20 to 30 minutes.)

Lightly oil a large bowl, transfer the dough to it, and turn the dough over. Cover with a plate and let it rest in a warm spot on the counter until it has doubled, about 1 hour.

Preheat the oven to 200°F (90°C).

Lightly flour the countertop and transfer the dough to the counter. Cut the dough in half with a knife or bench scraper and roll each piece into a log about 12 inches (30cm) long and 2 to 3 inches (5cm to 7.5cm) in diameter. Cut each log into 4 equal pieces and roll them into balls.

Adding as much flour as you need to keep the dough from sticking, roll each ball into a round or oblong shape about ¼ inch (6mm) thick and 6 to 7 inches (15cm to 18cm) in diameter. (Don't worry about making them into a perfect shape; irregularity is fine here. If you'd like, you can lightly brush off any excess flour before cooking them; this will make them slightly neater looking but is completely optional.)

Heat a cast-iron or other heavy skillet over medium heat for several minutes. Pour in 1 tablespoon of the sunflower oil, let it heat for a few seconds, then add one of the rounds. Cook until the bing is deeply browned in spots on one side, 1 to 2 minutes. Flip and cook until deeply browned on the other side, 1 to 2 minutes. (The dough will dramatically bubble and puff in parts as it cooks.) Transfer to a sheet pan, brush with olive oil, sprinkle with flaky salt, if using, and place in the warm oven while you cook the remaining bing.

Repeat with the remaining pieces of dough, adding another 1 tablespoon of oil before cooking each piece and transferring each to the sheet pan, brushing with oil, and sprinkling with salt. (If you'd like to speed up the process even more, you can get into the rhythm of cooking one bing while you roll out the next.)

Serve warm.

Pumpkin Chapatis

Chapati is a staple laminated flatbread commonly served with meals in Kenya and made using only flour, water, fat, and salt. (The bread's origin is Indian, and it came to East Africa with Indian immigrant laborers during British colonialism.) In this version, traditional in some regions, pumpkin or squash is used instead of water to yield an incredibly soft and colorful flatbread. The dough is laminated to give tender and flaky layers. Chapati-making requires much patience, but also yields high reward.

Makes 4 chapatis (4 servings)

Time: Weekend

Storage: Refrigerate for up to 1 week or freeze for up to 3 months. Reheat in a dry, hot skillet for 10 to 15 seconds per side.

- 3 cups (405g) bread flour, plus more as needed and for dusting the work surface
- 1½ teaspoons fine sea salt
- ¾ cup plus 2 tablespoons (215g) canned unsweetened pumpkin puree
- 6 tablespoons sunflower or other neutral oil, plus more for oiling your hands
- 1 tablespoon water, plus more as needed

IN A LARGE BOWL, use your hands to mix together the flour and salt to combine. Make a well in the center, adding the pumpkin puree and 1 tablespoon of the oil, using your dominant hand to mix. Add the water and continue to mix until a loose dough forms, adding more water, 1 tablespoon at a time, if the dough is too crumbly to hold together add more flour, 2 tablespoons at a time, if it's too sticky. (Some brands of canned pumpkin have more moisture than others, so you'll need to adjust to compensate.)

Lightly flour a work surface. Once the dough begins to pull together, turn it out onto the work surface and begin to knead. If the dough is sticky, add flour a little at a time while you knead until the dough is tacky, like Play-Doh. Continue to knead the dough until elastic and fairly smooth, about 5 minutes.

Divide the dough into 4 equal portions. Lightly oil your hands and shape the dough into balls. Cover with a clean kitchen towel and allow to rest for 30 minutes to relax the dough.

Working with 1 piece at a time, roll out the dough as thin as possible: ⅛ inch (3mm) or less. Don't worry if the dough tears. If the dough is shrinking as you roll, cover to allow it to rest for about 10 minutes and try rolling again.

Once the dough is stretched thin, coat the entire top side of the dough with about ½ tablespoon of oil. Working from the edge nearest you, tightly roll up the dough. Coil the long roll of dough into a spiral shape. Cover and repeat with the remaining pieces of dough. Allow to rest for another 30 minutes.

When ready to cook, heat a wide flat pan over medium-high heat.

While the pan is heating, roll out the dough, being sure to keep pieces covered. Lightly flour your hands and press down the piece of dough into a flat disk. Use a rolling pin to roll into a round ⅛ inch (3mm) thick, being sure to give the dough a quarter-turn after each roll to maintain a circular shape.

Cooking 1 chapati at a time, lightly brush the bottom of the pan with a scant 1 teaspoon or so of the oil. Carefully lay in a piece of chapati and lightly brush with more oil. It's ready to flip once it bubbles and the bottom has lightly browned, about 4 minutes. Cook on the other side until golden, 1 to 2 minutes. Keep the chapatis warm between 2 plates until ready to serve.

Whole Wheat Za'atar Man'oushe

Man'oushe (also called manakish or man'ousheh) is a popular Levantine flatbread commonly eaten for breakfast or lunch. It's chewy and fluffy, not unlike a pita, and often features a traditional za'atar oil topping.

This whole wheat version has a nutty taste (not to mention all the health benefits of whole-grain flour). The za'atar oil lends addictively herby, salty notes, with a nice variation of thanks to the sesame seeds. For a trendy take, swap out the za'atar for everything bagel seasoning.

Cut this man'oushe into triangles and serve it as part of a snack board with hummus and raw crunchy veg, slather it with an avocado-bean mash for breakfast, or top it like a pizza.

Makes 4 large flatbreads (4 to 8 servings)

Time: Weekend

Storage: Store leftovers in an airtight container at room temperature for up to 1 day, refrigerate for up to 1 week, or freeze for up to 3 months.

DOUGH

1¼ cups (295g) warm water

1 tablespoon maple syrup

1½ teaspoons active dry yeast

3¼ cups (405g) whole wheat flour, plus more for dusting and as needed

1 teaspoon fine sea salt

2 tablespoons extra-virgin olive oil

ZA'ATAR OIL

⅓ cup (35g) za'atar, homemade (page 44) or store-bought

½ cup (120ml) extra-virgin olive oil

MAKE THE DOUGH: In a bowl or measuring cup, combine ½ cup (118g) of the water, the maple syrup, and the yeast and whisk until the yeast is dissolved.

Meanwhile, in a large bowl, whisk together the flour and salt. Make a well in the center and pour in the oil, the yeast mixture, and remaining ¾ cup (177g) warm water. Stir until a shaggy dough forms and there are no large dry spots of flour left.

Turn the dough out onto a lightly floured surface (reserve the bowl) and gather into a ball. Knead until the dough is smooth, elastic, and no longer sticks to your hands, sprinkling on more flour if needed, about 5 minutes.

Lightly coat the bowl with the oil, place the dough inside, and cover with a kitchen towel. Let stand in a warm spot until the dough is doubled in size, about 1½ hours.

When the dough is almost ready, place 2 large sheet pans in the oven and preheat to 500°F (260°C).

Gently turn the dough out onto a lightly floured surface and divide into 4 equal portions. Gently form into balls, being careful not to deflate the dough. Cover with a towel and let stand for another 15 minutes.

While the dough is resting, make the za'atar oil: In a small bowl, stir together the za'atar and oil.

Working with 1 piece at a time, press the dough into a disk with your fingers. Pick up the disk by two edges and stretch the dough to a ¼-inch (6mm) thickness by rotating it with your hands and letting gravity pull it down (as you would with pizza dough).

Carefully place up to 2 rounds onto the hot sheet pans (or however many fit without touching). Quickly drizzle each round with za'atar oil, spread it into an even layer, and return to the oven. Repeat with the remaining dough and the second baking sheet.

Bake until the edges are dry and the dough is slightly puffed but still pale, about 5 minutes.

Transfer to a wire rack and serve warm or at room temperature.

Fluffy Whole Wheat Focaccia

Thanks to a generous amount of olive oil, this whole wheat focaccia is incredibly rich, but still delightfully fluffy with a crunchy exterior. It's so good, eat it on its own while it's still warm; it doesn't need any dips, toppers, or sidekicks. But if you want to gild the lily, see the toppings at right.

This recipe is adapted from Samin Nosrat, who got it from an Italian baker. What sets this Ligurian-style focaccia apart from others is drizzling the dough with a salt brine before the final proofing. The brine infuses the bread with an extra salty bite, which is partly why it's so satisfying to eat on its own.

Besides switching to instant yeast to streamline the process (and eliminate the need for sweetener to activate the yeast), this recipe subs half the original amount of all-purpose flour with whole wheat.

Makes one 18 × 13-inch focaccia (12 to 16 servings)

Time: Weekend

Storage: Store leftovers in an airtight container at room temperature for up to 2 days, refrigerate for up to 1 week, or freeze for up to 3 months.

DOUGH

3¼ cups (406g) all-purpose flour or bread flour

3¼ cups (405g) whole wheat flour, white whole wheat flour, or spelt flour

1 tablespoon fine sea salt

½ teaspoon instant yeast

2⅔ cups (630g) lukewarm water

¼ cup (60ml) extra-virgin olive oil

ASSEMBLY

4 tablespoons extra-virgin olive oil

¾ teaspoon fine sea salt

⅓ cup (80ml) lukewarm water

Toppings (see options at right)

Flaky sea salt

MAKE THE DOUGH: In a very large bowl, whisk together both flours, the fine salt, and yeast. Make a well in the center and add the water. Using a bowl scraper or rubber spatula, stir until all the flour is incorporated and a wet, shaggy dough forms. Add the oil and incorporate with a bowl scraper or your hands. The final dough should be soft, shiny, and sticky.

Cover the bowl tightly with beeswax wrap or a silicone bowl cover. Leave at room temperature until the dough is doubled in size and very bubbly, 9 to 14 hours. (If desired, you can transfer the dough to the fridge at this point and hold it for up to 24 hours, then bring it to room temperature for an hour before proceeding.)

To assemble: When the dough is ready, spread 2 tablespoons of the olive oil on a large sheet pan. Using a bowl scraper or rubber spatula, release the dough from the bowl and onto the pan, working gently to avoid deflating the dough. Drizzle the remaining 2 tablespoons oil on the dough and spread it with your hands to coat. Gently stretch the dough to the edges of the pan by placing your hands underneath and pulling outward. The dough might feel a little reluctant to get all the way out to the edges, but don't worry: It will relax eventually.

Rest the dough for 30 minutes, stretching the dough outward once or twice more while it's resting.

In a small cup, combine the fine salt and lukewarm water and stir to dissolve the salt to make a brine.

After the 30-minute rest, create dimples in the dough by pressing your fingers into the dough at an angle. Then drizzle the brine evenly on top. At this point, sprinkle on any toppings you wish to use.

Let the dough rest again until it looks light and puffy, about 45 minutes.

About 20 minutes before you're ready to bake, preheat the oven to 450°F (230°C).

Bake the focaccia until it is crisp and golden brown, 25 to 30 minutes.

Remove the focaccia from the oven and sprinkle with the flaky salt. Let cool in the pan for 10 minutes. Release the focaccia from the sheet pan by slipping a spatula underneath all the edges. Carefully transfer to a wire rack. Serve warm or at room temperature.

OPTIONAL TOPPINGS

- 1½ cups halved seedless grapes + 1 tablespoon roughly chopped rosemary
- 1 cup diced white onion + 2 medium vine tomatoes, thinly sliced
- 8 ounces wild mushrooms, torn and sauteed in olive oil until tender + ¾ cup shredded "cheese" + 1 tablespoon truffle oil

COOK'S NOTE: Start this recipe the night before you make it for breakfast or brunch the next day, or refrigerate the dough for up to 24 hours after the first rise and restart whenever it works for you.

13

DESSERTS & DRINKS

I don't know how many times I need to say this, but here we go again: Plant-based cooking is not health food. What do I mean? Well, that there's plenty of room for indulgences, and nowhere is that more obvious than in this chapter of sweets. Here's where you'll use vegan butters for flaky pie crusts and biscuits, silken tofu to make a custardy chocolate tart, aquafaba to make mousses and meringues, nut milks and nut butters to churn out creamy ice creams, and a host of smart techniques and ingredients to bake the best cookies and cakes you've ever had. In this chapter, variations abound, because once you've got a great cake, cookie, or ice cream base, you deserve a host of options for making it your own. This chapter is also where you'll raise a toast to the beauty of plant-based cocktails and other drinks. (Don't knock it till you try it, especially when aquafaba can take the place of egg whites in flips and foams!)

All-Purpose Dessert Pie Dough

Pie dough seems intimidating until you make it—it takes only a few ingredients, and the dough comes together in minutes. It's also a good practice to always make two crusts even if you need only one, because you can wrap the other one up and freeze it for later. When it comes to a dessert crust, recipe tester Kristen Hartke's recipe shows that it's worth it to add in just a little flavor that helps support the fillings; this one uses vanilla and chilled orange juice for the liquid, but you could just as easily add a little cinnamon to the dry ingredients and sub apple cider for the orange juice.

Makes two 12-inch crusts

Time: Weekday

Storage: Refrigerate for up to 1 week or freeze for up to 3 months; thaw frozen dough in the refrigerator for 24 hours before using.

- 1⅓ cups (166g) all-purpose flour, plus more for dusting
- 1⅓ cups (160g) whole wheat pastry flour
- 1 teaspoon fine sea salt
- 8 ounces (225g) unsalted vegan butter, chilled and cut into cubes
- ½ teaspoon vanilla extract (optional)
- 3 to 6 tablespoons chilled orange juice (see Note), plus more as needed

IN A FOOD PROCESSOR, combine the all-purpose flour, pastry flour, and salt and pulse to combine. Add half the butter cubes and pulse a few times, then add the remaining cubes and pulse until the mixture begins to look like sand with a few larger chunks of butter remaining. Add the vanilla and then drizzle in the orange juice, about 1 tablespoon at a time, while pulsing, just until the dough begins to come together in large clumps. Use more juice if needed to get the dough to come together. (If you don't have a food processor, you can use a large bowl and a fork or a pastry cutter, following the same steps above.)

Lightly dust a countertop with flour and turn the dough out onto it. Quickly pat into a round and fold in half, then pat out and fold again. Cut the dough in half, form each into a disk about 1 inch (2.5cm) thick, then wrap in parchment paper and chill in the refrigerator for at least 30 minutes before using.

COOK'S NOTE: To have really chilled orange juice, freeze 1 cup (240ml) of orange juice for 30 minutes before making the pie dough, then measure the tablespoons from that slightly icy cup of juice.

Raspberry Chocolate Pie

This easy chilled pie is the perfect taste of summer, stuffed with fresh raspberries and drizzled with dark chocolate. If you'd prefer white chocolate instead, feel free to sub that for the dark; it's lovely either way.

Makes one 9-inch pie (8 servings)

Time: Weekend

Storage: Refrigerate for up to 3 days.

Flour, for dusting

1 disk All-Purpose Dessert Pie Dough (page 404), chilled

5 cups (625g) fresh raspberries

2 tablespoons fresh lemon juice

2 tablespoons cornstarch

¼ cup (60ml) cold water

½ cup (100g) sugar

1 tablespoon finely grated lemon zest

¼ cup (60g) vegan dark chocolate chips, melted

Whipped coconut cream topping or vegan ice cream, for serving (optional)

ON A FLOUR-DUSTED COUNTERTOP, roll the chilled pie dough into a 12-inch (30cm) round. Place the dough into a 9-inch (23cm) deep-dish pie plate, gently pressing it into the corners of the dish without stretching. Trim the overhang to about ½ inch (1.3cm), fold under, then crimp the edges with a fork or your fingers. Place in the refrigerator to chill for 30 minutes. (You can wrap the dish in parchment for storage for up to 3 days.)

Preheat the oven to 425°F (220°C).

Prick the sides and bottom of the chilled pie shell all over with a fork, line with parchment and pie weights (dried rice or beans, coins, or clean pebbles), and bake until the crust is golden brown, 15 to 20 minutes. Remove from the oven and allow to cool completely on a rack while you prepare the filling.

In a 2-quart (2L) saucepan, combine 2 cups (250g) of the raspberries and the lemon juice and cook over medium heat for 2 to 3 minutes, mashing the raspberries with a spoon to help them soften. Pour the mashed raspberries into a sieve over a medium bowl and push them through the sieve to remove the seeds. Compost half the pulp and seeds, reserving the remainder. Return the strained raspberry puree to the saucepan along with the reserved pulp and seeds.

In a small bowl, whisk together the cornstarch and cold water. Set the raspberry mixture over medium heat, stir in the cornstarch slurry, then add the sugar and cook, stirring constantly, until the mixture is thickened and glossy, about 5 minutes. Stir in the lemon zest and remove from the heat to cool completely.

When both the crust and the raspberry puree have cooled, arrange the remaining 3 cups (375g) raspberries evenly in the base of the pie crust, then pour the raspberry puree over them, spreading it evenly across the top. Refrigerate the pie for 2 hours.

When the pie has chilled, drizzle the melted dark chocolate over the top of the pie, then refrigerate again for 20 minutes before serving.

Serve with vegan whipped coconut cream or vanilla ice cream, if desired.

Purple Sweet Potato Pie
(page 409) and Raspberry
Chocolate Pie (page 405)

Apple Pie with Salted Vanilla Sugar

It's a classic for good reason: Apple pies have it all, celebrating the natural sweet and tart flavor of a fruit that marries so well with warming spices. The touch of lightly salty sugar on the crust is the crowning glory.

Makes one 9-inch pie (8 servings)

Time: Weekend

Storage: The pie can be refrigerated for up to 1 week. The salted vanilla sugar can be stored in an airtight container at room temperature indefinitely.

2 disks All-Purpose Dessert Pie Dough (page 404), chilled

Flour, for dusting

FILLING

2½ pounds (1.1kg) tart apples, such as Granny Smith, peeled and sliced (about 8 cups)

2 tablespoons fresh lemon juice

¾ cup (150g) organic cane sugar

2 tablespoons all-purpose flour

2 tablespoons cornstarch

1 teaspoon ground cinnamon

1 teaspoon ground ginger

¼ teaspoon ground allspice

¼ teaspoon fine sea salt

¼ cup (60ml) apple cider

2 teaspoons vanilla extract

ASSEMBLY

2 tablespoons (28g) cold Soft Spreadable Butter (page 21) or cold store-bought vegan butter, diced in small pieces

1 tablespoon Nut Milk (page 17), Oat Milk (page 17), Soy Milk (page 75), or store-bought plant-based milk

1 tablespoon Salted Vanilla Sugar (recipe follows)

ON A FLOUR-DUSTED COUNTERTOP, roll the chilled pie dough into two 12-inch (30cm) rounds. Place one of them into a 9-inch (23cm) deep-dish pie plate, gently pressing it into the corners of the dish without stretching. Trim the overhang to about ½ inch (1.3cm).

Place the other 12-inch (30cm) round of dough on a sheet pan. Cover both with parchment and refrigerate for at least 30 minutes. (You can wrap them in parchment for storage for up to 3 days.)

Preheat the oven to 425°F (220°C).

When the pie shell has chilled, prick the dough all over with a fork, line with parchment and pie weights (dried rice or beans, coins, or clean pebbles), and bake until it just starts to become golden, about 10 minutes. Remove from the oven and allow to cool on a rack while you prepare the filling.

Reduce the oven temperature to 400°F (200°C). Line a baking sheet with parchment paper.

Make the filling: In a large bowl, toss the apples with the lemon juice until thoroughly coated.

In a small bowl, whisk together the sugar, flour, cornstarch, cinnamon, ginger, allspice, and salt. Sprinkle the mixture over the apples and stir to coat them. Stir in the apple cider and vanilla.

To assemble: Spoon the apple filling into the parbaked pie shell, then dot it with the pieces of vegan butter. Top with the second round of chilled pie dough, tucking the edges against the edges of the bottom crust to seal, then crimp the edges with your fingers or the tines of a fork. Using a sharp knife, cut a 1-inch (2.5cm) X in the center of the top crust, then brush the top of the pastry with the plant-based milk. Sprinkle all over with the salted vanilla sugar. Refrigerate the pie for 10 minutes.

Place the pie on the lined baking sheet and bake for 20 minutes.

Reduce the oven temperature to 375°F (190°C) and bake until you see the filling bubbling vigorously inside the pie, about 40 minutes. (It may bubble over the sides of the dish onto the parchment, but that's okay!) Check the pie after 30 minutes and cover the edges with foil or a pie shield to keep them from browning too quickly, if necessary.

Remove from the oven and allow to cool completely at room temperature before serving.

Salted Vanilla Sugar

In addition to sprinkling on pie crust, you'll find yourself sprinkling this on all manner of baked goods—even cinnamon toast!

Makes 1 cup

- 1 cup (200g) granulated sugar
- 2 tablespoons fine sea salt
- ½ vanilla bean, split lengthwise

IN A FOOD PROCESSOR, combine the sugar and salt. With the tip of a knife, scrape the vanilla seeds into the sugar. Process until evenly distributed. Stick the spent pod halves into the sugar, and store in an airtight container indefinitely.

Purple Sweet Potato Pie

Of course you can use sweet potatoes of any color to make this pie, but purple ones make it a show-stopper. If you love pumpkin pie, simply substitute 2½ cups (610g) canned pumpkin puree for the mashed sweet potatoes.

Makes one 9-inch pie (8 servings)

Time: Weekend

Storage: Refrigerate for up to 3 days; bring to room temperature before serving.

- 1½ pounds (680g) purple sweet potatoes, well-scrubbed
- Flour, for dusting
- 1 disk All-Purpose Dessert Pie Dough (page 404), chilled
- ¾ cup (120ml) canned full-fat coconut milk, plus more as needed
- ½ cup packed (110g) light brown sugar
- ¼ cup (64g) almond butter
- 2 tablespoons arrowroot powder
- 1 tablespoon finely grated orange zest
- 2 tablespoons orange juice
- 1 teaspoon fine sea salt
- 1 teaspoon vanilla extract
- 1 teaspoon ground cinnamon
- ½ teaspoon ground allspice
- Whipped coconut cream (optional), for serving

PREHEAT THE OVEN TO 425°F (220°C).

Prick the sweet potatoes all over with a fork and place on a sheet pan lined with compostable parchment paper. Bake until softened all over, 45 to 55 minutes, turning over halfway through.

Meanwhile, on a flour-dusted countertop, roll the chilled dough into a 12-inch (30cm) round. Transfer the dough to a 9-inch (23cm) deep-dish pie plate, gently pressing it into the corners of the dish without stretching. Trim the overhang to about ½ inch (1.3cm), fold under, then crimp the edges with a fork or your fingers. Transfer to the refrigerator to chill for 30 minutes. (You can wrap the dish in parchment and refrigerate for up to 3 days.)

When the sweet potatoes are done, remove them from the oven and allow to cool slightly, then slit them open with a sharp knife and scrape out all the flesh. Let it cool. Reserve the paper-lined sheet pan for baking the pie.

When the pie shell has chilled, prick the dough all over with a fork, line with parchment and pie weights (dried rice or beans, coins, or clean pebbles), and bake until it just starts to become golden, about 10 minutes. Remove from the oven and allow to cool on a rack while you prepare the filling.

In a blender, combine the cooled sweet potato flesh, coconut milk, brown sugar, almond butter, arrowroot, orange zest, orange juice, salt, vanilla, cinnamon, and allspice and briefly puree, just until smooth. (Avoid overblending to prevent the custard from becoming too gummy.) The consistency should be similar to pancake batter; if the mixture is overly thick, or too thick to blend, add more coconut milk, 1 tablespoon at a time, until it reaches the right consistency.

Place the pie dish on the same paper-lined sheet pan you used for the potatoes. Pour the sweet potato custard into the parbaked crust, tapping lightly to remove any bubbles and smoothing the top if necessary.

Bake for 15 minutes. Reduce the oven temperature to 350°F (180°C) and bake until the filling is starting to set and jiggle only slightly and the crust is lightly golden brown, another 15 minutes. Cover the edges of the crust with foil or a pie shield if starting to brown too much.

Allow to cool completely on a wire rack at room temperature, then refrigerate uncovered for 8 hours, or overnight. Serve with whipped coconut cream, if desired.

American Buttercream Four Ways

Some people don't like American buttercream because they find it overly sweet, but its thick, fluffy consistency is a classic for a reason. This recipe is from one of the smartest bakers I know, Alicia Kennedy, who once owned a vegan bakery on Long Island and now writes a popular newsletter, books, and articles from her home in Puerto Rico. Her technique provides very consistent results, regardless of the type of vegan butter used, though Miyoko's will provide a lovely tang and melting mouthfeel, as will the Soft Spreadable Butter (page 21). Extracts can change the flavor, and nut butter blends in seamlessly while amping up the richness.

Makes about 1¼ cups

Time: Weekday

Storage: Refrigerate for up to 14 days, or freeze for up to 3 months. Thaw and/or let come to room temperature before using to decorate a cake.

⅔ cup (150g) Soft Spreadable Butter (page 21) or store-bought unsalted or salted vegan butter

1½ cups (187g) organic powdered sugar, sifted

FLAVORING VARIATIONS

Vanilla: Seeds scraped from 1 split vanilla bean, or 1 teaspoon vanilla extract

Almond: 1 teaspoon almond extract + ¼ teaspoon vanilla extract

Coconut: 1 teaspoon coconut extract + ¼ teaspoon vanilla extract

Peanut butter: ½ teaspoon vanilla extract + 1 tablespoon natural peanut butter

IN A SMALL FOOD processor or a stand mixer fitted with the paddle, blend (or beat on medium-high speed) the butter until smooth and thick.

Scrape down the sides of the bowl. Add the powdered sugar and choice of flavoring. (If making peanut butter buttercream, don't add the peanut butter just yet.) Blend until smooth and fluffy, with no lumps of sugar or butter, scraping down the sides of the bowl again if needed. (If using the stand mixer, start on low to avoid puff-ups of the sugar, then work up to medium or medium-high speed.) For the peanut butter buttercream, add the peanut butter and blend until well incorporated.

Use immediately or transfer to an airtight container for storage.

Chocolate Bonbons with Tahini & Berries

This easy technique lets you make your own decadent chocolate bonbons at home with five simple ingredients. There's no frustrating tempering of the chocolate needed. You just combine coconut oil and cocoa powder to create a silky-smooth chocolate base, then fill them with tahini and raspberries and top with more of the chocolate mixture. These take just a few minutes to make, after which you pop them into the freezer. An hour later you'll be in chocolate heaven.

Feel free to experiment with a variety of nut butters and assorted fruits.

Sprinkling your bonbons with freeze-dried fruit gives these a colorful finish. If you don't have bonbon molds, you can use silicone ice cube trays.

Makes about 2 dozen 1-inch bonbons (fewer if you use larger molds)

Time: Weekday

Storage: Freeze leftovers in an airtight container for up to 1 month.

½ cup (120ml) virgin coconut oil, melted

5 tablespoons unsweetened cocoa powder

3 tablespoons agave syrup or maple syrup

Pinch of fine sea salt

¼ cup (60ml) runny tahini

6 fresh or frozen raspberries, broken into small pieces

Freeze-dried raspberries or strawberries (optional), crushed, for decorating

IN A SMALL BOWL, whisk together the coconut oil, cocoa powder, agave, and salt. Place two 12-cavity bonbon molds onto a flat tray or platter for stability.

Use a spoon to drizzle a small amount of chocolate mixture into the center of each cavity, followed by tahini and bits of raspberry. Top off the molds with more chocolate mixture to seal.

Transfer the tray to the freezer and freeze until solid, about 1 hour. Unmold the bonbons onto a plate when ready to serve and thaw for a few minutes before eating.

To decorate, sprinkle the freeze-dried fruit over the bonbons and serve.

Black Tahini Swirled Cheesecake

This pistachio-topped cheesecake is as delicious as it is pretty. While many vegan desserts are served raw and from the freezer, this one is baked like a traditional cheesecake. But because it is made without eggs, it doesn't require a water bath to achieve a super-creamy texture.

The gluten-free crust is made of toasted nuts and dates and pressed into a springform pan to act as a shell for the filling. A rich filling is swirled with ribbons of black tahini for a dramatic effect and subtle earthy flavor. Make this for your next holiday (or other special) event and dazzle your guests.

Makes one 8-inch cake (8 servings)

Time: Weekend

Storage: Refrigerate for up to 1 week or freeze for up to 1 month.

CRUST
Coconut or neutral oil, for the springform pan

1 cup (100g) pecan halves

¾ cup (95g) pistachios, plus more for topping

1⅓ cups (165g) pitted dates

½ teaspoon ground cinnamon

Pinch of fine sea salt

FILLING
24 ounces (680g) Velvety Tofu Cream Cheese (page 26; see Notes) or store-bought vegan cream cheese

1¼ cups (252g) canned unsweetened coconut cream (see Notes)

¾ cup (150g) organic cane sugar

¼ cup (30g) cornstarch

2 tablespoons fresh lemon juice

2 teaspoons vanilla extract

2 tablespoons black tahini (see Notes)

TOPPING
Chopped pistachios

PREHEAT THE OVEN TO 350°F (180°C). Lightly grease an 8-inch (20cm) springform pan with oil.

Make the crust: In a large dry skillet, toast the pecans and pistachios over medium-high heat, stirring or tossing frequently, until fragrant and browned, 4 to 5 minutes. Immediately transfer to a plate to cool.

Leave the oven on.

Transfer the cooled nuts to a food processor and add the dates, cinnamon, and salt. Process until the texture is mealy and the mixture holds together when you press some into a ball. Scoop the dough into the bottom of the springform and press it all the way up the sides of the springform pan, using your fingers to smooth and spread it evenly.

Make the filling: In a blender, combine the cream cheese, coconut cream, sugar, cornstarch, lemon juice, and vanilla. Puree on high speed until the mixture is super smooth.

Pour the filling into the crust, smoothing it over and spreading it evenly with a rubber spatula. (It's okay if it doesn't come all the way up to the top of the crust; you want a little room for it to puff up as it cooks, and for the garnishes.) Tap the pan lightly on the counter to remove any air bubbles. Using a spoon, drop splotches of black tahini on top of the batter. Use a toothpick or skewer to drag and swirl through the tahini, creating a marbled pattern.

Bake until the edges are set and the center is jiggly, 1 hour to 1 hour 10 minutes.

Transfer the cheesecake to a wire rack and let it cool to room temperature in the springform pan.

Cover the cake with a plate and transfer to the refrigerator to chill for at least 4 hours and up to 24 hours.

Run a knife around the edges and release the springform sides. Top the cake with pistachios and serve chilled.

COOK'S NOTES
- To use the Velvety Tofu Cream Cheese (page 26), double that recipe and save the leftovers to use as a spread.

- The coconut cream needs to be solid; if the brand you bought is separated into a solid layer on top and a watery layer beneath, use only the solid part, which might require starting with 2 (13.5-ounce/398ml) cans, and save the rest to blend in smoothies or use for overnight oats.

- If you can't easily find black tahini (or Asian black sesame paste), blend ½ cup (60g) black sesame seeds and 1 tablespoon toasted sesame oil in a mini food processor until smooth. Or you can use chocolate tahini or pomegranate molasses.

Aquafaba Cardamom Pavlovas

Traditionally, pavlova is a meringue-based dessert made from egg whites, but this recipe uses aquafaba, the viscous (and magical) liquid from a can (or cans) of chickpeas, which whips up easily with cream of tartar to hold stiff peaks just as egg whites would.

These cardamom-laced meringues (the aquafaba leaves them a light caramel color rather than snowy white) are baked at a low temperature until firm; leaving them to cool completely in the oven prevents any cracking. To finish, top them with a whipped rosewater coconut cream and fresh berries, for an elegant dessert made all the more surprising by its main ingredient.

Makes twelve 4-inch meringues or two 9-inch meringues

Time: Weekend

Storage: Once topped with the cream and berries, these are best eaten freshly made. But you can store the plain meringues in an airtight container at room temperature for up to 2 days before topping and serving.

¾ cup (180ml) aquafaba, from 1 or 2 (15-ounce/425g) cans no-salt-added chickpeas

½ teaspoon cream of tartar

½ cup (100g) organic cane sugar

½ teaspoon ground cardamom

1 teaspoon vanilla extract

2 (13.6-ounce/403ml) cans unsweetened coconut cream, preferably Native Forest or Thai Kitchen, refrigerated for 24 hours (see Note)

1 tablespoon agave syrup or maple syrup

1 teaspoon rose water

Fresh berries, for serving

PREHEAT THE OVEN TO 250°F (120°C). Line two large baking sheets with parchment paper.

In a stand mixer fitted with the whisk, combine the aquafaba and cream of tartar. Beat on high speed until stiff peaks form, about 10 minutes. While the mixer is running, add the sugar, 1 tablespoon at a time, then the cardamom, beating until the mixture becomes glossy. Beat in the vanilla extract.

Using a spoon, drop 12 big dollops of meringue onto the lined pans. Use the back of the spoon to shape the meringues into 4-inch (10cm) disks. Alternatively, make two larger 9-inch (23cm) meringues.

Bake until the meringues are dry to the touch, about 2 hours. Turn off the oven, prop open the oven door slightly, and let the meringues cool completely.

While the meringues are cooling, wash and dry the mixer bowl and whisk attachment and store in the freezer to chill.

When ready to serve, transfer the coconut cream to the chilled mixer bowl. Using the chilled whisk attachment, beat on medium-high speed until small peaks form, 1 to 2 minutes. Add the agave and rose water, beating until incorporated.

To serve, top each meringue with the whipped coconut cream and fresh berries.

COOK'S NOTE: If using canned full-fat coconut milk instead of coconut cream, refrigerate 4 (13.5-ounce/398ml) cans. Use a spoon to scoop out the thick layer of coconut cream that has separated to the top of the can and transfer it to your mixer bowl, saving the coconut water for another use (such as in smoothies).

Empanadas de Piña

These sweet golden pineapple empanadas, coated in cinnamon sugar, are the perfect treat for an afternoon snack or dessert. This recipe calls for making fresh pineapple filling, but you can also fill them with strawberry preserves, vegan cajeta, coconut cream, and even piloncillo-sweetened pumpkin puree. The addition of beer to the dough results in a light and flaky consistency. The dough also makes amazing savory empanadas; just omit the sugar or reduce it to ½ teaspoon.

This recipe will leave you with a little extra filling; treat it like pineapple jam, spreading it on toast or English muffins or dolloping it on your favorite plant-based yogurt.

Makes 6 servings (15 empanadas)

Time: Weekend

Storage: Refrigerate leftovers for up to 1 week or freeze for up to 3 months. To make ahead, freeze the dough for up to 2 months before you make the empanadas.

DOUGH

2 cups (250g) all-purpose flour, plus more as needed and for dusting

¼ teaspoon fine sea salt

¼ teaspoon baking powder

1 tablespoon organic cane sugar

9 tablespoons (128g) unsalted vegan butter, cubed, at room temperature

⅓ cup (80ml) Negra Modelo beer or another dark lager

FILLING

Scant 3 cups (454g) cubed fresh pineapple

⅓ cup (65g) plus 1 tablespoon organic cane sugar

1 tablespoon water

1 tablespoon cornstarch

½ teaspoon vanilla extract

ASSEMBLY

2 tablespoons Nut Milk (page 17), Oat Milk (page 17), Soy Milk (page 75), or store-bought plain plant-based milk

1 tablespoon maple syrup

1 cup (200g) organic cane sugar

3 tablespoons ground cinnamon

MAKE THE DOUGH: In a large bowl, combine the flour, salt, baking powder, and sugar. Add the butter and rub it in between your fingers until fine crumbs form. Make a well in the center of the bowl and add the beer. Using your hand, slowly begin to incorporate the flour into the beer, bringing the dough together. Knead the dough for 5 to 6 minutes, adding more flour a little at a time if needed, until the dough is smooth and no longer sticky. Place in an airtight silicone bag and refrigerate for 30 minutes.

While the dough is chilling, make the filling: In a medium saucepan, combine the pineapple and sugar. Bring to a simmer over medium heat, stirring occasionally. Reduce the heat to low and cook until the pineapple softens and releases its juices, about 15 minutes. In a small bowl, whisk together the water, cornstarch, and vanilla. Pour it into the pot, stir to incorporate, and simmer until the mixture starts to thicken, 1 to 2 minutes. Remove from the heat and let cool completely.

Preheat the oven to 350°F (180°C). Line a sheet pan with parchment paper or a silicone baking mat.

To assemble: Divide the dough into 15 equal portions (about 28g each). Lightly flour a surface and roll out each portion to a round ¼ inch (6.4mm) thick, turning the dough as you go to form an even round. Place 1 tablespoon of the filling in the center of each round. Brush water around half of the outer edge of each round and fold the dough over the filling, making the edges meet. Pinch the edges to seal and crimp with a fork.

In a small bowl, combine the milk and maple syrup. Line up the empanadas in the sheet pan and brush with the glaze.

Bake until the bottoms are golden brown, 15 to 20 minutes. Remove from the oven and let cool slightly.

In a large bowl, whisk together the sugar and the cinnamon. Toss the empanadas in the cinnamon sugar to coat and serve warm.

Chocolate Cake
Four Ways

If it's not utterly moist, buoyant, and soft, chocolate cake is a waste of time. Luckily, this recipe provides such a wonderfully soft cake that it needs to be refrigerated before decorating or else it will simply fall apart under the weight of a frosting knife. That's what makes it really good, though, as well as adaptable to changes like the addition of banana, coconut flakes, or a nut-based flour that can give you the sense of eating a beloved candy bar (see Variations at right).

Makes one 8-inch cake or 12 cupcakes

Time: Weekday

Storage: Store in an airtight container at room temperature for up to 3 days or freeze for up to 2 months.

Refined coconut oil, for the pan

1¼ cups (300ml) Nut Milk (page 17), Oat Milk (page 17), or store-bought plain plant-based milk

1 teaspoon apple cider vinegar

⅔ cup (160ml) refined coconut oil, melted and still warm

1¼ cups (250g) organic cane sugar

2 teaspoons vanilla extract

1¾ cups (218g) all-purpose flour

⅓ cup (30g) cocoa powder

1 teaspoon baking powder

1½ teaspoons baking soda

¼ teaspoon fine sea salt

POSITION A RACK IN the middle of the oven and preheat the oven to 350°F (180°C). Use a little coconut oil to grease an 8-inch (20cm) cake pan. Line the bottom of the pan with a round of parchment paper. (If making cupcakes, line 12 cups of a muffin tin with cupcake liners.)

In a small bowl or liquid measuring cup with a spout, whisk together the milk and vinegar.

In a large, microwave-safe bowl, whisk together the warm melted coconut oil, sugar, and vanilla until smooth. (If the coconut oil starts to solidify and form lumps, microwave on high, for just a few seconds at a time, to remelt it, and whisk again.) In another bowl, whisk together the flour, cocoa, baking powder, baking soda, and salt.

Add the milk to the coconut oil/sugar mixture and whisk until thoroughly combined. Add the flour mixture to the wet ingredients and whisk until a thick batter has formed without lumps.

Pour the batter into the prepared pan (or divide evenly among the muffin cups).

Bake until the top is firm to the touch and a toothpick inserted into the center comes out clean, 35 to 40 minutes (about 30 minutes for the cupcakes).

Let the cake cool in the pan on a wire rack to room temperature before removing for serving or storage.

If you want to frost the cake, wrap it in beeswax wrap and refrigerate for at least 2 hours or up to 3 days. Frost immediately after removing it from the refrigerator, and let it come to room temperature for at least 2 hours before serving. If you freeze the cake, let it thaw in the refrigerator before frosting.

VARIATIONS

Chocolate-Coconut Cake

Use full-fat canned coconut milk instead of any other plant-based milk. Use virgin coconut oil instead of refined. Stir 1 cup (85g) unsweetened shredded coconut into the batter before pouring into the pan and baking.

Chocolate-Banana Cake

Whisk ½ cup (113g) mashed ripe banana into the wet ingredients.

Chocolate-Hazelnut or Chocolate-Almond Cake

Whisk ½ cup (60g) hazelnut or almond flour plus 2 tablespoons cornstarch or arrowroot powder into the dry ingredients.

LET VEGAN BAKING SET YOU FREE

By Alicia Kennedy

I never intended to become a vegan baker. What happened was that I had taken up baking as a hobby, and then I decided to become vegan. I panicked a bit, thinking I would lose my new pastime, but figured I could buy all the vegan baking books on the market and just keep going. After all, that was how I had been learning how to bake in the first place.

I did that, and I baked some cakes, but I wasn't happy with how they were coming out. When I put cornstarch in a vanilla cake to replace the egg, I tasted corn. Chocolate cake made with canola oil turned out dry. None of the margarines on the market in the early 2010s were up to par, either. I knew, though, that it had to be possible: I knew I could figure out a way to bake all the same kinds of cakes and cookies I had been making without animal products. It would just take some research—and, I would quickly find out, some science.

Soon I knew the solid and milk-fat contents of butter and was replicating it with coconut oil and coconut milk. Arrowroot starch became my go-to egg replacement, because it totally lacks flavor. I started to understand how flaxseed meal, mixed with water, could work as an egg, too, and in which recipes its nutty wholesomeness fit best. Agar-agar became my friend and foe, as I worked it into various creamy desserts with varied results. When aquafaba emerged into the vegan consciousness as a miracle replacement for egg whites, I couldn't quite understand the hype until it made the perfect royal icing for which agar had been a temperamental solution. Miyoko's Creamery came out with cultured plant-based butter toward the end of the 2010s, and suddenly I no longer had to make my own.

In short, I've been deep into the evolution of vegan baking over the last decade, trying every new ingredient. What has always been my ultimate goal, though, is clarity of flavor, and through all of my experiments, I discovered that vegan baking encourages you to tinker, because you have so many more options for even the most basic ingredients. By allowing you to make so many more decisions, it actually gives you more autonomy. Vegan baking allows for endless adaptation.

In my freezer, I have arrowroot starch, flaxseed meal, and raw cashews. In my cabinets, there is an array of milks: coconut, almond, macadamia, and oat. In my pantry, there is flavorful virgin coconut oil, a neutral refined version, and olive oil. I don't need eggs, cream, or dairy butter because I can replace them all in a multitude of ways. Rather than being restrained by vegan baking, I am liberated by it.

Vegan baking, despite being a phrase made up of two words that often intimidate the uninitiated, is easy, adaptable, and simple because of its diversity. Traditionally, a baker's kitchen will always be stocked with the same kinds of dairy butter and milk or eggs around. When baking without animal products, though, I can choose to make a chocolate chip walnut cookie even nuttier by using a mix of flaxseed meal and water as the binder. When I want to make a coconut cake, I can use virgin oil as my fat to amp up that flavor and full-fat coconut milk as the liquid; when I want my cake to taste like vanilla, I use refined coconut oil. If I need a neutral cream, I soak and blend cashews—but I could also add them to a cookie, if I want to. Ingredients that are malleable and have varied applications mean, ultimately, a more affordable and less environmentally taxing way of baking.

Of course, people often don't believe vegan baking could be affordable. Many think it will require buying a bunch of strange, expensive ingredients at a specialized health food store on the outskirts of town—and maybe it will require a trip to a natural foods store, but only once every few months instead of requiring you to run out for milk or eggs every time the urge to make a cake strikes. For someone who normally eats farmers market eggs or local butter, baking in this nontraditional way means not burying those expensive ingredients in a baked good where they're not the star attraction. This approach means, simply, consuming fewer animal products of higher quality, even if not always eating a plant-based diet.

Egg substitutes such as arrowroot, flaxseed meal, cornstarch, agar-agar, and more all have long shelf lives if they're stored in cool, dark places. When I want a cake to taste like pumpkin or banana, though, I just use a puree of each: ¼ cup per egg, goes the rule. Aquafaba, that once-flashy egg white replacement, cuts down on food waste by using up a by-product of canned chickpeas. Nondairy milks, too, whether in a box or can, are easy to store and have on hand, and there is such variety that you never have to choose the same nut or grain. Relying on these ingredients rather than their nonvegan counterparts becomes an easy way to support biodiverse land use, which is key to stopping the rapid global warming we're experiencing as a result of climate change.

Baking with a diverse array of ingredients also means that whatever is local can easily be incorporated into the process. Where I live in Puerto Rico, coconuts are obviously abundant, and some farmers are making coconut oil that I'm able to put in my cakes. There is breadfruit, too, and when it's really ripe, I can puree it and use it in place of pumpkin for a different texture. Plantains that have turned black can replace mashed banana. There is no restriction in baking without using animal products; instead, I find abundance and adaptability.

It's true that when someone is new to baking with coconut oil, for example, even when it's refined and odorless, there is a palate adjustment. But I have found that the taste of dairy butter and the funk of dairy milk overwhelm me when I occasionally try a traditional treat to see what all the fuss is about.

The palate evolves, just as our approach to baking can. If there's one thing I've learned in my years of frustration and euphoria in the kitchen testing out new recipes, it's that vegan baking allows ample room for mistakes and innovations alike. No one knows what the future of how we eat will hold: The only promise of vegan baking is that it will change, that it will adapt.

Alicia Kennedy is the author of *No Meat Required: The Cultural History and Culinary Future of Plant-Based Eating.*

Chocolate Chip Cookies
and Rocky Road Cookies

Chocolate Chip Cookies Four Ways

A solid chocolate chip cookie recipe can be hard to come by, despite its simplicity. Maintaining simplicity, though, is key to letting the right flavors sing. This base recipe from writer/baker Alicia Kennedy provides a crisp edge and gooey center, and it allows for endless variation, from the addition of nuts or marshmallows to the swapping of some flour for cocoa powder for a texture that is brownie-like in its fudgy decadence. The quality of the butter here makes all the difference, which is why Alicia recommends using a cultured vegan butter like the one from Miyoko's Creamery. The molasses of the dark brown sugar and the bounty of chocolate chips really shine against its tangy richness. This dough can be frozen for up to 3 months or kept tightly covered in the refrigerator for up to 2 weeks.

Makes 30 cookies

Time: Weekend

Storage: Refrigerate in an airtight container for up to 1 week.

8 ounces (225g) cold vegan butter, such as Miyoko's

1 cup (200g) organic cane sugar

1 cup packed (220g) dark brown sugar

3 cups (375g) all-purpose flour

2 tablespoons arrowroot powder

¾ teaspoon baking soda

½ teaspoon fine sea salt

½ cup (120ml) Nut Milk (page 17), Oat Milk (page 17), Soy Milk (page 75), or store-bought plain plant-based milk

1 cup (240g) chocolate chips

Flaky sea salt (optional), for finishing

IN A STAND MIXER fitted with the paddle (or in a bowl using an electric hand mixer with whisks), beat the butter on medium-high speed until smooth. Add the cane sugar and brown sugar and beat until the mixture is well combined and has a sandy texture.

In a medium bowl, whisk together the flour, arrowroot, baking soda, and salt.

With the mixer on medium speed, add the dry ingredients in three additions, mixing just until each addition is incorporated before adding more. With the mixer running, pour in the milk in a stream and beat until incorporated.

When the dough comes together into a ball around the paddle, add the chocolate chips and beat until combined.

Cover the bowl and transfer it to the refrigerator to chill for at least 1 hour. (If desired, you can refrigerate the dough for up to 2 weeks or freeze for up to 3 months.)

Position racks in the bottom and upper third of the oven and preheat the oven to 350°F (180°C). Line two large baking sheets with parchment paper.

Using a 1-tablespoon-size scoop, form the dough into balls and place them 2 inches (5cm) apart on the parchment paper. Sprinkle with flaky sea salt, if using.

Bake the sheets until the cookies are set and have a matte finish, about 12 minutes, switching racks and rotating the pans front to back about halfway through the baking time.

Let the cookies cool on the pans on a wire rack before moving the cookies to a serving platter.

VARIATIONS

Walnut Chocolate Chip Cookies

Add 1 cup (120g) chopped walnuts with the chocolate chips.

Double-Chocolate Hazelnut Cookies

Reduce the all-purpose flour to 2½ cups (315g). Whisk 1⅓ cups (120g) cocoa powder into the dry ingredients. Add 1 cup (115g) chopped hazelnuts with the chocolate chips. Note that the double chocolate will not spread as much as the other cookies.

Rocky Road Cookies

Reduce the all-purpose flour to 2½ cups (315g). Whisk 1⅓ cups (120g) cocoa powder into the dry ingredients. Add 1 cup (120g) chopped walnuts and 1 cup (80g) mini vegan marshmallows with the chocolate chips. Note that these double chocolate cookies will not spread as much as the others.

Chocolate-Lime Olive Oil Cake with Mango Curd & Chocolate Ganache

This cake is perfect for a treasured friend's birthday or when you just want to impress the hell out of someone. It's got everything—moist layers that taste even more chocolatey thanks to coffee, lusciously creamy mango filling, and a truly decadent ganache. It's the kind of cake that people take a bite of and say, "Are you sure this is vegan?"

Makes one 8-inch layer cake

Time: Weekend

Storage: Refrigerate for up to 3 days. The components can all be stored separately before serving: Refrigerate the mango curd and well-wrapped cake layers for up to 1 week. Refrigerate the ganache for up to 2 weeks. Freeze the cake layers for up to 3 months. Thaw the cake layers and warm the ganache to the melting point on the stove or in the microwave, allowing it to cool to room temperature before using.

MANGO CURD

1½ cups (300g) diced fresh or thawed frozen mango

1 cup (240ml) canned full-fat coconut milk

½ cup (100g) organic cane sugar

2 tablespoons cornstarch

2 tablespoons fresh lime juice

½ teaspoon grated fresh ginger

½ teaspoon fine sea salt

3 tablespoons coconut oil, refined or unrefined

CAKE

Vegetable oil or cooking spray and cocoa powder, for the pans

1½ cups (188g) all-purpose flour

¾ cup packed (165g) light brown sugar

¾ cup (150g) organic cane sugar

¾ cup (70g) Dutch process cocoa powder, sifted

1½ teaspoons baking soda

½ teaspoon fine sea salt

¾ cup (180ml) brewed coffee

¾ cup (180ml) water

½ cup (120ml) olive oil

1 tablespoon red wine vinegar

2 teaspoons grated lime zest

1 teaspoon vanilla extract

CHOCOLATE GANACHE

½ cup (120ml) canned full-fat coconut milk

1¼ cups (177g) bittersweet vegan chocolate chips

1 teaspoon light agave syrup

½ teaspoon ground ginger

¼ teaspoon fine sea salt

OPTIONAL DECORATION

1 fresh mango, sliced into thin wedges, or other fruit

Sliced candied ginger

2 or 3 sprigs fresh mint

MAKE THE MANGO CURD: Do this the day before you want to serve the cake (or up to 1 week in advance). In a blender or food processor, combine the mango, coconut milk, sugar, cornstarch, lime juice, ginger, and salt and puree until very smooth. Set a sieve over a stainless steel saucepan and pour in the mixture to remove any remaining pieces of pulp.

Set the saucepan over medium heat and cook, stirring constantly, until it begins to boil and thicken, about 5 minutes. Remove from the heat and add the coconut oil, stirring until completely melted and blended into the curd.

Let the curd cool in the pan for 10 minutes, then pour into an airtight container and allow to cool to room temperature, uncovered, before sealing and refrigerating overnight so it sets completely.

Preheat the oven to 350°F (180°C). Lightly brush or spray two 8-inch (20cm) round cake pans with oil, lining the bottoms with rounds of parchment paper and brushing/spraying the parchment paper with more oil. If you are not using nonstick cake pans, you can also lightly dust the interior of the pans with cocoa powder.

In a large bowl, whisk together the flour, brown sugar, cane sugar, cocoa powder, baking soda, and salt until combined. Add the coffee, water, olive oil, vinegar, lime zest, and vanilla and whisk until smooth. Pour into the prepared pans.

Bake until the top is springy, the edges have come away from the sides of the pan, and a cake tester or toothpick inserted in the center comes out mostly clean, with no more than a few crumbs sticking to it, 30 to 35 minutes.

RECIPE CONTINUES ON NEXT PAGE

Remove from the oven and cool in the pans on a wire rack for 20 minutes. The cakes are a little fragile, so loosen the edges of the cakes gently, if necessary, then cover each with a plate, hold on to both, and invert them to turn each cake out onto a plate. Gently transfer the cakes to the rack to cool completely.

While the cakes are cooling, make the chocolate ganache: In a microwave-safe bowl, microwave the coconut milk until hot, about 1 minute. Stir in the chocolate chips until completely melted and combined. Add the agave syrup, ground ginger, and salt and whisk until glossy. Let cool for 5 minutes before using.

To assemble the cake, place one cake layer on a serving plate. Whisk the mango curd to loosen, then spoon it into the center and use an offset spatula to spread it evenly to the edges of the cake. Place the second cake layer on top of the curd. Spread the chocolate ganache evenly across the top using an offset spatula. At this point the cake can be refrigerated, or kept at a cooler room temperature, for a few hours until ready to serve.

When ready to serve, garnish the top of the cake with fresh fruit, candied ginger, and sprigs of mint, if desired.

COOK'S NOTE: You'll want to plan ahead for this one: Make the mango curd at least the day before, because it needs to set overnight in the refrigerator.

Chocolate Cinnamon Tart

In this creamy chocolate pie, all of the lusciousness comes from silken tofu (no, you can't taste it) blended with melted chocolate. There are lots of versions of tofu cream pies out there, but this one is a standout with a bit more chocolate (which makes for a firmer set), some ground cinnamon for warm depth, and a date-nut crust. That crust, which is pleasantly crumbly and not too sweet, is gluten-free and requires no rolling or chilling. While using a tart pan with a removable bottom makes this looks extra fancy—and slice neatly—you can also make it in a standard pie dish.

The coconut whipped cream, while optional, makes a welcome addition, cutting through some of the chocolate's richness. If you do want to make it, try to chill your coconut cream for at least 8 hours; this makes it much more willing to whip.

Makes one 9-inch tart (8 servings)

Time: Weekend

Storage: Refrigerate for up to 4 days or freeze for up to 3 weeks. Served from the freezer, it will be firm but mousse-y, like a fudge pop. Let thaw at room temperature for 10 to 15 minutes before serving.

1¾ cups (175g) raw pecans

¾ teaspoon fine sea salt, plus more to taste

3½ ounces (100g) pitted Medjool dates (about 7)

2 tablespoons cocoa powder, preferably Dutch process

1 teaspoon vanilla extract

1½ teaspoons ground cinnamon, plus more to taste and more for sprinkling

10 ounces (285g) dairy-free chocolate (60% to 70% cacao), coarsely chopped (about 2 cups)

1 (14-ounce/397g) block silken tofu, patted dry

3 tablespoons maple syrup, plus more to taste

2 tablespoons Nut Milk (page 17), Oat Milk (page 17), or store-bought plain plant-based milk

½ cup (120ml) canned coconut cream (optional), preferably chilled for at least 8 hours

PREHEAT THE OVEN TO 350°F (180°C).

Spread the pecans on a sheet pan, transfer to the oven, and toast, tossing once, until slightly darkened in color and fragrant, 9 to 11 minutes. Immediately transfer to a plate to cool slightly, at least 5 minutes.

Reduce the oven temperature to 300°F (150°C).

Measure out ¼ cup (25g) of the pecans and set aside for finishing the tart. Transfer the remaining 1½ cups (150g) pecans to a food processor, along with ¼ teaspoon of the salt. Pulse in short bursts until a coarse meal forms. Add the dates, cocoa powder, ½ teaspoon of the vanilla, and ½ teaspoon of the cinnamon and process, stopping to scrape down the bowl as needed, until you have large, moist clumps that hold together when squeezed, about 1 minute.

Press into a 9-inch (23cm) tart pan with a removable bottom in a thin, even layer (it's easiest if you start with the sides first). (Alternatively, press into a 9-inch/23cm pie plate.)

Bake until the crust is slightly darker and looks and feels dry to the touch, 12 to 15 minutes. Transfer to a rack to cool while you make the filling.

Melt the chocolate in a double-boiler or by microwaving in 20-second increments. Stir until smooth and melted. Let cool slightly.

In a food processor or blender, combine the tofu, maple syrup, milk, remaining ½ teaspoon vanilla, remaining 1 teaspoon cinnamon, and remaining ½ teaspoon salt. Puree, scraping down the sides as needed, until very smooth. Add the melted chocolate and process until very smooth. Taste and season with more salt, maple syrup, and/or cinnamon as desired.

Transfer to the tart shell and spread into an even layer. Transfer to the refrigerator and chill, uncovered, for at least 2 hours, until firm.

When ready to serve, if you want the topping, transfer the chilled coconut cream to a stand mixer fitted with the whisk (or in a deep bowl using an electric hand mixer). Beat until it holds soft peaks, 1 to 2 minutes.

Coarsely chop the reserved pecans and scatter around the perimeter of the tart.

Serve slices with a dollop of coconut cream and another sprinkling of cinnamon.

Churros & Hot Chocolate

In Mexico, churros are a popular street food. They can be dusted with cinnamon sugar or filled with cajeta, chocolate, or strawberry jam. And contrary to some recipes you see, they aren't always made with egg: just flour, water, sugar, and a little oil. This version from blogger Dora Stone adds a cornstarch slurry to approximate the lighter texture and softer interior of the eggy versions.

The perfect pairing for these freshly fried crisp churros is a cup of artisanal Mexican hot chocolate. Unlike cocoa powder, which is the by-product of the separation of the cocoa butter from the cacao beans, good Mexican ground chocolate uses the whole bean (resulting in a deep, rich chocolate flavor), combined with sugar and cinnamon and formed into tablets.

Makes 4 to 6 servings

Time: Weekday

Storage: Refrigerate leftovers for up to 3 days.

CHURROS
1¾ cups plus 2 tablespoons (450ml) water
⅓ cup (75g) unsalted vegan butter
1 tablespoon organic cane sugar
¼ teaspoon fine sea salt
1¼ cups (156g) all-purpose flour, sifted
⅔ cup (85g) cornstarch
1 tablespoon baking powder
Neutral vegetable oil, for frying

CINNAMON SUGAR
1 cup (200g) organic cane sugar
3 tablespoons ground cinnamon

HOT CHOCOLATE
4 cups (950ml) Nut Milk (page 17), Oat Milk (page 17), Soy Milk (page 75), or store-bought plain plant-based milk
5 to 6 ounces (140g to 170g) Mexican chocolate tablets, such as Hernán, Ibarra, or Taza

MAKE THE CHURROS: In a medium saucepan, combine 1 cup plus 2 tablespoons (270ml) of the water, the butter, sugar, and salt and bring to a boil over high heat. Reduce the heat to medium-low and add the flour all at once. Stir vigorously with a wooden spoon until the dough begins to separate from the sides of the pot, about 2 minutes. Remove the pot from the heat.

In a small bowl, combine the remaining ¾ cup (180ml) water, the cornstarch, and baking powder, and whisk until smooth. Scrape the cornstarch slurry into the pot with the dough, stirring vigorously with a wooden spoon until it is completely incorporated and the dough is smooth.

Transfer the dough to a piping bag fitted with a large star tip (see Note).

Set a wire rack inside a sheet pan beside the stovetop. Pour 3 inches (7.5cm) neutral oil into a Dutch oven or other deep, heavy pot and heat the oil over medium-high heat until it reaches 365°F (185°C).

Set out a large sheet of parchment paper. Pipe ribbons of dough 4 inches (10cm) long onto the paper, using kitchen shears to cut the batter at the end of the star tip. Use the paper to slide a few of the ribbons into the hot oil, avoiding overcrowding, and fry until golden brown, using a slotted spoon or spider to turn them as needed, about 2 minutes on each side. Transfer from the oil to the wire rack over the sheet pan to drain.

Meanwhile, make the cinnamon sugar: In a large bowl, whisk together the sugar and cinnamon.

Let the churros cool for 5 minutes, then toss in the cinnamon sugar to coat and transfer to a serving platter. Repeat with the rest of the dough.

While the churros are cooling, make the hot chocolate: In a large saucepan, heat the milk over medium heat until it just starts to lightly steam. Add the Mexican chocolate tablets. Whisk until the chocolate dissolves, but be careful not to overheat it or the milk or it will overflow. Remove from the heat and froth the chocolate with a molinillo (a traditional wooden Mexican whisk) or an immersion blender. Serve with the churros while hot and frothy.

COOK'S NOTE: If you don't have a piping bag and/or star tip, which results in the most traditional shape, cut off the corner of a large silicone zip-top bag, or look up videos on how to make a piping bag out of parchment paper, and use that instead.

Carob Brownies

Carob, made from the seeds of a Mediterranean fruit, is often touted as a caffeine-free chocolate substitute, but its naturally fruity sweet flavor does not have the bitterness of chocolate and deserves to be enjoyed on its own merit. In this recipe, carob molasses—a common ingredient in Middle Eastern cooking—adds even more depth of flavor, while tahini and espresso powder bring balance to the sweetness. Carob chips, which can be found in many natural foods stores, help bring a little fudgy quality to these otherwise delightfully cakey brownies.

Makes 9 brownies

Time: Weekday

Storage: Store leftovers in an airtight container at room temperature for up to 3 days or refrigerate for up to 1 week.

Neutral oil, for the pan

2 cups (250g) all-purpose flour

1 scant cup (103g) carob powder

1 teaspoon baking powder

½ teaspoon fine sea salt

½ teaspoon ground cinnamon

1 cup (240ml) hot water

¼ cup (80g) carob molasses or regular molasses

2 tablespoons black tahini or regular tahini (see Note)

1 teaspoon instant espresso powder

1½ teaspoons vanilla extract

½ teaspoon almond extract

½ cup (100g) organic cane sugar

¼ cup (60ml) grapeseed or other neutral oil

⅓ cup (80g) carob chips

POSITION A RACK IN the middle of the oven and preheat the oven to 350°F (180°C). Lightly oil an 8-inch (20cm) square baking pan.

In a large bowl, whisk together the flour, carob powder, baking powder, salt, and cinnamon.

In a medium bowl, whisk together the water, molasses, tahini, espresso powder, vanilla, and almond extract until well combined. Whisk in the sugar and oil until smooth.

Make a well in the center of the flour mixture and slowly pour in the wet ingredients, folding with a large spoon or rubber spatula until the dry ingredients are completely combined. Fold in the carob chips. Pour the batter evenly into the prepared pan, smoothing the top. Tap the pan lightly on the counter to remove any air bubbles

Bake until a wooden skewer or cake tester comes out with just a few crumbs attached, 20 to 25 minutes.

Allow the brownies to cool in the pan on a rack for 2 hours, then remove them from the pan to cool on the rack for an additional hour. Cut into 9 squares (in a 3 × 3 grid) and serve.

COOK'S NOTE: If you're wondering what else you might do with the rest of the black tahini you may have bought for this recipe, try the Black Tahini Swirled Cheesecake (page 413).

Frozen Cardamom Coconut Ice Box Cake

A mashup of Italian semifreddo and a retro American ice box cake, this dessert uses aquafaba meringue plus coconut cream and sweetened condensed coconut milk as a base. Flavored with cardamom and almond extract, the cream is then layered with vegan graham crackers, which soften in the freezer rather than the traditional refrigerator (which was called an "ice box" before electric versions were popularized). Topped with swooshes of sweetened, whipped coconut cream and lightly salted, roasted coconut chips, this dessert can wow guests at occasions both casual and special.

Make sure to plan so you can refrigerate the ingredients (aquafaba, coconut cream, and sweetened condensed coconut milk) that need to be cold. Since the cake needs to freeze overnight, make it at least the day before serving.

Makes 6 to 8 servings

Time: Weekend

Storage: Rewrap and return the cake to the freezer for up to 3 months. (The coconut cream topping will become a little icy in texture, but it's still tasty.)

CAKE

½ cup (120ml) aquafaba (from one 15-ounce/425g can no-salt-added chickpeas), refrigerated overnight

3 tablespoons organic powdered sugar

¼ teaspoon cream of tartar

½ cup (120ml) coconut cream (from one 13.6-ounce/403ml can), refrigerated overnight

1 cup (240ml) sweetened condensed coconut milk, homemade (page 22) or store-bought

¾ teaspoon almond extract

½ teaspoon ground cardamom

⅛ teaspoon fine sea salt

10 full sheets (155g total) vegan graham crackers, such as Nabisco Grahams Original, broken into 4 small rectangles

TOPPING

1 (13.6-ounce/403ml) can coconut cream, refrigerated overnight

¼ cup (30g) organic powdered sugar

One (3.17-ounce/90g) bag lightly salted, toasted coconut chips, such as Dang brand (see Notes)

MAKE THE CAKE: Line a 9 × 5-inch (23cm × 13cm) loaf pan with compostable plastic wrap or crisscrossed strips of compostable parchment paper, with at least 3 inches (7.5cm) of overhang on each side. Place in the freezer until ready to use.

In a stand mixer fitted with the whisk, combine the aquafaba, powdered sugar, and cream of tartar. Beat on high speed until stiff peaks form, 3 to 4 minutes. Transfer to a medium bowl.

Wipe out the stand mixer bowl, add the coconut cream, and beat on medium-high until it starts to lighten in texture, 3 to 4 minutes. Add the sweetened condensed coconut milk, almond extract, cardamom, and salt and beat for another 2 minutes. Remove the bowl from the stand mixer, add half of the aquafaba meringue, and gently fold into the coconut cream mixture. Add the remaining half and gently fold to combine.

Dollop about a cup of the coconut aquafaba mixture into the bottom of the chilled lined loaf pan, spreading it into an even layer. Add one layer of graham crackers, breaking the crackers to fit in the nooks and crannies. Spread another ½-inch (1.3cm) layer of the cream mixture and then layer more graham crackers. Repeat the process, ending with a cream layer, until the loaf pan is full. Fold the wrap over the top (taping the parchment if needed to secure) and freeze overnight.

Make the topping: About 15 minutes before serving, scoop the solid coconut cream off the top of the can of coconut cream, reserving the clear coconut liquid for another use, and place in the bowl of a stand mixer. Beat on medium-high speed until it lightens in texture and doubles in size, 4 to 5 minutes. Add the powdered sugar, scraping down the sides, and beat for another 30 seconds to 1 minute to combine.

To serve, remove the frozen ice box cake from the loaf pan and, moving swiftly, unwrap and transfer to a serving platter. Slather the top with the whipped coconut cream and sprinkle generously with the coconut chips. Serve immediately.

COOK'S NOTES

- If you can't find toasted coconut chips, buy the largest flaked coconut you can find and toast it in a dry skillet over medium heat, stirring frequently, until lightly browned.

- To cut the cake, first dip a serrated knife in very hot water and quickly wipe dry with a clean kitchen towel. Repeat as necessary.

Citrus Cream Bars

Orange creamy frozen pops, meet lemon bars. The key to this recipe is rubbing the orange and lemon zests into the cane sugar, which helps release their essential oils and all the citrusy goodness they have to offer (plus, your kitchen will smell insanely good). The filling is based on shelf-stable packages of firm or extra-firm silken tofu, typically Mori-Nu brand. That brings creaminess, while a generous dose of vanilla lends that orange-cream flavor. Bring to picnics, potlucks, and barbecues and wait for the oohs and aahs to follow. (Yes, people will ask you for the recipe.)

Makes 30 (2-inch-square) servings

Time: Weekend

Storage: Refrigerate for up to 5 days or freeze for up to 3 months.

CRUST

8 ounces (225g) vegan graham crackers (about 15 full cracker sheets), such as Nabisco Grahams Original

6 tablespoons (75g) organic cane sugar

¼ teaspoon fine sea salt

A few gratings of fresh nutmeg

8 tablespoons (112g) Soft Spreadable Butter (page 21) or store-bought vegan butter, melted

FILLING

2 cups (400g) organic cane sugar

4 teaspoons finely grated orange zest (from 2 oranges)

1 tablespoon finely grated lemon zest (from 3 lemons)

½ cup (120ml) fresh orange juice (from 2 to 3 oranges)

½ cup (120ml) fresh lemon juice (from 3 to 4 lemons)

2 (12.3-ounce/349g) packages firm or extra-firm silken tofu

½ cup (65g) organic powdered sugar, plus more for finishing

¼ cup (30g) cornstarch

2 teaspoons vanilla extract

¼ teaspoon fine sea salt

PREHEAT THE OVEN TO 350°F (180°C). Line a quarter-sheet pan or 9 × 13-inch (23cm × 33cm) pan with parchment paper.

Make the crust: In a food processor, blend the graham crackers into a medium-fine powder. Add the cane sugar, salt, and nutmeg and pulse a few times to combine. Add the melted butter and continue pulsing until incorporated. Transfer to the parchment-lined pan and press evenly along the bottom of the pan using the bottom of a measuring cup.

Bake until the crust is browning along the edges and smells toasty, 12 to 14 minutes. Allow to cool for at least 10 minutes. Leave the oven on.

Meanwhile, make the filling: In a medium bowl, combine the cane sugar, orange zest, and lemon zest. Using your fingers, rub the citrus zests into the sugar.

Wipe the food processor clean. Transfer the citrus sugar to the food processor and add the orange juice, lemon juice, tofu, powdered sugar, cornstarch, vanilla, and salt. Blend until smooth.

Pour the filling into the slightly cooled crust and knock the pan on the counter a couple of times to remove any air bubbles.

Bake until set, 35 to 45 minutes. (Firm tofu will take a little longer to set than extra-firm.) Let cool to room temperature, then transfer to the refrigerator and cool completely.

When ready to serve, sift a generous layer of powdered sugar over the top and cut into 30 pieces roughly 2 inches (5cm) square.

Salted Baklava

Baklava, the honey-soaked pastry that hails from Greece and the Middle East, is easily veganized by letting Wildflower Cider Syrup (page 35) stand in for the honey. The apple undertone benefits from some extra spice, and the extra sprinkle of flaky salt just before serving reinforces the lightly salted filling. The cider syrup also adds a delectable tang to a dessert that can sometimes suffer from cloying sweetness, but if you don't have time to make it, feel free to substitute light agave syrup for a more conventional flavor. Be sure to completely cool the syrup before pouring it over the hot-from-the-oven baklava, and then be sure to wait as long as possible before serving; the longer the syrup has to soak into the pastry, the stickier—and more delightful—it will be!

Makes sixteen 2-inch pieces (8 servings)

Time: Weekend

Storage: Refrigerate in an airtight container for up to 2 weeks or freeze, tightly wrapped, for up to 4 months.

- 1¼ cups (300ml) Wildflower Cider Syrup (page 35) or light agave syrup
- 1 large piece of fresh orange zest, about 1 × 3 inches (2.5cm × 7.5cm)
- 4 green cardamom pods, lightly crushed
- 6 black peppercorns, lightly cracked
- 2 cups (200g) walnuts
- 1 cup (140g) salted roasted almonds
- ¼ cup (50g) organic cane sugar
- ¼ cup packed (55g) light brown sugar
- 1 teaspoon ground cinnamon
- 1 teaspoon grated orange zest
- ½ teaspoon ground cardamom
- Olive oil, for brushing
- 12 phyllo sheets (from a 1-pound/454g box)
- ½ teaspoon flaky sea salt

PREHEAT THE OVEN TO 375°F (190°C).

In a small saucepan, combine the syrup, orange zest, cardamom pods, and peppercorns and bring to a simmer over medium heat. Cook for 5 minutes to meld the flavors. Remove from the heat and allow to cool completely. Strain out the orange zest, cardamom pods, and peppercorns and refrigerate the spiced soaking syrup until the baklava has cooked.

To make the filling, in a food processor, combine the walnuts, almonds, and both sugars and pulse until the nuts are well chopped but not finely ground (there should still be visible chunks), up to 1 minute. Transfer the mixture to a bowl and stir in the cinnamon, orange zest, and cardamom.

Trim the phyllo sheets down into 8-inch (20cm) squares. Keep them covered as you work so they don't dry out. Brush 1 tablespoon olive oil all over the interior of an 8-inch (20cm) square baking pan. For a "layer": Lay 1 square of phyllo inside the pan and brush about 1 teaspoon of olive oil all over the phyllo, top with a second square of phyllo and brush it with another 1 teaspoon of olive oil. Spread one-quarter of the nut filling evenly on top of the phyllo. Repeat this layer three more times, brushing each square of phyllo with 1 teaspoon olive oil. Top the nut filling with a final 4 sheets of phyllo, brushing each sheet with some oil, and then brush the top square of phyllo with 1 tablespoon olive oil.

Use a sharp knife (serrated works well) to cut horizontal lines about 2 inches (5cm) apart and about halfway down through the layers, trying to avoid dragging the knife and potentially disrupting the layers. Repeat with lines, also 2 inches (5cm) apart, either on a diagonal to create a diamond pattern, or perpendicular to make squares.

Bake until the top is golden brown and crisp, about 30 minutes. Transfer to a wire rack.

Pour the spiced soaking syrup over the warm baklava, making sure to get it in all the cut lines, and using a brush if need be to coat the top layer of the phyllo. Cool completely, for at least 1 hour but preferably overnight, so the syrup can soak into all the layers.

To serve, use a sharp knife to cut all the way through the lines that you cut prior to baking, to create individual pieces. Sprinkle lightly with flaky salt just before serving.

Fruit Curd Three Ways

Curd is wonderful to fill layer cakes or sandwich between shortbread cookies. It's also a good glaze for a single-layer cake, thanks to its bright, sweet acidity. This is a way of preserving lemons or limes when they are at their best, most abundant, and freshest for a taste of seasonality whenever the mood or occasion strikes. We also include instructions for a particularly vibrant passion fruit variation, and if you can get your hands on passion fruit pulp, you have to try it. Make sure to measure out all your ingredients beforehand, as the process goes quickly once you start.

Note that while you can use other vegan butters for this, we strongly prefer Earth Balance, which gives a wonderfully silky result; curd made with other brands, or with coconut oil, is plenty tasty but might be a little grainy.

Makes about 1 cup

Time: Weekday

Storage: Store in an airtight container in the fridge for up to 3 weeks.

1 tablespoon cornstarch

½ cup (120ml) fresh lemon or lime juice (from 2 to 3 lemons or 3 to 5 limes)

6 tablespoons (85g) unsalted vegan butter, preferably Earth Balance, cut into cubes

¼ cup (50g) organic cane sugar

1 teaspoon finely grated lemon or lime zest (from 1 lemon or 1 to 2 limes)

¼ teaspoon ground turmeric (if making lemon curd) or matcha powder (if making lime curd), for color (optional)

PUT THE CORNSTARCH IN a small bowl next to the stove.

In a small saucepan, combine the juice, butter, sugar, zest, and the turmeric or matcha (if using). While whisking constantly, heat over medium heat until the butter melts, the sugar dissolves, and a few wisps of steam start to rise.

Use a measuring spoon to transfer about 2 tablespoons of the juice mixture to the bowl with the cornstarch in it and whisk until smooth. Use a silicone spatula to scrape all the slurry back into the saucepan and immediately whisk to thoroughly combine. Use the spatula to gently stir, scraping back and forth along the bottom of the pan, until the mixture thickens, about 3 minutes. (The spatula will leave an exposed path on the bottom of the pan for a split second before it disappears.)

Remove from the heat and pour into a heatproof container (such as a small glass jar) and let cool to room temperature. As it cools, whisk occasionally to keep the butter from separating, then transfer to the refrigerator. (The curd will become more pudding-like in the fridge and loosen at room temperature.)

VARIATION

Passion Fruit Curd

Instead of citrus zest or juice, heat ½ cup (113g) passion fruit pulp (with seeds) with the sugar. After the sugar dissolves, whisk in 2 tablespoons fresh lemon juice. Press the mixture through a fine-mesh sieve into a bowl to remove the seeds. Wipe out the saucepan and return the mixture to the pan before adding the vegan butter and continuing.

Frozen Lime Pie

Frozen lime pie seems to contain the essence of summer in every bite, with the same satisfaction as ice cream but in pie form. The creamy filling in this pie uses cashews and coconut milk as a base with plenty of fresh lime juice and zest for zing. (If you want to make it closer to a traditional key lime pie, use key lime juice, of course.) A nut and date mixture forms a cinnamony gluten-free crust that might just beat the traditional graham cracker one. The secret is to toast the nuts first, which keeps it crunchy with a deeper flavor.

Once the pie is formed, it gets chilled in the freezer until firm, then thawed a little before serving time. Since it keeps well in the freezer, you can sneak in a slice after dinner anytime you please—and return the rest to the freezer for another night.

Makes one 9-inch pie (8 servings)

Time: Weekend

Storage: Freeze for up to 1 month, preferably without the coconut topping.

FILLING
1 cup (130g) raw cashews
Boiling water
¾ cup (180ml) canned full-fat coconut milk (see Note)
¼ cup (60ml) melted coconut oil, refined or unrefined
4 teaspoons grated lime zest
½ cup (120ml) fresh lime juice (from 4 limes)
⅓ cup (80ml) light agave syrup

CRUST
Coconut or neutral oil, for the pie dish
¾ cup (75g) raw pecans
¾ cup (105g) raw almonds
1 cup (125g) pitted Medjool dates
½ teaspoon ground cinnamon
Pinch of fine sea salt

TOPPING
½ cup (120ml) unsweetened coconut cream, preferably Thai Kitchen, chilled for 24 hours, or 1 (13.5-ounce/400ml) full-fat coconut milk (see Note)
1 teaspoon agave or maple syrup
½ teaspoon vanilla extract
Lime wheels and grated lime zest, for garnish

MAKE THE FILLING: In a small bowl, cover the cashews with the hot water and let sit for 30 minutes to soften, then drain and transfer to a blender. Add the coconut milk, coconut oil, lime zest, lime juice, and agave syrup and blend on high until smooth and creamy.

Make the crust: Grease a 9-inch (23cm) pie dish with some oil. In a dry skillet, toast the pecans and almonds over medium-high heat, stirring occasionally, until browned, 3 to 4 minutes. Transfer immediately to a plate to let cool.

Transfer the nuts to a food processor and add the dates, cinnamon, and salt and pulse until mealy in texture. Measure out 1 tablespoon of the mixture and set aside for garnish. Press the rest of the mixture into the pie dish, smoothing and spreading it evenly with the back of a spoon.

Pour the filling into the crust and tap on the counter to release air bubbles. Cover and freeze until firm, 3 to 4 hours. Remove from the freezer to thaw for 15 to 30 minutes before serving time.

While your pie is thawing, chill a stand mixer bowl and whisk (or a stainless steel bowl and electric hand mixer beaters) in the freezer for 10 minutes. Remove from the freezer, add the coconut cream to the bowl, and beat on medium-high speed until it lightens in texture and doubles in volume, 4 to 5 minutes. Add the agave and vanilla, beating until incorporated.

Decorate the pie with dollops of the whipped coconut cream and top with lime wheels. Sprinkle with the reserved crust mixture and some lime zest.

COOK'S NOTE: If using canned coconut milk instead of coconut cream for the topping, after it chills, use a spoon to scoop out the thick layer of coconut cream that has separated to the top of the can (you should have about ½ cup/120ml) and save the coconut water for another use, such as in smoothies.

Tahini Ice Cream

At chef Michael Rafidi's wonderful DC café, Yellow, he offers a tahini soft serve that is so creamy, as soon as I heard it was vegan, I had to see if he would share the recipe. To my delight, he did, and it works so well that this simple six-ingredient recipe has become the inspiration for all sorts of flavor variations: You can stud the ice cream with black sesame seeds, swirl pomegranate molasses into it, or add cocoa and/or melted chocolate (which turns into shreds, aka stracciatella, as it churns). Whichever variation you choose (or none at all), I recommend you start with this homemade oat milk, which is more concentrated than the one on page 17, and which thickens and gets a little sticky when you heat it, adding to the silkiness.

As always when making ice cream at home, be sure to prepare your equipment in advance: Freeze the ice cream maker insert for at least 24 hours, and also freeze a nonreactive 9 × 5-inch (23cm × 13cm) loaf pan or other freezer-safe storage container, preferably with a lid, for the ice cream. This helps you maintain the optimal texture by preventing the ice cream from melting after you process it and before you freeze it solid.

Makes 1 quart

Time: Weekend

Storage: Freeze in an airtight container for up to 3 months.

- 1 cup (90g) rolled oats
- 3 cups (700ml) filtered water
- 1¼ cups (250g) organic cane sugar
- ¾ cup (180ml) well-stirred tahini
- 1½ teaspoons vanilla paste or extract
- ¾ teaspoon fine sea salt

SET A BOWL OVER an ice bath consisting of half water and half ice.

In a high-powered blender, combine the oats and water and blend on high speed for about 30 seconds, until smooth.

Set a sieve over a large saucepan and arrange a nut-milk bag on top. Pour the milk into the bag, tie it closed, and squeeze the oat milk through the bag and sieve and into the pan. (Usually I avoid squeezing much when making oat milk, but for this use, the gelatinous quality that results from blending and squeezing helps the texture of the ice cream.) You should have about 3 cups (700ml). Reserve the leftover pulp for another use, such as in smoothies.

Set the saucepan over medium heat, bring the oat milk to a simmer, then whisk in the sugar, tahini, vanilla, and salt.

Pour the mixture through a fine-mesh sieve into the bowl set over the ice bath, and use a rubber spatula to press it all the way through. Clean the spatula, then stir the mixture, scraping the bottom and sides of the bowl often, until it feels cool to the touch. You might need to refresh the ice in the ice bath a time or two. (Alternatively, transfer the mixture to the refrigerator, cover, and chill overnight.)

Process the mixture in your ice cream maker according to the manufacturer's instructions, until it is as thick as soft serve. Immediately transfer it to the frozen loaf pan or other container. Press parchment paper directly onto the surface, cover with foil or the container lid, and freeze until solid, at least 8 hours or more.

VARIATIONS

Tahini Ice Cream with Pomegranate Swirl

After churning, pack one-third of the ice cream into a storage container and drizzle ¼ cup (60ml) pomegranate molasses over it. Use a chopstick or butter knife to draw shallow lines through, creating a swirl pattern. Repeat with another one-third of the ice cream and another ¼ cup (60ml) molasses. End with the remaining one-third of the ice cream, leaving it plain on top.

Tahini Black Sesame Ice Cream

While the ice cream is churning, sprinkle in ½ cup (60g) black sesame seeds.

Chocolate Tahini Ice Cream

Before whisking the sugar and tahini into the oat milk, stir ⅓ cup (30g) Dutch process cocoa powder into the sugar.

Tahini Stracciatella Ice Cream

Melt 3 ounces (85g) bittersweet chocolate and let it cool to room temperature. While the ice cream is churning, slowly drizzle in the melted chocolate.

COOK'S NOTE: If you'd like to use store-bought oat milk, make sure it's unsweetened and has as few ingredients as possible, and whisk in a slurry of 1 tablespoon cornstarch dissolved in 1 tablespoon warm water after you whisk in the sugar and tahini.

Dreamy Nut or Seed Butter Ice Cream

Michael Rafidi's brilliant Tahini Ice Cream (opposite) got me thinking: Would the same technique and basic proportions work with other nut butters? Countless batches later, I'm happy to report: It sure does. I like to turn the nuts into both a nut butter and a nut milk, and to save some roasted nuts for churning right into the ice cream, tripling down on the flavor. This is how you can turn five ingredients (including water and salt!) into luscious pistachio, hazelnut, peanut butter, pecan, or walnut ice cream—or even ice cream made from pumpkin or sunflower seeds.

As always when making ice cream at home, be sure to prepare your equipment in advance: Freeze the ice cream maker insert for at least 24 hours, and also freeze a nonreactive 9 × 5-inch (23cm × 13cm) loaf pan or other freezer-safe storage container, preferably with a lid, for the ice cream. This helps you maintain the optimal texture by preventing the ice cream from melting after you process it and before you freeze it solid.

Makes 1 quart

Time: Weekend

Storage: Freeze in an airtight container for up to 3 months.

3½ cups (830ml; see Notes) raw pistachios, skin-on hazelnuts (see Notes), peanuts, pecans, walnuts, pumpkin seeds, or sunflower seeds

3 cups (700ml) filtered water

1¼ cups (250g) organic cane sugar

¾ teaspoon fine sea salt

1½ teaspoons vanilla paste or extract

COVER 1 CUP (240ML) OF the nuts or seeds with enough water to cover by 2 inches (5cm), cover, and soak overnight. Rinse and drain.

Preheat the oven to 300°F (150°C).

In a high-powered blender, combine the drained nuts or seeds and the 3 cups (700ml) water. Blend until smooth, at least 1 minute. Pour the mixture into a nut-milk bag set over a bowl, close the bag, and squeeze and twist to extract as much of the liquid as possible. Save the pulp for smoothies or to add to muffin or pancake batter.

On a large sheet pan, spread out the remaining 2½ cups (600ml) nuts or seeds. Toast until deeply browned and very fragrant, 10 to 20 minutes, depending on the variety of nuts or seeds. Remove and immediately transfer ¾ cup (180ml) of the nuts or seeds to a bowl and set aside. Transfer the remaining 1¾ cups (420ml) nuts or seeds to a food processor and process until the nuts or seeds form a ball, anywhere from 2 to 6 minutes. Use a spatula to scrape down the sides and break up the ball and continue processing until the mixture turns smooth and liquid, 1 to 4 minutes. Measure out ¾ cup (180ml) of the nut/seed butter and save any extra for spreading on toast or eating however you'd like.

Set a bowl over an ice bath consisting of half water and half ice.

In a saucepan, bring the nut or seed milk to a simmer over medium heat. Whisk in the nut/seed butter, sugar, and salt. Whisk for a minute or two until the sugar and salt are fully dissolved.

Pour the mixture into the bowl set over the ice bath and stir, scraping the bottom and sides of the bowl often, until it feels cool to the touch. You might need to refresh the ice in the ice bath a time or two. Stir in the vanilla. (Alternatively, transfer the mixture to the refrigerator, cover, and chill overnight.)

Process the mixture in an ice cream maker according to the manufacturer's instructions until it is as thick as soft serve.

While the ice cream is churning, very coarsely chop the reserved ¾ cup (180ml) toasted nuts, leaving them in big pieces. (If you're using seeds, don't chop them.)

When the ice cream is thick, pour in all but a handful of the chopped nuts or whole seeds and let the ice cream finish churning. Immediately transfer it to the frozen loaf pan or other container, and sprinkle with the remaining chopped nuts. Press parchment paper directly onto the surface, cover with foil or the container lid, and freeze until solid, at least 8 hours or more.

COOK'S NOTES

- The gram weight of 1 cup will vary by the nut or seed, so it's easier to use the volume measure of 830 milliliters. The per-cup weight of the nuts will range from 100 grams (pecans, walnuts) to 150 grams (peanuts), with everything else in between.

- Many recipes call for you to peel hazelnuts before or after roasting, but I like the touch of bitterness the skins impart here, especially since that flavor is tempered by the cold.

From left to right: Tahini Black Sesame Ice Cream (page 436), Almost-Any-Fruit Ice Cream (page 440) made with strawberries, and Dreamy Nut or Seed Butter Ice Cream (page 437) made with pistachios.

Almost-Any-Fruit Ice Cream

My *Washington Post* colleague Becky Krystal had a stroke of genius when she researched the best way to make a peach ice cream. She amped up the flavor of a fruit puree with one of her (and my) favorite ingredients: freeze-dried peaches. I've since used that technique with just about every fruit I can find in both fresh and freeze-dried form—berries, mangoes, pineapple—and with every one of them, it works so well to dial in the flavor of each fruit's essence. I like to blend most of the jammy fruit into the ice cream base but save some of it for layering, which lends the ice cream more visual and textural interest—and pops of flavor. This ice cream base is the same one I used for Red Bean Ice Cream in my book *Cool Beans*; it's a veganized version of recipes from ice cream entrepreneur Jeni Britton Bauer.

As always when making ice cream at home, be sure to prepare your equipment in advance: Freeze the ice cream maker insert for at least 24 hours, and also freeze a nonreactive 9 × 5-inch (23cm × 13cm) loaf pan or other freezer-safe storage container, preferably with a lid, for the ice cream. This helps you maintain the optimal texture by preventing the ice cream from melting after you process it and before you freeze it solid.

Makes about 1½ quarts

Time: Weekend

Storage: Freeze for up to 3 months.

2 pounds (910g) pitted and chopped stone fruit, berries, peeled mango, or peeled pineapple

1 cup (200g) organic cane sugar

2 cups (260g) raw cashews, soaked for at least 2 hours (or as long as overnight) and drained

1½ cups (350ml) water

½ ounce (14g) freeze-dried fruit (the same as the fresh fruit you choose)

2 tablespoons fresh lemon juice

4 tablespoons Velvety Tofu Cream Cheese (page 26) or store-bought vegan cream cheese

2 tablespoons cornstarch

2 tablespoons light corn syrup

¼ teaspoon fine sea salt

SET A BOWL OVER an ice bath consisting of half water and half ice.

In a large saucepan, combine the chopped fruit and ½ cup (100g) of the sugar. Bring to a simmer over medium-high heat, adjust the heat to maintain gentle bubbles, and cook, stirring frequently, until the fruit has turned almost jammy, 15 to 25 minutes.

Transfer the fruit to a stainless steel bowl that will fit inside the ice bath and stir until the mixture is cool to the touch.

In a high-powered blender, combine the cashews and 1½ cups (350ml) water and blend until smooth, scraping down the sides of the blender as needed.

Transfer one-quarter of the fruit mixture to a bowl, cover, and refrigerate until you're ready to layer and freeze the ice cream. Transfer the remaining three-quarters of the fruit mixture to the blender along with the freeze-dried fruit, lemon juice, the remaining ½ cup (100g) sugar, cream cheese, cornstarch, corn syrup, and salt and blend until very smooth. Scrape down the sides of the blender as needed.

Refresh the ice bath with more ice. Transfer the ice cream base to a stainless steel bowl that will fit inside the ice bath and stir until the mixture is very cold to the touch. (Alternatively, transfer the mixture to the refrigerator, cover, and chill overnight.)

Process in an ice cream maker according to the manufacturer's instructions until it is as thick as soft serve.

Scoop one-quarter of the base into the chilled loaf pan, then dollop with one-third of the reserved jammy fruit. Repeat twice more, layering the base and then the fruit, and end with a layer of the base. Press parchment paper onto the top of the ice cream, cover with a lid, and freeze until firm, about 2 hours.

Red Beans & Shaved Ice

Entire restaurants in Korea are devoted to nothing more than perfecting paht bingsu, the quintessential Korean dessert. What started out as a fairly humble refresher on a hot summer day (i.e., shaved ice and sweet red beans) has transformed into a decadent post-meal treat. Still, the nice thing about paht bingsu, as Joanne Lee "The Korean Vegan" Molinaro demonstrates with this recipe, is that it's fairly easy to prepare and requires only a strong blender to "shave" the ice. Beyond that, you can really add whatever fruits and other toppings your fearless imagination comes up with, going for a variety of tastes and textures. One eating tip: This will taste better after you've allowed some of the ice to melt, so the flavors have a chance to mingle.

Makes 4 servings

Time: Weekday

Storage: Not recommended.

½ cup (120ml) canned full-fat coconut milk

1½ teaspoons maple syrup

8 cups (2L) ice

2 cups (470ml) canned sweet red beans with their liquid (aka paht or ogura-an; see Notes)

1 cup (125g) fresh raspberries

½ cup (120ml) mini mochi rice cakes or balls (see Notes), your favorite flavor

2 cups (430g) Tahini Ice Cream (page 436) or store-bought plant-based vanilla ice cream

IN A LIQUID MEASURING cup with a pourable spout, whisk together the coconut milk and maple syrup until smooth.

In a high-powered blender, blend the ice on medium-high until it has the consistency of shaved, about 1 minute. Divide among four serving bowls.

Pour 2 tablespoons of the coconut milk mixture over each bowl of ice. Dividing evenly, top each with sweet red beans, raspberries, mini mochi rice cakes, and a scoop of ice cream. Drizzle any remaining coconut milk mixture over the top of each bowl.

Let sit for a few minutes to let some of the ice start to melt, and serve cold.

COOK'S NOTES

- If you don't have access to a great Asian market to find the sweetened red beans, you can make them by draining one 15-ounce/425g can adzuki beans and simmering them with 1 cup (200g) sugar for a few minutes until a syrup forms.

- Look for mini mochi rice cakes/balls at Nuts.com and other online sources.

Panetón Loaf Cake

Panettone, the traditional Christmas and New Year cake from Italy, might be even more popular in Peru, where it's called panetón. Food writer Nico Vera remembers visiting family in Lima during the holidays and seeing vendors pile pyramids of panetón on street corners and in supermarkets. The traditional cake calls for a sourdough starter, plus eggs and butter, and is baked in a tall pan that is hung upside down to cool, giving it a cottony, light texture. To make it vegan and streamline its preparation for the home cook, this recipe draws inspiration from Timothy Pakron's hummingbird cake in *Mississippi Vegan* and Isa Chandra Moskowitz's lemon-blueberry loaf in *Isa Does It*, but adds vermouth, cinnamon, orange, and pineapple to evoke the flavors of Peruvian panetón in loaf-cake form. In keeping with Nico's family tradition, enjoy the cake with vegan hot chocolate, such as Tahini Hot Chocolate (page 468) or the Mexican hot chocolate with the churros (page 427).

Makes 1 loaf (8 to 10 servings)

Time: Weekend

Storage: Keep in a sealed container at room temperature for up to 4 days, refrigerate for up to 7 days, or freeze for up to 3 months.

Cooking spray
⅓ cup (55g) canned pineapple chunks, drained
½ cup (120ml) Oat Milk (page 17) or store-bought plain oat milk
2 tablespoons unsweetened applesauce
¾ cup (150g) organic cane sugar
¼ cup (60ml) canola oil
2 tablespoons sweet vermouth, such as Dolin Rouge
2 teaspoons grated orange zest
1 teaspoon grated lemon zest
1 tablespoon fresh lemon juice
1 teaspoon vanilla extract
2 cups (250g) plus 1 tablespoon all-purpose flour
2½ teaspoons baking powder
1 teaspoon ground cinnamon
½ teaspoon fine sea salt
¼ cup (33g) assorted candied fruit

PREHEAT THE OVEN TO 350°F (180°C). Mist an 8 × 4-inch (20cm × 10cm) loaf pan with cooking spray.

In a tall container (or an immersion blender cup), combine the pineapple chunks, oat milk, and applesauce. Use an immersion blender to puree the mixture into a smooth sauce. (Alternatively, you can use a mini food processor.)

Transfer the puree to a large bowl and add the sugar, oil, vermouth, orange zest, lemon zest, lemon juice, and vanilla. Use a whisk to mix thoroughly. Sift in 2 cups (250g) of the flour, the baking powder, cinnamon, and salt. Stir until smooth, but don't overmix. Toss the candied fruit with the remaining 1 tablespoon flour, and fold it into the batter.

Use a spatula to transfer the thick batter into the pan. Bake until the top browns, the sides begin to pull away from the pan, and a skewer inserted into the center comes out clean, 50 minutes to 1 hour.

Remove the pan from the oven and let the cake cool in the pan for about 20 minutes. Run a knife around the edges of the cake and turn it out onto a wire rack to cool for at least 1 hour.

Serve warm or at room temperature.

Oatmeal Cookies

An oatmeal cookie doesn't need to remind you of breakfast, though there's nothing wrong with eating one or three with morning coffee. In this recipe, arrowroot powder provides the binding work that in nonvegan recipes is accomplished by eggs, and a little cinnamon provides a light spice that works whether the cookie is plain, flecked with coconut, or bursting with raisins or nuts. Getting personal is how you can find your preferred oatmeal cookie, but what's a constant is the nutty wholesomeness of the oats themselves—comforting and nostalgic, dressed up any way you like.

Makes 18 (without add-ins) to 24 (with add-ins) cookies

Time: Weekend

Storage: Store leftovers in an airtight container for up to 2 weeks or freeze for up to 3 months. You can also freeze the formed dough balls for up to 3 months and bake them directly from frozen, adding a few minutes to the baking time as needed.

⅔ cup (150g) vegan butter

¾ cup (150g) organic cane sugar

⅓ cup packed (75g) dark brown sugar

½ teaspoon vanilla extract

1½ cups (135g) rolled oats

1¼ cups (156g) all-purpose flour

3 tablespoons arrowroot powder

½ teaspoon baking soda

½ teaspoon ground cinnamon

1½ tablespoons Nut Milk (page 17), Oat Milk (page 17), Soy Milk (page 75), or store-bought plant-based milk

Optional add-ins: 1 cup (weight varies) unsweetened fine shredded coconut, chopped nuts of your choice, and/or raisins

IN A STAND MIXER fitted with the paddle, beat the butter on medium-high speed until smooth. Add both sugars and the vanilla and continue beating until light and fluffy. Scrape down the sides of the bowl.

In a bowl, whisk together the oats, flour, arrowroot, baking soda, and cinnamon. Add to the mixer and beat on medium-low speed until well combined. With the mixer running, stream in the almond milk and beat until the dough comes together in a ball around the paddle.

Add the coconut flakes, nuts, and/or raisins, if using. Cover and transfer the dough to the refrigerator to chill for at least 1 hour and up to 24 hours.

Position racks in the top and bottom thirds of the oven and preheat the oven to 350°F (180°C). Line two large baking sheets with parchment paper.

Use a 2-tablespoon cookie scoop (or a #30 disher) and your hands to form the dough into balls. Place the balls on the sheet pans 2 inches (5cm) apart.

Bake until dry to the touch on top and just starting to turn very light golden brown on the very edges, 15 to 17 minutes, switching racks and rotating the sheets front to back halfway through. (If you like softer, chewier cookies, err on the side of baking them less, and if you like them crisper, bake them longer.)

Let cool on the pans on wire racks for 10 minutes. Serve warm or transfer the cookies directly to the racks to continue cooling.

Any-Berry Mousse

I wrote in my book *Cool Beans* that mousse might be the easiest, smartest use of aquafaba, and I stand by that. In that book, I used it to make a simple plant-based version of Julia Child's chocolate mousse; it's particularly simple because of the setting powers of chocolate. But with the help of coconut cream and agar-agar, a vegan alternative to gelatin, it can also help make a fabulous berry mousse. Note that while this recipe is still pretty simple, you do need to build in a little chilling time, so you might want to make this the morning of (or the day before) you plan to serve it.

Makes 4 servings

Time: Weekend

Storage: Refrigerate the mousse for up to 3 days.

1 (13.6-ounce/403ml) can coconut cream, preferably Thai Kitchen

10 ounces (285g) raspberries, strawberries, or blackberries, or individually frozen berries (thawed to room temperature), plus more for garnish

½ cup (100g) plus 3 tablespoons sugar

½ teaspoon agar-agar powder

½ cup (120ml) aquafaba (from one 15-ounce/425g can no-salt-added chickpeas, shaken well)

½ teaspoon cream of tartar

Pinch of fine sea salt

PLACE THE CAN OF coconut cream in the freezer to chill, along with a stainless steel bowl.

In a medium saucepan, combine the berries and ½ cup (100g) of the sugar. Heat over medium heat, stirring, until the mixture comes to a simmer. Use an immersion blender to puree until smooth. (Or transfer to a food processor to puree, then return to the pan over medium heat).

Sprinkle the agar-agar over the mixture and whisk until the agar-agar has fully dissolved. Bring the mixture to a gentle boil and cook for 3 minutes, using a silicone spatula to frequently scrape the bottom of the pan to prevent scorching. (This is the minimum boiling time needed for the agar-agar to disperse, hydrate, and set.)

Take the metal bowl from the freezer and transfer the berry mixture to the bowl. Set up an ice bath (half ice, half water) in a larger bowl. Set the bowl with the berry mixture in the ice bath and stir until the mixture is cool to the touch and gently set. (If it's too firm, mash it well with a fork until it's loosened, which will help it combine with the coconut cream.)

Remove the can of coconut cream from the freezer and scoop the thickest part (the cream) into another bowl, reserving the thin liquid for another use, such as in smoothies. Add 1 tablespoon of the sugar and use an electric hand mixer to beat the cream on high speed until smooth and thick. Measure out ⅓ cup (80ml) of the whipped coconut cream into a small bowl, cover, and refrigerate until ready to serve. Add the chilled berry mixture to the rest of the coconut cream and beat until smooth.

Rinse and dry the mixer beaters. In another deep bowl, using the mixer, beat the aquafaba on high speed until it foams, thickens, and turns white. Add the cream of tartar and salt and beat until it forms soft peaks. (Be patient; this could take several minutes.) Add the remaining 2 tablespoons sugar and beat until the aquafaba turns glossy and forms stiff peaks.

Dollop the aquafaba into the bowl with the berry-coconut mixture and gently fold until just combined. Divide among four 6-ounce (180ml) ramekins, glasses, or other serving dishes, cover with small plates, and refrigerate until set, at least 2 hours and up to 3 days.

When ready to serve, whisk the reserved coconut cream to loosen, then dollop it on the mousses, garnish with berries, and serve cold.

Strawberries & Cream Cake

Lots of bakeries—Korean, Japanese, even American—sell petite cakes topped with whipped cream and fruit. This recipe uses aquafaba to bring the fluff. Here you whip it to stiff peaks, just like egg whites or heavy cream, to form the foundation of a frosting for this otherwise simple but dreamy cake.

Makes 6 to 8 servings

Time: Weekend

Storage: The assembled cake is best eaten when freshly made, but the unfrosted cake can be refrigerated for up to 1 week or frozen for up to 3 months before frosting and assembly. The frosting can be frozen for up to 1 month.

CAKE

Cooking spray or neutral vegetable oil, for the pan

¾ cup (180ml) Nut Milk (page 17), Oat Milk (page 17), Soy Milk (page 75), or store-bought plain plant-based milk

1½ teaspoons distilled white vinegar

1⅓ cups (166g) all-purpose flour

2 teaspoons baking powder

¼ teaspoon baking soda

¼ teaspoon fine sea salt

3 tablespoons (42g) unsalted vegan butter, at room temperature

½ cup (100g) organic cane sugar

3 tablespoons aquafaba (from canned no-salt-added chickpeas)

1 tablespoon vanilla extract

FROSTING

7 tablespoons aquafaba (from canned no-salt-added chickpeas)

¼ cup (50g) organic cane sugar

½ teaspoon agar-agar powder

½ teaspoon cream of tartar

¼ cup (31g) organic powdered sugar

1½ teaspoons vanilla extract

5 large strawberries, hulled and chopped into small pieces

10 large strawberries, hulled and halved lengthwise

MAKE THE CAKE: Preheat the oven to 350°F (180°C). Line a 7-inch (18cm) round cake pan with a round of parchment paper and mist with cooking spray or brush lightly with oil.

In a small bowl or liquid measuring cup with a spout, stir together the plant-based milk and the vinegar (see Note).

In a medium bowl, sift together the flour, baking powder, baking soda, and salt.

In a stand mixer fitted with the whisk (or in a bowl using an electric hand mixer), combine the butter and cane sugar and beat on high speed until fluffy and light, about 2 minutes. Add the milk/vinegar mixture, aquafaba, and vanilla. Beat until smooth.

Turn off the mixer, add the dry ingredients, and beat on medium-low until incorporated. Scrape down the sides of the bowl as needed.

Transfer the batter to the prepared cake pan. Tap the pan lightly on the counter to remove any air bubbles.

Bake until a toothpick inserted in the center comes out clean, 20 to 25 minutes.

Let the cake cool in the pan on a wire rack for 15 minutes, then turn the cake out onto the rack and let it cool to room temperature.

While the cake is cooling, make the frosting: In a small saucepan, combine the aquafaba, cane sugar, and agar-agar and bring to a gentle boil over medium heat. Boil for 3 minutes, stirring constantly, to prevent clumping. Transfer to a small but deep bowl and let cool to room temperature.

Using an electric hand mixer, beat the aquafaba/sugar mixture on high until the mixture forms stiff peaks, 7 to 8 minutes. Add the cream of tartar, powdered sugar, and vanilla. Continue beating on high until the frosting is stiff and glossy, 3 to 5 minutes. Gently fold in the chopped strawberries.

Once the cake has cooled, scoop a small amount of frosting onto it and spread a layer on the top and sides of the cake. Follow with the remaining frosting, using an offset spatula or the back of a spoon to spread it and swoosh it evenly around the top of the cake. Line the bottom perimeter of the cake with the halved strawberries, standing them upright.

Refrigerate the cake for 4 to 6 hours to let the frosting set. Remove it from the refrigerator about 20 minutes before serving.

COOK'S NOTE: Feel free to substitute ¾ cup (180ml) Tangy Coconut Cashew Buttermilk (page 23) for the mixture of plant-based milk and vinegar.

Tropical Banana Bread

This super-moist, gluten-free banana bread boasts some tropical twists: coconut and passion fruit puree, the latter of which gives this bread a tangy brightness. Coating the pan with coconut flakes and sesame seeds keeps the bread from sticking, while also creating a chewy-but-crisp crust reminiscent of a macaroon. Finish your loaf with a cashew/passion fruit drizzle, which makes for a healthier (and possibly better) alternative to frosting.

Makes one 9 × 5-inch loaf (8 to 12 servings)

Time: Weekend

Storage: Store leftovers in an airtight container at room temperature for up to 5 days, or freeze for up to 3 months. The finished bread can also be stored for up to 2 days before topping with the drizzle and garnishing just before serving.

BANANA BREAD
Melted coconut oil, for the loaf pan

⅓ cup (30g) plus 2 tablespoons fine unsweetened shredded coconut

1 tablespoon black sesame seeds

1¾ cups (280g) white rice flour (not sweet rice flour)

½ teaspoon baking powder

½ teaspoon baking soda

¾ teaspoon fine sea salt

½ cup (120ml) melted virgin coconut oil

¾ cup (150g) coconut sugar or organic cane sugar

1 cup (225g) mashed very ripe (spotted black) bananas (from 2 to 3 bananas)

¼ cup (60ml) passion fruit or guava puree, fresh or thawed frozen (see Note)

⅓ cup (80ml) Creamy Coconut Yogurt (page 23) or store-bought plain almond or coconut yogurt

⅔ cup (160ml) canned full-fat coconut milk

1 ripe banana, halved lengthwise

PASSION FRUIT DRIZZLE
¼ cup (35g) raw cashews

Boiling water

¼ cup (60ml) passion fruit or guava puree, fresh or thawed frozen

¼ cup (60ml) canned full-fat coconut milk

1 tablespoon agave syrup or maple syrup

1 fresh passion fruit (optional), for garnish

MAKE THE BANANA BREAD: Preheat the oven to 375°F (190°C). Lightly grease a 9 × 5-inch (23cm × 13cm) loaf pan with coconut oil.

In a small bowl, mix together 2 tablespoons of the shredded coconut and the sesame seeds. Pour the mixture into the loaf pan and shake around to coat the inside.

In a large bowl, combine the remaining ⅓ cup (30g) shredded coconut, the rice flour, baking powder, baking soda, and salt.

In a bowl, using an electric mixer, beat the coconut oil with the sugar on medium speed until fluffy, 1 to 2 minutes. Reduce the speed to low and add half of the flour mixture. Once combined, add the mashed bananas, passion fruit puree, yogurt, and coconut milk. Add the remaining flour mixture and mix until just combined. Scrape the batter into the pan and smooth out the top.

Bake until the bread begins to set on top, about 12 minutes. Remove the pan from the oven. Leave the oven on and reduce the oven temperature to 350°F (180°C).

Top the bread with the banana halves, lightly pressing into the surface. Return to the oven and bake until golden and a tester inserted into the center comes out clean, 45 to 55 minutes.

Let the bread cool completely in the pan. Run a knife around the inside of the pan to release the bread. Turn out onto a wire rack.

While the bread is baking and/or cooling, make the passion fruit drizzle: In a small bowl, cover the cashews with the hot water and let soak for 30 minutes to soften.

Drain the cashews and transfer to a food processor. Add the passion fruit puree, coconut milk, and agave and blend until silky and smooth. Refrigerate it while the bread bakes and cools.

To serve, generously drizzle the cooled loaf with the passion fruit mixture. If desired, add pops of fresh passion fruit pulp here and there before cutting.

COOK'S NOTE: Look for passion fruit or guava puree in the freezer section of international grocery stores; thaw before using.

Rice Pudding with Apricots, Pistachios & Pomegranate

To make this simple dessert, you simmer Arborio rice (known for making creamy risotto) with coconut milk, sugar, and orange zest. While you can use store-bought coconut milk, homemade is really the way to go here. Store-bought canned coconut milk, even the light variety, is far thicker and richer than the kind you can make at home. Use the recipe for Nut Milk (page 17) to make coconut milk in just a few extra minutes, using 2 cups (180g) unsweetened flaked or shredded coconut for the 4 cups (950ml) water, and this rice pudding will be just the right amount of rich and refreshing. (Or, in a pinch, instead of canned coconut milk, use the unsweetened coconut milk beverage that comes in a refrigerated carton.)

The pudding gets most of its sweetness from dried apricots, which are hydrated in boiling water, then blended with orange juice into a gorgeous puree.

Makes 4 servings

Time: Weekend

Storage: Refrigerate the pudding and puree separately for up to 4 days.

⅔ cup (85g) dried apricot halves

1 cup (240ml) boiling water

¾ cup (145g) Arborio rice

4 cups (950ml) homemade coconut milk
(see Nut Milk, page 17)

2 (4-inch/10cm) strips of orange zest

1 tablespoon organic cane sugar

½ teaspoon fine sea salt

½ cup (120ml) freshly squeezed orange juice

1 teaspoon vanilla extract

Crushed pistachios, pomegranate seeds, and orange zest, for garnish

IN A HEATPROOF BOWL, combine the apricots and boiling water. Cover with a plate or lid and soak the apricots until they are soft and hydrated, about 10 minutes.

While the apricots are hydrating, in a medium saucepan, combine the rice, coconut milk, orange zest strips, sugar, and salt. Bring to a boil over medium heat, reduce to a simmer and cook, stirring occasionally, until the rice is tender but the mixture is still very loose, 10 to 15 minutes. The pudding will thicken significantly as it cools.

Drain the apricots and transfer them to a blender. Add the orange juice and blend at low speed, gradually increasing to medium, until creamy, about 30 seconds. Pour the puree into a container, cover, and refrigerate until chilled, about 4 hours.

When the pudding is ready, discard the orange zest and stir in the vanilla. Transfer to a container, cover, and refrigerate until chilled, about 4 hours.

To serve, spoon the rice pudding into a bowl or glass. Add a dollop of the apricot puree and top with the pistachios, pomegranate seeds, and orange zest.

Quinoa Oat Milk Pudding

Arroz con leche, or rice pudding, is ubiquitous in Latinx food culture, but countries around the world—Asia, the Middle East, Europe—prepare their own versions. Spanish colonial foodways introduced arroz con leche to Peru, and the dessert is most popular in Lima, where families often serve it with a purple corn pudding to make a *combinado*, or dessert combo. This variation features the ancestral Incan mother grain, quinoa, instead of rice. Oat milk offers its creamy texture, while star anise and cinnamon bring the kind of familiar warmth that will remind you of the sweet comforts of home.

Makes about 1⅓ cups (2 servings)

Time: Weekday

Storage: Refrigerate for up to 3 days.

½ cup (85g) white quinoa

1¾ cups (420ml) Oat Milk (page 17) or store-bought plain oat milk

Strips of zest from 1 small orange

1 cinnamon stick

1 whole star anise

¼ cup (50g) organic cane sugar

¼ teaspoon vanilla extract

Lemon zest, for garnish

IN A 2-QUART (2L) saucepan, combine the quinoa, 1½ cups (350ml) of the oat milk, orange zest, cinnamon stick, and star anise. Bring to a simmer over medium heat, reduce the heat to low, and cook, stirring occasionally, until the quinoa is cooked and liquid reduced, about 15 minutes.

Stir in the sugar, vanilla, and remaining ¼ cup (60ml) oat milk. Stir for about 5 minutes to achieve a creamy consistency. Remove from the heat.

Remove and compost the cinnamon stick, star anise, and orange zest. Serve the pudding warm in small ramekins and garnish with lemon zest.

Strawberry Cream Cheese Brownies

Here's an easy way to take brownies to the next level: Swirl the top with cream cheese and strawberry jam. The base brownies are bittersweet and fudgy, while the marbled topping offers two counterpoints: tartness from the cream cheese and sweetness (plus a wonderfully sticky glaze) from the jam.

Makes 9 brownies

Time: Weekday

Storage: Store in an airtight container at room temperature for up to 2 days, refrigerate for up to 1 week, or freeze, well wrapped, for up to 3 months.

Neutral oil, such as grapeseed, for the pan

1 cup (240g) Velvety Tofu Cream Cheese (page 26) or store-bought vegan cream cheese, such as Kite Hill or Miyoko's

¾ cup (150g) plus 1 tablespoon organic cane sugar

1¼ cups (300ml) hot water

2 teaspoons vanilla extract

1 teaspoon instant espresso powder

⅓ cup (80ml) grapeseed or other neutral oil

1¾ cups (218g) all-purpose flour

1 cup (95g) cocoa powder

1 teaspoon baking powder

½ teaspoon ground cinnamon

½ teaspoon fine sea salt

⅓ cup (85g) bittersweet vegan chocolate chips

½ cup (120ml) strawberry jam, stirred to loosen

POSITION A RACK IN the middle of the oven and preheat the oven to 350°F (180°C). Lightly oil an 8-inch (20cm) square baking pan.

In a small bowl, whisk the cream cheese to loosen, add 1 tablespoon of the sugar, and whisk to combine.

In a medium bowl, whisk together the hot water, vanilla, and espresso powder. Whisk in the remaining ¾ cup (150g) sugar and the oil until the sugar dissolves.

In a large bowl, whisk together the flour, cocoa powder, baking powder, cinnamon, and salt. Make a well in the center and slowly pour in the sugar/oil mixture, stirring with a rubber spatula or wooden spoon until smooth. Stir in the chocolate chips.

Scrape the batter evenly into the prepared pan, smoothing the top. Spoon large dollops of the cream cheese all over the top of the batter, about 1 inch (2.5cm) apart, then spoon dollops of the strawberry jam on top of the cream cheese. Drag a toothpick through the dollops, going ½ inch (1.3cm) or so into the batter underneath, to create a marbled pattern.

Bake until a skewer inserted along the edges comes out clean, but in the center comes out with a small bit of wet batter or crumbs, 30 to 35 minutes.

Transfer the pan to a wire rack and let the brownies cool in the pan for at least 30 minutes to 1 hour. Cut into 9 squares (in a 3 × 3 grid) to serve.

Sweet Potato Crème Brûlée

This dessert exemplifies the easy elegance that can be found in using an everyday ingredient in a classic and elevated way. Sweet potatoes are roasted with a heavy shower of orange zest and brown sugar, then blitzed and zinged with warm autumnal spices and creamy, nutty coconut milk. Cornstarch imparts the smooth textural density of a traditional crème brûlée, and of course another sprinkling of sugar gets torched for that signature crunchy topping. Serve this in individual 1-cup (240ml) ramekins, or in one big batch if desired.

Makes 6 servings

Time: Weekend

Storage: Refrigerate for up to 5 days.

2 large sweet potatoes (about 1 pound/450g each), scrubbed and halved lengthwise

1 tablespoon melted coconut oil, refined or unrefined

2 tablespoons finely grated orange zest (from 1 large navel orange)

¼ cup packed (55g) plus 1 teaspoon light brown sugar

1 (13.5-ounce/400ml) can full-fat coconut milk

1 teaspoon vanilla extract

½ teaspoon Angostura bitters (optional)

½ teaspoon fine sea salt

½ teaspoon ground cinnamon

1 teaspoon cornstarch

2 teaspoons cold water

¼ cup organic cane sugar

PREHEAT THE OVEN TO 400°F (200°C).

Brush the cut sides of the 4 sweet potato halves with the melted coconut oil. Sprinkle each half with 1½ teaspoons of the orange zest and ¼ teaspoon brown sugar. Place the sweet potato halves, cut-side down, on a large sheet pan.

Roast until very tender, about 40 minutes.

Transfer the sweet potatoes to a plate and let them sit until cool enough to handle, at least 10 to 15 minutes. Remove and compost the sweet potato skins (or save for a snack!) and transfer the flesh to a blender.

Add the coconut milk, vanilla, bitters (if using), salt, cinnamon, and remaining ¼ cup (55g) brown sugar. Blend on low for 1 minute. Then blend on medium-high speed until the mixture is very smooth, about 2 minutes.

While it is blending, in a small bowl, make a slurry by combining the cornstarch and cold water and whisking with a fork until smooth.

Transfer the sweet potato mixture to a medium saucepan. (If it's lumpy, press it through a fine-mesh sieve first.) Add the slurry and whisk to combine. Heat over medium-low heat, stirring constantly, until the mixture—which is already thick—bubbles and thickens a little more, 5 to 7 minutes.

While the mixture is cooking, set six 1-cup (240ml) single-serve ramekins on a sheet pan or platter.

Using a ladle, divide the sweet potato mixture among the ramekins. Transfer to the refrigerator and refrigerate, uncovered, for 2 hours to cool, or freeze for 1 hour. (If desired, you can instead pour the mixture into one 6-cup/1.4L bowl for serving.)

To serve, sprinkle 2 teaspoons granulated sugar on the surface of each ramekin. Use a kitchen torch to flambé the sugar until it melts and a hard golden crust forms. Allow the sugared crust to cool for at least 2 minutes before serving.

Pumpkin Cake with American
Buttercream (page 410)

Vanilla Cake Four Ways

Vanilla cake can go in so many directions, with very simple replacements—but that's just the magic of vegan baking. Arrowroot powder in the base of this recipe works as a flavorless egg replacement so that the vanilla extract takes center stage, but swapping it for mashed ripe banana or pumpkin puree takes the same recipe to completely different places. The coconut variation requires a change in the milk and the use of virgin coconut oil rather than the odorless refined; mixing the cane and brown sugar also deepens the tropical flavor, as the molasses evokes an aged rum.

Makes one 8-inch cake or 12 cupcakes

Time: Weekday

Storage: Keep covered at room temperature for up to 3 days. Freeze in an airtight container for up to 2 months.

Coconut oil, for the pan

1¼ cups (300ml) Nut Milk (page 17), Soy Milk (page 17), Oat Milk (page 75), or store-bought plain plant-based milk

1 teaspoon apple cider vinegar

1 cup (200g) organic cane sugar

½ cup (120ml) refined coconut oil, melted and still warm, plus more for greasing the pan

2 teaspoons vanilla extract

1⅔ cups (207g) all-purpose flour

2 tablespoons arrowroot powder

¾ teaspoon baking powder

½ teaspoon baking soda

¼ teaspoon fine sea salt

POSITION A RACK IN the middle of the oven and preheat the oven to 350°F (180°C). Use a little coconut oil to grease an 8-inch (20cm) cake pan, then line the bottom of the pan with a round of parchment. (For cupcakes, line 12 cups of a muffin tin with paper liners.)

In a small bowl or liquid measuring cup with a spout, whisk together the milk and vinegar.

In a large bowl, whisk together the sugar, coconut oil, and vanilla until smooth. (If the coconut oil starts to solidify and form lumps, microwave on high, for just a few seconds at a time, to remelt it, and whisk again.) In another bowl, whisk together the flour, arrowroot, baking powder, baking soda, and salt.

Add the milk to the wet ingredients and whisk until all is combined. Add the dry ingredients to the wet and whisk until a thick batter has formed without lumps.

Pour the batter into the prepared pan. (Or divide the batter evenly among the muffin cups.)

Bake until a toothpick stuck into the center comes out clean, 30 to 35 minutes for the cake (about 20 to 25 minutes for the cupcakes).

Transfer the pan to a wire rack and let the cake cool to room temperature in the pan before removing for serving or storage.

COOK'S NOTE: If you want to frost the cake, wrap it in beeswax wrap and refrigerate for at least 2 hours or up to 3 days. Frost immediately after removing it from the refrigerator, and let it come to room temperature for at least 2 hours before serving. If you freeze the cake, let it thaw in the refrigerator before frosting.

VARIATIONS

Banana Cake

Omit the arrowroot. Whisk ½ cup (110g) mashed very ripe banana into the wet ingredients.

Pumpkin Cake

Omit the arrowroot. Whisk ½ cup (120g) unsweetened pumpkin puree into the wet ingredients. Whisk 1 teaspoon pumpkin pie spice into the dry ingredients.

Coconut Cake

Instead of any other nondairy milk, use 1¼ cups (300ml) canned full-fat coconut milk. Instead of refined coconut oil, use virgin coconut oil. Omit ½ cup (100g) of the cane sugar and replace with ½ cup packed (110g) light brown sugar. Stir 1 cup (85g) unsweetened shredded coconut into the batter before pouring into the pan and baking.

Persimmon Biscuits

Persimmons are among the most delicious fruits you will ever eat: intensely sweet and packed with flavor, nutrients, and fiber. Of the two widely available types of persimmons, Fuyu (which looks like a squat miniature pumpkin) and Hachiya (which looks like an oblong tomato), the latter will also give you a mouthful of moisture-absorbing tannin if you eat it when it's unripe, making it hard to swallow, much less enjoy. This recipe uses the fruit to make tender biscuits, and skirts the whole is-it-ripe-enough issue by relying on dried persimmons, or gotgam as they are called in Korea. The fruits are in season in late fall and winter, but these delightful biscuits, with just a hint of sweetness, can be made and enjoyed year-round.

Makes 16 servings
___

Time: Weekday
___

Storage: Refrigerate the persimmon puree for up to 5 days or freeze for up to 6 months. Refrigerate the biscuits for up to 1 week or freeze for up to 6 months.

½ cup (42g) chopped dried persimmons

½ cup (120ml) water, plus more as needed

½ cup (120ml) plus 2 tablespoons Nut Milk (page 17), Oat Milk (page 17), Soy Milk (page 75), or store-bought plain plant-based milk

1 tablespoon apple cider vinegar

2½ cups (313g) all-purpose flour, plus more for dusting

¼ cup (50g) organic cane sugar

2 teaspoons baking powder

½ teaspoon baking soda

Pinch of fine sea salt

4 tablespoons (56g) cold unsalted vegan butter, cut into small cubes, plus more for greasing a pan

¼ cup (60g) Creamy Coconut Yogurt (page 23) or store-bought vegan sour cream

Softened vegan butter, for the pan

PREHEAT THE OVEN TO 350°F (180°C).

In a blender or mini food processor, combine the persimmons and water and blend, adding more water 1 to 2 tablespoons at a time if needed to get the blades moving. Transfer to a liquid measuring cup. You should have ½ cup plus 1 tablespoon puree; stir in a little water if needed to reach that amount.

In a large bowl, whisk together the plant-based milk and vinegar (see Note). Reserve 1 tablespoon of the persimmon puree, and transfer the remaining ½ cup to the milk/vinegar mixture and whisk until smooth.

In a food processor, combine the flour, sugar, baking powder, baking soda, and salt and process briefly until combined. Add the butter and sour cream and pulse until the texture is pebbly, about 20 times.

Transfer the flour mixture to the bowl of liquid ingredients and use a spoon or rubber spatula to slowly incorporate the mixture until just barely combined.

Generously dust a work surface with flour. Turn the dough out onto the surface (it will be pretty sticky). Gently fold the dough in half, rotate it 90 degrees, and fold in half again. Continue folding and rotating, sprinkling with flour as needed to prevent sticking, for about 2 minutes.

Form the dough into a roughly 7-inch (18cm) square 1 inch (2.5cm) thick. Using a sharp knife, cut the square evenly into quarters, then cut each of those 4 pieces into quarters again to yield 16 square biscuits.

Lightly grease a large sheet pan with some butter. Transfer the biscuits to the pan, leaving at least ½ inch (1.3cm) of space between them.

In a small bowl, whisk together the remaining 1 tablespoon of persimmon puree and the remaining 2 tablespoons milk. Brush the top of the biscuits with the mixture.

Bake until the biscuits have risen and the tops are golden brown, about 25 minutes. Serve warm or at room temperature.

COOK'S NOTE: If you have the Tangy Coconut Cashew Buttermilk (page 23) on hand, use that instead of the plant-based milk/vinegar mixture.

Creamy Chia Pudding

All hail the power of chia seeds! Not only are they nutritional powerhouses, they have a gelling ability that seems magical, which makes them so useful in creating plant-based puddings. I got the idea from Wayne Coates's 2012 book *Chia* to grind the seeds up so the pudding is smooth, but if you'd rather leave them whole, blend the other ingredients first and stir in the seeds before refrigerating the pudding. This recipe works with a variety of fruit and other ingredients; just be sure to taste and adjust the sweetener and/or citrus juice to dial in the balance you love.

Makes 4 to 6 servings

Time: Weekend

Storage: Refrigerate for up to 3 days.

3½ cups (830ml; see Notes) peeled, chopped, and otherwise prepped ripe fruit, such as berries, stone fruit, mango, or pineapple

1 (13.5-ounce/400ml) can full-fat coconut milk, shaken well

½ cup (80g) chia seeds, preferably white (see Notes), or ⅓ cup (40g) ground chia

2 tablespoons agave syrup or Wildflower Cider Syrup (page 35), plus more to taste

1 tablespoon fresh lemon or lime juice, plus more to taste

1 teaspoon vanilla extract

¼ teaspoon fine sea salt

2 teaspoons finely grated fresh lemon or lime zest, for garnish

Toasted nuts, for garnish

IN A HIGH-POWERED BLENDER, combine 3 cups (700ml) of the fruit, the coconut milk, chia seeds, agave syrup, citrus juice, vanilla, and salt. Blend for 1 to 2 minutes to form a smooth pudding. Taste and add more agave syrup and/or citrus juice as needed.

Divide the pudding among individual cups or transfer to a large container. Cover and refrigerate until cold and set to the texture of custard, about 8 hours.

Garnish with the citrus zest, nuts, and remaining ½ cup (120ml) fruit. Serve cold.

COOK'S NOTES

- The gram weight of 3½ cups will vary with the fruit, so it's easier to use the volume measure. However, the weights will be somewhere in the range of 125 to 165 grams per cup.

- Using white chia seeds will help ensure a more vibrant color for the fruit puddings, but if you can find only black ones, use them; the taste is identical, and both the black and white chia seeds thicken liquids in the same way.

VARIATIONS

Chocolate Chia Pudding

Omit the fruit and use 2 cups (470ml) water and ½ cup (47g) Dutch process cocoa powder. For the citrus juice, use 2 tablespoons orange juice instead of lemon or lime. Garnish with orange zest, chocolate shavings, cacao nibs, and almonds or hazelnuts.

Peanut Butter Chia Pudding

Omit the fruit, citrus juice, and citrus zest. Use 2 cups (470ml) water and ½ cup (125g) creamy peanut butter. Garnish with crushed peanuts. Swirl in 4 tablespoons jam for a PB&J effect if you'd like.

Chestnut Bread

Korean and Japanese bakeries have all sorts of breads, but none is more popular than milk bread, fluffy and impossibly tender. Sort of like a brioche, the bread peels off in lovely layers, and stays soft for days. The secret to its texture is in the starter, which is based on a cooked flour/water paste called tangzhong. Chestnut bread is essentially milk bread stuffed with chestnuts, a snack-time favorite in Korea that add a little nutty heartiness to this recipe. It goes beautifully with fruit preserves and coffee.

You'll need to plan ahead for this recipe, as the starter needs to be refrigerated for between 3 and 24 hours.

Makes one 9 × 5-inch loaf (8 to 10 servings)

Time: Weekend

Storage: Refrigerate for up to 1 week.

TANGZHONG
2 tablespoons bread flour
½ cup (120ml) water

DOUGH
Softened vegan butter, for the bowl and pan
2¾ cups (370g) bread flour, plus more for dusting your hands and the countertop
3 tablespoons organic cane sugar
2¾ teaspoons soy milk powder
2¼ teaspoons instant yeast
1½ teaspoons fine sea salt
¾ teaspoon baking powder
⅓ cup (80ml) Nut Milk (page 17), Oat Milk (page 17), Soy Milk (page 75), or store-bought plain plant-based milk
5 tablespoons aquafaba (from one 15-ounce/425g can no-salt-added chickpeas)
2 tablespoons plus 1 teaspoon (33g) unsalted vegan butter
5 ounces (140g) peeled roasted chestnuts, cut into ½-inch (1.3cm) pieces (1 cup)

GLAZE
1 tablespoon Nut Milk (page 17), Oat Milk (page 17), Soy Milk (page 75), or store-bought plain plant-based milk
1 teaspoon maple syrup

MAKE THE TANGZHONG: In a nonstick pan over medium-low heat, stir together the flour and water. Cook, stirring constantly, until the mixture is smooth, thick, and paste-like, about 10 minutes. Transfer to a small airtight container and refrigerate for at least 3 hours and up to 24 hours.

Remove the tangzhong from the refrigerator and let it sit at room temperature for 1 hour before making the dough.

Make the dough: Use a little vegan butter to grease a large bowl and a 9 × 5-inch (23cm × 13cm) nonstick loaf pan.

In a stand mixer fitted with the paddle, combine the flour, sugar, soy powder, yeast, salt, and baking powder. Mix on low speed to combine. Add the plant-based milk, aquafaba, and the tangzhong. Beat on medium speed until a dough begins to form. Add the vegan butter, increase the speed to medium-high, and beat until the dough is smooth, bouncy, and a little sticky, 10 to 12 minutes.

Dust your hands with flour and shape the dough into a ball. Transfer it to the greased bowl, cover with a plate, and set it in a warm place until the dough has doubled and when you poke it with a finger, it leaves a clean hole that does not readily bounce back, 1 hour 15 minutes to 1½ hours.

Lightly flour a work surface.

Punch down the dough, turn it out onto the work surface and divide it into 3 equal pieces. Cover two of the pieces with a clean kitchen towel to keep them from drying out. Fold the remaining piece in half, flip it over, and fold it in half once more. Using both hands, shape the piece into a compact ball, taking care to handle the dough as little as possible. Repeat for the other two pieces of dough, cover with the towel, and let them rest for about 15 minutes.

Working with one piece of the dough at a time, use a rolling pin to flatten the ball into a long oval, about 8 × 4 inches (20cm × 10cm). Position the dough so that it is horizontal (one of the long sides is facing you). Sprinkle one-third of the chestnuts over the dough. Take the long bottom edge and roll the dough up from the bottom like a jelly roll or cinnamon roll. Use your fingers to pinch and seal the ends and the seam.

Gently rotate the roll so that it is now vertical (one of the short sides is facing you). Starting from the bottom, roll the dough up again, this time into a very thick log. Gently transfer the roll into your greased loaf pan, seam-side down. Repeat for the remaining two pieces of dough, nestling them against one another in the pan.

Cover the pan with the kitchen towel and let it proof until the dough rises enough to peek over the edge of the pan and is firm to the touch, 25 to 40 minutes. (Be careful not to let it proof for too long.)

While the dough is proofing, preheat the oven to 350°F (180°C).

Make the glaze: In a small bowl, mix together the milk and maple syrup. When the dough is ready, gently brush the glaze all over the top of the dough.

Bake until the top is golden brown, about 45 minutes.

Remove from the oven and let the bread cool in the pan for 15 minutes. Use an offset spatula or small knife to help gently remove the bread from the pan and transfer to a wire rack to cool completely before cutting and serving.

Royal Icing Four Ways

Royal icing is the easiest way to decorate cake or cookies, and it is a wonderful reason to save aquafaba from cans of chickpeas. This recipe stands up well to food coloring and is thick enough to pipe onto cookies for holiday decorations. Glaze cakes with it, too. Traditional royal icing calls for egg whites or meringue powder, but using aquafaba makes for an excellent use of something that could go to waste and it is a seamless replacement for the egg white.

Makes 2 cups

Time: Weekday

Storage: Store in an airtight container in the fridge for up to 2 weeks.

- 4 cups (500g) organic powdered sugar
- ½ cup (100g) aquafaba (from one 15-ounce/425g can no-salt-added chickpeas)
- 1 teaspoon vanilla extract

MEASURE THE POWDERED SUGAR into a bowl, then whisk in the aquafaba and vanilla until combined.

VARIATIONS

Chocolate Royal Icing

Whisk ½ cup (47g) cocoa powder with the sugar before adding the aquafaba and vanilla.

Lemon Royal Icing

Whisk 2 tablespoons grated lemon zest and 1 tablespoon lemon juice in with the aquafaba and vanilla.

Orange Royal Icing

Whisk 2 tablespoons grated orange zest and 1 tablespoon orange juice in with the aquafaba and vanilla.

Shortbread Four Ways

Shortbread has a short list of ingredients by its very nature, but, as this recipe shows, that's what makes it endlessly adaptable to any season and any flavor profile. It's wonderful to dress these cookies up with Royal Icing (page 459), make sandwich cookies with a little bit of jam or Fruit Curd (page 434), or simply dust them with powdered sugar to snack on with afternoon coffee or tea. Change up the spice blends, add different extracts, and use different sugars for varied results.

Makes 24 cookies

Time: Weekend

Storage: Store in an airtight container at room temperature for up to 3 days, or freeze for up to 1 month. The dough can be frozen for up to 3 months before shaping and baking.

> 7 ounces (200g) store-bought vegan butter, such as Miyoko's
> ½ cup (100g) organic cane sugar
> 1 teaspoon vanilla extract
> 2½ cups (315g) all-purpose flour

IN A STAND MIXER fitted with the paddle (or in a bowl using an electric hand mixer fitted with whisk), beat the butter on medium-high speed until smooth. Add the sugar and vanilla and beat until the mixture is well combined, with a sandy texture. Reduce the mixer speed to low and add the flour in three parts, beating each time until combined before adding more, and continue to beat until the dough comes together around the paddle.

Transfer the dough to a piece of parchment paper and use the paper to help you shape it into a cylinder about 2 inches (5cm) in diameter or square off the cylinder to make a 2-inch rectangular log. Keeping it wrapped in the parchment, transfer to the refrigerator, and chill for at least 1 hour.

Position racks in the top and bottom thirds of the oven and preheat the oven to 350°F (180°C). Line two sheet pans with parchment paper.

Slice the dough into ½-inch (1.3cm) rounds and transfer them to the lined sheet pans, 1 inch (2.5cm) apart. (If the dough becomes very soft, place the sheets with cut cookies into the fridge for 15 to 30 minutes to firm up again.)

Bake the cookies until matte on top and golden brown on the bottom, about 12 minutes, rotating the sheets top to bottom and front to back halfway through the baking time.

Transfer the sheet pans to wire racks and let the cookies cool fully on the pans before serving or storing.

VARIATIONS

Chocolate Shortbread

Reduce the all-purpose flour to 2 cups (250g) and whisk ⅔ cup (60g) cocoa powder into the flour before adding to the butter/sugar mixture.

Chai Masala Shortbread

Whisk 2 teaspoons ground chai masala into the flour before adding to the butter/sugar mixture.

Gingerbread-Spiced Shortbread

Replace the cane sugar with ½ cup packed (90g) dark brown sugar and ½ cup (150g) blackstrap molasses. Increase the all-purpose flour to 2¾ cups (345g). Whisk 2 teaspoons gingerbread spice* into the flour before adding to the butter/sugar mixture.

*If you don't have gingerbread spice, use this:
¾ teaspoon each ground cinnamon + ground ginger,
¼ teaspoon each ground allspice + grated nutmeg,
⅛ teaspoon each ground black pepper + ground cloves.

Opposite: Dough ready to bake for, from left, Chai Masala Shortbread, Chocolate Shortbread, and Vanilla Shortbread

Master Kombucha

I've been making my own kombucha for so many years I can practically do it in my sleep. Once you get the hang of it, it can become part of your routine, too, and if you're a commercial kombucha buyer like I used to be, you'll marvel at how much money you can save. Kombucha, for the uninitiated, is fermented tea, and while some of the purported health benefits are obviously exaggerated, what's clear is that it gives you all the many benefits of drinking tea and consuming probiotics. Better yet, it's simply delicious, especially when you flavor it to your liking.

You make kombucha by brewing a strong tea, sweetening it in a big jug, then adding a SCOBY (symbiotic colony of bacteria and yeast) and letting it work its magic for a week or two. Then you transfer it to smaller bottles, add flavorings, and seal it up for a secondary fermentation. Similar to traditionally made champagne, it gets fizzy under pressure, providing natural carbonation.

The sugar is needed for that fermentation and fizz, so don't reduce it. Also, don't use flavored tea (or herbal tea), and don't add any flavorings to the first fermentation, or your kombucha may not brew correctly.

The secondary fermentation is when you get creative with your flavorings. I've tried many techniques, including the popular method of adding a little fruit juice. But after much trial and error, I've settled on the use of freeze-dried fruit because of the intense concentration of its flavor and because it's shelf-stable, meaning I can have a half-dozen or so options at the ready without needing to make a trip to the market. I also always use crystallized ginger, because it adds that punch of ginger spice and brings with it just a pinch of extra sugar to jump-start the carbonation.

You'll need some special equipment for this, but it's relatively inexpensive, long-lasting, and well worth it. Note that I highly recommend bottles that have a twist-style cap, not a flip-top cap, because if your kombucha does its job and gets really bubbly, the twist-style caps let you open the bottle gradually, releasing a little of the pressure at a time and (hopefully) preventing an eruption. Take it from me; once you've wiped kombucha off your ceiling a time or two, you figure out a solution. My favorite online sources for kombucha equipment are CulturesforHealth.com and Fermentaholics.com.

The most important ingredient is the SCOBY itself. You can grow one from scratch with unflavored store-bought kombucha, vinegar, and time, but I think it's a lot easier to ask around to see if anyone you know might give you one. (You need to "cast off" part of your SCOBY virtually every time you make kombucha, as with a sourdough starter, so you'll have plenty to give away.) Even easier, you can order one online: Look for fresh, not dehydrated, and it'll save you time getting it going.

THE EQUIPMENT

A 1-gallon (3.8L) wide-mouth glass jar for the first fermentation

Three 32-ounce (950ml) amber growler-style kombucha bottles with airtight polycone-insert twist caps for the second fermentation

Temperature strip

Coffee filter or tight-woven cloth (such as from a clean T-shirt)

Rubber band

Heating mat (if your kitchen is particularly cool and/or you're making kombucha in the winter)

A funnel that fits the kombucha bottles

Makes three 32-ounce bottles (12 servings, plus more to start the next batch)

Time: Project

Storage: Refrigerate for up to 3 weeks.

12 cups (2.8L) filtered water, plus more as needed (you'll use less in subsequent batches)

2 tablespoons loose unflavored black or green tea leaves (not herbal), or a mixture, or 8 tea bags

1 cup (200g) organic cane sugar

1 SCOBY, plus any liquid that comes with it

½ cup (85g) chopped crystallized ginger

½ cup packed (17g) organic freeze-dried fruit (such as Natierra), preferably raspberry, strawberry, pineapple, mango, or blueberry, or a combination, broken up if needed to fit into the bottles

Optional flavor enhancers (see page 464)

IN A SMALL SAUCEPAN, heat 2 cups (470ml) of the water to 212°F (100°C) if using black tea (or a combination); or to 175°F (79°C) if using green tea. Add the tea, let steep for 10 minutes, then strain out the leaves or remove the tea bags.

RECIPE CONTINUES ON NEXT PAGE

Wash the 1-gallon (3.8L) jar with hot, soapy water, dry, then pour the tea into the gallon jar and add the sugar. Swirl or stir until the sugar dissolves. Add the remaining 10 cups (2.4L) water, then add the SCOBY and any liquid that came with it, plus more water as needed to fill the jug up to the bottom of its neck. Top the jar with a coffee filter or a tightly woven cloth and secure with a rubber band.

Place the jar out of direct sunlight in a spot that can maintain a temperature of 75° to 85°F (24° to 29°C). (If your house is too cool for that, use a heating mat until the kombucha reaches that temperature, checking it by sticking a temperature strip on the side of the jar.)

Let the kombucha ferment for 1 to 3 weeks, depending on the temperature. (The warmer it is, the faster the kombucha will ferment.) Start tasting it after 1 week. When it's pleasantly tart but not vinegary—it tastes like unflavored kombucha rather than sweet tea—it's ready to bottle.

Wash the 32-ounce (950ml) jars and lids with hot, soapy water, and dry them.

To each bottle, add the crystallized ginger and freeze-dried fruit, plus any optional flavor enhancers.

Transfer the SCOBY to a clean dish, remove the bottom layer of the SCOBY, and give to a friend, compost, or save to add to a smoothie or two. Stir the kombucha in the gallon jar, then use a funnel to fill each of the 32-ounce (950ml) jars with kombucha, coming as close to the top of the jar as possible, leaving 1 inch (2.5cm) or less of headspace. (Reserve the remaining 2 to 3 cups/470ml to 700ml of kombucha for the next batch.) Tightly screw on the caps and put them in a cool, dark place for secondary fermentation.

To start another batch, wash and dry the gallon jar, then make the tea, sweeten it, and this time add 10 cups (2.4L) water plus the reserved 2 to 3 cups (470ml to 700ml) of kombucha and the SCOBY. (If you want to take a break between batches, you can refrigerate the 2 to 3 cups of kombucha with the SCOBY in a jar with an airtight lid; it will go dormant while waiting for its next tea-fermenting adventure.)

After 1 to 2 days, very carefully and slowly open one of the 32-ounce jars: If it sounds fizzy when you start to unscrew the lid, sit the bottle in a bowl to catch any kombucha that might run out. Continue gradually unscrewing it, going particularly slowly if you can feel pressure, and stopping to let the pressure escape—and any kombucha to flow into the bowl. Keep at this until you're able to fully remove the lid. Pour some kombucha to enjoy, tightly reseal the bottle, and transfer it to the refrigerator, where it will keep for weeks. (If the kombucha did not fizz at all when you started to unscrew the lid, retighten it and leave it at room temperature for another day, and check again.)

OPTIONAL FLAVOR ENHANCERS

1 split vanilla bean, cut into 3 pieces: particularly good with raspberry or strawberry

¼ cup (9g) dried tulsi (holy basil) or basil: good with strawberry

2 whole star anise pods, broken to fit if needed: good with pineapple

¼ teaspoon green cardamom seeds or 3 whole pods: good with mango

1 teaspoon dried lavender: good with blueberry

¼ teaspoon pink or black peppercorns: good with strawberry

Chamomile Bourbon Milk Punch

During one of food writer Nico Vera's visits to London, he was initiated into the world of clarified milk punches—a combination of hot milk, alcohol, sugar, citrus, water, and tea or spices—and was immediately hooked. The citrus curdles the milk, and carefully straining the solids clarifies the cocktail. In addition to the visual appeal, the process smooths the drink by removing harsh tannins in the ingredients. Back home stateside, he set to work on his own plant-based version using coconut milk for the clarifying (which also adds a rich, creamy mouthfeel). Here, bourbon evokes his tasting trips to Kentucky and Louisiana, and the chamomile tea syrup wonderfully balances the whiskey and lime. Using room-temperature, instead of hot, coconut milk produces smaller curds, which helps with the straining process. Begin preparing the punch a day in advance and allot an hour or two for filtering; it might seem slow going, but it's worth the wait.

Makes about 2 cups (6 servings)

Time: Weekend

Storage: Refrigerate for up to 2 weeks.

- ¾ cup (180ml) water
- 2 bags chamomile tea
- ⅓ cup (65g) organic cane sugar
- ¾ cup (180ml) bourbon
- ½ cup (120ml) fresh lime juice, strained
- ½ cup (120ml) canned full-fat coconut milk, at room temperature
- Large ice cubes
- 6 strips lime peel, for garnish

IN A SMALL SAUCEPAN, bring the water to a boil over high heat. Turn off the heat, add the tea bags, and steep for 8 minutes. Remove and compost the tea bags. Bring the liquid to a simmer, add the sugar, and stir until the sugar dissolves, about 2 minutes. Remove from the heat and let the syrup cool for at least 1 hour before using. (At this point, if you want to make the drinks later, you can refrigerate the syrup for up to 1 week in a sealed container.)

In a tall sealable jar, combine the bourbon, chamomile tea syrup, lime juice, and coconut milk. Seal the jar and refrigerate overnight, about 9 hours. The coconut milk will curdle into small pieces and float to the top.

Line a large fine-mesh sieve with cheesecloth or a nut-milk bag and set it over a large mixing bowl. Slowly pour all of the refrigerated mixture through the sieve and let it drip through. (Don't press or squeeze.) Let the solid coconut milk curds collect in the sieve; they help with the filtering process. Strain the filtered liquid two more times. Allot 1 to 2 hours for the filtering process. (See photo, page xii.) The result should be a slightly opaque concoction with a hint of color from the chamomile tea.

To serve, pour 2 to 3 fluid ounces (60ml to 90ml) of the milk punch into a glass with a large ice cube. Garnish with an expressed lime peel.

Tusán Pisco Sour

The Pisco Sour is Peru's national drink: a shaken, century-old concoction of grape brandy, lime juice, simple syrup, and egg whites, all topped with aromatic bitters. In this variation, the flavors of Chinese five-spice infuse the syrup. The drink pays homage to the first-generation Chinese Peruvians, or Tusán, and their ancestors—the Chinese indentured workers who migrated from Canton to Peru in the mid-nineteenth century. Here, frothy aquafaba replaces egg whites to make the cocktail vegan, and the aromatic garnish of vanilla extract with the syrup deepens the flavor of the drink. Using a blender creates a thick foam and crushes the ice cubes to chill the drink. To obtain the proper dilution, it's important to use ice cubes that are 1 fluid ounce (30ml) by volume, or with 1¼-inch (3cm) sides.

Makes 4 servings

Time: Weekday

Storage: Best enjoyed immediately; storage not recommended.

CHINESE FIVE-SPICE SYRUP & BITTERS

½ cup (120ml) water

½ cup (100g) organic cane sugar

2 cinnamon sticks

3 whole star anise pods

5 whole cloves

5 black peppercorns

2 teaspoons aniseed or fennel seeds

1 tablespoon vanilla extract

COCKTAILS

1 cup (240ml) pisco, Quebranta varietal or Acholado blend

½ cup (120ml) fresh lemon juice

½ cup (120ml) aquafaba (from no-salt-added canned chickpeas)

4 ice cubes (1 fluid ounce/30ml volume each)

MAKE THE CHINESE FIVE-SPICE syrup: In a small saucepan, combine the water, sugar, cinnamon stick, star anise, cloves, peppercorns, and aniseed. Bring to a boil over medium heat, then reduce the heat to a simmer and cook for 10 minutes, stirring to dissolve the sugar. Let cool to room temperature, about 30 minutes.

Strain the syrup into a glass jar. Compost the cinnamon stick, star anise, cloves, peppercorns, and aniseed. (If you want to make the syrup ahead of time, you can refrigerate it for up to 1 week in a sealed container.)

Make the bitters: In a small bowl or bottle fitted with an eyedropper, stir or shake together the vanilla and 1 tablespoon of the Chinese five-spice syrup.

Make the cocktails: In a blender, combine the pisco, lemon juice, remaining Chinese five-spice syrup, aquafaba, and ice cubes. Blend on high for 30 seconds to make a thick foam and crush the ice. Pour into four old-fashioned glasses. Use a small spoon, straw, or an eyedropper to sprinkle each drink generously with bitters.

Tahini Hot Chocolate

This mug will only be as wonderful as the tahini you put in it. You need to start with tahini that you'd be happy to eat by the spoonful out of the jar. (I suggest Soom brand!) Whisking tahini and water together, you get a surprisingly creamy, nutty base to showcase your favorite dark chocolate. It's rich—a little goes a long way—and it's best enjoyed immediately. If you are making it for more than two people, it doubles and triples easily.

Makes 1¾ cups (2 servings)

Time: Weekday

Storage: Not recommended.

2 tablespoons organic cane sugar

¼ cup (25g) Dutch process cocoa powder

¼ teaspoon vanilla extract

3 tablespoons tahini

Pinch of fine sea salt

1½ cups (350ml) warm water

½ ounce (14g) vegan dark chocolate, chopped

IN A SMALL SAUCEPAN, combine the sugar, cocoa, vanilla, tahini, and salt. Add about ¼ cup (60ml) of the water and whisk until the mixture is smooth, with no lumps of cocoa or tahini. Add the remaining water and whisk until combined.

Heat over medium heat, whisking occasionally until hot, about 150°F (66°C). Add the chopped chocolate, whisk to melt, and serve.

Quick Ginger "Beer"

True, long-fermented ginger beer is delicious and praiseworthy—but it requires an unwavering commitment to the cause. This quick version, on the other hand, is remarkably tasty—and doesn't require toil, tedium—or yeast. Deep flavors develop from a 24-hour rest in the refrigerator, offering a beverage punchier and more brazen than anything store-bought. Perhaps best of all, this makes for the perfect backdrop for all those big-batch weekend cocktails, alcoholic or NA.

Makes about 7 cups (4 servings)

Time: Weekend

Storage: Refrigerate for up to 5 days, without the sparkling water, and add it just before serving.

- 1 pound (450g) fresh ginger, peeled (see Note)
- 1¼ cups (250g) organic cane sugar
- 4 teaspoons finely grated lime zest (from 2 limes)
- ¼ cup (60ml) fresh lime juice (from 2 limes)
- 2 whole cloves
- 4 cups (950ml) water
- 2 teaspoons Angostura bitters
- 2 cups (470ml) sparkling water
- Ice cubes
- Lime wedges, for garnish

COARSELY GRATE THE GINGER using a box grater, or cut into chunks. Transfer to a food processor and pulse until the ginger is coarsely chopped but not pasty.

In a large bowl with a lid (or a pitcher with a lid), combine the grated ginger, sugar, lime zest, lime juice, and cloves. Mash together using a muddler or a wooden spoon to get the juices flowing. Pour the water over the ginger mixture. Cover and refrigerate for 24 hours.

Press through a fine-mesh sieve into another bowl or pitcher, pressing down on the ingredients to ensure all the liquid is extracted. Compost the solids. Stir in the bitters and add the sparkling water. Serve over ice, garnished with lime wedges.

COOK'S NOTE: The easiest way to peel fresh ginger is to use a teaspoon and scrape it along the peel.

Carrot & Cardamom Shake

This bright and nuanced alternative to your typical smoothie goes the distance in delivering an unexpectedly warm-flavored—but still cold and refreshing—any-time-of-day beverage. Carrots and cardamom have long been a favorite union, and here they shine, amped up by the sweetness of banana, zing from fresh ginger, and nutty heft from almonds. A secondary benefit: This shake is a nutritional powerhouse, too.

Makes 1 to 2 servings

Time: Weekday

Storage: Freeze for up to 2 months.

- 1 ripe banana, sliced and frozen
- 2 medium carrots (2 ounces/60g each), scrubbed and quartered
- 1½ cups (350ml) Nut Milk (page 17), Oat Milk (page 17), Soy Milk (page 75), or store-bought plant-based milk
- 1-inch (2.5cm) piece fresh ginger, peeled
- 1 teaspoon ground cardamom
- ¼ teaspoon ground clove
- ¼ cup (25g) slivered or sliced almonds, plus more (optional) for garnish
- 2 tablespoons maple syrup

IN A BLENDER, COMBINE all the ingredients and blend on high speed until smooth. Garnish with slivered or sliced almonds, if desired, and serve immediately.

BIBLIOGRAPHY

Ancient Grains for Modern Meals by Maria Speck

Artisan Vegan Cheese by Miyoko Schinner

The Art of Fermentation by Sandor Katz

Asian Tofu by Andrea Nguyen

At Home in the Whole Food Kitchen by Amy Chaplin

By Any Greens Necessary by Tracye McQuirter

Chloe Flavor by Chloe Coscarelli

The Complete Plant-Based Cookbook by America's Test Kitchen

Cool Beans by Joe Yonan

Crossroads by Tal Ronnen

Don't Count the Tortillas by Adán Medrano

East Meets Vegan by Sasha Gill

The First Mess Cookbook by Laura Wright

The Food of Sichuan by Fuchsia Dunlop

Food52 Vegan by Gena Hamshaw

The Glorious Vegetables of Italy by Domenica Marchetti

Grist by Abra Berens

The Homemade Vegan Pantry by Miyoko Schinner

The Homesick Texan Cookbook by Lisa Fain

I Dream of Dinner by Ali Slagle

In Bibi's Kitchen by Hawa Hassan

Japan: The Vegetarian Cookbook by Nancy Singleton Hachisu

Kansha by Elizabeth Andoh

The Korean Vegan by Joanne Lee Molinaro

La Vida Verde by Jocelyn Ramirez

Minimalist Baker's Everyday Cooking by Dana Shultz

A Modern Way to Eat by Anna Jones

The Moosewood Cookbook by Mollie Katzen

The New Vegetarian Cooking for Everyone by Deborah Madison

Our Fermented Lives by Julia Skinner

Plant-Based India by Dr. Sheil Shukla

Plenty by Yotam Ottolenghi

Provecho by Edgar Castrejón

River Cottage Veg by Hugh Fearnley-Whittingstall

Ruffage by Abra Berens

Sababa by Adeena Sussman

Salud! by Eddie Garza

The Sioux Chef's Indigenous Kitchen by Sean Sherman

Six Seasons by Joshua McFadden

The Southern Vegetarian by Amy Lawrence and Justin Fox Burks

Spicebox Kitchen by Linda Shiue

Super Natural Cooking by Heidi Swanson

Sweet Potato Soul by Jenné Claiborne

Tenderheart by Hetty Lui McKinnon

Ten Talents by Rosalie and Frank Hurd

Vegan Baking for Beginners by JL Fields

The Vegan Cake Bible by Sara Kidd

The Vegan Chinese Kitchen by Hannah Che

Vegan Chocolate by Fran Costigan

Veganomicon by Isa Chandra Moscowitz and Terry Romero

Vegan Richa's Indian Kitchen by Richa Hingle

Vegetable Kingdom by Bryant Terry

Vegetable Literacy by Deborah Madison

Vegetable Revelations by Steven Satterfield

Vegetables by James Peterson

Vegetables Illustrated by America's Test Kitchen

Vegetable Simple by Eric Ripert

Vegetables Unleashed by José Andrés

The Vegetarian Flavor Bible by Karen Page

Veggie Burgers Every Which Way by Lukas Volger

Whole Food Cooking Every Day by Amy Chaplin

World Vegetarian by Madhur Jaffrey

ACKNOWLEDGMENTS

This is the biggest, most ambitious book I've written, and, fittingly, it required the highest level of teamwork and coordination of any of my projects. I'm so grateful for everyone who helped.

First and foremost, that would be my agent, David Black, and my editor at Ten Speed Press, Kelly Snowden. Both of you immediately understood what I was after and worked tirelessly to help me achieve it. Thank you for keeping me sane—or at least saner than I would have otherwise been. And thank you, Kelly, for believing in me enough to put the power of my favorite publisher behind me as I followed my ambitions.

The visuals dream team of photographer Erin Scott and food stylist Lillian Kang: You will forever have my gratitude for your flexibility and willingness to step up in the wake of tragedy, and I can't wait to work together again. Your ability to combine humor and collegiality with unbeatable efficiency and a true sense of artistry was the main reason we were able to tame "The Beast"! Erin, your finesse in bouncing around that gorgeous California light until it hit just so, your exquisite taste in props, your commitment

to seeing not just the dish in front of us but also how it fits into the entire breadth of the project: I'm in awe. And Lillian, you know I wanted to work with you again since the last time, and thank you for making it happen. Your way with a swoosh, your ability to make something look perfectly imperfect in a way that makes readers swoon without being intimidated, and all the incredible flicking and dripping that I named "Pollocking": You make it look easy, even while working tirelessly. I'm proud to call you both my friends.

Even though we lost photographer Aubrie Pick to cancer just as we were preparing to shoot this book, we all felt her watching over us as we worked (sometimes through tears). Memories of Aubrie's energy and spirit pushed us to do what we know she would have done: make the most beautiful book possible. May she rest in peace.

Thanks, too, to workhorse styling assistants Paige Arnett and Allison Fellion for cranking out the food, and to photo assistants Tamer Abu-Dayyeh and Brad Knilans for helping manage so many technical aspects (and, in Tamer's case, for pro hand-modeling advice).

The efficiency at the photo shoot was aided in no small part by genius art director Betsy Stromberg, who spent weeks upon weeks just organizing the shot list. The book map created and continually updated by Betsy and Gabby Ureña Matos was a lifesaver, and Betsy's design work is not only breathtakingly elegant and clean, but it also helped fit way too many recipes in way too little space. Thank you not only for tolerating my cover input, Betsy, but also for using it as a jumping-off point to create something I am so proud to have my name on.

Thank you to Gabby, project editor Kim Keller, and production editor Patricia Shaw for keeping the train chugging along—and to Kim, particularly, for being a beacon of calm in those moments when I got just plain lost in the weeds. Copy editor Kate Slate, thank you for smoothing out all the rough edges while keeping my voice, and for asking the perfect questions along the way. I would say your work seems like magic, but I know how painstaking it can be to get things right.

I couldn't have done this project without the contributors I worked with to develop recipes. It was so much fun to brainstorm with each one of you, then watch as you channeled my taste and my mission, and then experience the delectable results. Thank you, thank you, thank you.

I would be nowhere—fast!—without Sheri Codiana, the spreadsheet queen, who took on yet again the daunting task of managing this project from the start and acted as an excellent sounding board during my best and worst moments.

Perhaps the most crucial work in ensuring workable recipes is testing, and I had some of the best in the business: Lead tester Kristen Hartke, with whom I appear to share a palate (and who also developed recipes), was available virtually anytime I needed her, ready with her notes—and a scale—to answer any of my questions. Kara Elder and Nicole Perry helped Kristen manage the incredible load.

My *Washington Post* colleagues have helped in innumerable ways, really, but I'll try to enumerate them anyway. The most important is the patience and flexibility they offered as I tried (and mostly succeeded) to fit this huge project on top of a full-time job. But they also inspire and teach me every day. To Ann Maloney, Matt Brooks, Tim Carman, Tom Sietsema, Daniela Galarza, Becky Krystal, Aaron Hutcherson, Emily Heil, Olga Massov, Anna Rodriguez, Liz Seymour, Krissah Thompson, Jim Webster, and Mitch Rubin: You are, simply, the best.

Last but not least, thank you to my family, most of all my sister Rebekah, whose wisdom in the plant-based kitchen (and the garden) has informed my work for decades; and to my husband, Carl, for being a willing taster and, best of all, an understanding, supportive spouse who tolerates my disappearing into my office for days on end, especially during crunch times. And there were plenty of those.

To our son, Isaiah, thank you for being part of our crazy crew. I know it's supposed to be the other way around, but I can't help it: I hope to, one day, make you proud.

INDEX

Note: Page references in *italics* indicate recipe photographs.

Index

481

For Karin Leigh Orr, whose open heart I miss every day, 1963–2023

Typefaces: Monotype's Eloquence and Gelion

Library of Congress Cataloging-in-Publication Data
Names: Yonan, Joe, author. Title: Mastering the
art of plant-based cooking : vegan recipes, tips,
and techniques / by Joe Yonan. Identifiers: LCCN
2023046372 (print) | LCCN 2023046373 (ebook) | ISBN
9781984860644 (hardcover) | ISBN 9781984860651
(ebook) Subjects: LCSH: Vegan cooking. | Cooking
(Natural foods) | LCGFT: Cookbooks. Classification:
LCC TX837 .Y653 2024 (print) | LCC TX837 (ebook) |
DDC 641.5/6362—dc23/eng/20231220
LC record available at https://lccn.loc.gov/2023046372
LC ebook record available at https://lccn.loc.
gov/2023046373

Hardcover ISBN: 978-1-9848-6064-4
eBook ISBN: 978-1-9848-6065-1

Printed in China

Acquiring editor: Kelly Snowden
Project editors: Kelly Snowden, Kim Keller, and
Gabby Ureña Matos
Production editors: Patricia Shaw and Liana Faughnan
Art director & designer: Betsy Stromberg
Production designers: Mara Gendell and Faith Hague
Production manager: Serena Sigona
Prepress color manager: Nick Patton
Food stylist: Lillian Kang
Food stylist assistants: Paige Arnett and Allison Fellion
Prop stylist: Erin Scott
Photo assistants: Tamer Abu-Dayyeh and Brad Knilans
Copy editor: Kate Slate
Proofreader: Nancy Inglis
Indexer: Elizabeth Parson
Publicist: David Hawk
Marketer: Andrea Portanova

10 9 8 7 6 5 4 3 2 1

First Edition